M000004896

to Ron,
best regards,
Ron Turner
4/19/05

AS TOLD

THE JOURNALS OF THE LEWIS AND CLARK EXPEDITION

Edited by
Ronald R. Turner
and
Gregory P. Turner

THE NARRATIVE PRESS
HISTORICAL ADVENTURE & EXPLORATION

Ron Turner, a retired orthopedic surgeon with a lifelong interest in Lewis and Clark, wrote a syndicated weekly newspaper column for ten years and taught English Composition at the university level. He has recently edited a 1908 cookbook and is now working on a true-crime story and a biography. He lives with his wife in Ohio.

His son and co-editor, **Greg Turner**, received his journalism degree from Boston University and is currently the business editor for a daily newspaper near Boston. He lives with his wife in Massachusetts.

The Narrative Press
P.O. Box 2487, Santa Barbara, California 93120 U.S.A.
Telephone: (800) 315-9005 Web: www.narrativepress.com

ISBN 1-58976-235-5 (Paperback)

Produced in the United States of America

Contents

Introduction

It is a rare treat to encounter a tale of adventure which, as it unfolds, is as unpredictable to the authors as it is to the involved reader hanging on every word. Whether Meriwether Lewis ponders the mood of an approaching Indian tribe or William Clark agonizes over the scarcity of food for his men, the eventual outcome is invariably uncertain. Like Columbus, but unlike today's astronauts, they never knew what lay ahead. So it is with the journals of the Lewis and Clark Expedition. We readers defy icy mountain ranges and challenge vicious rapids vicariously—if not simultaneously—with these early-1800s explorers. Their hopes and fears become our own; we empathize fully with the experiences and drama of the first white men to venture west of the Mississippi under the authority of the United States.

Indeed, hopes were fulfilled and fears were realized. While the Shoshones brought horses and information to assist the expedition's passage through the Bitterroot Mountains, the Teton Sioux brought almost nothing but anguish. Appetites sated by the successful hunting of huge herds of elk and buffalo were offset by days with little but roots and dried fish. Balmy weather and favorable winds contrasted with hailstorms, subzero temperatures and flash floods. Calm evenings spent writing descriptions of newly discovered flora and fauna paled in comparison with fierce battles with grizzlies, rattlesnakes and mosquitoes. This was a camping trip *in extremis,* and only the thoroughness of the journals—the diligent record-keeping of the men themselves—permits us to live this adventure as it happened.

Yet the journals in their original form, while of unquestionable historic value and written in the colorful language of their time, yield slow, burdensome and sometimes confusing reading. Although Nicholas Biddle paraphrased the journals in 1815, nearly one hundred years lapsed before Reuben Gold Thwaites published them in their entirety for the first time, in seven volumes plus a volume of maps. Bernard DeVoto's condensed version was introduced in 1953, and this was followed by a complete edition by Gary Moulton in 1988. The editors of the current rendering have provided a reader-friendly alternative with updated language for easier comprehension of this historic American saga.

For an overview, Lewis and Clark began their voyage near St. Louis in May of 1804, ascended the Missouri River, and stopped at Fort Mandan in present-day North Dakota, where they wintered in 1804-05. (Until they reached the Rocky Mountains more than a year later, the entire trip would be upstream, against the current, and for this they would utilize four modes of river travel: oars, sails, poles, and tow lines.) The following spring they completed their trip up the Missouri, crossed the Bitterroot Range of the Rocky Mountains, and traveled down the Clearwater, Snake and Columbia rivers to the Pacific Ocean. Here they spent the winter of 1805-06 at Fort Clatsop in today's Oregon. Then, in the spring of 1806, they returned up the Columbia, back across the mountains and, after significant variations that included the Yellowstone River, down the Missouri to St. Louis. In all, they covered 8,000 miles.

An earlier chain of events had fortuitously expanded the territory of the United States for the expedition. Louisiana, that huge area which included the western Mississippi River watershed (and therefore the Missouri River drainage basin as well), west to the Continental Divide, was ceded to Spain by France in 1762. According to a treaty,[1] however, France forced Spain to retrocede that territory in 1800. But Napoleon, because of preoccupations elsewhere, found himself unable to defend the region and feared Great Britain would take Louisiana. "It was primarily to deny her [Great Britain] such an enormous increase in wealth and power that Napoleon determined to sell Louisiana to the United States."[2] The famous Louisiana Purchase of April 1803, for the sum of $15 million, opened up the west to the United States, permitting the Lewis and Clark Expedition—the Corps of Discovery—to voyage westward on its own soil. West of the Rockies lay the Oregon Territory (including present-day Idaho, Washington and Oregon) to which the United States had laid partial claim through Captain Robert Gray's exploration of the mouth of the Columbia in 1792. So geopolitically, at least, potential travel within the United States extending to the Pacific Ocean had become a reality.

This, of course, dovetailed nicely with President Thomas Jefferson's plans to search for a water route to the Pacific—the sought-after Northwest Passage. Jefferson not only wanted to expand the territory of the United States, thereby securing its position as a continental as well as a coastal power, but he also desired to obtain more efficient trade routes. At the time, importers of silk and other important goods from China, after sailing across the Pacific, had to endure the rounding

---

1. Treaty of San Ildefonso

2. DeVoto, Bernard, ed., *The Journals of Lewis and Clark,* Houghton Mifflin, 1952, p. xxxi.

of Cape Horn and then venture north to America's populated east coast. So a water route from the Columbia, across a hopefully short portage, and down the Missouri, Mississippi and Ohio rivers to the east coast, would significantly shorten both time spent and distance traveled.

In 1801 Jefferson had begun to plan the investigation of America's uncharted West. Essential to his plan was finding a leader of men, an experienced woodsman, a confident diplomat, and a wilderness scientist—all in one person. For this position he selected Meriwether Lewis and made him his personal secretary the same year. Lewis had, in fact, requested to join a less ambitious westward expedition in 1792, but instead joined the army, spent time on the frontier with Indians, served in a rifle company under his future co-explorer, William Clark, and eventually rose to the rank of captain. Then, in January of 1803, Jefferson sent a secret message to Congress requesting $2,500 for the undertaking. The request was approved.

Without hesitating, Lewis ordered provisions and weapons from an arsenal in Harper's Ferry, Virginia (now West Virginia), bought scientific equipment, maps and medical supplies, and studied celestial navigation and botany in Philadelphia. In June he received his specific instructions from Jefferson. (See "Jefferson's Instructions to Lewis.")

In the same month, Lewis requested his recently re-enlisted friend, William Clark, to join him on the expedition at the rank of captain. (See "Letters Between Lewis and Clark.") Although Clark had reentered the army as a lieutenant, it was agreed privately that he would be known as captain to the corps members and that the two of them would jointly lead the expedition. With Clark's cartographic and diplomatic capabilities, and Lewis's naturalist background, and with both men having had wilderness experience with the Indians, the pair complemented each other ideally in a venture that would require a vast diversity of skills.

A Boston newspaper, the *New England Palladium,* announced, "It is reported, that capt. Lewis, the president's private secretary, is about to proceed to our south-western frontier on political business." But the business was more than political; it was largely commercial: to control the maritime commerce with China and corner the northern fur trade then controlled by Great Britain. In all fairness, however, Jefferson was also quintessentially inquisitive in matters both scientific and sociologic. The president was genuinely interested in discovering new plants and animals and uncovering the nature of unknown cultures.

Later in the summer of 1803, in Pittsburgh, Lewis struggled to have a 55-foot keelboat built. He also bought two pirogues, or large canoes, and hired French *engagés* to navigate the vessels downstream to Louisville. Here Clark, with recruits of his own, joined the assemblage and by the fall of 1803 they had reached St. Louis.

In September newspapers were taking a slightly different slant. Again, from the *New England Palladium:*

An expedition is expected to leave this place [Louisville] shortly, under the direction of Capt. William Clark and Mr. Lewis, (private secretary to the President), to proceed through the immense wilderness of Louisiana, to the Western or Pacific Ocean. The particular objects of this undertaking are at present matters of conjecture only: But we have good reason to believe that our government intend [sic] to encourage settle- ments and establish sea-ports on the coast of the Pacific Ocean.

Forty-eight men headed out in November and established a winter training camp at Camp Dubois just north of St. Louis across from the mouth of the Missouri River in present-day Illinois. Here the Corps would hone their skills in preparation for dealing with all aspects of the frontier.

And by now the press was better informed. From a November 1803, edition of the *New England Palladium:*

It is . . . certain that they [Lewis and Clark] will ascend the main branch of the Missisippi [sic] as far as possible; and it is probable they will then direct their course to the Missouri, and ascend it . . . . About 60 men will compose the party.

The actual voyage began on May 14, 1804, and at this point the reader is invited to follow the adventure in the journals themselves. "Most hours of most days, the captains were in their quarters, at their writing desks, dipping their quills into their inkstands, writing and drawing, candles providing the only illumination, smoke from the wet wood on the fire in the air, everything cold and damp. They wrote on. They were the writingest explorers of all time."[3]

• • •

The editors' purpose was not to re-write the journals into scholarly prose but rather to clarify them for swifter understanding. All of the changes and insertions were intended to ease the burden of reading the journal entries without altering their meaning, flavor, or tone. We

3. Ambrose, Stephen E., *Lewis & Clark: Voyage of Discovery,* National Geographic Society, 1998, p. 184.

wished to maintain the "voices" of the narrators while streamlining the flow with the judicious use of commas, paragraphs, spelling corrections, and accepted language modernizations. Subjects and verbs were altered to agree, sentence beginnings were capitalized, omitted words were inserted in brackets, and run-on sentences were disunited.

Spelling was a major concern. One view, expressed by DeVoto ("The spellings of the original are a large part of its charm . . . .")[4] and Stephen Ambrose ("They delighted our eyes with their idiosyncratic spelling . . . .")[5] has merit. Many readers, however, prefer to move more briskly through the text without pausing to puzzle out meanings and definitions. Thus "cewed" became "queued," "squar" became "squaw," "suckceed" became "succeed," and "raped" became "wrapped." In the original, nautical directions were often abbreviated "S.S.," meaning starboard, and "L.S.," or "Lard. side," meaning larboard; these were changed to starboard (right) and port (left), respectively.

The editors also found that the spelling of personal, tribal, and river names was often erratic and unpredictable. "[Clark] did manage to take the last name of Toussaint Charbonneau . . . and spell it at least fifteen different ways, not once correctly."[6] In an effort to minimize reader confusion, we adopted the most commonly accepted spellings for each, and maintained those spellings throughout the text. Since nomenclature often became exceedingly complicated when, for instance, the Gros Ventres tribe is also referred to as the Big Bellies, Minnetarees, and Hidatsa, we hope the studious reader will forgive any unintentional editorial lapses.

Because Lewis often produced enormously long, unwieldy paragraphs and Clark frequently wrote choppy, multi-subject ones, the editors adopted certain conventions for clarification and consistency. Weather notes, health status, dialogue, significant time jumps, and landscape and wildlife descriptions were set off individually. This sometimes resulted in one-sentence paragraphs (which our fourth-grade teachers taught was unconscionable), but here DeVoto would probably agree: "I have repeatedly indented paragraphs . . . where none are set off in the original."[7]

Of prime importance to the editors was to retain the flavor of the original journals. Colorful "non-words" were preserved: the "gladey"

4. DeVoto, *Ibid.*, p. xv.

5. Ambrose, Stephen E., in DeVoto, *Ibid.*, p. viii.

6. Betts, Robert B., "A Salute to the Ingenious Spelling and Grammar of William Clark," from *We Proceeded On,* vol. 6, no. 4, November, 1980.

7. DeVoto, *Ibid.*, p. xv.

region, the "mirey" river bottom, and we "nooned it" on shore. And most usage idiosyncrasies were kept as written:

answered as: worked like, or was used for
determined: decided
suffered: allowed
indifferent: inferior
interview: encounter
overtake: catch up with
passed (the river): crossed (the river)
evening: after noon
council: advice, or a serious discussion
overset (the boat): overturned (the boat)

To illustrate some of these changes, this section from the original,

"rained last night as usial and the greater part of this day, the men complete Chimneys & Bunks to day, in the evening a Chief and 4 men come of the Clotsop nation chief Co-ma-wool we sent out R. Fields & Collins to hunt and order Drewyer, Shannon & Labiach to set out early to morrow to hunt, Jo Fields, Bratten, & Gibson to make salt at Point Addams, Willard & Wiser, to assist them in carrying the Kittles &c. to the Ocian, and all the others to finish the Pickets and gates. worm weather I saw a Musquetor which I showed Capt. Lewis"

was updated to:

[It] rained last night as usual and the greater part of this day.

The men completed chimneys and bunks today.

In the evening a chief and four men came of the Clatsop nation, chief Comowool.

We sent out Reubin Field and Collins to hunt and ordered Drouillard, Shannon and Labiche to set out early tomorrow to hunt, Joseph Field, Bratton and Gibson to make salt at Point Adams, Willard and Wiser to assist them in carrying the kettles, etc., to the ocean, and all the others to finish the pickets and gates.

[It was] warm weather.

I saw a mosquito which I showed [to] Captain Lewis.

The members of the Corps of Discovery did not discover the sought-after commercially useful all-water route to the Pacific; such a passage did not exist. Nor did the friendly relations with most of the Indian tribes they encountered last. Yet, in the minds of most, the journey was a success.

Lewis and Clark and their men cleared the way for America's development west of the Mississippi. In 1811, for example, John Jacob Astor's agents followed nearly the same route to open the fur trade at the mouth of the Columbia. This and subsequent migration permitted the United States to claim the Oregon Country and become truly continental. Also of significance were the scientific discoveries, including nearly two hundred previously unknown plants, more than one hundred new animals, and two dozen Indian cultures. At last, the West had become tangible. "It [the expedition] satisfied desire and it created desire: the desire of a westering nation. That, the increase of our cultural heritage, the beginning of knowledge of the American West, must be accounted the most important result of the Lewis and Clark expedition."[8]

The editors hope that this version of the original journals of the Lewis and Clark Expedition will provide incentive enough for the majority of readers to indulge themselves in this epic of immense historic importance.

Ronald R. Turner, MD
Gregory P. Turner

8. DeVoto, *Ibid.*, p. lx.

Prologue

A. Jefferson's Instructions to Lewis

To Meriwether Lewis, Esq., Captain of the 1st regiment of infantry of the United States of America:

The object of your mission is to explore the Missouri River and such principal stream of it by its communication with the Pacific Ocean may offer the most direct and practicable water communication across this continent, for the purposes of commerce.

Specifically, Lewis was to begin at the mouth of the Missouri and note, by celestial observation, the latitude and longitude of river mouths, rapids, islands, and mountains. He was also to chart the expedition's water and land courses by dead reckoning.[9] *He was to receive from the Secretary of War:*

- *authority to engage and command ten to twelve volunteers*
- *arms and ammunition for ten to twelve men*
- *boats, tents, and other traveling gear*
- *medicines*[10] *and surgical instruments*
- *light articles for presents and barter with the Indians*
- *instruments for celestial observation*

To assist in future trade, Lewis was to obtain information about the people he encountered, including:

- *names and populations of nations and their interrelationships*
- *physical characteristics*
- *occupations*
- *language, traditions, religions, laws, and morality*
- *food, clothing, and accommodations*
- *diseases and remedies*
- *articles of trade possessed and needed*

---

9. using compass direction, time, and distance
10. including "kinepox" for smallpox prevention

In his relationships with the natives, he was to:

- *remain friendly and conciliatory*
- *indicate the innocence of the expedition*
- *acquaint them with the position, extent, desire for commerce, and peaceful intent of the United States*
- *encourage the chiefs to visit Washington at public expense*[11]

He was also to note:

- *the climate*
- *the contour, cover growth, and soil of the land*
- *animals and vegetables, particularly new ones*
- *mineral deposits*

Regarding personal safety, Lewis was directed to terminate the expedition if superior forces were encountered.[12] *Prior to departure, he was to name a successor (who was to name a successor, etc.) to command the expedition.*

Lewis was to communicate "at seasonal intervals" and to put into "cypher whatever might do injury if betrayed." Notes were to be duplicated[13] *and sent to settlements at St. Louis, Cahokia and St. Genevieve and thence to the war office in Washington. Farther upriver, they could be sent by trusted traders or Indians.*

At the Pacific Ocean, Lewis was determine whether furs could be sent as expeditiously to the head of the Missouri (transcontinentally) as by the current route (circumnavigation via the Cape of Good Hope or Cape Horn). If a ship was discovered, two men were to return by sea with a copy of the notes; if return by land seemed risky, all were to accompany the ship.

Upon returning to the United States, Lewis was to:

---

11. "If any of them should wish to have some of their young people brought up with us and taught such arts as may be useful to them, we will receive, instruct, and take care of them." (Jefferson)

12. "In the loss of yourselves, we should lose also the information you will have acquired." (Jefferson)

13. "guard by multiplying them" (Jefferson)

- *discharge any men requesting it*
- *return to Washington with his notes*

Given under my hand at the city of Washington, this 20th day of June, 1803,

Th. Jefferson,
Pr. U.S. of America

B. Letters Between Lewis and Clark

Sunday, June 19, 1803

Dear Clark:

From the long and uninterrupted friendship and confidence which has subsisted between us, I feel no hesitation in making to you the following communication under the fullest impression that it will be held by you inviolably secret.

During the last session of Congress a law was passed, in conformity to a private message of the President of the United States, entitled "An act making an appropriation for extending the external commerce of the United States." The object of this act as understood by its framers was to give the sanction of the government to exploring the interior of the continent of North America, or that part of it bordering on the Missouri and Columbia rivers.

I am armed with the authority of the government of the United States for my protection, so far as its authority or influence extends; in addition to which the further aid has been given me of liberal passports from the ministers both of France and England.

I shall embark at Pittsburgh with a party of recruits, eight or nine in number, intended only to manage the boat, and are not calculated on as a permanent part of my detachment. When descending the Ohio, it shall be my duty by enquiry to find out and engage some good hunters, stout, healthy, unmarried men, accustomed to the woods, and capable of bearing bodily fatigue in a pretty considerable degree. Should any young men answering this description be found in your neighborhood, I would thank you to give information of them on my arrival at the Falls of the Ohio.

The present season being already so far advanced, I do not calculate on getting farther than two or three hundred miles up the Missouri before the commencement of the ensuing winter.

You must know in the first place that very sanguine expectations are at this time formed by our government that the whole of that immense country watered by the Mississippi and its tributaries [and the] Missouri inclusive, will be the property of the United States in less than twelve months from this date. But here let me again impress you with the necessity of keeping this matter a perfect secret.

Thus, my friend, you have, so far as leisure will at this time permit me to give it to you, a summary view of the plan [and] the means and the objects of this expedition.

If, therefore, there is anything under these circumstances in this enterprise which would induce you to participate with me in its fatigues, its dangers and its honors, believe me there is no man on earth whom I should feel equal pleasure in sharing them as with yourself.

I make this communication to you with the privity of the president, who expresses an anxious wish that you would consent to join me in this enterprise. He has authorized me to say that in the event of your accepting this proposition, he will grant you a captain's commission which, of course, will entitle you to the pay and emoluments attached to that office and will, equally with myself, entitle you to such portion of land as was granted to officers of similar rank for their Revolutionary services. The commission with which he proposes to furnish you is not to be considered temporary but permanent, if you wish it. Your situation, if joined with me in this mission, will, in all respects, be precisely such as my own.

Pray write to me on this subject as early as possible and direct to me at Pittsburgh.

With sincere and affectionate regard,
your friend and humble servant,
Meriwether Lewis

• • •

Sunday, July 17, 1803
Clarksville[14]
Dear Lewis:

I received by yesterday's mail your letter of the 19th ult.,[15] the contents of which I received with much pleasure.

The enterprise and mission [are] such as I have long anticipated and am much pleased with and, as my situation in life will admit of my absence the length of time necessary to accomplish such an undertaking, I will cheerfully join you in an "official character" and partake of the dangers, difficulties and fatigues, and I anticipate the honors and rewards should we be successful in accomplishing it.

---

14. Kentucky
15. abbreviation for *ultimo*: in the preceding month

This is an immense undertaking fraught with numerous difficulties but, my friend, I can assure you that no man lives with whom I would prefer to undertake and share the difficulties of such a trip than as yourself.

I shall endeavor to engage temporarily such men as I think may answer our purpose, but holding out the idea as stated in your letter, the subject of which has been mentioned in Louisville several weeks ago.

With every assurance of sincerity in every respect,
and with affection, your faithful and humble servant,

W. C.[16]

• • •

Sunday, July 24, 1803
Louisville
Dear Lewis:

I am arranging my matters so as to detain but a short time after your arrival here, well-convinced of the necessity of getting as far as possible up the _____[17] this fall to accomplish the object as laid down by yourself and which I highly approve of.

My friend, I join you with hand and heart and anticipate advantages which will certainly arrive from the accomplishment of [a] so vast, hazardous, and fatiguing enterprise. You, [no] doubt, will inform the president of my determination to join you in an "official character," as mentioned in your letter. The credentials necessary for me to be furnished with had best be forwarded to this place and, if we set out before their arrival, to Kaskaskia.

I have temporarily engaged some men for the enterprise of a description calculated to work and go through those labors and fatigues which will be necessary. Several young men (gentlemen's sons) have applied to accompany us. As they are not accustomed to labor, and as that is a very essential part of the services required of the party, I am cautious in giving them any encouragement.

The newspaper accounts seem to confirm the report of war in Europe and the cession of Louisiana to the United States.

Pray let me hear from you as often as possible.

Yours,
W. C.

• • •

16. William Clark
17. indicates blank space in original journal

Wednesday, August 3, 1803
Pittsburgh
Dear Clark:

Be assured I feel myself much gratified with your decision, for I could neither hope, wish, or expect from a union with any man on earth more perfect support or further aid in the discharge of the several duties of my mission than that, which I am confident, I shall derive from being associated with yourself.

If a good hunter or two could be conditionally engaged I would think them an acquisition. They must, however, understand that they will not be employed for the purposes of hunting exclusively, but must bear a portion of the labor in common with the party.

The cession of Louisiana is now no secret. On the 14th of July, the president received the treaty from Paris, by which France has ceded to the United States Louisiana, according to the bounds to which she had a right, [for a] price [of] 11¼ millions of dollars, besides paying certain debts of France to our citizens, which will be from one to four millions. The Western people may now estimate the value of their possessions.

I have been detained much longer than I expected but shall be with you by the last of this month.

Your sincere friend and obedient servant,
Meriwether Lewis

Note—Write and direct to me at Cincinnati.

• • •

Wednesday, September 28, 1803
Cincinnati
Dear Clark:

After a most tedious and laborious passage from Pittsburgh, I have, at length, reached this place. It was not until the 31st of August that I was enabled to take my departure from that place owing to the unpardonable negligence and inattention of the boat builders who, unfortunately for me, were a set of most incorrigible drunkards, and with whom neither threats, entreaties, nor any other mode of treatment which I could devise, had any effect. As an instance of their tardiness, it may suffice to mention that they were twelve days in preparing my poles and oars.

I am much pleased with the measures you have taken relative to the engaging the men you mention. Your ideas in the subject of judicious selection of our party perfectly comport with my own.

There is a party of soldiers, six or eight in number, now at [Fort] Massac waiting my arrival. They were selected from the troops in the state of Tennessee. I am also authorized to select by voluntary engagement any men from the posts of Massac and Kaskaskia. From these I think we shall be enabled to form our party without much difficulty. Four or five French water-men, I conceive, will be essential; this we can do, I presume, very readily at St. Louis.

The amount of the monthly compensation (or $10) which you have mentioned to the men is precisely what I have calculated on. I shall clothe and subsist the men I have with me. This will, of course, form a proper charge against the United States.

Adieu and believe me,
your very sincere friend and associate,
Meriwether Lewis

• • •

Wednesday, May 2, 1804
St. Louis
Dear friend:

The pay of the men will commence from the dates of their last enlistments and will be made up to the last of November, 1804, at the regular wages of soldiers and sergeants, etc., including the bounty of such as are entitled to it, which is not the case with those whose former enlistments do not expire before the said 31st of November. Other receipt rolls will be made out for five dollars per month as an advance on the score of clothing and provisions not furnished by the government. This [is] to commence with those enlisted in Kentucky from the dates of their enlistments [and with] all others from the 1st of January, 1804.

Your sincere friend,
M. Lewis, in haste

• • •

Sunday, May 6, 1804
St. Louis
My dear friend:

I send you, herewith enclosed, your commission accompanied by the Secretary of War's letter. It is not such as I wished or had reason to expect, but so it is. [I will give you] a further explanation when I join you.[18] I think it will be best to let none of our party, or any other persons, know anything about the grade. You will observe that the grade

18. Congress would not approve Clark's promotion to the rank of captain

has no effect upon your compensation, which, by G_d, shall be equal to my own.

I send you, by Colter and Reed, two hundred pounds of tallow which you will be so good as to have melted with fifty pounds of hog lard, cooled in small vessels, and put into some of those small kegs which were intended for whiskey. Not a keg can be obtained in St. Louis.

I hope all matters will be in readiness for my departure from this place. Damn Manuel[19] and triply damn Mr. B.[20] They give me more vexation and trouble than their lives are worth. I have dealt very plainly with these gentlemen. In short, I have come to an open rupture with them. I think them both great scoundrels, and they have given me abundant proofs of their unfriendly dispositions towards our government and its measures. These gentlemen (no, I will scratch it out) these puppies are not unacquainted with my opinions, and I am well informed that they have engaged some hireling writer to draft a petition and remonstrance to Gov. Claibourne[21] against me. Strange, indeed, that men, to appearance in their senses, will manifest such strong symptoms of insanity as to be whetting knives to cut their own throats.

I have determined to take two horses on with me: the one which is at camp and the one the men now bring you.

Adieu, it is late,
Your sincere friend,
M. Lewis

C. Letter from Sergeant Ordway to his Parents

Sunday, April 8, 1804
Honored parents:

I am now on an expedition to the westward, through the interior parts of North America, with Captain Lewis and Captain Clark. We are to ascend the Missouri River with a boat as far as it is navigable, and then go by land to the Western Ocean, if nothing prevents. We expect to be gone eighteen months or two years, and if we make great discoveries, as we expect, the United States has promised to make us great rewards.

---

19. Manuel Lisa, a Spaniard and dissatisfied supplier for the expedition who "sent a petition to the authorities protesting Lewis's high-handedness and other shortcomings" (Ambrose, *UC*, p. 134)

20. Francis Marie Benoit, Lisa's partner

21. of the Louisiana Territory

For fear of accidents, I wish to inform you that I left two hundred dollars in cash and, if I should not live to return, my heirs can get that and all the pay due me from the U.S. government.

I will write next winter if I have a chance.

Sergeant John Ordway

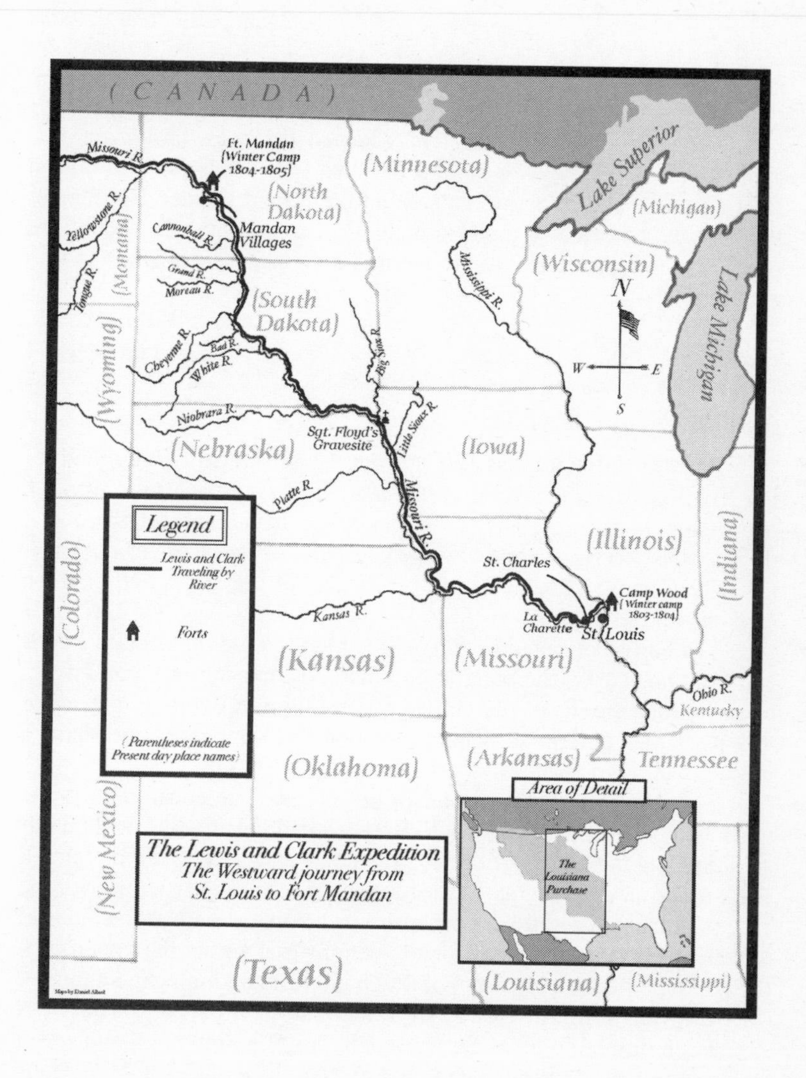
(CANADA)
Missouri R.
Ft. Mandan
(Winter Camp
1804-1805)
(Minnesota)
Lake Superior
(Michigan)
(North
Dakota)
Yellowstone R.
(Montana)
Cannonball R.
Mandan
Villages
Mississippi R.
(Wisconsin)
Lake Michigan
Grand R.
Moreau R.
Tongue R.
(South
Dakota)
N
W
E
S
(Wyoming)
Cheyenne R.
Bad R.
White R.
Big Sioux R.
Niobrara R.
Little Sioux R.
Sgt. Floyd's
Gravesite
(Nebraska)
(Iowa)
Platte R.
Missouri R.
Legend
Lewis and Clark
Traveling by
River
Forts
(Parentheses indicate
Present day place names)
(Illinois)
(Indiana)
(Colorado)
St. Charles
Camp Wood
(Winter camp
1803-1804)
Kansas R.
La
Charette
St. Louis
(Kansas)
(Missouri)
Ohio R.
Kentucky
(Oklahoma)
(Arkansas)
Tennessee
Area of Detail
The
Louisiana
Purchase
(New Mexico)
The Lewis and Clark Expedition
The Westward journey from
St. Louis to Fort Mandan
(Texas)
(Louisiana)
(Mississippi)

1: Spring, 1804

The swiftness of the current wheeled the boat, broke our tow rope, and was nearly over-setting the boat. All hands jumped out on the upper side and bore on that side until the sand washed from under the boat and wheeled on the next bank. By the time she wheeled a third time, [we] got a rope fast to her stern and by means of swimmers was carried to shore.

Captain William Clark,
May 24, 1804

Monday, May 14, 1804:

Private Patrick Gass: We left our establishment at the mouth of the River du Bois, or Wood River, a small river which falls into the Mississippi on the east side, a mile below the Missouri, and proceeded up the Missouri on our intended voyage of discovery, under the command of Captain Clark. Captain Lewis was to join us in two or three days on our passage.

The corps consisted of forty-three men (including Captain Lewis and Captain Clark, who were to command the expedition): part [were] of the regular troops of the United States and part [were] engaged for this particular enterprise. The expedition was embarked on board a bateau[22] and two pirogues.[23]

The day was showery, and in the evening we encamped on the north bank six miles up the river. Here we had leisure to reflect on our situation and the nature of our engagements and, as we had all entered this service as volunteers, to consider how far we stood pledged for the success of an expedition, which the government had projected and which had been undertaken for the benefit [of] and at the expense of the Union. Of course, [it was] of much interest and high expectation.

Captain William Clark: [It] rained the early part of the day.

I determined to go as far as St. Charles,[24] a French village seven leagues[25] up the Missouri, and wait at that place until Captain Lewis

22. the Lewis-designed 55-foot keelboat
23. open boats: one 41-foot red, and one 35-foot white
24. in Missouri
25. twenty-one miles (one league equals three miles)

could finish the business in which he was obliged to tend to at St. Louis and join me by land from that place.

I set out at 4:00 p.m. in the presence of many of the neighboring inhabitants and proceeded on under a gentle breeze up the Missouri to the upper point of the first island, four miles. We camped on the island which is situated close on the right (or starboard) side and opposite a small creek called Cold Water. A heavy rain [came] this afternoon.

Tuesday, May 15, 1804:

Captain Meriwether Lewis: It rained during the greater part of last night and continued until 7:00 a.m., after which the party proceeded.

The barge[26] ran foul there several times on logs, and in one instance it was with much difficulty [that] they could get her off. Happily, no injury was sustained, though the barge was several minutes in imminent danger. This was caused by her being too heavily laden in the stern. Persons accustomed to the navigation of the Missouri, and the Mississippi, also, below the mouth of this river, uniformly take the precaution to load their vessels heaviest in the bow when they ascend the stream in order to avoid the danger incident to running foul of the concealed timber, which lies in great quantities in the beds of these rivers.

Clark: At 9:00 we set out and proceeded nine miles past two islands and camped on the starboard side at a Mr. Piper's Landing opposite an island.

[It was] a fair afternoon. I saw a number of goslings today on the shore. The water is excessively rapid and the banks are falling in.

Wednesday, May 16, 1804:

Clark: [We] passed a remarkable coal hill on the port side, called by the French "Carbonere;" this hill appears to contain a great quantity of coal. From this hill the village of St. Charles may be seen at 12 o'clock. A number of spectators, French and Indians, flocked to the bank to see the party. This village is about one mile in length, situated on the north side of the Missouri at the foot of a hill from which it takes its name, Petit Coteau, or Little Hill. This village contains about one hundred houses, most of them small and indifferent, and about four hundred fifty inhabitants, chiefly French. These people appear poor, polite, and harmonious.

26. keelboat

Private Joseph Whitehouse: This place is an old French village situated on the north side of the Missouri. [They] are dressy, polite people and [are] Roman Catholics.

Friday, May 18, 1804:

Whitehouse: [We] passed the evening very agreeably, dancing with the French ladies, etc.

Monday, May 21, 1804:

Clark: [We spent] all the early part of the day arranging our party and procuring the different articles necessary for them at this place. [We] set out at 3:30 under three cheers from the gentlemen on the bank and proceeded three miles on to the head of the island (which is situated on the starboard side). Soon after we set out today, [we encountered] a hard wind from the west-southwest accompanied by a hard rain which lasted with short intervals all night.

Wednesday, May 23:

Whitehouse: We set out a 6:00 a.m. and proceeded on very well. [We] passed some inhabitants called Boone's[27] Settlement. [We] passed a noted place called Cave Tavern in a cliff of rocks.

Clark: Captain Lewis ascended the hill, which has peninsulas projecting in ragged points to the river, and was near falling from a peninsula of rocks three hundred feet [when] he caught [himself] at twenty feet, saving himself by the assistance of his knife.

Thursday, May 24, 1804:

Clark: [We] passed a very bad part of the river called The Devil's Raceground; this is where the current sets against some projecting rocks for half a mile on the port[28] side. [We] passed between an island and the port shore—a narrow pass. Above this island is a very bad part of the river. We attempted to pass up under the port bank, which was falling in so fast that the evident danger obliged us to cross between the starboard side and a sand bar in the middle of the river. We hove up near the head of the sand bar; the same moving and backing caused us to run on the sand.

The swiftness of the current wheeled the boat, broke our tow rope, and was nearly over-setting the boat. All hands jumped out on the upper side and bore on that side until the sand washed from under

27. Daniel Boone (Eide, p. 25)

28. left

the boat and wheeled on the next bank. By the time she wheeled a third time, [we] got a rope fast to her stern and by means of swimmers was carried to shore. When her stern was down while in the act of swinging a third time into deep water near the shore, we returned to the island where we [had] set out and ascended under the bank, which I have just mentioned as falling in.

Friday, May 25, 1804:

Clark: [We] camped at the mouth of a creek called La Charette above a small French village[29] of seven houses and as many families. [We] settled at this place to be convenient to hunt and trade with the Indians. Here we met with M. Loisel[30] immediately down from Cedar Island situated in the country of the Sioux four hundred leagues up. He gave us a good deal of information and some letters. He informed us that he saw no Indians on the river below the Poncas.

Saturday, May 26, 1804:

Detachment orders: The sergeants[31] are directed each to keep a separate journal from day to day of all passing occurrences and such other observations on the country, etc., as shall appear to them worthy of notice.

The day after tomorrow, lyed corn and grease will be issued to the party, the next day pork and flour, and the day following, Indian meal and pork. Provisions will continue to be issued to the party until further orders. No pork is to be issued when we have fresh meat on hand.

Meriwether Lewis, Captain
William Clark, Captain

Thursday, May 31, 1804:

Clark: [It] rained the greater part of last night. The wind from the west raised and blew with great force until 5:00 p.m., which obliged us to lay by.

A cajaux[32] of bearskins and peltries[33] came down from the Grand Osage; one Frenchman, one Indian, and a squaw. They had letters from the man Mr. Chouteau sent to that part of the Osage nation

---

29. near present-day Marthasville, Missouri (Schmidt, p. 16)
30. Régis Loisel, an experienced St. Louis trader with the Missouri Company (DeVoto)
31. Floyd and Ordway
32. raft
33. pelts, especially raw, undressed skins

[that had] settled on [the] Arkansas River. Mentioning that, his letter was committed to the flames, the Indians not believing that the Americans had possession of the country. They disregarded St. Louis and their supplies, etc.

Several rats of considerable size were caught in the woods today. Captain Lewis went out to the woods and found many curious plants and shrubs. One deer [was] killed this evening.

2: Summer, 1804

The water of this river, or some other cause, throws out a greater proportion of sweat than I could suppose could pass through the human body. Those men that do not work at all will wet a shirt in a few minutes and those who work, the sweat will run off in streams.

Captain William Clark,
July 6, 1804

Saturday, June 2, 1804:

Clark: George Drouillard[34] and John Shields, who we had sent with the horses by land on the north side, joined us this evening much worsted, they being absent seven days and depending on their gun. The greater part of the time [they experienced] rain. They were obliged to raft or swim many creeks. These men gave a flattering account of the country commencing below the first hill on the north side and extending parallel with the river for thirty or forty miles. The two [passed through] muddy rivers and some fine springs and streams.

Our hunters killed several deer today.

Monday, June 4, 1804:

Sergeant Charles Floyd: [It is as] beautiful a piece of land as I ever saw [with] level land on both sides.

Our hunters killed eight deer.

We came ten miles.

Tuesday, June 5, 1804:

Clark: After jerking[35] the meat killed yesterday and crossing the hunting party, we set out at 6:00. At 11:00 [we] brought to a small caissee[36] in which were two Frenchmen from eighty leagues up the Kansas River where they wintered and caught a great quantity of bea-

---

34. spelled "Drewyer" by the captains, he apparently signed his name "Drouilliard" (Bakeless, p. 31) but most historians write "Drouillard" (e.g., Ambrose, *UC*)

35. cutting meat into long, thin strips and drying in the sun or curing by exposing to smoke

36. cargo boat (Bakeless, p. 30)

ver, the greater part of which they lost by fire from the prairies. These men informed [us] that the Kansas nation is now out in the plains hunting buffalo; they hunted last winter on this river.

[We] passed a projecting rock, on which was painted a figure, and a creek, at two miles above, called Little Manitou Creek. From the painted rock [we] passed a small creek on the port side opposite a very bad sand bar of several miles in extent, which we named Sand Creek. Here my servant, York, swam to the sand bar to gather greens for our dinner; [he] returned with a sufficient quantity [of] wild cresses or tongue grass. We passed up for two miles on the port side of this sand [bar] and were obliged to return, the water uncertain and the quicksand moving. We had a fine wind but could not make use of it, our mast being broken.

We passed between two small islands in the middle of the current and round the head of three [encountered] a rapid current for one mile. [We] camped on the starboard side opposite a large island in the middle of the river. One pirogue did not get up for two hours.

Our scout discovered the fresh sign of about ten Indians. I expect that these Indians are on their way to war against the Osage nation; probably they are the Sauks.

Thursday, June 7, 1804:

Clark: A short distance above the mouth of a creek are several curious paintings and a carving on the projecting rock of limestone, inlaid with white, red and blue flint, of a very good quality. The Indians have taken of this flint great quantities.

We landed at this inscription[37] and found it a den of rattlesnakes. We had not landed three minutes before three very large snakes were observed in the crevices of the rocks and killed.

Saturday, June 9, 1804:

Clark: We got fast on a snag soon after we set out, which detained us a short time. [We] passed the upper point of the island. Several small channels ran out of the river below a bluff and prairie (called the Prairie of Arrows) where the river is confined within the width of three hundred yards.

Opposite the lower point of the second island on the starboard side, we had liked to have stove our boat in going round a snag. Her stern struck a log underwater and she swung round on the snag with her broadside to the current, exposed to the drifting timber. By the active exertions of our party, we got her off in a few minutes without

37. above Rocheport, Missouri, at the mouth of Moniteau Creek (Schmidt, p. 17)

injury and crossed to the island, where we camped. Seeing them and the banks, [we were] too uncertain to send her over.

Tuesday, June 12, 1804:

Clark: At 1:00 we brought to two caissees, one loaded with furs and peltries, the other with grease. We purchased three hundred pounds of grease, and finding that old Mr. Dorion[38] was of the party, we questioned him until it was too late to go farther and concluded to camp for the night. These people inform nothing of much information.

[We] concluded to take old Dorion back as far as the Sioux nation, with a view to get some of their chiefs to visit the President of the United States (this man being a very confidential friend of those people, he having resided with the nation twenty-odd years) and to accompany them on.

Sunday, June 17, 1804:

Clark: We set out early and proceeded on one mile and came to [in order] to make oars and repair our cable and tow rope, etc., etc., which was necessary for the boat and pirogues. [We] sent out Sergeant Pryor[39] and some men to get ash timber for oars, and sent some men to make a tow rope out of the cords of a cable which had been provided by Captain Lewis at Pittsburgh for the cable of the boat.

George Drouillard, our hunter, and one man came in with two deer and a bear, and also a young horse they had found in the prairie; this horse has been in the prairie a long time and is fat. I suppose he has been left by some war party against the Osage. This is a crossing place for the war parties against that nation from the Sauks, Iowas, and Sioux.

The party is much afflicted with boils and several have dysentery, which I contribute to the water, which is muddy.

The country about this place is beautiful on the river, rich and well-timbered on the starboard side. About two miles back, a prairie comes which is rich and interspersed with groves of timber. The country rises at seven or eight miles still farther back and is rolling. On the port side the highlands and prairie come in [to] the bank of the river and continue back, well-watered and abounding in deer, elk, and bear.

The ticks and mosquitoes are very troublesome.

---

38. Pierre Dorion, Sr., a fifty-five-year-old Frenchman with a Yankton Sioux wife and fluent in the Sioux language (DeVoto)

39. Nathaniel Pryor

Friday, June 29, 1804:

Clark: Orderly Book:

Ordered—A court martial will sit this day at 11:00, to consist of five members, for the trial of John Collins and Hugh Hall, confined on charges exhibited against them by Sergeant Floyd.

The court convened agreeable to order and proceeded to the trial of the prisoners, viz.:[40]

John Collins [is] charged "with getting drunk on his post this morning out of whiskey put under his charge as a sentinel, and for suffering Hugh Hall to draw whiskey out of the said barrel intended for the party."

To this charge the prisoner pled not guilty.

The court, after mature deliberation on the evidence adduced, etc., is of the opinion that the prisoner is guilty of the charge exhibited against him, and does therefore sentence him to receive one hundred lashes on his bare back.

Hugh Hall was brought before the court charged "with taking whiskey out of a keg this morning, which whiskey was stored on the bank (and under the charge of the guard), contrary to all order, rule, or regulation."

To this charged the prisoner pled guilty.

The court finds the prisoner guilty and sentences him to receive fifty lashes on his bear back.

Saturday, June 30, 1804:

Clark: Deer [are] to be seen in every direction and their tracks are as plenty as hogs about a farm.

Wednesday, July 4, 1804:

Clark: The plains of this country[41] are covered with copses of trees spreading their lofty branches over pools, springs, or brooks of fine water. Groups of shrubs covered with the most delicious fruit [are] to be seen in every direction and nature appears to have exerted herself to beautify the scenery by flowers delicately and highly flavored, raised above the grass, which strikes and perfumes the sensation.

Floyd: A snake bit Joseph Field on the side of the foot, which swelled much. [We] applied barks[42] to cure [it].

---

40. abbreviation for *videlicet:* that is, or "namely; used to introduce examples, lists, or items

41. near Doniphan, Kansas (Schmidt, p. 24)

42. probably a poultice of Peruvian bark (DeVoto)

[We] passed a creek on the south side about fifteen yards wide coming out of an extensive prairie. As the creek has no name and this day is the Fourth of July, we named this Independence Creek.

Friday, July 6, 1804:

Sergeant John Ordway: We set out early this morning. The weather is very warm. The sweat pours off the men in streams. A whippoorwill perched on the boat for a short time.

Clark: The water of this river, or some other cause, throws out a greater proportion of sweat than I could suppose could pass through the human body. Those men that do not work at all will wet a shirt in a few minutes and those who work, the sweat will run off in streams.

Thursday, July 12, 1804:

Floyd: [We] set out early this morning and proceeded on. [We] came to [at] about 12:00 p.m. for the purpose of resting one or two days.[43] Our object in delaying here is to take some observations and rest the men, who are much fatigued.

Arms and ammunition [were] inspected and all [were] in good order.

The men are all sick.

Clark: Orderly Book:

The commanding officers constituted themselves a court martial for the trial of such prisoners as are guilty of capital crimes and, under the rules of war, punishable by DEATH.

Alexander Willard was brought forward charged with lying down and sleeping on his post whilst a sentinel on the night of the 11th instant[44] (by John Ordway, Sergeant of the Guard).

To this charge the prisoner pleads guilty of lying down and not guilty of going to sleep.

The court, after duly considering the evidence adduced, is of the opinion that the prisoner, Alexander Willard, is guilty of every part of the charge [and] does sentence him to receive one hundred lashes on his bare back, at four different times.

Saturday, July 14, 1804:

Clark: [We had] some hard showers of rain this morning [which] prevented our setting out until 7:00.

---

43. south of present-day Rulo, Nebraska, at the mouth of the Big Nemaha River; the island on which they camped is now gone (Schmidt, p. 24)

44. the current month

At 7:30, the atmosphere became suddenly darkened by a black and dismal-looking cloud. At the time we were in a situation (not to be bettered) near the upper point of the Sand Island, on which we lay, and the opposite shore. The bank was falling in and lined with snags as far as we could see down.

In this situation the storm, which passed over an open plain from the northeast, struck our boat on the starboard quarter and would have thrown her up on Sand Island [and] dashed [her] to pieces in an instant had not the party leaped out on the port side and kept her off with assistance of the anchor and cable until the storm was over. The waves washed over her windward side and she would have filled with water if the lockers had not been covered with tarpaulin, [which] threw the water and prevented any quantity [from] getting into the bilge of the boat.

In this situation we continued about forty minutes when the storm suddenly ceased and the river became instantaneously as smooth as glass. The two pirogues during this storm were in a similar situation with the boat about half a mile above.

Several men [are] unwell with boils, felons, etc.

The river falls a little.[45]

Thursday, July 19, 1804:

Whitehouse: As we came along shore, there were two large catfish [that] had hold of each other. One of the Frenchmen shot the two [with] the first shot.

The men pulled a great quantity of wild cherries [and] put them in the barrel of whiskey.

[We] rowed twelve miles.

Friday, July 20, 1804:

Clark: It is worthy of observation to mention that our party has been much healthier on the voyage than parties of the same number are in any other situation. Tumors have been troublesome to them all.

From this evening's encampment a man may walk to the Pawnee village on the south bank of the Platte River in two days and to the Otos in one day. All these Indians are situated on the south bank of the Platte River. As these Indians are now out in the prairies following and hunting the buffalo, I fear we will not see them.

---

45. near Nebraska's Indian Cave State Park (Schmidt, p. 24)

Saturday, July 21, 1804:

Clark: [We] set out early under a gentle breeze from the southeast [and] proceeded on very well. [We] passed a willow island on the port side opposite a bad sand bar. Some highlands covered with timber [were on the] port side. In this hill is limestone and cemented rock of shale, etc. In high water, the opposite side is cut through by several small channels forming small islands. A large sand bar [is] opposite the hill.

At 7:00 the wind lulled and it commenced raining. [We] arrived at the lower mouth of the great River Platte[46] at 10:00, about three miles above the hill of woodland. The same range of highland continues within three-fourths of a mile of the mouth below.

This great river, being much more rapid than the Missouri, forces its current against the opposite shore. The current of this river comes with great velocity, rolling its sands into the Missouri, filling up its bed and compelling it to encroach on the north shore. We found great difficulty in passing around the sand at the mouth of this river.

Captain Lewis and I, with six men in a pirogue, went up this great river Platte about two miles. [We] found the current very rapid, rolling over sands, passing through different channels, none of them more than five or six feet deep and about nine hundred yards wide at the mouth. I am told by one of our party who wintered two winters on this river that "it is much wider above, and does not rise more than five or six feet." [It] spreads very wide and from its rapidity and rolling sands cannot be navigated with boats or pirogues.

The Indians pass this river in skin boats which are flat and will not turn over. The Otos, a small nation, reside on the south side ten leagues up [and] the Pawnees on the same side five leagues higher up.

About ten leagues up this river on the south side, a small river comes into the Platte called Salt River. The water [is] so brackish that it can't be drunk at some seasons.

We proceeded on to get a good place to camp and delay a few days. [We] camped for the night on the port side.

A very hard wind [blew] from the northwest.

I went on shore, starboard side, and proceeded up one mile through high bottom open land.

A great number of wolves [were] about this evening.

---

46. near today's Plattsmouth, Missouri (Schmidt, p. 25)

Sunday, July 22, 1804:

Clark: [We] came to and formed a camp on the starboard side[47] above a small willow island and opposite the first hill which approached the river on the port side and [was] covered with timber of oak, walnut, elm, etc., etc.

This being a good situation and much nearer the Otos town than the mouth of the Platte, we concluded to delay at this place a few days and send for some of the chiefs of that nation to let them know of the change of government, the wishes of our government to cultivate friendship with them, the objects of our journey, and to present them with a flag and some small presents.

Some of our provisions in the French pirogue being wet, it became necessary to dry them a few days.

The wind [blew] hard from the northwest.

Five deer [were] killed today.

The river rose a little.

Monday, July 23, 1804:

Clark: [It was] a fair morning.

[We] set a party to look for timber for oars [and] two parties to hunt.

At 11:00 [we] sent off George Drouillard and Pierre Cruzatte[48] with some tobacco to invite the Otos, if at their town, and Pawnees, if they saw them, to come and talk with us at our camp, etc., etc. (At this season the Indians on this river are in the prairies hunting the buffalo, but from some signs of hunters near this place and the plains being on fire near their towns, [we] induce a belief that they, this nation, have returned to get some green corn or roasting ears.)

[We] raised a flagstaff, sunned and dried our provisions, etc.

I commenced copying a map of the river below to send to the President [of the] United States.

Five deer [were] killed today.

One man [has] a tumor on his breast.

[We] prepared our camp; the men put their arms in order.

Wednesday, July 25, 1804:

Clark: White Catfish Camp - [It was] a fair morning.

Several hunters [went] out today.

---

47. across the river from present-day Bellevue, Nebraska (Schmidt, p. 26)

48. son of a French father and an Omaha mother; fluent in the Omaha language; a skilled waterman (Ambrose, *UC*, p. 138)

At 2:00 Drouillard and Pierre [Cruzatte] returned from the Oto village and informed [us] that no Indians were at their town. They saw some fresh signs of a small party but could not find them.

Two deer [were] killed today. One turkey [and] several grouse [were] seen today.

Thursday, July 26, 1804:

Clark: White Catfish Camp - The wind [was] blustering and hard from the south all day which blew the clouds of sand in such a manner that I could not complete my map in the tent. The boat rolled in such a manner that I could do nothing in that and was compelled to go to the woods and combat the mosquitoes.

I opened the tumor of a man on the left breast which discharged half a pint.

Five beaver [were] caught near the camp, the flesh of which we made use of.

This evening we found very pleasant.

Only one deer [was] killed today.

Friday, July 27, 1804:

Clark: White Catfish Camp - I took one man, Reubin Field, and walked on shore[49] with a view of examining some mounds on the port side of the river. These mounds I found to be of different height, shape and size, some composed of sand, some earth and sand. The highest [was] next to the river, all of which covered about two hundred acres of land in a circular form. On the side from the river [were] a low bottom and small pond. The Otos formerly lived here. I did not get to the boat until after night.

[There was] a beautiful breeze from the northwest this evening which would have been very agreeable had the mosquitoes been tolerably pacific but they were raging all night, some about the size of house flies.

Saturday, July 28, 1804:

Clark: The guard came in and informed [me] they heard two guns to the southwest.

The highland approaches in the first bend to the left. We camped on the starboard side below the point of an island.[50]

---

49. at present-day Omaha, Nebraska (Schmidt, p. 27)
50. just north of today's Council Bluffs, Iowa (Schmidt, p. 27)

George Drouillard brought in a Missouri Indian which he met while hunting in the prairie. This Indian is one of the few remaining of that nation and lives with the Otos. His camp [is] about four miles from the river. He informs [us] that the "great gang" of the nation was hunting the buffalo in the plains. His party was small, consisting only of about twenty lodges. Miles farther [there was] another camp where there was a Frenchman who lived in the nation. This Indian appeared sprightly and appeared to make use of the same pronunciation as the Osage, calling a chief "Inea."

Sunday, July 29, 1804:

Clark: [We] sent a Frenchman, La Liberté,[51] with the Indian to [the] Oto camp to invite the Indians to meet us on the river above.

We stopped to dine under some high trees near the highland on the port side. In a few minutes [we] caught three very large catfish, one nearly white. These fish are in great plenty on the sides of the river and very fat. A quart of oil came out of the surplus fat of one of these fish.

Above this highland and on the starboard side [we] passed much falling timber, apparently the ravages of a dreadful hurricane which had passed obliquely across the river from northwest to southeast, about twelve months since. Many trees were broken off near the ground, the trunks of which were sound and four feet in diameter.

Monday, July 30, 1804:

Clark: [We] set out this morning early [and] proceeded on to a clear open prairie on the port side on a rise of about seventy feet higher than the bottom, which is also a prairie (both forming bluffs to the river) of high grass, plum bush and grapes, etc., and situated above high water. In a small grove of timber at the foot of the rising ground between these two prairies and below the bluffs of the high prairie, we came to and formed a camp,[52] intending to wait the return of the Frenchman and Indians. The white horse which we found near the Kansas River died last night.

[We] posted our guard and sent out four men. Captain Lewis and I went up the bank and walked a short distance in the high prairie. This prairie is covered with grass of ten or twelve inches in height, [the] soil [is] of good quality, and at the distance of about a mile still farther back, the country rises about eighty or ninety feet higher and is one continuous plain as far as can be seen. From the bluff on the second

---

51. an employee of the party

52. beneath the bluff at present-day Fort Atkinson (Nebraska) State Historic Park; since 1804, the river has shifted a few miles east (Schmidt, p. 28)

rise immediately above our camp, the most beautiful prospect of the river up and down and the country opposite presented itself which I ever beheld. The river meandered the open and beautiful plains interspersed with groves of timber, and each point [was] covered with tall timber such as willow, cotton, some mulberry, elm, sycamore, linden, and ash. (The groves contain hickory, walnut, coffee nut, and oak, in addition.)

Joseph Field killed and brought in an animal called by the French "brarow"[53] and by the Pawnees "cho car tooch." This animal burrows in the ground and feeds on flesh (prairie dogs), bugs, and vegetables. His shape and size is like that of a beaver; his head, mouth, etc., are like a dog's with short ears; his tail and hair like that of a ground hog, and longer and lighter. His belly is white and the hair short [with] a white streak from his nose to his shoulders. The toenails of his forefeet are an inch and three-quarters long and [the] feet [are] large. The nails of his hind feet [are] three-fourths of an inch long; the hind feet [are] small and [the] toes crooked. His legs are short and, when he moves, [they are] just sufficient to raise his body above the ground. He is of the bear species. We have his skin stuffed.

Joseph and Reubin Field did not return this evening.

Several men [have] very bad boils.

Catfish are caught in any part of the river. Turkeys, geese, and a beaver [were] killed and caught.

Everything [is] in prime order [and the] men [are] in high spirits.

[It is] a fair, still evening.

[A] great number of mosquitoes [are about] this evening.

Tuesday, July 31, 1804:

Floyd: We lay by for to see the Indians who we expect [are] here to see the captains.

I am very sick and have been for some time but have recovered my health again.

The Indians have not come yet.

This place is called Council Bluffs.

Wednesday, August 1, 1804:

Clark: [It was] a fair morning.

[We] dispatched two men after the horses [that were] lost yesterday [and] one man back to the place from which the messenger was sent for the Otos to see if any Indians were or had been there since our

---

53. actually, *blaireau*, French for "badger"

departure. He returned and informed [us] that no person had been there since we left.

The prairie, which is situated below our camp, is above the high water level and richly covered with plums, currants (like those of the U.S.), raspberries, and grapes of different kinds. [It] also produces a variety of plants and flowers not common in the United States.

The Indians [have] not yet arrived. We fear something amiss with our messenger or them.

This being my birthday, I ordered a saddle of fat venison, an elk fleece, and a beavertail to be cooked, and a dessert of cherries, plums, raspberries, currants, and grapes of a superior quality.

Thursday, August 2, 1804:

Clark: The two men, Drouillard and Colter,[54] returned with the horses loaded with elk. They found these horses about twelve miles in a southerly direction from camp.

At sunset, Mr. Fairfong[55] and a part of the Oto and Missouri nation came to camp. Among these Indians, six were chiefs (not the principal chiefs). Captain Lewis and I met [with] these Indians and informed them we were glad to see them and would speak to them tomorrow. [We] sent them some roasted meat, pork, flour, and meal. In return, they sent us watermelons.

Every man [was] on his guard and ready for anything.

Friday, August 3, 1804:

Clark: [We] made up a small present for these people in proportion to their consequence and a package with a medal to accompany a speech for the grand chief.

After breakfast we collected these Indians under an awning of our mainsail. In the presence of our party, [we] paraded and delivered a long speech to them expressive of our journey, the wishes of our government, some advice to them, and directions [on] how they were to conduct themselves. The principal chief for the nation[56] being absent, we sent him the speech, flag, medal, and some clothes. After hearing what they had to say, [we] delivered a medal of Second Grade, one for the Otos and one for the Missouri, and presented four medals of a Third Grade to the inferior chiefs, two for each tribe. (Those two parts of nations, Otos and Missouri, now residing together, are of about two

---

54. Private John Colter
55. a trader residing among the Otos (DeVoto)
56. Little Thief (Ambrose, *UC*, p. 156)

hundred fifty men, the Otos composing two-thirds and the Missouri one-third part.)

These chiefs all delivered a speech acknowledging their approbation to the speech and promising to pursue the advice and directions given them [and] that they were happy to find that they had fathers which might be depended on, etc.

We gave them a canister of powder and a bottle of whiskey and delivered a few presents to the whole after giving a breechclout,[57] some paint, gartering, and a medal to those we made chiefs. After Captain Lewis's shooting the air gun[58] a few shots (which astonished these natives), we set out and proceeded on five miles on a direct line.

The man La Liberté, whom we sent for the Otos, has not come up. He left the Otos town one day before the Indians. This man has either tired his horse or lost himself in the plains. Some Indians are to hunt for him.

The situation of our last camp, Council Bluffs or Handsome Prairie (twenty-five days from this to Santa Fe), appears to be a very proper place for a trading establishment and fortification. The soil of the bluff [is] well adapted for brick. [There is] a great deal of timber above in the two points, and many other advantages of a small nature and, I am told, central to several nations, e.g., one day's march from the Oto town, one day and a half from the great Pawnee village, two days from the Omaha towns, two and one-fourth days from the Loups village, and convenient to the country through which bands of the Sioux hunt. Perhaps no other situation is as well-calculated for a trading establishment. The air is pure and healthy so far as we can judge.

Ordway: This morning the two captains held a council with the [Oto] Indians and made six chiefs under the American government. They all received their medals and other presents with great kindness and thankfulness. They made some very sensible speeches, smoked, and drank with us. [They] shook hands and parted.

The prepared speech that the captains repeated to each tribe they encountered:

Children. Your old fathers, the French and the Spaniards, have gone beyond the great lake towards the rising sun, from whence they never intend returning to visit their former red children.

Children. The great chief of the seventeen great nations of America, impelled by his parental regard for his newly adopted children on

57. breechcloth or loincloth

58. a long-barreled rifle that fired by compressed air, like a BB gun

the troubled waters, has sent us out to clear the road and make it a road of peace.

Children. Know that the great chief who has offered you the hand of unalterable friendship is the great Chief of the Seventeen Nations of America, whose cities are as numerous as the stars of the heavens, and whose people, like the grass of your plains, cover the wide, extended country to where the land ends and the sun rises from the face of the great waters. He will serve you and not deceive you.

Children. You are to live in peace with all the white men, neither wage war against the red men, your neighbors. Injure not the persons of any traders who visit you under the protection of your Great Father's flag.

Children. Do these things which your Great Father advises and be happy lest by one false step you should bring down upon your nation the displeasure of your Great Father who could consume you as the fire consumes the grass of the plains.

Children. Follow his counsels and you will have nothing to fear because the Great Spirit will smile upon your nation and, in future ages, will make you outnumber the trees of the forest.

Saturday, August 4, 1804:

Clark: [We] proceeded on [and] passed through between snags which were quit across the river, the channel [being] confined within two hundred yards. [On] one side [was] a sand point [and] on the other a bend. The banks [were] washing away and trees [were] falling in constantly for one mile.[59] Above this place are the remains of an old trading establishment [on the] port side where Pierre Cruzatte, one of our hands, stayed two years and traded with the Omaha.

Reed,[60] a man who went back to camp for his knife, has not joined us.

Here the highlands are some distance from the river on both sides and at this place the highlands are at least twelve or fifteen miles apart. The range of highland on the starboard side appears to contain some timber. That on the port side appears to be entirely clear of anything but what is common in an open plain. Some scattering timber or wood is to be seen in the ravines and where the creeks pass into the hill. The points and wetlands contain tall timber back of the willows which are generally situated back of a large sand bar from the points.

---

59. near present-day De Soto National Wildlife Refuge in Nebraska (Schmidt, p. 29)
60. Private Moses B. Reed

Monday, August 6, 1804:

Clark: Reed has not yet come up; neither has La Liberté, the Frenchman who we sent to the Indian camps a few miles below Council Bluffs.

Tuesday, August 7, 1804:

Clark: [We] set out late this morning [with the] wind from the north.

At 1:00 [we] dispatched George Drouillard, Reubin Field, William Bratton, and Francis Labiche back after the deserter Reed with [the] order [that] if he did not give up peacefully to put him to death, etc.; to go to the Oto's village and enquire for La Liberté and bring him to the Omaha village; also, with a speech on the occasion to the Otos and Missouri and directing a few of their chiefs to come to the Omaha and we would make peace between them and the Omaha and the Sioux; [and] a string of wampum[61] and a carrot of tobacco.

[We] proceeded on and camped on the starboard side.

Monday, August 13, 1804:

Clark: We formed a camp on a sand bar on the port side and detached Sergeant Ordway, Pierre Cruzatte, George Shannon, Werner,[62] and Carson to the Omaha village[63] with a flag and some tobacco to invite the nation to see and talk with us tomorrow.

We took some lunar observations this evening.

The air [was] pleasant.

Tuesday, August 14, 1804:

Clark: The men sent to the Omaha town last evening have not returned. We conclude to send a spy to know the cause of their delay.

At about 12:00 the party returned and informed us that they could not find the Indians nor any fresh sign; those people have not returned from their buffalo hunt. Those people, having no houses, no corn, or anything more than the graves of their ancestors to attach them to the old village, continue in pursuit of the buffalo longer than others who have greater attachments to their native village.

The ravages of the smallpox (which swept off four hundred men and women and children in proportion) have reduced this nation not

---

61. beads of polished shells strung in strands, belts, or sashes

62. Private William Werner

63. Tonwontonga, or "Large Village," one mile north of today's Homer, Nebraska (Schmidt, p. 30)

exceeding three hundred men and left them to the insults of their weaker neighbors, which before were glad to be on friendly terms with them. I am told [that] when this fatal malady was among them, they carried their frenzy to very extraordinary lengths, not only of burning their village but they put their wives and children to death with a view of their all going together to some better country. They bury their dead on the top of high hills and raise mounds on the top of them. The cause or way these people took the smallpox is uncertain; the most probable [is] from some other nation by means of a war party.

Wednesday, August 15, 1804:

Clark: Camp three miles northeast of the Omaha village - In my absence, Captain Lewis sent Mr. Dorion, the Sioux interpreter, and three men to examine a fire which threw up an immense smoke from the prairies on the northeast side of the river and at no great distance from camp. The object of this party was to find some bands of Sioux which the interpreter thought were near the smoke and get them to come in.

In the evening this party returned and informed [us] that the fire arose from some trees which had been left burning by a small party of Sioux who had passed several days ago. The wind setting from that point blew the smoke from that point over our camp.

Our party [is] all in [good] health and spirits.

The men sent to the Otos and in pursuit of the deserter Reed have not yet returned or joined our party.

Friday, August 17, 1804:

Clark: At 6:00 this evening Labiche, one of the party sent to the Otos, joined [us] and informed [us] that the party was behind with one of the deserters, Moses B. Reed, and the three principal chiefs of the nations. La Liberté they caught, but he deceived them and got away.

The object of these chiefs coming forward is to make a peace with the Omaha through us. As the Omaha are not at home, this great object cannot be accomplished at this time. [We] set the prairies on fire to bring the Omaha and Sioux if any were near, this being the usual signal.

Saturday, August 18, 1804:

Clark: [It was] a fine morning. [The] wind [was] from the southeast.

In the after part of the day, the party with the Indians arrived.[64] We met them under a shade near the boat and after a short talk we gave them provisions to eat and proceeded to the trial of Reed.

He confessed that he "deserted and stole a public rifle, shot pouch, powder, and ball" and requested [that] we would be as favorable with him as we could consistent with our oaths—which we were, and only sentenced him to run the gauntlet four times through the party and that each man with nine switches should punish him, and for him not to be considered in [the] future as one of the party.

The three principal chiefs petitioned for [the] pardon of this man. After we explained the injury such men could do [to] them by false representations, and [after] explaining the customs of our country, they were all satisfied with the propriety of the sentence and were witness to the punishment, after which we had some talk with the chiefs about the origin of the war between them and the Omaha, etc., etc.

Captain Lewis's birthday [was today]. The evening was closed with an extra gill[65] of whiskey and a dance until 11:00.

Sunday, August 19, 1804:

Clark: The main chief breakfasted with us and begged for a sun glass.[66] These people are all naked, covered only with breechclouts, blankets, or buffalo robes, the flesh side painted with different colors and figures.

At 10:00 we assembled the chiefs and warriors, nine in number, under an awning and Captain Lewis explained the speech sent to the nation from Council Bluffs by Mr. Fairfong. The three chiefs and all the men or warriors made short speeches approving the advice and council their Great Father had sent them, and concluded by giving themselves some credit for their acts.

We then brought out the presents and gave all some small articles and eight carrots of tobacco. We gave one small medal to one of the chiefs and a certificate to the others of their good intentions.

One of these Indians, after receiving his certificate, delivered it again to me. Big Blue Eyes, the chief, petitioned for the certificate again. We would not give [him] the certificate, but rebuked them very roughly for having in object goods, and not peace, with their neighbors. This language they did not like at first, but at length all petitioned for us to give back the certificate to Big Blue Eyes. He came forward

64. a few miles downriver from Dakota City, Nebraska (Schmidt, p. 32)
65. four ounces
66. magnifying glass

and made a plausible excuse. I then gave the certificate to the great chief to bestow it to the most worthy; they gave it to him.

We showed them many curiosities and the air gun, which they were much astonished at. These people begged much for whiskey.

Sergeant Floyd is taken very bad all at once with a bilious colic.[67] We attempt to relieve him without success as yet. He gets worse and we are much alarmed at his situation; all attention to him.

Gass: This day Sergeant Floyd became very sick and remained so all night. He was seized with a complaint somewhat like a violent colic.

Wednesday, August 20, 1804:

Clark: Sergeant Floyd [is] much weaker and no better. [He has] no pulse and nothing will stay a moment on his stomach. [We] passed two islands and at the first bluff on the starboard side, Sergeant Floyd died with a great deal of composure. Before his death, he said to me, "I am going away. I want you to write me a letter."

We buried him on the top of the bluff a half-mile below a small river, to which we gave his name. He was buried with the honors of war [and] much lamented.

A cedar post with the name:

Sergeant C. Floyd

died here

20th of August

1804

was fixed at the head of his grave. This man at all times gave us proof of his firmness and determined resolution to do service to his country and honor to himself.

After paying all the honor to our deceased brother, we camped in the mouth of Floyd's River, about thirty yards wide.

[It was] a beautiful evening.

Whitehouse: He was laid out in the most decent manner possible. We dug a grave on the top of a round knob[68] and buried the deceased with the honors of war. The funeral ceremony [was] performed, etc. We named this hill Sergeant Floyd's Bluff.[69]

---

67. which suggests a perforated appendix (Chuinard; DeVoto; Ambrose, *UC*, p. 160)
68. now marked by the Sergeant Floyd Monument in Sioux City, Iowa (Schmidt, p. 33)

Friday, August 22, 1804:

Clark: At three miles we landed at a bluff where the two men sent with the horses were waiting with two deer. By examination this bluff contained alum, copper, cobalt, pyrites, an alum rock soft, and sandstone.

Captain Lewis, in proving the quality of those minerals, was near poisoning himself by the fumes and taste of the cobalt, which had the appearance of soft isinglass. Copper and alum are very poisonous. Captain Lewis took a dose of salts to work off the effects of the arsenic.[70]

Thursday, August 23, 1804:

Clark: I walked on shore[71] and killed a fat buck.

Joseph Field [was] sent out to hunt. [He] came to the boat and informed [us] that he had killed a buffalo in the plain ahead. Captain Lewis took twelve men and had the buffalo brought to the boat in the next bend to the starboard side.

The wind blew hard [from the] west and raised the sands off the bar in such clouds that we could scarcely see. This sand, being fine and very light, stuck to everything it touched and in the plain for a half a mile every spire of grass was covered with the sand or dust.

Friday, August 24, 1804:

Clark: In a northerly direction from the mouth of this creek in an immense plain, a high hill[72] is situated and appears [to be] of a conic form and, by the different nations of Indians in this quarter, is supposed to be the residence of devils that are in human form with remarkably large heads and about eighteen inches high, [and] that are very watchful and are armed with sharp arrows with which they can kill at a great distance. They are said to kill all persons who are so hardy as to attempt to approach the hill.

They state that tradition informs them that many Indians have suffered by these little people and, among others, three Omaha men fell as sacrifice to their merciless fury not many years since. So much do the Omaha, Sioux, Otos, and other neighboring nations believe this

---

69. Floyd's death was the only fatality of the expedition. Gass was appointed [actually, elected; the first election held west of the Mississippi (Ambrose, *UC*, p. 161)] sergeant to replace the rank. Robert Frazier was then enlisted in the permanent party to fill the vacancy. (DeVoto)

70. camped for the night near present-day Elk Point, South Dakota (Schmidt, p. 36)

71. near present-day Vermillion, South Dakota (Schmidt, p. 36)

72. Spirit Mound, six miles north of Vermillion (Schmidt, p. 37)

fable that no consideration is sufficient to induce them to approach the hill.

Saturday, August 25, 1804:

Clark: [It was] a cloudy morning.

Captain Lewis and I concluded to go and see the mound which was viewed with such terror by all the different nations in this quarter. We selected nine men to go along. From the top of this highland, the country is level and open as far as can be seen except [for] some few rises at a great distance and the mound, which the Indians call Mountain of Little People, or Spirits.

At four miles we crossed the creek, twenty-three yards wide in an extensive valley, and continued on at two miles further. Our dog[73] was so heated and fatigued we were obliged to send him back to the creek.

At 12:00 we arrived at the hill. Captain Lewis [was] much fatigued from the heat—the day it being very hot and he being in a debilitated state from the precautions he was obliged to take to prevent the effects of the cobalt and mineral substance which had like to have poisoned him two days ago. His want of water, and several of the men complaining of great thirst, determined us to make for the first water. We proceeded on to the place [where] we camped last night and stayed all night.

The regular form of this hill would in some measure justify a belief that it owed its origin to the hand of man, but as the earth and loose pebbles and other substances of which it is composed bore an exact resemblance to the steep ground which borders on the creek in its neighborhood, we concluded it was most probably the production of nature.

The only remarkable characteristic of this hill admitting it to be a natural production is that it is insulated or separated a considerable distance from any other, which is very unusual in the natural order or disposition of the hills.

The surrounding plains are open, void of timber, and level to a great extent, hence the wind, from whatever quarter it may blow, drives with unusual force over the naked plains and against this hill. The insects of various kinds are thus involuntarily driven to the mound by the force of the wind or fly to its leeward side for shelter. The small birds whose food they are consequently resort in great numbers to this place in search of them, particularly the small brown martin of which we saw a vast number hovering on the leeward side of the hill. When we approached them in the act of catching these insects, they were so

73. a black Newfoundland, named Seaman

gentle that they did not quit the place until we had arrived within a few feet of them.

One evidence which the Indians give for believing this place to be the residence of some unusual spirits is that they frequently discover a large assemblage of birds about this mound. [This] is, in my opinion, a sufficient proof to produce in the savage mind a confident belief of all the properties [to] which they ascribe it.

From the top of this mound we beheld a most beautiful landscape. Numerous herds of buffalo were seen feeding in various directions. The plain to north northwest and northeast extends without interruption as far as can be seen.

The boat under the command of Sergeant Pryor proceeded on in our absence (after jerking the elk I killed yesterday) [for] six miles and camped on the port side.

Reubin Field brought in five deer. George Shannon killed an elk buck.

[There was] some rain this evening.

We set the prairies on fire as a signal for the Sioux to come to the river.

Tuesday, August 28, 1804:

Clark: John Shields and Joseph Field, who were sent back to look for Shannon and the horses, joined us and informed [us] that Shannon had the horses and that they could not overtake him. This man not being a first-rate hunter, we determined to send one man[74] in pursuit of him with some provisions.[75]

Thursday, August 30, 1804:

Whitehouse: About 9:00 the Indians were brought across the river in our pirogue. Our captains counseled with them, read a speech to them, and made five of them chiefs, and gave them all some merchandise, etc., etc. They received them very thankfully, divided them out amongst themselves, and played on their jews'-harps, sang, etc.

Captain Lewis shot his air gun, told them that there was medicine in her, and that she would do great execution. They were all amazed at the curiosity.

---

74. Private John Colter (DeVoto)
75. they camped downstream from today's Gavins Point Dam (Schmidt, p. 38)

3: Fall, 1804

The chief said [that] he had warriors, too, and if we were to go on, they would follow us and kill [us] and take the whole of us by degrees.

Sergeant John Ordway,
September 25, 1804

Tuesday, September 4, 1804:

Ordway: The water[76] shoots into the Missouri very swiftly and has thrown the sand out, which makes a sand bar and shoals from the mouth a considerable distance.

We saw two deer and large flocks of geese up the mouth of this river.

Thursday, September 6, 1804:

Ordway: Colter came to the boat. [He] had not found Shannon.

Friday, September 7, 1804:

Ordway: They attempted to drown several of these prairie dogs out of their holes, but they caught but one, which they brought in alive. Shields killed a prairie dog, which was cooked for the captains' dinner. They are a curious animal.

Tuesday, September 11, 1804:

Clark: He[77] shot away what few bullets he had with him. Thus a man had liked to have starved to death in a land of plenty for the want of bullets or something to kill his meat.

---

76. of the Niobrara River (Schmidt, p. 40)
77. Shannon

Friday, September 14, 1804:

Ordway: John Shields killed a very large white rabbit or hare[78] of a different description that anyone ever [has] yet seen in the States.

Captain Clark joined us. [He] had killed a curious animal resembling a goat. It was three feet high [and] resembles a deer in some parts. The legs [are] like a deer, [the] feet like a goat, [and] horns like a goat, only forked.[79] Such an animal was never yet known in [the] United States.

The captain had the skins of the hare and goat stuffed in order to send back to the city of Washington, the bones and all.

Sunday, September 16, 1804:

Lewis: This morning [we] set out at an early hour. [We] came to at one and a half after 7:00 a.m. on the port side shore, one and one-fourth miles above the mouth of a small creek, which we named Corvus,[80] in consequence of having killed a beautiful bird of that genus near it.

Monday, September 17, 1804:

Lewis: Having for many days past confined myself to the boat, I determined to devote this day to amuse myself on shore with my gun and view the interior of the country lying between the river and Corvus Creek.[81] Accordingly, before sunrise, I set out with six of my best hunters, two of whom I dispatched to the lower side of Corvus Creek, two with orders to hunt the bottoms and woodland on the river, while I retained two others to accompany me in the intermediate country.

One-quarter of a mile in rear of our camp, which was situated in a fine open grove of cottonwood, [we] passed a grove of plum trees loaded with fruit and now ripe. [I] observed but little difference between this fruit and that of a similar kind common to the Atlantic states. The trees are smaller and more thickly set. This forest of plum trees garnishes a plain about twenty feet more elevated than that on which we were encamped.

This plain extends with the same breadth from the creek below to the distance of near three miles above, parallel with the river, and it is entirely occupied by the burrows of the barking squirrel[82] heretofore described. This animal appears here in infinite numbers. The shortness

78. white-tailed jackrabbit (Ambrose, *UC*, p. 166)
79. pronghorn (Ambrose, *UC*, p. 166)
80. the Latin designation for the black-billed magpie (Ambrose, *UC*, p. 167)
81. at present-day Oacoma, South Dakota (Schmidt, p. 42)
82. prairie dog (DeVoto)

and verdure of [the] grass gives the plain the appearance throughout its whole extent of [a] beautiful bowling green in fine order; its aspect is southeast.

A great number of wolves of the small kind, hawks, and some polecats[83] were to be seen. I presume that these animals feed on this squirrel.

[I] found the countryside in every direction for about three miles [to be] intersected with deep ravines and steep irregular hills of one hundred to two hundred feet high. At the tops of these hills the country breaks of as usual into a fine level plain extending as far as the eye can reach.

From this plain I had an extensive view of the river below and the irregular hills which border the opposite sides of the river and creek. The surrounding country had been burned about a month before and young grass has now sprung up to a height of four inches, presenting the live green of the spring. To the west, a high range of hills stretch across the country from north to south and appeared distant about twenty miles. They are not very extensive as I could plainly observe their rise and termination. No rock appeared on them and the sides were covered with verdure similar to that of the plains.

This scenery, already rich, pleasing and beautiful, was still further heightened by immense herds of buffalo, deer, elk, and antelope which we saw in every direction feeding on the hills and plains. I do not think I exaggerate when I estimate the number of buffalo which could be comprehended at one view to amount to three thousand. My object was, if possible, to kill a female antelope, having already procured a male.

I pursued my route on this plain to the west flanked by my two hunters until eight in the morning, when I made the signal for them to come to me, which they did shortly after. We rested ourselves about half an hour and regaled ourselves on half a biscuit each and some jerks of elk, which we had taken the precaution to put in our pouches in the morning before we set out, and drank of the water of a small pool which had collected on this plain from the rains which had fallen some days before. We had now, after various windings in pursuit of several herds of antelope which we had seen on our way, made the distance of about eight miles from our camp.

We found the antelope extremely shy and watchful insomuch that we had been unable to get a shot at them. I had this day an opportunity of witnessing the agility and the superior fleetness of this animal, which was to me really astonishing. I had pursued and twice surprised a small herd of seven. In the first instance they did not discover me

83. skunks

distinctly and therefore did not run at full speed, though they took care before they rested to gain an elevated point where it was impossible to approach them under cover except in one direction, and that happened to be in the direction from which the wind blew towards them. [As] bad as the chance to approach them was, I made the best of my way towards them, frequently peeping over the ridge with which I took care to conceal myself from their view. The male, of which there was but one, frequently encircled the summit of the hill on which the females stood in a group as if to look out for the approach of danger. I got within about two hundred paces of them when they smelled me and fled.

I gained the top of the eminence on which they stood as soon as possible, from where I had an extensive view of the country. The antelope, which had disappeared in a steep ravine, now appeared at the distance of about three miles on the side of a ridge which passed obliquely across me and extended about four miles.

As soon as these antelope gained the distance at which they had again appeared to my view, I doubted at first that they were the same that I had just surprised, but my doubts soon vanished when I beheld the rapidity of their flight along the ridge before me. It appeared rather the rapid flight of birds than the motion of quadrupeds. I think I can safely venture the assertion that the speed of this animal is equal if not superior to that of the finest blooded courser.

Tuesday, September 18, 1804:

Sergeant Gass: Yesterday Captain Lewis, while hunting, killed a bird not common in the States. It is like a magpie and is a bird of prey.

Ordway: George Drouillard killed a prairie wolf.[84] [It was] some larger than a fox, with long teeth, and of a different description from any in the States. The bones of the wolf were taken apart and saved, as well as the skin in order to send back to the States next spring with the other curiosities we have.

Thursday, September 20, 1804:

Whitehouse: At 2:00 we proceeded on past a long range of bluffs on [the] north side of a dark color. Out of these, and others of the same kind, is where the Missouri gets its muddy color, for this earth melts like sugar.

---

84. coyote (DeVoto)

Friday, September 21, 1804:

Clark: At half past one o'clock this morning, the sand bar on which we camped began to undermine and give way, which alarmed the sergeant on guard. The motion of the boat awakened me. I got up and by the light of the moon observed that the sand had given way both above and below our camp and was falling in fast. I ordered all hands on as quick as possible and pushed off. We had pushed off but a few minutes before the bank under which the boat and pirogues lay gave way, which would certainly have sunk both the pirogues.

By the time we made the opposite shore, our camp fell in. We made a second camp for the remainder of the night and at daylight proceeded on to the gorge of this great bend[85] and breakfasted.

We sent a man to measure (step off) the distance across the gorge; he made it two thousand yards. The distance around is thirty miles. The hills extend through the gorge and are about two hundred feet above the water.

In the bend, as also the opposite sides both above and below the bend, is a beautiful inclined plain in which there are great numbers of buffalo, elk, and goats in view feeding and sipping on those plains. Grouse, larks, and the prairie bird are common in those plains.

We camped at the lower point of the mock island on the starboard side. This [is] now connected with the mainland. It has the appearance of one being an island detached from the mainland covered with tall cottonwood. We saw some camps and tracks of the Sioux which appear to be old, three or four weeks ago.

One Frenchman, I fear, has got an abscess on his thigh; he complains very much; we are making every exertion to relieve him.

The prairies in this quarter contain great quantities of prickly pear.

Saturday, September 22, 1804:

Clark: [We] passed an island situated nearest the starboard side immediately above the last, called Cedar Island. This island is about one and a half miles long and nearly as wide [and is] covered with cedar. On the south side of this island Mr. Loisel, a trader from St. Louis, built a fort of cedar and a good house to trade with the Sioux, and wintered last winter. About this fort I observed a number of Indian camps in a conical form. They fed their horses on cotton limbs, [it] appears.

---

85. the Big Bend, or Grand Detour; near today's Lower Brule, South Dakota (Schmidt, p. 43)

Here our hunters joined us, having killed two deer and a beaver. They complain much of the mineral substances in the barren hills over which they passed destroying their moccasins.

Sunday, September 23, 1804:

Clark: [We] set out under a gentle breeze from the southeast. [We] passed a small island situated in a bend to the port side called Goat Island. A short distance above the upper point, a creek of twelve yards wide comes in on the starboard side. We observed a great smoke to the southwest. I walked on shore and observed buffalo in great herds at a distance.

The river is nearly straight for a great distance, wide and shoal. [We] passed a creek on the starboard side sixteen yards wide we call Reubin Creek, as Reubin Field found it. [We] camped on the starboard side below the mouth of a creek on the port side.

Three Sioux boys came to us, swam the river, and informed [us][86] that the band of Sioux called the Tetons, of eighty lodges, were camped at the next creek above and sixty lodges more a short distance above. We gave those boys two carrots of tobacco to carry to their chiefs with directions to tell them that we would speak to them tomorrow.

Captain Lewis walked on shore this evening.

Reubin Field killed a doe goat.

Monday, September 24, 1804:

Clark: [We] set out early.

[It was] a fair day; the wind [was] from the east.

[We] passed the mouth of [a] creek on the port side called Creek on High Water. [We] passed a large island on the port side about two and a half miles long on which Colter had camped and killed four elk.

The wind [was] fair from the southeast.

We prepared some clothes and a few medals for the chiefs of the Teton band of Sioux which we expect to see today at the next river. [We] observed a great deal of stone on the sides of the hills on the starboard side. We saw one hare today.

[We] prepared all things for action in case of necessity.

Our pirogues went to the island for the meet. Soon after, the man[87] on shore ran up the bank and reported that the Indians had stolen the horse. We soon after met five Indians and anchored out some distance and spoke to them. [We] informed them we were friends and

86. via sign language and Drouillard (Ambrose, *UC*, p. 168)

87. John Colter (Schmidt, p. 44)

wished to continue so but were not afraid of any Indians. Some of their young men had taken the horse sent by their Great Father for their chief, and we would not speak to them until the horse was returned to us again.

[We] passed an island on the starboard side, on which we saw several elk, about one and a half miles long, called Good Humored Island. [We] came to about one and a half miles above, off the mouth of a small river about seventy yards wide, called by Mr. Evans[88] the Little Missouri River.

The tribes of the Sioux called the Teton are camped about two miles up on the northwest side and we shall call the river after that nation, Teton.[89] This river is seventy yards wide at the mouth of water and has a considerable current. We anchored off the mouth.[90]

The French boatman's pirogue came up early in the day. The other did not get up until the evening soon after we had come to. I went and smoked with the chiefs who came to see us here all well. We prepared to speak with the Indians tomorrow at which time, we are informed, the Indians will be here.

The Frenchman who had for some time been sick began to bleed, which alarmed him.

Two-thirds of our party camped on board, the remainder with the guard on shore.

Tuesday, September 25, 1804:

Clark: All [are] well. [We] raised a flagstaff and made an awning or shade on a sand bar in the mouth of [the] Teton River for the purpose of speaking with the Indians under [it]. The boat crew [was] on board at seventy yards distance from the bar. The five Indians, which we met last night, continued.

About 11:00 the first and second chiefs came. We gave them some of our provisions to eat. They gave us great quantities of meat, some of which was spoiled. We feel much at a loss for the want of an interpreter; the one we have can speak but little.

[We] met in council at 12:00 and after smoking, agreeable to usual custom, Captain Lewis proceeded to deliver a speech which we were obliged to curtail for want of a good interpreter. All our party paraded. [We] gave a medal to the grand chief called, in Indian, Un ton gar sar bar, in French, Buffle Noir, [or] Black Buffalo. [He is] said to

---

88. John Evans, an assistant to explorer James MacKay, who had mapped as far as the Mandan villages (Ambrose, *UC*, p. 125)

89. now the Bad River (DeVoto)

90. at present-day Pierre, South Dakota (Schmidt, p. 45)

be a good man. The second chief [was] Torto hon gar, or the Parti sin, or Partisan, bad. The third was the Buffle de Médecine;[91] his name is Tar ton gar wa ker. [The] First Considerable Man [was] War zing go, [and the] Second Considerable Man, Second Bear—Mato co que par.

[We] invited these chiefs on board to show them our boat and such curiosities as were strange to them. We gave them one-fourth of a glass of whiskey, which they appeared to be very fond of. [They] sucked the bottle after it was out and soon began to be troublesome. One, the second chief, assumed drunkenness as a cloak for his rascally intentions. I went with these chiefs in one of the pirogues with five men—three [of ours] and two Indians who left the boat with great reluctance—to shore with a view of reconciling these men to us.

As soon as I landed the pirogue, three of their young men seized the cable of the pirogue in which we had presents, etc. The chief's soldier hugged the mast and the second chief was very insolent both in words and gestures, pretending drunkenness and staggered up against me, declaring I should not go on, stating he had not received presents sufficient from us. His gestures were of such a personal nature I felt myself compelled to draw my sword and made a signal to the boat to prepare for action.

At this motion Captain Lewis ordered all under arms in the boat. Those with me also showed a disposition to defend themselves and me. The grand chief then took hold of the rope and ordered the young warriors away. I felt myself warm and spoke in very positive terms. Most of the warriors appeared to have their bows strung and took out their arrows from the quiver.

As I, being surrounded, was not permitted to return, I sent all the men except two interpreters to the boat. The pirogue soon returned with about twelve of our determined men ready for any event. This movement caused a number of the Indians to withdraw at a distance. Their treatment to me was very rough and, I think, justified roughness on my part. They all left my pirogue and counseled with themselves. The result I could not learn and nearly all went off.

After remaining in this situation some time, I offered my hand to the first and second chiefs, who refused to receive it. I turned off and went with my men on board the pirogue. I had not proceeded more than ten paces before the first chief, third [chief], and two brave men waded in after me. I took them in and went on board.

We proceeded on about one mile and anchored out off a willow island. [We] placed a guard on shore to protect the cooks, and a guard in the boat. [We] fastened the pirogues to the boat. I call this island Bad Humored Island as we were in a bad humor.

---

91. Buffalo Medicine

Ordway: [It was] a clear and pleasant morning. All things [were] made ready to receive the band of the Sioux nation of Indians called the tribe of Tetons.

About 10:00 a.m. they came flocking in from both sides of the river. When thirty-odd were selected under the American colors, Captain Lewis and Captain Clark went out to speak and treat with them. [They] gave the three chiefs three new medals and one American flag, some knives and other small articles of goods, and gave the head chief, Black Buffalo, a red coat and a cocked hat and feather, etc., [and], likewise, some tobacco. We had no good interpreter, but the old Frenchman[92] could make them understand tolerably well but they did not appear to talk much until they had got the goods, and then they wanted more and said we must stop with them or leave one of the pirogues with them, as that was what they expected.

Captain Lewis showed them the air gun [and] shot it several times. Then the captains brought the three chiefs and one warrior they had with them. [They] gave the warrior a certificate. Then [they] showed the chiefs some curiosities [and] gave them a drum. They brought a quantity of fat buffalo meat and offered [it to] us. The captains accepted some of it and gave them pork in return.

Then the captains told them that we had a great ways to go and that we did not wish to be detained any longer. They then began to act as if they were intoxicated. With some difficulty Captain Clark got them to shore. They then began to show some signs of stopping or attempting to stop us. One of them stayed on board the pirogue when Captain Clark and the chiefs went out of it. The head chief, Black Buffalo, seized hold of the cable of the pirogue and sat down. Captain Clark spoke to all the party to stand to their arms. Captain Lewis, who was on board, ordered every man to his arms. The large swivel [was] loaded immediately with sixteen musket balls in it; the two other swivels [were] loaded well with buckshot [and] each of them manned.

Captain Clark used moderation with them [and] told them that we must and would go on and would go [and] that we were not squaws but warriors. The chief said [that] he had warriors, too, and if we were to go on they would follow us and kill [us] and take the whole of us by degrees, or that he had another party or lodge above this [and] that they were able to destroy us. Then Captain Clark told them that we were sent by their Great Father, the President of the U.S., and that if they misused us that he or Captain Lewis could by writing to him have them all destroyed, as it were, in a moment.

They then requested that their women and children see the boat, as they never saw such a one. The captain told them that we could not

92. Cruzatte

go far as the day was far spent, but we would let them see that they should not stop us and that we should go a short distance and can camp for the night. The chief then let go [of] the cable and said that he was sorry to have us go for his women and children were naked and poor and wished to get some goods, but he did not think we were merchants nor that we were loaded with goods, but he was sorry to have us leave them so soon [and that] they wished to come on board. Captain Clark took the chief and warriors on board to stay all night with them.

We then set off and proceeded on about one mile and camped anchored out [with] the guard and cooks on shore, etc. The Indians camped on [the] starboard side. Our camp was on a willow island in the middle of the river, at our starboard side.

Whitehouse: They are, or appear as yet, to be the most friendly people I ever saw, but they will steal and plunder if they can get an opportunity. About fifteen days ago, they had a battle with the Omaha. They killed sixty-five men and took twenty-five women prisoners. They took the sixty-five scalps and had them hung on small poles, which their women held in their hands when they danced.

We saw them have one dance this evening. They had drums and whistles for music. They kept it up until 1:00, dancing war dances round the fire, which was curious to us.

Wednesday, September 26, 1804:

Clark: [We] set out early. [We] proceeded on and came to by the wish of the chiefs for to let their squaws and boys see the boat and suffer them to treat us well. Great numbers of men, women, and children [were] on the banks viewing us.

These people show great anxiety. They appear sprightly, generally ill-looking, and not well made; their legs and arms [are] small generally. They grease and black themselves [and] when they dress [they] make use of hawks' feathers about their heads. The men [wear] a robe and each a polecat's skin for to hold their bois roulé[93] for smoking. [They are] fond of dress and show, [and] badly armed with fusils,[94] etc. The squaws are cheerful, fine-looking women, not handsome, [with] high cheeks, dressed in skins [and] a petticoat and robe which folds back over their shoulders, with long wool. [They] do all their laborious work and, I may say, [are] perfect slaves to the men, as [are] all squaws of nations much at war, or where the women are more numerous than the men.

---

93. kinnikinnik: Indian tobacco rolled with leaves or bark, and a fine palindrome
94. light flintlock muskets

After coming to, Captain Lewis and five men went on shore with the chiefs, who appeared disposed to make up and be friendly. After Captain Lewis had been on shore about three hours, I became uneasy for fear of deception and sent a sergeant to see him and know his treatment which, he reported, was friendly and they were preparing for a dance this evening. They made frequent solicitations for us to remain one night only and let them show their good disposition towards us. We determined to remain.

After the return of Captain Lewis, I went on shore. On landing I was received on an elegant painted buffalo robe and taken to the village by six men and was not permitted to touch the ground until I was put down in the grand council house on a white dressed robe. I saw several Omaha prisoners and spoke to the chiefs [that] it was necessary to give those prisoners up and become good friends with the Omaha if they wished to follow the advice of their Great Father.

I was in several lodges neatly formed as before mentioned as to the Bois Brulé[95] tribe. I was met by about ten well-dressed young men who took me up in a robe highly decorated and sat me down by the side of their chief on a dressed robe in a large council house. This house formed a three-fourths circle of skins, well-dressed and sewn together. Under this shelter about seventy men sat forming a circle. In front of the chiefs a plaque of six feet [in] diameter was clear and the pipe of peace [was] raised on sticks under which there was swans down scattered. On each side of this circle [were] two pipes, the two flags of Spain, and the flag we gave them in front of the grand chief. A large fire was near in which provisions were cooking; in the center [were] about four hundred pounds of excellent buffalo beef as a present for us.

Soon after they sat me down, the men went for Captain Lewis. [They] brought him in the same way and placed him also by the chief. In a few minutes an old man rose and spoke approvingly [of] what we had done and informed us of their situation, requesting us to take pity on them and which was answered. The great chief then rose with great state, [speaking] to the same purpose as far as we could learn and then, with great solemnity, took up the pipe of peace and, after pointing it to the heavens, the four quarters of the globe and the earth, he made some dissertation, lit it, and presented the stem to us to smoke.

When the principal chief spoke with the pipe of peace, he took in one hand some of the most delicate parts of the dog, which was prepared for the feast, and made a sacrifice to the flag. After a smoke had taken place, and a short harangue to his people, we were requested to take the meal. Then [they] put before us the dog which they had been

95. Yankton Sioux

cooking, and pemmican,[96] and ground potato[97] in several platters. Dog, Sioux think, [is a] great dish, used on festivals. [We] ate little of [the] dog; [the] pemmican and potatoes [were] good.

We smoked for an hour [until] dark and all was cleared away. A large fire [was] made in the center [and] about ten musicians played on tambourines made of hoops and skin stretched, [using] long sticks with deer and goat hooves tied so as to make a jingling noise, and many others of a similar kind. These men began to sing and beat on the tambourines. The women came forward, highly decorated in their way with the scalps and trophies of war of their fathers, husbands, brothers or near connections, and proceeded to dance the war dance, which they did with great cheerfulness until about 12:00, when we informed the chiefs that they were fatigued, etc. They then retired and we, accompanied by four chiefs, returned to our boat. They stayed with us all night.

These people have some brave men which they make use of as soldiers. These men attend to the police of the village, correct all errors. I saw one of them today whip two squaws who appeared to have fallen out. When he approached, all about appeared to flee with great terror. At night they keep two, three, four, [or] five men at different distances walking around [the] camp singing the occurrences of the night.

All the men [are] on board one hundred paces from shore. [The] wind is from the southeast, moderate. One man [is] very sick on board with a dangerous abscess on his hip. All [are] in [good] spirits this evening.

In this tribe I saw twenty-five squaws and boys taken thirteen days ago in a battle with the Omaha. In this battle they destroyed forty lodges, killed seventy-five men and some boys and children, and took forty-eight prisoners, women and boys which they promised both Captain Lewis and myself shall be delivered up to Mr. Dorion at the Yankton tribe.

These are a wretched and dejected looking people. The squaws appear low and coarse, but this is an unfavorable time to judge them.

We gave our Omaha interpreter some few articles to give [to] those squaws in his name, such as awls, needles, etc., etc.

I saw and ate pemmican, the dog, [and] ground potatoes made into a kind of hominy, which I thought but little inferior. I also saw a spoon made of a horn of an animal of the sheep kind; the spoon will hold two quarts.

---

96. lean dried strips of meat pounded into a paste, mixed with fat and berries, and pressed into small cakes

97. "prairie turnip" or "Indian breadfruit:" turnip-like roots that could be eaten raw or cooked; usually braided into strings and dried (DeVoto)

Thursday, September 27, 1804:

Clark: I rose early after a bad night's sleep.

[I] found the chiefs all up and the bank, as usual, lined with spectators. We gave the two great chiefs a blanket apiece—or rather they took off, agreeable to their custom, the ones they [were] lying on—and each one [a] peck of corn.

After breakfast Captain Lewis and the chiefs went on shore as a very large part of their nation was coming in, the disposition of whom I did not know.

One of us being sufficient on shore, I wrote a letter to Mr. Pierre Dorion and prepared a medal and some certificates and sent [them] to Captain Lewis.

At 2:00 Captain Lewis returned with four chiefs and a brave man named "War cha pa," or On His Guard. When the friends of these people die, they run arrows through their flesh above and below their elbows as a testimony of their grief.

After staying about half an hour, I went with them on shore; these men left the boat with reluctance. I went first to the second chief's lodge where a crowd came around. After speaking on various subjects I went to a principal man's lodge [and] from there to the grand chief's lodge. After a few minutes he invited me to a lodge within the circle, in which I stayed with all their principal men until the dance began, which was similar to the one of last night performed by their women with poles on which scalps of their enemies were hung. Some [had] the guns, spears, and war implements of their husbands in their hands.

Captain Lewis came on shore and we continued until we were sleepy and returned to our boat. The second chief and one principal man accompanied us. These two Indians accompanied me on board in the small pirogue; Captain Lewis, with a guard, [was] still on shore. The man who steered, not being much accustomed to steer, passed the bow of the boat and the pirogue came broadside against the cable and broke it, which obliged me to order in a loud voice all hands up and at their oars.

My preemptory order to the men and the bustle of their getting to their oars alarmed the chiefs, together with the appearance of the men on shore, as the boat turned. The chief hollered and alarmed the camp or town, informing them that the Omaha were about attacking them.

In about ten minutes the bank was lined with men armed, the first chief at their head. About two hundred men appeared and after about a half an hour returned all but about sixty men who continued on the bank all night. The chiefs continued all night with us.

This alarm I, as well as Captain Lewis, considered as the signal of their intentions (which was to stop our proceeding on our journey and, if possible, rob us). We were on our guard all night. The misfortune of the loss of our anchor obliged us to lie under a falling bank much exposed to the accomplishment of their hostile intentions.

Pierre Cruzatte, our bowman who could speak Omaha, informed us in the night that the Omaha prisoners informed him [that] we were to be stopped. We showed as little signs of a knowledge of their intentions as possible. [We] all prepared on board for anything which might happen. We kept a strong guard all night in the boat; no sleep.

Ordway: Sergeant Gass informed me, as he was at the village today, that he counted eighty lodges (of the Teton tribe) which contain ten persons each, which were built round with poles about fifteen or twenty feet high and covered with dressed buffalo hides painted, some of them red, etc.

The dance lasted until about 12:00 at night, at which time the captains returned to the boat. [They] brought with them two chiefs. The men all returned, also.

An accident happened as they came on board by the neglect of the men at the helm of the pirogue who steered her above the big boat. She swung around with the current and she came full force down against the bow of the barge [and] broke the cable of her. We found we were all afloat. [We] roused all hands and got safely to shore on [the] starboard side.

The Indians, hearing us and expecting that the Omaha Indians had come to attack us, all ran to our assistance on the bank of the river and fired several guns for an alarm only. I, being on duty, sat up the remaining part of the night and had all the party on their guards.

Friday, September 28, 1804:

Clark: [We] made many attempts in different ways to find our anchor but could not; the sand had covered it. From the misfortune of last night our boat was laying at shore in a very unfavorable situation. After finding that the anchor could not be found, we determined to proceed on.

With great difficulty [we] got the chiefs out of our boat, and when we were about [to] set out, the class called the soldiers took possession of the cable. The first chief was still on board and intended to go a short distance up with us. I told him the men of his nation [were] sitting on the cable. He went out and told Captain Lewis, who was at the bow, [that] the men who [were] sitting on the rope were soldiers and wanted tobacco. Captain Lewis would not agree to be forced into anything. The second chief demanded a flag and tobacco which we refused to give stating proper reasons to them for it. [I] took the port fire from the gunner, spoke so as to touch his pride. The chief gave the tobacco to his soldiers and he jerked the rope from them and handed it to the bowman. We then set out under a breeze from the southeast.

About two miles up we observed the third chief on shore beckoning to us. We took him on board. He informed us [that] the rope was held by the order of the second chief who was a double-spoken man.

Soon after we saw a man coming full speed through the plains. [He] left his horse and proceeded across a sand bar near the shore. We took him on board and observed that he was the son of the chief we had on board. We sent by him a talk to the nation stating the cause of our hoisting the red flag under the white. If they were for peace, stay at home and do as we had directed them. If they were for war or were determined to stop us, we were ready to defend ourselves.

We halted one hour and a half on the starboard side and made a substitute of stones for an anchor. [We] refreshed our men and proceeded on about two miles higher up and came to a very small sand bar in the middle of the river and stayed all night.

I am very unwell for want of sleep. [I am] determined to sleep tonight if possible.

The men cooked and we rested well.

Ordway: [It was] a clear and pleasant morning.

Captain Clark went with the pirogues early.

This morning [we went] to hunt for [the] anchor. [We] searched some time with the boat hook and poles [but] could not find it. They took a cord and put sinkers to the middle and took each end to the two pirogues and dragged the river diligently a long time but could not find it.

[We] took breakfast about 10:00. The whole lodge of Indians was waiting on the bank to see us start, as we intended [as] if the incident had not happened last night.

We gave up the idea of finding our anchor.

We then were about to set off. Some of the chiefs were on board insisting on our staying until the others came. We told them we could not wait any longer. They then did not incline to let us go on. They said we might return back with what we had or remain with them, but we could not go up the Missouri any farther. About two hundred Indians were then on the bank. Some had firearms, some had spears, some had a kind of cutlass, and all the rest had bows and steel- or iron-pointed arrows. Several of the warriors sat by the cord where our boat, the big barge, was tied. The two pirogues were tied on the outside of the barge.

Captain Clark was speaking to the chiefs in the cabin.

Captain Lewis asked the chiefs if they were going out of the boat. They did not incline to. Then Captain Lewis came out [and] ordered every man to his place [and] ordered the sail hoisted. One man went out [and] untied the cord which the warrior had in his hand. Then two or three more of their warriors caught hold of the cord and tied it faster than before. Captain Lewis then appeared to be angry and told [them] to go out of the boat, and the chief then went out and said we are sorry to have you go, but if you will give us one carrot of tobacco we will be willing for you to go on and will not try to stop you. Captain Lewis gave it to them.

The head chief said then that we must give him one more carrot of tobacco, more for his warriors who held the cord, and then we might go.

Both of our captains told him that we did not mean to be trifled with, nor would not humor them anymore, but would give him one carrot more for the warriors if he would be a man of his word and stand to his word like a man.

The chief said he was mad, too, to see us stand so much for one carrot of tobacco. If we would give it we might go on. Captain Lewis gave it to him. He then took the cord in his hand and gave it to us.

We then set off under a gentle breeze which happened to be favorable. We proceeded on past bottom prairie on [the] south side, highland on [the] north side. [We] went four miles and halted. We fixed two large stones to our boats to answer as anchors as we did not intend to camp on shore again until we got to another nation.

Saturday, September 29, 1804:

Clark: [We] proceeded on. At 9:00 we observed the second chief and two principal men [and] one man and a squaw on shore. They wished to go up with us as far as the other part of their band which, they said, was on the river ahead not far distant. We refused, stating very sufficient reasons and were plain with them on the subject.

Sunday, September 30, 1804:

Clark: [We] set out this morning early. [We] had not proceeded on far before we discovered an Indian running after us. He came up with us at 7:00 and requested to come on board and go up to the Arikaras.[98] We refused to take any of that band on board. If he chose to proceed on shore it was very well.

Soon after, I discovered on the hills at a great distance great numbers of Indians which appeared to be making to the river above us. We proceeded on under a double reefed sail, and some rain.

---

98. a tribe they will meet upriver

At 9:00 [we] observed a large band of Indians, the same which I had before seen on the hills, encamping on the bank [on] the port side. We came to on a sand bar, [ate] breakfast and proceeded on. [We] cast the anchor opposite their lodge at about one hundred yards distant and informed the Indians, which we found to be a part of the band we had before seen, that [we] took them by the hand, and sent to each chief a carrot of tobacco.

We proceeded on under a very stiff breeze from the southeast. The stern of the boat got fast on a log and the boat turned and was very near filling before we got her righted, the waves being very high. The chief on board was so frightened at the motion of the boat which, in its rocking, caused several loose articles to fall on the deck from the lockers, [that] he ran off and hid himself.

[When] we landed, he got his gun and informed us [that] he wished to return, that all things were clear for us to go, [and that] we would not see any more Tetons, etc.

We repeated to him what had been said before and advised him to keep his men away. [We] gave him a blanket, a knife, and some tobacco, smoked a pipe, and he set out. We also set sail and came to at a sand bar and camped.

[It was] a very cold evening; all [stayed] on guard.

Sand bars are so numerous that it is impossible to describe them and [I] think it [is] unnecessary to mention them.

Monday, October 1, 1804:

Clark: [We] continued on, with the wind immediately ahead, and came to on a large sand bar in the middle of the river. We saw a man opposite to our camp on the port side which we discovered to be a Frenchman. A little off from shore among the willows we observed a house. We called to them to come over. A boy came in a canoe and informed [us] that two Frenchmen were at the house with goods to trade with the Sioux, which he expected down from the Arikaras every day. Several large parties of Sioux set out from the Arikaras for this place to trade with these men.

This Mr. Jean Vallé[99] informs us that he wintered last winter three hundred leagues up the Cheyenne River under the Black Mountains.[100] He informs [us] that this river is very rapid and difficult even for pirogues to ascend and when rising the swells are very high. One hundred leagues up it forks; one fork comes from the south, the other at forty leagues above; the forks enter the Black Hills. The country

99. from an influential St. Louis fur-trading family (DeVoto)

100. Black Hills (DeVoto)

from the Missouri to the Black Hills is much like the country on the Missouri: less timber and a great proportion of cedar.

The Black Hills, he says, are very high and some parts of them have snow on them in the summer. No beaver [are] on [the] Cheyenne River. On the [Black] Hills [are] great numbers of goat and a kind of animal with large circular horns;[101] this animal is nearly the size of an elk. White bears[102] are also plentiful.

Tuesday, October 2, 1804:

Clark: [We] observe great caution this day, expecting [that] the Sioux intentions [are] somewhat hostile towards our progression.

The river [is] not so rapid as below the Cheyenne [and] its width [is] nearly the same.

[We made] twelve miles.

Friday, October 5, 1804:

Clark: [There was] frost this morning.

We set out early and proceeded on past a small creek on the port side.

At 7:00 [we] heard some yells. [We] proceeded on [and] saw three Indians of the Teton band. They called to us to come on shore [and] begged [for] some tobacco. We answered them as usual and proceeded on.

In the evening [we] passed a small island situated close to the port side. At the head of this island a large creek comes in on the port side. [We] saw white brants[103] [so] we call this creek White Brant Creek. I walked on the island [and] found it covered with wild rye. I shot a buck [and] saw a large gang of goats on the hills opposite. One buck [was] killed [and] also a prairie wolf this evening. The highland [is] not so high as below, [the] river about the same width, the sand bars as numerous, the earth black, and many of the bluffs have the appearance of being on fire.

We came to and camped on a mud bar making from the starboard side.

The evening is calm and pleasant.

[We] refreshed the men with a glass of whiskey.

---

101. the Rocky Mountain sheep, or bighorn (DeVoto)

102. grizzlies; the captains often used "white," "brown," or even "gray," for "grizzly"

103. small dark wild geese, often with a black head and neck

Sunday, October 7, 1804:

Clark: At the mouth of this river[104] we saw the tracks of [a] white bear which was very large. I walked up this river a mile. Below the mouth of this river are the remains of an Arikaras village, or wintering camp, fortified in a circular form of about sixty lodges, built in the same form of those passed yesterday. This camp appears to have been inhabited last winter. Many of their willow and straw mats, baskets, and buffalo skin canoes remain intact within the camp.

From this river we proceeded on under a gentle breeze from the southwest. At 10:00 we saw two Indians on the starboard side. They asked for something to eat and informed us they were part of the Buffle de Médecine lodge on their way to the Arikaras.

[We] passed a willow island in a bend to the starboard side. At five miles, [we] passed a willow island on the starboard side.

The wind [was] hard from the south.

In the evening I walked on an island nearly [in] the middle of the river called Grouse Island. One of the men killed a she-blaireau[105] [and] another man killed a black-tail deer, the largest doe I ever saw (black under her breast). This island is nearly one and one-fourth miles square, no timber, high, and covered with grass [and] wild rye and contains great numbers of grouse.

We proceeded on a short distance above the island and camped on the starboard side.

[It was] a fine evening.

Monday, October 8, 1804:

Clark: [We] passed the mouth of a river[106] called by the Arikaras "We tar hoo" on the port side. This river is one hundred twenty yards wide, the water of which at this time is confined within twenty yards, discharging but a small quantity, throwing out mud with [a] small proportion of sand. Great quantities of the red berries, resembling currants, are on the river in every bend.

[We] proceeded on past the lower point of an island close on the port side. Two of our men discovered the Arikaras village about [in] the center of the island on the port side on the main shore. This island is about three miles long [and] separated from the port side by a channel of about sixty yards wide [and] very deep. The island is covered with fields where these people raise their corn, tobacco, beans, etc., etc. Great numbers of these people came on the island to see us pass.

---

104. the Moreau (DeVoto)
105. female badger
106. Grand River (DeVoto)

We passed above the head of the island and Captain Lewis, with two interpreters and two men, went to the village. I formed a camp of the French [boatmen] and the guard on shore with one sentinel on board of the boat at anchor.

[It was] a pleasant evening.

All things [are] arranged both for peace or war.

This village is situated [at] about the center of a large island near the port side and near the foot of some high, bald, uneven hills. Several Frenchmen came up with Captain Lewis in a pirogue, one of which is a Mr. Gravelines,[107] a man well-versed in the language of this nation, and gave us some information relative to the country, nation, etc.

Tuesday, October 9, 1804:

Clark: River Maropa - [It was] a windy, rainy night, and cold, so much so [that] we could not speak with the Indians today. The three great chiefs and many others came to see us today. We gave them some tobacco and informed them we would speak on tomorrow.

The day continued cold and windy [with] some rain.

Several canoes of skins passed down from the two villages a short distance above and many came to view us all day. [They were] much astonished at my black servant who did not lose the opportunity of displaying his powers, strength, etc., etc. This nation never saw a black man before.

Several hunters came in with loads of meat. I observed several canoes made of a single buffalo skin,[108] with three squaws, cross the river today in waves as high as I ever saw them on this river, quite uncomposed.

I have a slight pleurisy this evening; very cold, etc., etc.

Ordway: All the nation made a great deal of him.[109] The children would follow after him and, if he turned towards them, they would run from him and holler as if they were terrified and afraid of him.

Wednesday, October 10, 1804:

Clark: We prepared all things [to be] ready to speak to the Indians.

Mr. Tabeau[110] and Mr. Gravelines came to breakfast with us.

---

107. a trader (one of Loisel's employees) who had been living with the Arikaras for thirteen years (Ambrose, *UC*, p. 179, and DeVoto)

108. bull boats; hide is stretched over a bowl-shaped willow frame (Ambrose, *UC*, p. 179)

109. York

At 1:00 the chiefs all assembled and after some little ceremony the council commenced. We informed them what we had told the others before, i.e., Otos and Sioux. [We] met three chiefs, one for each village. [We] gave them presents. After the council was over, we shot the air gun which astonished them much. They then departed and we rested secure all night.

These Indians were much astonished at my servant; they never saw a black man before. [They] all flocked around him and examined him from top to toe. He carried on the joke and made himself more terrible than we wished him to do.

These Indians are not fond of spirituous liquor of any kind.

Thursday, October 11, 1804:

Clark: At 11:00 we met the grand chief[111] in council and he made a short speech thanking us for what we had given him and his nation, promising to attend to the council we had given him, and informed us the road was open and no one dare shut it, and we might depart at pleasure.

At 1:00 we set out for the upper villages. At one mile [we] took in the second chief[112] and came to off the second village, separated from the third by a creek. After arranging all matters, we walked up with the second chief to his village and sat talking on various subjects until late.

We also visited the upper, or third, village, each of which gave us something to eat in their way, and a few bushels of corn, beans, etc., etc.

After being treated by every civility by these people, who are both poor and dirty, we returned to our boat at about 10:00 p.m., informing them before we departed that we would speak to them tomorrow at their separate villages. These people gave us to eat bread made of corn and beans [and] also corn and beans boiled, a large bean, which they rob the mice of the prairie, which is rich and very nourishing; [they] also [gave us] squashes, etc.

All [is] tranquil.

Friday, October 12, 1804:

Clark: We sat some time before the council commenced. This man spoke at some length, declaring his disposition to believe and pursue our councils, his intention of going to visit his Great Father. [He]

---

110. Pierre-Antoine Tabeau, a trader with another island village (Ambrose, *UC*, p. 179)

111. Crow at Rest (Ambrose, *UC*, p. 180)

112. Hay (Ambrose, *UC*, p. 180)

acknowledged the satisfaction in receiving the presents, etc., raising a doubt as to the safety in passing the nations below, particularly the Sioux, [and] requested us to take a chief of their nation and make a good peace with [the] Mandans and nations above.

After answering those parts of the second chief's speech which required it, which appeared to give general satisfaction, we went to the village of the third chief.[113] This chief spoke very much in the same style on nearly the same subjects as the other chief who sat by his side, more sincerely and pleasantly. After we had answered his speech and [had] given them some account of the magnitude and power of our country, which pleased and astonished them very much, we returned to our boat. The chiefs accompanied us on board. We gave them some sugar, a little salt, and a sun glass. [We] set two on shore; the third proceeded on with us to the Mandans.

The nation of the Arikaras is about six hundred men (Mr. Tabeau says, I think, five hundred men) able to bear arms. A great proportion of them have fusils. They appear to be peaceful. Their men [are] tall and proportioned. [Their] women [are] small and industrious, raise great quantities of corn, beans, simlins,[114] etc., [and] also tobacco for the men to smoke. They collect all the wood and do the drudgery as [is] common amongst savages.

The corruption of the language of the different tribes has so reduced the language that the different villages do not understand all the words of the others. These people are dirty, kind, poor and extravagant, possessing national pride, not beggarly, [and] receive what is given with great pleasure. [They] live in warm houses, large and built in an octagon form, forming a cone at [the] top which is left open for the smoke to pass. These houses are generally thirty or forty feet [in] diameter, covered with earth on poles [with] willows and grass to prevent the earth [from] passing through.

These people express an inclination to be at peace with all nations. The Sioux, who trade the goods which they get off the British traders for their corn and [have] great influence over the Arikaras, poison their minds and keep them in perpetual dread.

A curious custom with the Sioux, as well as the Arikaras, is to give handsome squaws to those whom they wish to show some acknowledgment. The Sioux we got clear of without taking their squaws; they followed us with squaws [for] two days. The Arikaras we put off during the time we were at the towns, but two handsome young squaws were sent by a man to follow us. They came up this evening and persisted in their civilities.

---

113. Hawk's Feather (Ambrose, *UC*, p. 180)

114. summer squash

Dress of the men of this nation is simply a pair of moccasins, leggings, flap in front, and a buffalo robe, with their hair, arms, and ears decorated. The women wore moccasins, leggings fringed, and a shirt of goat skins, some with sleeves. This garment is long and generally white and fringed, tied at the waist, with a robe.

Sunday, October 14, 1804:

Clark: The punishment of this day[115] alarmed the Indian chief very much. He cried aloud (or effected to cry). I explained the cause of the punishment and the necessity [of it], [and] he thought examples were also necessary and he himself had made them by death. His nation never whipped even their children from their birth.

Monday, October 15, 1804:

Clark: At sunset we arrived at a camp of Arikaras of ten lodges on the starboard side. We came to and camped near them.

Captain Lewis and I went with the chief who accompanied us to the huts of several of the men, all of whom smoked and gave us something to eat [and] also some meat to take away. These people were kind and appeared to be much pleased at the attention paid [to] them.

These people are much pleased with my black servant.

Their women [are] very fond of caressing our men, etc.

Thursday, October 18, 1804:

Clark: [We] set out early [and] proceeded on. At six miles [we] passed the mouth of La Boulet (or Cannon Ball) River,[116] about one hundred forty yards wide on the port side. Above the mouth of the river, great numbers of stone, perfectly round with fine grit, are in the bluff and on the shore. The river takes its name from these stones which resemble cannon balls. The water of this river is confined within forty yards.

We met two Frenchmen in a pirogue descending from hunting; [they] complained of the Mandans robbing them of four traps, their furs, and several other articles. These men were in the employ of our Arikara interpreter, Mr. Gravelines. They turned and followed us.

[We] saw great numbers of goats on the starboard side coming to the river. Our hunters killed four of them. Some ran back and others

---

115. John Newman was found guilty of insubordination, sentenced to seventy-five lashes, and discharged ("discarded," according to Ambrose, *UC*, p. 181) from the army. (DeVoto)

116. at present-day Cannon Ball, North Dakota

crossed and proceeded on their journey to the Black Hills. [We] passed a small creek on the port side one mile above the last and camped on a sand bar on the port side.

Opposite to us we saw a gang of buffalo bulls which we did not think worthwhile to kill. Our hunters killed four goats, six deer, four elk and a pelican, and informed [us] that they saw in one gang two hundred and forty-eight elk. (I walked on shore in the evening with a view to see some of those remarkable places mentioned by Evans, none of which I could find.)

The country in this quarter is generally level and fine. [There are] some high, short hills and some ragged ranges of hills at a distance.

The Arikaras are not fond of spirituous liquors, nor do they appear to be fond of receiving any or thankful for it. They say we are no friends or we would not give them what makes them fools.

Saturday, October 20, 1804:

Clark: [We] camped on the port side above a bluff containing coal of an inferior quality. This bank is immediately above the old village of the Mandans. The country is fine [and] the high hills at a distance [have] gradual ascents. I killed three deer. The timber [is] confined to the bottoms as usual which is much larger than below.

[There are] great numbers of buffalo, elk, deer, and goats. Our hunters killed ten deer and a goat today and wounded a white bear. I saw several fresh tracks of these animals which are three times as large as a man's track.

The wind [blew] hard all day from the northeast and east.

Great numbers of buffalo [were] swimming [in] the river. I observed near all large gangs of buffalo wolves, and when the buffalo move, these animals follow and feed on those that are killed by accident or those that are too poor or fat to keep up with the gang.

Sunday, October 21, 1804:

Gass: We had a disagreeable night of sleet and hail. It snowed during the forenoon but we proceeded early on our voyage.

Monday, October 22, 1804:

Clark: Last night at 1:00 I was violently and suddenly attacked with the rheumatism in the neck which was so violent I could not move. Captain [Lewis] applied a hot stone wrapped in flannel which gave me some temporary ease.

We set out early; the morning [was] cold.

At 7:00 we came to at a camp of Teton Sioux on the port side. These people, twelve in number, were naked and had the appearance of war. We have every reason to believe that they are going or have been to steal horses from the Mandans. They tell two stories. We gave them nothing. After taking breakfast, [we] proceeded on.

My neck is yet very painful, at times spasms.

The hunters killed a buffalo bull. They said [that] out of about three hundred buffalo which they saw, they did not see one cow. [There are] a great deal of beaver seen; several [are] caught every night.

Wednesday, October 24, 1804:

Clark: [We] set out early. [It was] a cloudy day [with] some little snow in the morning.

I am something better of the rheumatism in my neck.

[It is] a beautiful country on both sides of the river. The bottoms are covered with wood. We have seen no game on the river today—a proof of the Indians hunting in the neighborhood. [We] passed an island on the starboard side made by the river cutting through a point, by which the river is shortened several miles.

On this island we saw one of the grand chiefs of the Mandans,[117] with five lodges hunting. This chief met the chief of the Arikaras, who accompanied us with great cordiality and ceremony smoked the pipe. Captain Lewis, with the interpreter,[118] went with the chiefs to his lodges at one mile distant. After his return, we admitted the grand chief and his brother for a few minutes on our boat.

[We] proceeded on a short distance and camped on the starboard side below the old village of the Mandans and Arikaras. Soon after our landing, four Mandans came from a camp above. The Arikaras chief went with them to their camp.

Thursday, October 25, 1804:

Clark: [It was] a cold morning.

[We] set our early under a gentle breeze from the southeast by east. [We] proceeded on [and] passed the third old village of the Mandans which has been deserted for many years. This village was situated on an eminence of about forty feet above the water on the port side. Back for several miles is a beautiful plain at a short distance above this old village.

---

117. Big White (Ambrose, *UC*, p. 183)

118. Gravelines (Ambrose, *UC*, p. 183)

On a continuation of the same eminence was situated the Arikaras village which has been evacuated only six years.

Several parties of Mandans rode to the river on the starboard side to view us. Indeed, they are continually in sight satisfying their curiosities as to our appearance, etc.

We are told that the Sioux have lately fallen in with and stolen the horses of the Hidatsa.[119] On their way home they fell in with the Assiniboines, who killed them and took the horses. A Frenchman[120] has lately been killed by the Indians on the track to the trading establishment on the Assiniboine River in the north of this place (or British fort). This Frenchman had lived many years with the Mandans.

[The] river [is] full of sand bars and we are at a great loss to find the channel of the river [and] frequently run on the sand bars, which delays us much. [We] passed a very bad riffle[121] of rocks in the evening by taking the port side of a sand bar and camped on a sand point on the starboard side opposite a high hill on the port side.

Several Indians came to see us this evening, amongst others the son of the late great chief of the Mandans. This man has his two little fingers off. On inquiring [about] the cause, [we] were told it was customary for this nation to show their grief by some testimony of pain and that it was not uncommon for them to take off two smaller fingers of the hand at the second joints and sometimes more, with other marks of savage affection.

Reubin Field [is] with the rheumatism in his neck and Pierre Cruzatte [is] with the same complaint in his legs; the party [is] otherwise well. As to myself, I feel but slight symptoms of that disorder at this time.

Friday, October 26, 1804:

Clark: [We] proceeded on. [We] saw numbers of the Mandans on shore. We set the Arikaras chief on shore and we proceeded on to the camp of two of their grand chiefs where we delayed a few minutes with the chiefs and proceeded on, taking two of their chiefs on board and some of the heavy articles of his household, such as earthen pots and corn. [We] proceeded on.

At this camp [we] saw a Mr. McCracken, an Englishman from the North West Company.[122] This man came nine days ago to trade for horses and buffalo robes; one other man came with him.

---

119. also known as the Minnetarees; often called the "Big Bellies," or "Gros Ventres," by Lewis and Clark (DeVoto)

120. Ménard; probably the first *engagé* of a British fur company to reach the Mandans (DeVoto)

121. a shallows extending across a stream bed and causing broken water

The Indians continued on the banks all day.

[There is] but little wood on this part of the river. [There are] many sand bars and bad places [with] water much divided between them.

We came to and camped on the port side about half a mile below the first Mandan town on the port side. Soon after our arrival, many men, women, and children flocked down to see us. Captain Lewis walked to the village with the principal chiefs and our interpreters.

My rheumatic complaint [was] increasing [so] I could not go. I smoked with the chiefs who came after. These people appeared much pleased with the corn mill which we were obliged to use and was fixed in the boat.

Saturday, October 27, 1804:

Clark: [We] came to at the village on the port side. This village is situated on an eminence of about fifty feet above the water in a handsome plain. It contains ____[123] houses in a kind of picket work. The houses are round and very large, containing several families and also their horses, which are tied on one side of the entrance. I walked up and smoked a pipe with the chiefs of the villages. They were anxious that I would stay and eat with them. My indisposition prevented my eating, which displeased them until a full explanation took place. I returned to the boat and sent two carrots of tobacco for them to smoke, and proceeded on.

[We] passed the second village and camped opposite the village of the Anahaways, which is situated on an eminence in a plain on the port side.

We met with a Frenchman by the name of Jessaume[124] [who] we employ as an interpreter. This man has a wife and children in the village. Great numbers on both sides flocked down to the bank to view us as we passed. We sent three twists of tobacco by three young men to the villages above, inviting them to come down and council with us tomorrow.

Many Indians came to view us. Some stayed all night in the camp of our party. We procured some information of Mr. Jessaume of the chiefs of the different nations.

Gass: This village contains forty or fifty lodges, built in the manner of those of the Arikaras. Some of the children have fair hair.

---

122. Hugh McCracken, actually an Irishman and former soldier in the British Army (DeVoto)

123. signifies a blank space in the original journals

124. René Jessaume, a trader from the second Mandan village who had lived with them for fifteen years (Ambrose, *UC*, p. 184)

Sunday, October 28, 1804:

Clark: Many of the Hidatsa and Anahaways came to see us and hear the council. The wind, being so violently hard from the southwest, prevented our going into council. (Indeed, the chiefs of the Mandans from the lower village could not cross.)

We made up the presents and entertained several of the curious chiefs who wished to see the boat, which was very curious to them, viewing it as great medicine, as they also viewed my black servant.

The Black Cat, grand chief of the Mandans, Captain Lewis and I, with an interpreter,[125] walked up the river about one and a half miles. We had several presents from the women of corn, boiled hominy, soft corn, etc., etc. I presented a jar to the chief's wife, who received it with much pleasure.

Our men [are] very cheerful this evening.

We sent the chiefs of the Hidatsa to smoke a pipe with the grand chief of the Mandans in his village and told them we would speak tomorrow.

Monday, October 29, 1804:

Clark: [It was] a fair, fine morning.

After breakfast we were visited by the old chief of the Hidatsa. This man was old and had transferred his power to his son who was then out at war against the Shoshone Indians[126] who inhabit the Rocky Mountains. We collected the chiefs and commenced a council under an awning and our sails stretched around to keep out as much wind as possible. We delivered a long speech, the substance of which [was] similar to what we had delivered to the nations below. The old chief of the Hidatsa was very restless before the speech was half ended. [We] observed that he could not wait long, that his camp was exposed to the hostile Indians, etc., etc. He was rebuked by one of the chiefs for his uneasiness at such a time as the present.

We, at the end of the speech, mentioned the Arikaras who accompanied us to make a firm peace. They all smoked with him. (I gave this chief a dollar of the American coin as a medal, with which he was much pleased.) In council we presented him with a certificate of his sincerity and good conduct, etc. We also spoke about the fur which was taken from two Frenchmen by a Mandan and informed [them] of our intentions of sending [it] back [to] the French hands.

After the council we gave the presents with much ceremony and put the medals on the chiefs. We intended to make, viz., one for each

125. Jessaume

126. also called the Snake Indians

town to whom we gave coats, hats and flags, one grand chief [of] each nation to whom we gave medals with the president's likeness. In council we requested them to give us an answer tomorrow, or as soon as possible, to some points which required their deliberation. After the council was over, we shot the air gun, which appeared to astonish the natives much. The greater part then retired soon after. An iron or steel corn mill which we gave to the Mandans was very thankfully received.

The prairie was set on fire (or caught by accident) by a young man of the Mandans. The fire went with such velocity that it burned to death a man and [a] woman who could not get to any place of safety. One man, a woman, and child [were] much burned and several narrowly escaped the flame.

A boy, half-white, was saved unhurt in the midst of the flame. These ignorant people say this boy was saved by the Great Medicine Spirit because he was white. The cause of his being saved was [because] a green buffalo skin was thrown over him by his mother, who perhaps had more foresight for the protection of her son, and less for herself, than those who escaped the flame. The fire did not burn under the skin, leaving the grass around the boy.

This fire passed our camp last night about 8:00 p.m. It went with great rapidity and looked tremendous.

We sent the presents intended for the grand chief of the Hidatsa, and the presents, flag and wampum by the old chief, and those intended for the chief of the lower village by a young chief.

Tuesday, October 30, 1804:

Clark: I took eight men in a small pirogue and went up the river as far as the first island, about seven miles, to see if a situation could be got on it for our winter quarters. [We] found the wood on the island, as also on the point above, [to be] so distant from the water that I did not think that we could get a good wintering ground there, and as all the white men here informed us that wood was scarce, as well as game above, we determined to drop down a few miles near wood and game.

On our return, [we] found many Indians at our camp. [We] gave the party a dram.[127] They danced, as is very common in the evening, which pleased the savages much.

Wednesday, October 31, 1804:

Clark: The grand chief of the Mandans came dressed in the clothes we had given with his two small sons and requested to see the men dance, which they very readily gratified him in.

---

127. an eighth of an ounce

The wind blew hard all the afterpart of the day from the northeast and continued all night to blow hard from that point. In the morning it shifted [to the] northwest.

Captain Lewis wrote to the North West Company's agent on the Assiniboine River, about nine days' march north of this place.

Thursday, November 1, 1804:

Clark: Mr. McCracken, a trader, set out at 7:00 to the fort on the Assiniboine. By him [we] sent a letter (enclosing a copy of the British minister's protection) to the principal agent of the company.

At about 10:00 the chiefs of the lower village came and after a short time informed us [that] they wished that we would call at their village and take some corn. They said that they would make peace with the Arikaras. They never made war against them but after the Arikaras killed their chiefs, they killed them like the birds and were tired of killing them and would send a chief and some brave men to the Arikaras to smoke with that people.

Friday, November 2, 1804:

Clark: This morning at daylight I went down the river with four men to look for a proper place to winter. [We] proceeded down the river three miles and found a place[128] well supplied with wood and returned.

Many Indians [came] to view us today.

Saturday, November 3, 1804:

Clark: We commenced building our cabins. [We] sent down in a pirogue six men to hunt [and] enlisted one man. [We] set the French who intend to return[129] to building a pirogue. Mr. Jessaume, with his squaw and children, came down to live as interpreter. We received[130] a horse for our service.

The men were indulged with a dram this evening.

Two beaver [were] caught this morning and one trap [was] lost.

Sunday, November 4, 1804:

Clark: We continued to cut down trees and raise our houses.

A Mr. Charbonneau,[131] interpreter for the Hidatsa nation, came to see us and informed [us] that he came down with several Indians

---

128. fourteen miles west of Washburn, North Dakota (Schmidt, p. 54)

129. to St. Louis

130. hired (DeVoto)

from a hunting expedition up the river to hear what we had told the Indians in council. This man wished to [be] hired as an interpreter.

Monday, November 5, 1804:

Ordway: All hands [are] splitting out puncheons[132] for to lay the loft which we intend covering over with earth to make the huts more warm and comfortable.

Tuesday, November 6, 1804:

Clark: Fort Mandan - Last night late we were awakened by the sergeant of the guard to see a northern light which was light, not red, and appeared to darken and sometimes nearly obscured, and open. Many times [it] appeared in light streaks and other times a great space light, and containing floating columns which appeared to approach each other and retreat, leaving the lighter space. At no time [was it] of the same appearance.[133]

Mr. Joseph Gravelines, our Arikara interpreter, Paul Primaut, La Jeunesse,[134] and two French boys who came with us set out in a small pirogue. On their return to the Arikara nation and the Illinois, Mr. Gravelines has instructions to take on the Arikaras in the spring, etc.

[We] continued to build the huts out of cottonwood timber, etc., this being the only timber we have.

Saturday, November 10, 1804:

Clark: [We] continued to build our fort.

Numbers of Indians came to see us. A chief, half-Pawnee, came and brought a side of a buffalo. In return we gave some few small things to himself and wife and son. He crossed the river in the buffalo skin canoe and the squaw took the boat on her back and proceeded on to the town three miles.

The day [was] raw and [there was a] cold wind from the north-west.

The geese continue to pass in gangs, as also the brant to the south; some ducks also pass.

---

131. Toussaint Charbonneau, a French trader living with the Hidatsa; one of his squaws was Sacagawea, meaning "Bird Woman"

132. wooden uprights used in structural framing

133. the Northern Lights

134. Baptiste La Jeunesse, the "patroon" in charge of the red pirogue (Bakeless, p. 103)

Sunday, November 11, 1804:

Clark: [We] continued at work at the fort. Two men cut themselves with an ax.

The large ducks pass to the south.

An Indian gave me several rolls of parched meat. Two squaws[135] of the Rocky Mountains, purchased from the Indians by a Frenchman, came down. The Mandans [are] out hunting the buffalo.

Monday, November 12, 1804:

Clark: Early this morning Big White, principal chief of the lower village of the Mandans, came down. He packed about one hundred pounds of fine meat on his squaw for us.

Three men [are] sick with the ____.

The interpreter says that the Mandan nation, as they (old men) say, came out of a small lake where they had gardens. Many years ago they lived in several villages on the Missouri low down. The smallpox destroyed the greater part of the nation and reduced them to one large village and some small ones. All the nations, before this malady, were afraid of them. After they were reduced, the Sioux and other Indians waged war and killed a great many, and they moved up the Missouri. Those Indians still continued to wage war and they moved still higher until [they] got in the country of the Arikaras. With this nation, they lived in friendship many years, inhabiting the same neighborhood until that people waged war. They moved up near the Anahaways and Winataras, where they now live in peace with those nations.

The Mandans speak a language peculiar to themselves, very much ____. They can raise about three hundred and fifty men, the Winataras about eighty, and the Hidatsa about six hundred or six hundred and fifty men. The Mandans and Sioux have the same word for water. The Hidatsa, or Minnetarees, and Crow[136] Indians speak nearly the same language and the presumption is [that] they were originally the same nation. The Crow Indians have four hundred lodges and about twelve hundred men and follow the buffalo or hunt for their subsistence in the plains and on the Côte Noire[137] and Rocky Mountains, and are at war with the Sioux and Shoshone Indians.

The Hidatsa and Anahaways are at war with the Shoshone Indians and Sioux and were at war with the Arikaras until we made peace a few days past. The Mandans are at war with all who make war only,

---

135. the younger was Sacagawea (DeVoto)

136. called "Raven" by Lewis and Clark

137. Black Hills

and wish to be at peace with all nations; [they are] seldom the aggressors.

Tuesday, November 13, 1804:

Clark: The ice began to run in the river [at] 10:30 p.m.

We rose early and unloaded the boat before breakfast, except the cabin, and stored away in a storehouse.

[It] snowed all day. The ice ran thick and [the] air [was] cold.

Friday, November 16, 1804:

Clark: [We have] a very white frost. All the trees [are] all covered with ice; [it is] cloudy.

All the men moved into the huts, which are not finished.

The Assiniboines are at the Hidatsa camp. Some trouble [is] likely to take place between them from the loss of horses, etc., as is said by an old Indian who visited us with four buffalo robes and corn to trade for a pistol which we did not let him have.

[The] men [were] employed until late in daubing their huts. Some horses [were] sent down to stay in the woods near the fort to prevent the Assiniboines [from] stealing them.

Sunday, November 18, 1804:

Clark: The Black Cat came to see us. He made great inquiries respecting our fashions. He also stated the situation of their nation. He mentioned that a council had been held the day before and it was thought advisable to put up with the recent insults of the Assiniboines and Crees until they were convinced [of] what had been told them by us. Mr. Evans had deceived them and we might also. He [had] promised to return and furnish them with guns and ammunition.

We advised them to remain at peace and that they might depend upon getting supplies through the channel of the Missouri but it required time to put the trade in operation. The Assiniboines, etc., have the trade of these nations in their power and treat them badly, as the Sioux do the Arikaras, and they cannot resent, for fear of losing their trade.

Tuesday, November 20, 1804:

Clark: We this day moved into our huts, which are now completed. This place, which we call Fort Mandan, is situated in a point of low ground on the north side of the Missouri, covered with tall and heavy cottonwood. The works consist of two rows of huts or sheds, forming an angle where they join each other. Each row contains four rooms of fourteen feet square and seven feet high, with plank ceiling, and the roof slanting so as to form a loft above the rooms, the highest part of which is eighteen feet from the ground. The backs of the huts form a wall of that height and, opposite the angle, the place of the wall is supplied by picketing. In the area are two rooms for stores and provisions.

The latitude by observation is forty-seven degrees, twenty-one minutes, and forty-seven seconds, and the computed distance from the mouth of the Missouri is sixteen hundred miles.

In the course of the day, several Indians came down to partake of our fresh meat. Among the rest, three chiefs of the second Mandan village [came]. They informed us that the Sioux on the Missouri about the Cheyenne River threaten to attack them this winter [and] that these Sioux are much irritated at the Arikaras for having made peace through our means with the Mandans, and have lately ill-treated three Arikaras who carried the pipe of peace to them, by beating them and taking away their horses.

We gave them assurances that we would protect them from all their enemies.

November____, 1804:

Lewis: Fort Mandan,

1,609 miles above the entrance of the Missouri

Dear Mother,

The near approach of winter, the low state of the water, and the known scarcity of timber which exists on the Missouri for many hundreds of miles determined my friend and companion, Captain Clark, and myself to fortify ourselves and remain for the winter in the neighborhood of the Mandans who are the most friendly and well-disposed savages that we have yet met with.

You may expect me in Albemarle[138] about the last of next September twelve months. I request that you will give yourself no uneasiness with respect to my fate, for I assure you that I feel myself perfectly as safe as I should do in Albemarle, and the only difference between three or four thousand miles and one hundred thirty is that I cannot have the pleasure of seeing you as often as I did while at Washington.

---

138. Albemarle County, Virginia

Thursday, November 22, 1804:

Clark: I was alarmed about 10:00 by the sentinel, who informed [me] that an Indian was about to kill his wife in the interpreter's fire about sixty yards below the works. I sent down and spoke to the fellow about the rash act which he was [about to] commit and forbade any act of the kind near the fort. Some misunderstanding took place between this man and his wife about eight days ago, and she came to this place and continued with the squaws of the interpreters. Two days ago she returned to the village. In the evening of the same day, she came to the interpreter's fire apparently much beaten and stabbed in three places.

We directed that no man of this party have any intercourse with this woman under the penalty of punishment. He, the husband, observed that one of our sergeants slept with his wife and if he wanted her he would give her to him. We directed the sergeant[139] to give the man some articles, at which time I told the Indian that I believed not one man of the party had touched his wife except the one he had given the use of her for a night in his own bed. No man of the party should touch his squaw, or the wife of any Indian, nor did I believe they [should] touch a woman if they knew her to be the wife of another man, and advised him to take his squaw home and live happily together in [the] future.

The grand chief continued [with us] all day.

[It was] a warm day [and a] fair afternoon.

[We heard] many Indian anecdotes. Our chief and his family stayed all night.

Ordway: [It was] pleasant and warm.

The pirogue returned towards evening with about twelve bushels of mixed colored corn in ears, which the natives took out of the ground where they bury it in holes in their village.

Tuesday, November 27, 1804:

Clark: Captain Lewis returned from the villages with two chiefs and a Considerable Man with the party who accompanied him. The Hidatsa were alarmed at the tales told [to] them by the Mandans, viz., that we intended to join the Sioux to cut off them in the course of the winter. Many circumstances combined to give force to those reports, i.e., the movements of the interpreters and their families to the fort, the strength of our works, etc., etc. All these reports were contradicted by Captain Lewis with a conviction on the minds of the Indians of the falsity of those reports.

139. Ordway (DeVoto)

Seven traders arrived from the fort on the Assiniboine from the North West Company, one of which, Lafrance, took [it] upon himself to speak unfavorably of our intentions, etc. The principal, Mr. Larocque[140] (and Mr. MacKenzie[141]) were informed of the conduct of their interpreter and the consequences if they did not put a stop to unfavorable and ill-founded assertions, etc., etc.

The two chiefs [were] much pleased with their treatment and the cheerfulness of the party, who danced to amuse them, etc., etc.

The river fell by two inches. [It was] very cold and began to snow at 8:00 p.m. and continued all night.

Wednesday, November 28, 1804:

Clark: [The] river [is] full of floating ice. [It] began to snow at 7:00 a.m. and continued all day.

At 8:00, the Black Cat came to see us. After showing these chiefs many things which were curiosities to them and giving [them] a few presents of curious handkerchiefs, arm bands and paint, with a twist of tobacco, they departed at 1:00 much pleased. At parting, we had some little talk on the subject of the British trader, Mr. Larocque, giving [them] medals and flags, and [we] told these chiefs to impress it on the minds of their nations that these symbols were not to be received by any from them, without they wished to incur the displeasure of their Great American Father.

[It was] a very disagreeable day. No work [was] done today.

Thursday, November 29, 1804:

Clark: The depth of the snow is various in the woods, about thirteen inches. The river [is] closed at the village above.

Mr. Larocque and one of his men came to visit us. We informed him what we had heard of his intentions of making chiefs, etc., and forbade him to give medals or flags to the Indians. He denied having any such intention. We agreed that one of our interpreters[142] should speak for him on [the] condition [that] he did not say anything more than what tended to trade alone.

Sergeant Pryor, in taking down the mast, put his shoulder out of place. We made four trials before we replaced it.

---

140. François Antoine Larocque, leader of this North West Company party (DeVoto)

141. Charles MacKenzie, Larocque's clerk (DeVoto)

142. Charbonneau

Friday, November 30, 1804:

Clark: This morning at 8:00, an Indian called from the other side and informed [us] that he had something of consequence to communicate. We sent a pirogue for him and he informed us as follows, viz., "Five men of the Mandan nation out hunting in a southwest direction about eight leagues were surprised by a large party of Sioux and Arikaras; one man was killed and two wounded with arrows and nine horses [were] taken. Four of the Anahaway nation were missing and they expected to be attacked by the Sioux, etc., etc."

We thought it well to show a disposition to aid and assist them against their enemies, and I determined to go to the town with some men and, if the Sioux were coming to attack the nation, to collect the warriors from each village and meet them. I crossed the river in about an hour after the arrival of the Indian express with twenty-three men, including the interpreters, and flanked the town and came up on the back part.

The Indians, not expecting to receive such strong aid in so short a time, were much surprised and a little alarmed at the formidable appearance of my party. I explained to the nation [that] the cause of my coming in this formidable manner to their town was to assist and [to] chastise the enemies of our dutiful children. I requested the grand chief to repeat the circumstances as they happened, which he did as was mentioned by the express in the morning. I then informed them that if they would assemble their warriors and those of the different towns, I would go to meet the army of Sioux, etc., [and] chastise them for taking the blood of our dutiful children, etc.

After a conversation of a few minutes amongst themselves, one chief said [that] they now saw that what we had told them was the truth, [that] when we expected the enemies of their nation were coming to attack them or had spilled their blood, we were ready to protect them and kill those who would not listen to our good talk. His people had listened to what we had told them and carelessly went out to hunt in small parties, believing themselves to be safe from the other nations, and have been killed by the Arikaras and Sioux.

"I knew," said he, "that the Arikaras were liars and told the old chief who came with you (to confirm a peace with us) that his people were liars and bad men and that we killed them like the buffalo when we pleased. We had made peace several times and your nation has always commenced the war. We do not want to kill you and will not suffer you to kill us or steal our horses. We will make peace with you as our two fathers have directed, and they shall see that we will not be the aggressors, but we fear the Arikaras will not be at peace long.

"My father, those are the words I spoke to the Arikaras in your presence. You see they have not opened their ears to your good councils but have spilled our blood. Two Arikaras whom we sent home this day for fear of our people killing them in their grief informed us when they came here several days ago that two towns of the Arikaras were making their moccasins[143] and that we had best take care of our horses, etc.

"My father, the snow is deep and it is cold; our horses cannot travel through the plains. Those people who have spilled our blood have gone back. If you will go with us in the spring after the snow goes off, we will raise the warriors of all the towns and nations around about us, and go with you."

I told this nation that we should be always willing and ready to defend them from the insults of any nation who would dare to come to do them injury during the time we would remain in their neighborhood, and requested that they would inform us of any party who may at any time be discovered by their patrols or scouts.

I was sorry that the snow in the plains had fallen so deep since the murder of the young chief by the Sioux as [to] prevent their horses from traveling. I wished to meet those Sioux and all others who will not open their ears but make war on our dutiful children, and let you see that the warriors of your Great Father will chastise the enemies of his dutiful children, the Mandans, Anahaways and Hidatsa, who have opened their ears to his advice.

After about two hours [of] conversation on various subjects, all of which tended towards their situation, etc., I informed them [that] I should return to the fort. The chief said [that] they all thanked me very much for the fatherly protection which I showed towards them, that the village had been crying all night and day for the death of the brave young man who fell, but now they would wipe away their tears and rejoice in their Father's protection and cry no more.

I then paraded and crossed the river on the ice, and came down on the north side. The snow [was] so deep it was very fatiguing. [I] arrived at the fort after night [and] gave a little taffee[144] to my party.

---

143. preparing for war (DeVoto)

144. rum (Bakeless, p. 111)

4: Winter, 1804-5

About 5:00 this evening, one of the wives of Charbonneau [Sacagawea] was delivered of a fine boy. It is worthy of remark that this was the first child which this woman had borne and, as is common in such cases, her labor was tedious and the pain violent.

Meriwether Lewis,
February 11, 1805

Saturday, December 1, 1804:

Clark: In the evening, a Mr. G. Henderson arrived in the employ of the Hudson's Bay Company, sent to trade with the Gros Ventres, or Big Bellies, so-called by the French traders.

December 6, 1804:

Gass: In the night, the river froze over, and in the morning was covered with solid ice an inch and a half thick.

Friday, December 7, 1804:

Clark: Big White, grand chief of the first village, came and informed us that a large drove of buffalo was near and his people were waiting for us to join them in a chase. Captain Lewis took fifteen men and went out [and] joined the Indians who were, at the time he got up, killing the buffalo on horseback with arrows, which they did with great dexterity. His party killed ten buffalo, five of which we got to the fort by the assistance of a horse, in addition to what the men packed on their backs. One cow was killed on the ice after drawing her out of a vacancy in the ice in which she had fallen, and [we] butchered her at the fort. Those we did not get in were taken by the Indians under a custom which is established amongst them, i.e., any person seeing a buffalo lying without an arrow sticking in him, or some particular mark, takes possession.

The river closed opposite the fort last night, one-and-a-half inches thick. The thermometer stood this morning at one degree below zero.

Three men [were] frostbitten badly today.

Saturday, December 8, 1804:

Clark: The thermometer stood at twelve degrees below zero, which is forty-four degrees below the freezing point.

Several men returned a little frostbitten, one of the men with his feet badly frostbitten. My servant's feet [were] also frostbitten and his p___s a little.

Monday, December 10, 1804:

Ordway: The weather gets colder very fast so that the sentinel had to be relieved every hour.

Tuesday, December 11, 1804:

Clark: [It is] twenty-one degrees below zero and getting colder. The sun shows and reflects two images, the ice floating in the atmosphere being so thick that the appearance is like a fog dispersing.

Wednesday, December 12, 1804:

Clark: I line my gloves and have a cap made of the skin of the Louservia (lynx) (or wild cat of the north), the fur [of which is] nearly three inches long.

The weather is so cold that we do not think it prudent to turn out to hunt in such cold weather, or at least until our constitutions are prepared to undergo this climate. I measured the river from bank to bank on the ice and make it five hundred yards.

Ordway: [It was] clear and cold. The frost was white in the guard chimney where there was a fire kept all last night. It is several degrees colder this morning than it has been before so that we did nothing but get wood for our fires. Our rooms are very close and warm so we can keep ourselves warm and comfortable, but the sentinel who stood out in the open weather had to be relieved every hour all day.

Thursday, December 13, 1804:

Clark: The thermometer stands this morning at twenty degrees below zero. [It is] a fine day.

[I] find it impossible to make an observation with an artificial horizon.

Sunday, December 16, 1804:

Clark: Mr. Heney,[145] from the establishment on River Assiniboine, with a letter from Mr. Charles Chaboillez,[146] one of the company, arrived in six days. Mr. Chaboillez, in his letter, expressed a great anxiety to serve us in anything in his power.

A root [was] described by Mr. Heney for the cure of a mad dog.

Mr. Larocque, a clerk of the North West Company, and Mr. George Bunch, a clerk of the Hudson's Bay Company, accompanied Mr. Heney from the village.

Gass: Three of the traders from the North West Company came to our fort and brought a letter to our commanding officers. They remained with us all night. The object of the visits we received from the North West Company was to ascertain our motives for visiting that country and to gain information with respect to the change of government.

Monday, December 17, 1804:

Clark: [It was] a very cold morning forty-five degrees below zero.

We found Mr. Heney [to be] a very intelligent man from whom we obtained some sketches of the country between the Mississippi and Missouri and some sketches from him, which he had obtained from the Indians to the west of this place [and] also the names and characters of the Sioux, etc.

About 8:00 p.m. the thermometer fell to seventy-four degrees below the freezing point.

The Indian chiefs sent word that buffalo were in our neighborhood.

Whitehouse: [It was] a cold day. Sergeant Gass fixed a horse sled for one of the North West Company traders to go to their forts.

Tuesday, December 18, 1804:

Ordway: [It was] very cold last night so that the sentinel had to be relieved every half hour.

Clark: Mr. Heney and Mr. Larocque left us for the Hidatsa camp.

[We] sent out seven men to hunt for the buffalo; they found the weather too cold and returned.

I employ myself making a small map of connections, etc.

[I] sent Jessaume to the main chief of the Mandans to know the cause of his detaining or taking a horse of Charbonneau, our Hidatsa interpreter, which we found was through the rascality of one Lafrance, a trader from the North West Company.

---

145. Hugh Heney, one of Loisel's partners (DeVoto)

146. an agent for the North West Company (Bakeless, p. 114)

Friday, December 21, 1804:

Clark: The Indian whom I stopped from committing murder on his wife, through jealousy of one of our interpreters, came and brought his two wives and showed great anxiety to make up with the man with whom his jealousy sprang.

A woman brought a child with an abscess on the lower part of the back and offered as much corn as she could carry for some medicine. Captain Lewis administered, etc.

Saturday, December 22, 1804:

Clark: A number of squaws and men dressed in squaw's clothes[147] came with corn to sell to the men for little things. We procured two horns of the animal the French call the Rocky Mountain sheep.

Tuesday, December 25, 1804:

Clark: Christmas - I was awakened before day by a discharge of three platoons from the party and the Frenchmen. The men [were] merrily disposed. I gave them all a little taffee and permitted three cannons [to be] fired at raising our flag. Some men went out to hunt and others to dance and continued until 9:00 p.m. when the frolic ended, etc.

Ordway: We fired the swivels at daybreak and each man fired one round. Our officers gave the party a drink of taffee. We had the best to eat that could be had and continued firing, dancing and frolicking during the whole day. The savages did not trouble us as we had requested them not to come as it was a great medicine day with us. We enjoyed a merry Christmas during the day and evening until 9:00—all in peace and quietness.

Whitehouse: We ushered in the morning with a discharge of the swivel gun and one round of small arms of all the party, then another from the swivel. Then Captain Clark presented a glass of brandy to each man of the party. We hoisted the American flag and each man had another glass of brandy. The men prepared one of the rooms and commenced dancing.

At 10:00 we had another glass of brandy [and] at 1:00 a gun was fired as a signal for dinner.

---

147. homosexuals; the Indians believed that they had been directed by a medicine vision to dress and act as women; they suffered no loss of status (DeVoto)

[At] half past two another gun was fired to assemble at the dance and so we kept it up in a jovial manner until 8:00 at night, all without the company of the female sex.

Monday, December 31, 1804:

Clark: Fort Mandan - A number of Indians [are] here every day. Our blacksmith [is] mending their axes, hoes, etc., etc., for which the squaws bring corn for payment.

Tuesday, January 1, 1805:

Clark: The day was ushered in by the discharge of two cannons. We suffered sixteen men with their music to visit the first village for the purpose of dancing by, as they said, the particular request of the chiefs of that village.

About 11:00 I, with an interpreter and two men, walked up to the village. (My views were to allay some little misunderstanding which had taken place through jealousy and mortification as to our treatment towards them.) I found them much pleased at the dancing of our men. I ordered my black servant to dance, which amused the crowd very much and somewhat astonished them that so large a man should be active, etc., etc.

A chief returned from a mission on which they had been sent to meet a large party (one hundred fifty) of Hidatsa who were on their way down from their camps ten miles above to revenge on the Sioux tribe [for] an injury which they had received by a Sioux man stealing a Hidatsa girl. Those chiefs gave the pipe and turned the party back after delivering up the girl, which the Sioux chief had taken and given to them for that purpose.

I returned in the evening. At night the party, except six, returned with three robes and thirteen strings of corn which the Indians had given them.

The day was warm; [the] thermometer [stood at] thirty-four degrees above zero. Some few drops of rain [fell] about sunset. At dark it began to snow and snowed the greater part of the night.

Ordway: We went up to the first village of Mandans to dance, as it had been their request. [We] carried with us a fiddle and a tambourine and a sounding horn. As we arrived at the entrance of the village, we fired one round, then the music played. [We] loaded again [and] then marched to the center of the village and fired again, [and] then commenced dancing. A Frenchman danced on his head and all danced round him for a short time. Then [we] went into a lodge and danced awhile, which pleased them very much. They then brought victuals from different lodges and some buffalo robes, which they made us a present of. So we danced in different lodges until late in the afternoon. Then a part of the men returned to the fort. The remainder stayed all night in the village.

Saturday, January 5, 1805:

Clark: I employ myself drawing a connection of the country from what information I have received.

[There was] a buffalo dance for three nights past in the first village, a curious custom. The old men arrange themselves in a circle and after smoking a pipe which is handed [to] them by a young man, dress up for the purpose. The young men, who have their wives back of the circle, [each] go to one of the old men with a whining tone and request the old man to take his wife (who presents herself naked except [for] a robe) and ____ (or sleep with her). The girl then takes the old man (who very often can scarcely walk) and leads him to a convenient place for the business, after which they return to the lodge. If the old man (or a white man) returns to the lodge without gratifying the man and his wife, he offers her again and again. It is often the case that after the second time, without kissing, the husband throws a new robe over the old man, etc., and begs him not to despise him and his wife. (We sent a man to this medicine dance last night; they gave him four girls.) All this is to cause the buffalo to come near so that they may kill them.

Monday, January 7, 1805:

Gass: Captain Lewis and eleven more of us went out and saw the prairie covered with buffalo and the Indians on horseback killing them. They killed thirty or forty and we killed eleven of them. They shoot them with bows and arrows and have their horses trained [so] that they will advance very near and suddenly wheel and fly off in case the wounded buffalo attempts an attack.

Wednesday, January 9, 1805:

Clark: [It is] a cold day; [the] thermometer [stands at] twenty-one degrees below zero.

Great numbers of Indians go to kill cows.

Little Crow[148] [ate] breakfast with us.

Several Indians called at the fort nearly frozen.

---

148. second chief (under Big White) of the first Mandan village (Ambrose, *UC*, p. 183)

Ordway: [It is] blustery and exceedingly cold. A number of the savages [were] out hunting the buffalo again and came in towards evening with their horses loaded with meat and told us that two of their young men were frozen to death in the prairie.

Thursday, January 10, 1805:

Clark: Last night was excessively cold. The mercury this morning stood at forty degrees below zero, which is seventy-two degrees below the freezing point.

We had one man out last night who returned about 8:00 this morning.

The Indians of the lower village turned out to hunt for a man and a boy who had not returned from the hunt of yesterday, and borrowed a sleigh to bring them in, expecting to find them frozen to death. About 10:00 the boy, about thirteen years of age, came to the fort with his feet frozen; [he] had lain out last night without [a] fire with only a buffalo robe to cover him. The dress which he wore was a pair of cabra[149] (antelope) leggings, which are very thin, and moccasins. We had his feet put in cold water and they are coming to.

Soon after the arrival of the boy, a man came in who had also stayed out without [a] fire, and very thinly clothed. This man was not the least injured. Customs and the habits of these people have inured them to bear more cold than I thought it possible for man to endure.

Monday, January 14, 1805:

Whitehouse: [I] killed one buffalo, a wolf and two porcupines, and I got my feet so frozen that I could not walk to the fort.

Ordway: George Shannon came in this evening and informed us that Whitehouse had his feet frostbitten and could not come in without a horse.

Wednesday, January 16, 1805:

Whitehouse: [It is] quite warm for the time of year, and pleasant. The snow melted fast. I came to the fort and two more men with me. My feet got some easier.

Clark: One of the first war chiefs of the Hidatsa nation came to see us today with one man and his squaw to wait on him. We shot the air gun and gave two shots with the cannon, which pleased him very much.

---

149. Spanish for *cabretta*: light, soft leather from sheepskins

Four men of ours who had been hunting returned; one [was] frostbitten.

This war chief gave us a chart in his way of the Missouri. He informed us of his intentions of going to war in the spring against the Shoshone Indians.

We advised him to look back at the number of nations who had been destroyed by war and reflect upon what he was about to do, observing, if he wished the happiness of his nation, he would be at peace with all. By that, by being at peace and having plenty of goods amongst them and a free intercourse with those defenseless nations, they would get on easy terms a greater number of horses and that nation would increase. If he went to war against those defenseless people, he would displease his Great Father and he would not receive that protection and care from him as other nations who listened to his word.

This chief, who is a young man twenty-six years old, replied that if his going to war against the Shoshone Indians would be displeasing to us he would not go, [that] he had horses enough.

Saturday, January 19, 1805:

Whitehouse: Two men [were] sent with three horses down the river for meat to the hunting camp, which is about thirty miles distant from the fort. The way they go [is] on the ice.

Sunday, January 20, 1805:

Whitehouse: Some of the men went up to the villages. When they were done eating, they[150] gave a bowl of victuals to a buffalo head which they worshipped. [They] eat this so that the live ones may come in [so] that we may get a supply of meat.

Some of them and, indeed, the most of them have strange and uncommon ideas [and are] but very ignorant of our forms and customs, but quick and sensible in their own way and in their own conceit, etc., etc.

Saturday, January 26, 1805:

Clark: [It is] a very fine, warm day.

One man [has] taken violently bad with the pleurisy. [We] bleed and apply those remedies common to that disorder.

---

150. the Mandans

Sunday, January 27, 1805:

Clark: [We] attempted to cut our boat and canoes out of the ice, a difficult task, I fear, as we found water between the ice.

I bled the man with the pleurisy today, and sweated him. Captain Lewis took off the toes of one foot of the boy who got frostbitten some time ago.

Wednesday, January 30, 1805:

Ordway: Sergeant Gass [was] sent up the river to another bluff in order to look for another kind of stone that would not split with heat. He brought one home and heated it. As soon as it was hot it burst asunder. So we gave up that plan.

Clark: Mr. Larocque paid us a visit and we gave him an answer, respecting the request he made when last here, of accompanying us on our journey, etc. ([We] refused.)

Sunday, February 3, 1805:

Lewis: The situation of our boat and pirogues is now alarming. They are firmly enclosed in the ice and almost covered with snow. The ice which encloses them lies in several strata of unequal thickness which are separated by streams of water. This is peculiarly unfortunate because as soon as we cut through the first stratum of ice, the water rushes up and rises as high as the upper surface of the ice and thus creates such a depth of water as renders it impracticable to cut away the lower strata, which appear firmly attached to, and confining, the bottom of the vessels.

The instrument we have hitherto used has been the ax only with which we have made several attempts that proved unsuccessful. We then determined to attempt freeing them from the ice by means of boiling water which we proposed heating in the vessels by means of hot stones, but this expedient proved also fruitless as every species of stone which we could procure in the neighborhood partook so much of the calcareous genus that they burst into small particles on being exposed to the heat of the fire.

We now determined as the derriere resort to prepare a parcel of iron spikes and attach them to the end of small poles of convenient length and endeavor, by means of them, to free the vessels from the ice. We have already prepared a large rope of elk skin and a windlass, by means of which we have no doubt of being able to draw the boat on the bank, provided we can free it from the ice.

Monday, February 4, 1805:

Lewis: Captain Clark set out with a hunting party consisting of sixteen of our command and two Frenchmen who, together with two others, have established a small hut and resided this winter within the vicinity of Fort Mandan under our protection. Our stock of meat, which we had procured in the months of November and December, is now nearly exhausted. Captain Clark therefore determined to continue his route down the river even as far as the River Cannonball unless he should find a plenty of game nearer. The men transported their baggage on a couple of small wooden sleighs drawn by themselves and took with them three pack horses. No buffalo have made their appearance in our neighborhood for some weeks.

Wednesday, February 6, 1805:

Lewis: The blacksmiths take a considerable quantity of corn today in payment for their labor. The blacksmiths have proved a happy resource to us in our present situation as I believe it would have been difficult to have devised any other method to have procured corn from the natives.[151]

Thursday, February 7, 1805:

Lewis: The sergeant of the guard reported that the Indian women (wives to our interpreters) were in the habit of unbarring the fort gate at any time of the night and admitting their Indian visitors. I therefore directed a lock to be put to the gate and ordered that no Indians but those attached to the garrison should be permitted to remain all night within the fort or admitted during the period which the gate had been previously ordered to be kept shut, which was from sunset until sunrise.

Saturday, February 9, 1805:

Lewis: [We were] visited by Mr. MacKenzie, one of the North West Company clerks.

This evening a man by the name of Howard,[152] whom I had given permission to go to the Mandan village, returned after the gate was shut and rather than call to the guard to have it opened, scaled the works. An Indian who was looking on shortly after followed his exam-

---

151. John Shields, a blacksmith, cut up old stove pieces that could be traded with the Indians for corn; the Indians would then make arrow points or buffalo-hide scrapers. (Ambrose, *UC*, p. 199)

152. Private Thomas P. Howard

ple. I convinced the Indian of the impropriety of his conduct and explained to him the risk he had run of being severely treated. The fellow appeared much alarmed. I gave him a small piece of tobacco and sent him away. Howard I had committed to the care of the guard with a determination to have him tried by a court-martial for his offense. This man is an old soldier, which still heightens this offense.

Monday, February 11, 1805:

Lewis: About 5:00 this evening, one of the wives of Charbonneau[153] was delivered of a fine boy.[154] It is worthy of remark that this was the first child which this woman had borne and, as is common in such cases, her labor was tedious and the pain violent. Mr. Jessaume informed me that he had frequently administered a small portion of the rattle of the rattlesnake which, he assured me, had never failed to produce the desired effect, that of hastening the birth of a child. Having the rattle of a snake by me, I gave it to him and he administered two rings of it to the woman, broken in small pieces with the fingers, and added to a small quantity of water. Whether this medicine was truly the cause or not, I shall not undertake to determine, but I was informed that she had not taken it more than ten minutes before she brought forth.

Wednesday, February 13, 1805:

Clark: I returned last night from a hunting party much fatigued, having walked thirty miles on the ice and through points of woodland in which the snow was nearly knee-deep.

Friday, February 15, 1805:

Clark: At 10:00 p.m. last night, the men that dispatched yesterday for the meat returned and informed us that as they were on their march down at the distance of about twenty-four miles below the fort (George Drouillard, Frazier,[155] Silas Goodrich, and Newman,[156] with a broken gun), about one hundred five Indians, which they took to be Sioux, rushed on them and cut their horses from the sleighs, two of which they carried off in great haste. The third horse was given up to the party by the intercession of an Indian who assumed some authority on the occasion, probably more through fear of himself or some of the

---

153. Sacagawea

154. Jean Baptiste Charbonneau, nicknamed "Pomp" by the captains

155. Private Robert Frazier, usually spelled "Frasure" by the captains

156. Private John Newman

Indians being killed by our men who were not disposed to be robbed of all they had tamely. They also forced two of the men's knives and a tomahawk. The men obliged them to return the tomahawk; the knives they ran off with.

We dispatched two men to inform the Mandans, and if any of them chose to pursue those robbers, to come down in the morning and join Captain Lewis, who intended to set out with a party of men very early. By 12:00 the chief of the second village,[157] Big White, came down and soon after, one other chief and several men. The chief observed that all the young men of the two villages were out hunting and but very few guns were left.

Captain Lewis set out at sunrise with twenty-four men to meet those Sioux, etc. Several Indians accompanied him, some with bows and arrows, some with spears and battle axes, [and] two with fusils.

One chief of the Mandans returned from Captain Lewis' party nearly blind. This complaint is, as I am informed, common at this season of the year and [is] caused by the reflection of the sun on the ice and snow. It is cured by gently sweating the part affected, by throwing snow on a hot stone.

Saturday, February 16, 1805:

Clark: At dusk, two of the Indians who went down with Captain Lewis returned. Soon after, two others and one man (Howard), with his feet frostbitten, [returned] and informed [us] that the Indians who committed the robbery of the two horses were so far ahead that they could not be overtaken. They left a number of pairs of moccasins, which the Mandans knew to be Sioux moccasins.

Captain Lewis and [the] party proceeded on down. The meat I left at my last camp was taken.

Thursday, February 21, 1805:

Clark: [It was] a delightful day. [We] put out our clothes to sun.

[We were] visited by Big White and Big Man. They informed me that several men of their nation were gone to consult their medicine stone, about three days' march to the southwest, to know what was to be the result of the ensuing year. They have great confidence in this stone and say that it informs them of everything which is to happen, and visit it every spring and sometimes in the summer. They, having arrived at the stone, give it smoke and proceed to the woods at some distance to sleep. The next morning [they] return to the stone and find marks, white and raised, on the stone representing the peace or war

157. actually, the first village

which they are to meet with and other changes which they are to meet. This stone has a level surface of about twenty feet in circumference, [is] thick and porous, and no doubt has some mineral qualities affected by the sun.

Captain Lewis returned with two sleighs loaded with meat. After finding that he could not overtake the Sioux war party (who had, in their way, destroyed all the meat at one deposit which I had made, and burned the lodges), [he] determined to proceed on to the lower deposit, which he found had not been observed by the Sioux. He hunted two days, killed thirty-six deer and fourteen elk, several of them so meager that they were unfit for use. The meat which he killed and that in the lower deposit, amounting to about three thousand pounds, was brought up on two sleighs. One, drawn by sixteen men, had about twenty-four hundred pounds on it.

Saturday, February 23, 1805:

Clark: All hands [were] employed in cutting the pirogues loose from the ice, which was nearly even with their top. We found great difficulty in effecting this work owing to the different divisions of ice and water.

The father of the boy, whose feet were frozen near this place, and nearly cured by us, took him home in a sleigh.

Monday, February 25, 1805:

Clark: We fixed a windlass and drew up the two pirogues on the upper bank and attempted [to draw up] the boat, but the rope, which we had made of elk skins, proved too weak and broke several times.

Tuesday, February 26, 1805:

Clark: [It was] a fine day.

[We] commenced very early in making preparations for drawing up the boat on the bank. At sunset, by repeated exertions the whole day, we accomplished this troublesome task. Just as we were fixed for hauling the boat, the ice gave way near us for about one hundred yards in length. A number of Indians [were] here today to see the boat rise on the bank.

Thursday, February 28, 1805:

Clark: [It was] a fine morning.

Two men of the North West Company arrived with letters, and also a root and top of a plant, presented by Mr. Heney, for the cure of mad dogs, snakes, etc. This root is found on the highlands and ascent of hills. The way of using it is to scarify the part when bitten, to chew or pound an inch, or more if the root is small, and apply it to the bitten part, renewing it twice a day. The bitten person is not to chew nor swallow any of the root for it might have [a] contrary effect.

[We] sent out sixteen men to make four pirogues. Those men returned in the evening and informed [us] that they found trees they thought would answer.

Mr. Gravelines, two Frenchmen, and two Indians arrived from the Arikaras nation with letters from Mr. Antoine Tabeau informing us of the peaceable dispositions of that nation towards the Mandans and Hidatsa and their avowed intentions of pursuing our council and advice. They express a wish to visit the Mandans to know if it will be agreeable to them to admit the Arikaras to settle near them and join them against their common enemy, the Sioux.

Mr. Gravelines informs [us] that the Sisseton Sioux and the three upper bands of the Tetons, with the Yanktons of the north,[158] intend to come to war in a short time against the nations in this quarter and will kill every white man they see. Mr. Tabeau also informs [us] that Mr. Cameron, of St. Peter's River, has put arms into the hands of the Sioux to revenge the death of three of his men killed by the Chippewas lately, and that the band of Tetons which we saw is disposed to do as we have advised them, through the influence of their chief, Black Buffalo.

Mr. Gravelines further informs [us] that the party which robbed us of the two horses lately were all Sioux, one hundred six in number. They called at the Arikaras on their return. The Arikaras, being displeased at their conduct, would not give them anything to eat, that being the greatest insult they could peaceably offer them, and upbraided them.

Ordway: The Sioux savages who robbed our men of the two horses were one hundred six in number and they had a mind to kill our men and then they held a counsel. But while they were doing that, our men were off and got clear.

Mr. Tabeau,[159] a Frenchman, sent a letter up to the commanding officers and Mandan chiefs to keep a good lookout, for he had heard the Sioux say that they should surely come to war in the spring against us and [the] Mandans.

---

158. all are bands of Sioux

159. Antoine Tabeau, an Arikara trader (Eide, p. 47)

5: Spring, 1805

We were now about to penetrate a country at least two thousand miles in width, on which the foot of civilized man had never trodden. The good or evil it had in store for us was for experiment yet to determine, and these little vessels contained every article by which we were to expect to subsist or defend ourselves. Entertaining as I do the most confident hope of succeeding in a voyage which had formed a darling project of mine for the last ten years, I could but esteem this moment of my departure as among the most happy of my life.

Captain Meriwether Lewis,
April 7, 1805

Saturday, March 2, 1805:

Clark: Mr. Larocque, a clerk of the North West Company, visited us. He has lately returned from the establishments on the Assiniboine River with merchandise to trade with Indians. Mr. Larocque informs us [that] the North West and XY Companies have joined, and the head of the North West Company is dead, Mr. McTavish of Montreal.

Saturday, March 9, 1805:

Clark: [It was] a cloudy, cold and windy morning [with the] wind from the north. I walked up to see the party that is making pirogues, about five miles above this; the wind [was] hard and cold. On my way up, I met the main chief of the Hidatsa,[160] with four Indians, on their way to see us. I requested him to proceed on to the fort where he would find Captain Lewis. I should be there myself in [the] course of a few hours. [I] sent the interpreter back with him and proceeded on myself to the canoes [and] found them nearly finished, the timber very bad.

After visiting all the pirogues where I found a number of Indians, I went to the upper Mandan village and smoked a pipe with the chief and returned.

On my return, [I] found the Hidatsa chief about setting out on his return to his village, having received of Captain Lewis a medal, arm-

160. Le Borgne, the One-Eyed Man (DeVoto)

bands, a flag, shirt scarlet, etc., etc., etc., for which he was much pleased. Two guns were fired for this great man.

Tuesday, March 12, 1805:

Clark: Our interpreter, Charbonneau, determines on not proceeding with us as an interpreter under the terms mentioned yesterday. He will not agree to work, let our situation be what it may, nor stand a guard, and if miffed with any man, he wishes to return when he pleases, [and] also have the disposal of as much provisions as he chooses to carry. [That is] inadmissible, and we suffer him to be off the engagement, which was only verbal.

Date approximated:

Lewis: Mr. Garreau, a Frenchman who has lived many years with the Arikaras and Mandans, showed us the process used by those Indians to make beads.[161] The discovery of this art these nations are said to have derived from the Shoshone Indians who had been taken prisoners by the Arikaras. The art is kept a secret by the Indians among themselves and is yet known to but a few of them. The Indians are extremely fond of the large beads formed by this process. They use them as pendants to their ears, or hair, and sometimes wear them about their necks.

Sunday, March 17, 1805:

Clark: Mr. Charbonneau sent a Frenchman of our party to say that he was sorry for the foolish part he had acted and, if we pleased, he would accompany us agreeably to the terms we had proposed and do everything we wished him to do, etc., etc. He had requested me some through our French interpreter two days ago to excuse his simplicity and take him into the service. After he had taken his things across the river, we called him in and spoke to him on the subject. He agreed to our terms and we agreed that he might go on with us, etc., etc.

Tuesday, March 19, 1805:

Clark: [It was a] cold, windy day [and] cloudy. [We had] some little snow last night.

[We were] visited today by Big White and Little Crow, [and] also a man and his wife with a sick child; I administered for the child. We

161. ordinary glass trade beads were pulverized, heated, and remolded into larger beads (DeVoto)

are told that two parties are gone to war from the Hidatsa and [that] one other party [was] going to war shortly.

Wednesday, March 20, 1805:

Clark: I, with all the men who could be spared from the fort, went to [the] canoes. There I found a number of Indians. The men carried four to the river, about one and a half miles through the bottom.

I visited the chief of the Mandans in the course of the day and smoked a pipe with him and several old men.

Thursday, March 21, 1805:

Clark: The men carried the remaining canoes[162] to the river and all, except three left to take care [of] and complete the canoes, returned to the fort with their baggage.

On my return today to the fort, I came on the points of the high hills. [I] saw an immense quantity of pumice stone on the sides and foot of the hills, and immense beds of pumice stone near the tops of them, with evident marks of the hills having once been on fire. I collected some of the different sorts, i.e., stone, pumice stone and a hard earth, and put them into a furnace. The hard earth melted and glazed; the other two and the hard clay became a pumice stone glazed.

Saturday, March 23, 1805:

Clark: After breakfast, Mr. Larocque and Mr. MacKenzie and the chiefs and men of the Hidatsa left us. In the forepart in the evening a little rain [fell], the first this winter.

Sunday, March 24, 1805:

Clark: [We] saw swans and wild geese flying northeast this evening.

Monday, March 25, 1805:

Clark: But few Indians visited us today, the ice having broken up in several places. The ice began to break away this evening and was near destroying our canoes as [it was] descending to the fort.

---

162. the six "canoes" or "pirogues" were cottonwood dugouts; they were to replace the too-deep keelboat which was to return to St. Louis (DeVoto)

Friday, March 29, 1805:

Clark: I observed extraordinary dexterity of the Indians in jumping from one cake of ice to another, for the purpose of catching the buffalo as they float down. Many of the cakes of ice which they pass over are not two feet square.

The plains are on fire in view of the fort on both sides of the river.

Saturday, March 30, 1805:

Clark: All [of] the party [are] in high spirits. They pass but few nights without amusing themselves dancing, possessing perfect harmony and good understanding towards each other.

[They are] generally healthy except venereal complaints which are very common amongst the natives, and the men catch it from them.

Wednesday, April 3, 1805:

Clark: Mr. Larocque and Mr. MacKenzie, clerks to the North West Company, visit us. We are all day engaged [in] packing up sundry articles[163] to be sent to the President of the U.S.

Friday April 5, 1805:

Gass: Some readers will perhaps expect [us], when we are about to renew our voyage, to give some account of the fair sex of the Missouri and entertain them with narratives of feats of love, as well as of arms. Though we could furnish a sufficient number of entertaining stories and pleasant anecdotes, we do not think it prudent to swell our journal with them, as our views are directed to more useful information. Besides, we are yet ignorant of the dangers which may await us.

It may be observed generally that chastity is not very highly esteemed by these people and that the severe and loathsome effects of certain French principles are not uncommon amongst them. The fact is that the women are generally considered an article of traffic, and indulgences are sold at a very moderate price. As proof of this, I will just mention that, for an old tobacco box, one of our men was granted the honor of passing a night with the daughter of the head chief of the Mandan nation. An old bawd[164] with her punks[165] may also be found in some of the villages on the Missouri as well as in the large cities of polished nations.

---

163. including plant and animal specimens, Indian artifacts, live animals, letters, and reports

164. madam

165. prostitutes

Sunday, April 7, 1805:

Lewis: Having on this day at 4:00 p.m. completed every arrangement necessary for our departure, we dismissed the barge and crew with orders to return without loss of time to St. Louis. A small canoe with two French hunters accompanied the barge. These men had ascended the Missouri with us the last year as engagés. The barge crew consisted of six soldiers and two ____ Frenchmen. Two Frenchmen and an Arikara Indian also take their passage in her as far as the Arikara villages, at which place we expect Mr. Tabeau to embark with his peltry who in that case will make an addition of two, perhaps four, men to the crew of the barge.[166]

We gave Richard Warfington, a discharged corporal, the charge of the barge and crew, and confided to his care likewise our dispatches to the government, letters to our private friends, and a number of articles to the President of the United States.

One of the Frenchmen, by the name of Gravelines, an honest, discrete man and an excellent boatman, is employed to conduct the barge as a pilot. We have therefore every hope that the barge, and with her our dispatches, will arrive safe at St. Louis. Mr. Gravelines, who speaks the Arikara language extremely well, has been employed to conduct a few of the Arikara chiefs to the seat of government who have promised us to descend in the barge to St. Louis with that view.

At the same moment that the barge departed from Fort Mandan, Captain Clark embarked with our party and proceeded up the river. As I had no exercise for several weeks, I determined to walk on shore as far as our encampment of this evening.

Our vessels consisted of six small canoes and two large pirogues. This little fleet, although not quite so respectable as those of Columbus or Captain Cook, was still viewed by us with as much pleasure as those deservedly famed adventurers ever beheld theirs, and I dare say with quite as much anxiety for their safety and preservation.

We were now about to penetrate a country at least two thousand miles in width, on which the foot of civilized man had never trodden. The good or evil it had in store for us was for experiment yet to determine, and these little vessels contained every article by which we were to expect to subsist or defend ourselves. However, as the state of mind in which we are generally gives the coloring to events, when the imagination is suffered to wander into futurity, the picture which now presented itself to me was a most pleasing one. Entertaining as I do the most confident hope of succeeding in a voyage which had formed a

166. in addition, Reed and Newman, who had been discharged (DeVoto)

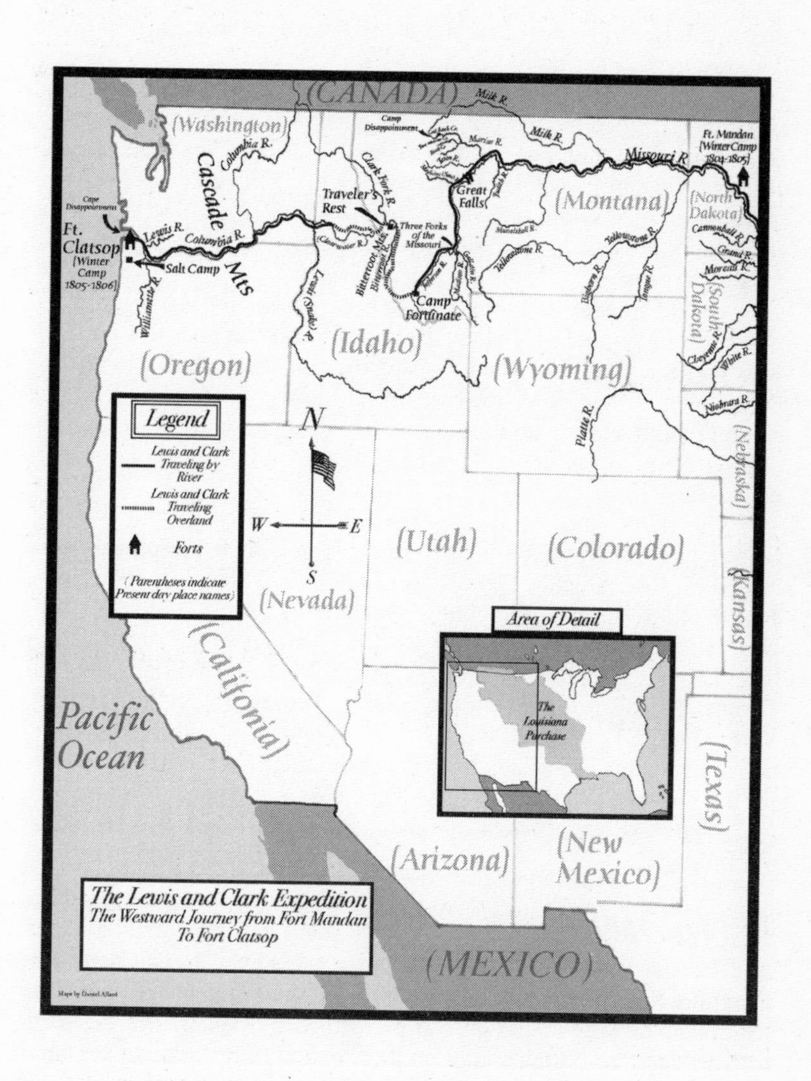
(CANADA)
(Washington)
(Montana)
(North Dakota)
(South Dakota)
(Idaho)
(Oregon)
(Wyoming)
(Nebraska)
(Utah)
(Colorado)
(Kansas)
(Nevada)
(California)
(Texas)
(Arizona)
(New Mexico)
(MEXICO)
Pacific Ocean
Cascade Mts
Ft. Clatsop (Winter Camp 1805-1806)
Salt Camp
Traveler's Rest
Three Forks of the Missouri
Camp Fortunate
Great Falls
Ft. Mandan (Winter Camp 1804-1805)
Missouri R.
Milk R.
Columbia R.
Lewis R.
Platte R.
Legend
Lewis and Clark Traveling by River
Lewis and Clark Traveling Overland
Forts
(Parentheses indicate Present day place names)
N
S
W
E
Area of Detail
The Louisiana Purchase
The Lewis and Clark Expedition
The Westward Journey from Fort Mandan To Fort Clatsop

darling project of mine for the last ten years, I could but esteem this moment of my departure as among the most happy of my life.

The party is in excellent health and spirits, zealously attached to the enterprise, and anxious to proceed. Not a whisper of murmur or discontent [is] to be heard among them, but all act in unison and with the most perfect harmony.

Captain Clark, myself, the two interpreters,[167] and the woman and child[168] sleep in a tent of dressed skins. This tent is in the Indian style, formed of a number of dressed buffalo skins sewn together with sinews. It is cut in such [a] manner that when folded double, it forms the quarter of a circle and is left open at one side. Here it may be attached or loosened at pleasure by strings which are sewn to its sides for the purpose.

Clark: Sunday at 4:00 p.m., the boat, in which were six soldiers, two Frenchmen and an Indian, all under the command of a corporal who had the charge of [the] dispatches, etc., and a canoe with two Frenchmen, set out down the river for St. Louis. At the same time, we set out on our voyage up the river in two pirogues and six canoes and proceeded on to the first village of Mandans and camped on the starboard side.

Our party consists of Sergeants Nathaniel Pryor, John Ordway, Patrick Gass, Privates William Bratton, John Colter, Joseph and Reubin Field, John Shields, George Gibson, George Shannon, John Potts, John Collins, Joseph Whitehouse, Richard Windsor, Alexander Willard, Hugh Hall, Silas Goodrich, Robert Frazier, Pierre Cruzatte, Baptiste Lepage,[169] Francis Labiche, Hugh McNeal, William Werner, Thomas P. Howard, Peter Wiser, John B. Thompson, and my servant, York, George Drouillard, who acts as a hunter and interpreter, Charbonneau and his Indian squaw to act as an interpreter and interpretress for the Shoshone Indians, one Mandan, and Charbonneau's infant.

Ordway: We all went on board, fired the swivel, and set off on our journey.

Tuesday, April 9, 1805:

Lewis: When we halted for dinner, the squaw busied herself in searching for the wild artichokes which the mice collect and deposit in large hoards. This operation she performed by penetrating the earth with a sharp stick about some small collection of driftwood. Her labor soon proved successful and she procured a good quantity of these

---

167. Drouillard and Charbonneau

168. Sacagawea and Pomp

169. previously a French trapper (Ambrose, *UC*, p.213)

roots. The flavor of this root resembles that of the Jerusalem artichoke and the stalk of the weed which produces it is also similar.

Clark: I saw a mosquito today. Great numbers of brant [are] flying up the river. The maple and elm have budded, and cottonwood and arrowwood [are] beginning to bud. But few resident birds or water fowl which I have seen as yet. [I] saw great numbers of geese feeding in the prairies on the young grass. I saw flowers in the prairies today. Juniper grows on the sides of the hills and runs on the ground.

Wednesday, April 10, 1805:

Lewis: At the distance of twelve miles from our encampment of last night, we arrived at the lower point of a bluff on the port side. About one-and-a-half miles down this bluff from this point, the bluff is now on fire and throws out considerable quantities of smoke which has a strong sulfurous smell.

At 1:00 p.m. we overtook three French hunters who had set out a few days before us with a view of trapping beaver. They had taken twelve since they left Fort Mandan. These people avail themselves of the protection which our numbers will enable us to give them against the Assiniboines who sometimes hunt on the Missouri, and intend ascending with us as far as the mouth of the Yellowstone River and continue there [to] hunt up that river. This is the first essay of a beaver hunter of any description on this river above the villages. The beaver these people have already taken are by far the best I have ever seen.

Saturday, April 13, 1805:

Lewis: The wind was in our favor after 9:00 a.m. and continued favorable until 3:00 p.m. We therefore hoisted both the sails in the white pirogue, consisting of a small square sail, and spritsail, which carried her at a pretty good gait until about 2:00 in the afternoon when a sudden squall of wind struck us and turned the pirogue so much on the side as to alarm Charbonneau, who was steering at the time. In this state of alarm, he threw the pirogue with her side to the wind when the spritsail jibing was as near oversetting the pirogue as it was possible to have missed. The wind, however, abated for an instant [and] I ordered Drouillard to the helm and the sails to be taken in, which was instantly executed, and the pirogue, being steered before the wind, was again placed in a state of security.

This accident was very near costing us dearly. Believing this vessel to be the most steady and safe, we had embarked on board of it our instruments, papers, medicine, and the most valuable part of the merchandise which we had still in reserve as presents for the Indians. We had also embarked on board ourselves, with three men who could not swim, and the squaw with the young child, all of whom, had the pirogue overset, would most probably have perished as the waves were high and the pirogue upwards of two hundred yards from the nearest shore.

Just above the entrance of the Little Missouri, the Great Missouri is upwards of a mile in width, though immediately at the entrance of the former it is not more than two hundred yards wide and so shallow that the canoes passed it with setting poles.

We found a number of carcasses of the buffalo lying along the shore which had been drowned by falling through the ice in winter and lodged on shore by the high water when the river broke up about the first of this month.

We saw also many tracks of the white bear of enormous size along the river shore and about the carcasses of the buffalo on which, I presume, they feed. We have not as yet seen one of these animals [even] though their tracks are so abundant and recent. The men, as well as ourselves, are anxious to meet with some of these bears.

The Indians give a very formidable account of the strength and ferocity of this animal which they never dare to attack but in parties of six, eight, or ten persons, and are even then frequently defeated with the loss of one or more of their party. The savages attack this animal with their bows and arrows and the indifferent guns with which the traders furnish them. With these they shoot with such uncertainty and at so short a distance that unless shot through [the] head or heart, [the] wound [is] not mortal. They frequently miss their aim and fall a sacrifice to the bear. This animal is said more frequently to attack a man on meeting with him than to flee from him. When the Indians are about to go in quest of the white bear, previous to their departure they paint themselves and perform all those superstitious rites commonly observed when they are about to make war upon a neighboring nation.

[We] observed more bald eagles on this part of the Missouri than we have previously seen. [We] saw the small hawk, frequently called the sparrow hawk, which is common to most parts of the United States. Great quantities of geese are seen feeding in the prairies. [We] saw a large flock of white brant, or geese with black wings, pass up the river. There were a number of gray brant with them.

Sunday, April 14, 1805:

Lewis: Where the land is level, it is uniformly fertile, consisting of a dark loam intermixed with a proportion of fine sand. It is generally covered with a short grass resembling very much the bluegrass. The mineral appearances still continue. Considerable quantities of bituminous water, about the color of strong lye, trickles down the sides of the hills. This water partakes of the taste of Glauber salts[170] and slightly of alum.

While the party halted to take dinner today, Captain Clark killed a buffalo bull. It was meager and we therefore took the marrow bones and a small proportion of the meat only.

[We] passed an island above which two small creeks fall in on [the] port side. The upper creek [is] largest, which we called Charbonneau's Creek after our interpreter who encamped several weeks on it with a hunting party of Indians. This was the highest point to which any white man had ever ascended except two Frenchmen (one of whom, Lepage, was now with us) who, having lost their way, straggled a few miles farther, though to what place precisely I could not learn.

Thursday, April 18, 1805:

Clark: After breakfast I ascended a hill and observed that the river made a great bend to the south. I concluded to walk through the point about two miles and take Charbonneau with me. He had taken a dose of salts, etc. His squaw followed on with her child. When I struck the next bend of the river, [I] could see nothing of the party. [I] left this man and his wife and child on the river bank and went out to hunt.

[I] killed a young buck elk and a deer. The elk was tolerable meat, the deer very poor. [I] butchered the meat and continued until near sunset before Captain Lewis and the party came up. They were detained by the wind which rose soon after I left the boat, from the northwest, and blew very hard until very late in the evening. [I] saw several old Indian camps. The game, such as buffalo, elk, antelope and deer, [were] very plenty.

Friday, April 19, 1805:

Clark: The wind [blew] so hard from the northwest that we were fearful of entering our canoes in the river. [We] laid by all day on the starboard side in a good harbor.[171]

The prairies appear to green [and] the cottonwood trees begin to leaf. [We] saw some plum bushes in full bloom. The beaver of this river are much larger than usual. [We saw] a great deal of [the] signs of the large bear.

---

170. a strong laxative

171. near Lewis and Clark State Park in North Dakota (Schmidt, p. 66)

Saturday, April 20, 1805:

Clark: We set out at 7:00 [and] proceeded on. Soon after we set out, a bank fell in near one of the canoes which liked to have filled her with water. The wind became hard and [the] waves so rough that we proceeded with our little canoes with much risk. Our situation was such after setting out that we were obliged to pass round the first point or lay exposed to the blustering winds and waves. In passing round the point, several canoes took in water, as also our large pirogue, but without injuring our stores, etc., much.

A short distance below our camp, I saw some rafts on the starboard side near which an Indian woman was scaffolded in the Indian form of deposing their dead and fallen down. She was or had been raised about six feet, enclosed in several robes tightly laced around her, with her dog sleigh, her bag of different colored earths paint, small bones of animals, beaver, nails, and several other little trinkets, [and] also a blue jay. Her dog was killed and lay near her.

Captain Lewis joined me soon after I landed and informed me [that] he had walked several miles higher and in his walk killed two deer and wounded an elk and a deer. Our party shot in the river four beaver and caught two which were very fat and much admired by the men. After we landed, they killed three elk, four geese, and two deer. We had some of our provisions, etc., which we got a little wet, aired.

The wind continued so hard that we were compelled to delay all day.

[We] saw several buffalo lodged in the driftwood which had been drowned in the winter in passing the river.

Monday, April 22, 1805:

Lewis: [We] set out at an early hour this morning. [We] proceeded pretty well until breakfast when the wind became so hard ahead that we proceeded with difficulty even with the assistance of our tow lines.

The party halted and Captain Clark and I walked to the White Earth River[172] which approaches the Missouri very near at this place, being about four miles above its entrance. We found that it contained more water than streams of its size generally do at this season. The water is much clearer than that of the Missouri. The banks of the river are steep and not more than ten or twelve feet high. The bed seems to be composed of mud altogether. The salts, which have been before mentioned as common on the Missouri, appear in great quantities along the banks of this river which are, in many places, so thickly cov-

172. now the Little Muddy River, near Williston, North Dakota (Schmidt, p. 66)

ered with them that they appear perfectly white. Perhaps it has been from this white appearance of its banks that the river has derived its name. This river is said to be navigable nearly to its source, which is at no great distance from the Saskatchewan, and I think from its size, the direction it seems to take, and the latitude of its mouth that there is very good ground to believe that it extends as far north as latitude fifty degrees. This stream passes through an open country generally.

Coal or carbonated wood, pumice, stone, lava, and other mineral appearances still continue. The coal appears to be of better quality. I exposed a specimen of it to the fire and found [that] it burned tolerably well. It afforded but little flame or smoke but produced a hot and lasting fire.

I ascended to the top of the cut bluff this morning from whence I had a most delightful view of the country, the whole of which, except the valley formed by the Missouri, is void of timber or underbrush, exposing to the first glance of the spectator immense herds of buffalo, elk, deer, and antelope feeding in one common and boundless pasture. We saw a number of beaver feeding on the bark of the trees along the verge of the river, several of which we shot, [and] found them large and fat.

Walking on shore this evening, I met with a buffalo calf which attached itself to me and continued to follow close at my heels until I embarked and left it. It appeared alarmed at my dog, which was probably the cause of its so readily attaching itself to me.

Captain Clark informed me that he saw a large drove of buffalo pursued by wolves today [and] that they, at length, caught a calf which was unable to keep up with the herd. The cows only defend their young so long as they are able to keep up with the herd and seldom return any distance in search of them.

Thursday, April 25, 1805:

Lewis: The water froze on the oars this morning as the men rowed. About 10:00 a.m. the wind began to blow so violently that we were obliged to lay to.

My dog had been absent during the last night and I was fearful we had lost him altogether. However, much to my satisfaction, he joined us at 8:00 this morning.

Knowing that the river was crooked from the reports of the hunters who were out yesterday, and believing that we were at no very great distance from the Yellowstone River, I determined, in order as much as possible to avoid detention, to proceed by land with a few men to the entrance of that river and make the necessary observations to determine its position.

Accordingly, I set out at 11:00 on the port side, accompanied by four men. When we had proceeded about four miles, I ascended the hills from whence I had a most pleasing view of the country, particularly of the wide and fertile valleys formed by the Missouri and the Yellowstone rivers which occasionally, unmasked by the wood on their borders, disclose their meanderings for many miles in their passage through these delightful tracts of country. I determined to encamp on the bank of the Yellowstone River, which made its appearance about two miles south of me.

The whole face of the country was covered with herds of buffalo, elk, and antelope. Deer are also abundant, but keep themselves more concealed in the woodland. The buffalo, elk, and antelope are so gentle that we pass near them while feeding without appearing to excite any alarm among them. And when we attract their attention, they frequently approach us more nearly to discover what we are and, in some instances, pursue us a considerable distance, apparently with that view. We encamped on the bank of the Yellowstone River two miles south of its confluence with the Missouri.

Ordway: [We] saw large gangs of buffalo swimming the river just before our canoes and we would not shoot them as we had meat enough on board.

Friday, April 26, 1805:

Lewis: This morning I dispatched Joseph Field up the Yellowstone River with orders to examine it as far as he could conveniently, and return the same evening, while I proceeded down the river with one man in order to take a view of the confluence of this great river with the Missouri, which we found to be two miles distant on a direct line northwest from our encampment.

The bottom land on the lower side of the Yellowstone River near its mouth, for about one mile in width, appears to be subject to inundation while that on the opposite side of the Missouri, and the point formed by the junction of these rivers, is of the common elevation, say from twelve to eighteen feet above the level of the water, and, of course, not liable to overflow except in extreme high water, which does not appear to be very frequent. There is more timber in the neighborhood of the junction of these rivers and on the Missouri as far below as the White Earth River than there is on any part of the Missouri above the entrance of the Cheyenne River to this place.

About 12:00 I heard the discharge of several guns at the junction of the rivers which announced to me the arrival of the party with Captain Clark. I afterward learned that they had fired on some buffalo which they met with at that place, and of which they killed a cow and several calves. The latter are now fine veal.

After I had completed my observations in the evening, I walked down and joined the party at their encampment on the point of land formed by the junction of the rivers. [I] found them all in good health and much pleased at having arrived at this long wished- for spot, and in order to add in some measure to the general pleasure, which seemed to pervade our little community, we ordered a dram to be issued to each person. This soon produced the fiddle, and they spent the evening with much hilarity, singing and dancing, and seemed as perfectly to forget their past toils as they appeared regardless of those to come.

Captain Clark measured these rivers just above their confluence. [He] found the bed of the Missouri five hundred twenty yards wide, the water occupying three hundred thirty [yards, and] its channel deep. The Yellowstone River, including its sand bar, [was] eight hundred fifty-eight yards [wide], of which the water occupied two hundred ninety-seven yards; the deepest part [was] twelve feet. It was falling at this time and appeared to be nearly at its summer tide.

The Indians inform [us] that the Yellowstone River is navigable for pirogues and canoes nearly to its source in the Rocky Mountains, and that in its course near these mountains it passes within less than half a day's march of a navigable part of the Missouri, River Platte and, I think, probably with some of the south branch of the Columbia River. The water of this river is turbid, though does not possess as much sediment as that of the Missouri.

Saturday, April 27, 1805:

Lewis: Although the game is very abundant and gentle, we only kill as much as is necessary for food. I believe that two good hunters could conveniently supply a regiment with provisions.

For several days past, we have observed a great number of buffalo lying dead on the shore, some of them entire, and others partly devoured by the wolves and bear. These animals either drowned during the winter in attempting to pass the river on the ice, or by swimming across, at present, to bluff banks where they are unable to ascend and, feeling themselves too weak to return, remain and perish for the want of food. In this situation, we met with several little parties of them.

Beaver are very abundant. The party kills several of them every day. The eagles, magpies, and geese have their nests in trees adjacent to each other. The magpie, particularly, appears fond of building near the eagle, as we scarcely see an eagle's nest unaccompanied by two or three magpie's nests within a short distance. The bald eagles are more abundant here than I ever observed them in any part of the country.

Sunday, April 28, 1805:

Lewis: [We] set out this morning at an early hour. The wind was favorable and we employed our sails to advantage. Captain Clark walked on shore this morning and I proceeded with the party.

We saw great quantities of game today consisting of the common and mule deer, elk, buffalo, and antelope, [and] also four brown bears, one of which was fired on and wounded by one of the party, but we did not get it. The beaver have cut great quantities of timber. [We] saw a tree nearly three feet in diameter that had been felled by them.

Monday, April 29, 1805:

Lewis: I walked in shore[173] with one man. About 8:00 a.m. we fell in with two brown or yellow bears,[174] both of which we wounded. One of them made his escape. The other, after my firing on him, pursued me seventy or eighty yards but fortunately had been so badly wounded that he was unable to pursue me so closely as to prevent my charging my gun. We again repeated our fire and killed him.

It was a male, not fully grown. We estimated his weight at three hundred pounds, not having means of ascertaining it precisely. The legs of this bear are somewhat longer than those of the black, as are its talons and tusks incomparably larger and longer. The testicles, which in the black bear are placed pretty well back between the thighs and contained in one pouch like those of the dog and most quadrupeds, are in the yellow or brown bear placed much farther forward and are suspended in separate pouches[175] from two to four inches asunder. Its color is yellowish brown, the eyes small, black and piercing. The front of the forelegs near the feet is unusually black. The fur is finer, thicker and deeper than that of the black bear. These are all the particulars in which this animal appeared to me to differ from the black bear.

It is a much more furious and formidable animal, and will frequently pursue the hunter when wounded. It is astonishing to see the wounds they will bear before they can be put to death. The Indians may well fear this animal, equipped as they generally are with their bows and arrows or indifferent fusils, but in the hands of skillful riflemen they are by no means as formidable or dangerous as they have been represented.

---

173. near present-day Culbertson, Montana (Schmidt, p. 67)

174. grizzlies

175. never subsequently verified scientifically

The game is still very abundant. We can scarcely cast our eyes in any direction without perceiving deer, elk, buffalo, or antelope. The quantity of wolves appears to increase in the same proportion. They generally hunt in parties of six, eight, or ten. They kill a great number of the antelope at this season. The antelope are yet meager and the females are big with young. The wolves take them most generally in attempting to swim the river. In this manner my dog caught one, drowned it, and brought it on shore. They are but clumsy swimmers, though on land when in good order, they are extremely fleet and durable. We have frequently seen the wolves in pursuit of the antelope in the plains. They appear to decoy a single one from a flock and then pursue it, alternately relieving each other until they take it.

On joining Captain Clark, he informed me that he had seen a female and fawn of the bighorned animal, that they ran for some distance with great apparent ease along the side of the river bluff where it was almost perpendicular. Two of the party fired on them while in motion without effect.

We took the flesh of the bear on board and proceeded.

Captain Clark walked on shore this evening, killed a deer, and saw several of the bighorned animals.

Thursday, May 2, 1805:

Clark: The wind blew very hard all the last night. This morning about sunrise, [it] began to snow (the thermometer [stood] at twenty-eight above zero) and continued until about 10:00, at which time it ceased.

The wind continued hard until about 2:00 p.m. The snow which fell today was about one inch deep. A very extraordinary climate, to behold the trees green and flowers spread on the plain, and snow an inch deep.

We set out about 3:00 and proceeded on about five and a half miles and encamped on the starboard side. The evening [was] very cold [and] ice [was] freezing to the oars.

I shot a large beaver and Drouillard [shot] three in walking on the bank. The flesh of these animals the party is fond of eating, etc.

Whitehouse: At daylight it began to snow and blow so that we did not set off this morning. The men who were out hunting found several pieces of red cloth at an Indian camp where, we expect, they left last winter for a sacrifice to their maker, as that is their form of worship, as they have some knowledge of the Supreme Being, and anything above their comprehension they call Big Medicine.

Lewis: The flesh of the beaver is esteemed a delicacy among us. I think the tail a most delicious morsel; when boiled it resembles in flavor the fresh tongues and sounds[176] of the codfish and is usually sufficiently large to afford a plentiful meal for two men.

Friday, May 3, 1805:

Clark: We set out rather later this morning than usual owing to [the] weather being very cold. [There was] a frost last night and the thermometer stood this morning at twenty-six above zero, which is six degrees below freezing. The ice that was on the kettle kept near the fire last night was one-fourth of an inch thick. The snow is all or nearly all off the low bottoms; the hills are entirely covered.

Three of our party found in the back of a bottom three pieces of scarlet cloth, one brace[177] in each, which had been left as a sacrifice near one of their sweat houses.

On the port side, we passed today a curious collection of bushes tied up in the shape of [a] fascine,[178] about ten feet [in] diameter, which must have been left also by the natives as an offering to their medicine which, they are convinced, protected or gave them relief near the place.

The wind continued to blow hard from the west, although not sufficiently so to detain us.

Great numbers of buffalo, elk, deer, antelope, beavers, porcupines, and water fowl [were] seen today, such as geese, ducks of different kinds, and a few swans.

Saturday, May 4, 1805:

Clark: The rudder irons of our large pirogue broke off last night, the replacing of which detained us this morning until 9:00, at which time we set out.

The country on each side of the Missouri is rich, high, and beautiful. The bottoms are extensive with a great deal of timber on them. All the forepart of this day, the woodland bordered the river on both sides. In the afterpart of [this day, there was a] beautiful ascending plain on the starboard side.

We encamped on the starboard side a little above. [We] saw great numbers of animals of different kinds on the banks.

We have one sick man.

The river has been falling for several days past. It now begins to rise a little; the rate of rise and fall is from one to three inches in twenty-four hours.

---

176. air bladders

177. an arm span's length (DeVoto)

178. a long bundle of sticks bound together

Sunday, May 5, 1805:

Clark: We set out very early and had not proceeded far before the rudder irons of one of the pirogues broke, which detained us a short time.

Captain Lewis walked on shore this morning and killed a deer.

After breakfast, I walked on shore [and] saw great numbers of buffalo and elk. [I] saw also a den of young wolves and a number of grown wolves[179] in every direction. The country on both sides is as yesterday: handsome and fertile. The river [is] rising and [the] current [is] strong.

In the evening we saw a brown or grizzly bear on a sand beach.[180] I went out with one man, George Drouillard, and killed the bear, which was [a] very large and terrible looking animal, which we found very hard to kill. We shot ten balls into him before we killed him, and five of those balls [went] through his lungs. This animal is the largest of the carnivorous kind I ever saw.

Lewis: It was a most tremendous looking animal, and extremely hard to kill. Notwithstanding he had five balls through his lungs and five others in various parts, he swam more than half the distance across the river to a sand bar and it was at least twenty minutes before he died. He did not attempt to attack, but fled and made the most tremendous roaring from the moment he was shot.

We had no means of weighing this monster. Captain Clark thought he would weigh five hundred pounds. For my own part, I think the estimate too small by one hundred pounds. He measured eight feet, seven and a half inches from the nose to the extremity of the hind feet, five feet, ten and a half inches around the breast, one foot, eleven inches around the middle of the arm, and three feet, eleven inches around the neck. His talons, which were five in number on each foot, were four and three-eighths inches in length. He was in good order. We therefore divided him among the party and made them boil the oil and put it in a cask for future use. The oil is as hard as hog's lard when cool, much more so than that of the black bear.

This bear differs from the common black bear in several respects: its talons are much longer and more blunt; its tail [is] shorter; its hair, which is of a reddish or bay brown, is longer, thicker, and finer than that of the black bear; his liver, lungs and heart are much larger even in proportion with his size; the heart particularly was as large as that of a

---

179. gray wolves (Ambrose, *UC*, p. 217)

180. near present-day Wolf Point, Montana (Schmidt, p. 68)

large ox; his maw[181] was also ten times the size of [the] black bear, and was filled with flesh and fish.

The party killed two elk and a buffalo today, and my dog caught a goat, which he overtook by superior fleetness. The goat, it must be understood, was with young and extremely poor.

Monday, May 6, 1805:

Lewis: [We] saw a brown bear swim the river above us; he disappeared before we could get in reach of him. I find that the curiosity of our party is pretty well satisfied with respect to this animal. The formidable appearance of the male bear killed on the 5th, added to the difficulty with which they die when even shot through the vital parts, has staggered the resolution of several of them. Others, however, seem keen for action with the bear. I expect these gentlemen will give us some amusement shortly as the bears soon begin now to copulate.

[We] saw a great quantity of game of every species common here. Captain Clark walked on shore[182] and killed two elk. They were not in very good order. We therefore took a part of the meat only. It is now only amusement for Captain Clark and myself to kill as much meat as the party can consume.

Wednesday, May 8, 1805:

Lewis: We nooned it just above the entrance of a large river which discharges on the starboard side. I took the advantage of this leisure moment and examined the river about three miles. I have no doubt but it is navigable for boats, pirogues and canoes, for the latter probably a great distance. From the quantity of water furnished by this river, it must water a large extent of country. Perhaps this river also might furnish a practicable and advantageous communication with the Saskatchewan River. It is sufficiently large to justify a belief that it might reach to that river if its direction be such. The water of this river possesses a peculiar whiteness, being about the color of a cup of tea with the admixture of a tablespoonful of milk. From the color of its water, we called it Milk River. We think it possible that this may be the river called by the Hidatsa "The River That Scolds At All Others."

Captain Clark, who walked this morning on the port shore, ascended a very high point opposite to the mouth of this river. He informed me that he had a perfect view of this river and the country through which it passed for a great distance, probably fifty or sixty miles, [and] that the river from its mouth bore northwest for twelve or

181. stomach

182. near present-day Oswego, Montana (Schmidt, p. 68)

fifteen miles when it forked, the one [fork] taking a direction nearly north and the other to the west of northwest. Captain Clark could not be certain, but thought he saw the smoke and some Indian lodges at a considerable distance up Milk River.

Thursday, May 9, 1805:

Lewis: Captain Clark killed two bucks and two buffalo. I also killed one buffalo which proved to be the best meat; it was in tolerable order. We saved the best of the meat, and from the cow I killed, we saved the necessary materials for making what our right-hand cook, Charbonneau, calls the "boudin blanc,"[183] and immediately set him about preparing them for supper.

This white pudding we all esteem [to be] one of the greatest delicacies of the forest. It may not be amiss, therefore, to give it a place. About six feet of the lower extremity of the large gut of the buffalo is the first morsel that the cook makes love to. This he holds fast at one end with the right hand, while with the forefinger and thumb of the left he gently compresses it and discharges what he says is not good to eat, but of which in the sequel we get a moderate portion.

The muscle lying underneath the shoulder blade next to the back, and the filets, are next sought. These are kneaded up very fine with a good portion of kidney suet. To this composition is then added a just proportion of pepper and salt and a small quantity of flour.

Thus far advanced, our skillful operator, Charbonneau, seizes his receptacle, which has never once touched the water, for that would entirely destroy the regular order of the whole procedure. You will not forget that the side you now see is that covered with a good coat of fat, provided the animal be in good order. The operator seizes the receptacle, I say, and tying it fast at one end, turns it inward and begins now, with repeated revolutions of the hand and arm, and a brisk motion of the finger and thumb, to put in what he says is "bon pour manger."[184] Thus, by stuffing and compressing, he soon distends the receptacle to the utmost limits of its power of expansion, and, in the course of its longitudinal progress, it drives from the other end of the receptacle a much larger portion of the ____ than was previously discharged by the finger and thumb of the left hand in a former part of the operation.

Thus, when the sides of the receptacle are skillfully exchanged, the outer for the inner, and all is completely filled with something good to eat, it is tied at the other end, but not cut off, for that would make the pattern too scant. It is then baptized in the Missouri with two

---

183. literally, *white black pudding*

184. good to eat

dips and a flirt, and bobbed into the kettle from whence, after it be well boiled, it is taken and fried with bear oil until it becomes brown, when it is ready to assuage the pangs of a keen appetite or such, as travelers in the wilderness are seldom at a loss for.

Whitehouse: [It was] clear and pleasant. We set off at sunrise and proceeded on. [It was] about nine degrees Celsius. We halted to take breakfast.

The game is getting so plentiful and tame in this country that some of the men went up near enough to club them.

Tuesday, May 14, 1805:

Lewis: One of the party wounded a brown bear very badly, but being alone, did not think [it] proper to pursue him.

In the evening, the men in two of the rear canoes discovered a large brown bear lying in the open grounds[185] about three hundred paces from the river, and six of them went out to attack him, all good hunters.

They took the advantage of a small eminence which concealed them and got within forty paces of him unperceived. Two of them reserved their fires as had been previously concerted, [and] the four others fired nearly at the same time and put each his bullet through him. Two of the balls passed through the bulk of both lobes of his lungs. In an instant, this monster ran at them with open mouth. The two who had reserved their fires discharged their pieces at him as he came towards them. Both of them struck him: one only slightly, and the other, fortunately, broke his shoulder. This, however, only retarded his motion for a moment only. The men, unable to reload their guns, took to flight.

The bear pursued and had very nearly overtaken them before they reached the river. Two of the party betook themselves to a canoe; the others separated and concealed themselves among the willows, reloaded their pieces, [and] each discharged his piece at him as they had an opportunity. They struck him several times again but the guns served only to direct the bear to them.

In this manner he pursued two of them separately so close that they were obliged to throw aside their guns and pouches and throw themselves into the river, although the bank was nearly twenty feet perpendicular. So enraged was this animal that he plunged into the river only a few feet behind the second man he had compelled to take refuge in the water, when one of those who still remained on shore shot him through the head and finally killed him.

---

185. near Hell Creek Recreational Area in Montana (Schmidt, p. 69)

They then took him on shore and butchered him when they found eight balls had passed through him in different directions. The bear, being old, the flesh was indifferent. They therefore only took the skin and fleece; the latter made us several gallons of oil.

It was after the sun had set before these men came up with us where we had been halted by an occurrence, which I have now to recapitulate and which although happily passed without ruinous injury, I cannot recollect but with the utmost trepidation and horror. This is the upsetting and narrow escape of the white pirogue.

It happened, unfortunately for us this evening, that Charbonneau was at the helm of this pirogue instead of Drouillard, who had previously steered her. Charbonneau cannot swim and is, perhaps, the most timid waterman in the world. Perhaps it was equally unlucky that Captain Clark and myself were both on shore at that moment, a circumstance which rarely happened. And though we were on the shore opposite to the pirogue, [we] were too far distant to be heard or to do more than remain spectators of her fate. In this pirogue were embarked our papers, instruments, books, medicine, a great part of our merchandise and, in short, almost every article indispensably necessary to further the views, or insure the success of the enterprise in which we are now launched to the distance of two thousand two hundred miles.

Suffice it to say that the pirogue was under sail when a sudden squall of wind struck her obliquely and turned her considerably. The steersman, alarmed, instead of putting her before the wind, lufted her up into it. The wind was so violent that it drew the brace of the squaresail out of the hand of the man who was attending it, and instantly upset the pirogue, and would have turned her completely topsy-turvy had it not have been from the resistance made by the awning against the water.

In this situation, Captain Clark and myself both fired our guns to attract the attention, if possible, of the crew, and order the halyards to be cut and the sail hauled in, but they did not hear us. Such was their confusion and consternation at this moment that they suffered the pirogue to lie on her side for half a minute before they took the sail in. The pirogue then righted, but had filled within an inch of the gunwales.

Charbonneau, still crying to his god for mercy, had not yet recollected the rudder, nor could the repeated orders of the bowman, Cruzatte, bring him to his recollection until he threatened to shoot him instantly if he did not take hold of the rudder and do his duty.

The waves, by this time, were running very high but the fortitude, resolution, and good conduct of Cruzatte saved her. He ordered two of the men to throw out the water with some kettles that, fortunately, were convenient, while he and two others rowed her ashore, where she arrived scarcely above the water. We now took every article out of her and laid them to drain as well as we could for the evening, bailed out the canoe, and secured her. There were two other men besides Charbonneau on board who could not swim and who, of course, must also have perished had the pirogue gone to the bottom.

While the pirogue lay on her side, finding I could not be heard, I for a moment forgot my own situation and involuntarily dropped my gun, threw aside my shot pouch, and was in the act of unbuttoning my coat before I recollected the folly of the attempt I was about to make, which was to throw myself into the river and endeavor to swim to the pirogue. The pirogue was three hundred yards distant, the waves so high that a pirogue[186] could scarcely live in any situation, the water excessively cold, and the stream rapid. Had I undertaken this project, therefore, there was a hundred to one but what I should have paid the forfeit of my life for the madness of my project but this, had the pirogue been lost, I should have valued but little. After having all matters arranged for the evening as well as the nature of the circumstances would permit, we thought it a proper occasion to console ourselves and cheer the spirits of our men and, accordingly, took a drink of grog and gave each man a gill of spirits.

Thursday, May 16, 1805:

Lewis: The morning was fair and the day proved favorable to our operations. By 4:00 in the evening, our instruments, medicine, merchandise, provisions, etc., were perfectly dried, repacked, and put on board the pirogue.

The loss we sustained was not so great as we had first apprehended. Our medicine sustained the greatest injury, several articles of which were entirely spoiled, and many others considerably injured. The balance of our losses consisted of some garden seeds, a small quantity of gunpowder, and a few culinary articles which fell overboard and sunk. The Indian woman, to whom I ascribe equal fortitude and resolution with any person on board at the time of the accident, caught and preserved most of the light articles which were washed overboard.

In the early part of the day, two of our men fired on a panther, a little below our encampment, and wounded it. They informed us that it was very large, had just killed a deer and partly devoured it, and [was] in the act of concealing the balance as they discovered him. This

---

186. Lewis probably meant "person" here

morning, a white bear tore Labiche's coat, which he had left in the plains.

Friday, May 17, 1805:

Lewis: We employed the tow line the greater part of the day. The banks were firm and shore bald which favored the use of the cord. I find this method of ascending the river, when the shore is such as will permit it, the safest and most expeditious mode of traveling, except with sails in a steady and favorable breeze.

The great number of large beds of streams [that are] perfectly dry, which we daily pass, indicates a country but badly watered which, I fear, is the case with the country through which we have been passing for the last fifteen or twenty days.

Captain Clark walked on shore this evening and killed an elk. Buffalo are not so abundant as they were some days past. The party with me killed a female brown bear; she was but meager and appeared to have suckled young very recently.

Captain Clark narrowly escaped being bitten by a rattlesnake in the course of his walk. The party killed one this evening at our encampment which, he informed me, was similar to that he had seen. This snake is smaller than those common to the Middle Atlantic States, being about two feet, six inches long. It is of a yellowish brown color on the back and sides, variegated with one row of oval spots of a dark brown color lying transversely over the back from the neck to the tail, and [has] two other rows of small circular spots of the same color which garnish the sides along the edge of the scuta.[187] Its belly contains one hundred seventy-six scuta on the belly and seventeen on the tail.

Captain Clark saw an Indian fortified camp this evening which appeared to have been recently occupied, from which we concluded it was probable that it had been formed by a war party of the Hidatsa who left their village in March last with a view to attack the Blackfoot Indians in consequence of their having killed some of their principal warriors the previous autumn.

We were roused late at night by the sergeant of the guard and warned of the danger we were in from a large tree that had taken fire and which leaned immediately over our lodge. We had the lodge removed and a few minutes after, a large proportion of the top of the tree fell on the place the lodge had stood. Had we been a few minutes later, we should have been crushed to atoms. The wind blew so hard that notwithstanding the lodge was fifty paces distant from the fire, it

---

187. broad, thickened scales, usually on the belly of a snake

sustained considerable injury from the burning coals which were thrown on it. The party was much harassed also by this fire, which communicated to a collection of fallen timber and could not be extinguished.

Sunday, May 19, 1805:

Clark: [It was] a very cold night. The mercury stood at thirty-eight at 8:00 this morning. [There is] a heavy dew, which is the second I have seen this spring. The fog (which was the first) was so thick this morning that we could not set out until the sun was about two hours up, at which time a small breeze sprung up from the east which cleared off the fog, and we proceeded on by means of the cord.

The hills are high and rugged, the country as yesterday.

I walked on shore with two men. We killed a white or gray bear. Notwithstanding that it was shot through the heart, it ran at its usual pace near a quarter of a mile before it fell.

Captain Lewis' dog was badly bitten by a wounded beaver and was near bleeding to death.

After killing the bear, I continued my walk alone and killed three deer and a beaver. Finding that the pirogues were below, I ascended the highest hill I could see, from the top of which I saw the mouth of Musselshell River and the meanderings of the Missouri for a long distance. I also saw a high mountain in a westerly direction, bearing south southwest, about forty or fifty miles distant.

In the evening, the river was very crooked and much more rapid, and containing more sawyers[188] than any which we have passed above the River Platte.

Captain Lewis walked on shore this afternoon and killed an elk, buck, and a beaver. I killed three deer at dinner. The hunters killed three other deer today. Several beaver [were] also killed.

We camped on the starboard side in a bottom of small cottonwood.

Monday, May 20, 1805:

Lewis: The hunters returned this evening and informed us that the country continued much the same in appearance as that [which] we saw where we were or broken, and that about five miles above the mouth of Musselshell River,[189] a handsome river of about fifty yards in width discharged itself into the Musselshell River on the starboard,

---

188. trees, or parts of a trees, that protrude above the surface of a body of water

189. near Crooked Creek Recreational Area in Montana

or upper, side. This stream we called Sâh-câ-ger we-âh,[190] or Bird Woman's River, after our interpreter, the Shoshone woman.

Clark: [It was] a fine morning [with the] wind from the north-east.

[The] river [is] falling a little.

We set out about 7:00 and proceeded on very well, as usual by the assistance of the cord. [We] passed some very swift water; [the] river [is] narrow and crooked.

At 11:00 [we] arrived at the mouth of Musselshell River on the port side, and formed a camp for the present, having passed a large creek, about four miles below on the port side, which we call Blowing Fly Creek, from the immense quantities of those insects which gather on our meat in such numbers that we are obliged to brush them off what we eat.

[The] Musselshell River falls in on [the] port side, 2,270 miles up from the mouth of the Missouri. [It] contains a greater proportion of water than rivers of its size below. I measured it and found it to be one hundred ten yards wide, the water of a greenish-yellow color, and appears to be navigable for small craft. The Hidatsa inform us that this river heads in the first of the Rocky Mountains and passes through a broken country. Its head [is] at no great distance from the Yellowstone River. The country about this river [is] as described yesterday.

The Missouri, at the mouth of [the] Musselshell River, is two hundred twenty-two yards wide, with a smooth current. The Missouri water is not so muddy as below, but retains nearly its usual color, and the sand [is] principally confined to the points.

I killed two deer and an elk. The hunters killed an elk and several deer, merely for their skins, to make leggings. [We] sent men out in every direction.

The country [is] generally very broken [with] some level plains up the Musselshell River. The bottoms of the Musselshell River are well-timbered, as [are] also [the bottoms of] a small river which falls into that river on the upper side, five miles above its mouth. The hills on the port side contain scattering pine and cedar.

Wednesday, May 22, 1805:

Clark: The wind continued to blow so violently hard [that] we did not think it prudent to set out until it lulled a little. About 10:00 we set out. The morning [was] cold.

Captain Lewis walked out before dinner and killed a deer.

---

190. Sacagawea

I walked out after dinner and ascended a butte a few miles off to view the country, which I found rolling and of a very rich, sticky soil, producing but little vegetation of any kind, except the prickly pear, but little grass, and that very low. [There was] a great deal of scattering pine on the port side, and some few on the starboard side. Game [is] not so abundant as below.

The river continues about the same width; [there are] fewer sand bars and [the] current [is] more regular. [The] river falls about an inch a day.

We camped on the starboard side, earlier than we intended, on account of saving the oil of a bear which the party killed late this afternoon.

Many of the creeks which appear to have no water near their mouths have streams of running water higher up, which rise and waste in the sand or gravel. The water of these creeks is so much impregnated with the salt substance that it cannot be drunk with pleasure.

Thursday, May 23, 1805:

Clark: [There was] a severe frost last night. The thermometer stood at the freezing point this morning, i.e., thirty-two above zero. [The] wind [is] southwest. The water freezes on the oars [and there is] ice on the edge of the river.

A mountain, which appears to be sixty or seventy miles long, bearing east and west, is about twenty-five miles distant from this river.

I walked on shore and killed four deer and an elk and a beaver. In the evening, we killed a large fat bear, which we unfortunately lost in the river. After being shot, [it] took [to] the water and was carried under a drift.

[We] passed, in [the] course of this day, three islands, two of them covered with tall timber and a third with willows.

The afterpart of this day was warm and the mosquitoes troublesome.

[We] saw but five buffalo, a number of elk and deer, and five bears and two antelope today.

The river [is] beginning to rise, and the current [is] more rapid than yesterday.

Saturday, May 25, 1805:

Clark: I walked on shore and killed a female ibi,[191] or bighorn animal. In my absence, Drouillard and Bratton killed two others. This animal is a species peculiar to this upper part of the Missouri. The head and horns of the male, which Drouillard killed today, weighed twenty-seven pounds. It was somewhat larger than the male of the common deer.

The body [is] rather thicker, deeper, and not so long in proportion to its height as the common deer. The head and horns of the male are remarkably large compared with the other parts of the animal. The whole form is much more delicate than that of the common goat, and there is a greater disparity in the size of the male and female than between those of either the deer or goat. The bone above the eye is remarkably prominent. The head, nostrils, and division of the upper lip are precisely in form like the sheep.

Their legs resemble the sheep more than any other animal with which I am acquainted, though they are more delicately formed. Like the sheep, they stand forward in the knee, and the lower joint of the foreleg is smallest where it joins the knee. The hoof is black and large in proportion, is divided, very open, and roundly pointed at the toe, like the sheep. [It] is much hollowed and sharp on the under edge, like the Scotch goat. [It] has two small hoofs behind each foot below the ankle, as the goat, sheep, and deer have.

The belly, inner side of the legs, and the extremity of the rump and buttocks, for about two inches half around the butt of the tail, are white, as is also the tail, except just at its extremity on the upper side, which is of a dark brown. The tail is about three inches in length, covered with short hair, or at least not longer than that of the body. The outer part of the animal is of a dusky brown, or rather a lead-colored light brown.

The animal is now shedding its winter coat, which is thick [and] not quite as long as that of the deer, and appears to be intermixed with a considerable quantity of fine fur which lies next to the skin and [is] concealed by the coarser hair. The shape of the hair itself is cylindrical, as that of the antelope, but is smaller, shorter, and not [as] compressed or flattened as that of the deer's winter coat. I believe this animal only sheds its hair once a year.

It has eight fore teeth in the under jaw, and no canine teeth. The horns are large at their base, and occupy the crown of the head almost entirely. They are compressed, bent backwards and lunated.[192] The

191. Clark may have meant ibex; actually, a bighorn, or Rocky Mountain sheep (Ambrose, *UC*, p. 226)

surface, swelling into wavy rings which, encircling the horn, continue to succeed each other from the base to the extremity, and becoming less elevated and more distant as they recede from the head. The horn, for about two-thirds of its length, is filled with a porous bone which is united with the frontal bone. The horns of the female are small, but are also compressed and bent backwards and encircled with a succession of wavy rings. The horn is of a light brown color. When dressed, it is almost white, extremely transparent, and very elastic. This horn is used by the natives in constructing their bows. I have no doubt of its elegance and usefulness in hair combs, and might probably answer as many valuable purposes to civilized man as it does to the native Indians, who form their water cups, spoons, and platters of it.

The females have already brought forth their young. Indeed, from the size of the young, I suppose that they produce them early in March. They have from one to two at birth. They feed on grass but principally on the aromatic herbs which grow on the cliffs and inaccessible heights which they frequent most commonly. The places they generally collect to lodge is the crannies or crevices of the rocks in the face of inaccessible precipices where the wolf nor bear can reach them and where, indeed, man himself would in many instances find a similar deficiency. Yet these animals bound from rock to rock and stand apparently in the most careless manner on the side of precipices of many hundred feet. They are very shy, and quick of both scent and sight.

In my walk of this day, I saw mountains on either side of the river at no great distance. These mountains appeared to be detached, and not ranges as laid down by the Hidatsa. I also think I saw a range of high mountains at a great distance to the south southwest, but am not certain as the horizon was not clear enough to view it with certainty. The appearance of the salts and bituminous still continue.

We saw a polecat today, being the first which we have seen for some time past.

The air of this quarter is pure and healthy.

The water of the Missouri tasted not quite so muddy as it is below. Notwithstanding the last rains have raised the river a little, it is less muddy than it was before the rain.

Sunday, May 26, 1805:

Lewis: [We] proceeded principally by the tow line, using the oars merely to pass the river, in order to take advantage of the shores. [There are] scarcely any bottoms to the river. The hills [are] high and

192. crescent-shaped

jutting in on both sides to the river in many places. The stone, tumbling from these cliffs and brought down by the rivulets, became more troublesome today.

Captain Clark walked on shore this morning and ascended to the summit of the river hills. He informed me on his return that he had seen mountains on both sides of the river, running nearly parallel with it and at no great distance, [and] also an irregular range of mountains on the port side about fifty miles distant, the extremities of which bore west and northwest from this station. He also saw in the course of his walk some elk, several herds of the bighorn, and the large hare. The latter is common to every part of this open country. Scarcely any timber [is] to be seen except the few scattering pines and spruce which crown the high hills or, in some instances, grow along their sides.

In the afterpart of the day, I also walked out and ascended the river hills, which I found sufficiently fatiguing. On arriving to the summit of one of the highest points in the neighborhood, I thought myself well repaid for my labor, as from this point I beheld the Rocky Mountains[193] for the first time. I could only discover a few of the most elevated points above the horizon, the most remarkable of which, by my pocket compass, I found bore north sixty-five degrees west, being a little to the north of the northwest extremity of the range of broken mountains seen this morning by Captain Clark.

These points of the Rocky Mountains were covered with snow and the sun shone on them in such [a] manner as to give me the most plain and satisfactory view. While I viewed these mountains, I felt a secret pleasure in finding myself so near the head of the heretofore conceived boundless Missouri. But when I reflected on the difficulties which this snowy barrier would most probably throw in my way to the Pacific, and the sufferings and hardships of myself and party in them, it, in some measure, counterbalanced the joy I had felt in the first moments in which I gazed on them. But as I have always held, it [is] a crime to anticipate evils. I will believe it [to be] a good, comfortable road until I am compelled to believe differently.

Late this evening, we passed a very bad rapids which reached quite across the river. The party had considerable difficulty in ascending it, although they doubled their crews and used both the rope and the pole. While they were passing this rapids, a female elk and its fawn swam down through the waves, which ran very high, hence the name of Elk Rapids, which they instantly gave this place. These are the most considerable rapids which we have yet seen on the Missouri and, in short, the only place where there has appeared to be a sudden descent.

193. actually, the detached Little Rocky Mountains of northern Montana (DeVoto)

This is truly a desert, barren country, and I feel myself still more convinced of its being a continuation of the Black Hills. We have continued every day to pass more or less old stick lodges of the Indians in the timbered points; there are two even in this little bottom where we lie.

Monday, May 27, 1805:

Gass: [This is] the most dismal country I ever beheld.

Tuesday, May 28, 1805:

Clark: [It is] a cloudy morning [with] some few drops of rain, and very smoky.

The shoal places are very numerous and some [are] bad to get around. We have to make use of the cords and poles and our tow ropes are, all except one, of elk skin, and stretch and sometimes break, which endangers the pirogues or canoes, as it immediately turns, and if any rock should chance to be below, the rapidity of the current would turn her over if she should chance to strike the rock. We observe great caution at those places.

I saw great numbers of the bighorn animals, one of which I killed. Their fawns are nearly half-grown. One of the party saw a very large bear.

[We] picked up on the shore a pole which had been made use of by the natives for [a] lodge pole, and hauled by dogs. It is new and is a certain sign of the Indians being on the river above. A football and several other articles are also found to substantiate this opinion.

At 1:00 we had a few drops of rain and some thunder, which is the first thunder we have had since we set out from Fort Mandan.

Wednesday, May 29, 1805:

Lewis: Last night we were all alarmed by a large buffalo bull which swam over from the opposite shore, and coming alongside of the white pirogue, climbed over it to land. He then [became] alarmed [and] ran up the bank in full speed directly towards the fires and was within eighteen inches of the heads of some of the men who lay sleeping before the sentinel could alarm him or make him change his course. Still more alarmed, he now took his direction immediately towards our lodge, passing between four fires and within a few inches of the heads of one range of the men as they yet lie sleeping. When he came near the tent, my dog saved us by causing him to change his course a second time, which he did by turning a little to the right, and was quickly out of sight, leaving us by this time all in an uproar with our guns in our hands, enquiring of each other the cause of the alarm which, after a few moments, was explained by the sentinel. We were happy to find no one hurt.

The next morning, we found that the buffalo, in passing the pirogue, had trodden on a rifle which belonged to Captain Clark's black man who had negligently left her in the pirogue. The rifle was much bent. He had also broken the spindle [and] pivot and shattered the stock of one of the blunderbusses[194] on board. With this damage I felt well content, happy indeed, that we had sustained no further injury. It appears that the white pirogue, which contains our most valuable stores, is attended by some evil genie.

This morning we set out at an early hour and proceeded as usual by the cord. At the distance of two and a half miles, [we] passed a handsome river which discharged itself on the port side. I walked on shore and ascended this river about a mile and a half in order to examine it. The water of this river is clearer much than any we have met, with great abundance of the argali, or bighorn, animals in the high country through which this river passes. Captain Clark, who ascended this river much higher than I did, has thought [it] proper to call it Judith's River.[195]

On the Missouri, just above the entrance of the Judith River, I counted the remains of the fires of one hundred twenty-six Indian lodges which appeared to be of [a] very recent date, perhaps twelve or fifteen days. Captain Clark also saw a large encampment just above the entrance of this river, on the starboard side, of [a] rather older date; probably they were the same Indians. The Indian woman with us examined the moccasins which we found at these encampments and informed us that they were not of her nation, the Shoshone Indians, but she believed they were some of the Indians who inhabit the country on this side of the Rocky Mountains and north of the Missouri, and I think it most probable that they were the Hidatsa of Fort de Prairie.[196]

Today we passed, on the starboard side, the remains of a vast many mangled carcasses of buffalo which had been driven over a precipice of one hundred twenty feet by the Indians and perished. The water appeared to have washed away a part of this immense pile of slaughter, and still there remained the fragments of at least a hundred carcasses. They created a most horrid stench. In this manner, the Indians of the Missouri destroy vast herds of buffalo at a stroke.

For this purpose, one of the most active and fleet young men is selected and disguised in a robe of buffalo skin, having also the skin of

---

194. short firearms with large bores and flaring muzzles

195. after Julia (Judy) Hancock of Virginia, whom Clark later married (DeVoto)

196. the Fall Indians, or Atsina, allied with the Blackfeet (DeVoto)

the buffalo's head, with the ears and horns, fastened on his head in [the] form of a cap. Thus comparisoned, he places himself at a convenient distance between a herd of buffalo and a precipice proper for the purpose, which happens in many places on this river for miles together. The other Indians now surround the herd on the back and flanks and, at a signal agreed on, all show themselves at the same time, moving forward towards the buffalo. The disguised Indian, or decoy, has taken care to place himself sufficiently nigh the buffalo to be noticed by them when they take to flight and, running before them, they follow him in full speed to the precipice, the cattle behind driving those in front over and, seeing them go, do not look or hesitate about following until the whole are precipitated down the precipice, forming one common mass of dead and mangled carcasses.

The decoy, in the meantime, has taken care to secure himself in some cranny or crevice of the cliff which he had previously prepared for that purpose. The part of the decoy, I am informed, is extremely dangerous. If they are not very fleet runners, the buffalo tread them underfoot and crush them to death and sometimes drive them over the precipice also, where they perish in common with the buffalo.

We saw a great many wolves in the neighborhood of these mangled carcasses. They were fat and extremely gentle. Captain Clark, who was on shore, killed one of them with his espontoon.[197]

Soon after we landed, it began to blow and rain and, as there was no appearance of even wood enough to make our fires for some distance above, we determined to remain here until the next morning and, accordingly, fixed our camp and gave each man a small dram. Notwithstanding the allowance of spirits we issued did not exceed one-half gill per man, several of them were considerably affected by it. Such are the effects of abstaining for some time from the use of spirituous liquors. They were all very merry.

Thursday, May 30, 1805:

Clark: The rain commenced yesterday evening and continued moderately through the course of the night. More rain has now fallen than we have experienced since the 15th of September last.

The rain continued this morning and the wind [was] too high for us to proceed until about 11:00, at which time we set out and proceeded on with great labor. We were obliged to make use of the tow rope, and the banks were so muddy and slippery that the men could scarcely walk. Notwithstanding, we proceeded on as well as we could. [The] wind [was] hard from the northwest.

197. a spear and ax combined (Bakeless, p. 146)

In attempting to ascend a rapids, our tow cord broke and we turned without injury. These rapids or shoal points are numerous and difficult, one being at the mouth of every stream.

Some little rain [fell] at times all day. One man ascended the high country, and it was raining and snowing on those hills. The day has proven to be raw and cold.

We discover, in several places, old encampments of large bands of Indians, a few weeks past, and appear to be making up the river. These Indians we believe to be the Blackfoot Indians, or Hidatsa, who inhabit the heads of the Saskatchewan and north of this place, and trade a little in the Fort de Prairie establishments.

Lewis: Many circumstances indicate our near approach to a country whose climate differs considerably from that [in] which we have been for many months. The air of the open country is astonishingly dry as well as pure. I found by several experiments that a tablespoon of water exposed to the air in a saucer would evaporate in thirty-six hours. My ink stand so frequently becoming dry put me on [to] this experiment. I also observed [that] the well-seasoned case of my sextant shrank considerably and the joints opened.

Gass: I remarked, as a singular circumstance, that there is no dew in this country, and very little rain. Can it be owing to the want of timber?

Ordway: This country may, with propriety, be called the Deserts of North America, for I do not conceive [that] any part of it can ever be settled as it is deficient of water except in this river, and deficient of timber, and too steep to be tilled.

Friday, May 31, 1805:

Lewis: This morning we proceeded at an early hour with the two pirogues, leaving the canoes and crews to bring on the meat of the two buffalo that were killed last evening and which had not been brought in as it was late and a little off the river. Soon after we got under way, it began to rain and continued until meridian,[198] when it ceased but still remained cloudy through the balance of the day.

The obstructions of rocky points and riffles still continue as yesterday. At these places, the men are compelled to be in the water, even to their armpits, and the water is yet very cold, and so frequent are these points that they are one-fourth of their time in the water. Added to this, the banks and bluffs along which they are obliged to pass are so slippery and the mud so tenacious that they are unable to wear moccasins and, in that situation, [they are] dragging the heavy burden of a

198. when the sun is at its highest point in the sky (about noon)

canoe and walking occasionally for several hundred yards over the sharp fragments of rocks which tumble from the cliffs and garnish the borders of the river. In short, their labor is incredibly painful and great, yet these faithful fellows bear it without a murmur.

The tow rope of the white pirogue, the only one, indeed, of hemp and that on which we most depended, gave way today at a bad point. The pirogue swung and but slightly touched a rock, yet was very near oversetting. I fear her evil genie will play so many pranks with her that she will go to the bottom some of these days.

The hills and river cliffs which we passed today exhibit a most romantic appearance.[199] The bluffs of the river rise to the height of from two to three hundred feet and [are], in most places, nearly perpendicular. They are formed of remarkably white sandstone which is sufficiently soft to give way readily to the impression of water. Two or three thin horizontal strata of white freestone, on which the rains or water make no impression, lie embedded in these cliffs of soft stone near the upper part of them. The earth on the top of these cliffs is a dark, rich loam which, forming a gradually ascending plain, extends back from one-half a mile to a mile where the hills commence and rise abruptly to a height of about three hundred feet more.

The water, in the course of time, in descending from these hills and plains on either side of the river, has trickled down the soft sand cliffs and worn it into a thousand grotesque figures which, with the help of a little imagination and an oblique view, at a distance are made to represent elegant ranges of lofty freestone buildings, having their parapets well-stocked with statuary. Columns of various sculpture, both grooved and plain, are also seen supporting long galleries in front of those buildings.

In other places, on a much nearer approach and with the help of less imagination, we see the remains or ruins of elegant buildings, some columns standing and almost entire with their pedestals and capitals, others retaining their pedestals but deprived by time or accident of their capitals, some lying prostrate and broken, others in the form of vast pyramids of conic structure bearing a series of other pyramids on their tops, becoming less as they ascend, and finally terminating in a sharp point. Niches and alcoves of various forms and sizes are seen at different heights as we pass. The thin strata of hard freestone intermixed with the soft sandstone seems to have aided the water in forming this curious scenery.

As we passed on, it seemed as if those scenes of visionary enchantment would never have an end. For here it is, too, that nature presents to the view of the traveler vast ranges of walls of tolerable

199. The White Cliffs Area of Montana (Schmidt, p. 71)

workmanship. So perfect, indeed, are these walls that I should have thought that nature had attempted here to rival the human art of masonry had I not recollected that she had first begun her work. These walls rise to the height, in many places, of one hundred feet, are perpendicular with two regular faces, and are from one to twelve feet thick. Each wall retains the same thickness at top which it possesses at bottom.

Clark: In many places we observe on either side of the river extraordinary walls of a black cemented stone which appear to be regularly placed, one stone on the other. These walls commence at the waters edge and, in some places, meet at right angles.

Gass: We passed some very curious cliffs and rocky peaks in a long range. Some of them [are] two hundred feet high and not more than eight feet thick. They seem as if [they were] built by the hand of man, and are so numerous that they appear like the ruins of an ancient city.

6: June, 1805

About 2:00 p.m. I reached the camp [and] *found the Indian woman extremely ill and much reduced by her indisposition. This gave me some concern as well for the poor object herself, then with a young child in her arms, as from the consideration of her being our only dependence for a friendly negotiation with the Shoshone Indians, on whom we depend for horses to assist us in our portage from the Missouri to the Columbia River.*

Captain Meriwether Lewis,
June 16, 1805

Sunday, June 2, 1805:

Lewis: The wind blew violently last night and was attended by a slight shower of rain.

The morning was fair and we set out at an early hour. [We] employed the cord, as usual, the greater part of the day. The current was strong though regular, and the banks afforded us good towing. The wind was hard and against us, yet we proceeded with infinitely more ease than the two preceding days.

The river bluffs still continue to get lower and the plains leveler and more extensive. The timber on the river increases in quantity.

Game [is] becoming more abundant this morning and I thought it best now to lose no time or suffer an opportunity to escape in providing the necessary quantity of elk skins to cover my leather boat, which I now expect I shall be obliged to use shortly. Accordingly, I walked on shore most of the day with some of the hunters for that purpose and killed six elk, two buffalo, two mule deer, and a bear. These animals were all in good order. We therefore took as much of the meat as our canoes and pirogues could conveniently carry.

The bear was very near catching Drouillard. It also pursued Charbonneau, who fired his gun in the air as he ran, but fortunately eluded the vigilance of the bear by secreting himself very securely in the bushes until Drouillard finally killed it by a shot in the head, the only shot, indeed, that will conquer the ferocity of these tremendous animals.

We came to on the port side in a handsome bottom of small cottonwood timber opposite to the entrance of a very considerable river[200] but, it being too late to examine these rivers minutely tonight, we determined to remain here until the morning and, as the evening was favorable, to make some observations.

Whitehouse: [We] camped at a fork of the river. We could not determine which one was the Missouri.

Monday, June 3, 1805:

Lewis: This morning early, we passed over and formed a camp on the point formed by the junction of the two large rivers. Here, in the course of the day, I continued my observations.

An interesting question was now to be determined: which of these rivers was the Missouri, or that river which the Hidatsa call "Amahte Arzzha," or Missouri, and which [was the one] they had described to us as approaching very near to the Columbia River? To mistake the stream at this period of the season, two months of the traveling season having now elapsed, and to ascend such stream to the Rocky Mountains, or perhaps much farther, before we could inform ourselves whether it did approach the Columbia or not, and then be obliged to return and take the other stream, would not only lose us the whole of this season, but would probably so dishearten the party that it might defeat the expedition altogether. Convinced we were that the utmost circumspection and caution were necessary in deciding on the stream to be taken.

To this end, an investigation of both streams was the first thing to be done: to learn their widths, depths, comparative rapidity of their currents, and thence the comparative bodies of water furnished by each. Accordingly, we dispatched two light canoes, with three men in each, up those streams. We also sent out several small parties by land with instructions to penetrate the country as far as they conveniently can, permitting themselves time to return this evening and endeavor, if possible, to discover the distant bearing of these rivers by ascending the rising grounds.

Between the time of my a.m. and meridian observations, Captain Clark and I strolled out to the top of the heights in the fork of these rivers from whence we had an extensive and most enchanting view. The country in every direction around us was one vast plain in which innumerable herds of buffalo were seen attended by their shepherds, the wolves. The solitary antelope, which now had their young, were dis-

200. actually, this is the stream called the "River That Scolds At All Others" by the Hidatsa (DeVoto)

tributed over its face. Some herds of elk were also seen. The verdure perfectly clothed the ground [and] the weather was pleasant and fair.

To the south we saw a range of lofty mountains which we supposed to be a continuation of the South Mountains, stretching themselves from southeast to northwest [and] terminating abruptly about southwest from us. These were partially covered with snow. Behind these mountains, and at a great distance, a second and more lofty range of mountains appeared to stretch across the country in the same direction with the others, reaching from west to the north of northwest where their snowy tops lost themselves beneath the horizon. This last range was perfectly covered with snow. The direction of the rivers could be seen but little way, soon losing the break of their channels to our view in the common plain.

On our return to camp, we bore a little to the left and discovered a handsome little river falling into the north fork on the port side about one and a half miles above our camp. This little river has as much timber in its bottom as either of the larger streams.

We took the width of the two rivers [and] found the left hand, or south fork, three hundred seventy-two yards and the north fork two hundred. The north fork is deeper than the other, but its current [is] not so swift. Its waters run in the same boiling and rolling manner which has uniformly characterized the Missouri throughout its whole course so far. Its waters are of a whitish-brown color [and] very thick and turbid, also characteristic of the Missouri. While the south fork is perfectly transparent, runs very rapid but with a smooth unriffled surface, [and] its bottom [is] composed of round and flat smooth stones like most rivers issuing from a mountainous country, the bed of the north fork [is] composed of some gravel, but principally mud. In short, the air and character of this river is so precisely that of the Missouri below that the party, with very few exceptions, has already pronounced the north fork to be the Missouri.

I and Captain Clark, not quite so precipitative, have not yet decided, but if we were to give our opinions, I believe we should be in the minority, certain it is that the north fork gives the coloring matter and character which is retained from hence to the Gulf of Mexico. I am confident that this river rises in and passes a great distance through an open plain country. I expect that it has some of its sources on the eastern side of the Rocky Mountains south of the Saskatchewan, but that it does not penetrate the first range of the mountains, and that much the greater part of its sources are in a northwardly direction towards the lower and middle parts of the Saskatchewan, in the open plains. Convinced I am that if it penetrated the Rocky Mountains to any great distance, its waters would be clearer, unless it should run an immense distance, indeed, after leaving those mountains through these level plains in order to acquire its turbid hue.

What astonishes us a little is that the Indians, who appeared to be so well-acquainted with the geography of this country, should not have mentioned this river on [the] right hand if it be not the Missouri. The River That Scolds At All Others, as they call it, if there is in reality such a one, ought, agreeably to their account, to have fallen in a considerable distance below. And, on the other hand, if this right-hand, or north fork, be the Missouri, I am equally astonished at their not mentioning the south fork, which they must have passed in order to get to those large falls which they mention on the Missouri. Thus have our cogitating faculties been busily employed all day.

Those who have remained at camp today have been busily engaged in dressing skins for clothing, notwithstanding that many of them have their feet so mangled and bruised with stones and rough ground over which they passed barefoot that they can scarcely walk or stand. At least it is with great pain they do either. For some days past, they were unable to wear their moccasins. They have fallen off considerably, but notwithstanding the difficulties past, or those which seem now to menace us, they still remain perfectly cheerful.

In the evening, the parties whom we had sent out returned agreeably to instructions. The parties who had been sent up the rivers in canoes informed [us] that they ascended some distance and had then left their canoes and walked up the rivers a considerable distance farther, barely leaving themselves time to return. The north fork was not so rapid as the other, and afforded the easiest navigation of course. Six feet appeared to be the shallowest water of the south branch, and five feet that of the north. Their accounts were by no means satisfactory, nor did the information we acquired bring us nigher to the decision of our question, or determine us which stream to take.

Captain Clark and I concluded to set out early the next morning, with a small party each, and ascend these rivers until we could perfectly satisfy ourselves of the one which it would be most expedient for us to take on our main journey to the Pacific. Accordingly, it was agreed that I should ascend the right-hand fork and he the left. I gave orders to Sergeant Pryor, Drouillard, Shields, Windsor, Cruzatte, and Lepage to hold themselves in readiness to accompany me in the morning. Captain Clark also selected Reubin and Joseph Field, Sergeant Gass, Shannon, and his black man, York, to accompany him. We agreed to go up those rivers one day and a half's march, or farther if it should appear necessary to satisfy us more fully of the point in question. I take my octant with me, also; this I confide to Lepage.

Whitehouse: Our officers and all the men differ in their opinions of which river to take. The captains gave each man a dram of ardent spirits.

Wednesday, June 5, 1805:

Clark: [There was] some little rain and snow last night. The mountains to our southeast [are] covered with snow this morning. [The] air [is] very cold and [it is] raining a little.

We saw eight buffalo opposite; they made two attempts to cross [but] the water being so swift they could not.

About the time we were setting out, three white bears approached our camp. We killed the three and ate part of one, and set out and proceeded on, north twenty degrees west, eleven miles.

[We] struck the river at many places in this distance to a ridge on the north side from the top of which I could plainly see a mountain to the south and west covered with snow at a long distance. The mountains opposite to us, to the southeast, are also covered with snow this morning. A high ridge from these mountains approached the river on the southeast side, forming some cliffs of hard, dark stone. From the ridge, at which place I struck the river last, I could discover that the river runs west of south a long distance and has a strong, rapid current. As this river continued its width, depth and rapidity, and the course west of south, going up farther would be useless. I determined to return. [I] marked my name in a tree [on the] north side near the ridge where the little river breaks through.

Thursday, June 6, 1805:

Lewis: I now became well convinced that this branch of the Missouri had its direction too much to the north for our route to the Pacific, and therefore determined to return the next day after taking an observation of the degrees meridian altitude[201] in order to fix the latitude of the place.

The forepart of the last evening was fair, but in the latter part of the night [it] clouded up and continued so with short intervals of sunshine until a little before noon when the whole horizon was overcast and I, of course, [was] disappointed in making the observation which I much wished. I had sent Sergeant Pryor and Windsor early this morning with orders to proceed up the river to some commanding eminence and take its bearing as far as possible.

In the meantime, the four others and I were busily engaged in making two rafts on which we proposed descending the river. We had

---

201. the angular measurement between the horizon and the sun at meridian

just completed this work when Sergeant Pryor and Windsor returned, it being about noon. They reported that they had proceeded from hence south seventy west, six miles, to the summit of a commanding eminence from whence the river on their left was about two-and-a-half miles distant, that a point of its port side bluff which was visible, bore south eighty west, distant about fifteen miles, that the river on their left bent gradually around to this point, and from thence seemed to run northwardly.

We now took dinner and embarked with our plunder and five elk skins on the rafts but were soon convinced that this mode of transportation was hazardous, particularly with these rafts, they being too small and slender. We wet a part of our baggage and were near losing one of our guns. I therefore determined to abandon the rafts and return as we had come, by land. I regretted much being obliged to leave my elk skins, which I had wanted to assist in forming my leather boat, those [that] we had prepared at Fort Mandan being injured in such [a] manner that they would not answer.

Ordway: About 2:00 p.m. Captain Clark and his party returned to camp. [They] had been about forty miles up the south fork and Captain Clark thinks it will be the best course for us to go.

Friday, June 7, 1805:

Lewis: It continued to rain almost without intermission last night and, as I expected, we had a most disagreeable and restless night. Our camp possessing no allurements, we left our watery beds at an early hour and continued our route down the river. It still continues to rain. The wind [is] hard from the northeast and cold.

The ground [is] remarkably slippery, insomuch that we were unable to walk on the sides of the bluffs where we had passed as we ascended the river. Notwithstanding the rain that has now fallen, the earth of these bluffs is not wet to a greater depth than two inches. In its present state, it is precisely like walking over frozen ground which has thawed to [a] small depth, and slips equally as bad. This clay not only appears to require more water to saturate it, as I before observed, than any earth I ever observed, but when saturated it appears, on the other hand, to yield its moisture with equal difficulty.

In passing along the face of one of these bluffs today, I slipped at a narrow pass of about thirty yards in length, and but for a quick and fortunate recovery by means of my espontoon, I should [have] been precipitated into the river down a craggy precipice of about ninety feet.

I had scarcely reached a place on which I could stand with tolerable safety, even with the assistance of my espontoon, before I heard a voice behind me cry out, "God, God, Captain, what shall I do?" On turning about, I found it was Windsor who had slipped and fallen about the center of this narrow pass and was lying prostrate on his belly with his right hand, arm, and leg over the precipice, while he was holding on with the left arm and foot as well as he could, which appeared to be with much difficulty. I discovered [that] his danger and the trepidation which he was in gave me still further concern, for I expected every instant to see him lose his strength and slip off.

Although much alarmed at his situation, I disguised my feelings and spoke very calmly to him, and assured him that he was in no kind of danger, to take the knife out of his belt behind him with his right hand and dig a hole with it in the face of the bank to receive his right foot, which he did, and then raised himself to his knees. I then directed him to take off his moccasins and to come forward on his hands and knees, holding the knife in one hand and the gun in the other. This he happily effected and escaped. Those who were some little distance behind returned by my orders and waded the river at the foot of the bluff where the water was breast deep.

It was useless, we knew, to attempt the plains on this part of the river in consequence of the numerous steep ravines which intersected and which were quite as bad as the river bluffs. We therefore continued our route down the river, sometimes in the mud and water of the bottomlands, at others in the river to our breasts and, when the water became so deep that we could not wade, we cut footsteps in the face of the steep bluffs with our knives and proceeded.

We continued our disagreeable march through the rain, mud, and water until late in the evening, having traveled only about eighteen miles, and encamped in an old Indian stick lodge which afforded us a dry and comfortable shelter.

During the day we had killed six deer, some of them in very good order, although none of them had yet entirely discarded their winter coats. We had reserved and brought with us a good supply of the best pieces. We roasted and ate a hearty supper of our venison, not having tasted a morsel before during the day.

I now laid myself down on some willow boughs to a comfortable night's rest and felt, indeed, as if I were fully repaid for the toil and pain of the day. So much will a good shelter, a dry bed, and [a] comfortable supper revive the spirits of the weary, wet, and hungry traveler.

Saturday, June 8, 1805:

Lewis: The whole of my party to a man, except myself, was fully persuaded that this river was the Missouri, but being fully of [the] opinion that it was neither the main stream nor that which it would be advisable for us to take, I determined to give it a name, and in honor of Miss Maria Wood,[202] called it Maria's River.[203]

It is true that the hue of the waters of this turbulent and troubled stream but illy comport with the pure celestial virtues and amiable qualifications of that lovely fair one, but on the other hand, it is a noble river, one destined to become, in my opinion, an object of contention between the two great powers of America and Great Britain with respect to the adjustment of the northwestwardly boundary of the former. And that it will become one of the most interesting branches of the Missouri in a commercial point of view I have but little doubt, as it abounds with animals of the fur kind, and most probably furnishes a safe and direct communication to that productive country of valuable furs exclusively enjoyed at present by the subjects of his Britannic Majesty.

In addition to which it passes through a rich, fertile, and one of the most beautifully picturesque countries that I ever beheld, through the wide expanse of which innumerable herds of living animals are seen, its borders garnished with one continuous garden of roses, while its lofty and open forests are the habitation of [a] myriad of feathered tribes who salute the ear of the passing traveler with their wild and simple, yet sweet and cheerful, melody.

I arrived at camp about 5:00 in the evening much fatigued where I found Captain Clark and the balance of the party waiting our return with some anxiety for our safety, having been absent nearly two days longer than we had engaged to return.

Captain Clark plotted the courses of the two rivers as far as we had ascended them. I now began, more than ever, to suspect the veracity of Mr. Fidler[204] or the correctness of his instruments. For I see that Arrowsmith,[205] in his late map of North America,[206] has laid down a remarkable mountain in the chain of the Rocky Mountains called the Tooth, nearly as far south as latitude forty-five degrees, and this is said to be from the discoveries of Mr. Fidler. We are now within a hundred miles of the Rocky Mountains, and I find from my observation of the third instance that the latitude of this place is forty-seven degrees, twenty-four minutes, twelve-point-eight seconds.

The river must therefore turn much to the south between this and the Rocky Mountains to have permitted Mr. Fidler to have passed

202. Lewis's cousin (Ambrose, *UC*, p. 233)
203. now called the Marias River
204. Peter Fidler, a Hudson's Bay Company surveyor and explorer (DeVoto)
205. Aaron Arrowsmith, a London cartographer (DeVoto)
206. 1795 and 1796 editions (DeVoto)

along the eastern border of these mountains as far south as nearly forty-five degrees without even seeing it. But from hence, as far as Captain Clark had ascended the south fork, or Missouri, being the distance of fifty-five miles, its course is south twenty-nine degrees west, and it still appeared to bear considerably to the west of south as far as he could see it.

I think, therefore, that we shall find that the Missouri enters the Rocky Mountains to the north of forty-five degrees. We did take the liberty of placing his discoveries, or at least the southern extremity of them, about a degree farther north in the sketch which we sent on to the government this spring, merely from the Indian information of the bearing from Fort Mandan of the entrance of the Missouri into the Rocky Mountains, and I rather suspect that actual observation will take him at least another degree farther north.

Ordway: So our captains conclude to ascend the south fork. They named the north fork River Maria and the middle or little river [they] named Teton River. The water and bottoms, in every respect of each, resemble the Missouri below the Forks, only smaller.

Sunday, June 9, 1805:

Lewis: We determined to deposit at this place the large red pirogue [and] all the heavy baggage which we could possibly do without, and some provisions, salt, tools, powder, and lead, etc. Accordingly, we set some hands to digging a hole, or cellar, for the reception of our stores. These holes in the ground, or deposits, are called by the engagés "caches."

Today we examined our maps and compared the information derived as well from them as from the Indians, and fully settled in our minds the propriety of adopting the south fork for the Missouri as that which it would be most expedient for us to take. These ideas, as they occurred to me, I endeavored to impress on the minds of the party, all of whom, except Captain Clark, being still firm in the belief that the north fork was the Missouri and that which we ought to take.

They said very cheerfully that they were ready to follow us anywhere we thought proper to direct, but that they still thought the other was the river, and that they were afraid that the south fork would soon terminate in the mountains and leave us at a great distance from the Columbia.

Finding them so determined in this belief, and wishing that if we were in error to be able to detect it and rectify it as soon as possible, it was agreed between Captain Clark and myself that one of us should set out with a small party by land up the south fork, and continue our route up it until we found the falls or reached the snowy mountains, by which means we should be enabled to determine this question pretty accurately.

This expedition I preferred undertaking as Captain Clark is the best waterman, etc., and determined to set out the day after tomorrow. I wished to make some further observations at this place, and as we had determined to leave our blacksmith's bellows and tools here, it was necessary to repair some of our arms, and particularly my air gun, the main spring of which was broken, before we left this place. These and some other preparations will necessarily detain us two, perhaps three, days.

I felt myself very unwell this morning and took a portion of salts from which I feel much relief this evening.

Most of the men are busily engaged dressing skins for clothing.

In the evening, Cruzatte gave us some music on the violin and the men passed the evening dancing, singing, etc., and were extremely cheerful.

Whitehouse: Towards evening we had a frolic. The officers gave the party a dram, the fiddle [was] played, and they danced late, etc.

Monday, June 10, 1805:

Clark: We drew up our large pirogue into the middle of a small island in the north fork and covered her with bushes after making her fast to the trees [and] branded several trees to prevent the Indians [from] injuring her.

Sacagawea, our Indian woman, [is] very sick; I bled her.

We determined to ascend the south fork, and Captain Lewis selected four men, George Drouillard, Gibson, Joseph Field and Silas Goodrich, to accompany him, and determined to set out in the morning.

The afternoon, or night, [was] cloudy [with] some rain. [The] river [is] rising a little.

Tuesday, June 11, 1805:

Lewis: At 8:00 a.m. I swung my pack and set forward with my little party. [We] proceeded to the point where Rose River, a branch of Maria's River, approaches the Missouri so nearly. From this height, we discovered a herd of elk on the Missouri just above us to which we descended and soon killed four of them.

We butchered them and hung up the meat and skins in view of the river, but before the meal was prepared, I was taken with such violent pain in the intestines that I was unable to partake of the feast of marrowbones. My pain still increased, and towards evening was attended with a high fever. Finding myself unable to march, I determined to prepare a camp of some willow boughs and remain all night.

Having brought no medicine with me, I resolved to try an experiment with some simples[207] and the chokecherry, which grew abundantly in the bottom, first struck my attention. I directed a parcel of the small twigs to be gathered, stripped of their leaves, cut into pieces of about two inches in length, and boiled in water until a strong, black decoction[208] of an astringent, bitter taste was produced. At sunset I took a pint of this decoction and, about an hour after, repeated the dose. By 10:00 in the evening I was entirely relieved from pain and, in fact, every symptom of the disorder forsook me. My fever abated, a gentle perspiration was produced, and I had a comfortable and refreshing night's rest.

Goodrich, who is remarkably fond of fishing, caught several dozen fish of two different species.

Thursday, June 13, 1805:

Lewis: We again ascended the hills of the river and gained the level country.[209] The country through which we passed for the first six miles, though more rolling than that we had passed yesterday, might still with propriety be deemed a level country. Our course, as yesterday, was generally southwest. The river, from the place we left it, appeared to make a considerable bend to the south.

From the extremity of this rolling country, I overlooked a most beautiful and level plain of great extent, or at least fifty or sixty miles. In this there were infinitely more buffalo than I had ever before witnessed at a view.

Nearly in the direction I had been traveling, or southwest, two curious mountains presented themselves of square figures, the sides rising perpendicularly to the height of two hundred fifty feet, and appeared to be formed of yellow clay. Their tops appeared to be level plains.

Fearing that the river bore to the south and that I might pass the falls if they existed between this and the snowy mountains, I altered my course nearly to the south, leaving those insulated hills to my right, and proceeded through the plain. I sent Field on my right and Drouillard and Gibson on my left with orders to kill some meat and join me at the river where I should halt for dinner.

---

207. medicinal plants
208. reduction or extract
209. near present-day Fort Benton, Montana (Schmidt, p. 72)

I had proceeded on this course about two miles, with Goodrich at some distance behind me, when my ears were saluted with the agreeable sound of a fall of water and, advancing a little farther, I saw the spray arise above the plain like a column of smoke, which would frequently disappear again in an instant, caused, I presume, by the wind, which blew pretty hard from the southwest. I did not, however, lose my direction to this point, which soon began to make a roaring too tremendous to be mistaken for any cause short of the Great Falls of the Missouri. Here I arrived about 12:00, having traveled, by estimate, about fifteen miles.

I took my position on the top of some rocks about twenty feet high, opposite the center of the falls. This chain of rocks appears to have formed a part of those over which the waters tumbled, but in the course of time has been separated from it to the distance of one hundred fifty yards, lying parallel to it and an abutment, against which the water, after falling over the precipice, beats with great fury. This barrier extends on the right to the perpendicular cliff which forms that border of the river, but to the distance of one hundred twenty yards next to the cliff, it is but a few feet above the level of the water, and here the water, in very high tides, appears to pass in a channel of forty yards next to the higher part of the ledge of rocks. On the left, it extends within eighty or ninety yards of the port side cliff, which is also perpendicular. Between this abrupt extremity of the ledge of rocks and the perpendicular bluff, the whole body of water passes with incredible swiftness.

Immediately at the cascade, the river is about three hundred yards wide. About ninety or a hundred yards from this, next to the port side bluff, is a smooth, even sheet of water falling over a precipice of at least eighty feet.

The remaining part, of about two hundred yards on my right, forms the grandest sight I ever beheld. The height of the falls is the same as the other, but the irregular and somewhat projecting rocks below receives the water in its passage down and breaks it into a perfect white foam which assumes a thousand forms in a moment, sometimes flying up in jets of sparkling foam to the height of fifteen or twenty feet and are scarcely formed before large rolling bodies of the same beaten and foaming water is thrown over and conceals them. In short, the rocks seem to be most happily fixed to present a sheet of the whitest beaten froth for two hundred yards in length and about eighty feet perpendicular.

The water, after descending, strikes against the abutment before mentioned, or that on which I stand, and seems to reverberate, and being met by the more impetuous current, it rolls and swells into half-formed billows of great height, which rise and again disappear in an instant.

The abutment of rock defends a handsome little bottom of about three acres which is diversified and agreeably shaded with some cottonwood trees. In the lower extremity of the bottom, there is a very thick grove of the same kind of trees which are small. In this woods there are several Indian lodges formed of sticks. A few small cedars grow near the ledge of rocks where I rest. Below the point of these rocks at a small distance, the river is divided by a large rock which rises several feet above the water and extends downward with the stream for about twenty yards.

About a mile before the water arrives at the pitch, it descends very rapidly and is confined on the port side by a perpendicular cliff of about one hundred feet. On the starboard side, it is also perpendicular for about three hundred yards above the pitch where it is then broken by the discharge of a small ravine down which the buffalo have a large beaten road to the water, for it is but in very few places that these animals can obtain water near this place owing to the steep and inaccessible banks.

About three hundred yards below me, there is another abutment of solid rock with a perpendicular face and about sixty feet high which projects from the starboard side at right angles to the distance of one hundred thirty-four yards, and terminates the lower part nearly of the bottom before mentioned, there being a passage around the end of this abutment, between it and the river, of about twenty yards. Here the river again assumes its usual width, soon spreading to near three hundred yards, but still continues its rapidity. From the reflection of the sun on the spray, or mist, which arises from these falls, is a beautiful rainbow produced which adds not a little to the beauty of this majestically grand scenery.

After writing this imperfect description, I again viewed the falls and was so much disgusted with the imperfect idea which it conveyed of the scene that I determined to draw my pen across it and begin again, but then reflected that I could not perhaps succeed better than penning the first impressions of the mind.

I retired to the shade of a tree where I determined to fix my camp for the present and dispatch a man in the morning to inform Captain Clark and the party of my success in finding the falls, and settle in their minds all further doubts as to the Missouri. The hunters now arrived loaded with excellent buffalo meat and informed me that they had killed three very fat cows about three-fourths of a mile from hence.

I walked down the river about three miles to discover, if possible, some place to which the canoes might arrive or at which they might be drawn on shore in order to be taken by land above the falls, but returned without effecting either of these objects. The river was one continuous scene of rapids and cascades which I readily perceived could not be encountered with our canoes, and the cliffs still retained their perpendicular structure and were from one hundred fifty to two hundred feet high. In short, the river appears here to have worn a channel, in the process of time, through a solid rock.

My fare is really sumptuous this evening: buffalo humps, tongues and marrowbones, fine trout, parched meal, pepper and salt, and a good appetite. The last is not considered the least of the luxuries.

Friday, June 14, 1805:

Lewis: I descended the hill and directed my course to the bend of the Missouri near which there was a herd of at least a thousand buffalo. Here I thought it would be well to kill a buffalo and leave him until my return from the river, and if I then found that I had not time to get back to camp this evening, to remain all night here, there being a few sticks of driftwood lying along shore which would answer for my fire and a few scattering cottonwood trees a few hundred yards below which would afford me at least the semblance of a shelter. Under this impression, I selected a fat buffalo and shot him very well, through the lungs.

While I was gazing attentively on the poor animal discharging blood in streams from his mouth and nostrils, expecting him to fall every instant, and having entirely forgotten to reload my rifle, a large white, or rather brown, bear had perceived and crept on me within twenty steps before I discovered him. In the first moment, I drew up my gun to shoot, but at the same instant recollected that she was not loaded, and that he was too near for me to hope to perform this operation before he reached me, as he was then briskly advancing on me. It was an open level plain, not a bush within miles nor a tree within less than three hundred yards of me. The river bank was sloping and not more than three feet above the level of the water. In short, there was no place by means of which I could conceal myself from this monster until I could charge my rifle.

In this situation, I thought of retreating in a brisk walk as fast as he was advancing until I could reach a tree about three hundred yards below me, but I had no sooner turned myself about but he pitched at me, open-mouthed and full speed. I ran about eighty yards and found he [had] gained on me fast. I then ran into the water. The idea struck me to get into the water to such depth that I could stand and he would be obliged to swim, and that I could, in that situation, defend myself with my espontoon. Accordingly, I ran hastily into the water about waist deep and faced about, and presented the point of my espontoon. At this instant he arrived at the edge of the water within about twenty feet of me. The moment I put myself in this attitude of defense, he suddenly wheeled about as if frightened, declined to combat on such unequal grounds, and retreated with quite as great precipitation as he had just before pursued me.

As soon as I saw him run in that manner, I returned to the shore and charged my gun, which I had still retained in my hand throughout this curious adventure. I saw him run through the level open plain about three miles until he disappeared in the woods on Medicine River.[210] During the whole of this distance he ran at full speed, sometimes appearing to look behind him as if he expected pursuit.

I now began to reflect on this novel occurrence and endeavored to account for this sudden retreat of the bear. I at first thought that perhaps he had not smelled me before he arrived at the water's edge so near me, but I then reflected that he had pursued me for about eighty or ninety yards before I took [to] the water and, on examination, saw the ground torn with his talons immediately on the impression of my steps. The cause of his alarm still remains with me mysterious and unaccountable. So it was, and I felt myself not a little gratified that he had declined the combat. My gun reloaded, I felt confidence once more in my strength.

In returning through the level bottom of Medicine River, and about two hundred yards distant from the Missouri, my direction led me directly to an animal that I at first supposed was a wolf. But on nearer approach, or about sixty paces distant, I discovered that it was not. Its color was a brownish-yellow. It was standing near its burrow, and when I approached it thus nearly, it couched itself down like a cat, looking immediately at me as if it designed to spring on me. I took aim at it and fired. It instantly disappeared in its burrow. I loaded my gun and examined the place, which was dusty, and saw the track, from which I am still further convinced that it was of the tiger kind.[211] Whether I struck it or not I could not determine, but I am almost confident that I did. My gun is true and I had a steady rest by means of my espontoon which I have found very serviceable to me in this way in the open plains.

It now seemed to me that all the beasts of the neighborhood had made a league to destroy me, or that some fortune was disposed to amuse herself at my expense, for I had not proceeded more than three

210. present-day Sun River

211. probably a wolverine (Ambrose, *UC*, p. 239), or a cougar (Bakeless, p. 187)

hundred yards from the burrow of this tiger cat before three bull buffalo, which were feeding with a large herd about half a mile from me on my left, separated from the herd and ran full speed towards me. I thought at least to give them some amusement, and altered my direction to meet them. When they arrived within a hundred yards, they made a halt, took a good view of me, and retreated with precipitation.

I then continued my route homeward past the buffalo which I had killed, but did not think it prudent to remain all night at this place which really, from the succession of curious adventures, wore the impression on my mind of enchantment. At some times, for a moment, I thought it might be a dream, but the prickly pears which pierced my feet very severely once in a while, particularly after it grew dark, convinced me that I was really awake and that it was necessary to make the best of my way to camp.

Clark: [It is] a fine morning.

The Indian woman complained all night, and excessively bad this morning. Her case is somewhat dangerous. Two men [have] the toothache, two with tumors, and one man with a tumor and a slight fever.

[We] passed the camp Captain Lewis made the first night, at which place he had left part of two bear, their skins, etc. [The] three men with tumors went on shore and stayed out all night. One of them killed two buffalo, a part of which we made use of for breakfast.

The current [is] excessively rapid, more so as we ascend. We find great difficulty in getting the pirogue and canoes up in safety; [the] canoes take in water frequently.

At 4:00 this evening, Joseph Field returned from Captain Lewis with a letter for me. Captain Lewis dates his letter from the Great Falls of the Missouri, which Field informs me is about twenty miles in advance and about ten miles above the place I left the river the time I was up last week.

Saturday, June 15, 1805:

Clark: We set out at the usual time and proceeded on with great difficulty as the river is more rapid. We can hear the falls this morning very distinctly.

Our Indian woman is sick and low-spirited. I gave her the bark and applied it externally to her region which revived her much.

The current [is] excessively rapid and difficult to ascend. [There are] great numbers of dangerous places, and the fatigue which we have to encounter is incredible. The men [are] in the water from morning until night hauling the cord and boats, walking on sharp rocks and round slippery stones which alternately cut their feet and throw them down. Notwithstanding all this difficulty, they go with great cheerfulness. Added to these difficulties, the rattlesnakes [are] innumerable and require great caution to prevent being bitten.

Sunday, June 16, 1805:

Lewis: At noon the men arrived, and shortly after I set out with them to rejoin the party. We took with us the dried meat, consisting of about six hundred pounds, and several dozen dried trout.

About 2:00 p.m. I reached the camp [and] found the Indian woman extremely ill and much reduced by her indisposition. This gave me some concern as well for the poor object herself, then with a young child in her arms, as from the consideration of her being our only dependence for a friendly negotiation with the Shoshone Indians, on whom we depend for horses to assist us in our portage from the Missouri to the Columbia River.

I now informed Captain Clark of my discoveries with respect to the most proper side for our portage, and of its great length, which I could not estimate at less than sixteen miles. Captain Clark had already sent two men this morning to examine the country on the starboard side of the river. He now passed over with the party to that side and fixed a camp about a mile below the entrance of a creek where there was a sufficient quantity of wood for fuel, an article which can be obtained but in few places in this neighborhood.

After discharging the loads, four of the canoes were sent back to me which, by means of strong ropes, we hauled above the rapids and passed over to the south side from whence, the water not being rapid, we can readily convey them into the creek by means of which we hope to get them on the high plain with more ease. One of the small canoes was left below this rapids in order to pass and repass the river for the purpose of hunting as well as to procure the water of the sulfur spring, the virtues of which I now resolved to try on the Indian woman.

Captain Clark determined to set out in the morning to examine the country and survey the portage and discover the best route. As the distance was too great to think of transporting the canoes and baggage on the men's shoulders, we selected six men and ordered them to look out [for] some timber this evening, and early in the morning to set about making a parcel of truck wheels in order to convey our canoes and baggage over the portage. We determined to leave the white pirogue at this place and substitute the iron boat, and also to make a further deposit of a part of our stores.

I found that two doses of bark and opium which I had given her[212] since my arrival had produced an alteration in her pulse for the

---

212. Sacagawea

better; [it was] now much fuller and more regular. I caused her to drink the mineral water altogether. When I first came down, I found that her pulse was scarcely perceptible—very quick, frequently irregular—and attended with strong nervous symptoms, that of twitching of the fingers and leaders[213] of the arm. Now the pulse has become regular, much fuller, and a gentle perspiration has taken place. The nervous symptoms have also in a great manner abated, and she feels herself much freer from pain.

She complains principally of the lower region of the abdomen. I therefore continued the cataplasms[214] of bark and laudanum which had been previously used by my friend, Captain Clark. I believe her disorder originated principally from an obstruction of the menses in consequence of taking cold.[215]

Monday, June 17, 1805:

Lewis: Captain Clark set out early this morning with five men to examine the country and survey the river and portage as had been concerted last evening.

I set six men at work to prepare four sets of truck wheels with couplings, tongues and bodies, that they might either be used without the bodies for transporting our canoes, or with them in transporting our baggage. We were fortunate enough to find one cottonwood tree just below the entrance of Portage Creek that was large enough to make our carriage wheels about twenty-two inches in diameter. Fortunate, I say, because I do not believe that we could find another of the same size, perfectly sound, within twenty miles of us. The cottonwood which we are obliged to employ in the other parts of the work is extremely illy calculated, for it being soft and brittle. We have made two axles of the mast of the white pirogue, which I hope will answer tolerably well, though it is rather small.

The Indian woman [is] much better today. I have still continued the same course of medicine. She is free from pain, clear of fever, her pulse [is] regular, and [she] eats as heartily as I am willing to permit her, of broiled buffalo well-seasoned with pepper and salt, and rich soup of the same meat. I think, therefore, that there is every rational hope of her recovery.

---

213. tendons

214. poultices

215. possibly chronic pelvic inflammatory disease, secondary to gonorrheal infection (Chuinard, pp. 287-9)

Ordway: Two hunters [went] out in order to get elk skins to cover, or bottom, our iron boat when we get about the Falls, as we will stand in need of it, as we [will] leave our largest craft at this place.

Tuesday, June 18, 1805:

Clark: This evening one man, Alexander Willard, [while] going for a load of meat at one hundred seventy yards distance on an island, was attacked by a white bear and, very near being caught, [was] pursued within forty yards of the camp, where I was with one man. I collected three others of the party and pursued the bear (who had pursued my track from a buffalo I had killed on the island at about three hundred yards distance and chanced to meet Willard) for fear of his attacking one man, Colter, at the lower point of the island. Before we had gotten down, the bear had alarmed the man and pursued him into the water. At our approach he retreated, and we relieved the man in the water. I saw the bear but the bushes were so thick that I could not shoot him, and it was nearly dark.

Thursday, June 20, 1805:

Clark: I directed stakes to be cut to stick up in the prairie to show the way for the party to transport the baggage, etc., etc. We set out early on the portage. Soon after we set out, it began to rain, and continued a short time.

We proceeded on through a tolerable level plain and found the hollow of a deep ravine to obstruct our route as it could not be passed with canoes and baggage for some distance above the place we struck it. I examined it for some time and, finding it late, determined to strike the river and take its course and distance to camp, which I accordingly did.

The wind [was] hard from the southwest. [It was] a fair afternoon. The river on both sides [is] cut with ravines, some of which pass through steep cliffs into the river. The country above the falls and up the Medicine River is level, with low banks. A chain of mountains [is] to the west, some part of which, particularly those to the northwest and southwest, are covered with snow and appear very high.

I saw a rattlesnake in an open plain two miles from any creek or woods.

When I arrived at camp, [I] found all well, with quantities of meat. The canoes Captain Lewis had carried up the creek one and three-fourths miles to a good place to ascend the land, and taken up.

Not having seen the Shoshone Indians or knowing, in fact, whether to calculate on their friendship or hostility, we have conceived our party sufficiently small, and therefore have concluded not to dispatch a canoe with a party of our men to St Louis as we have intended early in the spring. We fear also that such a measure might also discourage those who would in such case remain, and might possibly hazard the fate of the expedition. We have never hinted to anyone of the party that we had such a scheme in contemplation, and all appear perfectly to have made up their minds to succeed in the expedition or perish in the attempt. We all believe that we are about to enter on the most perilous and difficult part of our voyage, yet I see no one repining. All appear ready to meet those difficulties which await us with resolution and becoming fortitude.

The mountains to the northwest and west of us are still entirely covered, are white and glitter with the reflection of the sun. I do not believe that the clouds that prevail at this season of the year reach the summits of those lofty mountains. And if they do, the probability is that they deposit snow only, for there has been no perceptible diminution of the snow which they contain since we first saw them. I have thought it probable that these mountains might have derived their appellation of Shining Mountains from their glittering appearance when the sun shines in certain directions on the snow which covers them.

During the time of my being on the plains and above the falls, I, as also all my party, repeatedly heard a noise which proceeded from a direction a little to the north of west. [It was] a loud noise and resembled precisely the discharge of a piece of ordinance of six pounds at the distance of five or six miles. I was informed of it several times by the men, Joseph Field particularly, before I paid any attention to it, thinking it was thunder most probably which they had mistaken. At length walking in the plains yesterday near the most extreme southeast bend of the river above the falls, I heard this noise very distinctly. It was perfectly calm, clear, and not a cloud to be seen. I halted and listened attentively about two hours, during which time I heard two other discharges, and took the direction of the sound with my pocket compass, which was as nearly west from me as I could estimate from the sound.

I have no doubt but if I had leisure I could find from whence it issued. I have thought it probable that it might be caused by running water in some of the caverns of those immense mountains, on the principle of the blowing caverns. But in such case the sounds would be periodical and regular, which is not the case with this, being sometimes heard once only and at other times several discharges in quick succession. It is heard also at different times of the day and night. I am at a great loss to account for this phenomenon. I well recollect hearing the Hidatsa say that these Rocky Mountains make a great noise, but they could not tell me the cause. Neither could they inform me of any remarkable substance or situation in these mountains which would authorize a conjecture of a probable cause of this noise.

Sunday, June 23, 1805:

Clark: The men have to haul with all their strength, weight and art, many times every man all catching the grass and knobs and stones with their hands to give them more force in drawing on the canoes and loads and, notwithstanding the coolness of the air, [are] in high perspiration, and [at] every halt [the men] are asleep in a moment, many limping from the soreness of their feet.

Monday, June 24, 1805:

Whitehouse: [It was] a fair morning.

We hauled out the last canoe. [We] set out early with a wagon and baggage. [We] had some difficulty in getting the loading up on the high plains. We hoisted a sail in the largest canoe, which helped us [as] much as four men hauling at the cord with a harness. [We] passed through high, smooth, delightful plains.

Wednesday, June 26, 1805:

Lewis: The mosquitoes are extremely troublesome to us.

This morning early, I dispatched Joseph Field and Drouillard in one of the canoes up the river to hunt elk. [I] set Frazier at work to sew the skins together for the covering of the boat. Shields and Gass I sent over the river to search a small timbered bottom on that side opposite to the islands for timber and bark. And myself I assign the duty to cook as well for those present as for the party which I expect again to arrive this evening from the lower camp. I collected my wood and water, boiled a large quantity of excellent dried buffalo meat, and made each man a large suet dumpling by way of a treat.

About 4:00 p.m. Shields and Gass returned with a better supply of timber than they had yet collected, though not by any means enough. They brought some bark, principally of the cottonwood, which I found was too brittle and soft for the purpose. For this article I find my only dependence is the sweet willow, which has a tough and strong bark. Shields and Gass had killed seven buffalo in their absence, the skins of which and a part of the best of the meat they brought with them. If I cannot procure a sufficient quantity of elk skin, I shall substitute those of the buffalo.

Late in the evening, the party arrived with two more canoes and another portion of the baggage. Whitehouse, one of them much heated and fatigued on his arrival, drank a very hearty draught[216] of water and was taken almost instantly extremely ill. His pulse was full and I therefore bled him plentifully, from which he felt great relief. I had no other instrument with which to perform this operation but my penknife; however, it answered very well.

The wind being from the southeast today and favorable, the men made considerable progress by means of their sails.

At the lower camp, Captain Clark selected the articles to be deposited in the cache, consisting of my desk, which I had left for that purpose and in which I had left some books, my specimens of plants, minerals, etc., collected from Fort Mandan to this place, [and] also two kegs of pork, half a keg of flour, two blunderbusses, half a keg of fixed ammunition, and some other small articles belonging to the party which could be dispensed with. [We] deposited the swivel and carriage under the rocks a little above the camp near the river.

Thursday, June 27, 1805:

Lewis: The party returned early this morning for the remaining canoe and baggage.

Whitehouse was not quite well this morning. I therefore detained him, and about 10:00 a.m. set him at work with Frazier sewing the skins together for the boat. Shields and Gass continued the operation of shaving and fitting the horizontal bars of wood in the sections of the boat. The timber is so crooked and indifferent that they make but little progress. For myself, I continued to act the part of cook in order to keep all hands employed.

Some elk came near our camp and we killed two of them.

At 1:00 p.m. a cloud arose to the southwest and shortly after came on attended with violent thunder, lightening, and hail, etc.

Soon after this storm was over, Drouillard and Joseph Field returned. They were about four miles above us during the storm. The hail was of no uncommon size where they were. They had killed nine elk and three bears during their absence. One of the bears was the largest by far that we have yet seen. The skin appears to me to be as large as a common ox.

While hunting, they saw a thick, brushy bottom on the bank of the river where, from the tracks along shore, they suspected that there were bears concealed. They therefore landed without making any noise and climbed a leaning tree and placed themselves on its branches

216. British variation of *draft*

about twenty feet above the ground. When thus securely fixed, they gave a whoop, and this large bear instantly rushed forward to the place from whence he had heard the human voice issue. When he arrived at the tree, he made a short pause and Drouillard shot him in the head. It is worthy of remark that these bears never climb. The forefeet of this bear measured nine inches across and the hind feet eleven and three-fourths inches in length, exclusive of the talons, and seven inches in width.

A bear came within thirty yards of our camp last night and ate up about thirtyweight[217] of buffalo suet which was hanging on a pole. My dog seems to be in a constant state of alarm with these bears and keeps barking all night.

Saturday, June 29, 1805:

Clark: [There was] a little rain very early this morning; afterwards [it was] clear.

Finding that the prairie was so wet as to render it impossible to pass on to the end of the portage, [we] determined to send back to the top of the hill at the creek for the remaining part of the baggage left at that place yesterday, leaving one man to take care of the baggage at this place.

I determined myself to proceed to the falls and take the river. Accordingly, we all set out. I took my servant and one man; Charbonneau, our interpreter, and his squaw accompanied.

Soon after I arrived at the falls, I perceived a cloud which appeared black and threatened immediate rain. I looked out for a shelter but could see no place without being in great danger of being blown into the river if the wind should prove as turbulent as it is at some times. About one-fourth of a mile above the falls, I observed a deep ravine in which were shelving rocks, under which we took shelter near the river, and placed our guns, the compass, etc., etc., under a shelving rock on the upper side of the creek in a place which was very secure from rain.

The first shower was moderate, accompanied with a violent wind, the effects of which we did not feel.

Soon after, a torrent of rain and hail fell more violently than ever I saw before. The rain fell like one volley of water falling from the heavens and gave us time only to get out of the way of a torrent of water which was pouring down the hill in the river with immense force, tearing everything before it, taking with it large rocks and mud. I took my gun and shot pouch in my left hand, and with the right,

---

217. a hundredweight equals 100 pounds, so perhaps thirty pounds

scrambled up the hill, pushing the interpreter's wife (who had her child in her arms) before me, the interpreter himself making attempts to pull up his wife by the hand, much scared and nearly without motion. We at length reached the top of the hill safe where I found my servant in search of us, greatly agitated for our welfare.

Before I got out of the bottom of the ravine, which was a flat, dry rock when I entered it, the water was up to my waist and wet my watch. I scarcely got out before it raised ten feet deep with a torrent which was terrible to behold, and by the time I reached the top of the hill [there was] at least fifteen feet [of] water.

I directed the party to return to the camp at the run as fast as possible to get to our lode where clothes could be got to cover the child whose clothes were all lost, and the woman who was but just recovering from a severe indisposition, and was wet and cold; I was fearful of a relapse. I caused her, as also the others of the party, to take a little spirits, which my servant had in a canteen, which revived them very much.

On arrival at the camp on the willow run, [we] met the party who had returned in great confusion to the run, leaving their loads in the plain, the hail and wind being so large and violent in the plains, and them naked. They were much bruised and some nearly killed. One [was] knocked down three times and others, without hats or anything on their heads, [were] bloody and complained very much. I refreshed them with a little grog.

Soon after, the run began to rise and rose six feet in a few minutes. I lost at the river in the torrent the large compass, an elegant fusil, tomahawk, umbrella, shot pouch and horn with powder and ball, [and] moccasins, and the woman lost her child's bier[218] and clothes, bedding, etc. The compass is a serious loss as we have no other large one.

Whitehouse: In the afternoon there arose a storm of hard wind and rain and amazingly large hail. At our camp we measured and weighed some of them and Captain Lewis made a bowl of ice punch of one of them. They were seven inches in circumference and weighed three ounces.

Sunday, June 30, 1805:

Clark: The two men dispatched in search of the articles lost yesterday returned and brought the compass, which they found in the mud and stones near the mouth of the ravine. No other articles [were] found. The place I sheltered under [was] filled up with huge rocks.

---

218. a framework for carrying; here, a rawhide shoulder pack and cradle (DeVoto)

Lewis: I began to be extremely impatient to be off as the season is now wasting apace. Nearly three months have now elapsed since we left Fort Mandan and [we have] not yet reached the Rocky Mountains. I am therefore fully persuaded that we shall not reach Fort Mandan again this season, if we even return from the ocean to the Shoshone Indians.

7: July, 1805

We began to feel considerable anxiety with respect to the Shoshone Indians. If we do not find them or some other nation who has horses, I fear the successful issue of our voyage will be very doubtful or, at all events, much more difficult in its accomplishment.

Captain Meriwether Lewis,
July 27, 1805

Wednesday, July 3, 1805:

Ordway: The men not otherwise directed are dressing skins to make themselves moccasins as they have about worn them all out in the plains. One pair of good moccasins will not last more than about two days.

Thursday, July 4, 1805:

Ordway: [It was] a beautiful, clear, pleasant, warm morning. It being the Fourth of Independence, we drank the last of our ardent spirits, except a little reserved for sickness. The fiddle [was] put in order and the party amused themselves, dancing all the evening until about 10:00 in a civil and jovial manner.

Monday, July 8, 1805:

Whitehouse: About 9:00 a.m. Captain Clark and all the men that could be spared from camp set out for to go down to the Falls hunting. I remained in camp making leather, clothes, etc. The rest of the men at camp were employed in making coal and tallow and beeswax mixed, and payed[219] over the leather on the iron boat,[220] etc..

Tuesday, July 9, 1805:

Lewis: We caulked the canoes and put them in the water, and also launched the boat. She lay like a perfect cork on the water. Five men would carry her with the greatest ease. I now directed seats to be fixed

---

219. coated with waterproof material
220. called *The Experiment*

in her and oars to be fitted. The men loaded the canoes in readiness to depart.

Just at this moment, a violent wind commenced and blew so hard that we were obliged to unload the canoes again. A part of the baggage in several of them got wet before it could be taken out.

The wind continued violent until late in the evening, by which time we discovered that a greater part of the composition had separated from the skins and left the seams of the boat exposed to the water, and she leaked in such [a] manner that she would not answer. I need not add that this circumstance mortified me not a little. And to prevent her leaking without pitch was impossible with us, and to obtain this article was equally impossible. Therefore, the evil was irreparable.

I now found that the section formed of the buffalo hides on which some hair had been left answered much the best purpose. This leaked but little, and the parts which were well covered with hair, about one-eighth of an inch in length, retained the composition perfectly and remained sound and dry. From these circumstances, I am persuaded that had I formed her with buffalo skins singed not quite as close as I had done those I employed, that she would have answered even with this composition. But to make any further experiments in our present situation seemed to me madness. The buffalo had principally deserted us, and the season was now advancing fast. I therefore relinquished all further hope of my favorite boat, and ordered her to be sunk in the water, that the skins might become soft in order the better to take her in pieces tomorrow, and deposited the iron frame at this place, as it could probably be of no further service to us.

Ordway: So we sank her in the water so that she might be the easier taken to pieces tomorrow. Our officers conclude to build two canoes more so that we can carry all our baggage without the iron boat. About ten men got ready to go up the river to build two canoes.

Friday, July 12, 1805:

Lewis: [The] mosquitoes [are] extremely troublesome to me today, nor is a large gnat less troublesome, which does not sting but attacks the eye in swarms and compels us to brush them off or have our eyes filled with them.

Sunday, July 14, 1805:

Clark: [It was] a fine morning, and warm. [The] mosquitoes and gnats [are] very troublesome.

The canoes arrived at 12:00 and [were] unloaded to dry, etc. [We] finished and launched the two canoes.

[There was] some rain this afternoon.

All [are] preparing to set out on tomorrow.

Monday, July 15, 1805:

Lewis: We arose very early this morning. [We] assigned the canoes their loads and had them put on board. We now found our vessels eight in number, all heavily laden notwithstanding our several deposits, though it is true we have now a considerable stock of dried meat and grease. We find it extremely difficult to keep the baggage of many of our men within reasonable bounds. They will be adding bulky articles of but little use or value to them.

At 10:00 a.m. we once more saw ourselves fairly under way much to my joy and, I believe, [to] that of every individual who composes the party. I walked on shore and killed two elk, near one of which the party halted and dined. In order to lighten the burden of the canoes, I continued my walk all the evening and took our only invalids, Potts and Lepage, with me. We passed the river near where we dined and just above the entrance of a beautiful river eighty yards wide, which falls in on the port side. In honor of Mr. Robert Smith, the Secretary of the Navy, we called [it] Smith's River.

Drouillard wounded a deer, which ran into the river. My dog pursued [it], caught it, drowned it, and brought it to shore at our camp.

The prickly pear is now in full bloom and forms one of the beauties as well as [one of] the greatest pests of the plains. The sunflower is also in bloom and is abundant. This plant is common to every part of the Missouri from its entrance to this place.[221] The lamb's-quarters,[222] wild cucumber, sand rush,[223] and narrow dock[224] are also common here.

The river is from one hundred to one hundred fifty yards wide. [There is] more timber on the river than below the falls for a great distance. On the banks of the river, there are many large banks of sand, much elevated above the plains on which they lie. [They] appear as if they had been collected in the course of time from the river by the almost incessant southwest winds; they always appear on the sides of the river opposite to those winds.

---

221. at Ulm, Montana (Schmidt, p. 77)
222. goosefoot with a waxy or powdery coating
223. a tufted marsh plant; stems are used in bottoming chairs and plaiting mats
224. coarse, weedy plants in the buckwheat family

Tuesday, July 16, 1805:

Lewis: Drouillard killed a buffalo this morning near the river and we halted and breakfasted on it. Here, for the first time, I ate of the small guts of the buffalo cooked over a blazing fire in the Indian style, without any preparation of washing or other cleansing, and found them very good.

After breakfast, I determined to leave Captain Clark and [the] party and go on to the point where the river enters the Rocky Mountains and make the necessary observations against their arrival. Accordingly, I set out with the two invalids, Potts and Lepage, and Drouillard.

Clark: [It was] a fair morning after a very cold night [and] heavy dew.

[I] dispatched one man back for an ax left a few miles below, and set out early. [We] passed about forty small camps which appeared to be abandoned about ten or twelve days. [I] suppose they were Shoshone Indians. A few miles above, I saw the poles standing in their position of a very large lodge of sixty feet [in] diameter, and the appearance of a number of leather lodges about. This sign was old and appeared to have been last fall. [There were a] great number of buffalo.

The river is not so wide as below, from one hundred to one hundred fifty yards wide, and deep, [and] crowded with islands, and crooked. Some scattering timber [is] on its edge, such as cottonwood, cotton willow, willow, and box elder. The shrubs are arrowwood, redwood, choke cherry, red berries, gooseberries, serviceberries, red and yellow currants, [and] a species of shomake,[225] etc.

I camped on the head of a small island near the starboard shore at the Rocky Mountains.[226] This range of mountains appears to run northwest and southeast and is about eight hundred feet higher than the water in the river, [and is] faced with a hard black rock. The current of the river from the Medicine River to the mountain is gentle, [the] bottoms [are] low and extensive, and its general course is south ten degrees west, about thirty miles on a direct line.

Wednesday, July 17, 1805:

Clark: [We] set out early this morning and crossed the rapids at the island called Pine Rapids with some difficulty. At this rapids, I came up with Captain Lewis and [the] party. [We] took a meridian altitude, and we took some lunar observations, etc., and proceeded on.

---

225. possibly "sumac"

226. at the foot of the Big Belt Mountains (DeVoto)

The immense, high precipices oblige all [of] the party to pass and repass the river from one point to another. The river [is] confined in many places in a very narrow channel from seventy to one hundred twenty yards wide, [the] bottoms [are] narrow without timber, and [in] many places the mountains approach on both sides. The river [is] crooked, [the] bottoms [are] narrow, [and the] cliffs [are] high and steep.

I ascended a spur of the mountain, which I found to be high and difficult of access, containing pitch pine and covered with grass. Scarcely any game [are] to be seen. The yellow currants [are] now ripe, [and] also the fuzzy red choke cherries [are] getting ripe. [The] purple currants are also ripe. [We] saw several ibex, or mountain rams, today.

Thursday, July 18, 1805:

Lewis: Previous to our departure, [we] saw a large herd of the big-horned animals on the immensely high and nearly perpendicular cliff opposite to us. On the face of this cliff, they walked about and bounded from rock to rock with apparent unconcern, where it appeared to me that no quadruped could have stood and from which, had they made one false step, they must have been precipitated at least five hundred feet. This animal appears to frequent such precipices and cliffs where, in fact, they are perfectly secure from the pursuit of the wolf, bear, or even man himself.

At the distance of two and a half miles, we passed the entrance of a considerable river on the starboard side. [It is] about eighty yards wide, being nearly as wide as the Missouri at that place. Its current is rapid and [the] water extremely transparent. The bed is formed of small, smooth stones of flat, rounded, or other figures. Its bottoms are narrow but possess as much timber as the Missouri. The country is mountainous and broken through which it passes. It appears as if it might be navigated, but to what extent must be conjectural. This handsome, bold, and clear stream we named in honor of the Secretary of War, calling it Dearborn's River.[227]

As we were anxious now to meet with the Shoshones, or Snake, Indians as soon as possible in order to obtain information relative to the geography of the country and also, if necessary, some horses, we thought it better for one of us, either Captain Clark or myself, to take a small party and proceed on up the river some distance before the canoes in order to discover them should they be on the river, before the daily discharge of our guns, which was necessary in procuring subsis-

---

227. for Henry Dearborn

tence for the party, should alarm and cause them to retreat to the mountains and conceal themselves, supposing us to be their enemies who visit them, usually by the way of this river. Accordingly, Captain Clark set out this morning after breakfast with Joseph Field, Potts, and his servant, York.

We proceeded on tolerably well. The current [was] stronger than yesterday. We employed the cord and oars principally, though sometimes the setting pole.

Clark: After breakfast, I took Joseph Field, Potts, and my servant [and] proceeded on. The country [was] so hilly that we gained but little on the canoes until in the evening I passed over a mountain on an Indian road, by which route I cut off several miles of the meanderings of the river. The road which passes this mountain is wide and appears to have been dug in many places.

We camped on a small run of clear, cold water.

Mosquitoes [were] very troublesome [in] the forepart of the evening.

I saw many fine springs and streams of running water which sink and rise alternately in the valleys. The water of these streams is fine. These streams, which run off into the river, are dammed up by the beaver from near their mouths [to] up as high as I could see up them.

Friday, July 19, 1805:

Lewis: This morning we set out early and proceeded on very well, though the water appears to increase in velocity as we advance. The current has been strong all day and obstructed with some rapids, though these are but little broken by rocks and are perfectly safe. The river [is] deep and from one hundred to one hundred fifty yards wide.

I walked along shore today and killed an antelope.

Whenever we get a view of the lofty summits of the mountains, the snow presents itself, although we are almost suffocated in this confined valley with heat.

This evening, we entered much the most remarkable cliffs that we have yet seen. These cliffs rise from the water's edge on either side perpendicularly to the height of twelve hundred feet. Every object here wears a dark and gloomy aspect. The towering and projecting rocks in many places seem ready to tumble on us. The river appears to have forced its way through this immense body of solid rock for the distance of five and three-fourths miles, and where it makes its exit below, has thrown on either side vast columns of rocks mountains high.

The river appears to have worn a passage just the width of its channel, or one hundred fifty yards. It is deep from side to side, nor is there in the first three miles of this distance a spot, except one of a few yards, in extent on which a man could rest the sole of his foot. Several fine springs burst out at the water's edge from the interstices of the rocks. It happens, fortunately, that although the current is strong, it is not so much so but what it may be overcome with the oars, for there is here no possibility of using either the cord or setting pole.

It was late in the evening before I entered this place and was obliged to continue my route until sometime after dark before I found a place sufficiently large to encamp my small party. At length, such a one occurred on the port side where we found plenty of light wood and pitch pine. This rock is a black granite below and appears to be of a much lighter color above and, from the fragments, I take it to be flint of a yellowish-brown and light cream-colored yellow. From the singular appearance of this place, I called it the Gates of the Rocky Mountains.

Clark: I proceeded on in an Indian path. [The] river [is] very crooked. [We] passed over two mountains. [We] saw several Indian camps which they have left this spring. [We] saw trees peeled and found poles, etc.

At 11:00 I saw a gang of elk [and], as we had no provisions, concluded to kill some. [We] killed two and dined, being obliged to substitute dry buffalo dung in place of wood.

This evening [we] passed over cream-colored flint which has rolled down from the cliffs into the bottoms. The cliffs contain flint, a dark gray stone, and a reddish-brown intermixed, and no one cliff is solid rock. All the rocks of every description are in small pieces [and] appear to have been broken by some convulsion.

My feet are very much bruised and cut [from] walking over the flint, and constantly stuck full of prickly pear thorns. I pulled out seventeen by the light of the fire tonight.[228]

Mosquitoes [are] very troublesome.

Saturday, July 20, 1805:

Lewis: About 10:00 a.m. we saw the smoke arise as if the country had been set on fire up the valley of this creek, about seven miles distant. We were at a loss to determine whether it had been set on fire by the natives as a signal among themselves on discovering us, as is their custom, or whether it had been set on fire by Captain Clark and [his] party accidentally. The first, however, proved to be the fact; they had, unperceived by us, discovered Captain Clark's party or mine, and

---

228. on the west side of present-day Hauser Lake, created by the Hauser Dam (Schmidt, p. 84)

had set the plain on fire to alarm the more distant natives, and fled themselves farther into the interior of the mountains.

This evening we found the skin of an elk and part of the flesh of the animal which Captain Clark had left near the river at the upper side of the valley where he ascended the mountain, with a note informing me of his transactions and that he should pass the mountains which lie just above us and wait our arrival at some convenient place on the river. The other elk which Captain Clark had killed we could not find.

About 2:00 in the evening, we had passed through a range of low mountains, and the country became more open again, though still broken and untimbered, and the bottoms [were] not very extensive.

We encamped on the port side near a spring on a high bank. The prickly pears are so abundant that we could scarcely find room to lie.

Sunday, July 21, 1805:

Lewis: [We] set out early this morning and passed a bad rapids where the river enters the mountain about one mile from our camp of last evening. The cliffs [are] high and covered with fragments of broken rocks.

The current [is] strong. We employed the tow rope principally [and] also the poles, as the river is not now so deep but rather wider and much more rapid. Our progress was, therefore, slow and laborious.

We saw three swans this morning which, like the geese, have not yet recovered the feathers of the wing and could not fly. We killed two of them; the third escaped by diving and passed down with the current. They had no young ones with them; [we] therefore presume they do not breed in this country. These are the first we have seen on the river for a great distance. We daily see great numbers of geese with their young who are perfectly feathered except the wings, which are deficient in both young and old. My dog caught several today, as he frequently does. The young ones are very fine but the old geese are poor and unfit for use.

[We] saw several of the large brown, or sandhill, cranes today with their young. The young crane is as large as a turkey and cannot fly. They are of a bright red bay color, or that of the common deer at this season.

The grass near the river is lofty and green. That of the hillsides and high open ground is perfectly dry and appears to be scorched by the heat of the sun. The country was rough, mountainous, and much as that of yesterday until towards evening when the river entered a beautiful and extensive plain country of about ten or twelve miles wide, which extended upwards farther than the eye could reach. This valley is bounded by two nearly parallel ranges of high mountains which have their summits partially covered with snow. Below the snowy region, pine succeeds and reaches down their sides, in some parts to the plain, but much the greater portion of their surfaces is uncovered with timber and exposes either a barren, sterile soil covered with dry, parched grass, or black and rugged rocks.

The river, immediately on entering this valley, assumes a different aspect and character. It spreads to a mile and upwards in width [and is] crowded with islands, some of them large. [It] is shallow enough for the use of the setting pole in almost every part, and [is] still more rapid than before.

Clark: [It is] a fine morning.

Our feet [are] so bruised and cut that I determined to delay for the canoes and, if possible, kill some meat by the time they arrived.

Small birds are plenty. [There are] some deer, elk, goats, and ibex, [but] no buffalo in the mountains.

These mountains are high and a great proportion of them [are] rocky. [The] valleys [are] fertile. I observed, on the highest pinnacles of some of the mountains to the west, snow lying in spots. Some, still farther north, are covered with snow and can't be seen from this point.

Monday, July 22, 1805:

Lewis: The river, being divided into such a number of channels by both large and small islands, I found it impossible to lay it[229] down correctly following one channel only in a canoe and, therefore, walked on shore.

I [was] met with great quantities of a small onion about the size of a musket ball, and some even larger. They were white, crisp, and well-flavored. I gathered about half a bushel of them before the canoes arrived. I halted the party for breakfast, and the men also gathered considerable quantities of those onions.

In the afternoon, I killed an otter which sunk to the bottom on being shot, a circumstance unusual with that animal. The water was about eight feet deep yet so clear that I could see it at the bottom. I swam in and obtained it by diving. I halted the party here for dinner.

I placed my thermometer in a good shade, as was my custom, about 4:00 p.m., and after dinner set out without it and had proceeded nearly a mile before I recollected it. I sent Sergeant Ordway back for it; he found it and brought it on. The mercury stood at eighty degrees above zero. This is the warmest day, except one, which we have experienced this summer.

---

229. the course

The Indian woman recognized the country and assures us that this is the river on which her relations live, and that the Three Forks are at no great distance. This piece of information has cheered the spirits of the party, who now begin to console themselves with the anticipation of shortly seeing the head of the Missouri, yet unknown to the civilized world.

Late this evening, we arrived at Captain Clark's camp on the starboard side of the river. We took them on board with the meat they had collected and proceeded a short distance and encamped on an island. Captain Clark's party had killed a deer and an elk today, and ourselves one deer and an antelope only. Although Captain Clark was much fatigued, his feet yet blistered and sore, he insisted on pursuing his route in the morning, nor would he consent willingly to my relieving him at that time by taking a tour of the same kind. Finding him anxious, I readily consented to remain with the canoes. He ordered Frazier and Joseph and Reubin Field to hold themselves in readiness to accompany him in the morning. Charbonneau was anxious to accompany him and was accordingly permitted.

The mosquitoes and gnats [are] more than usually troublesome to us this evening.

Tuesday, July 23, 1805:

Lewis: Captain Clark left us, with his little party of four men, and continued his route on the starboard side of the river.

About 10:00 a.m. we came up with Drouillard who had separated from us yesterday evening and lain out all night, not being able to find where we had encamped. He had killed five deer, which we took on board.

I ordered the canoes to hoist their small flags in order that should the Indians see us, they might discover that we were not Indians nor their enemies.

We made great use of our setting poles and cords, the use of both which the river and banks favored. Most of our small sockets were lost, and the stones were so smooth that the points of their poles slipped in such [a] manner that it increased the labor of navigating the canoes very considerably.

Clark: [We] proceeded on an Indian road through a wide valley which the Missouri passes, about twenty-five miles, and camped on the bank of the river. I saw no fresh sign of Indians today.

[There were] great numbers of antelope, some deer, and a large gang of elk.

Wednesday, July 24, 1805:

Lewis: The adjacent mountains commonly rise so high as to conceal the more distant and lofty mountains from our view. I fear every day that we shall meet with some considerable falls or obstruction in the river, notwithstanding the information of the Indian woman to the contrary, who assures us that the river continues much as we see it. I can scarcely form an idea of a river running to great extent through such a rough, mountainous country without having its stream intercepted by some difficult and dangerous rapids or falls. We daily pass a great number of small rapids or riffles which descend one, two, or three feet in one hundred fifty yards, but we are rarely incommoded with fixed or standing rocks, and although [it is] strong, rapid water, [it] is nevertheless quite practicable and by no means dangerous.

Our trio of pests still invades and obstructs us on all occasions. These are the mosquitoes, eye gnats, and prickly pears, equal to any three curses that ever poor Egypt labored under, except the Muhammadan yoke. The men complain of being much fatigued. Their labor is excessively great. I occasionally encourage them by assisting in the labor of navigating the canoes, and have learned to "push a tolerable good pole," in their phrase.

Thursday, July 25, 1805:

Clark: [It was] a fine morning.

We proceeded on a few miles to the Three Forks of the Missouri. These three forks are nearly of [the same] size. The north fork appears to have the most water and must be considered as the one best calculated for us to ascend. [The] middle fork is quite as large, about ninety yards wide. The south fork is about seventy yards wide and falls in about four hundred yards below the middle fork. These forks appear to be very rapid and contain some timber in their bottoms which are very extensive.

On the north side, the Indians have lately set the prairies on fire, the cause I can't account for. I saw one horse track going up the river, about four or five days past.

After breakfast (which we made on the ribs of a buck killed yesterday), I wrote a note informing Captain Lewis [of] the route I intended to take, and proceeded on up the main north fork through a valley. The day [was] very hot.

We camped on the same side. We ascended starboard twenty miles on a direct line up the north fork. Charbonneau, our interpreter, [was] nearly tired out, one of his ankles failing him.

The bottoms are extensive and tolerable [and the] land [is] covered with tall grass and prickly pears. The hills and mountains are high, steep, and rocky. The river [is] very much divided by islands. [There are] some elk, bear, and deer, and some small timber on the islands. [There are] great quantities of currants, red, black, yellow, and purple, [and] also mountain currants, which grow on the sides of cliffs, inferior in taste to the others, having [a] sweet, piney flavor, and are red and yellow. Choke cherries, baie rouge,[230] and the red berries also abound.

Mosquitoes [were] very troublesome until the mountain breeze sprang up, which was a little after night.

Friday, July 26, 1805:

Lewis: [The] current [is] strong with frequent riffles. [We] employed the cord and setting poles, the oars scarcely ever being used.

The highlands are thin, meager soil covered with dry, low sedge and a species of grass,[231] the dry seeds of which are armed with a long, twisted, hard beard at the upper extremity, while the lower point is a sharp subulate[232] firm point beset at its base with little stiff bristles standing with their points in a contrary direction to the subulate point to which they answer as a barb and serve also to press it forward when once entered a small distance. These barbed seeds penetrate our moccasins and leather leggings and give us great pain until they are removed. My poor dog suffers with them excessively. He is constantly biting and scratching himself as if in a rack of pain.

Clark: I determined to leave Charbonneau and one man who had sore feet to rest, and proceed on with the other two to the top of a mountain twelve miles distant west, [and] from thence view the river and valleys ahead.

We, with great difficulty and much fatigue, reached the top at 11:00. From the top of this mountain, I could see the course of the north fork about ten miles, meandering through a valley, but could discover no Indians or sign which was fresh. I could also see some distance up the small river below, and also the middle fork. After satisfying myself, [I] returned to the two men by an old Indian path. On this path and in the mountain, we came to a spring of excessively cold water which we drank rather freely of as we were almost famished. Notwithstanding the precautions of wetting my face, hands, and feet, I soon felt the effects of the water.

---

230. red berry

231. needle grass

232. linear and tapering to a fine point

We continued through a deep valley without a tree to shade us, scorching with heat, to the men who had killed a poor deer. I was fatigued [and] my feet [had] several blisters and [were] stuck with prickly pears. I ate but very little.

[I] determined to cross to the middle fork and examine that. We crossed the Missouri, which was divided by a very large island. The first part was knee deep, the other waist deep and very rapid.

Lewis: Here Charbonneau was very near being swept away by the current and cannot swim. Captain Clark, however, risked himself and saved his life.

Clark: I felt myself very unwell and took up camp on the little river three miles above its mouth and near the place it falls into the bottom.

[There were] a few drops of rain this evening.

Saturday, July 27, 1805:

Lewis: We set out at an early hour and proceeded on but slowly, the current still so rapid that the men are in a continual state of their utmost exertion to get on, and they begin to weaken fast from this continual state of violent exertion.

At 9:00 a.m. [we were] at the junction of the southeast fork of the Missouri and the country opens suddenly to extensive and beautiful plains and meadows which appear to be surrounded in every direction with distant and lofty mountains. Supposing this to be the Three Forks of the Missouri,[233] I halted the party on the port side shore for breakfast and walked up the southeast fork about one-half mile and ascended the point of a high limestone cliff from whence I commanded a most perfect view of the neighboring country. From east to south between the southeast and middle forks, a distant range of lofty mountains ran their snow-clad tops above the irregular and broken mountains which lie adjacent to this beautiful spot. Between the middle and southeast forks, near their junction with the southwest fork, there is a handsome site for a fortification.

After making a draft of the connections and meanderings of these streams, I descended the hill and returned to the party, took breakfast, and ascended the southwest fork one and three-fourths miles, and encamped at a port side bend in a handsome, level, smooth plain just below a bayou, having passed the entrance to the middle fork one-half a mile. Here I encamped to wait the return of Captain Clark and to give the men a little rest, which seemed absolutely necessary to them.

233. now the site of Missouri Headwaters State Park in Montana (Schmidt, p. 86)

At the junction of the southwest and middle forks, I found a note which had been left by Captain Clark informing me of his intended route, and that he would rejoin me at this place provided he did not fall in with any fresh sign of Indians, in which case he intended to pursue until he overtook them, calculating on my taking the southwest fork, which I most certainly prefer, as its direction is much more promising than any other.

Believing this to be an essential point in the geography of this western part of the continent, I determined to remain at all events until I obtained the necessary data for fixing its latitude, longitude, etc. After fixing my camp, I had the canoes all unloaded and the baggage stowed away and securely covered on shore, and then permitted several men to hunt. I walked down to the middle fork and examined and compared it with the southwest fork but could not satisfy myself which was the largest stream of the two. In fact, they appeared as if they had been cast in the same mold, there being no difference in character or size. Therefore, to call either of these streams the Missouri would be giving it a preference which its size does not warrant, as it is not larger than the other. They are each ninety yards wide.

In these meadows, I saw a number of the duck, mallard, with their young which are now nearly grown.

At 3:00 p.m. Captain Clark arrived very sick with a high fever on him, and much fatigued and exhausted. He informed me that he was very sick all last night, had a high fever and frequent chills, and constant aching pains in all his muscles. This morning, notwithstanding his indisposition, he pursued his intended route to the middle fork about eight miles, and finding no recent sign of Indians, rested about an hour and came down the middle fork to this place. Captain Clark thought himself somewhat bilious and had not had a passage for several days. I prevailed on him to take a dose of Rush's pills, which I have always found sovereign in such cases, and to bathe his feet in warm water and rest himself.

Captain Clark's indisposition was a further inducement for my remaining here a couple of days. I therefore informed the men of my intention, and they put their deerskins in the water in order to prepare them for dressing tomorrow.

We began to feel considerable anxiety with respect to the Shoshone Indians. If we do not find them or some other nation who has horses, I fear the successful issue of our voyage will be very doubtful or, at all events, much more difficult in its accomplishment. We are now several hundred miles within the bosom of this wild and mountainous country, where game may rationally be expected shortly to become scarce and subsistence precarious, without any information with respect to the country, not knowing how far these mountains continue, or where to direct our course to pass them to advantage or intercept a navigable branch of the Columbia. Or even were we on such a one, the probability is that we should not find any timber within these mountains large enough for canoes, if we judge from the portion of them through which we have passed.

However, I still hope for the best, and intend taking a tramp myself in a few days to find these yellow gentlemen, if possible. My two principal consolations are that from our present position, it is impossible that the southwest fork can head with the waters of any other river but the Columbia, and that if any Indians can subsist in the form of a nation in these mountains with the means they have of acquiring food, we can also subsist.

Sunday, July 28, 1805:

Lewis: Both Captain Clark and I corresponded in opinion with respect to the impropriety of calling either of these streams the Missouri, and accordingly agreed to name them after the President of the United States and the secretaries of the Treasury and State, having previously named one river in honor of the secretaries of War and Navy. In pursuance of this resolution, we called the southwest fork, that which we mean to ascend, Jefferson's River, in honor of that illustrious personage, Thomas Jefferson. The middle fork we called Madison's River, in honor of James Madison,[234] and the southeast fork we called Gallatin's River, in honor of Albert Gallatin.[235]

The two first are ninety yards wide, and the last is seventy yards. All of them run with great velocity and throw out large bodies of water. Gallatin's River is rather more rapid than either of the others, is not quite as deep, but from all appearances may be navigated to a considerable distance. Captain Clark, who came down Madison's River yesterday and has also seen Jefferson's some distance, thinks Madison's rather the most rapid, but it is not as much so, by any means, as Gallatin's. The beds of all these streams are formed of smooth pebble and gravel, and their waters [are] perfectly transparent. In short, they are three noble streams.

There is timber enough here to support an establishment, provided it be erected with brick or stone, either of which would be much cheaper than wood as all materials for such a work are immediately at the spot. There are several small sand bars along the shores, at no great

---

234. Secretary of State
235. Secretary of the Treasury

distance, of very pure sand, and the earth appears as if it would make good brick.

I had all our baggage spread out to dry this morning. And the day proving warm, I had a small bower,[236] or booth, erected for the comfort of Captain Clark. Our leather lodge, when exposed to the sun, is excessively hot.

All those who are not hunting, although much fatigued, are busily engaged in dressing their skins, making moccasins, leggings, etc., to make themselves comfortable.

The mosquitoes are more than usually troublesome; the gnats are not as much so.

In the evening about 4:00, the wind blew hard from southwest and after some little time brought on a cloud attended with thunder and lightning, from which we had a fine refreshing shower which cooled the air considerably. The showers continued, with short intervals, until after dark.

In the evening, the hunters all returned. They had killed eight deer and two elk; some of the deer were in excellent order.

Our present camp is precisely on the spot that the Shoshone Indians were encamped at the time the Hidatsa of the Knife River first came in sight of them five years since. From hence they retreated about three miles up Jefferson's River and concealed themselves in the woods. The Hidatsa pursued [them], attacked them, killed four men, four women [and] a number of boys, and made prisoners of all the females and four boys.

Sacagawea, our Indian woman, was one of the female prisoners taken at that time, though I cannot discover that she shows any emotion of sorrow in recollecting this event, or of joy in being restored to her native country. If she has enough to eat and a few trinkets to wear, I believe she would be perfectly content anywhere.

Whitehouse: Captain Clark [is] very unwell. We built a bower for his comfort. The party, in general, [is] much fatigued. Several [are] lame.

I am employed making the chief part of the clothing for the party.

Tuesday, July 30, 1805:

Lewis: Captain Clark, being much better this morning, and having completed my observations, we reloaded our canoes and set out, ascending Jefferson's River. Charbonneau, his woman, two invalids, and I walked through the bottom on the port side of the river about four and a half miles when we again struck it at the place the woman

236. shelter made with tree boughs or vines twined together

informed us that she was taken prisoner. Here we halted until Captain Clark arrived, which was not until after 1:00 p.m., the water being strong and the river extremely crooked. We dined and again proceeded on.

As the river now passed through the woods, the invalids got on board together with Charbonneau and the Indian woman.

I passed the river and continued my walk on the starboard side. [I] saw a vast number of beaver in many large dams which they had made. I directed my course to the high plain to the right, which I gained after some time with much difficulty and wading [on] many beaver dams [up] to my waist in mud and water. I would willingly have joined the canoes, but the brush was so thick, the river crooked, and [the] bottoms intercepted in such [a] manner by the beaver dams, that I found it useless to attempt to find them, and therefore proceeded on up the river in order to intercept it where it came near the plain and would be more collected into one channel.

At length, about sunset, I arrived at the river, only about six miles from my calculation on a direct line from the place I had left the canoes, but I thought they were still below me. I found the river was divided where I reached it by an island and was therefore fearful that they might pass without seeing them, and went down to the lower point of the large island.

Here I discovered a small island, close under the shore on which I was. I passed the narrow channel to the small island and examined the gravelly bar along the edge of the river for the tracks of the men, knowing from the appearance of the river at this place that if they had passed, they would have used the cord on the side where I was. I saw no tracks and was then fully convinced that they were below me. I fired my gun and hallooed but could hear nothing of them.

By this time it was getting dark. A duck lit on shore in about forty steps of me and I killed it. Having now secured my supper, I looked for a suitable place to amuse myself in combating the mosquitoes for the balance of the evening. I found a parcel of driftwood at the head of the little island on which I was and immediately set it on fire, and collected some willow brush to lie on. I cooked my duck, which I found very good, and after eating it, lay down, and should have had a comfortable night's lodge but for the mosquitoes which infested me all night.

Late at night, I was awakened by the noise of some animal running over the stony bar on which I lay, but did not see it. From the weight with which it ran, I supposed it to be either an elk or a brown bear.

Wednesday, July 31, 1805:

Lewis: This morning I waited at my camp very impatiently for the arrival of Captain Clark and party. I observed by my watch that it was 7:00 a.m. and they had not come in sight. I now became very uneasy and determined to wait until 8:00, and if they did not arrive by that time, to proceed on up the river, taking it as a fact that they had passed my camp some miles last evening.

Just as I set out to pursue my plan, I discovered Charbonneau walking up shore some distance below me, and waited until he arrived. I now learned that the canoes were behind. They arrived shortly after. Their detention had been caused by the rapidity of the water and the circuitous route of the river.

They halted and breakfasted, after which we all set out again, and I continued my walk on the starboard shore. The river now becomes more collected; the islands, though numerous, are generally small. The river continues [to be] rapid and is from ninety to one hundred twenty yards wide [and] has a considerable quantity of timber in its bottoms. Towards evening, the bottoms became much narrower and the timber much more scant.

This evening, just before we encamped, Drouillard discovered a brown bear enter a small copse of bushes on the port side. We surrounded the place and searched the brush, but he had escaped in some manner unperceived, but how we could not discover.

Nothing [was] killed today and our fresh meat is out. When we have a plenty of fresh meat, I find it impossible to make the men take any care of it, or use it with the least frugality, though I expect that necessity will shortly teach them this art.

The mountains on both sides of the river at no great distance are very lofty.

We have a lame crew just now: two with tumors or bad boils on various parts of them, one with a bad stone bruise, one with his arm accidentally dislocated but fortunately well-replaced, and a fifth has strained his back by slipping and falling backwards on the gunwale of the canoe.

The latter is Sergeant Gass. It gives him great pain to work in the canoe in his present situation, but he thinks he can walk with convenience. I therefore selected him as one of the party to accompany me tomorrow, being determined to go in quest of the Shoshone Indians. I also directed Drouillard and Charbonneau to hold themselves in readiness. Charbonneau thinks that his ankle is sufficiently recovered to stand the march, but I entertain my doubts of the fact. He is very anxious to accompany me and I therefore indulge him.

8: August, 1805

These men then advanced and embraced me very affectionately in their way, which is by putting their left arm over your right shoulder, clasping your back while they apply their left cheek to yours. Both parties now advanced, and we were all caressed and besmeared with their grease and paint until I was heartily tired of the national hug.

Captain Meriwether Lewis,
August 13, 1805

Thursday, August 1, 1805:

Lewis: At half after 8:00 a.m., we halted for breakfast and, as had been previously agreed on between Captain Clark and myself, I set out with three men in quest of the Shoshone Indians. The men I took were the two interpreters, Drouillard and Charbonneau, and Sergeant Gass. The route we took lay over a rough, high range of mountains[237] on the north side of the river. The river entered these mountains a few miles above where we left it.

Captain Clark recommended this route to me from a belief that the river, as soon as it passed the mountains, bore to the north of west, he having a few days before ascended these mountains to a position from which he discovered a large valley passing between the mountains and which bore to the northwest. This, however, proved to be the inlet of a large creek which discharged itself into the river just above this range of mountains, the river bearing to the southwest. We were, therefore, thrown several miles out of our route. As soon as we discovered our mistake, we directed our course to the river, which we at length gained about 2:00 p.m., much exhausted by the heat of the day, the roughness of the road, and the want of water.

The mountains are extremely bare of timber, and our route lay through the steep valleys exposed to the heat of the sun without shade, and scarcely a breath of air. And to add to my fatigue in this walk of about eleven miles, I had taken a dose of Glauber salts in the morning in consequence of a slight dysentery with which I had been afflicted for several days. Being weakened by the disorder and the operation of

237. the Tobacco Root Mountains (DeVoto)

the medicine, I found myself almost exhausted before we reached the river.

I felt my spirits much revived on our near approach to the river at the sight of a herd of elk, of which Drouillard and I killed two. We then hurried to the river and allayed our thirst. I ordered two of the men to skin the elk and bring the meat to the river, while I and the other prepared a fire and cooked some of the meat for our dinner.

We made a comfortable meal of the elk and left the balance of the meat on the bank of the river for the party with Captain Clark. This supply was no doubt very acceptable to them as they had had no fresh meat for nearly two days except one beaver, game being very scarce and shy. We had seen a few deer and some goats, but had not been fortunate enough to kill any of them. After dinner, we resumed our march and encamped about six miles above the starboard side of the river.

Shortly after I left Captain Clark this morning, he proceeded on and passed through the mountains. They formed tremendous cliffs of ragged and nearly perpendicular rocks. The lower part of this rock is of the black granite before mentioned, and the upper part a light-colored freestone. These cliffs continue for nine miles and approach the river very closely on either side. He found the current very strong. Captain Clark killed a bighorn on these cliffs which he and [his] party dined on. After passing this range of mountains, he entered this beautiful valley in which we also were. Just at the upper side of the mountain, there is a bad rapids. Here the tow line of our canoe broke in the chute of the rapids and swung on the rocks and had very nearly upset.

Whitehouse: It being Captain Clark's birthday, he ordered some flour [to be] given out to the party.

Friday, August 2, 1805:

Lewis: We resumed our march this morning at sunrise. Finding that the river still bore to the south, I determined to pass it, if possible, in order to shorten our route.

This we effected by wading the river about five miles above our encampment of the last evening. We found the current very rapid, waist deep, and about ninety yards wide, [and the] bottom smooth pebbles with a small mixture of coarse gravel. This is the first time I ever dared to wade the river, though there are many places between this and the forks where I presume it might be attempted with equal success.

The valley along which we passed today, and through which the river winds its meandering course, is from six to eight miles wide and consists of a beautiful level plain with but little timber, and that confined to the verge of the river. The land is tolerably fertile, and is either black or dark yellow loam, covered with grass from nine inches to two feet high. The plain ascends gradually on either side of the river to the bases of two ranges of high mountains. The tops of these mountains are yet covered partially with snow, while we in the valley are nearly suffocated with the intense heat of the midday sun. The nights are so cold that two blankets are not more than sufficient covering.

Soon after passing the river this morning, Sergeant Gass lost my tomahawk in the thick brush and we were unable to find it. I regret the loss of this useful implement. However, accidents will happen in the best families, and I consoled myself with the recollection that it was not the only one we had with us.

The bones of the buffalo and their excrement of an old date are to be met with in every part of this valley, but we have long since lost all hope of meeting with that animal in these mountains.

[There has been] no recent appearance of Indians. The Indians in this part of the country appear to construct their lodges with the willow boughs and brush. They are small, of a conic figure, and have a small aperture on one side through which they enter.

We continued our route up this valley on the port side of the river until sunset, at which time we encamped on the port side bank of the river,[238] having traveled twenty-four miles. We had brought with us a good stock of venison of which we ate a hearty supper. I feel myself perfectly recovered of my indisposition, and do not doubt being able to pursue my route tomorrow with the same comfort I have done today.

Captain Clark continued his route early this morning. The rapidity of the current was such that his progress was slow. In short, it required the utmost exertion of the men to get on, nor could they resist this current by any other means than that of the cord and pole. In the course of the day, they passed some villages of burrowing squirrels, saw a number of beaver dams and the inhabitants of them, many young ducks, both of the mallard and the red-headed fishing duck, geese, several rattlesnakes, black woodpeckers, and a large gang of elk. They found the river much crowded with islands, both large and small, and passed a small creek on the starboard side which we called Birth Creek.[239]

Captain Clark discovered a tumor rising on the inner side of his ankle this evening which was painful to him.

They encamped in a level bottom on the port side.

---

238. near present-day Waterloo, Montana (Schmidt, p. 89)

239. for Clark's August 1 birthday

Saturday, August 3, 1805:

Lewis: [We] set out early this morning, or before sunrise. [We] still continued our march through the level valley on the port side of the river. The valley [was] much as yesterday, only rather wider. I think it [is] twelve miles wide, though the plains near the mountains rise higher and are more broken, with some scattering pine near the mountains. In the leveler parts of the plain and river bottoms, which are very extensive, there is no timber except a scant proportion of cottonwood near the river. The mountains continue high on either side of the valley and are but scantily supplied with timber. Small pine appears to be the prevalent growth. It is of the pitch kind, with a short leaf.

At 11:00 a.m. Drouillard killed a doe and we halted about two hours and breakfasted, and then continued our route until night without halting, when we arrived at the river in a level bottom which appeared to spread to [a] greater extent than usual. From the appearance of the timber, I supposed that the river forked above us and [I] resolved to examine this part of the river minutely tomorrow.

This evening, we passed through a high plain for about eight miles, covered with prickly pears and bearded grass, though we found this even better walking than the wide bottoms of the river which we passed in the evening. We encamped on the river bank on [the] port side[240] having traveled, by estimate, twenty-three miles.

Captain Clark set out this morning as usual. He walked on shore a small distance this morning and killed a deer. In the course of his walk, he saw a track which he supposed to be that of an Indian from the circumstance of the large toes turning inward. He pursued the track and found that the person had ascended a point of a hill from which his camp of the last evening was visible. This circumstance also confirmed the belief of its being an Indian who had thus discovered them and ran off.

They found the river, as usual, much crowded with islands [and] the current more rapid and much more shallow than usual. In many places they were obliged to double-man the canoes and drag them over the stone and gravel. This morning they passed a small creek on [the] starboard side at the entrance of which Reubin Field killed a large panther. We called the creek, after that animal, Panther Creek.[241] They also passed a handsome little stream on [the] port side which is formed of several large springs which rise in the bottoms and along the base of the mountains with some little rivulets from the melting snows. In the

240. the Twin Bridges, Montana area (Schmidt, p. 90)
241. now Pipestone Creek (DeVoto)

evening they passed a very bad rapids where the bed of the river is formed entirely of solid rock, and encamped on an island just above.

The men were compelled to be a great proportion of their time in the water today. They have had a severe day's labor and are much fatigued.

Sunday, August 4, 1805:

Lewis: Charbonneau complains much of his leg and is the cause of considerable detention to us. Captain Clark's ankle became so painful to him that he was unable to walk.

Monday, August 5, 1805:

Lewis: Drouillard missed his step and had a very dangerous fall. He sprained one of his fingers and hurt his leg very much. The men were so much fatigued today that they wished much that navigation was at an end, that they might go by land.

Tuesday, August 6, 1805:

Lewis: About five miles above the forks, I heard the whooping of the party to my left and changed my route towards them. On my arrival, [I] found that they had taken the rapid fork[242] and learned from Captain Clark that he had not found the note which I had left for him at that place and the reasons which had induced him to ascend this stream. It was easiest and more in our direction and appeared to contain as much water. He had, however, previous to my coming up with him, met Drouillard who informed him of the state of the two rivers and was on his return. One of their canoes had just overset and all the baggage [was] wet, the medicine box among other articles, and several articles lost, a shot pouch and horn, with all the implements for one rifle lost and never recovered.

I walked down to the point where I waited their return. On their arrival, [I] found that two other canoes had filled with water and wet their cargoes completely. Whitehouse had been thrown out of one of these canoes as she swung in a rapid current and the canoe had rubbed him and pressed him to the bottom as she passed over him and, had the water been inches shallower, must inevitably have crushed him to death. Our parched meal, corn, Indian presents, and a great part of our most valuable stores were wet and much damaged on this occasion.

To examine, dry, and arrange our stores was the first object. We therefore passed over to the port side opposite to the entrance of the

---

242. the Big Hole River (Schmidt, p. 90)

rapid fork where there was a large gravelly bar that answered our purposes. Wood was also convenient and plenty. Here we fixed our camp and unloaded all our canoes and opened and exposed to dry such articles as had been wet.

A part of the load of each canoe consisted of leaden canisters of powder which were not in [the] least injured, though some of them had remained upwards of an hour underwater. About twenty pounds of powder which we had in a tight keg, or at least [in] one which we thought sufficiently so, got wet and entirely spoiled. This would have been the case with the others had it not have been for the expedient which I had fallen on of securing the powder by means of the lead, having the latter formed into canisters which were filled with the necessary proportion of powder to discharge the lead when used, and those canisters well-secured with corks and wax.

In this country, the air is so pure and dry that any vessel, however well-seasoned the timber may be, will give way or shrink unless it is kept full of some liquid.

We found that three deerskins, which we had left at a considerable height on a tree, were taken off which we supposed had been done by a panther.

We sent out some men to hunt this evening; they killed three deer and four elk which gave us a plentiful supply of meat once more.

Shannon had been dispatched up the rapid fork this morning to hunt by Captain Clark before he met with Drouillard or learned his mistake in the rivers. When he returned, he sent Drouillard in search of him but he rejoined us this evening and reported that he had been several miles up the river and could find nothing of him. We had the trumpet sounded and fired several guns but he did not join us this evening. I am fearful he is lost again. This is the same man who was separated from us [for] fifteen days as we came up the Missouri and subsisted nine days of that time on grapes only.

Whitehouse is in much pain this evening with the injury one of his legs sustained from the canoe today at the time it upset and swung over on him. Captain Clark's ankle is also very painful to him.

We would have given the party a day's rest somewhere near this place [even] had not this accident happened, as I had determined to take some observations to fix the latitude and longitude of these forks. Our merchandise, medicine, etc., are not sufficiently dry this evening; we covered them securely for the evening.

We believe that the northwest, or rapid, fork is the drain of the melting snows of the mountains, and that it is not as long as the middle fork, and does not at all seasons of the year supply anything like as much water as the other, and that about this season it rises to its greatest height. This last appears from the apparent bed of the river which is now overflowed, and the water, in many places, spreads through old channels which have their bottoms covered with grass that has grown this season and is such as appears on the parts of the bottom not inundated. We therefore determined that the middle fork was that which ought, of right, to bear the name we had given to the lower portion, or "River Jefferson," and called the bold, rapid, and clear stream "Wisdom," and the more mild and placid one which flows in from the southeast "Philanthropy,"[243] in commemoration of two of those cardinal virtues which have so eminently marked their deservedly celebrated character through life.

Wednesday, August 7, 1805:

Lewis: [I] dispatched Reubin Field in search of Shannon.

Our stores were now so much exhausted that we found we could proceed with one canoe less. We therefore drew out one of them into a thicket of brush and secured her in such [a] manner that the water could not take her off should the river rise to the height where she is.

My air gun was out of order and her sights had been removed by some accident. I put her in order and regulated her. She shot again as well as she ever did.

At 1:00 all our baggage was dry. We therefore packed it up, reloaded the canoes, and the party proceeded with Captain Clark up Jefferson's River.

I remained with Sergeant Gass to complete the observation of equal altitudes and joined them in the evening at their camp on the port side. We had a shower of rain which continued about forty minutes, attended with thunder and lightening. This shower wet me perfectly before I reached the camp. The clouds continued during the night in such [a] manner that I was unable to obtain any lunar observations.

This evening, Drouillard brought in a deer which he had killed.

We have not heard anything from Shannon yet. We expect that he has pursued Wisdom River upwards for some distance, probably killed some heavy animal, and is waiting our arrival.

Thursday, August 8, 1805:

Lewis: At noon, Reubin Field arrived and reported that he had been up Wisdom River some miles above where it entered the mountain and could find nothing of Shannon. He had killed a deer and an antelope.

243. today's Beaverhead, Big Hole, and Ruby rivers, respectively (DeVoto)

[A] great quantity of beaver, otter, and muskrats [are] in these rivers. Two of the hunters we sent out this morning returned at noon [and] had killed each a deer and an antelope.

We used the setting poles today almost altogether.

We encamped on the port side where there was but little timber [and] were obliged to use willow brush for fuel. The rose bushes and briars were very thick.

The hunters brought in another deer this evening.

The tumor on Captain Clark's ankle has discharged a considerable quantity of matter but is still much swollen and inflamed and gives him considerable pain.

[We] saw a number of geese, ducks, and some cranes today. The former began to fly.

The evening again proved cloudy, much to my mortification, and prevented my making any lunar observations.

The Indian woman recognized the point of a high plain to our right which she informed us was not very distant from the summer retreat of her nation on a river beyond the mountains which runs to the west. This hill, she says, her nation calls the Beaver's Head from a conceived resemblance of its figure to the head of that animal. She assures us that we shall either find her people on this river or on the river immediately west of its source which, from its present size, cannot be distant.

As it is now all important with us to meet with these people as soon as possible, I determined to proceed tomorrow with a small party to the source of the principal stream of this river and pass the mountains to the Columbia, and down that river until I find the Indians. In short, it is my resolution to find them or some others who have horses [even] if it should cause me a trip of one month. For without horses, we shall be obliged to leave a great part of our stores of which, it appears to me, that we have a stock already sufficiently small for the length of the voyage before us.

Friday, August 9, 1805:

Clark: [It was] a fine morning. [The] wind [was] from the northeast.

We proceeded on very well. [The] rapid places [are] more numerous than below.

Shannon, the man whom we lost on Wisdom River, joined us, having returned to the forks and pursued us up after pursuing Wisdom River one day.

Captain Lewis and three men[244] set out after breakfast to examine the river above, find a portage, if possible, [and] also the Shoshone

Indians. I should have taken this trip had I been able to march, from the raging fury of a tumor on my ankle muscle.

In the evening, [it] clouded up and [there were] a few drops of rain.

[We] encamped on the port side near a low bluff.

The river [was] today as yesterday.

The three hunters could kill only two antelope today [as] game of every kind [is] scarce.

Ordway: Captain Lewis, Shields, Drouillard and McNeal set out to go on ahead a long distance to make discoveries in hopes to find Indians, etc.

We came eighteen miles.

Saturday, August 10, 1805:

Lewis: After passing a large creek at about five miles, we fell in with a plain Indian road which led towards the point that the river entered the mountains; we therefore pursued the road. I sent Drouillard to the right to kill a deer which we saw feeding, and halted on the river under an immensely high perpendicular cliff of rocks where it entered the mountains. Here we kindled a fire and waited for Drouillard. He arrived in about an hour and a half, or at noon, with three deerskins and the flesh of one of the best of them.

We cooked and ate a hasty meal and departed, returning a short distance to the Indian road which led us the best way over the mountains which are not very high but are rugged and approach the river closely on both sides. From the number of rattlesnakes about the cliffs at which we halted, we called them the Rattlesnake Cliffs.

The river below the mountains is rapid, rocky, very crooked, much divided by islands, and withal shallow. After it enters the mountains, its bends are not so circuitous and its general course [is] more direct, but it is equally shallow, less divided, [and] more rocky and rapid. We continued our route along the Indian road which led us sometimes over the hills and again in the narrow bottoms of the river until, at the distance of fifteen miles from the Rattlesnake Cliffs, we arrived in a handsome, open, and level valley where the river divided itself nearly into two equal branches. Here I halted and examined these streams and readily discovered from their size that it would be vain to attempt the navigation of either any farther.

Here, also, the road forked, one leading up the valley of each of these streams. I therefore sent Drouillard on one and Shields on the other to examine these roads for a short distance and to return and

244. Drouillard, Shields, and McNeal (DeVoto)

compare their information with respect to the size and apparent plainness of the roads, as I was now determined to pursue that which appeared to have been the most traveled this spring.

In the meantime, I wrote a note to Captain Clark informing him of the occurrences which had taken place, recommending it to him to halt at this place until my return, and informing him of the route I had taken which, from the information of the men on their return, seemed to be in favor of the southwest, or left-hand, fork which is rather the smallest.

Accordingly, I put up my note on a dry willow pole at the forks and set out up the southeast fork. After proceeding about one-and-a-half miles, I discovered that the road became so blind that it could not be that which we had followed to the forks of Jefferson's River. Neither could I find the tracks of the horses which had passed early in the spring along the other. I therefore determined to return and examine the other myself, which I did, and found that the same horses had passed up the west fork which was rather the largest and more in the direction that I wished to pursue. I therefore did not hesitate about changing my route but determined to take the western road. I now wrote a second note to Captain Clark informing him of this change and sent Drouillard to put it with the other at the forks and waited until he returned.

There is scarcely any timber on the river above the Rattlesnake Cliffs nor is there anything larger than willow brush in sight of these forks. Immediately in the level plain between the forks and about one-half a mile distance from them stands a high rocky mountain, the base of which is surrounded by the level plain. It has a singular appearance. The mountains do not appear very high in any direction, though the tops of some of them are partially covered with snow. This convinces me that we have ascended to a great height since we have entered the Rocky Mountains, yet the ascent has been so gradual along the valleys that it was scarcely perceptible by land.

I do not believe that the world can furnish an example of a river running to the extent which the Missouri and Jefferson's rivers do through such a mountainous country and at the same time [be] so navigable as they are. If the Columbia furnishes us such another example, a communication across the continent by water will be practicable and safe. But this I can scarcely hope from a knowledge of its having in its comparatively short course to the ocean the same number of feet to descend which the Missouri and Mississippi have from this point to the Gulf of Mexico.

Sunday, August 11, 1805:

Lewis: The track which we had pursued last evening soon disappeared. I therefore resolved to proceed to the narrow pass on the creek about ten miles west in hopes that I should again find the Indian road at that place. Accordingly, I proceeded through the level plain directly to the pass. I now sent Drouillard to keep near the creek to my right, and Shields to my left, with orders to search for the road which, if they found [it], were to notify me by placing a hat in the muzzle of their gun. I kept McNeal with me.

After having marched in this order for about five miles, I discovered an Indian on horseback about two miles distant coming down the plain towards us. With my glass, I discovered from his dress that he was of a different nation from any that we had yet seen and was satisfied of his being a Shoshone. [In] his arms were a bow and quiver of arrows, and [he] was mounted on an elegant horse, without a saddle, and [held] a small string which was attached to the under jaw of the horse which answered as a bridle.

I was overjoyed at the sight of this stranger and had no doubt of obtaining a friendly introduction to his nation provided I could get near enough to him to convince him of our being white men. I therefore proceeded towards him at my usual pace. When I had arrived within about a mile, he made a halt, which I did also, and unloosening my blanket from my pack, I made him a signal of friendship known to the Indians of the Rocky Mountains and those of the Missouri, which is by holding the mantle or robe in your hands at two corners, and then throwing it up in the air higher than the head, bringing it to the earth as if in the act of spreading it, [and] thus repeating three times. This signal of the robe has arisen from a custom, among all those nations, of spreading a robe or skin for their guests to sit on when they are visited.

This signal had not the desired effect. He still kept his position and seemed to view Drouillard and Shields, who were now coming in sight on either hand, with an air of suspicion. I would willingly have made them halt but they were too far distant to hear me, and I feared to make any signal to them lest it should increase the suspicion in the mind of the Indian of our having some unfriendly design upon him.

I therefore hastened to take out of my sack some beads, a looking glass, and a few trinkets which I had brought with me for this purpose and, leaving my gun and pouch with McNeal, advanced unarmed towards him. He remained in the same steadfast posture until I arrived [with]in about two hundred paces of him when he turned his horse about and began to move off slowly from me.

I now called to him in as loud a voice as I could command, repeating the word "tab-ba-bone," which in their language signifies "white man."[245] But looking over his shoulder, he still kept his eye on Drouillard and Shields who were still advancing, neither of them having sagacity enough to recollect the impropriety of advancing when they saw me thus in parley with the Indian.

I now made a signal to these men to halt. Drouillard obeyed but Shields, who afterwards told me that he did not observe the signal, still kept on. The Indian halted again and turned his horse about as if to wait for me, and I believe he would have remained until I came up with him had it not been for Shields who still pressed forward. When I arrived within about one hundred fifty paces, I again repeated the word "tab-ba-bone" and held up the trinkets in my hands, and stripped up my shirt sleeve to give him an opportunity of seeing the color of my skin, and advanced leisurely towards him. But he did not remain until I got nearer than about one hundred paces when he suddenly turned his horse about, gave him the whip, leaped the creek, and disappeared in the willow brush in an instant, and with him vanished all my hopes of obtaining horses for the present.

I now felt quite as much mortification and disappointment as I had pleasure and expectation at the first sight of this Indian. I felt sorely chagrined at the conduct of the men, particularly Shields, to whom I principally attributed this failure in obtaining an introduction to the natives.

We now set out on the track of the horse, hoping by that means to be led to an Indian camp, the trail of inhabitants of which, should they abscond, we should probably be enabled to pursue to the body of the nation to which they would most probably fly for safety. This route led us across a large island framed by nearly an equal division of the creek in this bottom.

After passing to the open ground on the north side of the creek, we observed that the track made out towards the high hills about three miles distant in that direction. I thought it probable that their camp might probably be among those hills and that they would reconnoiter us from the tops of them, and that if we advanced hastily towards them, they would become alarmed and probably run off.

I therefore halted in an elevated situation near the creek, had a fired kindled of willow brush, cooked and took breakfast. During this leisure, I prepared a small assortment of trinkets consisting of some moccasin awls, a few strands of several kinds of beads, some paint, a looking glass, etc., which I attached to the end of a pole and planted it near our fire in order that should the Indians return in search of us they

---

245. many believe the phrase meant "stranger," or possibly even "enemy" (e.g., Ambrose, *UC*, p. 256, and Bakeless, p. 225)

might, from this token, discover that we are friendly and white persons.

Before we had finished our meal, a heavy shower of rain came on, with some hail, which continued about twenty minutes and wet us to the skin. After this shower, we pursued the track of the horse, but as the rain had raised the grass which he had trodden down, it was with difficulty that we could follow it.

We pursued it, however, about four miles, it turning up the valley to the left under the foot of the hills. We passed several places where the Indians appeared to have been digging roots today, and saw the fresh tracks of eight or ten horses, but they had been wandering about in such a confused manner that we not only lost the track of the horse which we had been pursuing, but could make nothing of them.

In the head of this valley, we passed a large bog covered with tall grass and moss in which were a great number of springs of cold, pure water. We now turned a little to the left along the foot of the high hills and arrived at a small branch on which we encamped for the night. After meeting with the Indian today, I fixed a small flag of the U.S. to a pole, which I made McNeal carry, and planted [it] in the ground where we halted or encamped.

Monday, August 12, 1805:

Lewis: This morning I sent Drouillard out as soon as it was light to try and discover what route the Indians had taken. He followed the track of the horse we had pursued yesterday to the mountains where it had ascended, and returned to me in about an hour and a half.

I now determined to pursue the base of the mountains which form this cove to the southwest in the expectation of finding some Indian road which leads over the mountains. Accordingly, I sent Drouillard to my right and Shields to my left with orders to look out for a road or the fresh tracks of horses, either of which we should first meet with I had determined to pursue.

At the distance of about four miles, we passed four small rivulets near each other on which we saw some recent bowers, or small conic lodges, formed with willow brush. Near them, the Indians had gathered a number of roots, from the manner in which they had torn up the ground, but I could not discover the root which they seemed to be in search of.

Near this place, we fell in with a large and plain Indian road which came into the cove from the northeast and led along the foot of the mountains to the southwest, obliquely approaching the main stream which we had left yesterday. This road we now pursued to the southwest. At five miles, it passed a stout stream which is a principal fork of the main stream and falls into it just above the narrow pass between the two cliffs before mentioned and which we now saw below us. Here we halted and breakfasted on the last of our venison, having yet a small piece of pork in reserve.

After eating, we continued our route through the low bottom of the main stream along the foot of the mountains. On our right, the valley, for five miles farther in a southwesterly direction, was two to three miles wide. The main stream now, after discarding two streams on the left in this valley, turns abruptly to the west through a narrow bottom between the mountains. The road was still plain. I therefore did not despair of shortly finding a passage over the mountains and of tasting the waters of the great Columbia this evening.

At the distance of four miles farther, the road took us to the most distant fountain of the waters of the mighty Missouri, in search of which we have spent so many toilsome days and restless nights. Thus far, I had accomplished one of those great objects on which my mind had been unalterably fixed for many years. Judge, then, of the pleasure I felt in allaying my thirst with this pure and ice-cold water which issues from the base of a low mountain or hill of a gentle ascent for one-half a mile. The mountains are high on either hand [and] leave this gap[246] at the head of this rivulet through which the road passes. Here I halted a few minutes and rested myself.

Two miles below, McNeal had exultingly stood with a foot on each side of this little rivulet and thanked his god that he had lived to bestride the mighty, and heretofore deemed endless, Missouri.

After refreshing ourselves, we proceeded on to the top of the dividing ridge[247] from which I discovered immense ranges of high mountains[248] still to the west of us, with their tops partially covered with snow. I now descended the mountain about three-fourths of a mile, which I found much steeper than on the opposite side, to a handsome, bold, running creek of cold clear water. Here I first tasted the water of the great Columbia River.[249]

After a short halt of a few minutes, we continued our march along the Indian road which led us over steep hills and deep hollows to a spring on the side of a mountain where we found a sufficient quantity of dry willow brush for fuel. Here we encamped for the night, having traveled about twenty miles. As we had killed nothing during the day,

---

246. Lemhi Pass, on today's Montana-Idaho border (DeVoto)

247. the Continental Divide

248. the Bitterroot Range of the Rocky Mountains (DeVoto)

249. actually, a tributary (Lemhi) of a tributary (Salmon) of a tributary (Snake) of the Columbia (Bakeless, p. 228)

we now boiled and ate the remainder of our pork, having yet a little flour and parched meal.

This morning Captain Clark set out early. [He] found the river shoally, rapid, shallow, and extremely difficult. The men [were] in the water almost all day. They are getting weak, sore, and much fatigued. They complained of the fatigue to which the navigation subjected them and wished to go by land. Captain Clark encouraged them and pacified them.

Tuesday, August 13, 1805:

Lewis: At the distance of five miles, the road, after leading us down a long descending valley for two miles, brought us to a large creek about ten yards wide. This we passed and, on rising the hill beyond it, had a view of a handsome little valley to our left of about a mile in width through which, from the appearance of the timber, I conjectured that a river passed.

We had proceeded about four miles through a wavy plain parallel to the valley, or river bottom, when, at the distance of about a mile, we saw two women, a man, and some dogs on an eminence immediately before us. They appeared to view us with attention and two of them, after a few minutes, sat down as if to wait our arrival. We continued our usual pace towards them. When we arrived within half a mile of them, I directed the party to halt and, leaving my pack and rifle, I took the flag which I unfurled, and advanced singly towards them. The women soon disappeared behind the hill. The man continued until I arrived within a hundred yards of him and then likewise absconded, though I frequently repeated the word "tab-ba-bone" sufficiently loud for him to have heard it.

I now hastened to the top of the hill where they had stood but could see nothing of them. The dogs were less shy than their masters; they came about me pretty close. I therefore thought of tying a handkerchief about one of their necks, with some beads and other trinkets, and then let them loose to search [for] their fugitive owners, thinking by this means to convince them of our pacific disposition towards them, but the dogs would not suffer me to take hold of them. They, also, soon disappeared.

I now made a signal for the men to come on. They joined me and we pursued the back track of these Indians which led us along the same road which we had been traveling. The road was dusty and appeared to have been much traveled lately, both by men and horses.

We had not continued our route more than a mile when we were so fortunate as to meet with three female savages. The short and steep ravines which we passed concealed us from each other until we arrived within thirty paces. A young woman immediately took to flight; an elderly woman and a girl of about twelve years old remained. I instantly laid by my gun and advanced towards them. They appeared much alarmed but saw that we were too near for them to escape by flight. They therefore seated themselves on the ground, holding down their heads as if reconciled to die, which they expected, no doubt, would be their fate.

I took the elderly woman by the hand and raised her up, repeated the word "tab-ba-bone," and stripped up my shirt sleeve to show her my skin to prove to her the truth of the assertion that I was a white man, for my face and hands, which have been constantly exposed to the sun, were quite as dark as their own. They appeared instantly reconciled, and the men [were] coming up. I gave these women some beads, a few moccasin awls, some pewter looking-glasses, and a little paint.

I directed Drouillard to request the old woman to recall the young woman who had run off to some distance by this time, fearing she might alarm the camp before we approached, and might so exasperate the natives that they would perhaps attack us without enquiring who we were. The old woman did as she was requested, and the fugitive soon returned almost out of breath. I bestowed an equivalent portion of trinkets on her with the others.

I now painted their tawny cheeks with some vermilion which, with this nation, is emblematic of peace. After they had become composed, I informed them by signs that I wished them to conduct us to their camp [and] that we were anxious to become acquainted with the chiefs and warriors of their nation. They readily obeyed and we set out, still pursuing the road down the river.

We had marched about two miles[250] when we met a party of about sixty warriors, mounted on excellent horses, who came in nearly full speed. When they arrived, I advanced towards them with the flag, leaving my gun with the party about fifty paces behind me. The chief and two others, who were a little in advance of the main body, spoke to the women and they informed them who we were and exultingly showed the presents which had been given them.

These men then advanced and embraced me very affectionately in their way, which is by putting their left arm over your right shoulder, clasping your back while they apply their left cheek to yours, and frequently vociferate the word "âh-hi-e, âh-hi-e," that is, I am much pleased, I am much rejoiced. Both parties now advanced, and we were all caressed and besmeared with their grease and paint until I was heartily tired of the national hug.

---

250. near Tendoy, Idaho, just west of Lemhi Pass (Schmidt, p. 98)

I now had the pipe lit and gave them smoke. They seated themselves in a circle around us and pulled off their moccasins before they would receive or smoke the pipe. This is a custom among them, as I afterwards learned, indicative of a sacred obligation of sincerity in their profession of friendship given by the act of receiving and smoking the pipe of a stranger. Or which is as much as to say that they wish they may always go barefoot if they are not sincere, a pretty heavy penalty if they are to march through the plains of their country.

After smoking a few pipes with them, I distributed some trifles among them, with which they seemed much pleased, particularly with the blue beads and vermilion. I now informed the chief that the object of our visit was a friendly one, that after we should reach his camp I would undertake to explain to him fully those objects, who we were, from whence we had come, and whither we were going, that in the meantime I did not care how soon we were in motion, as the sun was very warm and no water [was] at hand. They now put on their moccasins and the principal chief, Cameahwait,[251] made a short speech to the warriors. I gave him the flag which, I informed him, was an emblem of peace among white men, and now that it had been received by him, it was to be respected as the bond of union between us.

I desired him to march on, which he did, and we followed him. The dragoons moved on in squadron in our rear. After we had marched about a mile in this order, he halted them and gave a second harangue, after which six or eight of the young men rode forward to their encampment, and no further regularity was observed in the order of march.

I afterwards understood that the Indians we had first seen this morning had returned and alarmed the camp. These men had come out armed cap à pie[252] for action, expecting to meet with their enemies, the Hidatsa of Fort de Prairie, whom they call Pahkees. They were armed with bows, arrows, and shields, except three whom I observed with small pieces such as the North West Company furnishes the natives, which they had obtained from the Rocky Mountain Indians on the Yellowstone River, with whom they are at peace.

On our arrival at their encampment on the river[253] in a handsome level and fertile bottom at the distance of four miles from where we had first met them, they introduced us to a lodge made of willow brush, and an old leather lodge which had been prepared for our reception by the young men which the chief had dispatched for that purpose.

251. meaning "The One Who Never Walks"

252. head to toe

253. the Lemhi, near Sandy Creek (Schmidt, p. 99)

Here we were seated on green boughs and the skins of antelope. One of the warriors then pulled up the grass in the center of the lodge, forming a small circle of about two feet in diameter. The chief next produced his pipe and native tobacco and began a long ceremony of the pipe when we were requested to take off our moccasins, the chief having previously taken off his, as well as all the warriors present. This we complied with.

The chief then lit his pipe at the fire kindled in this little magic circle and, standing on the opposite side of the circle, uttered a speech of several minutes in length at the conclusion of which he pointed the stem to the four cardinal points of the heavens, first beginning at the east and ending with the north. He now presented the pipe to me as if desirous that I should smoke, but when I reached my hand to receive it, he drew it back and repeated the same ceremony three times, after which he pointed the stem first to the heavens, then to the center of the magic circle, smoked himself with three whiffs, and held the pipe until I took as many as I thought proper. He then held it to each of the white persons, and then gave it to be consumed by his warriors.

I now explained to them the objects of our journey, etc. All the women and children of the camp were shortly collected about the lodge to indulge themselves with looking at us, we being the first white persons they had ever seen. After the ceremony of the pipe was over, I distributed the remainder of the small articles I had brought with me among the women and children.

By this time it was late in the evening and we had not tasted any food since the evening before. The chief informed us that they had nothing but berries to eat, and gave us some cakes of serviceberries and choke cherries which had been dried in the sun.

Of these I made a hearty meal, and then walked to the river, which I found about forty yards wide, very rapid, clear, and about three feet deep.[254] Cameahwait informed me that this stream discharged itself into another, doubly as large, at the distance of half a day's march, which came from the southwest.[255] But he added on further enquiry that there was but little more timber below the junction of those rivers than I saw here, and that the river was confined between inaccessible mountains, was very rapid and rocky, insomuch that it was impossible for us to pass either by land or water down this river to the great lake where the white men lived, as he had been informed.

This was unwelcome information, but I still hoped that this account had been exaggerated with a view to detain us among them. As to timber, I could discover not any that would answer the purpose

---

254. the Lemhi River (Schmidt, p. 99)

255. the Salmon River (Ambrose, *UC*, p. 270)

of constructing canoes or, in short, more than was barely necessary for fuel.

These people had been attacked by the Hidatsa[256] of Fort de Prairie this spring and about twenty of them killed and taken prisoner. In this occasion, they lost a great part of their horses and all their lodges except that which they had erected for our accommodation. They were now living in lodges of a conic figure made of willow brush.

I still observe a great number of horses feeding in every direction around their camp, and therefore entertain but little doubt but we shall be enabled to furnish ourselves with an adequate number to transport our stores, even if we are compelled to travel by land over these mountains.

On my return to my lodge, an Indian called me in to his bower and gave me a small morsel of the flesh of an antelope boiled and a piece of a fresh salmon roasted, both [of] which I ate with a very good relish. This was the first salmon I had seen and perfectly convinced me that we were on the waters of the Pacific Ocean.

This evening the Indians entertained us with their dancing nearly all night. At 12:00 I grew sleepy and retired to rest, leaving the men to amuse themselves with the Indians. I observed no essential difference between the music and manner of dancing among this nation and those of the Missouri. I was several times awakened in the course of the night by their yells, but was too much fatigued to be deprived of a tolerable sound night's repose.

Wednesday, August 14, 1805:

Lewis: In order to give Captain Clark time to reach the forks of Jefferson's River, I concluded to spend this day at the Shoshone camp and obtain what information I could with respect to the country. As we had nothing but a little flour and parched meal to eat except the berries with which the Indians furnished us, I directed Drouillard and Shields to hunt a few hours and try to kill something.

The Indians furnished them with horses, and most of their young men also turned out to hunt. I was very much entertained with a view of this Indian chase. It was after a herd of about ten antelope, and about twenty hunters. It lasted about two hours, and considerable part of the chase in view from my tent. About 1:00 p.m. the hunters returned, had not killed a single antelope, and their horses [were] foaming with sweat. My hunters returned soon after and had been equally unsuccessful. I now directed McNeal to make me a little paste

256. actually, the Atsina (DeVoto)

with the flour, and added some berries to it, which I found very palatable.

The means I had of communicating with these people was by way of Drouillard, who understood perfectly the common language of gesticulation, or signs, which seems to be universally understood by all the nations we have yet seen. It is true that this language is imperfect and liable to error, but is much less so than would be expected. The strong parts of the ideas are seldom mistaken.

I now told Cameahwait that I wished him to speak to his people and engage them to go with me tomorrow to the forks of Jefferson's River where our baggage was, by this time, arrived with another chief and a large party of white men who would wait my return at that place, that I wished them to take with them about thirty spare horses to transport our baggage to this place where we would then remain some time among them and trade with them for horses and, finally, concert our future plans for getting on to the ocean, and of the trade which would be extended to them after our return to our homes.

He complied with my request and made a lengthy harangue to his village. He returned in about an hour and a half and informed me that they would be ready to accompany me in the morning. I promised to reward them for their trouble.

Drouillard, who had a good view of their horses, estimated them at four hundred. Most of them are fine horses. Indeed, many of them would make a figure on the south side of [the] James River, or the land of fine horses. I saw several with Spanish brands on them and some mules which, they informed me, they had also obtained from the Spaniards. I also saw a bridle bit of Spanish manufacture and sundry other articles which, I have no doubt, were obtained from the same source.

Notwithstanding the extreme poverty of these poor people, they are very merry [and] they danced again this evening until midnight. Each warrior keeps one or more horses tied by a cord to a stake near his lodge both day and night, and [they] are always prepared for action at a moment's warning. They fight on horseback altogether.

I observed that the large flies are extremely troublesome to the horses, as well as ourselves.

Thursday, August 15, 1805:

Lewis: This morning I arose very early and as hungry as a wolf. I had eaten nothing yesterday except one scant meal of the flour and berries, except the dried cakes of berries, which did not appear to satisfy my appetite as they appeared to do those of my Indian friends.

I found, on enquiry of McNeal, that we had only about two pounds of flour remaining. This I directed him to divide into two equal parts and to cook the one half this morning in a kind of pudding with the berries as he had done yesterday, and reserve the balance for the evening. On this new-fashioned pudding, four of us breakfasted, giving a pretty good allowance also to the chief who declared it the best thing he had tasted for a long time. He took a little of the flour in his hand, tasted and examined it very scrutinizingly, and asked me if we made it of roots. I explained to him the manner in which it grew.

I hurried the departure of the Indians. The chief addressed them several times before they would move. They seemed very reluctant to accompany me. I, at length, asked the reason and he told me that some foolish persons among them had suggested the idea [that] we were in league with the Pahkees and had come on in order to decoy them into an ambuscade[257] where their enemies were waiting to receive them but that, for his part, he did not believe it. I readily perceived that our situation was not entirely free from danger as the transition from suspicion to the confirmation of the fact would not be very difficult in the minds of these ignorant people who have been accustomed from their infancy to view every stranger as an enemy.

I told Cameahwait that I was sorry to find that they had put so little confidence in us, that I knew they were not acquainted with white men and therefore could forgive them, [and] that among white men it was considered disgraceful to lie or entrap an enemy by falsehood. I told him [that] if they continued to think thus meanly of us that they might rely on it that no white men would ever come to trade with them or bring them arms and ammunition, and that if the bulk of his nation still entertained this opinion, I still hoped that there were some among them that were not afraid to die, that were men and would go with me and convince themselves of the truth of what I had asserted, that there was a party of white men waiting my return, either at the forks of Jefferson's River or a little below coming on to that place, in canoes loaded with provisions and merchandise. He told me for his own part he was determined to go, that he was not afraid to die.

I soon found that I had touched him on the right string. To doubt the bravery of a savage is at once to put him on his mettle. He now mounted his horse and harangued his village a third time, the purport of which, as he afterwards told me, was to inform them that he would go with us and convince himself of the truth or falsity of what we had told him, if he was certain he should be killed, that he hoped there were some of them who heard him, were not afraid to die with him, and if there were, to let him see them mount their horses and prepare to set out.

---

257. ambush

Shortly after this harangue, he was joined by six or eight only, and with these I smoked a pipe, and directed the men to put on their packs, being determined to set out with them while I had them in the humor.

At half after 12:00 we set out. Several of the old women were crying and imploring the Great Spirit to protect their warriors, as if they were going to inevitable destruction.

We had not proceeded far before our party was augmented by ten or twelve more, and before we reached the creek which we had passed in the morning of the 13th, it appeared to me that we had all the men of the village, and a number of women, with us. This may serve in some measure to illustrate the capricious disposition of these people, who never act but from the impulse of the moment. They were now very cheerful and gay, and two hours ago they looked as surly as so many imps of Saturn.

When we arrived at the spring on the side of the mountain where we had encamped on the 12th, the chief insisted on halting to let the horses graze, with which I complied, and gave the Indians smoke. They are excessively fond of the pipe but have it not much in their power to indulge themselves with even their native tobacco, as they do not cultivate it themselves.

After remaining about an hour, we again set out, and by engaging to make compensation to four of them for their trouble, obtained the privilege of riding with an Indian myself, and a similar situation for each of my party. I soon found it more tiresome riding without stirrups than walking and, of course, chose the latter, making the Indian carry my pack.

About sunset, we reached the upper part of the level valley of the cove which we now called Shoshone Cove.[258] The grass being burned on the north side of the river, we passed over to the south and encamped near some willow brush about four miles above the narrow pass between the hills, noticed as I came up the cove. The river[259] was here about six yards wide, and frequently dammed up by the beaver.

I had sent Drouillard forward this evening, before we halted, to kill some meat, but he was unsuccessful and did not rejoin us until after dark. I now cooked and divided among six of us to eat the remaining pound of flour stirred in a little boiling water.

---

258. now mostly covered by the Clark Canyon Reservoir (Ambrose, *UC*, p. 264)
259. present-day Horse Prairie Creek (Ambrose, *UC*, p. 274)

Friday, August 16, 1805:

Lewis: I sent Drouillard and Shields before this morning in order to kill some meat, as neither the Indians nor ourselves had anything to eat.

I informed the chief of my view in this measure, and requested that he would keep his young men with us lest, by their whooping and noise, they should alarm the game and we should get nothing to eat, but so strongly were their suspicions exited by this measure, that two parties of discovery immediately set out, one on each side of the valley, to watch the hunters as, I believe, to see whether they had not been sent to give information of their approach to an enemy that they still persuaded themselves was lying in wait for them. I saw that any further effort to prevent their going would only add strength to their suspicions and, therefore, said no more.

After the hunters had been gone about an hour, we set out. We had just passed through the narrows when we saw one of the spies coming up the level plain under whip. The chief paused a little and seemed somewhat concerned. I felt a good deal so myself, and began to suspect that by some unfortunate accident that perhaps some of their enemies had straggled hither at this unlucky moment. But we were all agreeably disappointed on the arrival of the young man to learn that he had come to inform us that one of the white men had killed a deer.

In an instant they all gave their horses the whip, and I was taken nearly a mile before I could learn what were the tidings. As I was without stirrups and an Indian [was] behind me, the jostling was disagreeable. I therefore reined up my horse and forbid the Indian to whip him, who had given him the lash at every jump for a mile, fearing he should lose a part of the feast. The fellow was so uneasy that he left me the horse, dismounted, and ran on foot at full speed, I am confident, [for] a mile.

When they arrived where the deer was, which was in view of me, they dismounted and ran in, tumbling over each other like a parcel of famished dogs, each seizing and tearing away a part of the intestines which had been previously thrown out by Drouillard, who [had] killed it.

The scene was such when I arrived, that had I not have had a pretty keen appetite myself, I am confident I should not have tasted any part of the venison shortly. Each one had a piece of some description and all [were] eating most ravenously. Some were eating the kidneys, the melt,[260] and liver, and the blood [was] running from the corners of their mouths. Others were in a similar situation with the

260. spleen

paunch and guts, but the exuding substance, in this case, from their lips was of a different description.

One of the last who attracted my attention on particularly had been fortunate in his allotment, or rather active in the division. He had provided himself with about nine feet of the small guts, one end of which he was chewing on, while with his hands he was squeezing the contents out at the other. I really did not, until now, think that human nature ever presented itself in a shape so nearly allied to the brute creation.

I viewed these poor, starved devils with pity and compassion. I directed McNeal to skin the deer and reserve a quarter. The balance I gave the chief to be divided among his people. They devoured the whole of it nearly, without cooking.

I now bore obliquely to the left in order to intercept the creek where there was some brush to make a fire, and arrived at this stream where Drouillard had killed a second deer. Here, nearly the same scene was enacted. A fire being kindled, we cooked and ate and gave the balance of the two deer to the Indians who ate the whole of them, even to the soft parts of the hoofs.

Drouillard joined us at breakfast with a third deer. Of this, I reserved a quarter and gave the balance to the Indians. They all appeared now to have filled themselves and were in a good humor.

This morning early, soon after the hunters set out, a considerable part of our escort became alarmed and returned; twenty-eight men and three women only continued with us. After eating, and suffering the horses to graze about two hours, we renewed our march and, towards evening, arrived at the lower part of the cove. Shields killed an antelope on the way, a part of which we took, and gave the remainder to the Indians.

Being now informed of the place at which I expected to meet Captain Clark and the party, they insisted on making a halt, which was complied with. We now dismounted, and the chief, with much ceremony, put tippets[261] about our necks such as they themselves wore. I readily perceived that this was to disguise us, and owed its origin to the same cause already mentioned. To give them further confidence, I put my cocked hat with feather on the chief, and my overshirt being of the Indian form, my hair disheveled, and skin well-browned with the sun, I wanted no further addition to make me a complete Indian in appearance. The men followed my example and we were soon completely metamorphosed.

I again repeated to them the possibility of the party not having arrived at the place which I expected they were, but assured them

261. fur coverings for the shoulders with long ends that hang in front

[that] they could not be far below, lest by not finding them at the forks, their suspicions might arise to such height as to induce them to return precipitately. We now set out and rode briskly within sight of the forks, making one of the Indians carry the flag [so] that our own party should know who we were.

When we arrived in sight at the distance of about two miles, I discovered to my mortification that the party had not arrived, and the Indians slackened their pace. I now scarcely knew what to do, and feared every moment when they would halt altogether. I now determined to restore their confidence, cost what it might, and therefore gave the chief my gun, and told him that if his enemies were in those bushes before him that he could defend himself with that gun, that for my own part, I was not afraid to die, and if I deceived him, he might make what use of the gun he thought proper or, in other words, that he might shoot me. The men also gave their guns to other Indians, which seemed to inspire them with more confidence.

They sent their spies before them at some distance, and when I drew near the place, I thought of the notes which I had left, and directed Drouillard to go with an Indian man and bring them to me, which he did, the Indian seeing him take the notes from the stake on which they had been placed.

I now had recourse to a stratagem in which I thought myself justified by the occasion but which, I must confess, set a little awkward. It had its desired effect.

After reading the notes which were the same I had left, I told the chief that when I had left my brother chief with the party below where the river entered the mountains, that we both agreed not to bring the canoes higher up than the next forks of the river above us, wherever this might happen, that there he was to wait my return should he arrive first, and that in the event of his not being able to travel as fast as usual from the difficulty of the water, that he was to send up to the first forks above him and leave a note informing me where he was, that this note was left here today, and that he informed [me] that he was just below the mountains and was coming slowly up, and added that I should wait here for him, but if they did not believe me, that I should send one of their young men with him, that I and two others would remain with them at this place.

This plan was readily adopted and one of the young men offered his services. I promised him a knife and some beads as a reward for his confidence in us.

Most of them seemed satisfied, but there were several that complained of the chief's exposing them to danger unnecessarily and said that we told different stories. In short, a few were much dissatisfied.

I wrote a note to Captain Clark by the light of some willow brush and directed Drouillard to set out early, being confident that there was not a moment to spare. The chief and five or six others slept about my fire, and the others hid themselves in various parts of the willow brush to avoid the enemy whom they were fearful would attack them in the course of the night.

I now entertained various conjectures myself with respect to the cause of Captain Clark's detention and was even fearful that he had found the river so difficult that he had halted below the Rattlesnake Cliffs. I knew that if these people left me that they would immediately disperse and secrete themselves in the mountains where it would be impossible to find them, or at least in vain to pursue them, and that they would spread the alarm to all other bands within our reach and, of course, we should be disappointed in obtaining horses which would vastly retard and increase the labor of our voyage and, I feared, might so discourage the men as to defeat the expedition altogether.

My mind was, in reality, quite as gloomy all this evening as the most affrighted Indian, but I affected cheerfulness to keep the Indians so who were about me. We finally lay down, and the chief placed himself by the side of my mosquito bier. I slept but little, as might be well expected, my mind dwelling on the state of the expedition which I have ever held in equal estimation with my own existence, and the fate of which appeared at this moment to depend in a great measure upon the caprice of a few savages who are ever as fickle as the wind.

I had mentioned to the chief several times that we had with us a woman of his nation who had been taken prisoner by the Hidatsa, and that by means of her I hoped to explain myself more fully than I could do signs. Some of the party had also told the Indians that we had a man with us who was black and had short, curling hair. This had excited their curiosity very much, and they seemed quite as anxious to see this monster as they were the merchandise which we had to barter for their horses.

Saturday, August 17, 1805:

Lewis: We made them sensible of their dependence on the will of our government for every species of merchandise, as well for their defense and comfort, and apprised them of the strength of our government and its friendly dispositions towards them.

We also gave them as a reason why we wished to penetrate the country as far as the ocean to the west of them was to examine and find out a more direct way to bring merchandise to them, that as no trade could be carried on with them before our return to our homes, that it was mutually advantageous to them as well as to ourselves that they should render us such aids as they had in their power to furnish in order to hasten our voyage and, of course, our return home, that such were their horses to transport our baggage, without which we could not subsist, and that a pilot to conduct us through the mountains was also necessary if we could not descend the river by water, but that we did not ask [for] either their horses or services without giving a satisfactory compensation in return, that at present we wished them to collect as many horses as were necessary to transport our baggage to their village on the Columbia where we would then trade with them at our leisure for such horses as they could spare us.

The chief thanked us for friendship towards himself and nation and declared his wish to serve us in every respect, that he was sorry to find that it must yet be some time before they could be furnished with firearms, but said they could live as they had done heretofore until we brought them as we had promised. He said they had not horses enough with them at present to remove our baggage to their village over the mountains, but that he would return tomorrow and encourage his people to come over with their horses, and that he would bring his own and assist us. This was complying with all we wished at present.

We next enquired who were chiefs among them. Cameahwait pointed out two others whom he said were chiefs. We gave him a medal of the small size with the likeness of Mr. Jefferson, the President of the United States, in relief on one side and clasped hands with a pipe and tomahawk on the other. To the other chiefs we gave each a small medal which was struck in the presidency of George Washington, Esq. We also gave small medals of the last description to two young men whom the first chief informed us were good young men and much respected among them. We gave the first chief a uniform coat, shirt, a pair of scarlet leggings, a carrot of tobacco, and a few small articles. We also distributed a good quantity [of] paint, moccasin awls, knives, beads, looking glasses, etc., among the other Indians, and gave them a plentiful meal of lyed corn which was the first they had ever eaten in their lives. They were much pleased with it.

Every article about us appeared to excite astonishment in their minds. The appearance of the men, their arms, the canoes, our manner of working them, the black man, York, and the sagacity of my dog were equally objects of admiration. I also shot my air gun which was so perfectly incomprehensible that they immediately denominated it the great medicine.

Captain Clark and I now concerted measures for our future operations, and it was mutually agreed that he should set out tomorrow morning with eleven men furnished with axes and other necessary tools for making canoes, their arms, accouterments, and as much of their baggage as they could carry, [and] also to take the Indians, Charbonneau, and the Indian woman with him, that on his arrival at the Shoshone camp he was to leave Charbonneau and the Indian woman to hasten the return of the Indians with their horses to this place, and to proceed himself with the eleven men down the Columbia in order to examine the river, and if he found it navigable and could obtain timber, to set about making canoes immediately.

In the meantime, I was to bring the party and baggage to the Shoshone camp, calculating that by the time I should reach that place that he would have sufficiently informed himself with respect to the state of the river, etc., as to determine [for] us whether to prosecute our journey from thence by land or water. In the former case, we should want all the horses which we could purchase, and in the latter, only to hire the Indians to transport our baggage to the place at which we made canoes.

Sunday, August 18, 1805:

Lewis: This morning, while Captain Clark was busily engaged in preparing for his route, I exposed some articles to barter with the Indians for horses, as I wished a few at this moment to relieve the men who were going with Captain Clark from the labor of carrying their baggage, and also one to keep here in order to pack the meat to camp which the hunters might kill. I soon obtained three very good horses for which I gave a uniform coat, a pair of leggings, a few handkerchiefs, three knives, and some other small articles, the whole of which did not cost more than about twenty dollars in the United States. The Indians seemed quite as well pleased with their bargain as I was. The men also purchased one for an old checked shirt, a pair of old leggings, and a knife. Two of those I purchased Captain Clark took on with him.

At 10:00 a.m., Captain Clark departed with his detachment and all the Indians except two men and two women, who remained with us.

After their departure this morning, I had all the stores and baggage of every description opened and aired and began the operation of forming the packages in proper parcels for the purpose of transporting them on horseback. The rain in the evening compelled me to desist from my operations. I had the raw hides put in the water in order to cut them in thongs proper for lashing the packages and forming the necessary gear for pack horses, a business which I fortunately had not to learn on this occasion. I had the net arranged and set this evening to catch some trout which we could see in great abundance at the bottom of the river.

This day I completed my thirty-first year and conceived that I had, in all human probability, now existed about half the period which I am to remain in this sublunary world. I reflected that I had as yet done but little, very little, indeed, to further the happiness of the human race or to advance the information of the succeeding generation. I viewed with regret the many hours I have spent in indolence, and now sorely feel the want of that information which those hours would have given me had they been judiciously expended. But since they are past and cannot be recalled, I dash from me the gloomy thought, and resolve in the future to redouble my exertions, and at least [to] endeavor to promote those two primary objects of human experience, by giving them the aid of that portion of talents which nature and fortune have bestowed on me, or in [the] future to live for *mankind* as I have heretofore lived for *myself.*

Clark: At 10:00, I set out accompanied by the Indians, except three, [and] the interpreter and wife.

The forepart of the day [was] warm. At 12:00, it became hazy, with a mist of rain. [The] wind [was] hard from the southwest, and cold, which increased until night. The rain ceased in about two hours.

We proceeded on through a wide, level valley without wood, except willows and shrubs, for fifteen miles and encamped at a place the highlands approach within two hundred yards in two points. The river here [was] only ten yards wide. Several small streams [were] branching out on each side below.

All the Indians proceeded on except the three chiefs and two young men.

Monday, August 19, 1805:

Lewis: The Shoshones[262] may be estimated at about one hundred warriors, and about three times that number of women and children. They have more children among them than I expected to have seen among a people who procure subsistence with such difficulty. There are but few very old persons, nor did they appear to treat these with much tenderness or respect.

The man is the sole proprietor of his wives and daughters, and can barter or dispose of either as he thinks proper. A plurality of wives is common among them, but these are not generally sisters as with the Hidatsa and Mandans, but are purchased of different fathers.

The father frequently disposes of his infant daughters in marriage to men who are grown or to men who have sons for whom they think proper to provide wives. The compensation given in such cases usu-

262. this band only (DeVoto)

ally consists of horses or mules, which the father receives at the time of contract and converts to his own use. The girl remains with her parents until she is conceived to have obtained the age of puberty which, with them, is considered to be about the age of thirteen or fourteen years. The female at this age is surrendered to her sovereign lord and husband agreeably to contract, and with her is frequently restored by the father quite as much as he received in the first instance in payment for his daughter, but this is discretionary with the father.

Sacagawea had been thus disposed of before she was taken by the Hidatsa, or had arrived to the years of puberty. The husband was yet living with this band. He was more than double her age and had two other wives. He claimed her as his wife, but said that as she had had a child by another man, who was Charbonneau, that he did not want her.

They seldom correct their children, particularly the boys who become masters of their own acts. They give as a reason that it cows and breaks the spirit of the boy to whip him, and that he never recovers his independence of mind after he is grown.

They treat their women but with little respect, and compel them to perform every species of drudgery. They collect the wild fruits and roots, attend to the horses or assist in that duty, cook, dress the skins and make all their apparel, collect wood and make their fires, arrange and form their lodges and, when they travel, pack the horses and take charge of all the baggage. In short, the man does little else except attend his horses, hunt, and fish.

The man considers himself degraded if he is compelled to walk any distance. And if he is so unfortunately poor as only to possess two horses, he rides the best himself and leaves the woman, or women if he has more than one, to transport their baggage and children on the other, and to walk if the horse is unable to carry the additional weight of their persons.

The chastity of their women is not held in high estimation and the husband will, for a trifle, barter the companion of his bed for a night, or longer if he conceives the reward adequate, though they are not so importunate that we should caress their women as the Sioux were, and some of their women appear to be held more sacred than in any nation we have seen.

I have requested the men to give them no cause of jealousy by having connection with their women without their knowledge which, with them, strange as it may seem, is considered as disgraceful to the husband as clandestine connections of a similar kind are among civilized nations. To prevent this mutual exchange of good offices altogether I know it impossible to effect, particularly on the part of our young men whom some months abstinence have made very polite to these tawny damsels. No evil has yet resulted, and I hope will not from these connections.

Notwithstanding the late loss of horses which this people sustained by the Hidatsa, the stock of the band may be very safely estimated at seven hundred, of which there are perhaps about forty colts and half that number mules. Their arms, offensive and defensive, consist in the bow and arrows, shields, some lances, and a weapon, called by the Chippewa who formerly used it, the "pog-gar-mag-gon."[263] In fishing they employ wires, gigs, and fishing hooks. The salmon is the principal object of their pursuit. They snare wolves and foxes.

I was anxious to learn whether these people had the venereal, and made the enquiry through the interpreter and his wife. The information was that they sometimes had it, but I could not learn their remedy. They most usually die with its effects. This seems a strong proof that these disorders, both gonorrhea and Lues venera,[264] are native disorders of America, though these people have suffered much by the smallpox, which is known to be imported, and perhaps those other disorders might have been contracted from other Indian tribes who, by a round of communications, might have obtained [them] from the Europeans since it was introduced into that quarter of the globe but so much detached, on the other hand, from all communication with the whites, that I think it most probable that these disorders are original with them.

From the middle of May to the first of September these people reside on the waters of the Columbia where they consider themselves in perfect security from their enemies, as they have not as yet ever found their way to this retreat. During this season, the salmon furnish the principal part of their subsistence, and as this fish either perishes or returns about the first of September, they are compelled at this season, in search of subsistence, to resort to the Missouri, in the valleys of which there is more game even than within the mountains.

Here they move slowly down the river in order to collect and join other bands, either of their own nation or the Flatheads and, having become sufficiently strong as they conceive, venture on the eastern side of the Rocky Mountains into the plains, where the buffalo abound. But they never leave the interior of the mountains while they can obtain a scanty subsistence, and always return as soon as they have acquired a good stock of dried meat in the plains. When this stock is consumed, they venture again into the plains, thus alternately obtaining their food at the risk of their lives, and retiring to the mountains while they consume it. These people are now on the eve of their depar-

263. war club (DeVoto); see also Lewis's August 23 entry

264. syphilis

ture for the Missouri and inform us that they expect to be joined at or about the three forks by several bands of their own nation and a band of the Flatheads.

Clark: [It was] a very cold morning [with] frost to be seen.

We set out at 7:00 and proceeded on through a wide, level valley. This valley continues five miles and then becomes narrow. We proceeded on up the main branch, with a gradual ascent to the head, and passed over a low mountain and descended a steep descent to a beautiful stream, passed over a second hill of a very steep ascent, and through a hilly country for eight miles, and encamped on a small stream.

The Indians with us we were obliged to feed. One man met me with a mule and Spanish saddle to ride. I gave him a waistcoat. A mule is considered of great value among these people.

We proceeded on over a very mountainous country across the head of hollows[265] and springs.

Tuesday, August 20, 1805:

Lewis: I walked down the river about three-fourths of a mile and selected a place near the riverbank, unperceived by the Indians, for a cache, which I set three men to make, and directed the sentinel to discharge his gun if he perceived any of the Indians going down in that direction, which was to be the signal for the men at work on the cache to desist and separate, lest these people should discover our deposit and rob us of the baggage we intend leaving here. By evening the cache was completed unperceived by the Indians, and all our packages made up.

The pack-saddles and harnesses are not yet complete. In this operation, we find ourselves at a loss for nails and boards. For the first, we substitute thongs of rawhide, which answer very well, and for the last, had to cut off the blades of our oars and use the plank of some boxes, which have heretofore held other articles, and put those articles into sacks of rawhide which I have had made for the purpose. By this means I have obtained as many boards as will make twenty saddles, which I suppose will be sufficient for our present exigencies. I made up a small assortment of medicines, seeds, etc., which I have collected between this place and the Falls of the Missouri, which I shall deposit here.

I now prevailed on the chief to instruct me with respect to the geography of his country. This he undertook very cheerfully by delineating the rivers on the ground. But I soon found that his information

---

265. small valleys

fell far short of my expectation or wishes. He drew the river on which we now are,[266] to which he placed two branches just above us which he showed me from the openings of the mountains were in view. He next made it discharge itself into a large river[267] which flowed from the southwest about ten miles below us, then continued this joint stream in the same direction of this valley, or northwest, for one day's march, and then inclined it to the west for two more days' march.

Here he placed a number of heaps of sand on each side which, he informed me, represented the vast mountains of rock, eternally covered with snow, through which the river passed, that the perpendicular and even jutting rocks so closely hemmed in the river that there was no possibility of passing along the shore, that the bed of the river was obstructed by sharp pointed rocks, [that] the rapidity of the stream [was] such that the whole surface of the river was beaten into perfect foam as far as the eye could reach, [and] that the mountains were also inaccessible to man or horse. He said that this being the state of the country in that direction, that he nor none of his nation had ever been farther down the river than these mountains.

I then enquired [about] the state of the country on either side of the river, but he could not inform me. He said there was an old man of his nation a day's march below who could probably give me some information of the country to the northwest, and referred me to an old man then present for that to the southwest. The chief further informed me that he had understood from the Pierced-Nose Indians,[268] who inhabit this river below the Rocky Mountains, that it ran a great way towards the setting sun and finally lost itself in a great lake of water which was illy tasted, and where the white men lived.

I next commenced my enquiries of the old man to whom I had been referred for information relative [to] the country southwest of us. This he depicted with horrors and obstructions scarcely inferior to those just mentioned.

He informed me that the band of this nation to which he belonged resided at the distance of twenty days' march from hence, not far from the white people with whom they traded for horses, mules, cloth, metal, beads, and the shells which they wore as ornaments, being those of a species of pearl oyster, that the course to his relations was a little to the west of south, that in order to get to his relations, the first seven days we should be obliged to climb over steep and rocky mountains where we could find no game to kill or anything but roots, such as a fierce and warlike nation lived on, whom he called the Broken Mocca-

266. the Lemhi (DeVoto)
267. the Salmon (DeVoto)
268. the Nez Percé

sins, or Moccasins With Holes, and said inhabited those mountains and lived like the bear of other countries among the rocks, and fed on roots or the flesh of such horses as they could take or steal from those who passed through their country, that in passing this country the feet of our horses would be so much wounded with the stones [that] many of them would give out.

The next part of the route was about ten days through a dry and parched sandy desert[269] in which there is no food at this season for either man or horse, and in which we must suffer, if not perish, for the want of water, that the sun had now dried up the little pools of water which exist through this desert plain in the spring season and had also scorched all the grass, that no animal inhabited this plain on which we could hope to subsist, that about the center of this plain a large river passed from southeast to northwest which was navigable but afforded neither salmon nor timber, that beyond this plain three or four days' march, his relations lived in a country, tolerably fertile and partially covered with timber, on another large river which ran in the same direction of the former, that this last discharged itself into a large river on which many numerous nations lived with whom his relations were at war, but whether this last discharged itself into the great lake or not, he did not know, that from his relations it was yet a great distance to the Great or Stinking Lake, as they call the ocean, that the way which such of his nation as had been to the Stinking Lake traveled was up the river on which they lived and over to that on which the white people lived, which last they knew discharged itself into the ocean, and that this was the way which he would advise me to travel if I was determined to proceed to the ocean, but would advise me to put off the journey until the next spring, when he would conduct me.

I thanked him for his information and advice, and gave him a knife with which he appeared to be much gratified.

From this narrative, I was convinced that the streams of which he had spoken as running through the plains and that on which his relations lived were southern branches of the Columbia, heading with the rivers Apostles and Colorado, and that the route he had pointed out was to the Vermilion Sea, or Gulf of California.

I therefore told him that this route was more to the south than I wished to travel, and requested to know if there was no route on the left of this river on which we now are, by means of which I could intercept it below the mountains through which it passes, but he could not inform me of any except that of the barren plain which, he said, joined the mountains on that side and through which it was impossible

---

269. the lava plains of southern Idaho along the Snake River (DeVoto)

for us to pass at this season, even if we were fortunate enough to escape from the Broken Moccasin Indians.

I now asked Cameahwait by what route the Nez Percé Indians who, he informed me, inhabited this river below the mountains, came over to the Missouri. This, he informed me, was to the north, but added that the road was a very bad one as he had been informed by them, and that they had suffered excessively with hunger on the route, being obliged to subsist for many days on berries alone, as there was no game in that part of the mountains which were broken, rocky, and so thickly covered with timber that they could scarcely pass.

However, knowing that Indians had passed, and did pass, at this season on that side of this river to the same below the mountains, my route instantly settled in my own mind, provided the account of this river should prove true on an investigation of it, which I was determined should be made before we would undertake the route by land in any direction. I felt perfectly satisfied that if the Indians could pass these mountains with their women and children, that we could also pass them, and that if the nations on this river below the mountains were as numerous as they were stated to be, that they must have some means of subsistence which it would be equally in our power to procure in the same country. They informed me that there was no buffalo on the west side of these mountains, that the game consisted of a few elk, deer, and antelope, and that the natives subsisted on fish and roots principally.

In this manner, I spent the day smoking with them and acquiring what information I could with respect to their country.

They informed me that they could pass to the Spaniards by the way of the Yellowstone River in ten days. I can discover that these people are by no means friendly to the Spaniards. Their complaint is that the Spaniards will not let them have firearms and ammunition, that they put them off by telling them that if they suffer them to have guns, they will kill each other, thus leaving them defenseless and an easy prey to their bloodthirsty neighbors to the east of them who, being in possession of firearms, hunt them up and murder them without respect to sex or age, and plunder them of their horses on all occasions. They told me that to avoid their enemies who were eternally harassing them, that they were obliged to remain in the interior of these mountains at least two-thirds of the year where they suffered, as they then saw great hardships for the want of food, sometimes living for weeks without meat and only a little fish, roots, and berries.

"But this," added Cameahwait, with his fierce eyes and lank jaws grown meager for the want of food, "would not be the case if we had guns. We could then live in the country of buffalo and eat as our enemies do, and not be compelled to hide ourselves in these mountains, and live on roots and berries as the bears do. We do not fear our enemies when placed on an equal footing with them."

I told them that the Hidatsa, Mandans, and Arikaras of the Missouri had promised us to desist from making war on them, and that we would endeavor to find the means of making the Hidatsa of Fort de Prairie, or as they call them, Pahkees, desist from waging war against them also, that after our finally returning to our homes towards the rising sun, white men would come to them with an abundance of guns and every other article necessary to their defense and comfort, and that they would be enabled to supply themselves with these articles on reasonable terms in exchange for the skins of the beaver, otter, and ermine so abundant in their country. They expressed great pleasure at this information and said they had been long anxious to see the white men that traded guns, and that we might rest assured of their friendship, and that they would do whatever we wished them.

Clark: Shoshone Indians - [We] set out at half past 6:00 and proceeded on (met many parties of Indians) through a hilly country to the camp of the Indians on a branch of the Columbia River. Before we entered this camp, a ceremonious halt was requested by the chief, and I smoked with all that came around, for several pipes.

We then proceeded on to the camp and I was introduced into the only lodge they had which was pitched in the center for my party. All the other lodges [were] made of bushes.

After a few Indian ceremonies, I informed the Indians [of] the object of our journey, our good intentions towards them, my concern for their distressed situation, what we had done for them in making a peace with the Hidatsa, Mandans, Arikaras, etc., for them, and requested them all to take over their horses and assist Captain Lewis across, etc., also informing them [of] the object of my journey down the river, and requested a guide to accompany me, all of which was repeated by the chief to the whole village.

These poor people could only raise a salmon and a little dried choke cherries for us. Half the men of the tribe, with the chief, turned out to hunt the antelope.

At 3:00, after giving a few small articles as presents, I set out, accompanied by an old man as a guide. I endeavored to procure as much information from these people as possible without much success, they being but little acquainted or affecting to be so. I left one man to purchase a horse and overtake me, and proceeded on through a wide, rich bottom on a beaten road eight miles. [We] crossed the river and encamped on a small run. I left our interpreter and his woman to accompany the Indians to Captain Lewis tomorrow, the day they informed me they would set out.

Gass: They are the poorest and most miserable nation I ever beheld, having scarcely anything to subsist on except berries and a few fish. They have a great many fine horses and nothing more.

We had a long talk with them and they gave us very unfavorable accounts with respect to the rivers.

Ordway: The two Indians at our camp behave very well and their squaws mend our moccasins. [They] are as friendly as any savages we have yet seen.

Our hunters returned in the afternoon but had killed nothing. The game [is] scarce.

Wednesday, August 21, 1805:

Lewis: This morning was very cold, the ice one-fourth of an inch thick on the water which stood in the vessels exposed to the air. Some wet deerskins that had been spread on the grass last evening are stiffly frozen. The ink freezes in my pen. The bottoms are perfectly covered with frost, insomuch that they appear to be covered with snow.

This morning early, I dispatched two hunters to kill some meat, if possible, before the Indians arrive. Drouillard I sent with the horse into the cove for that purpose.

The party pursued their several occupations as yesterday. By evening, I had all the baggage, saddles, and harnesses completely ready for a march. After dark, I made the men take the baggage to the cache and deposit it. I believe we have been unperceived by the Indians in this movement.

Notwithstanding the coldness of the last night, the day has proved excessively warm.

Neither of the hunters returned this evening and I was obliged to issue pork and corn.

The moccasins of both sexes are usually the same and are made of deer, elk, or buffalo skin dressed without hair. Sometimes in the winter they make them of buffalo skin dressed with the hair on and turn the hair inwards, as the Mandans, Hidatsa, and most of the nations do who inhabit the buffalo country. The moccasin is formed with one seam on the outer edge of the foot, is cut open at the instep to admit the foot, and sewed up behind. In this respect they are the same with the Mandans. They sometimes ornament their moccasins with various figures wrought with the quills of the porcupine. Some of the dressy young men ornament the tops of their moccasins with the skins of polecats and trail the tail of that animal on the ground at their heels as they walk.

The robe of the woman is generally smaller than that of the man, but is worn in the same manner over the shoulders. The chemise is roomy and comes down below the middle of the leg. The upper part of this garment is formed much like the shirt of the men except the shoulder strap, which is never used with the chemise. In women who give suck, they are left open at the sides, nearly as low as the waist [and] in others, close as high as the sleeve. The sleeve underneath, as low as the elbow, is open, that part being left very full. The sides, tail, and upper part of the sleeves are deeply fringed and sometimes ornamented in a similar manner with the shirts of the men, with the addition of little patches of red cloth about the tail edged around with beads. The breast is usually ornamented with various figures of party colors, wrought with the quills of the porcupine. It is on this part of the garment that they appear to exert their greatest ingenuity. A girdle of dressed leather confines the chemise around the waist.

The leggings of the women reach as high as the knee and are confined with a garter below. The moccasin covers and confines its lower extremity. They are neither fringed nor ornamented. These leggings are made of the skins of the antelope, and the chemise usually of those of the large deer, bighorn, and the smallest elk.

The warriors, or such as [they] esteem themselves brave men, wear collars made of the claws of the brown bear, which are also esteemed of great value and are preserved with great care. These claws are ornamented with beads about the thick end, near which they are pierced through their sides and strung on a thong of dressed leather and tied about the neck, commonly with the upper edge of the talon next [to] the breast or neck, but sometimes are reversed.

It is esteemed by them an act of equal celebrity the killing one of these bears or an enemy, and with the means they have of killing this animal, it must really be a serious undertaking.

Clark: I entered a lodge and, after smoking with all who came about me, I went to see the place these people take the fish, a weir[270] across the creek in which there are stuck baskets set in different directions so as to take the fish either descending or ascending. Their method of taking fish with a gig, or bone, is with a long pole. About a foot from one end is a strong string attached to the pole. This string is a little more than a foot long and is tied to the middle of a bone from four to six inches long. One end [is] sharp, the other with a hole to fasten on the end of the pole with a barb to the large end. They fasten this bone on one end, and with the other, feel for the fish and turn and strike them so hard that the bone passes through and catches on the

270. a fence or enclosure set in a waterway for taking fish

opposite side, slips off the end of the pole, and holds the center of the bone.

These Indians are mild in their disposition, appear sincere in their friendship, [are] punctual and decided, [and are] kind with what they have to spare. They are excessively poor [with] nothing but horses. Their enemies, which are numerous on account of their horses and defenseless situation, have deprived them of tents and all the small conveniences of life. They have only a few indifferent knives, no ax, make use of [an] elk's horn sharpened to split their wood, no clothes except short leggings and robes of different animals, beaver, bear, buffalo, wolf, panther, ibex (sheep), deer, but most commonly the antelope skins which they wear loosely about them.

The women are held more sacred among them than any nation we have seen and appear to have an equal share in all conversation, which is not the case in any other nation I have seen. Their boys and girls are also admitted to speak, except in councils. The women do all the drudgery except fishing and taking care of the horses, which the men appear to take upon themselves.

The most sacred of all the ornaments of this nation are the seashells of various sizes and shapes and colors, of the bastard pearl kind which, they inform us, they get from the Indians to the south on the other side of a large fork of this river, in passing to which they have to pass through sandy and barren open plains without water, to which place they can travel in fifteen or twenty days. The men who passed by the forks informed me that the southwest fork was double the size of the one I came down, and I observed that it was a handsome river at my camp. I shall, in justice to Captain Lewis, who was the first white man ever on this fork of the Columbia, call this Louis's River.

Thursday, August 22, 1805:

Lewis: This morning early I sent a couple of men to complete the covering of the cache which could not be done well last night in the dark. They soon accomplished their work and returned.

Late last night Drouillard returned with a fawn he had killed and a considerable quantity of Indian plunder. The anecdote with respect to the latter is perhaps worthy of relation. He informed me that while hunting in the cove yesterday about 12:00, he came suddenly upon an Indian camp at which there were a young man, an old man, and a boy, and three women, that they seemed but little surprised at seeing him, and he rode up to them and dismounted, turning his horse out to graze. These people had just finished their repast on some roots. He entered into conversation with them by signs, and after twenty minutes one of the women spoke to the others of the party and they all went immediately and collected their horses, brought them to camp, and saddled them. At this moment, he thought he would also set out and continue his hunt, and accordingly walked to catch his horse at some little distance, and neglected to take up his gun which he [had] left at camp.

The Indians, perceiving him at the distance of fifty paces, immediately mounted their horses, the young man took the gun, and the whole of them left their baggage and laid whip to their horses, directing their course to the pass of the mountains. Finding himself deprived of his gun, he immediately mounted his horse and pursued. After running [after] them about ten miles, the horses of two of the women nearly gave out and the young fellow with the gun, from their frequent cries, slackened his pace, and being on a very fleet horse, rode around the women at a little distance.

At length Drouillard overtook the women, and by signs convinced them that he did not wish to hurt them. They then halted and the young fellow approached still nearer. He asked him for his gun, but the only part of the answer which he could understand was "pahkee," which he knew to be the name by which they called their enemies. Watching his opportunity when the fellow was off his guard, he suddenly rode alongside of him, seized his gun, and wrested her out of his hands. The fellow, finding Drouillard too strong for him and discovering that he must yield the gun, had [the] presence of mind to open the pan and cast the primer before he let the gun escape from his hands. Now finding himself divested of the gun, he turned his horse about and laid whip, leaving the women to follow him as well as they could.

At 11:00 a.m. Charbonneau, the Indian woman, Cameahwait, and about fifty men with a number of women and children arrived. They encamped near us.

After they had turned out their horses and arranged their camp, I called the chiefs and warriors together and addressed them a second time [and] gave them some further presents, particularly the second and third chiefs, who it appeared had, agreeably to their promise, exerted themselves in my favor.

Having no fresh meat and these poor devils half-starved, I had previously prepared a good meal for them all of boiled corn and beans, which I gave them as soon as the council was over and I had distributed the presents. This was thankfully received by them.

The chief wished that his nation could live in a country where they could provide such food. I told him that it would not be many years before the white men would put it in the power of his nation to live in the country below the mountains where they might cultivate corn, beans, and squashes. He appeared much pleased with the information. I gave him a few dried squashes which we had brought from the Mandans. He had them boiled and declared them to be the best thing he had ever tasted except sugar, a small lump of which it seems his sister Sacagawea had given him.

Late in the evening I made the men form a bush drag,[271] and with it, in about two hours, they caught five hundred twenty-eight very good fish, most of them large trout. Among them I now for the first time saw ten or a dozen of a white species of trout. They are of a silvery color, except on the back and head, where they are of a bluish cast. The scales are much larger than the speckled trout, but in their form, position of their fins, teeth, mouth, etc., they are precisely like them. They are not generally quite as large, but equally well-flavored. I distributed much the greater portion of the fish among the Indians.

I purchased five good horses from them very reasonably, or at least for about the value of six dollars apiece in merchandise. The Indians are very orderly and do not crowd about our camp nor attempt to disturb any article they see lying about. They borrow knives, kettles, etc., from the men and always carefully return them.

Clark: We set out early. [We] passed a small creek on the right at one mile, and the points of four mountains [which were] very steep, high, and rocky. The ascent of three was so steep that it is incredible to describe. The rocks in many places [were] loose and slipped from those mountains and are a solid bed of rugged, loose, white and dark brown, loose rock for miles. The Indian horses pass over these cliffs, hills, beds, and rocks as fast as a man [and] the three horses with me do not detain me any on account of those difficulties.

[We] passed two bold, running streams on the right, and a small river at the mouth of which several families of Indians were encamped and had several scaffolds of fish and berries drying. We alarmed them very much as they knew nothing of a white man being in their country, and at the time we approached their lodges, which were in a thick place of bushes, my guides were behind.

They offered everything they possessed (which was very little) to us. Some ran off and hid in the bushes. The first offer of theirs was elk tushes[272] from around their children's necks, salmon, etc. My guide attempted to pacify these people, and they set before me berries and fish to eat. I gave a few small articles to these frightened people, which added very much to their pacification, but not entirely, as some of the women and children cried during my stay of an hour at this place.

I proceeded on the side of a very steep and rocky mountain for three miles, and encamped on the lower point of an island. We attempted to gig fish without success; [we] caught but one small one.

271. trout net (Ambrose, *UC*, p. 281)

272. long pointed teeth

The last creek, or small river, is on the right side, and a road passes up it and over to the Missouri.

Ordway: Our interpreter, his wife, and one tribe of the Snake nation of Indians arrived here on horseback. They have come to trade horses with us. Captain Lewis counseled with them, made two of their principal men chiefs and gave [them] medals, and told them in council that the chief of the seventeen great nations of America had sent us to open the road and know their wants, etc., and told them that we wanted in return their beaver and other skins if they would take care to save them, etc. Captain Lewis traded with them and bought three fine horses and two half-breed mules for a little merchandise. They appear very kind and friendly. [They] do not offer to steal or pilfer anything from us. We trade any useless article. We lend them anything they want and they are very careful to return the same.

Friday, August 23, 1805:

Lewis: I wished to have set out this morning but the chief requested that I would wait until another party of his nation arrived, which he expected today. To this I consented from necessity.

I laid up the canoes this morning in a pond near the forks, [and] sunk them in the water and weighted them down with stones after taking out the plugs of the gage holes[273] in their bottoms, hoping by this means to guard against both the effects of high water and that of the fire which is frequently kindled in these plains by the natives. The Indians have promised to do them no intentional injury, and I believe they are too lazy, at any rate, to give themselves the trouble to raise them from their present situation in order to cut or burn them.

The metal which we found in possession of these people consisted of a few indifferent knives, a few brass kettles, some arm bands of iron and brass, a few buttons worn as ornaments in their hair, a spear or two of a foot in length, and some iron and brass arrow points which, they informed me, they obtained in exchange for horses from the Crow or Rocky Mountain Indians on the Yellowstone River. The bridlebits and stirrups they obtained from the Spaniards, though these were but few.

Many of them made use of flint for knives, and with this instrument skinned the animals they killed, dressed their fish, and made their arrows. In short, they used it for every purpose to which the knife is applied. This flint is of no regular form, and if they can only obtain a part of it, an inch or two in length that will cut, they are satisfied. They renew the edge by flecking off the flint by means of the point of an elk

273. drains (Bakeless, p. 249)

or deer horn. With the point of a deer or elk horn, they also form their arrow points of the flint with a quickness and neatness that is really astonishing.

We found no axes or hatchets among them. What wood they cut was done either with stone or elk horn. The latter they use always to rive, or split, their wood. Their culinary utensils, exclusive of the brass kettles before mentioned, consist of pots in the form of a jar made either of earth or of a white, soft stone which becomes black and very hard by burning, and is found in the hills near the Three Forks of the Missouri between Madison's and Gallatin's rivers. They have also spoons made of buffalo horn and those of the bighorn.

They sometimes make bows of the elk horn, and those also of the bighorn. Those of the elk horn are made of a single piece and covered on the back with glue and sinews, like those made of wood, and are frequently ornamented with a strand wrought of porcupine quills and sinews wrapped around them for some distance at both extremities. The bows of the bighorn are formed of small pieces laid flat and cemented with glue and rolled with sinews, after which they are also covered on the back with sinews and glue, and highly ornamented as they are much prized.

Forming the shield is a ceremony of great importance among them. This implement would, in their minds, be divested of much of its protecting power were it not inspired with those virtues by their older men and jugglers.[274] Their method of preparing it is thus: An entire skin of a bull buffalo two years old is first provided. A feast is next prepared and all the warriors, old men, and jugglers [are] invited to partake. A hole is sunk in the ground about the same in diameter with the intended shield, and about eighteen inches deep. A parcel of stones is now made red hot and thrown into the hole. Water is next thrown in and the hot stones cause it to emit a very strong, hot steam. Over this they spread the green skin which must not have been suffered to dry after [having been] taken off the beast. The flesh side is laid next to the ground and as many of the workmen as can reach it take hold on its edges and extend it in every direction.

As the skin becomes heated, the hair separates and is taken off with the fingers, and the skin continues to contract until the whole is drawn within the compass designed for the shield. It is then taken off and laid on a parchment hide where they pound it with their heels when barefoot. This operation of pounding continues for several days, or as long as the feast lasts, when it is delivered to the proprietor and declared by the jugglers and old men to be a sufficient defense against the arrows of their enemies, or even bullets, if [the] feast has been a

274. medicine priests (DeVoto)

satisfactory one. Many of them believe implicitly that a ball cannot penetrate their shields in consequence of certain supernatural powers with which they have been inspired by their jugglers.

The "pog-gar-mag-gon" is an instrument with a handle of wood covered with dressed leather, about the size of a whip handle, and twenty-two inches long. A round stone of two pounds weight is also covered with leather and strongly united to the leather of the handle by a thong of two inches long. A loop of leather united to the handle passes around the wrist. A very heavy blow may be given with this instrument.

They have also a kind of armor which they form with many folds of dressed antelope skin [and] unite with glue and sand. With this they cover their own bodies and those of their horses. These are sufficient against the effects of the arrow.

Their implements for making fire are nothing more than a blunt arrow and a piece of well-seasoned, soft, spongy wood such as the willow or cottonwood. The point of this arrow they apply to this dry stick so near one edge of it that the particles of wood which are separated from it by the friction of the arrow fall down by its side in a little pile. The arrow is held between the palms of the hand with the fingers extended, and being pressed as much as possible against the piece, is briskly rolled between the palms of the hands backwards and forwards by pressing the arrow downwards. The hands, of course, in rolling the arrow so descend. They bring them back with a quick motion and repeat the operation until the dust, by the friction, takes fire. The piece and arrow are then removed and some dry grass or rotted wood is added. In less than a minute, they will produce fire.

Clark: [We] proceeded on with great difficulty as the rocks were so sharp, large, and unsettled, and the hillsides steep, that the horses could with the greatest risk and difficulty get on. At four miles we came to a place the horses could not pass without going into the river. We passed one mile to a very bad riffle; the water [was] confined in a narrow channel and [was] beating against the left shore.

As we have no path farther, and the mountains jut so close as to prevent the possibility of horses proceeding down, I determined to delay the party here, and with my guide and three men, proceed on down to examine if the river continued bad or was practicable.

I set out with three men, directing those left to hunt and fish until my return. I proceeded on, sometimes in a small wolf path and at other times climbing over the rocks for twelve miles to a large creek on the right side. Above the mouth of this creek, for a short distance, is a narrow bottom and the first below the place I left my party.

The river, from the place I left my party to this creek, is almost one continued rapids, five very considerable rapids. The passage of either with canoes is entirely impossible as the water is confined between huge rocks and the current [is] beating from one against another for some distance below, etc., etc. At one of these rapids, the mountains close so close as to prevent a possibility of a portage without great labor in cutting down the side of the hill, removing large rocks, etc., etc. All the others may be passed by taking everything over slippery rocks, and the smaller ones passed by letting down the canoes empty with cords, as running them would certainly be productive of the loss of some canoes. Those difficulties and necessary precautions would delay us an immense time in which provisions would be necessary.

Below this creek, the lofty pine is thick in the bottom, hillsides, on the mountains, and up the runs. The river has much the resemblance of that above. [The] bends [are] shorter and [there is] no passing, after a few miles, between the river and the mountains, and the current [is] so strong that it [would be] dangerous crossing the river, and to proceed down it would render it necessary to cross almost at every bend. This river is about one hundred yards wide, and can be forded but in a few places.

Below, my guide and many other Indians tell me that the mountains [are] close and [there] is a perpendicular cliff on each side, and continues for a great distance, and that the water runs with great violence from one rock to the other on each side, foaming and roaring through rocks in every direction so as to render the passage of anything impossible. Those rapids which I had seen, he said, were small and trifling in comparison to the rocks and rapids below at no great distance, and the hills or mountains were not like those I had seen but like the side of a tree, straight up.

We proceeded on a well-beaten Indian path up this creek (Berry Creek) about six miles and passed over a ridge one mile to the river in a small valley, through which we passed, and ascended a spur of the mountain from which place my guide showed me the river for about twenty miles lower, and pointed out the difficulties.

Saturday, August 24, 1805:

Lewis: As the Indians who were on their way down the Missouri had a number of spare horses with them, I thought it probable that I could obtain some of them and therefore desired the chief to speak to them and inform me whether they would trade. They gave no positive answer, but requested to see the goods which I was willing to give in exchange. I now produced some battle-axes which I had made at Fort

Mandan, with which they were much pleased. Knives also seemed in great demand among them.

I soon purchased three horses and a mule. For each horse I gave an ax, a knife, [a] handkerchief, and a little paint, and for the mule, the addition of a knife, a shirt, [a] handkerchief, and a pair of leggings. At this price, which was quite double that given for the horses, the fellow who sold him made a merit of having bestowed on me one of his mules. I consider this mule a great acquisition.

These Indians soon told me that they had no more horses for sale, and I directed the party to prepare to set out. I had now nine horses and a mule, and two, which I had hired, made twelve. These I had loaded, and the Indian women took the balance of the baggage. I had given the interpreter some articles with which to purchase a horse for the woman which he had obtained.

At 12:00 we set out and passed the river below the forks, directing our route towards the cove along the track formerly mentioned. Most of the horses were heavily laden, and it appears to me that it will require at least twenty-five horses to convey our baggage along such roads as I expect we shall be obliged to pass in the mountains. I had now the inexpressible satisfaction to find myself once more underway with all my baggage and party. An Indian had the politeness to offer me one of his horses to ride, which I accepted with cheerfulness, as it enabled me to attend better to the march of the party.

I had reached the lower part of the cove when an Indian rode up and informed me that one of my men was very sick and unable to come on. I directed the party to halt at a small run which falls into the creek on the port side at the lower part of the cove, and rode back about two miles where I found Wiser very ill with a fit of the colic. I sent Sergeant Ordway, who had remained with him, for some water, and gave him a dose of the essence of peppermint and laudanum which, in the course of [a] half an hour or so, far recovered him that he was enabled to ride my horse, and I proceeded on foot and rejoined the party.

The sun was yet an hour high but the Indians, who had for some time impatiently waited my return, at length unloaded and turned out their horses and my party had followed their example. As it was so late, and the Indians had prepared their camp for the night, I thought it best to acquiesce, and determined also to remain. We had traveled only about six miles.

The few guns which the Shoshones have are reserved for war almost exclusively, and the bow and arrows are used in hunting.

I have seen a few skins among these people which have almost every appearance of the common sheep. They inform me that they find this animal on the high mountains to the west and southwest of them. It is about the size of the common sheep, [and] the wool is rather shorter and more intermixed with long hairs, particularly on the upper part of the neck. These skins have been so much worn that I could not form a just idea of the animal or its color. The Indians, however, inform me that it is white, and that its horns are lunated, compressed, twisted, and bent backward as those of the common sheep. The texture of the skin appears to be that of the sheep. I am now perfectly convinced that the sheep, as well as the bighorn, exist in these mountains.

Clark: I wrote a letter to Captain Lewis informing him of the prospects before us, and information received of my guide, which I thought favorable, etc., and stating two plans, one of which for us to pursue, etc., and dispatched one man and horse, and directed the party to get ready to march back. Every man appeared disheartened from the prospects of the river and nothing to eat.

I set out late and camped two miles above [with] nothing to eat but choke cherries and red haws,[275] which act in different ways so as to make us sick.

[The] dew [was] very heavy [and] my bedding wet. In passing around a rock, the horses were obliged to go deep into the water.

The plan I stated to Captain Lewis, if he agrees with me we shall adopt it, [is] to procure as many horses (one for each man) as possible, and to hire my present guide who I sent on to him to interrogate through the interpreter, and [to] proceed on by land to some navigable part of the Columbia River, or to the ocean, depending on what provisions we can procure by the gun added to the small stock we have on hand, depending on our horses as the last resort.

A second plan [is] to divide the party, one part to attempt this difficult river with what provisions we had, and the remainder to pass by land on horseback, depending on our guns, etc., for provisions, etc., and coming together occasionally on the river. The first of which I would be most pleased with, etc.

I saw several trees which would make small canoes, and by putting two together would make a sizeable one, all below the last Indian camp several miles.

Ordway: We had about twenty horses loaded with baggage and set out about 12:00 on our journey to cross the dividing mountains.

Sunday, August 25, 1805:

Lewis: This morning [we] loaded our horses and set out a little after sunrise. A few only of the Indians unengaged in assisting us went

275. the fruit of the hawthorn tree

on, as I had yesterday proposed to the chief. The others flanked us on each side and started some antelope which they pursued for several hours, but killed none of them. We proceeded within two miles of the narrow pass, or seven miles from our camp of last evening, and halted for dinner. Our hunters joined us at noon with three deer, the greater part of which I gave [to] the Indians.

Sometime after we had halted, Charbonneau mentioned to me with apparent unconcern that he expected to meet all the Indians from the camp on the Columbia tomorrow on their way to the Missouri. Alarmed at this information, I asked why he expected to meet them. He then informed me that the first chief had dispatched some of his young men this morning to this camp requesting the Indians to meet tomorrow, and that he and those with him would go on with them down the Missouri, and consequently leave me and my baggage on the mountain or thereabouts.

I was out of patience with the folly of Charbonneau who had not sufficient sagacity to see the consequences which would inevitably flow from such a movement of the Indians, and although he had been in possession of this information since early in the morning when it had been communicated to him by his Indian woman, yet he never mentioned it until the afternoon. I could not forbear speaking to him with some degree of asperity on this occasion. I saw that there was no time to be lost in having those orders countermanded, or that we should not, in all probability, obtain any more horses, or even get my baggage to the waters of the Columbia.

I therefore called the three chiefs together and, having smoked a pipe with them, I asked them if they were men of their words and whether I could depend on the promises they had made me. They readily answered in the affirmative. I then asked them if they had not promised to assist me with my baggage to their camp on the other side of the mountains, or to the place at which Captain Clark might build the canoes, should I wish it. They acknowledged that they had.

I then asked them why they had requested their people on the other side of the mountain to meet them tomorrow on the mountain where there would be no possibility of our remaining together for the purpose of trading for their horses, as they had also promised, that if they had not promised to have given me their assistance in transporting my baggage to the waters on the other side of the mountain, that I should not have attempted to pass the mountains but would have returned down the river, and that, in that case, they would never have seen anymore white men in their country, that if they wished the white men to be their friends and to assist them against their enemies from attacking them, that they must never promise us anything which they did not mean to perform, that when I had first seen them they had doubted what I told them about the arrival of the party of white men in canoes, that they had been convinced that what I told them on that occasion was true, why then would they doubt what I said on any other point?

I told them that they had witnessed my liberality in dividing the meat which my hunters killed with them and that I should continue to give such of them as assisted me a part of whatever we had ourselves to eat, and finally concluding by telling them [that] if they intended to keep the promises they had made me, to dispatch one of their young men immediately with orders to their people to remain where they were until our arrival.

The two inferior chiefs said that they wished to assist me and be as good as their word and that they had not sent for their people, that it was the first chief who had done so and they did not approve of the measure.

Cameahwait remained silent for some time. At length he told me that he knew he had done wrong but that he had been induced to that measure from seeing all his people hungry, but as he had promised to give me his assistance he would not, in [the] future, be worse than his word.

I then desired him to send immediately and countermand his orders. Accordingly, a young man was sent for this purpose and I gave him a handkerchief to engage him in my interest.

Monday, August 26, 1805:

Lewis: We collected our horses and set out at sunrise. We soon arrived at the extreme source of the Missouri. Here I halted a few minutes. The men drank of the water and consoled themselves with the idea of having, at length, arrived at this long wished-for point.

From hence, we proceeded to a fine spring on the side of the mountain where I had lain the evening before I first arrived at the Shoshone camp. Here I halted to dine and graze the horses, there being fine green grass on that part of the hillside, which was moistened by the water of the spring, while the grass on the other parts was perfectly dry and parched with the sun. I directed a pint of corn to be given [to] each Indian who was engaged in transporting our baggage, and about the same quantity to each of the men, which they parched, pounded, and made into soup.

One of the women who had been assisting in the transportation of the baggage halted at a little run about a mile behind us and sent on the two pack horses, which she had been conducting, by one of her female friends. I enquired of Cameahwait the cause of her detention and was informed by him, in an unconcerned manner, that she had halted to bring forth a child and would soon overtake us. In about an hour, the woman arrived with her newborn babe and passed us on her way to the camp, apparently as well as she ever was.

It appears to me that the facility and ease with which the women of the aborigines of North America bring forth their children is rather a gift of nature than depending, as some have supposed, on the habitude of carrying heavy burdens on their backs while in a state of pregnancy.

Cameahwait requested that we would discharge our guns when we arrived in sight of the village. Accordingly, when I arrived on an eminence above the village in the plain, I drew up the party at open order in a single rank and gave them a running fire, discharging two rounds. They appeared much gratified with this exhibition.

We then proceeded to the village, or encampment, of brush lodges, thirty-two in number. We were conducted to a large lodge, which had been prepared for me in the center of their encampment, which was situated in a beautiful, level, smooth, and extensive bottom near the river about three miles above the place I had first found them encamped. Here we arrived at 6:00 in the evening, arranged our baggage near my tent, and placed those of the men on either side of the baggage facing outwards.

I found Colter here who had just arrived with a letter from Captain Clark in which Captain Clark had given me an account of his peregrination and the description of the river and country, as before detailed. From this view of the subject, I found it a folly to think of attempting to descend this river in canoes and therefore determined to commence the purchase of horses in the morning from the Indians in order to carry into execution the design we had formed of passing the Rocky Mountains.

I now informed Cameahwait of my intended expedition overland to the great river, which lay in the plains beyond the mountains, and told him that I wished to purchase twenty horses of himself and his people to convey our baggage.

He observed that the Hidatsa had stolen a great number of their horses this spring but hoped his people would spare me the number I wished.

I also asked [for] another guide.

He observed that he had no doubt but the old man who was with Captain Clark would accompany us if we wished him [to], and that he was better informed of the country than any of them.

Matters being thus far arranged, I directed the fiddle to be played and the party danced very merrily, much to the amusement and gratification of the natives, though I must confess that the state of my own mind at this moment did not well accord with the prevailing mirth as I somewhat feared that the caprice of the Indians might suddenly induce them to withhold their horses from us, without which my hopes of prosecuting my voyage to advantage were lost.

Tuesday, August 27, 1805:

Ordway: In the evening the natives had a war dance. They were very merry but did not dance so regular as the Indians on the Missouri. Their women sang with them but did not dance any. They tell us that some of their horses will dance, but they have not brought them out yet.

Thursday, August 29, 1805:

Clark: I spoke to the Indians on various subjects, endeavoring to impress on their minds the advantage it would be to them for to sell us horses and expedite the journey the nearest and best way possibly. I purchased a horse for which I gave my pistol, one hundred balls, powder, and a knife.

Our hunters killed two deer near their camp today, two yesterday, and three the day before. This meat was a great treat to me as I had eaten none for eight days past.

Friday, August 30, 1805:

Ordway: [It was] a fine morning.

We got up all our horses. [We] bought eight more. [We] now have thirty in all. We got our loads ready.

The guide who has engaged with us to go on to the ocean tells us the road to the north of the river is rough and mountainous but said he could take us to where the tide comes up and [the] salt water.

[We] went about ten miles and camped.

Saturday, August 31, 1805:

Clark: I met an Indian on horseback who fled with great speed to some lodges below and informed them that the enemies were coming down armed with guns, etc.

We proceeded on the road on which I had descended as far as the first run[276] below and left the road and proceeded up the run in a tolerable road four miles and encamped in some old lodges.

---

276. Tower Creek (Eide, p. 101)

[We] proceeded on twenty-two miles today, four miles of which [was] up a run.

9: September, 1805

We proceeded on two miles and encamped opposite a small island. Here we were compelled to kill a colt for our men and selves to eat for the want of meat, and we named the south fork Colt Killed Creek. The Flathead name is Kooskooskee.

Captain William Clark,
September 14, 1805

Monday, September 2, 1805:

Clark: We set out early and proceeded on up the creek.[277] [We] crossed a large fork from the right and one from the left, and at eight miles left the road on which we were pursuing and which leads over to the Missouri, and proceeded up a west fork without a road.

[We] proceeded on through thickets in which we were obliged to cut a road, over rocky hillsides where our horses were in perpetual danger of slipping to their certain destruction, and up and down steep hills where several horses fell, some turned over, and others slipped down steep hillsides, [and] one horse [was] crippled and two gave out. With the greatest difficulty, risk, etc., we made five miles and encamped.[278]

Tuesday, September 3, 1805:

Clark: [The] hills [were] high and rocky on each side. In the afterpart of the day, the high mountains closed the creek on each side and obliged us to take on the steep sides of those mountains, so steep that the horses could scarcely keep from slipping down. Several slipped and injured themselves very much. With great difficulty, we made ____ miles and encamped[279] on a branch of the creek we ascended after crossing several steep points and one mountain. [There is] but little to eat.

At dusk, it began to snow [and] at 3:00 [there was] some rain.

---

277. the North Fork of the Salmon River (DeVoto)
278. near today's Gibbonsville, Idaho (Schmidt, p. 105)
279. along the Continental Divide, near Lost Trail Pass (Schmidt, p. 105)

The mountains to the east [are] covered with snow. We met with a great misfortune in having our last thermometer broken by accident. This day we passed over immense hills and some of the worst roads that ever horses passed. Our horses frequently fell.

[The] snow [was] about two inches deep when it began to rain, which terminated in a sleet storm.

Whitehouse: The mountains were so steep and rocky that several of the horses fell back among the rocks and were near killing them. [In] some places we had to cut the road through thickets of balsam fir.

We camped after a disagreeable day's march of only eleven miles, with much fatigue and hunger, as nothing has been killed this day, only two pheasants, and [we] have no meat of any kind.

[It] set in to raining hard at dark so we lay down and slept, wet, hungry and cold.

[We] saw snow on the tops of some of these mountains this day.

Wednesday, September 4, 1805:

Clark: [The] ground [is] covered with snow. We ascended a mountain and took a dividing ridge, which we kept for several miles, and fell on the head of a creek which appeared to run the course we wished to go.

[We] pursued our course down the creek to the forks, about five miles, where we met a party of the Flathead[280] nation of thirty-three lodges. [There were] about eighty men, four hundred total, and at least five hundred horses. These people received us friendlily, threw white robes over our shoulders, and smoked in the pipes of peace. We encamped with them and found them friendly. The chief harangued until late at night, smoked in our pipe, and appeared satisfied. I was the first white man who ever was on the waters of this river.[281]

Whitehouse: They tell us that we can go in six days to where white traders come and that they had seen bearded men who came [from] a river to the north of us, six days' march.

Thursday, September 5, 1805:

Clark: We assembled the chiefs and warriors and spoke to them with much difficulty as what we said had to pass through several languages[282] before it got into theirs, which is a gurgling kind of language, spoken much through the throat. In the course of the day, I

---

280. actually, Salish Indians; the captains used the name "Flatheads" generically, referring to all Northwest Indians (Ambrose, *UC*, p. 289)

281. Fish Creek (Eide, p. 102)

purchased eleven horses and exchanged seven, for which we gave a few articles of merchandise. These people possess elegant horses.

Whitehouse: These savages have the strangest language of any we have ever seen. They appear to us to have an impediment in their speech, or a brogue, or [a] burr on their tongue, but they are the [most] likable and honest savages we have ever yet seen. We take these savages to be the Welsh Indians, if there be any such, from the language. So Captain Lewis took down the names of everything in their language in order that it may be found out whether they are or whether they sprang or originated first from the Welsh or not.

Ordway: These natives are well-dressed, decent-looking Indians [and] light complexioned. They have the most curious language of any we have seen before. They talk as though they lisp or have a burr on their tongue. We suppose that they are the Welsh Indians, if there are any such.

Gass: This was a fine morning with a great white frost.

The Indian dogs are so hungry and ravenous that they ate four or five pairs of our moccasins last night.

We remained here all day and recruited our horses to forty, and three colts, and made four or five of this nation Indian chiefs. They are a very friendly people but they have nothing to eat but berries, roots, and such articles of food. They are the whitest Indians I ever saw.

Friday, September 6, 1805:

Clark: [We] crossed a small river from the right we call Clark's.[283] Soon after setting out, [there was] also a small creek from the north, all three forks coming together below our camp, at which place the mountains close on each side of the river. We proceeded on north thirty west. [We] crossed a mountain[284] and struck the river[285] several miles down, at which place the Indians had encamped two days before.

We proceeded on down the river, which is thirty yards wide, shallow and stony, crossing it several times, and encamped in a small bottom on the right side.

[It] rained this evening.

[There is] nothing to eat but berries, our flour [is] out, and [there is] but little corn.

---

282. the captains spoke English to Labiche, who spoke French to Charbonneau, who spoke Hidatsa to Sacagawea, who spoke Shoshone to a Shoshone boy living among the Salish, who spoke Salish to the Indians (DeVoto)

283. today's Bitterroot River (Ambrose, *UC*, p. 289)

284. Sula Peak (Schmidt, p. 106)

285. the East Fork of the Bitterroot River (Schmidt, p. 106)

The hunters killed two pheasants[286] only.

Whitehouse: Captain Lewis took down the names of everything in their language in order that it may be found out whether they are,[287] or whether they sprang or originated first from the Welsh or not.

Monday, September 9, 1805:

Lewis: The country in the valley of this river is generally a prairie and from five to six miles wide. At 12:00 we halted on a small branch which falls into the river on the east side, where we breakfasted on a scant proportion of meat which we had reserved from the hunt of yesterday, added to three geese which one of our hunters killed this morning.

We continued our route down the valley about four miles and crossed the river. It is here a handsome stream about one hundred yards wide and affords a considerable quantity of very clear water. The banks are low and its bed entirely gravel. The stream appears navigable, but from the circumstance of there being no salmon in it, I believe that there must be a considerable falls in it below.

Our guide[288] could not inform us where this river discharged itself into the Columbia River. He informed us that it continues its course along the mountains to the north as far as he knew it, and that not very distant from where we then were it formed a junction with a stream nearly as large as itself which took its rise in the mountains near the Missouri to the east of us and passed through an extensive valley, generally open prairie, which forms an excellent pass to the Missouri. The point of the Missouri where this Indian pass intersects it is about thirty miles above the Gates of the Rocky Mountains, or the place where the valley of the Missouri first widens into an extensive plain after entering the Rocky Mountains. The guide informed us that a man might pass to the Missouri, from hence by that route, in four days.

We continued our route down the west side of the river about five miles farther, and encamped on a large creek which falls in on the west. As our guide informed me that we should leave the river at this place, and the weather appearing settled and fair, I determined to halt the next day, rest our horses, and take some celestial observations. We called this creek Traveller's Rest.[289]

---

286. grouse (Schmidt, p. 104)
287. Welsh Indians
288. the Shoshone guide whom the captains called Old Toby (DeVoto)
289. also spelled "Traveler's;" just south of Lolo, Montana (Schmidt, p. 108)

Tuesday, September 10, 1805:

Lewis: The morning being fair, I sent out all the hunters and directed two of them to proceed down the river as far as its junction with the eastern fork which heads near the Missouri, and [to] return this evening. This fork of the river we determined to name the Valley Plain River. ([That is what] we called the eastern fork of Clark's River.) I think it most probable that this river continues its course along the Rocky Mountains northwardly as far [as], or perhaps beyond, the sources of Medicine River and then, turning to the west, falls into the Tacootchetessee.[290] The Hidatsa informed us that there was a large river west of, and at no great distance from, the sources of Medicine River, which passed along the Rocky Mountains from south to north.

This evening, one of our hunters returned accompanied by three men of the Flathead nation[291] whom he had met in his excursion up Traveller's Rest Creek. On first meeting him, the Indians were alarmed and prepared for battle with their bows and arrows, but he soon relieved their fears by laying down his gun and advancing towards them. The Indians were mounted on very fine horses of which the Flatheads have a great abundance. That is, each man in the nation possesses from twenty to a hundred head.

Our guide could not speak the language of these people, but soon engaged them in conversation by signs, or gesticulation, the common language of all the aborigines of North America. It is one understood by all of them and appears to be sufficiently copious to convey with a degree of certainty the outlines of what they wish to communicate.

In this manner we learned from these people that two men, who they supposed to be of the Shoshone nation, had stolen twenty-three horses from them, and that they were in pursuit of the thieves. They told us they were in great haste.

We gave them some boiled venison, of which they ate sparingly. The sun was now set [and] two of them departed after receiving a few small articles which we gave them, and the third remained, having agreed to continue with us as a guide, and to introduce us to his relations whom, he informed us, were numerous and resided in the plain below the mountains on the Columbia River, from whence, he said, the water was good and capable of being navigated to the sea, that some of his relations were at the sea last fall and saw an old white man who resided there by himself, and who had given them some handkerchiefs such as he saw in our possession. He said it would require five sleeps.

---

290. actually, the Fraser River (DeVoto)

291. probably Nez Percé (Ambrose, *UC*, p. 292)

Whitehouse: As our road next leads over a mountain to our left, our captains conclude to stay here this day to take observations, and for the hunters to kill meat to last us across the mountains, and for our horses to rest, etc.

Though the day is warm, the snow does not melt on the mountains a short distance from us. The snow makes them look like the middle of winter.

Wednesday, September 11, 1805:

Clark: The loss of two of our horses detained us until 3:00 p.m. Our Flathead Indian, being restless, thought [it] proper to leave us and proceed on alone.

[We] sent out the hunters to hunt in advance as usual.

We proceeded on up the Traveller's Rest Creek on the right side through a narrow valley and good road for seven miles, and encamped at some old Indian lodges.[292]

Nothing [was] killed this evening.

[The] hills on the right [are] high and rugged. The mountains of the left [are] high and covered with snow.

The day [was] very warm.

Whitehouse: [We] passed a tree on which were a number of shapes drawn on it with paint by the natives. A white bearskin hung on the same tree. We suppose this to be a place of worship among them.

[We] came about seven miles.

Thursday, September 12, 1805:

Clark: The road through this hilly country is very bad, passing over hills and through steep hollows, over fallen timber, etc., etc. [We] continued on and passed some most intolerable road on the sides of the steep, stony mountains, which might be avoided by keeping up the creek which is thickly covered with undergrowth and fallen timber.

[We] crossed a mountain eight miles, without water, and encamped on a hillside on the creek after descending a long, steep mountain. Some of our party did not get up until 10:00 p.m. [The] party and horses [were] much fatigued.

Friday, September 13, 1805:

Clark: At two miles [we] passed several springs which I observed the deer, elk, etc., had made roads to, and below one of the Indians had made a hole [in which] to bathe.[293] I tasted this water and

---

292. at the mouth of Woodman Creek (Schmidt, p. 109)

found it hot and not bad tasting. In further examination, I found this water nearly boiling hot at the places it spouted from the rocks. I put my finger in the water at first [and] could not bear it in a second.

My guide took a wrong road and took us out of our route three miles through an intolerable route.

After falling into the right road, I proceeded on through a tolerable route for about four or five miles, and halted to let our horses graze as well as wait for Captain Lewis who has not yet come up. We proceeded over a mountain to the head of the creek which we left to our left, and at six miles from the place I nooned it, we fell on a small creek from the left which passed through open glades,[294] some of which were one-half a mile wide. We proceeded down this creek about two miles to where the mountains closed on either side and encamped.

One deer and some pheasants [were] killed this morning. I shot four pheasants of the common kind, except the tail was black.

The road over the last mountain was thick, steep, and stony as usual. After passing the head of Traveller's Rest Creek, the road was very fine, level, open, and firm. [We saw] some mountains in view to the southeast and southwest covered with snow.

Saturday, September 14, 1805:

Clark: In the valleys it rained and hailed [and] on top of the mountains some snow fell.

We set out early and crossed a high mountain on the right of the creek for six miles to the forks of the Glade Creek.[295] We crossed to the left side at the forks, and crossed a very high, steep mountain for nine miles to a large fork from the left which appears to head in the snow-topped mountains southerly and southeasterly. I could see no fish, and the grass [was] entirely eaten out by the horses.

We proceeded on two miles and encamped opposite a small island at the mouth of a branch on the right side of the river which is at this place eighty yards wide, swift, and stony. Here we were compelled to kill a colt for our men and selves to eat for the want of meat, and we named the south fork Colt Killed Creek. The Flathead name is Kooskooskee.[296]

The mountains which we passed today [were] much worse than yesterday, the last excessively bad and thickly strewn with fallen tim-

293. today's Lolo Hot Springs (Ambrose, *UC*, p. 292-3)

294. today's Packer Meadows (Ambrose, *UC*, p. 293)

295. today's Pack Creek (Ambrose, *UC*, p. 293)

296. today's Lochsa River, in Idaho (Ambrose, *UC*, p. 293)

ber, and pine, spruce, fir, hackmatak,[297] and tamarack, [and] steep and stony.

Our men and horses [were] much fatigued.

Gass: None of the hunters killed anything except two or three grouse on which, without a miracle, it was impossible to feed thirty hungry men and upwards, besides some Indians. So Captain Lewis gave out some portable soup[298] which he had along to be used in cases of necessity. Some of the men did not relish this soup and agreed to kill a colt, which they immediately did, and set about roasting it, and which appeared to me to be good eating.

Ordway: [We] had nothing to eat but some portable soup. We being hungry for meat, as the soup did not satisfy, we killed a fat colt, which ate very well at this time.

Sunday, September 15, 1805:

Clark: [We] proceeded on down the right side of Colt Killed Creek, over steep points, rocky and bushy as usual, for four miles to an old Indian fishing place. Here the road leaves the river to the left and ascends a mountain, winding in every direction to get up the steep ascents and to pass the immense quantity of fallen timber which had been falling from different causes, i.e., fire and wind, and has deprived the greater part of the southerly sides of this mountain of its green timber.

Several horses slipped and rolled down steep hills which hurt them very much. The one which carried my desk and small trunk turned over and rolled down a mountain for forty yards and lodged against a tree [and] broke the desk. The horse escaped and appeared but little hurt. After two hours delay, we proceeded on up the mountain, steep and rugged as usual, [and] more timber near the top.

When we arrived at the top, as we conceived, we could find no water and concluded to camp[299] and make use of the snow we found on the top to cook the remains of our colt and make our soup.

[The] evening [was] very cold and cloudy.

Two of our horses gave out, poor and too much hurt to proceed on, and [were] left in the rear.

Nothing [was] killed today except two pheasants.

From this mountain, I could observe high, rugged mountains in every direction as far as I could see.

---

297. balsam poplar

298. a thick paste concocted by boiling down beef, eggs, and vegetables

299. present-day Snowbank Camp (Schmidt, p. 114)

Monday, September 16, 1805:

Clark: [It] began to snow about three hours before day, and continued all day. The snow in the morning [was] four inches deep on the old snow, and by night we found it from six to eight inches deep.

I walked in front to keep the road, and found great difficulty in keeping it as [in] many places the snow had entirely filled up the track, and obliged me to hunt several minutes for the track.

At 12:00 we halted on the top of the mountain to warm and dry ourselves a little as well as to let our horses rest and graze a little on some long grass which I observed. I have been wet and as cold in every part as I ever was in my life. Indeed, I was at one time fearful my feet would freeze in the thin moccasins which I wore.

After a short delay in the middle of the day, I took one man and proceeded on as fast as I could about six miles to a small branch passing to the right, halted,[300] and built fires for the party against their arrival which was at dusk. [They were] very cold and much fatigued. [We] killed a second colt which we all supped heartily on and thought it fine meat.

I saw four deer today and, what is singular, snapped[301] seven times at a large buck. It is singular as my gun has a steel fusil and never snapped seven times before. In examining her [I] found the flint loose.

To describe the road of this day would be a repetition of yesterday except the snow, which made it much worse.

Whitehouse: When we awoke this morning, to our great surprise, we were covered with snow which had fallen about two inches [during] the latter part of last night, and it continues a very cold snowstorm.

Captain Clark shot at a deer but did not kill it.

We mended up our moccasins. Some of the men without socks wrapped rags on their feet.

[We] loaded up our horses and set out without anything to eat and proceeded on. [We] could hardly see the old trail for the snow.

Tuesday, September 17, 1805:

Clark: The want of provisions, together with the difficulty of passing these immense mountains, has dampened the spirits of the party.

---

300. at today's Lonesome Cove (Schmidt, p. 114)

301. misfired

Wednesday, September 18, 1805:

Clark: [We] encamped on a bold running creek which I call Hungry Creek, as at that place we had nothing to eat.

Lewis: We dined and supped on a scant proportion of portable soup, a few canisters of which and a little bear oil and about twenty pounds of candles form our stock of provisions, the only resources being our guns and pack horses. The first is but a poor dependence in our present situation where there is nothing upon earth except ourselves and a few small pheasants, small grey squirrels, and a bluebird.

Ordway: Some places are so steep and rocky that some of our horses fell backwards and rolled twenty or thirty feet among the rocks, but [it] did not kill them.

We came to the highest part of the mountain [and] we halted. The mountains continue as far as our eyes could extend. They extend much farther than we expected.

Sunday, September 22, 1805:

Lewis: The pleasure I now felt in having triumphed over the Rocky Mountains and descending once more to a level and fertile country where there was every rational hope of finding a comfortable subsistence for myself and [the] party can be more readily conceived than expressed.

Whitehouse: These savages[302] were very glad to see us. The men, women, and children ran meeting us and seemed rejoiced to see us.

We camped near the village and the natives gave us such food as they had to eat, consisting of roots[303] of different kinds which were sweet and good. They are much like potatoes when cooked. The natives [also] gave us some excellent fat salmon to eat with the root, or potato, bread.

Monday, September 23, 1805:

Ordway: [It was] a fair morning. We purchased considerable salmon and camas roots from the natives. Also, they are fond of any kind of merchandise, but the blue beads they want mostly. Our officers gave the chiefs of this nation a flag [and] a medal. These natives have a great many horses and live well.

---

302. the Nez Percé

303. camas; plants of the lily family with edible bulbs

Tuesday, September 24, 1805:

Clark: Captain Lewis [was] scarcely able to ride on a gentle horse, which was furnished by the chief. Several men [were] so unwell that they were compelled to lie on the side of the road for some time. Others [were] obliged to be put on horses. I gave Rush's pills to the sick this evening.

Thursday, September 26, 1805:

Whitehouse: We formed our camp in a narrow plain on the bank of the river. [We] made a pen of pine bushes around the officer's lodge to put all our baggage in.

Some of the natives followed us with droves of horses.

Sunday, September 29, 1805:

Clark: [It was] a cool morning. [The] wind [was] from the south-west.

[The] men [are] sick as usual. Captain Lewis [is] very sick and most of the men [are] complaining very much of their bowels and stomach.

All the men that are able to work [are] at the canoes.

Drouillard killed two deer [and] Colter killed one deer.

The afterpart of this day [was] warm.

10: October, 1805

[We were] *nearly covered with fleas which were so thick amongst the straw and fish skins at the upper part of the portage, at which place the natives had been camped not long since, that every man of the party was obliged to strip naked during the time of taking over the canoes, that they might have an opportunity of brushing the fleas off their legs and bodies.*

Captain William Clark,
October 23, 1805

Tuesday, October 1, 1805:

Clark: [We] had examined and dried all our clothes and other articles, and laid out a small assortment of such articles as these Indians were fond of, to trade with them for some provisions (they are remarkably fond of beads).

[There was] nothing to eat except a little dried fish which the men complain of as working of them as much as a dose of salts. Captain Lewis [is] getting much better.

Several Indians visited us from the different tribes below, some from the main south fork.

Our hunters killed nothing today.

[It was a] warm evening.

Friday, October 4, 1805:

Clark: [There was] a cool wind from off the eastern mountains.

I displeased an Indian by refusing him a piece of tobacco which he took the liberty to take out of our sack. Three Indians visited us from the great river south of us.

The two men, Frazier and Goodrich, returned late from the village with fish, roots, etc., which they purchased. As our horse [was] eaten, we have nothing to eat except dried fish and roots, which disagree with us very much.

The afterpart of this day [was] very warm.

Captain Lewis [is] still sick but [is] able to walk about a little.

Saturday, October 5, 1805:

Clark: [We] had all our horses, thirty-eight in number, collected and branded. [We] cut off their fore tops and delivered them to the two brothers and one son of one of the chiefs who intends to accompany us down the river. To each of those men I gave a knife and some small articles, etc.

[There was] nothing to eat except dried fish and roots. Captain Lewis and I ate a supper of roots boiled which swelled us in such a manner that we were scarcely able to breathe for several hours.

[We] finished and launched two of our canoes this evening which proved to be very good.

Our hunters, with every diligence, could kill nothing. The hills [are] high and rugged and [the] woods too dry to hunt the deer, which is the only game in our neighborhood.

Sunday, October 6, 1805:

Clark: [We] had all our saddles collected, a hole dug, and in the night buried them [and] also a canister of powder and a bag of balls, at the place the canoe, which Shields made, was cut from the body of the tree. The saddles were buried on the side of a bend about one-half a mile below. All the canoes [were] finished this evening [and] ready to be put into the water.

I am taken very unwell with a pain in the bowels and stomach, which is certainly the effects of my diet, which lasted all night.

The river below this fork is called Kooskooskee.[304] It is clear, rapid, with shoals or swift places. The open country commences a few miles below this on each side of the river, on the port side below the first creek, with a few trees scattered near the river.

Monday, October 7, 1805:

Clark: I continue very unwell but [am] obliged to attend [to] everything. All the canoes [were] put into the water and loaded. [We] fixed our canoes as well as possible and set out. As we were about to set out, we missed both of the chiefs[305] who promised to accompany us. I also missed my pipe tomahawk which could not be found.

The afterpart of the day [was] cloudy.

[We] proceeded on past ten rapids which were dangerous. The canoe in which I was struck a rock and sprang a leak in the third rap-

---

304. at this point, it becomes today's Clearwater

305. Nez Percé: Twisted Hair and Tetoharsky (Ambrose, *UC*, p. 303)

ids. A short distance from the river, at two feet, four inches north of a dead-topped pine tree, [we] had buried two lead canisters of powder.

[We] had the canoes unloaded and examined, and mended a small leak which we discovered in a thin place in her side.

[We] passed several camps of Indians today.

Gass: We had four large canoes and one small one, to look ahead. About 3:00 in the afternoon we began our voyage down the river.

Tuesday, October 8, 1805:

Clark: [We] passed fifteen rapids, four islands, and a creek on the starboard side at sixteen miles just below which one canoe, in which Sergeant Gass was steering, was nearly turning over. She sprang a leak, or split open on one side, and [her] bottom filled with water and [she] sank on the rapids. The men, several of which could not swim, hung on to the canoe. I had one of the other canoes unloaded and, with the assistance of our small canoe and one Indian canoe, [we] took out everything and towed the empty canoe on shore. One man, Thompson, [was] a little hurt, [and] everything [was] wet, particularly the greater part of our small stock of merchandise.

[I] had everything opened and two sentinels put over them to keep off the Indians, who are inclined to thieve, having stolen several small articles. These people appeared disposed to give us every assistance in their power during our distress.

We passed several encampments of Indians on the islands and those near the rapids, in which places they took the salmon. At one of these camps we found our two chiefs who had promised to accompany us. We took them on board after the ceremony of smoking.

Ordway: One of the canoes struck a rock in the middle of the rapids and swung round and struck another rock and cracked her so that it filled with water. The waves roared over the rocks and some of the men could not swim. There they stayed in this doleful situation until we unloaded one of the other canoes and went and released them. Two Indians went in a canoe to their assistance, also.

Wednesday, October 9, 1805:

Clark: In examining our canoe, [we] found that by putting knees and strong pieces pinned to her sides and bottom, etc., she could be made fit for service by the time the goods dried. [I] set four men to work at her, Sergeants Pryor and Gass, Joseph Field, and Gibson, [and] others to collect resin. At 1:00, she was finished [and] stronger than ever.

The wet articles, not sufficiently dried to pack up, obliged us to delay another night. During the time, one man was trading for fish for our voyage.

At dark, we were informed that our old guide and his son had left us and had been seen running up the river several miles above. We could not account for the cause of his leaving us at this time without receiving his pay for the services he had rendered us or letting us know anything of his intention. We requested the chief[306] to send a horseman after our old guide to come back and receive his pay, etc., which he advised us not to do, as his nation would take his things from him before he passed their camps.

The Indians and our party were very merry this afternoon. A woman feigned madness, etc., etc., singular acts of this woman in giving in small portions all she had and if they were not received, she would scarify herself in a horrid manner, etc.

Captain Lewis [is] recovering fast.

Ordway: She began singing Indian and to giving all around her some camas roots and bracelets which hung about her. One of our party refused to take them from her. She then appeared angry [and] threw them in the fire. [She] took a sharp flint from her husband and cut both her arms in sundry places so that the blood gushed out. She scraped the blood in her hand and ate it, and so continued in this way about half an hour [and] then fainted, or went into a fit [for] some time, [and] then came to by their putting water on her.

Whitehouse: We were obliged to delay and prepare, or repair, the canoe which got stove last evening. [We] put the loading, merchandise, etc., out to dry.

The natives hung about us as though they wished to steal or pilfer something from us, so we had to keep two sentinels.

After dark we played the fiddle and danced a little. The natives were pleased to see us. One of their women was taken with the crazy fit by our fire.

Thursday, October 10, 1805:

Clark: At eight and a half miles lower, we arrived at the head of a very bad riffle, at which place we landed near eight lodges of Indians[307] on the port side to view the riffle, having passed two islands and six rapids, several of them very bad. After viewing this riffle, two canoes were taken over very well. The third stuck on a rock which took us an hour to get her off which was effected without her receiving

306. Twisted Hair

307. Nez Percé, or Pierced Nose

a greater injury than a small split in her side, which was repaired in a short time.

We purchased fish and dogs of these people, dined, and proceeded on.

Here we met with an Indian from the falls at which place, he says, he saw white people, and expressed an inclination to accompany us. We passed, a few miles above this riffle, two lodges and an Indian bathing in a hot bath made by hot stones thrown into a pond of water.

At five miles lower and sixty miles below the forks, [we] arrived at a large southerly fork which is the one we were on with the Snake, or Shoshone, nation. This south fork of Lewis's River has two forks which fall into it on the south. The country about the forks is an open plain on either side. I can observe at a distance on the lower port side a high ridge of thinly timbered country. The water of the south fork is a greenish-blue, the north as clear as crystal.

Immediately in the point is an Indian cabin, and in the south fork a small island. We came to on the starboard side below with a view to making some lunar observations. The night proved cloudy and we were disappointed.

The Indians came down all the courses of this river, on each side on horses, to view us as we were descending. [It is] worthy of remark that [there is] not one stick of timber on the river near the forks and but few trees for a great distance up the river we descended. I think Lewis's River[308] is about two hundred fifty yards wide, the Kooskooskee River about one hundred fifty yards wide, and the river below the forks about three hundred yards wide.

A misunderstanding took place between Charbonneau, one of our interpreters, and Joseph and Reubin Field, which appears to have originated in jest.

Our diet [is] extremely bad, having nothing but roots and dried fish to eat. All [of] the party has greatly the advantage of me in as much as they all relish the flesh of the dogs, several of which we purchased of the natives to add to our store of fish and roots, etc., etc.

The Chopunnish, or Pierced-Nose Indians, are stout, likable men, handsome women, and very dressy in their way. The dress of the men is a white buffalo robe, or elk skin, dressed with beads which are generally white, seashells and the mother of pearl hung to their hair and on a piece of otter skin about their necks, hair queued in two parcels hanging forward over their shoulders, feathers, and different colored paints which they find in their country, generally white, green, and light blue. Some few wore a shirt of dressed skins and long leggings

308. today's Snake

and moccasins painted, which appears to be their winter dress, with a plait of twisted grass about their necks.

The women dress in a shirt of ibex or goat skins which reach quite down to their ankles, with a girdle. Their heads are not ornamented. Their shirts are ornamented with quilled brass, small pieces of brass cut into different forms, beads, shells, and curious bones, etc.

The men expose those parts which are generally kept from view by other nations, but the women are more particular than any other nation which I have passed.

Their amusements appear but few. As their situation requires the utmost exertion to procure food, they are generally employed in that pursuit, all the summer and fall fishing for the salmon, the winter hunting the deer on snow shoes in the plains and taking care of their immense number of horses, and in the spring crossing the mountains to the Missouri to get buffalo robes and meat, etc., at which time they frequently meet with their enemies and lose their horses and many of their people.

Their disorders are but few, and those few of a scrofulous[309] nature. They make great use of sweating, the hot and cold baths. They are very selfish and stingy of what they have to eat or wear, and they expect in return something for everything given as presents or the services which they do, let it be however small, and fail to make those returns on their part.

Sunday, October 13, 1805:

Clark: The wife of Charbonneau, our interpreter, we find reconciles all the Indians as to our friendly intentions. A woman with a party of men is a token of peace.

Monday, October 14, 1805:

Clark: Our stern canoe turned broadside in a rapids. The canoe filled and sank. A number of articles floated out, the greater part of which were caught by two of the other canoes. Our loss of provisions is very considerable. All our roots were in the canoe that sank. Our loose powder was also in the canoe.

We found some split timber, the parts of a house which the Indians had very securely covered with stone. We have made it a point at all times not to take anything belonging to the Indians, even their wood. But at this time we are compelled to violate that rule and take a part of the split timber we find here for firewood, as no other is to be found in any direction.

---

309. scrofula: tuberculosis of the lymph glands, especially in the neck

Ordway: [We] came to another bad rapids at the head of an island. The canoe I had charge of ran fast on a rock. [A] considerable [amount] of the baggage washed overboard, but most of it was taken up below. She went off [all] of a sudden and left myself and three more standing on the rock half [a] leg deep in the rapid water.

Wednesday, October 16, 1805:

Clark: [It was] a cool morning.

[I was] determined to run the rapids. [I] put our Indian guide in front, our small canoe next, and the other four following each other. The canoes all passed over safely except the rear canoe, which ran fast on a rock at the lower part of the rapids. With the early assistance of the other canoes and the Indians, who were extremely alert, everything was taken out and the canoe got off without any injury further than the articles with which it was loaded getting all wet.

At fourteen miles [we] passed a bad rapids at which place we unloaded and made a portage of three-fourths of a mile, having passed four smaller rapids, three islands, and the parts of a house above.

I saw Indians and horses on the south side below. Five Indians came up the river in great haste. We smoked with them and gave them a piece of tobacco to smoke with their people, and sent them back. They set out in a run and continued to go as fast as they could run as far as we could see them.

After getting safely over the rapids and having taken dinner, [we] set out and proceeded on seven miles to the junction of this river[310] and the Columbia, which joins from the northwest. In every direction from the junction of these rivers, the country is one continued plain low and rises from the water gradually, except a range of high country on the opposite side about two miles distant from the Columbia.

We halted above the point on the Snake River to smoke with the Indians who had collected there in great numbers to view us. Here we met our two chiefs[311] who left us two days ago and proceeded on to this place to inform these bands of our approach and friendly intentions towards all nations, etc. We also met the two men who had passed us several days ago on horseback. One of them, we observed, was a man of great influence with these Indians [and] harangued them. After smoking with the Indians who had collected to view us, we formed a camp at the point near which place I saw a few pieces of driftwood.

---

310. the Snake

311. Twisted Hair and Tetoharsky

After we had our camp fixed and fires made, a chief came from his camp,[312] which was about one-fourth of a mile up the Columbia River, at the head of about two hundred men, singing and beating on their drumsticks and keeping time to the music. They formed a half-circle around us and sang for some time. We gave them all smoke and spoke to their chief as well as we could by signs, informing them of our friendly disposition to all nations and our joy in seeing those of our children around us. [We] gave the principal chief a large medal, shirt, and handkerchief, a second chief a medal of small size, and to the chief who came down from the upper villages, a small medal and handkerchief. The chiefs then returned with the men to their camp.

Soon after, we purchased for our provisions seven dogs. Some few of these people made us presents of fish and several returned and delayed with us until bedtime. The two old chiefs who accompanied us from the head of the river procured us some fuel, such as the stalks of weeds or plants and willow bushes. One man made me a present of about twenty pounds of very fat dried horse meat.

Thursday, October 17, 1805:

Clark: Several men and women offered dogs and fish to sell. We purchased all the dogs we could. The fish, being out of season and dying in great numbers in the river, we did not think [it] proper to use them. [We] sent out hunters to shoot the prairie cock, a large fowl which I have only seen on this river.

Captain Lewis took a vocabulary of the language of these people, who call themselves "Sokulk,"[313] and also one of the language of a nation residing on a westerly fork of the Columbia which mouths a few miles above this place, who call themselves "Chim-nâ-pum." Some few of this nation reside with the Sokulk nation.

I took two men in a small canoe and ascended the Columbia River ten miles to an island near the starboard shore on which two large mat lodges of Indians were drying salmon. The number of dead salmon on the shores and floating in the river is incredible to say—and at this season they have only to collect the fish, split them open, and dry them on their scaffolds on which they have great numbers. How far they have to raft their timber [which] they make their scaffolds of I could not learn, but there is no timber of any sort except small willow bushes in sight in any direction. From this island, the natives showed

312. the Wanapam (Schmidt, p. 122)

313. closely related to the Nez Percé; probably Yakima (DeVoto)

me the entrance of a large westerly fork, which they call "Tâpetâtt,"[314] at about eight miles distant.

The evening being late, I determined to return to the forks, at which place I reached at dark. [We] passed an island in the middle of the river at five miles at the head of which is a rapids, not dangerous. On the port side opposite to this rapids is a fishing place, three mat lodges, and great quantities of salmon on scaffolds drying. [We] saw great numbers of dead salmon on the shores and floating in the water [and] great numbers of Indians on the banks viewing me. Eighteen canoes accompanied me from the point.

The waters of this river are clear and a salmon may be seen at the depth of fifteen or twenty feet. West four miles to the lower point of a large island near the starboard side at two lodges, [we] passed three large lodges on the starboard side near which great numbers of salmon were drying on scaffolds.

One of these mat lodges I entered [and] found it crowded with men, women and children, and near the entrance of these houses I saw many squaws engaged in splitting and drying salmon. I was furnished with a mat to sit on, and one man set about preparing me something to eat. First he brought in a piece of a drift log of pine and, with a wedge of the elk horn and a mallet of stone curiously carved, he split the log into small pieces and laid it open on the fire on which he put round stones. A woman handed him a basket of water and a large salmon about half-dried. When the stones were hot, he put them into the basket of water with the fish, which was soon sufficiently boiled for use. It was then taken out, put on a platter of rushes neatly made, and set before me. They boiled a salmon for each of the men with me. During these preparations, I smoked with those about me who chose to smoke, which was but few, this being a custom these people are but little accustomed to and only smoke through form.

After eating the boiled fish, which was delicious, I set out and halted, or came to, on the island at the two lodges. Several fish were given to me, in return for which I gave small pieces of ribbon.

On my return, [I] found great numbers of the natives with Captain Lewis. [The] men [were] all employed in dressing their skins, mending their clothes, and putting their arms in the best order, the latter being always a matter of attention with us.

The dress of these natives differs but little from those on the Kooskooskee and Lewis's Rivers except the women, who dress very differently, inasmuch as those above wear long, leather shirts which are highly ornamented with beads, shells, etc., etc., and these on the main Columbia River only wear a truss or piece of leather tied around

314. the Yakima River (Schmidt, p. 123)

them at their hips and drawn tight between their legs and fastened before so as barely to hide those parts which are so sacredly hidden and secured by our women. These women are more inclined to corpulence than any we have yet seen. Their eyes are of a dusky black, their hair of a coarse black without ornaments of any kind, [and] braided as above.

These people appear to live in a state of comparative happiness. They take a greater share in the labor of the women than is common among savage tribes and, as I am informed, are content with one wife.

These people respect the aged with veneration. I observed an old woman in one of the lodges which I entered. She was entirely blind, as I was informed by signs, had lived more than one hundred winters, she occupied the best position in the house, and when she spoke, great attention was paid to what she said.

These people, as also those of the Flatheads which we had passed on the Kooskooskee and Lewis's rivers, are subject to sore eyes and many are blind of one and some of both eyes. This misfortune must be owing to the reflections of the sun, etc., on the waters in which they are continually fishing during the spring, summer, and fall, and the snows, during the winter seasons, in this open country where the eye has no rest.

I have observed amongst these, as well [as] in all other tribes which I have passed on these waters who live on fish, many of different sects who have lost their teeth about middle age. Some have their teeth worn to the gums, particularly those of the upper jaw, and the tribes generally have bad teeth.

The houses, or lodges, of the tribes of the main Columbia River are of large mats made of rushes. These houses are from fifteen to sixty feet in length, generally of an oblong square form, supported by poles on forks in the inner side, [and] six feet high. The top is covered also with mats, leaving a separation in the whole length of about twelve or fifteen inches wide, left for the purpose of admitting light and for the smoke of the fire to pass which is made in the middle of the house.

These people appear of a mild disposition and friendly disposed. They have in their huts, independent of their nets, gigs, and fishing tackle, each bows and large quivers or arrows on which they use flint spikes.

Friday, October 18, 1805:

Ordway: [It was] a clear, pleasant morning. We proceeded on down the great Columbia River, which is now very wide, about three-fourths of a mile, in general. The country, in general, [was] smooth plains for about ten miles down, then the barren hills made close to the river on each side.

Clark: The fish being very bad, those which were offered to us we had every reason to believe were taken up on the shore dead, we thought [it] proper not to purchase any. We purchased forty dogs for which we gave articles of little value, such as beads, bells, and thimbles, of which they appeared very fond.

At 4:00 we set out down the great Columbia accompanied by our two old chiefs. One young man wished to accompany us, but we had no room for more and he could be of no service to us.

We landed a few minutes to view a rapids. [We] passed this rapids, which was very bad, between two small islands, two still smaller near the port side. At this rapids on the starboard side, are two lodges of Indians drying fish. At two and one-half miles lower, [we] passed an island close under the starboard side on which were two lodges of Indians drying fish on scaffolds.

At sixteen miles the river passes into the range of high country, at which place the rocks project into the river from the high cliffs which are, on the port side, about one-third of the way across, and those of the starboard side about the same distance. The country rises here about two hundred feet above the water and is bordered with black, rigid rocks. At the commencement of this high country on the port side, a small rivulet[315] falls in which appears to have passed under the high country in its whole course. [We] saw a mountain,[316] bearing southwest, conical [in] form [and] covered with snow.

[We] passed four islands. At the upper point of the third is a rapids; on this island are two lodges of Indians, drying fish. On the fourth island, close under the starboard side, are nine large lodges of Indians drying fish on scaffolds as above. At this place we were called to land.

As it was near night and [there was] no appearance of wood, we proceeded on about two miles lower to some willows, at which place we observed a drift log. [We] formed a camp[317] on the port side under a high hill nearly opposite to five lodges of Indians.

Saturday, October 19, 1805:

Clark: The great chief Yellept,[318] two other chiefs, and a chief of a band below presented themselves to us very early this morning. Yellept is a bold, handsome Indian with a dignified countenance, about

315. the Walla Walla River (DeVoto)
316. Mount Hood (DeVoto)
317. in Washington, just north of the Oregon border (Schmidt, p. 123)
318. of the Wallawallas (Ambrose, *UC*, p. 303)

thirty-five years of age, about five feet, eight inches high, and well-proportioned. He requested us to delay until the middle of the day, that his people might come down and see us. We excused ourselves and promised to stay with him one or two days on our return, which appeared to satisfy him. Great numbers of Indians came down in canoes to view us before we set out, which was not until 9:00 a.m.

We proceeded on past an island close under the port side, about six miles in length. About four miles below this island, we arrived at the head of a very bad rapids. We came to on the port side to view the rapids before we would venture to run it. As the channel appeared to be close under the opposite shore and it would be necessary to lighten our canoes, I determined to walk down on the port side with the two chiefs, the interpreter and his woman, and directed the small canoe to proceed down on the port side to the foot of the rapids, which were about two miles in length.

I ascended a high cliff about two hundred feet above the water. From this place, I discovered a high mountain of immense height covered with snow. This must be one of the mountains laid down by Vancouver, as seen from the mouth of the Columbia River. From the course which it bears, which is west, I take it to be Mount St. Helens,[319] distant about one hundred twenty miles, [in] a range of mountains[320] in the direction crossing a conical mountain southwest, topped with snow.

I delayed at the foot of the rapids about two hours for the canoes which, I could see, met with much difficulty in passing down the rapids on the opposite side. [In] many places the men were obliged to get into the water and haul the canoes over shoals. I observed a great number of lodges on the opposite side at some distance below and several Indians on the opposite bank passing up to where Captain Lewis was with the canoes. Others I saw on a knob nearly opposite to me at which place they delayed but a short time before they returned to their lodges as fast as they could run.

I was fearful that these people[321] might not be informed of us. I determined to take the little canoe which was with me and proceed with the three men in it to the lodges. On my approach, not one person was to be seen except three men off in the plains, and they sheered off as I approached near the shore.

I landed in front of five lodges, which were at no great distance from each other, [and] saw no person. The entrances, or doors, of the

---

319. actually, Mount Adams (DeVoto, Bakeless, p. 270, and Ambrose, *UC*, p. 304)
320. the Cascades (DeVoto)
321. the Umatilla Indians, near Plymouth, Washington (Schmidt, p. 124)

lodges were shut with the same materials of which they were built: a mat.

I approached one with a pipe in my hand [and] entered a lodge which was the nearest to me. [I] found thirty-two persons, men, women and a few children, sitting promiscuously in the lodge in the greatest agitation. Some [were] crying and wringing their hands, others [were] hanging their heads. I gave my hand to them all and made signs of my friendly disposition and offered the men my pipe to smoke and distributed a few small articles which I had in my pockets. This measure pacified these distressed people very much.

I then sent one man into each lodge and entered a second myself, the inhabitants of which I found more frightened than those of the first lodge. I distributed sundry small articles amongst them and smoked with the men.

I then set myself on a rock and made signs to the men to come and smoke with me. Not one came out until the canoes arrived with the two chiefs, one of whom spoke aloud and, as was their custom, to all we had passed. The Indians came out and sat by me and smoked. They said we came from the clouds, etc., etc., and were not men, etc., etc.

[At] this time Captain Lewis came down with the canoes in which the Indians were. As soon as they saw the squaw wife of the interpreter, they pointed to her and informed those who continued yet in the same position I first found them. They immediately all came out and appeared to assume new life. The sight of this Indian woman, wife to one of our interpreters, confirmed [for] these people of our friendly intentions, as no woman ever accompanies a war party of Indians in this quarter. [We] dined and proceeded on.

[We] passed a small rapids and fifteen lodges below the five and encamped below an island close under the port side, nearly opposite to twenty-four lodges on an island near the middle of the river and the main starboard shore. Soon after we landed, which was at a few willow trees, about one hundred Indians came from the different lodges and a number of them brought wood which they gave us. We smoked with all of them, and two of our party, Pierre Cruzatte and Gibson, played on the violin, which delighted them greatly.

Their dress is similar to those at the fork except their robes are smaller and do not reach lower than the waist. Three-fourths of them have scarcely any robes at all. The women have only a small piece of a robe which covers their shoulders [and] neck and reaches down behind to their waists, with a tight piece of leather about the waist. The breasts are large and hang down very low [and are] illy shaped. [They have] high cheeks, flattened heads, and have but few ornaments.

Sunday, October 20, 1805:

Clark: We set out, leaving about two hundred of the natives at our encampment. [We] passed a rapids at seven miles, one at a short distance below. We passed a very bad rapids, a chain of rocks making from the starboard side and nearly choking the river up entirely with huge black rocks. [We passed] an island below close under the starboard side on which were four lodges of Indians drying fish. Here I saw a great number of pelicans on the wing, and black cormorants.

At 1:00 we landed on the lower point of an island. On the upper part of this island, we discovered an Indian vault. Our curiosity induced us to examine the method these natives practiced in depositing the dead. The vault was made by broad boards and pieces of canoes leaning on a ridge pole which was supported by two forks set in the ground, six feet in height, in an easterly and westerly direction, and about sixty feet in length and twelve feet wide. In it I observed great numbers of human bones of every description, particularly, in a pile near the center of the vault on the east end, twenty-one skull bones forming a circle on mats.

The westerly part of the vault appeared to be appropriated for those of more recent death, as many of the bodies of the deceased [were] wrapped up in leather robes [and] lay in rows on boards covered with mats, etc. We observed, independent of the canoes which served as covering, fishing nets of various kinds, baskets of different sizes, wooden bowls, robes, skins, trenchers,[322] and various kinds of trinkets in and suspended on the ends of the pieces forming the vault. We also saw the skeletons of several horses at the vault [with] a great number of bones about them, which convinced me that these animals were sacrificed, as well as the above articles, to the deceased.

After dinner, we proceeded on to a bad rapids at the lower point of a small island on which four lodges of Indians were situated drying fish. Here the high country commences again on the starboard side, leaving a valley of forty miles in width, from the Musselshell Rapids. [We] examined and passed this rapids close to the island.

At eight miles lower, [we] passed a large island near the middle of the river, a brook on the starboard side, and eleven islands all in view of each other below. A rivulet falls in on the port side behind a small island [and] a small rapids below. The starboard side is high, rugged hills, the port side a low plain, and not a tree to be seen in any direction except a few small willow bushes which are scattered partially on the sides of the bank.

---

322. wooden platters for serving food

The river today is about one-fourth of a mile in width. This evening, the country on the port side rises to the height of that on the starboard side, and is wavering.

We made forty-two miles today. The current [was] much more uniform than yesterday or the day before.

[We] killed two speckled gulls [and] several ducks of a delicious flavor.

Monday, October 21, 1805:

Ordway: [We] proceeded on. [We] passed river hills and cliffs of rocks on each side. [We] passed over a number of bad, rocky rapids where then river is nearly filled with high, dark-colored rocks. The water divided into narrow, deep channels [with] bad whirlpools.

We came about thirty-two miles.

Clark: [We] passed a small island at five and a half miles [and] a large one [at] eight miles in the middle of the river. [There was] some rapid water at the head and eight lodges of natives opposite its lower point on the starboard side.

We came to at these lodges [and] bought some wood and breakfast. These people received us with great kindness and examined us with much attention. Their employments, customs, dress, and appearance [are] similar to those above [and they] speak the same language. Here we saw two scarlet and a blue cloth blankets [and] also a sailor's jacket.

We got from these people a few pounded roots, fish, and acorns of white oak. These acorns they make use of as food, raw and roasted, and inform us they procure them of the natives who live near the falls below, which place they all describe by the term "Timm."

At two miles lower [we] passed a rapids [with] large rocks stringing into the river of large size. Opposite to this rapids on the starboard shore are situated two lodges of the natives drying fish. Here we halted a few minutes to examine the rapids before we entered them, which was our constant custom, and at all that were very dangerous [we] put out all who could not swim, to walk around.

After passing this rapids, we proceeded on past another rapids at five miles lower down. Above this rapids, [there were] many large rocks on each side at some distance from shore. A little below is a bad rapids which is badly crowded with huge rocks scattered in every direction, which renders the passage very difficult. A little above this rapids, on the port side, immense piles of rocks appear as if [they] slipped from the cliffs under which they lie. [We] passed great numbers of rocks in every direction scattered in the river.

[There were] five lodges a little below on the starboard side, and one lodge on an island near the starboard shore, opposite to which is a very bad rapids through which we found much difficulty in passing. The river is crowded with rocks in every direction. After passing this difficult rapids, we came to the mouth of a small river[323] on the port side.

Immediately above and below this little river commences a rapids which is crowded with large rocks in every direction. The passage [was] both crooked and difficult. We halted at a lodge to examine these numerous islands of rock which appeared to extend many miles below. Great numbers of Indians came in canoes to view us at this place.

After passing this rapids, which we accomplished without loss, winding through [or] between the huge rocks for about two miles, [we] proceeded on about two miles lower and landed and encamped near five lodges of natives drying fish. These are the relations of those at the Great Falls. They are poor and have but little wood, which they bring up the river from the falls, as they say. We purchased a little wood to cook our dog meat and fish. These people did not receive us at first with the same cordiality as those above. They appear to be the same nation, speak the same language with a little corruption of many words, dress and fish in the same way, all of whom have pierced noses, and the men, when dressed, wear a long, tapered piece of shell or bead put through the nose.

One of the old chiefs who accompanies us pointed out a place on the port side where they had a great battle not many years ago, in which many were killed on both sides.

One of our party, John Collins, presented us with very good beer made of the quamash[324] bread, which bread is the remains of what was laid in as a part of our stores of provisions at the first Flathead, or Nez Percé, nation at the head of the Kooskooskee River, which by being frequently wet, molded and soured, etc.

Tuesday, October 22, 1805:

Clark: [It was] a fine morning, calm and fair. We set out at 9:00.

[We] passed a very bad rapids at the head of an island close under the starboard side. Above this rapids on the starboard side, are six lodges of natives drying fish. At nine miles [we] passed a bad rapids at the head of a large island, of high and uneven rocks jutting over the water. [There was] a small island in a starboard bend opposite the

---

323. the John Day River (DeVoto)

324. camas

upper point on which I counted twenty parcels of dried and pounded fish.

On the main starboard shore opposite to this island, five lodges of Indians are situated [and] several Indians in canoes killing fish with gigs, etc. Opposite the center of this island of rocks, which is about four miles long, we discovered the entrance of a large river on the port side which appeared to come from the southeast. We landed at some distance above the mouth of this river, and Captain Lewis and I set out to view this river above its mouth.

We proceeded on past the mouth of this river, at which place it appears to discharge one-fourth as much water as runs down the Columbia. At two miles below this river [we] passed eight lodges on the lower point of the rock island. Below this island, on the main starboard shore, are sixteen lodges of natives. Here we landed a few minutes to smoke [near] the lower point of one island, opposite which heads in the mouth of Deschutes River, which I did not observe until after passing these lodges. About one-half mile lower, [we] passed six more lodges on the same side, and six miles below the upper mouth of Deschutes River, the commencement of the pitch of the Great Falls.[325]

Opposite, on the starboard side, are seventeen lodges of the natives. We landed and walked down, accompanied by an old man, to view the falls and the best route for to make a portage, which we soon discovered was much nearest on the starboard side, and the distance twelve hundred yards, one-third of the way on a rock, [and] about two hundred yards over a loose sand collected in a hollow blown by the winds from the bottoms, below which was disagreeable to pass, as it was steep and loose. At the lower part of these rapids, we arrived at five lodges of natives drying and preparing fish for market.

We returned, dropped down to the head of the rapids, and took every article except the canoes across the portage where I had formed a camp on an eligible situation for the protection of our stores from theft, which we were more fearful of than their arrows. We dispatched two men to examine the river on the opposite side and they reported that the canoes could be taken down a narrow channel on the opposite side after a short portage at the head of the falls, at which place the Indians take over their canoes. Indians assisted us over the portage with our heavy articles on their horses. The waters are divided into several narrow channels which pass through a hard, black rock, forming islands of rocks at this stage of the water.

On these islands of rocks, as well as at and about their lodges, I observed great numbers of stacks of pounded salmon neatly preserved in the following manner, i.e., after being sufficiently dried, it is

325. now submerged by The Dalles Dam (Schmidt, p. 126)

pounded between two stones fine, and put into a species of basket neatly made of grass and rushes, better than two feet long and one foot [in] diameter, which basket is lined with the skin of salmon stretched and dried for the purpose. In this it is pressed down as hard as possible. When full, they secure the open part with the fish skins, across which they fasten through the loops of the basket that part very securely and then, on a dry situation, they set those baskets [with] the corded part up.

Their common custom is to set seven as close as they can stand, and five on the top of them, and secure them with mats, which are wrapped around them and made fast with cords, and covered also with mats. Those twelve baskets, of from ninety to one hundred pounds each, form a stack. Thus preserved, those fish may be kept sound and sweet [for] several years, as these people inform me. Great quantities, as they inform us, are sold to the white people who visit the mouth of this river, as well as to the natives below.

Wednesday, October 23, 1805:

Clark: I, with the greater part of the men, crossed in the canoes to [the] opposite side above the falls and hauled them across the portage of four hundred fifty-seven yards, which is on the port side and certainly the best side to pass the canoes. I then descended through a narrow channel of about one hundred fifty yards wide, forming a kind of half-circle in its course of a mile, to a pitch of eight feet in which the channel is divided by two large rocks.

At this place, we were obliged to let the canoes down by strong ropes of elk skin which we had for that purpose. One canoe, in passing this place, got loose by the cords breaking and was caught by the Indians below. I accomplished this necessary business and landed safely with all the canoes at our camp below the falls by 3:00 p.m.

[We were] nearly covered with fleas which were so thick amongst the straw and fish skins at the upper part of the portage, at which place the natives had been camped not long since, that every man of the party was obliged to strip naked during the time of taking over the canoes, that they might have an opportunity of brushing the fleas off their legs and bodies.

Great numbers of sea otters [were] in the river below the falls. I shot one in the narrow channel today which I could not get.

Great numbers of Indians visited us both from above and below. One of the old chiefs,[326] who had accompanied us from the head of the river, informed us that he heard the Indians say that the nation

326. Twisted Hair (Ambrose, *UC*, p. 305)

below[327] intended to kill us. We examined all the arms, etc., [and] completed the ammunition to one hundred rounds. The natives left us earlier this evening than usual which gave a shadow of confirmation to the information of our old chief. As we are at all times and places on our guard, [we] are under no greater apprehension than is common.

I observed on the beach near the Indian lodges two beautiful canoes of different shape and size to what we had seen above: wide in the middle and tapering to each end, [and] on the bow curious figures were cut in the wood, etc. Captain Lewis went up to the lodges to see these canoes and exchanged our smallest canoe for one of them by giving a hatchet and [a] few trinkets to the owner who informed [him] that he [had] purchased it of a white man below for a horse. These canoes are neater made than any I have ever seen, and calculated to ride the waves and carry immense burdens. They are dug thin and are supported by cross pieces of about one inch [in] diameter [and] tied with strong bark through holes in the sides.

Gass: In high water there is nothing but rapids and the salmon can pass up without difficulty. The reason of this rise in the water below the falls is that for three miles down, the river is so confined by rocks (being not more than seventy yards wide) that is cannot discharge the water as fast as it comes over the falls, until what is deficient in breadth is made up in depth. About the great pitch, the appearance of the place is terrifying, with vast rocks, and the river below the pitch [is] foaming through different channels.

Thursday, October 24, 1805:

Clark: Our two old chiefs expressed a desire to return to their band from this place, saying that they could be of no further service to us as their nation extended no farther down the river than these falls, and as the nation below had expressed hostile intentions against us, would certainly kill them, particularly as they had been at war with each other. We requested them to stay with us two nights longer. Our views were to detain these chiefs with us until we should pass the next falls[328] which, we were told, were very bad and at no great distance below, that they might inform us of any designs of the natives and, if possible, to bring about a peace between them and the tribes below.

The first pitch of this falls is twenty feet perpendicular, then passing through a narrow channel for one mile to rapids of about [an] eight foot fall, below which the water has no perceptible fall but [is] very

327. the Chinooks (Ambrose, *UC*, p. 305)
328. The Dalles (DeVoto)

rapid. Captain Lewis and three men crossed the river and on the opposite side to view the falls, which he had not yet taken a full view of.

At 9:00 a.m. I set out with the party and proceeded on down a rapid stream of about four hundred yards wide. At two and a half miles, the river widened into a large basin to the starboard side on which there were five lodges of Indians. Here a tremendous black rock presented itself, high and steep, appearing to choke up the river. Nor could I see where the water passed farther than the current was drawn with great velocity to the port side of this rock at which place I heard a great roaring. I landed at the lodges and the natives went with me to the top of this rock, which makes from the starboard side, from the top of which I could see the difficulties we had to pass for several miles below. At this place the water of this great river is compressed into a channel[329] between two rocks not exceeding forty-five yards wide, and continues for one-fourth of a mile when it again widens to two hundred yards, and continues this width for about two miles when it is again interspersed by rocks. The whole of the current of this great river must, at all stages, pass through this narrow channel of forty-five yards wide.

As the portage of our canoes over this high rock would be impossible with our strength, and the only danger in passing through these narrows were the whorls and swells arising from the compression of water, and which I thought (as also our principal waterman, Pierre Cruzatte) by good steering, we could pass down safely. Accordingly, I determined to pass through this place, notwithstanding the horrid appearance of this agitated gut, swelling, boiling, and whirling in every direction which, from the top of the rock, did not appear as bad as when I was in it. However, we passed safely to the astonishment of all the Indians of the last lodges who viewed us from the top of the rock.

[We] passed one lodge below this rock and halted on the starboard side to view a very bad place, the current [being] divided by two islands of rocks, the lower of them large and in the middle of the river. This place being very bad, I sent by land all the men who could not swim and such articles as were most valuable to us, such as papers, guns, and ammunition, and proceeded down with the canoes, two at a time, to a village of twenty wood houses in a deep bend to the starboard side, below which was a rugged black rock.

The natives of this village received me very kindly, one of whom invited me into his house which I found to be large and commodious, and [they were] the first wooden houses in which Indians have lived since we left those in the vicinity of the Illinois. They are scattered

---

329. the Short Narrows (Ambrose, *UC*, p. 305)

promiscuously on an elevated situation near a mound of about thirty feet above the common level, which mound has some remains of houses and has every appearance of being artificial. One half of these houses is appropriated for the storing away [of] dried and pounded fish, which is the principal food, the other part next door is the part occupied by the natives who have beds raised on either side, with a fireplace in the center of this space. Each house appeared to be occupied by about three families. That part which is appropriated for fish was crowded with that article, and a few baskets of berries.

I dispatched a sufficient number of the good swimmers back for the two canoes above the last rapids and, with two men, walked down three miles to examine the river over a bed of rocks which the water, at very high floods, passes over. On these rocks I saw several large scaffolds on which the Indians dry fish. As this is out of season, the poles on which they dry those fish are tied up very securely in large bundles and put upon the scaffolds. I counted one hundred seven stacks of dried pounded fish in different places on these rocks which must have contained ten thousand pounds of neat fish. The evening [being] late, I could not examine the river to my satisfaction.

I returned through a rocky, open country infested with polecats to the village. The principal chief from the nation below, with several of his men, visited us and afforded a favorable opportunity of bringing about a peace and good understanding between this chief and his people and the two chiefs who accompanied us. Pierre Cruzatte played on the violin and the men danced, which delighted the natives who show every civility towards us. We smoked with these people until late at night, when everyone retired to rest.[330]

Friday, October 25, 1805:

Clark: Captain Lewis and I walked down to see the place the Indians pointed out as the worst place in passing through the gut, which we found difficult of passing without great danger, but as the portage was impracticable with our large canoes, we concluded to make a portage of our most valuable articles and run the canoes through.[331] Accordingly, on our return [we] divided the party, some to take over the canoes and others to take our stores across a portage of a mile to a place on the channel below this bad whorl and suck. With some others, I had fixed [them] on the channel with ropes to throw out to any who should unfortunately meet with difficulty in passing

330. near today's Horsethief Lake State Park (Schmidt, p. 127)

331. the Long Narrows (DeVoto)

through. [A] great number of Indians [were] viewing us from the high rocks under which we had to pass.

The three first canoes passed through very well, the fourth nearly filled with water, [and] the last passed through by taking in a little water. Thus safely below what I conceived to be the worst part of this channel, [I] felt myself extremely gratified and pleased.

We loaded the canoes and set out and had not proceeded more than two miles before the unfortunate canoe which [had] filled crossing the bad place above, ran against a rock and was in great danger of being lost. This channel is through a hard, rough, black rock, from fifty to one hundred yards wide, and swelling and boiling in a most tremendous manner.

We passed through a deep basin to the starboard side of one mile, below which the river narrows and is divided by a rock. The current we found quite gentle. Here we met with our two old chiefs who had been to a village below to smoke a friendly pipe, and at this place they met the chief and party from the village above on his return from hunting, all of whom were then crossing over their horses.

We landed to smoke a pipe with this chief whom we found to be a bold, pleasing-looking man of about fifty years of age, dressed in a war jacket, a cap, leggings, and moccasins. He gave us some meat, of which we had but little, and informed us [that] he, in his route, met with a war party of Shoshone Indians from the great river of the southeast which falls in a few miles above, and had a fight. We gave this chief a medal, etc., [and] had a parting smoke with our two faithful friends, the chiefs who [had] accompanied us from the head of the river (who had purchased a horse each with two robes and intended to return on horseback).

We proceeded on down. The water [was] fine, rocks in every direction for a few miles, when the river widened and became a beautiful, gentle stream of about half a mile wide. [There were] great numbers of the sea otters about these narrows, and both below and above. We came to under a high point of rocks on the port side below a creek of twenty yards wide and [with] much water. As it was necessary to make some celestial observations, we formed our camp[332] on the top of a high point of rocks which forms a kind of fortification in the point between the river and creek, with a boat guard.

Monday, October 28, 1805:

Clark: [It was] a cool, windy morning.

332. Fort Rock Camp, at present-day The Dalles, Oregon (Ambrose, *UC*, p. 307)

We loaded our canoes and set out at 9:00 a.m. As we were about to set out, three canoes from above and two from below came to view us. In one of those canoes I observed an Indian with [a] round hat [and] jacket, and [he] wore his hair queued.

We proceeded on. At four miles, we landed at a village of eight houses on the starboard side under some rugged rocks. I entered one of the houses in which I saw a British musket, a cutlass, and several brass tea kettles, of which they appeared very fond. [We] saw them boiling fish in baskets with stones. Here we purchased five small dogs, some dried berries, and white bread made of roots.

The wind rose and we were obliged to lay by all day at one mile below on the port side.

We had not been long on shore before a canoe came up with a man, woman and two children, who had a few roots to sell. Soon after, many others joined them from above. The wind, which was the cause of our delay, does not retard the motions of these people at all, as their canoes are calculated to ride the highest waves. They are built of white cedar or pine, very light, wide in the middle and taper at each end, with aprons, and heads of animals carved on the bow, which is generally raised.

[The] wind blew hard, accompanied with rain, all the evening. Our situation [was] not a very good one for an encampment, but such as it is, we were obliged to put up with [it]. The harbor is a safe one. We encamped on the sand, wet and disagreeable.

Tuesday, October 29, 1805:

Clark: [It was] a cloudy morning [with the] wind from the west, but not hard.

We set out at daylight and proceeded on about five miles.

[We] came to on the starboard side at a village of seven houses built in the same form and materials as those above. I observed in the lodge of the chief sundry articles which must have been procured from the white people, such as a scarlet and blue cloth, sword, jacket, and hat. I also observed two wide, split boards with images on them, cut and painted in imitation of a man.

The chief directed his wife to hand him his medicine bag which he opened and showed us fourteen fingers which, he said, were the fingers of his enemies which he had taken in war. This is the first instance I ever knew of the Indians taking any other trophies of their exploits off the dead bodies of their enemies except the scalp. The chief painted these fingers, with several other articles which were in his bag, red and securely put them back, having first made a short harangue which, I suppose, was bragging of what he had done in war.

We purchased twelve dogs, four sacks of fish, and some few ascid[333] berries. After breakfast, we proceeded on.

The mountains were high on each side, containing scattering pine, white oak and undergrowth, [and the] hillsides [were] steep and rocky. At four miles lower, we observed a small river falling in with great rapidity on the starboard side, below which was a village of eleven houses. Here we landed to smoke a pipe with the natives. We purchased four dogs and set out. (This village is of the same nation of the one we last passed.)

[We] proceeded on. The country on each side began to be thicker, timbered with pine and low white oak. [It was] very rocky and broken. [We] passed three large rocks in the river. The middle rock was large [and] long and had several square vaults on it. We call this rocky island the Sepulcher. The last river we passed we shall call the Cataract River, from the number of falls which the Indians say is on it.

[We] passed two lodges of Indians a short distance below the Sepulcher Island on the starboard side. [The] river [was] wide. At four miles, [we] passed two houses on the starboard side. Six miles lower, [we] passed four houses above the mouth of a small river forty yards wide on the port side. [There was] a thick, timbered bottom above and back of these houses. These are the first houses which we have seen on the south side of the Columbia River (and the access to these [is] difficult) for fear of the approach of their common enemies, the Snake Indians.[334]

Wednesday, October 30, 1805:

Clark: [It was] a cool morning. [There was] a moderate rain all the last night.

After eating a partial breakfast of venison, we set out. [We] saw four cascades caused by small streams falling from the mountains on the port side.

[There was] some rain.

We landed above the mouth of a small river on the starboard side and dined. John Shields killed a buck, and Labiche three ducks. Here the river widens to about one mile [with a] large sand bar in the middle [and] a great rock both in and out of the water. Large stones, or rocks, are also promiscuously scattered about in the river.

The day proved cloudy, dark, and disagreeable with some rain all day which kept us wet.

---

333. ascidia = pitcher-shaped

334. probably the Bannocks (DeVoto)

The country [consisted of] a high mountain on each side, thickly covered with timber, such as spruce, pine, cedar, oak, cottonwood, etc., etc.

I took two men and walked down three miles to examine the chute and river below. [We] proceeded along an old Indian path past an old village at one mile on an elevated situation. Captain Lewis saw one gun and several articles which must have been procured from the white people.

[It was] a wet, disagreeable evening. The only wood we could get to burn on this little island on which we have encamped was the newly discovered ash, which makes a tolerable fire.

Whitehouse: One-half mile above the falls is a village of about ten well-looking cabins covered with bark. These savages were surprised to see us. They signed to us that they thought that we had rained down out of the clouds.

Thursday, October 31, 1805:

Clark: [It was] a cloudy, rainy, disagreeable morning.

I proceeded down the river to view with more attention the rapids we had to pass on the river below. The two men with me, Joseph Field and Pierre Cruzatte, proceeded down to examine the rapids. The Great Chute,[335] which commenced at the island on which we encamped, continued with great rapidity and force through a narrow channel much compressed and interspersed with large rocks for half a mile. At a mile lower, [it] is a very considerable rapids at which place the waves are remarkably high.

[We] proceeded on in an old Indian path, two and a half miles by land through a thick woods and hillside, to the river where the Indians make a portage. From this place I dispatched Pierre Cruzatte (our principal waterman) back to follow the river and examine the practicability of the canoes passing, as the rapids appeared to continue down below as far as I could see. I, with Joseph Field, proceeded on.

The mountains, which are but low on the starboard side, leave the river and a level, stony, open bottom succeeds on the said starboard side for a great distance down. The mountains [are] high and rugged on the port side. This open bottom is about two miles.

A short distance below this village is a bad stony rapids, and [it] appears to be the last in view. I observed at this lower rapids the remains of a large and ancient village which I could plainly trace by the sinks in which they had formed their houses, as also those in which they had buried their fish.

---

335. the Cascades of the Columbia (Ambrose, *UC*, p. 307)

From this rapids to the lower end of the portage, the river is crowded with rocks of various sizes between which the water passes with great velocity creating, in many places, large waves. An island, which is situated near the port side, occupies about half the distance, the lower point of which is at this rapids.

Immediately below this rapids, the high water passes through a narrow channel through the starboard bottom, forming an island of three miles long and one wide. I walked through this island which I found to be very rich land, and had every appearance of having been, at some distant period, cultivated. At this time it is covered with grass interspersed with strawberry vines. I could not see any rapids below in the extent of my view, which was for a long distance down the river which, from the last rapids, widened and had every appearance of being affected by the tide. I determined to return to camp ten miles distant. A remarkable high, detached rock stood in a bottom on the starboard side near the lower point of this island on the starboard side about eight hundred feet high and four hundred paces around; we called [it] the Beacon Rock.[336]

One of the men shot a goose above this Great Chute. [It] was floating into the chute when an Indian observed it, plunged! into the water and swam to the goose and brought [it] in on shore at the head of the suck. As this Indian richly earned the goose, I suffered him to keep it, which he about half-picked and spitted it up with the guts in it to roast.

This Great Chute, or falls, is about half a mile, with the water of this great river compressed within the space of one hundred fifty paces, in which there are great numbers of both large and small rocks, water passing with great velocity, foaming and boiling in a most horrible manner, with a fall of about twenty feet. Below, it widens to about two hundred paces and [the] current [is] gentle for a short distance.

---

336. Castle Rock (DeVoto)

11: November, 1805

[There was] *great joy in* [our] *camp. We are in view of the ocean, this great Pacific Ocean, which we* [have] *been so long anxious to see, and the roaring, or noise, made by the waves breaking on the rocky shores (as I suppose) may be heard distinctly.*

Captain William Clark,
November 7, 1805

Friday, November 1, 1805:

Clark: [It was] a very cool morning [with the] wind hard from the northeast.

The Indians who arrived last evening took their canoes on their shoulders and carried them below the Great Chute. We set about taking our small canoe and all the baggage by land, nine hundred forty yards of bad, slippery and rocky way. The Indians, we discovered, took their loading the whole length of the portage, two and a half miles, to avoid a second chute, which appears very bad to pass, and through which they passed with their empty canoes.

[There are] great numbers of sea otters. They are so cautious that I with difficulty got a shot at one today which I must have killed, but could not get him, as he sunk.

We got all our baggage over the portage[337] of nine hundred forty yards, after which we got the four large canoes over by slipping them over the rocks on poles placed across from one rock to another and, at some places, along partial streams of the river. In passing those canoes over the rocks, etc., three of them received injuries which obliged us to delay to have them repaired.

Several Indian canoes arrived at the head of the portage. Some of the men, accompanied by those from the village, came down to smoke with us. They appear to speak the same language, with a little different accent.

I cannot learn certainly as to the traffic these Indians carry on below, if [from] white people or the Indians who trade with the whites, who are either settled or visit the mouth of this river. I believe mostly

337. near today's North Bonneville, Washington (Schmidt, p. 130)

with the latter, as their knowledge of the white people appears to be very imperfect, and the articles which they appear to trade mostly, i.e., pounded fish, beargrass, and roots, cannot be an object of commerce with furring merchants.

However, they get in return for those articles blue and white beads, copper kettles, brass arm bands, some scarlet and blue robes, and a few articles of old clothes. They prefer beads to anything and will part with the last mouthful or articles of clothing they have for a few of those beads. These beads they traffic with Indians still higher up this river for robes, skins, biscuitroot bread, beargrass, etc., who, in their turn, traffic with those under the Rocky Mountains for beargrass, camas roots, and robes, etc.

The natives of the waters of the Columbia appear healthy. Some have tumors on different parts of their bodies, and sore and weak eyes are common. Many have lost their sight entirely [and there are] great numbers with one eye out and frequently the other very weak. This misfortune I must again ascribe to the water, etc. They have bad teeth, which is not uncommon with Indians. Many have worn their teeth down and some quite into their gums. This I cannot satisfactorily account for. [I] do ascribe it in some measure to their method of eating their food, roots particularly, which they make use of as they are taken out of the earth, frequently nearly covered with sand. I have not seen any of their long roots offered for sale clear of sand.

They are rather below the common size [and with] high cheeks. [The] women [are] small and homely and have swelled legs and thighs, and their knees [are] remarkably large, which I ascribe to the method in which they sit on their hams. [They] go nearly naked, wearing only a piece of leather tied about their breast which falls down nearly as low as the waist, a small robe about three feet square, and a piece of leather tied about their breech. They have all flat heads in this quarter, both men and women.

They are dirty in the extreme, both in their person and cookery. [They] wear their hair loose, hanging in every direction. They ask high prices for what they sell and say that the white people below give great prices for everything, etc.

Their noses are all pierced, and when they are dressed, they have a long, tapered piece of white shell or wampum put through the nose. These shells are about two inches in length. I observed, in many of the villages which I have passed, the heads of the female children in the press, for the purpose of compressing their heads in their infancy into a certain form, between two boards.

Saturday, November 2, 1805:

Clark: [I] examined the rapids below us more particularly. The danger appearing too great to hazard our canoes loaded, [I] dispatched all the men who could not swim with loads to the end of the portage below. I also walked to the end of the portage with the carriers where I delayed until every article was brought over and [the] canoes arrived safely. Here we breakfasted and took a meridian altitude.

About the time we were setting out, seven squaws came over loaded with dried fish and beargrass neatly bundled up. Soon after, four Indian men came down over the rapids in a large canoe.

[We] passed a rapids at two miles and one at four miles opposite the lower point of a high island on the port side, and a little below [were] four houses on the starboard bank. [We passed] a small creek on the port side, opposite Strawberry Island, which heads below the last rapids. Opposite the lower point of this island, [we] passed three islands covered with tall timber opposite the Beaten Rock. These islands are nearest the starboard side.

Immediately below on the starboard side, [we] passed a village of nine houses which is situated between two small creeks and is of the same construction of those above. Here the river widens to nearly a mile, and the bottoms are more extensive and thickly timbered, as also the high mountains on each side, with pine, spruce pine, cottonwood, a species of ash, and alder.

At seventeen miles, [we] passed a rock near the middle of the river, about one hundred feet high and eighty feet in diameter. [We] proceeded on down a smooth, gentle stream of about two miles wide, in which the tide has its effect as high as the Beaten Rock, or the last rapids at Strawberry Island.

[We] saw great numbers of waterfowl of different kinds, such as swans, geese, white and gray brants, ducks of various kinds, gulls, and plovers. Labiche killed fourteen brant, Joseph Field three, and Collins one.

We encamped under a high projecting rock on the port side.[338] Here the mountains leave the river on each side which, from the Great Chute to this place, are high and rugged [and] thickly covered with timber, principally of the pine species. The bottoms below appear extensive and thickly covered with wood. [The] river here [is] about two and a half miles wide. Seven Indians in a canoe, on their way down to trade with the natives below, encamped with us. Those we left at the portage passed us this evening and proceeded on down.

---

338. near Rooster Rock State Park in Oregon (Schmidt, p.132)

The ebb tide rose here about nine inches; the flood tide must rise here much higher.

Sunday, November 3, 1805:

Clark: The fog [was] so thick this morning that we could not see a man fifty steps off. This fog detained us until 10:00, at which time we set out, accompanied by our Indian friends who are from a village near the Great Falls.

A mountain, which we suppose to be Mt. Hood, is south eighty-five degrees east, about forty-seven miles distant. This mountain is covered with snow and in the range of mountains which we have passed through, and is of a conical form but rugged.

[We] proceeded on to the center of a large island in the middle of the river which we call Diamond Island, from its appearance. Here we met fifteen Indian men in two canoes from below. They informed us [that] they saw three vessels below, etc., etc.

We landed on the north side of this Diamond Island and encamped. A canoe arrived from the village below the last rapids with a man, his wife and three children, and a woman who had been taken prisoner from the Shoshone Indians[339] on Clark's River. I sent the interpreter's wife, who is a Shoshone, or Snake, Indian of the Missouri, to speak to this squaw. They could not understand each other sufficiently to converse. This family, and the Indians we met from below, continued with us. Captain Lewis borrowed a small canoe of those Indians, and four men took her across to a small lake in the island.

Captain Lewis killed a swan and several ducks, which made our number of fowls this evening three swans, eight brants, and five ducks, on which we made a sumptuous supper. We gave the Indian who lent the canoe a brant and some meat to the others. One of those Indians, the man from the village near the lower rapids, has a gun with a brass barrel and cock, of which he prizes highly.

Note [that] the mountain we saw from near the forks proves to be Mount Hood.

Whitehouse: Towards evening we met several Indians in a canoe who were going up the river. They signed to us that in two sleeps we should see the ocean vessels and white people, etc., etc.

The country [is] lower and not so mountainous [and] the river more handsome.

---

339. probably a Bannock (DeVoto)

Monday, November 4, 1805:

Clark: Shannon set out early to walk on the island to kill something. He joined us at the lower point with a buck.

([The] tide rose last night eighteen inches perpendicularly at camp.)

Near the lower point of this Diamond Island is the head of a large island separated from a small one by a narrow channel, and both [are] situated nearest the port side.

On the main port shore, a short distance below the last island, we landed at a village of twenty-five houses. Twenty-four of those houses were thatched with straw and covered with bark; the other house was built of boards in the form of those above, except that it is above ground and about fifty feet in length. This village contains about two hundred men of the Skillute nation. I counted fifty-two canoes on the bank in front of this village, many of them very large and raised in [the] bow.

We recognized the man who overtook us last night. He invited us to a lodge in which he had some part, and gave us roundish roots about the size of a small Irish potato which they roasted in embers until they became soft. This root they call "wapatoo,"[340] the bulb of which the Chinese cultivate in great quantities called the "sagitta[341] folia," or common arrowhead. It has an agreeable taste and answers very well in place of bread. We purchased about four bushels of this root and divided it to our party.

At seven miles below this village, [we] passed the upper point of a large island nearest the port side, [and] a small prairie in which there is a pond opposite on the starboard [side]. Here I landed and walked on shore, about three miles. [There was] a fine, open prairie for about one mile, back of which the country rose gradually and woodland commenced.

[I] saw some elk and deer signs, and joined Captain Lewis at a place he had landed with the party for dinner. Soon after, several canoes of Indians from the village above came down, dressed for the purpose, I supposed, of paying us a friendly visit. They had scarlet and blue blankets, sailor jackets, overalls, shirts, and hats, independent of their usual dress. The most of them had either muskets or pistols and tin flasks to hold their powder. These fellows we found assuming and disagreeable. However, we smoked with them and treated them with every attention and friendship.

---

340. the edible root of the arrowhead plant

341. *Sagittaria*

During the time we were at dinner, these fellows stole my pipe tomahawk,[342] which they were smoking with. I immediately searched every man and the canoes but could find nothing of my tomahawk. While searching for the tomahawk, one of these scoundrels stole a capote[343] of one of our interpreters which was found stuffed under the root of a tree, near the place [where] they sat. We became much displeased with these fellows, which they discovered and moved off on their return home to their village, except two canoes which had passed on down.

[We] proceeded on [and] met a large and a small canoe from below with twelve men. The large canoe was ornamented with images carved in wood, the figures of a bear in front and a man in [the] stern, painted and fixed very neatly on the canoe, rising to nearly the height of a man. Two Indians, very finely dressed and with hats on, were in this canoe.

[We] passed the lower point of the island, which is nine miles in length, having passed two islands on the starboard side of this large island [and] three small islands at its lower point. The Indians make signs that a village is situated back of these islands on the port side, and I believe that a channel is still on the port side as a canoe passed in between the small islands and made signs that way, probably to traffic with some of the natives living on another channel.

At three miles lower and twelve leagues below Quicksand River, [we] passed a village of four large houses on the port side, near which we had a full view of Mount St. Helens,[344] which is perhaps the highest pinnacle in America. It bears north twenty-five degrees east, about ninety miles. This is the mountain I saw from the Musselshell Rapids on the nineteenth of October last covered with snow. It rises something in the form of a sugar loaf.

About a mile lower, [we] passed a single house on the port side and one on the starboard side. [We] passed a village on each side and camped near a house on the starboard side. We [had] proceeded on until one hour after dark with a view to get clear of the natives who were constantly about us and troublesome. Finding that we could not get shut of those people for one night, we landed and encamped on the starboard side. Soon after, two canoes came to us loaded with Indians. We purchased a few roots of them.

The Indians which we have passed today were of the Skillute nation in their language, and differ a little from those near and about the long narrows. Their dress differs but little, except they have more

---

342. which served as a weapon, camp ax, and tobacco pipe (Bakeless, p. 276)

343. a long, hooded, woolen blanket coat (Ambrose, *UC*, p. 310)

344. still actually Mt. Adams

of the articles procured from the white traders. They all have flattened heads, both men and women, [and] live principally on fish and wapatoo roots. They are thievishly inclined, as we experienced.

Tuesday, November 5, 1805:

Clark: [It] rained all the afterpart of last night [and] rain continued this morning.

I slept but very little last night for the noise kept up during the whole of the night by the swans, geese, white and gray brants, ducks, etc., on a small sand island close under the port side. They were immensely numerous and their noise horrid.

We met four canoes of Indians from below in which there were twenty-six Indians. One of these canoes was large and ornamented with images on the bow and stern. That in the bow was the likeness of a bear and in the stern, the picture of a man.

The day proved cloudy, with rain the greater part of it. We are all wet, cold and disagreeable.

I killed a grouse which was very fat and larger than common.

This is the first night which we have been entirely clear of Indians since our arrival on the waters of the Columbia River.

Wednesday, November 6, 1805:

Clark: [It] was a cool, wet, rainy morning. We set out early.

The Indians of the two lodges we passed today came in their canoes with sundry articles to sell. We purchased of them wapatoo roots, salmon, trout, and I purchased two beaver skins for which I gave five small fish hooks.

We overtook two canoes of Indians going down to trade. One of the Indians spoke a few words of English and said that the principal man who traded with them was Mr. Haley, and that he had a woman in his canoe who Mr. Haley was fond of, etc. He showed us a bow of iron and several other things which, he said, Mr. Haley gave him.

We came to to dine on a long, narrow island. [We] found the woods so thick with undergrowth that the hunters could not get any distance into the island. The redwood and greenbriers [were] interwoven and mixed with pine, alder, a species of beech, ash, etc.

We killed nothing today.

The Indians left us in the evening.

[The] river [was] about one mile wide, [and the] hills [were] high and steep on the starboard side.

We at length landed at a place which, by moving the stones, we made a place sufficiently large for the party to lie level on the smaller stones clear of the tide.

[It was] cloudy with rain all day.

We were all wet and disagreeable. [We] had large fires made on the stone and dried our bedding and killed the fleas which [had] collected in our blankets at every old village we encamped near.

Thursday, November 7, 1805:

Clark: [It was] a cloudy, foggy morning [with] some rain.

We set out early [and] proceeded under the starboard side under high, rugged hills with [a] steep ascent. The shore [was] bold and rocky. The fog [was] so thick [that] we could not see across the river.

Two canoes of Indians met [us] and returned with us to their village. They gave us to eat some fish and sold us fish, wapatoo roots, three dogs, and two otter skins, for which we gave fish hooks, principally, of which they were very fond.

These people call themselves "Wahkiakum" and speak a language different from the natives above with whom they trade for the wapatoo roots of which they make great use of as food. Their houses [are] differently built, raised entirely above ground [with] eaves about five feet from the ground, supported and covered in the same way of those above. [The] doors [are] about the same size, but in the side of the house in one corner. [There is] one fireplace and that [is] near the opposite end, around which they have their beds raised about four feet from the floor, which is of earth. Under their beds they store away baskets of dried fish, berries, and wapatoo. Over the fire they hang the fish as they take them and of which they do not make immediate use. Their canoes are of the same form as those above.

After delaying at this village one hour and a half, we set out, piloted by an Indian dressed in a sailor's dress, to the main channel of the river. The tide being in, we should have found much difficulty in passing into the main channel from behind these islands without a pilot. Here we saw great numbers of water fowl about these marshy islands. Here the high mountainous country approaches the river on the port side. [There was] a high mountain to the southwest about twenty miles. The high mountainous country continues on the starboard side.

About fourteen miles below the last village, we landed at a village of the same nation. It contained seven indifferent houses built in the same form as those above. Here we purchased a dog, some fish [and] wapatoo roots, and I purchased two beaver skins for the purpose of making me a robe, as the robe I have is rotten and good for nothing.

Opposite to this village, the high mountainous country leaves the river on the port side, below which the river widens into a kind of bay and is crowded with low islands subject to be covered by the tides.

We proceeded on about twelve miles below the village under a high mountainous country on the starboard side, [the] shore bold and rocky, and encamped[345] under a high hill on the starboard side opposite to a rock,[346] situated half a mile from the shore, about fifty feet high and twenty [in] diameter. We, with difficulty, found a place clear of the tide and sufficiently large to lie on, and the only place we could get was on round stones on which we laid our mats.

[The] rain continued moderately all day.

Two Indians accompanied us from the last village. They we detected in stealing a knife and returned.

[There was] great joy in [our] camp.[347] We are in view of the ocean, this great Pacific Ocean,[348] which we [have] been so long anxious to see, and the roaring, or noise, made by the waves breaking on the rocky shores (as I suppose) may be heard distinctly.

Friday, November 8, 1805:

Clark: [It was] a cloudy morning [with] some rain.

We did not set out until 9:00, having changed our clothing. Three Indians in a canoe overtook us with salmon to sell.

We came to at the remains of an old village at the bottom of this niche and dined. Here we saw great numbers of fowl. [We] sent out two men and they killed a goose and two canvasback ducks. Here we found great numbers of fleas which we treated with the greatest caution and distance.

After dinner the Indians left us and we took the advantage of a returning tide and proceeded on to the second point on the starboard side. Here we found the swells, or waves, so high that we thought it imprudent to proceed. We landed, unloaded, and drew up our canoes.

[There was] some rain all day at intervals.

We are all wet and disagreeable, as we have been for several days past, and our present situation [is] a very disagreeable one in as much as we have not level land sufficient for an encampment and for our baggage to lie clear of the tide. The high hills [are] jutting in so close and steep that we cannot retreat back, and the water of the river [is] too

345. in present-day Altoona, Washington (Schmidt, p. 133)

346. Pillar Rock (Schmidt, p. 133)

347. from Clark's personal field journal: "Ocian in view! O! the joy." (DeVoto, Schmidt, p. 133, and Ambrose, *UC*, p. 310)

348. actually only the Columbia River estuary (Ambrose, *UC*, p. 313, and Bakeless p. 277)

salty to be used. Added to this, the waves are increasing to such a height that we cannot move from this place. In this situation, we are compelled to form our camp between the height of the ebb and flood tides, and raise our baggage on logs.

We are not certain as yet if the white people who trade with these people, or from whom they procure their goods, are stationary at the mouth or [if they] visit this quarter at stated times for the purpose of traffic, etc. I believe the latter to be the most probable conjecture.

The seas rolled and tossed the canoes in such a manner this evening that several of our party were seasick.

Saturday, November 9, 1805:

Clark: The tide of last night did not rise sufficiently high to come into our camp but the canoes, which were exposed to the mercy of the waves, etc., which accompanied the returning tide, they all filled, and with great attention we saved them until the tide left them dry.

[The] wind [was] hard from the south and [it] rained hard all the forepart of the day.

At 2:00 p.m. the flood tide came in, accompanied with immense waves and heavy winds, [and] floated the trees and driftwood which were on the point on which we camped, and tossed them about in such a manner as to endanger the canoes very much. Every exertion and the strictest attention by every individual of the party were scarcely sufficient to save our canoes from being crushed by those monstrous trees, many of them nearly two hundred feet long and from four to seven feet through. Our camp [was] entirely underwater during the height of the tide.

Every man [was] as wet as water could make him all the last night and today all day, as the rain continued all day.

At 4:00 p.m. the wind shifted about to the southwest and blew with great violence immediately from the ocean for about two hours. Notwithstanding the disagreeable situation of our party, all wet and cold (and one which they have experienced for several days past), they are cheerful and anxious to see farther into the ocean.

The water of the river being too salty to use, we are obliged to make use of rain water. Some of the party, not accustomed to salt water, have made too free a use of it. On them it acts as a purgative.

At this dismal point, we must spend another night as the wind and waves are too high to proceed.

Sunday, November 10, 1805:

Clark: [It] rained very hard the greater part of the last night and continues this morning. The wind has laid and the swells have fallen. We loaded our canoes and proceeded on.

The wind rose from the northwest and the swells became so high [that] we were compelled to return about two miles to a place where we could unload our canoes, which was in a small bay on driftwood on which we had also to make our fires to dry ourselves as well as we could, the shore being either a cliff of perpendicular rocks or steep ascents to the height of four or five hundred feet.

We continued on this driftwood until about 3:00 when, the evening appearing favorable, we loaded and set out in hopes to turn the point[349] below and get into a better harbor, but finding [that] the waves and swells continued to rage with great fury below, we got a safe place for our stores and a much better one for the canoes to lie, and formed an encampment on drift logs in the same little bay under a high hill at the entrance of a small stream which we found very convenient on account of its water, as that of the river is brackish. The logs on which we laid are all on float every high tide.

The rain continued all day.

We are all wet [and] also our bedding and many other articles. We were all employed until late drying our bedding.

[There was] nothing to eat but pounded fish.

Monday, November 11, 1805:

Clark: [There was] a hard rain all the last night.

During the last tide, the logs on which we lay were all on float.

[We] sent out Joseph Field to hunt. He soon returned and informed us that the hills were so high and steep and thick with undergrowth and fallen timber that he could not get out any distance.

About 12:00 five Indians came down in a canoe. The wind [was] very high from the southwest, with [the] most tremendous waves breaking with great violence against the shores, [and] rain [was] falling in torrents. We are all wet as usual, and our situation is truly a disagreeable one. The great quantities of rain have loosened the stones on the hillsides and the small stones fall down upon us. Our canoes at one place [are] at the mercy of the waves, our baggage in another, and ourselves and party scattered on floating logs and such dry spots as can be found on the hillsides and crevices of the rocks.

---

349. Point Ellice (Schmidt, p. 135)

We purchased of the Indians thirteen red char[350] which we found to be an excellent fish. They are badly clad and illy made, small, and speak a language much resembling the last nation. One of these men had on a sailor's jacket and pantaloons, and made signs that he got these clothes from the white people who lived below the point, etc. These people left us and crossed the river (which is about five miles wide at this place) through the highest waves I ever saw a small vessel ride. These Indians are certainly the best canoe navigators I ever saw.

[It] rained all day.

Tuesday, November 12, 1805:

Clark: [There was] a tremendous wind from the southwest about 3:00 this morning, with lightening and hard claps of thunder, and hail, which continued until 6:00 a.m. when it became light for a short time. Then the heavens became suddenly darkened by a black cloud from the southwest and rained with great violence until 12:00.

The waves [were] tremendous, breaking with great fury against the rocks and trees on which we were encamped. Our situation was dangerous.

We took the advantage of a low tide and moved our camp around a point[351] to a small, wet bottom at the mouth of a brook which we had not observed when we came to this cove, from its being very thick and obscured by drift trees and thick bushes.

It would be distressing to see our situation, all wet and cold, our bedding also wet (and the robes of the party, which compose half the bedding, are rotten, and we are not in a situation to supply their places), in a wet bottom scarcely large enough to contain us, our baggage half a mile from us and [the] canoes at the mercy of the waves, although secured as well as possible, sunk with immense parcels of stone to weigh them down to prevent their dashing to pieces against the rocks. One got loose last night and was left on a rock a short distance below without receiving more damage than a split in her bottom.

Fortunately for us, our men are healthy.

Three men, Gibson, Bratton and Willard, attempted to go around the point below in our Indian canoe, much such a canoe as the Indians visited us in yesterday. They proceeded to the point from which they were obliged to return, the waves tossing them about at will.

I walked up the branch and gigged three salmon trout.

---

350. small-scaled trout

351. Point Ellice again

Wednesday, November 13, 1805:

Clark: [There were] some intervals of fair weather last night, [but the] rain continued this morning.

I walked up the brook and ascended the first spur of the mountain with much fatigue, the distance about three miles, through an intolerable thicket of small pine, a growth much resembling arrowwood, on the stems of which there are thorns. This growth [is] about twelve or fifteen feet high, interlocked into each other, and scattered over the high fern and fallen timber. Added to this, the hills were so steep that I was compelled to draw myself up by the assistance of those bushes. The timber on these hills are of the pine species, large and tall, many of them more than two hundred feet high and from eight to ten feet through at the stump.

The rain continued and [the] weather proved so cloudy that I could not see any distance.

On my return, we dispatched three men, Colter, Willard and Shannon, in the Indian canoe to get around the point, if possible, and examine the river and the bay below for a good harbor for our canoes to lie in safety, etc.

The tide at every flood tide came in with great fury. The rain continued all day.

[There was] nothing to eat but pounded fish which we keep as a reserve and use in situations of this kind.

Thursday, November 14, 1805:

Clark: [It] rained all the last night without intermission and this morning [the] wind blows very hard, but our situation is such that we cannot tell from what point it comes.

One of our canoes was much broken by the waves dashing it against the rocks.

Five Indians came up in a canoe through the waves which are very high and roll with great fury. They made signs to us that they saw three men we sent down yesterday. Only three of these Indians landed. The other two, which were women, played off in the waves, which induced me to suspect that they had taken something from our men below. At this time, one of the men, Colter, returned by land and informed us that these Indians had taken his gig and basket. I called to the squaws to land and give back the gig, which they would not do until a man ran with a gun as if he intended to shoot them when they landed, and Colter got his gig and basket.

Colter informed us that it was but a short distance from where we lay around the point to a beautiful sand beach which continued for a long way, that he had found a good harbor in the mouth of a creek near two Indian lodges, that he had proceeded in the canoe as far as he could for the waves, [and that] the other two men, Willard and Shannon, had proceeded on down.

Captain Lewis concluded to proceed on by land and find, if possible, the white people the Indians say are below and examine if a bay is situated near the mouth of this river, as laid down by Vancouver, in which we expect, if there are white traders to find them, etc. At 3:00 he set out with four men, Drouillard, Joseph and Reubin Field and Robert Frazier, in one of our large canoes, and five men to set them around the point on the sand beach. This canoe returned nearly filled with water, at dark, which it received by the waves dashing into it on its return, having landed Captain Lewis and his party safely on the sand beach.

The rain, etc., which has continued without a longer intermission than two hours at a time for ten days past, has destroyed the robes and rotted nearly one half of the few clothes the party has, particularly the leather clothes. If we have cold weather before we can kill and dress skins for clothing, the bulk of the party will suffer very much.

Friday, November 15, 1805:

Clark: [It] rained all the last night at intervals of sometimes of two hours. This morning it became cold and fair.

I prepared to set out, at which time the wind sprang up from the southeast and blew down the river, and in a few minutes raised such swells and waves breaking on the rocks at the point as to render it unsafe to proceed. I went to the point in an empty canoe and found it would be dangerous to proceed even in an empty canoe.

The sun shone until 1:00 p.m., which gave an opportunity for us to dry some of our bedding and examine our baggage, the greater part of which I found wet. Some of our pounded fish [was] spoiled. I had all the arms put in order and ammunition examined.

The rainy weather continued without a longer intermission than two hours at a time. From the fifth in the morning until the sixteenth are eleven days [of] rain, and the most disagreeable time I have experienced confined on a tempest coast wet where I can neither get out to hunt, return to a better situation, or proceed on. In this situation have we been for six days past.

Fortunately, the wind lay about 3:00. We loaded in great haste and set out past the blustering point below which is a sand beach[352] with a small marshy bottom for three miles on the starboard side, on which is a large village of thirty-six houses, deserted by the Indians,

352. present-day Fort Canby State Park (Ambrose, *UC*, p. 314)

and in full possession of the fleas. A small creek falls in at this village which waters the country for a few miles back.

Shannon and five Indians met me here. Shannon informed me [that] he met Captain Lewis some distance below and he took Willard with him and sent him to meet me. The Indians with him were rogues; they had, the night before, stolen both his and Willard's guns from under their heads. Captain Lewis and party arrived at the camp of these Indians at so timely a period that the Indians were alarmed and delivered up the guns, etc.

The tide meeting of me and the immense swells from the main ocean (immediately in front of us) raised to such a height that I concluded to form a camp on the highest spot I could find in the marshy bottom and proceed no farther by water, as the coast becomes very dangerous for crafts of the size of our canoes, and as the ocean is immediately in front and gives us an extensive view of it from Cape Disappointment to Point Adams, except three small islands off the mouth and southwest of us. My situation is in the upper part of Haley Bay.

Four Indians in a canoe came down with wapatoo roots to sell for which they asked blankets or robes, both of which we could not spare. I informed these Indians, all of which understood some English, that if they stole our guns, etc., the men would certainly shoot them. I treated them with great distance, and the sentinel which was over our baggage alarmed them very much. They all promised not to take any things, and if anything was taken by the squaws and bad boys, to return them, etc.

The waves became very high.

[The] evening [was] fair and pleasant.

Our men [are] all comfortable in the camps[353] they have made of the boards they found at the town above.

Saturday, November 16, 1805:

Whitehouse: We are now of the opinion that we cannot go any farther with our canoes, and I think that we are at an end of our voyage to the Pacific Ocean, and as soon as discoveries necessary are made, that we shall return a short distance up the river and provide ourselves with winter quarters.

---

353. near present-day Lewis and Clark Campsite State Park near Chinook, Washington (Schmidt, p. 135)

Sunday, November 17, 1805:

Clark: [It was] a fair, cool morning [with] wind from the east. The tide rises at this place eight feet, six inches, and comes in with great waves breaking on the sand beach on which we lay with great fury. Six hunters [went] out this morning in search of deer and fowl.

At half past 10:00 Captain Lewis returned, having traversed Haley Bay[354] to Cape Disappointment and the seacoast to the north for some distance. Several Chinook Indians followed Captain Lewis, and a canoe came up with roots, mats, etc., to sell. Those Chinooks made us a present of a root boiled, much resembling the common licorice in taste and size. In return for this root, we gave more than double the value to satisfy their craving disposition. It is a bad practice to receive a present from these Indians as they are never satisfied for what they receive in return if ten times the value of the articles they gave.

This Chinook nation is about four hundred souls, inhabits the country on the small rivers which run into the bay below us and on the ponds to the northwest of us, [and] lives principally on fish and roots. They are well-armed with fusils and sometimes kill elk, deer, and fowl.

Our hunters killed today three deer, four brants, and two ducks, and inform me they saw some elk sign.

I directed all the men who wished to see more of the main ocean to prepare themselves to set out with me early on tomorrow morning.

The principal chief of the Chinooks and his family came up to see us this evening.

Monday, November 18, 1805:

Clark: I set out with ten men and my man, York, to the ocean by land, i.e., Sergeants Ordway and Pryor, Joseph and Reubin Field, George Shannon, William Bratton, John Colter, Peter Wiser, Francis Labiche, and Toussaint Charbonneau, one of our interpreters, and York. I set out at daylight and proceeded on a sandy beach.

After dinner, [we went] to a small rock island in a deep niche, past a niche in which there was a drain from some ponds back. A bluff of yellow clay and soft stone [runs] from the river to the commencement of this niche. Below, the country rises to high hills of about eighty or ninety feet above the water. At three miles, [we] passed a niche. This rock island is small and at the south of a deep bend in which, the natives inform us, the ships anchor, and from whence they receive their goods in return for their pelts and elk skins, etc. This appears to be a very good harbor for large ships.

---

354. present-day Baker Bay

Here I found Captain Lewis's name on a tree. I also engraved my name, and by land, the day of the month and year, as also several of the men.

[We went] to the inner extremity of Cape Disappointment, passing a niche in which there is a small rock island. A small stream falls into this niche from a pond which is immediately on the seacoast, passing through a low isthmus. This cape is an elevated circular point covered with thick timber on the inner side and open grassy exposure next to the sea, and rises with a steep ascent to the height of about one hundred fifty or one hundred sixty feet above the level of the water. This cape, as also the shore both on the bay and seacoast, is a dark brown rock.

I crossed the neck of land, low and one-half of a mile wide, to the main ocean at the foot of a high, open hill projecting into the ocean and about one mile in circumference. I ascended this hill, which is covered with high, coarse grass, [and] descended to the north of it and camped. [We] walked nineteen miles today.

From Cape Disappointment, a high point of a mountain, which we shall call Clark's Point of View, bears south twenty degrees west about twenty-five miles. Point Adams is very low and is situated within the direction between those two high points of land. The water appears very shoal from off the mouth of the river for a great distance, and I cannot ascertain the direction of the deepest channel. The Indians point nearest the opposite side. The waves appear to break with tremendous force in every direction quite across. A large sand bar lies within the mouth nearest to Point Adams, which is nearly covered at high tide. [The] men appear much satisfied with their trip, beholding with astonishment the high waves dashing against the rocks and this immense ocean.

Tuesday, November 19, 1805:

Clark: Cape Disappointment at the entrance of the Columbia River into the Great South Sea, or Pacific Ocean

I arose early this morning from under a wet blanket caused by a shower of rain which fell in the latter part of the last night, and sent two men on ahead with directions to proceed on near the seacoast and kill something for breakfast, and that I should follow myself in about half an hour.

After drying our blankets a little, I set out with a view to proceed near the coast, the direction of which induced me to conclude that at the distance of eight or ten miles, the bay was at no great distance across. I overtook the hunters at about three miles. They had killed a small deer on which we breakfasted. It commenced raining and continued moderately until 11:00 a.m.

After taking a sumptuous breakfast of venison which was roasted on sticks [and] exposed to the fire, I proceeded on through rugged country of high hills and steep hollows to the commencement of a sandy coast which extended to a point of highland, distant nearly twenty miles. This point I have taken the liberty of calling after my particular friend Lewis. At the commencement of this sand beach, the highlands leave the seacoast in a direction to Chinook River, and do not touch the seacoast again below Point Lewis, leaving a low, pondy country, many places open with small ponds in which there is a great number of fowl. I am informed that the Chinook nation inhabits this low country and lives in large, wood houses on a river which passes through this bottom parallel to the seacoast and falls into the bay.

I proceeded on the sandy coast and marked my name on a small pine, the day of the month and year, etc., and returned to the foot of the hill. I saw a sturgeon which had been thrown on shore and left by the tide, ten feet in length, and several joints of the backbone of a whale, which must have foundered on this part of the coast.

After dining on the remains of our small deer, I proceeded to the bay, [a] distance [of] about two miles, thence up to the mouth of Chinook River two miles, crossed this little river in the canoe we left at its mouth, and encamped on the upper side in an open, sandy bottom.

Wednesday, November 20, 1805:

Clark: [There was] some rain last night.

[I] dispatched Labiche to kill some fowl for our breakfast. He returned in about two hours with eight large ducks, on which we breakfasted.

I proceeded on to the entrance of a creek near a cabin. No person being at this cabin, and two canoes lying on the opposite shore from us, I determined to have a raft made and send a man over for a canoe. A small raft was soon made, and Reubin Field crossed and brought over a canoe. This creek, which is the outlet of a number of ponds, is at this time (high tide) three hundred yards wide.

I proceeded on up the beach and was overtaken by three Indians. One of them gave me some dried sturgeon and a few wapatoo roots. I employed these Indians to take up one of our canoes which had been left by the first party that came down, for which service I gave them each a fishing hook of a large size.

On my way up I met several parties of Chinooks which I had not before seen. They were on their return from our camp. All these people appeared to know my determination of keeping every individual of their nation at a proper distance, as they were guarded and reserved in my presence, etc.

[I] found many of the Chinooks with Captain Lewis, of whom there were two chiefs, "Com-com-mo-ly" and "Chil-lar-la-wil," to whom we gave medals, and to one a flag. One of the Indians had on a robe made of two sea otter skins. The fur of them was more beautiful than any fur I had ever seen. Both Captain Lewis and I endeavored to purchase the robe with different articles. At length we procured it for a belt of blue beads which the squaw-wife of our interpreter, Charbonneau, [had] worn around her waist.

In my absence, the hunters had killed several deer and fowl of different kinds.

Thursday, November 21, 1805:

Clark: [It was] a cloudy morning.

Most of the Chinooks left our camp and returned home.

The wind blew hard from the southeast which, with the addition of the flood tide, raised very high waves which broke with great violence against the shore, throwing water into our camp. The forepart of this day [was] cloudy. At 12:00 it began to rain and continued all day moderately.

Several Indians visited us today of different nations, or bands, some of the Chiltz nation who reside on the seacoast near Point Lewis, several of the Clatsops who reside on the opposite side of the Columbia immediately opposite to us, and a chief from the Grand Rapids to whom we gave a medal.

An old woman and wife to a chief of the Chinooks came and made a camp near ours. She brought with her six young squaws I believe for the purpose of gratifying the passions of the men of our party, and receiving for those indulgences such small presents as she (the old woman) thought proper to accept of.

These people appear to view sensuality as a necessary evil and do not appear to abhor it as a crime in the unmarried state. The young females are fond of the attention of our men and appear to meet the sincere approbation of their friends and connections for thus obtaining their favors.

The women of the Chinook nation have handsome faces, [are] low and badly made, with large legs and thighs which are generally swelled from a stoppage of the circulation in the feet (which are small) by many strands of beads or curious strings which are drawn tight around the leg above the ankle. Their legs are also picked with different figures. I saw on the left arm of a squaw the following letters: "J. Bowman." All these are considered by the natives of this quarter as handsome decorations, and a woman without these decorations is considered as among the lower class. They wear their hair loose, hanging over their backs and shoulders. Many have blue beads threaded and hung from different parts of their ears and about their necks and around their wrists. Their dress otherwise is precisely like that of the nation of Wahkiakum, as already described.

Many of the men have blankets of red, blue, or spotted cloth, or the common three- and two-and-a-half-point[355] blankets, and sailors' old clothes which they appear to prize highly. They also have robes of sea otter, beaver, elk, deer, fox, and [a] cat common to this country which I have never seen in the United States. They also procure a robe from the natives above, which is made of the skins of a small animal about the size of a cat, which is light and durable and highly prized by these people. The greater numbers of the men of the Chinooks have guns and powder and ball. The men are low, homely, and badly made, [with] small crooked legs, large feet, and all of both sexes have flattened heads.

Many of the Chinooks appear to have venereal and pustular disorders. One woman whom I saw at the creek appeared all over in scabs and ulcers, etc.

We gave to the men each a piece of ribbon. We purchased cranberries, mats very neatly made of flags and rushes, some roots, salmon, and I purchased a hat made of splits[356] and strong grass which is made in the fashion which was common in the United States two years ago, [and] also small baskets to hold water, made of splits and straw. For these articles we gave high prices.

Friday, November 22, 1805:

Clark: [There was] a moderate rain all the last night, with wind. A little before daylight the wind, which was from the south-southeast, blew with such violence that we were almost overwhelmed with water blown from the river. This storm did not cease at day but blew with nearly equal violence throughout the whole day, accompanied with rain.

O! How horrible was the day. Waves [were] breaking with great violence against the shore, throwing water into our camp, etc. [We were] all wet and confined to our shelters.

Several Indian men and women crowded about the men's shelters today. We purchased a few wapatoo for which we gave armbands, and

---

355. points: lines woven into blankets to denote their size, from one to four (DeVoto)
356. strips of flexible wood used in making baskets

rings to the old squaw. These roots are equal to the Irish potato and are a tolerable substitute for bread.

The threat which I made to the men of this nation whom I first saw and an indifference towards them is, I am fully convinced, the cause of their conducting themselves with great propriety towards ourselves and party.

Saturday, November 23, 1805:

Clark: [It was] a calm, cloudy morning. [There was] a moderate rain the greater part of the last night.

Captain Lewis branded a tree with his name, date, etc. I marked my name, the day and year on an alder tree, [and] the party all cut the first letters of their names on different trees in the bottom.

In the evening seven Indians of the Clatsop nation came over in a canoe. They brought with them two sea otter skins for which they asked blue beads, etc., and such high prices that we were unable to purchase them without reducing our small stock of merchandise on which we depended for subsistence on our return up this river. Merely to try the Indian who had one of those skins, I offered him my watch, handkerchief, a bunch of red beads, and a dollar of the American coin, all of which he refused and demanded "ti-â-co-mo-shack," which is "chief beads," and the most common blue beads, but few of which we have at this time.

Sunday, November 24, 1805:

Clark: Being now determined to go into winter quarters as soon as possible, as a convenient situation to procure the wild animals of the forest, which must be our dependence for subsisting this winter, we have every reason to believe that the natives have not provisions sufficient for our consumption and, if they had, their prices are so high that it would take ten times as much to purchase their roots and dried fish as we have in our possession.

Most [of the] elk are on the opposite shore, and the greatest numbers of deer are up the river at some distance. Added to this, [is] a convenient situation to the sea coast where we could make salt, and a probability of vessels coming into the mouth of the Columbia (which, the Indians inform us, would return to trade with them in three months) from whom we might procure a fresh supply of Indian trinkets to purchase provisions on our return home. To the above advantages in being near the seacoast, one most striking one occurs to me, i.e., the climate, which must be, from every appearance, much milder than that above the first range of mountains. If this should be the case, it will most certainly be the best situation of our naked party dressed as they are altogether in leather.

Tuesday, November 26, 1805:

Clark: We are now descending to see if a favorable place should offer on the south side to winter, etc.

Thursday, November 28, 1805:

Clark: We are all wet, bedding and stores, having nothing to keep ourselves or stores dry. [Our] lodge [is] nearly worn out and the pieces of sails and tents [are] so full of holes and rotten. [The] wind [is] too high to go either back or forward and we have nothing to eat but a little pounded fish. This is our present situation! Truly disagreeable.

Saturday, November 30, 1805:

Clark: [There was] some rain and hail with intervals of fair weather.

Several men complain of a looseness and griping,[357] which I contribute to the diet [of] pounded fish mixed with salt water. I directed that in the future that the party mix the pounded fish with fresh water.

The squaw gave me a piece of bread made of flour, which she had reserved for her child and carefully kept until this time, [but] which had unfortunately gotten wet and a little sour. This bread I ate with great satisfaction, it being the only mouthful I had tasted for several months past.

My hunters killed three hawks, which we found fat and delicious. They saw three elk but could not get a shot at them. The fowlers[358] killed three black ducks with sharp, white beaks.

The Chinooks, Cathlahmahs, and others in this neighborhood bury their dead in their canoes. We cannot understand them sufficiently to make any inquiries relative to their religious opinions. From their depositing various articles with their dead, [they] believe in a state of future existence.

I walked on the point and observed rose bushes, different species of pine, a species of ash, alder, a species of wild crab laurel, and several species of undergrowth common to this lower part of the Columbia River. The hills on this coast rise high and are thickly covered with

---

357. sharp, spasmodic pains in the bowels

358. wildfowl hunters

lofty pine, many of which are ten and twelve feet through and more than two hundred feet high.

12: Winter, 1805-6

For as to the species of meat, I am not very particular. The flesh of the dog, the horse, the wolf, having from habit become equally familiar with any other, I have learned to think that if the cord be sufficiently strong which binds the soul and body together, it does not so much matter about the materials which compose it.

Captain Meriwether Lewis,
January 5, 1806

Sunday, December 1, 1805:

Clark: The immense seas and waves and this roaring have continued ever since our arrival in the neighborhood of the seacoast, which has been twenty-four days since we arrived in sight of the great Western (for I cannot say Pacific) Ocean, as I have not seen one pacific day since my arrival in its vicinity, and its waters are forming and perpetually break with immense waves on the sands and rocky coasts. [The wave are] tempestuous and horrible.

Tuesday, December 3, 1805:

Clark: I am still unwell and can't eat even the flesh of the elk.

[There was] some rain this evening.

I marked my name and the day of the month and year on a large pine tree immediately on this peninsula:

William Clark December 3rd 1805. By land from the U. States in 1804 & 1805.[359]

Wednesday, December 4, 1805:

Clark: My appetite has returned and I feel much better of my late complaint.

No account of Captain Lewis. I fear some accident has taken place in his craft or party.

---

359. verbatim journal entry

Thursday, December 5, 1805:

Clark: Captain Lewis returned with three men in the canoe and informed me that he thinks that a sufficient number of elk may be procured convenient to a situation on a small river.

Saturday, December 7, 1805:

Clark: [There was] some rain from ten to twelve last night. This morning [was] fair.

[We] had everything put on board the canoes and set out to the place Captain Lewis had viewed and thought well-situated for winter quarters.

After breakfast I delayed about half an hour before York came up, and then proceeded around this bay which I call Meriwether's Bay.[360] We ascended a river[361] three miles to the first point of high land on the west side. This situation is on a rise about thirty feet higher than the high tides, level and thickly covered with lofty pine. This is certainly the most eligible situation for our purposes.

Tuesday, December 10, 1805:

Clark: [It was] a cloudy, rainy morning.

Very early I arose and walked on the shore of the seacoast and picked up several curious shells. I saw Indians walking up and down the beach. One man came to where I was and told me (in English), the "sturgeon was very good." After amusing myself for about an hour on the edge of the raging seas, I returned to the houses.

One of the Indians pointed to a flock of brant. I walked down with my small rifle and killed two at about forty yards distance. On my return to the houses, two small ducks sat at about thirty steps from me. The Indians pointed at the ducks; they were near together. I shot at the ducks and accidentally shot the head of one off and every man came around [and] examined the duck, looked at the gun, the size of the ball, which was one hundred to the pound, and said in their own language [that they] do not understand this kind of musket, etc.

I proceeded on through a heavy rain to the camp at our intended fort [and] found Captain Lewis with all the men out cutting down trees for our huts, etc.

---

360. now Young's Bay (Eide, p. 153)

361. Lewis and Clark River (Eide, p. 153)

Thursday, December 12, 1805:

Clark: In the evening two canoes of Clatsops visited us. They brought with them wapatoo, a black, sweet root. These Indians appear well-disposed.

We gave a medal to the principal chief, named Con-ny-au, or Comowool. I can readily discover that they are close dealers and stickle for a very little. [They] never close a bargain except [when] they think they have the advantage. [They] value blue beads highly.

Friday, December 13, 1805:

Clark: The Clatsops leave us today.

We continued to put up the straight, beautiful balsam pine on our houses.

Tuesday, December 17, 1805:

Clark: All the men [were] at work about the houses. Some [were] chinking, daubing, cutting out doors, etc., etc.

Tuesday, December 24, 1805:

Clark: [There was a] hard rain at different times last night and all this day without intermission. [The] men [were] all employed in finishing their huts and moving into them.

Cuscalah came up in a canoe with his young brother and two squaws. As we had no files to part with, we each returned the present which we had received, which displeased Cuscalah a little. He then offered a woman to each of us, which we also declined accepting. The female party appeared highly disgusted at our refusing to accept of their favors, etc.

The expedition needed to decide where to spend the winter. The captains felt that the winter would be more severe upriver, back at the falls. At the mouth of the Columbia on its north side, they would have to deal with the thieving Chinooks who would charge high prices and empty their dwindling supply of trinkets. On the south side were the friendlier Clatsops and plentiful elk which were larger, easier to kill, and provided skins superior to the deer on the north side. The south side would also allow them to camp closer to the ocean and set up a salt-making site, and would increase the likelihood of meeting a trading vessel and obtain additional provisions.

With only John Shields dissenting, the vote, which included York and Sacagawea, was overwhelming: move to the south side.[362]

The party moved to Fort Clatsop[363] on December 7 and completed the fifty-foot square log stockade on January 1. The fortification consisted of seven cabins (three facing four) with a twenty-foot-wide parade ground between them. [from DeVoto]

Wednesday, December 25, 1805:

Clark: At daylight this morning, we were awakened by the discharge of the firearms of all our party and a salute, shouts, and a song which the whole party joined in under our windows, after which they retired to their rooms. [We] were cheerful all the morning.

After breakfast, we divided our tobacco which amounted to twelve carrots, one-half of which we gave to the men of the party who use tobacco, and to those who do not use it, we made a present of a handkerchief.

The Indians left us in the evening.

All the party [was] snugly fixed in their huts. I received a present of Captain Lewis of a fleece hosiery, shirt, drawers, and socks, a pair of moccasins of Whitehouse, a small Indian basket of Goodrich, two dozen white weasel tails of the Indian woman, and some black root of the Indians before their departure.

Drouillard informed me that he saw a snake pass across the path today.

The day proved showery, wet, and disagreeable. We would have spent this day, the Nativity of Christ, in feasting had we anything either to raise our spirits or even gratify our appetites. Our dinner consisted of poor elk, so much spoiled that we ate it through mere necessity, some spoiled pounded fish, and a few roots.

Ordway: [It is] rainy and wet, disagreeable weather. We all moved into our new fort, which our officers named Fort Clatsop after the name of the Clatsop nation of Indians who live nearest to us. The party saluted our officers by each man firing a gun at their quarters at daybreak this morning. They divided out the last of their tobacco among the men that used it and the rest they gave each a silk handkerchief as a Christmas gift to keep us in remembrance of it as we have no ardent spirits.

But all are in good health which we esteem more than all the ardent spirits in the world. We have nothing to eat but poor elk meat and no salt to season that with, but still keep in good spirits as we expect this to be the last winter that we will have to pass in this way.

---

362. "It was the first time in American history that a black slave had voted, the first time a woman had voted." (Ambrose, *UC*, p. 316)

363. on today's Lewis and Clark River, up from Young's Bay, in Oregon

Thursday, December 26, 1805:

Clark: [It] rained and blew hard last night, [with] some hard thunder. The rain continued as usual all day and [the] wind blew hard from the southeast.

Joseph Field finished a table and two seats for us.

We dried our wet articles and had the blankets fleaed. The fleas are so troublesome that I have slept but little for two nights past, and we have regularly to kill them out of our blankets every day for several past.

Many of the men have their powder wet by the horns being repeatedly wet.

[The] hut smokes very bad.

Friday, December 27, 1805:

Clark: [It] rained last night as usual and the greater part of this day.

The men completed chimneys and bunks today.

In the evening a chief and four men came of the Clatsop nation, chief Comowool.

We sent out Reubin Field and Collins to hunt and ordered Drouillard, Shannon and Labiche to set out early tomorrow to hunt, Joseph Field, Bratton and Gibson to make salt at Point Adams, Willard and Wiser to assist them in carrying the kettles, etc., to the ocean, and all the others to finish the pickets and gates.

[It was] warm weather.

I saw a mosquito which I showed to Captain Lewis.

These Indians gave us a black root they call "shan-na-tâh-que," a kind of licorice which they roast in embers and call "cul-ho-mo," a black berry the size of a cherry and dried which they call "shel-well," all of which they prize highly and make use of as food to live on, for which Captain Lewis gave the chief a cap of sheepskin, and I his son ear bobs, a piece of ribbon, a piece of brass, and two small fishing hooks, of which they were much pleased.

Those roots and berries are grateful to our stomachs as we have nothing to eat but poor elk meat, nearly spoiled. And this accident of spoiled meat is owing to warmth and the repeated rains which cause the meat to taint before we can get it from the woods.

[The] mosquitoes [are] troublesome.

Monday, December 30, 1805:

Ordway: We finished putting up our pickets and gates of the fort. A sentinel [was] placed in the fort to look out for the savages for our safety, etc.

Wednesday, January 1, 1806:

Lewis: This morning I was awakened at an early hour by the discharge of a volley of small arms which were fired by our party in front of our quarters to usher in the new year. This was the only mark of respect which we had it in our power to pay this celebrated day.

Our repast of this day, though better than that of Christmas, consisted principally in the anticipation of the first day of January 1807, when, in the bosom of our friends, we hope to participate in the mirth and hilarity of the day, and when, with the zest given by the recollection of the present, we shall completely, both mentally and corporally, enjoy the repast which the hand of civilization has prepared for us. At present, we were content with eating our boiled elk and wapatoo, and solacing our thirst with our only beverage, pure water.

Two of our hunters who set out this morning returned in the evening having killed two buck elks. They presented Captain Clark and me each a marrow bone and tongue, on which we supped.

[We were] visited today by a few of the Clatsops who brought some roots and berries for the purpose of trading with us.

We were uneasy with respect to two of our men, Willard and Wiser, who were dispatched on the 28th ult.[364] with the salt-makers, and were directed to return immediately. Their not having returned induces us to believe [that] it [is] probable that they have missed their way.

Our fortification being now completed, we issued an order for the more exact and uniform discipline and government of the garrison.

Clark: A list of the names of sundry persons who visit this part of the coast for the purpose of trade, etc., etc., in large vessels, all of which speak the English language, etc., as the Indians inform us:

MooreVisits them in a large, four-masted ship; they expect him in two moons to trade

One-eyed SkellieIn a large ship; long time gone

YouinIn a large ship and they expect him in one moon to trade with them

SwepetonIn a ship; they expect him in three months back to trade

MackeyIn a ship; they expect him back in one or two moons to trade with them

---

364. abbreviation for *ultimo:* in the preceding month

MeshipIn a ship; they expect him [in] two moons to trade

JacksonVisits them in a ship and they expect him back in three months to trade

BalchIn a ship and they expect him in three months to trade

Mr. HaleyVisits them in a ship and they expect him back to trade with them in three moons to trade; he is the favorite of the Indians (from the number of presents he gives) and has the trade principally with all the tribes

WashiltonIn a schooner; they expect him in three months to return and trade with them—a favorite

LemonIn a sloop and they expect him in three moons to trade with them

DavidsonVisits this part of the coast and river in a brig for the purpose of hunting the elk; returns when he pleases; he does not trade any; kills a great many elk, etc., etc.

FallawanIn a ship with guns; he fired on and killed several Indians; he does not trade now and they do not know when he will return; well done

Thursday, January 2, 1806:

Lewis: We are infested with swarms of fleas already in our new habitations. The presumption is therefore strong that we shall not divest ourselves of this intolerably troublesome vermin during our residence here.

Friday, January 3, 1806:

Clark: At 11:00 a.m. we were visited by our near neighbor, chief, or "tiá," Comowool, alias "Conia," and six Clatsops. They brought for sale some roots, berries, and three dogs, [and] also a small quantity of fresh blubber. This blubber, they informed us, they had obtained from their neighbors, the Killamucks, who inhabit the coast to the southeast. Near one of their villages, a whale had recently perished. This blubber the Indians eat and esteem it excellent food.

Our party, from necessity, has been obliged to subsist some length of time on dogs [and] has now become extremely fond of their flesh. It is worthy of remark that while we lived principally on the flesh of this animal, we were much more healthy, strong, and more fleshy than we have been since we left the buffalo country. As for my part, I have not become reconciled to the taste of this animal as yet.

Lewis: I have become so perfectly reconciled to the dog that I think it an agreeable food and would prefer it vastly to lean venison or elk.

Clark: [I] sent Sergeant Gass and George Shannon to the salt-makers, who are on the seacoast to the southwest of us,[365] to enquire after Willard and Wiser who have not yet returned.

Reubin Field, Potts, and Collins, the hunters who set out on the twenty-eighth ult., returned this evening after dark. They reported that they had been about fifteen miles up the river which falls into Meriwether's Bay to the east of us and had hunted the country a considerable distance to the east and had proved unsuccessful, having killed one deer and a few fowl, barely as much as subsisted them. This reminded us of the necessity of taking time by the forelock and keeping out several parties while we have yet a little meat beforehand.

Captain Lewis gave the chief, Comowool, a pair of satin breeches with which he appeared much pleased.

Saturday, January 4, 1806:

Lewis: Comowool and the Clatsops who visited us yesterday left us in the evening. These people, the Chinooks, and others residing in this neighborhood and speaking the same language, have been very friendly to us. They appear to be a mild inoffensive people but will pilfer if they have an opportunity to do so where they conceive themselves not liable to detection.

They are great hagglers in trade and, if they conceive you anxious to purchase, will be a whole day bargaining for a handful of roots. This I should have thought proceeded from their want of knowledge of the comparative value of articles of merchandise and the fear of being cheated, did I not find that they invariably refuse the price first offered them and afterwards very frequently accept a smaller quantity of the same article.

In order to satisfy myself on this subject, I once offered a Chinook my watch, two knives, and a considerable quantity of beads for a small, inferior sea otter skin which I did not much want. He immediately conceived it of great value, and refused to barter except [when] I would double the quantity of beads. The next day, with a great deal of importunity on his part, I received the skin in exchange for a few strands of the same beads he had refused the day before.

I therefore believe this trait in their character proceeds from an avaricious, all-grasping disposition. In this respect, they differ from all Indians I ever became acquainted with, for their dispositions invariably lead them to give whatever they are possessed of, no matter how

---

365. twenty miles south at Tillamook Head, near present-day Seaside, Oregon (Schmidt, p. 140)

useful or valuable, for a bauble which pleases their fancy, without consulting its usefulness or value.

Nothing interesting occurred today, or more so than our wapatoo being all exhausted.

Sunday, January 5, 1806:

Lewis: At 5:00 p.m. Willard and Wiser returned. They had not been lost as we apprehended. They informed us that it was not until the fifth day after leaving the fort that they could find a convenient place for making salt, that they had at length established themselves on the coast about fifteen miles southwest from this, near the lodge of some Killamuck families, that the Indians were very friendly and had given them a considerable quantity of the blubber of a whale which perished on the coast some distance southeast of them.[366]

Part of this blubber they brought with them. It was white and not unlike the fat of pork, though the texture was more spongy and somewhat coarser. I had a part of it cooked and found it very palatable and tender. It resembled the beaver or the dog in flavor. It may appear somewhat extraordinary, though it is a fact that the flesh of the beaver and dog possess a very great affinity in point of flavor.

These lads also informed us that Joseph Field, Bratton, and Gibson (the salt-makers) had, with their assistance, erected a comfortable camp, killed an elk and several deer, and secured a good stock of meat. They commenced the making of salt and found that they could obtain from three quarts to a gallon a day.

They brought with them a specimen of the salt of about a gallon. We found it excellent, fine, strong, and white. This was a great treat to myself and most of the party, having not had any since the twentieth ultimo. I say most of the party, for my friend, Captain Clark, declares it to be a mere matter of indifference with him whether he uses it or not. For myself, I must confess I felt a considerable inconvenience from the want of it.

The want of bread I consider as trivial, provided I get fat meat. For as to the species of meat, I am not very particular. The flesh of the dog, the horse, the wolf, having from habit become equally familiar with any other, I have learned to think that if the cord be sufficiently strong which binds the soul and body together, it does not so much matter about the materials which compose it.

Captain Clark determined this evening to set out early tomorrow with two canoes and twelve men in quest of the whale, or at all events

---

366. near Tillamook Head (Schmidt, p. 141)

to purchase from the Indians a parcel of the blubber. For this purpose, he prepared a small assortment of merchandise to take with him.

Monday, January 6, 1806:

Lewis: Captain Clark set out after an early breakfast with the party in two canoes as had been concerted the last evening. Charbonneau and his Indian woman were also of the party. The Indian woman was very importunate to be permitted to go and was, therefore, indulged. She observed that she had traveled a long way with us to see the great waters, and that now that monstrous fish was also to be seen. She thought it very hard [that] she could not be permitted to see either (she had never yet been to the ocean).

The Clatsops, Chinooks, Killamucks, etc., are very loquacious and inquisitive. They possess good memories and have repeated to us names, capacities of the vessels, etc., of many traders and others who have visited the mouth of this river. They are generally low in stature, proportionately small, rather lighter complected, and much more illy formed than the Indians of the Missouri and those of our frontier. They are generally cheerful but never gay.

With us, their conversation generally turns upon the subjects of trade, smoking, eating, or their women. About the latter, they speak without reserve in their presence, of their every part, and of the most familiar connection. They do not hold the virtue of their women in high estimation, and will even prostitute their wives and daughters for a fishing hook or a strand of beads.

Clark: The Chinook women are lewd and carry on sport publicly.

Lewis: In common with other savage nations, they make their women perform every species of domestic drudgery, but in almost every species of this drudgery, the men also participate. Their women are also compelled to gather roots and assist them in taking fish, which articles form much the greatest part of their subsistence. Notwithstanding the servile manner in which they treat their women, they pay much more respect to their judgment and opinions, in many respects, than most Indian nations. Their women are permitted to speak freely before them, and sometimes appear to command with a tone of authority. They generally consult them in their traffic and act in conformity to their opinions.

I think it may be established as a general maxim that these nations treat their old people and women with most deference and respect where they subsist principally on such articles that they can participate with the men in obtaining them, and that that part of the community is treated with least attention when the act of procuring subsistence devolves entirely on the men in the vigor of life.

It appears to me that nature has been much more deficient in her filial tie than in any other of the strong affections of the human heart and, therefore, think our old men, equally with our women, [are] indebted to civilization for their ease and comfort.

Among the Sioux, Assiniboines, and others on the Missouri who subsist by hunting, it is a custom when a person of either sex becomes so old and infirm that he or she is unable to travel on foot from camp to camp as they roam in search of subsistence, for the children or near relations of such [a] person to leave him or her without compunction or remorse. On these occasions they usually place within their reach a small piece of meat and a platter of water, telling the poor, old, superannuated wretch, for his consolation, that he or she has lived long enough, that it was time they should die and go to their relations who can afford to take care of them much better than they could. I am informed that this custom prevails even among the Hidatsa, Anahaways, and Arikaras when attended by their old people on their hunting excursions.

But in justice to these people, I must observe that it appeared to me at their villages that they provided tolerably well for their aged persons, and several of their feasts appear to have principally for their object a contribution for their aged and infirm persons.

This day I overhauled our merchandise and dried it by the fire, [having] found it all damp. We have not been able to keep anything dry for many days together since we arrived in this neighborhood; the humidity of the air has been so excessively great. Our merchandise is reduced to a mere handful and our comfort during our return the next year much depends on it. It is therefore almost unnecessary to add that we much regret the reduced state of this fund.

Tuesday, January 7, 1806:

Lewis: Last evening Drouillard visited his traps and caught a beaver and an otter. The beaver was large and fat. We have therefore fared sumptuously today. This we consider a great prize for another reason: it being a full-grown beaver, [it] was well-supplied with the materials for making bait with which to catch others.

To prepare beaver bait, the castor,[367] or bark stone, is taken as the base. This is gently pressed out of the bladder-like bag which contains it into a vial of four ounces with a wide mouth. If you have them, you

367. a bitter strong-smelling creamy orange-brown substance consisting of the secretions of the perineal glands of the beaver

will put from four to six stones in a vial of that capacity. To this you will add half a nutmeg, a dozen or fifteen grains of cloves, and thirty grains of cinnamon, finely pulverized. Stir them well together and then add as much ardent spirits to the composition as will reduce it [to] the consistency of mustard prepared for the table. When thus prepared, it resembles mustard precisely to all appearance. When you cannot procure a vial, a bottle made of horn or a tight earthen vessel will answer.

In all cases, it must be excluded from the air or it will soon lose its virtue. It is fit for use immediately [when] it is prepared, but becomes much stronger and better in about four or five days, and will keep for months provided it be perfectly secluded from the air.

When cloves are not to be had, use double the quantity of allspice, and when no spice can be obtained, [use] the bark of the root of sassafras. It appears to me that the principal use of the spices is only to give a variety to the scent of the bark stone and, if so, the mace, vanilla, and other sweet-smelling spices might be employed with equal advantage.

The male beaver has six stones, two of which contain a substance much like finely pulverized bark of a pale yellow color, and not unlike tanner's ooze in smell. These are called the bark stones, or castors. Two others which, like the bark stones, resemble small bladders, contain a pure oil of a strong, rank, disagreeable smell, and not unlike train oil. These are called the oil stones. And [there are] two others of generation.

The bark stones are about two inches in length, the others somewhat smaller. All are of a long oval form and lie in a bunch together between the skin and the root of the tail, beneath or behind the fundament with which they are closely connected and seem to communicate.

The pride of the female lies on the inner side, much like those of the hog. They have no further parts of generation that I can perceive, and therefore believe that, like the birds, they copulate with the extremity of the gut. The female have from two to four young ones at a birth and bring forth once a year only, which usually happens about the latter end of May and beginning of June. At this stage, she is said to drive the male from the lodge, who would otherwise destroy the young.

[We] dried our lodge and had it put away under shelter.

This is the first day during which we have had no rain since we arrived at this place.

Clark: Near the base of a high mountain I found our salt-makers and, with them, Sergeant Gass. George Shannon was out in the woods assisting Joseph Field and Gibson to kill some meat. The salt-makers had made a neat, close camp, convenient to wood, salt water, and the fresh water of the Clatsop River which, at this place, was within one hundred paces of the ocean. They were also situated near four houses of Clatsops and Killamucks who, they informed me, had been very kind and attentive to them.

I hired a young Indian to pilot me to the whale, for which service I gave him a file in hand and promised several other small articles on my return. [I] left Sergeant Gass and one man of my party, Werner, to make salt, and permitted Bratton to accompany me. We proceeded of the round, slippery stones under a high hill which projected into the ocean about four miles farther than the direction of the coast.

After walking for two and a half miles on the stones my guide made a sudden halt, pointed to the top of the mountain, and uttered the word "pe shack," which means bad, and made signs that we could not proceed any farther on the rocks, but must pass over that mountain. I hesitated a moment and viewed this immense mountain, the top of which was obscured in the clouds, and the ascent appeared to be almost perpendicular.

As the small Indian path, along which they had brought immense loads but a few hours before, led up this mountain and appeared to ascend in a sidling direction, I thought more than probable that the ascent might be tolerably easy and therefore proceeded on. I soon found that the path became much worse as I ascended, and at one place we were obliged to support and draw ourselves up by the bushes and roots for nearly one hundred feet, and after about two hours [of] labor and fatigue, we reached the top of this high mountain, from the top of which I looked down with astonishment to behold the height which we had ascended, which appeared to be almost perpendicular.

Here we met fourteen Indians, men and women, loaded with the oil and blubber of the whale. In the face of this tremendous precipice immediately below us, there was a stratum of white earth (which my guide informed me) [that] the neighboring Indians use to paint themselves, and which appears to me to resemble the earth of which the French porcelain is made.

Wednesday, January 8, 1806:

Lewis: The Clatsops, Chinooks, and others inhabiting the coast and country in this neighborhood are excessively fond of smoking tobacco. In the act of smoking, they appear to swallow it as they draw it from the pipe, and for many draughts together, you will not perceive the smoke which they take from the pipe. In the same manner also, they inhale it in their lungs until they become surcharged with this vapor, when they puff it out to a great distance through their nostrils and mouth. I have no doubt the smoke of the tobacco in this manner becomes much more intoxicating and that they do possess themselves of all its virtues in their fullest extent.

They frequently give us sounding proofs of its creating a dismorality of order in the abdomen. Nor are those light matters thought indelicate in either sex, but all take the liberty of obeying the dictates of nature without reserve.

These people do not appear to know the use of spirituous liquors, they never having once asked us for it. I presume therefore that the traders who visit them have never indulged them with the use of it. From whatever cause this may proceed it is a very fortunate occurrence, as well for the natives themselves, as for the quiet and safety of those whites who visit them.

Clark: We arrived on a beautiful sand shore.[368] [We] found only the skeleton of this monster on the sand. The whale was already pillaged of every valuable part by the Killamuck Indians, in the vicinity of whose village it lies on the strand where the waves and tide had driven up and left it. This skeleton measured one hundred five feet.

I returned to the village of five cabins on the creek [and] found the natives busily engaged boiling blubber, which they performed in a large, square wooden trough by means of hot stones. The oil, when extracted, was secured in bladders and the guts of the whale. The blubber, from which the oil was only partially extracted by this process, was laid by in their cabins in large flitches[369] for use. These flitches they usually expose to the fire on a wooden spit until it is pretty well warmed through and then eat it, either alone or with roots of rush dipped in the oil. The Killamucks, although they possessed large quantities of this blubber and oil, were so penurious that they disposed of it with great reluctance and in small quantities only, insomuch that my utmost exertion, aided by the party, with the small stock of merchandise I had taken with me, was not able to procure more blubber than about three hundred pounds, and a few gallons of oil.

Small as this stock is, I prize it highly and thank Providence for directing the whale to us, and think him much more kind to us than he was to Jonah, having sent this monster to be swallowed *by* us instead of swallowing *of* us, as Jonah's did.

Thursday, January 9, 1806:

Lewis: The persons who usually visit the entrance of this river for the purpose of traffic or hunting I believe are either English or

368. Cannon Beach, at the mouth of Ecola Creek (Schmidt, p. 141)
369. like sides of pork

Americans. The Indians informed us that they speak the same language with ourselves, and give us proofs of their veracity by repeating many words of English [such] as musket, powder, shot, knife, file, damned rascal, son of a bitch, etc.

Whether these traders are from Nootka Sound,[370] from some other late establishment on this coast, or immediately from the United States or Great Britain, I am at a loss to determine nor can the Indians inform us. The Indians whom I have asked in what direction the traders go when they depart from hence, or arrive here, always point to the southwest, from which it is presumable that Nootka cannot be their destination.

And as from Indian information, a majority of these traders annually visit them about the beginning of April and remain with them six or seven months, they cannot come immediately from Great Britain or the United States, the distance being too great for them to go and return in the balance of the year. From this circumstance I am sometimes induced to believe that there is some other establishment on the coast of America southwest of this place of which little is but yet known to the world, or it may be perhaps on some island in the Pacific Ocean between the continents of Asia and America to the southwest of us.

This traffic on the part of the whites consists in vending guns (principally old British or American muskets), powder, balls and shot, copper and brass kettles, brass teakettles and coffee pots, blankets from two to three points, scarlet and blue cloth (coarse), plates and strips and sheet copper and brass, large brass wire, knives, beads, tobacco, fishing hooks, buttons, and some other small articles, [and] also a considerable quantity of sailors' clothes, [such] as hats, coats, trousers, and shirts.

For these they receive in return from the natives dressed and undressed elk skins, skins of the sea otter, common otter, beaver, common fox, spuck,[371] and tiger cat, [and] also dried and pounded salmon in baskets, and a kind of biscuit which the natives make of roots, called by them "shappellel."[372]

The natives are extravagantly fond of the most common, cheap, blue and white beads of moderate size, or such that from fifty to seventy will weigh one pennyweight.[373] The blue is usually preferred to the white. These beads constitute the principal circulating medium with all the Indian tribes on this river. For these beads they will dis-

---

370. in southwest British Columbia on the west coast of Vancouver Island

371. infant otter

372. a bread made of roots baked in the sun (Bakeless, p. 291)

373. 1.555 grams, or 0.05 ounces

pose of any article they possess. The beads are strung on strands of a fathom[374] in length, and in that manner sold by the breadth or yard.

Clark: Last night about 10:00, while smoking with the natives, I was alarmed by a loud, shrill voice from the cabins on the opposite side. The Indians all ran immediately across to the village. My guide, who continued with me, made signs that someone's throat was cut. By enquiry, I found that one man, McNeal, was absent.

I immediately sent off Sergeant Nathaniel Pryor and four men in quest of McNeal, who they met coming across the creek in great haste, and informed me that the people were alarmed on the opposite side at something, but what he could not tell, [that] a man had very friendlily invited him to go and eat in his lodge, that the Indian had locked arms with him and went to a lodge in which a woman gave him some blubber, that the man invited him to another lodge to get something better, and [that] the woman held him by the blanket which he had around him. He, not knowing her object, freed himself and was going off when this woman, a Chinook, an old friend of McNeal's, and another ran out and hollered, and his pretended friend disappeared.

I immediately ordered every man to hold themselves in a state of readiness and sent Sergeant Pryor and four men to know the cause of the alarm, which was found to be a premeditated plan of the pretended friend of McNeal to assassinate him for his blanket and what few articles he had about him, which was found out by a Chinook woman who alarmed the men of the village who were with me in time to prevent the horrid act. This man was of another band at some distance, and ran off as soon as he was discovered.

Sunday, January 12, 1806:

Clark: This morning [I] sent out Drouillard and one man to hunt. They returned in the evening, Drouillard having killed seven elk. I scarcely know how we should subsist, I believe but badly, if it were not for the exertions of this excellent hunter. Many others also exert themselves, but not being acquainted with the best method of finding and killing the elk, and no other wild animals are to be found in this quarter, they are unsuccessful in their exertions.

At 2:00 p.m. Sergeant Gass and the men I left to assist the saltmakers in carrying in their meat arrived, [and] also the hunters which I directed to hunt in the point; they killed nothing.

We have heretofore divided the meat, when first killed, among the four messes, into which we have divided our party, leaving to each the care of preserving and distribution of using it. But we find that they

---

374. six feet

make such prodigal use of it when they happen to have a tolerable stock on hand that we are determined to adopt a different system with our present stock of seven elk. This is to jerk it and issue it to them in small quantities.

Monday, January 13, 1806:

Lewis: This evening we exhausted the last of our candles but fortunately [we] had taken the precaution to bring with us molds and wick, by means of which and some elk tallow in our possession, we do not yet consider ourselves destitute of this necessary article. The elk we have killed have a very small portion of tallow.

Tuesday, January 14, 1806:

Lewis: From the best estimate we were able to make as we descended the Columbia, we conceived that the natives inhabiting that noble stream, for some miles above the Great Falls to the Grand Rapids inclusive, annually prepare about thirty thousand pounds of pounded salmon for market.

But whether this fish is an article of commerce with the whites or is exclusively sold to and consumed by the natives of the seacoast, we are at a loss to determine. The first of these positions I am disposed to credit most, but still I must confess that I cannot imagine what the white merchant's object can be in purchasing this fish, or where they dispose of it. And on the other hand, the Indians in this neighborhood, as well as the Skillutes, have an abundance of dried salmon, which they take in the creeks and inlets, and I have never seen any of this pounded fish in their lodges which, I presume, would have been the case if they purchased this pounded fish for their own consumption.

The Indians who prepared this dried and pounded fish informed us that it was to trade with the whites, and showed us many articles of European manufacture which they obtained for it. It is true [that] they obtain these articles principally for their fish, but they trade with the Skillutes for them and not immediately with the whites. The intermediate merchants and carriers, the Skillutes, may possibly consume a part of this fish themselves and dispose of the balance of it to the natives of the seacoast, and from them obtain such articles as they again trade with the whites.

Thursday, January 16, 1806:

Lewis: We have plenty of elk beef for the present, and a little salt, our houses [are] dry and comfortable and, having made up our minds to remain until the first of April, everyone appears content with his situation and his fare.

It is true that we could even travel now on our return as far as the timbered country reaches, or to the falls of the river, but farther it would be madness for us to attempt to proceed until April as the Indians inform us that the snows lie knee deep in the plains of Columbia during the winter, and in these plains we could scarcely get as much fuel of any kind as would cook our provisions as we descended the river. And even were we happily over these plains and again in the woody country at the foot of the Rocky Mountains, we could not possibly pass that immense barrier of mountains, on which the snows lie in winter to the depth, in many places, of twenty feet.

In short, the Indians inform us that they are impracticable until about the first of June, at which time even there is an abundance of snow [and] but a scanty subsistence may be obtained for the horses. We should not, therefore, forward ourselves on our homeward journey by reaching the Rocky Mountains earlier than the first of June, which we can easily effect by setting out from hence on the first of April.

Friday, January 17, 1806:

Whitehouse: [It] continued stormy all last night and this morning [is] wet and rainy.

Sunday, January 19, 1806:

Whitehouse: This morning we had moderate showers of rain.

Ordway: The men in the fort are employed dressing elk skins for moccasins, etc.

Monday, January 20, 1806:

Lewis: [We were] visited this morning by three Clatsops who remained with us all day. The object of their visit was merely to smoke the pipe.

On the morning of the eighteenth, we issued six pounds of jerked elk per man. This evening, the sergeant reported that it was all exhausted. The six pounds have therefore lasted two days and a half only. At this rate, our seven elk will last us only three days longer, yet no one seems much concerned about the state of the stores. So much for habit. We have lately so frequently had our stock of provisions reduced to a minimum and sometimes [have] taken a small touch of fasting, that three days full allowance excites no concern. In these cases, our skill as hunters affords us some consolation, for if there is any game of any description in our neighborhood, we can track it up and kill it. Most of the party have become very expert with the rifle.

The Indians who visited us today understood us sufficiently to inform us that the whites did not barter for the pounded fish, that it was purchased and consumed by the Clatsops, Chinooks, Cathlahmahs, and Skillutes.

The native roots, which furnish a considerable proportion of the subsistence of the Indians in our neighborhood, are those of a species of thistle, fern, and rush, the licorice, and a small cylindrical root, the top of which I have not yet seen. This last resembles the sweet potato very much in its flavor and consistency.

Whitehouse: [It was] wet and rainy weather during the whole of this day.

Nothing material occurred worth mentioning.

Thursday, January 23, 1806:

Lewis: This morning [I] dispatched Howard and Werner to the camp of the salt-makers for a supply of salt.

The men of the garrison are still busily employed in dressing elk skins for clothing. They find great difficulty for the want of brains.[375] We have not soap to supply the deficiency, nor can we procure ashes to make the lye. None of the pines which we use for fuel affords any ashes. Extraordinary as it may seem, the green wood is consumed without leaving the residuum of a particle of ashes.

Friday, January 24, 1806:

Lewis: Drouillard and Baptiste Lepage returned this morning in a large canoe with Comowool and six Clatsops. They brought two deer and the flesh of three elk and one elk skin, having given the flesh of one other elk, which they killed, and three elk skins to the Indians as the price of their assistance in transporting the balance of the meat to the fort. These elk and deer were killed near Point Adams and the Indians carried them on their backs about six miles before the waves were sufficiently low to permit their being taken on board their canoes. The Indians remained with us all day.

The Indians witnessed Drouillard's shooting [of] some of those elk, which has given them a very exalted opinion of us as marksmen and the superior excellence of our rifles compared with their guns. This may probably be of service to us as it will deter them from any acts of hostility if they have ever meditated any such. My air gun also

375. brains of animals were used in the tanning process, rubbing them into the flesh side to make the pelt soft and pliable (DeVoto)

astonishes them very much. They cannot comprehend its shooting so often and without powder and think that it is "great medicine" which comprehends everything that is to them incomprehensible.

Monday, January 27, 1806:

Lewis: Goodrich has recovered from the Lues venera which he contracted from an amorous contact with a Chinook damsel. I cured him, as I did Gibson last winter, by the use of mercury. I cannot learn that the Indians have any simples which are sovereign specifics in the cure of this disease, and indeed I doubt very much whether any of them have any means of effecting a perfect cure. When once this disorder is contracted by them, it continues with them during life but always ends in decrepitude, death, or premature old age, though from the use of certain simples, together with their diet, they support this disorder with but little inconvenience for many years, and even enjoy a tolerable share of health, particularly so among the Chippewas, who I believe to be better skilled in the use of those simples than any nation of savages in North America.

The Chippewas use a decoction of the lobelia[376] and that of a species of sumac common to the Atlantic states and to this country near and on the western side of the Rocky Mountains. This is the smallest species of the sumac, readily distinguished by its winged rib, or common footstalk, which supports its oppositely pinnate leaves. These decoctions are drunk freely and without limitation. The same decoctions are used in cases of the gonorrhea, and are efficacious and sovereign. Notwithstanding that this disorder does exist among the Indians on the Columbia, yet it is witnessed in but few individuals, at least [in] the males who are always sufficiently exposed to the observations or inspection of the physician. In my whole route down this river, I did not see more than two or three with gonorrhea, and about double that number with the pox.

Wednesday, January 29, 1806:

Lewis: Nothing worthy of notice occurred today.

Our fare is the flesh of lean elk boiled with pure water and a little salt. The whale blubber, which we have used very sparingly, is now exhausted. On this food I do not feel strong, but enjoy the most perfect health. A keen appetite supplies, in a great degree, the want of more luxurious sauces or dishes, and still renders my ordinary meals not uninteresting to me, for I find myself sometimes enquiring of the cook whether dinner or breakfast is ready.

---

376. the leaves and tops of Indian tobacco

Saturday, February 1, 1806:

Lewis: They have but few axes among them, and the only tool usually employed in felling the trees, forming a canoe, or carving, etc., is a chisel formed of an old file about an inch or an inch and a half broad. This chisel has, sometimes, a large block of wood for a handle. They grasp the chisel just below the block with the right hand holding the edge down, while with the left they take hold of the top of the block and strike backhanded against the wood with the edge of the chisel.

A person would suppose that the forming of a large canoe with an instrument like this was the work of several years, but these people make them in a few weeks. They prize their canoes very highly. We have been anxious to obtain some of them for our journey up the river, but have not been able to obtain one as yet from the natives in this neighborhood.

Some of the large canoes are upwards of fifty feet long and will carry from eight to ten thousand pounds or from twenty to thirty persons, and some of them, particularly on the seacoast, are waxed, painted, and ornamented with curious images at [the] bow and stern. These images sometimes rise to the height of five feet.

Today we opened and examined all our ammunition, which had been secured in leaden canisters. We found twenty-seven of the best rifle powder, four of common rifle, three of glazed, and one of the musket powder in good order, perfectly as dry as when first put in the canisters, although the whole of it, from various accidents, has been for hours under the water. These canisters contain four pounds of powder each and eight of lead. Had it not have been for that happy expedient, which I devised, of securing the powder by means of the lead, we should not have had a single charge of powder at this time.

Three of the canisters which had been accidentally bruised and cracked, one of which was carelessly stopped, and a fifth that had been penetrated with a nail, were a little damaged. These we gave to the men to make dry. However, exclusive of those five, we have an abundant stock to last us back, and we always take care to put a proportion of it in each canoe to the end that should one canoe or more be lost, we should still not be entirely bereft of ammunition, which is now our only hope for subsistence and defense in a route of four thousand miles through a country exclusively inhabited by savages.

Tuesday, February 4, 1806:

Lewis: There are several species of fir in this neighborhood which I shall describe as well as my slender botanical skill will enable me and, for the convenience of comparison with each other, shall number them.

(No. 1) A species which grows to immense size, very commonly twenty-seven feet in the girth six feet above the surface of the earth and, in several instances, we have found them as much as thirty-six feet in the girth, or twelve feet [in] diameter, perfectly solid and entire. They frequently rise to the height of two hundred thirty feet, and one hundred and twenty or thirty of that height without a limb. This timber is white and soft throughout, and rives[377] better than any other species we have tried. The bark scales off in irregular, rounded flakes and is of a reddish-brown color, particularly of the younger growth. The stem of this tree is simple branching, ascending, not very diffuse, and proliferous.

The leaf of this tree is acerose,[378] one-tenth of an inch in width and three-fourths of an inch in length [and] is firm, stiff, and acuminate.[379] They are triangular, a little declining, thickly scattered on all sides of the bough, but respect the three upper sides only, and are also sessile, growing from little triangular pedestals of soft, spongy, elastic bark. At the junction of the boughs the bud-scales continued to encircle their respective twigs for several years. At least three years is common, and I have counted as many as the growth of four years beyond these scales. This tree affords but little resin. Its cone I have not yet had an opportunity to discover, although I have sought it frequently. The trees of this kind which we have felled have had no cones on them.[380]

Wednesday, February 5, 1806:

Lewis: Fir No. 2 is next in dignity in point of size. It is much the most common species. It may be said to constitute at least one-half of the timber in this neighborhood. It appears to be of the spruce kind. It rises to the height of one hundred sixty to one hundred eighty feet very commonly, and is from four to six feet in diameter, very straight, round, and regularly tapering. The bark is thin, of a dark color, and much divided with small longitudinal interstices. That of the boughs and young trees is somewhat smooth, but not so much so as the balsam fir nor that of the white pine of our country. The wood is white throughout and rather soft, but very tough, and difficult to rive. The trunk of this tree is a simple, branching, diffused stem, and not prolif-

377. splits
378. shaped like a needle
379. tapering to a slender point
380. the Sitka spruce (DeVoto)

erous as the pines and firs usually are but, like most other trees, it puts forth buds from the sides of the small boughs as well as their extremities. The stem usually terminates in a very slender, pointed top, like the cedar.

The leaves are petiolate,[381] the footstalk small, short, and oppressed, acerose rather more than half a line in width, and very unequal in length, the greatest length being little more than half an inch while others, intermixed on every part of the bough, are not more than one-fourth [of an inch] in length. [The leaves are] flat, with a small, longitudinal channel in the upper disk, which is of a deep green and glossy, while the under disk is of a whitish-green only. [They are] two-ranked, obtusely pointed, soft, and flexible. This tree affords but little resin. The cone is remarkably small, not larger than the end of a man's thumb, soft, flexible, and of an ovate form, produced at the ends of the small twigs.[382]

Friday, February 7, 1806:

Lewis: This evening we had what I call an excellent supper. It consisted of a marrow bone apiece and a brisket of boiled elk that had the appearance of a little fat on it. This, for Fort Clatsop, is living in high style.

In this neighborhood I observe the honeysuckle, common in our country. I first met with it on the waters of the Kooskooskee near the Nez Percé nation, and again below the Grand Rapids in the Columbian valley on tide-water.

The elder, also common to our country, grows in great abundance in the rich woodlands on this side of the Rocky Mountains, though it differs here in the color of its berry, this being of a pale sky blue, while that of the United States is a deep purple.

The seven bark, or nine bark as it is called in the United States, is also common in this quarter.

There is a species of huckleberry common to the piney lands from the commencement of the Columbian valley to the seacoast. It rises to the height of six or eight feet [and] is a simple, branching, somewhat diffuse stem. The main body, or trunk, is cylindrical and of a dark brown, while the collateral branches are green, smooth, square, and put forth a number of alternate branches of the same color, and form from the two horizontal sides only. The fruit is a small, deep purple berry, which the natives inform us is very good. The leaf is thin, of a pale green, and small, being three-fourths of an inch in length and

381. having a stalk or slender stem

382. the mountain hemlock (DeVoto)

three-eighths [of an inch] in width, oval, terminating more acutely at the apex than near the insertion of the footstalk which is at the base, veined, nearly entirely serrate but so slightly so that it is scarcely perceptible. [The] footstalks [are] short and their position with respect to each other is alternate and two-ranked, proceeding from the horizontal sides of the bough only.

The smallpox has destroyed a great number of the natives in this quarter. It prevailed about four years since among the Clatsops and destroyed several hundred of them. Four of their chiefs fell victim to its ravages. Those Clatsops are deposited in their canoes on the bay a few miles below us. I think the late ravages of the smallpox may well account for the number of remains of villages which we find deserted on the river and seacoast in this quarter.

Wednesday, February 12, 1806:

Lewis: This morning we were visited by a Clatsop man who brought with him three dogs as a remuneration for the elk which he and [the] nation had stolen from us some little time since. However, the dogs took alarm and ran off. We suffered him to remain in the fort all night.

Thursday, February 13, 1806:

Lewis: Yesterday we completed the operation of drying the meat and think we have a sufficient stock to last us this month. The Indians inform us that we shall have [a] great abundance of a small fish in March which, from their description, must be the herring. These people have also informed us that one Captain More, who sometimes touches at this place and trades with the natives of this coast, had on board of his vessel three cows, and that when he left them he continued his course along the northwest coast.

I think this [is] strong circumstantial proof that there is a settlement of white persons at Nootka Sound or some point to the northwest of us on the coast.

Friday, February 14, 1806:

Clark: I completed a map of the country through which we have been passing from the Mississippi at the mouth of [the] Missouri to this place. In the map, the Missouri, Jefferson's River, the southeast branch of the Columbia, or Lewis's River, [the] Kooskooskee, and [the] Columbia from the entrance of the southeast fork to the Pacific Ocean, as well as a part of Clark's River and our track across the Rocky Mountains are laid down by celestial observations and survey.

The rivers are also connected at their sources with other rivers, agreeably to the information of the natives, and the most probable conjecture arising from their capacities and the relative positions of their respective entrances which last have, with but few exceptions, been established by celestial observations.

We now discover that we have found the most practicable and navigable passage across the continent of North America. It is that which we have traveled, with the exception of that part of our route from the foot of the falls of the Missouri, or in the neighborhood of the entrance of the Rocky Mountains until we arrive on Clark's River at the entrance of Traveller's Rest Creek.

The distance between those two points would be traveled more advantageously by land, as the navigation of the Missouri above the falls is crooked, laborious, and five hundred twenty-one miles distant by which no advantage is gained, as the route which we are compelled to travel by land from the source of Jefferson's River to the entrance of Traveller's Rest Creek is two hundred twenty miles, being farther by about six hundred miles than that from the falls of the Missouri to the last mentioned point (Traveller's Rest Creek), and a much worse route if Indian information is to be relied on, which is from the Shoshone, or Snake, Indians and the Flatheads of the Columbia west of the Rocky Mountains.

From the same information, Clark's River, like that of the southeast branch of the Columbia which heads with Jefferson's and Madison's Rivers, cannot be navigated through the Rocky Mountains in consequence of falls and rapids, and as a confirmation of the fact, we discovered that there were no salmon in Clark's River, which is not the case in the southeast branch of the Columbia, although it is not navigable. Added to this, the Indians of different quarters further inform us that Clark's River runs in the direction of the Rocky Mountains for a great distance to the north before it discharges itself into the Columbia River.

From the same information, the Columbia, from the entrance of the southeast branch to the entrance of Clark's River, is obstructed with a great number of difficult and dangerous rapids (and the place [where] Clark's River comes out of the Rocky Mountains is a tremendous falls, etc., which there is no possibility of passing the mountains, either by land or water).

Considering, therefore, the dangers and difficulties attending the navigation of the Columbia in this part, as well as the circuitous and distant route formed by itself and that of Clark's River, we conceive, that even admitting that Clark's River, contrary to information, to be as navigable as the Columbia below its entrance, that the tract by land over the Rocky Mountains usually traveled by the natives, from the entrance of Traveller's Rest Creek to the forks of the Kooskooskee, is preferable, the same being a distance of one hundred eighty-four miles.

The inference therefore deduced from these premises is that the best and most practicable route across the continent is by way of the Missouri to the Falls, thence to Clark's River at the entrance of Traveller's Rest Creek, from thence up Traveller's Rest Creek to the forks, from whence you pursue a range of mountains which divides the waters of the two forks of this creek, and which still continues its westwardly course on the mountains, which divides the waters of the two forks of the Kooskooskee River to their junction, from thence to descend this river to the Columbia, and down the latter to the Pacific Ocean.

There is a large river[383] which falls into the Columbia on its south side, at what point we could not learn, which passes through those extensive Columbia plains from the southeast and, as the Indians inform us, heads in the mountains south of the head of Jefferson's River and at no great distance from the Spanish settlement, Multnomah, and that that fork, which heads with the Yellowstone River and waters of the Missouri, passes through those extensive plains in which there is no wood, and the river [is] crowded with rapids and falls, many of which are impassable.

The other, or westerly, fork passes near a range of mountains and is the fork on which live great numbers of Indian bands of the Shoshone, or Snake, Indians. This fork most probably heads with North River or the waters of California. This river may afford a practicable land communication with New Mexico by means of its western fork. This river cannot be navigable as an impracticable rapids is within one mile of its entrance into the Columbia, and we are fully persuaded that a route by this river, if practicable at all, would lengthen the distance greatly and encounter the same difficulties in passing the Rocky Mountains with the route by way of Traveller's Rest Creek and Clark's River.

Saturday, February 15, 1806:

Lewis: The quadrupeds of this country, from the Rocky Mountains to the Pacific Ocean, are first, the domestic animals, consisting of the horse and the dog only, [and] secondly, the native wild animals, consisting of the brown, white, or grizzly bear (which I believe to be [of] the same family with a merely accidental difference in point of

383. the Willamette

color), the black bear, the common red deer, the black-tailed fallow deer, the mule deer, elk, the large brown wolf, the small wolf of the plains, the large wolf of the plains, the tiger cat, the common red fox, black fox or fisher, silver fox, large red fox of the plains, small fox of the plains or kit fox, antelope, sheep, beaver, common otter, sea otter, mink, spuck, seal, raccoon, large grey squirrel, small brown squirrel, small grey squirrel, ground squirrel, sewelel, blaireau, rat, mouse, mole, panther, hare, rabbit, and polecat or skunk, all of which shall be severally noticed in the order in which they occur, as well as such others as I learn do exist and which have not been here recapitulated.

The horse is confined principally to the nations inhabiting the great plains of the Columbia, extending from latitude forty degrees to fifty degrees north, and occupying the tract of country lying between the Rocky Mountains and a range of mountains which pass the Columbia River about the Great Falls, or from longitude one hundred sixteen to one hundred twenty-one west.

In this extensive tract of principally untimbered country, so far as we have learned, the following natives reside (viz.) the Shoshone or Snake Indians, the Nez Percé, Sokulks, Cutssahnims, Chymnapums, Echelutes, Eneshuh, and Chilluckkittequaws, all of whom enjoy the benefit of that docile, generous, and valuable animal, the horse and all of them, except the three last, have immense numbers of them.

Their horses appear to be of an excellent race. They are lofty, elegantly formed, active, and durable. In short, many of them look like the fine English coursers and would make a figure in any country. Some of these horses are pied,[384] with large spots of white irregularly scattered and intermixed with the black, brown, bay, or some other dark color, but much the larger portion are of a uniform color with stars, snips,[385] and white feet, or in this respect, marked much like our best blooded horses in Virginia, which they resemble as well in fleetness and bottom, as in form and colors.

The natives suffer them to run at large in the plains, the grass of which furnishes them with the only subsistence, their masters taking no trouble to lay in a winter's store for them, but they even keep fat, if not much used, on the dry grass of the plains during winter. No rain scarcely ever falls in these plains, and the grass is short and but thin. The natives, except those near the Rocky Mountains, appear to take no pains in selecting their male horses from which they breed. In short, those of that description which I have noticed appeared the most indifferent.

384. patchy in color

385. white or light marks

Whether the horse was originally a native of this country or not, it is out of my power to determine as we cannot understand the language of the natives sufficiently to ask the question. At all events, the country and climate appear well-adapted to this animal. Horses are said to be found wild in many parts of this extensive plain country.

The several tribes of Shoshones who reside towards Mexico on the waters of the Multnomah River,[386] or particularly one of them called "Shâ-bo-bó-ah," have also a great number of mules which, among the Indians, I find are much more highly prized than horses. An elegant horse may be purchased of the natives in this country for a few beads or other paltry trinkets which, in the United States, would not cost more than one or two dollars. This abundance and cheapness of horses will be extremely advantageous to those who may hereafter attempt the fur trade to the East Indies by way of the Columbia River and the Pacific Ocean. The mules in the possession of the Indians are principally stolen from the Spaniards in Mexico. They appear to be large and fine, such as we have seen. Among the Shoshones of the upper part of the southeast fork of the Columbia, we saw several horses with Spanish brands on them which, we supposed, had been stolen from the inhabitants of Mexico.

Thursday, February 20, 1806:

Lewis: This forenoon we were visited by "Tâh-cum," a principal chief of the Chinooks, and twenty-five men of his nation. We had never seen this chief before. He is a good-looking man of about fifty years of age, rather larger in stature than most of his nation. As he came on a friendly visit, we gave himself and party something to eat and plied them plentifully with smoke. We gave this chief a small medal with which he seemed much gratified.

In the evening, at sunset, we desired them to depart, as is our custom, and closed our gates. We never suffer parties of such number to remain within the fort all night, for notwithstanding their apparent friendly disposition, their great avarice and hope of plunder might induce them to be treacherous.

At all events, we determined always to be on our guard as much as the nature of our situation will permit us, and never place ourselves at the mercy of any savages. We well know that the treachery of the aborigines of America, and the too great confidence of our countrymen in their sincerity and friendship has caused the destruction of many hundreds of us. So long have our men been accustomed to a friendly intercourse with the natives that we find it difficult to impress

---

386. non-existent (DeVoto)

on their minds the necessity of always being on their guard with respect to them. This confidence on our part we know to be the effect of a series of uninterrupted friendly intercourses, but the well-known treachery of the natives by no means entitles them to such confidence and we must check its growth in our own minds, as well as those of our men, by recollecting ourselves, and repeating to our men, that our preservation depends on never losing sight of this trait in their character, and being always prepared to meet it in whatever shape it may present itself.

Saturday, February 22, 1806:

Lewis: We were visited today by two Clatsop women and two boys who brought a parcel of excellent hats made of cedar bark and ornamented with beargrass.[387] Two of these hats had been made by measures which Captain Clark and I had given one of the women some time since with a request to make each of us a hat. They fit us very well and are in the form we desired them. We purchased all their hats and distributed them among the party. The woodwork and sculpture of these people, as well as these hats and their waterproof baskets, evince an ingenuity by no means common among the aborigines of America.

In the evening they returned to their village and Drouillard accompanied them in their canoe in order to get the dogs which the Clatsops have agreed to give in payment for the elk they stole from us some weeks since. These women informed us that the small fish began to run, which we suppose to be herring from their description. They also informed us that their chief, Conia, or Comowool, had gone up the Columbia to the valley in order to purchase wapatoo, a part of which he intended trading with us on his return.

One of our canoes broke the cord by which it was attached and was going off with the tide this evening. We sent Sergeant Pryor and a party after her who recovered and brought her back.

Our sick, consisting of Gibson, Bratton, Sergeant Ordway, Willard, and McNeal, are all on the recovery. We have not had as many sick at any one time since we left Wood River. The general complaint seems to be colds and fevers, something I believe of the influenza.

Sunday, February 23, 1806:

Lewis: The sea otter is found on the seacoast and in the salt water. This animal, when fully grown, is as large as a common mastiff dog. The ears and eyes are remarkably small, particularly the former,

---

387. of the lily family, with foliage resembling coarse blades of grass

which is not an inch in length, thick, fleshy, and pointed [and] covered with short hair. The tail is about ten inches in length, thick where it joins the body, and tapering to a very sharp point. In common with the body, it is covered with a deep fur; particularly on the under part the fur is not so long. The legs are remarkably short, and the feet, which have five toes each, are broad, large, and webbed. The legs are covered with fur and the feet with short hair. The body of this animal is long and nearly of the same thickness throughout. From the extremity of the tail to that of the nose, they will measure five feet or upwards. The color is a uniform dark brown and when in good order and season, perfectly black and glossy.

It is the richest and, I think, the most delicious fur in the world; at least I cannot form an idea of any more so. It is deep, thick, silky in the extreme, and strong. The inner part of the fur, when opened, is lighter than the surface in its natural position. There are some fine, black, and shining hairs intermixed with the fur which are rather longer and add much to its beauty. The nose, about the eyes, ears, and forehead in some of these otters is of a lighter color, sometimes a light brown.

Those parts in the young suckling otter of this species are sometimes of a cream-colored white, but always much lighter than the other parts. The fur of the infant otter is much inferior in point of color and texture to that of the full-grown otter, or even after it has been weaned. There is so great a difference that I have for some time supposed it a different animal. The Indians call the infant otter "spuck," and the full-grown, or such as had obtained a coat of good fur, "E-luck-ke." This still further confirmed the opinion of their being [a] distinct species, but I have since learned that the spuck is the young otter. The color of the neck, body, legs, and tail is a dark, lead brown.

Tuesday, February 25, 1806:

Clark: I purchased of the Clatsops this morning about half a bushel of small fish which they had caught about forty miles up the Columbia in their scooping nets. The rays of the fins are bony but not sharp, though somewhat pointed. The small fin on the back next to the tail has no rays of bone, being a thin, membranous pedicle. The fins next to the gills have eleven rays each. Those of the abdomen have eight each, those of the pinna ani are twenty and two half-formed in front, [and] that of the back has eleven rays. All the fins are of a white color.

The back is of a bluish dusky color, and that of the lower part of the sides and belly is of a silvery white. [There are] no spots on any part. The first gills next behind the eye are of a bluish cast, and the second of a light gold color, nearly white. The under jaw exceeds the upper, and the mouth opens to a great extent, folding like that of a herring. It has no teeth. The abdomen is obtuse and smooth, in this differing from the herring, shad, anchovy, etc., of the Malacapterygious order and class Clupea to which, however, I think it [is] more nearly allied than to any other, although it has not their acute and serrate abdomen, and the under jaw exceeding the upper. The scales of this little fish are so small and thin that without minute inspection, you would suppose they had none. They are filled with roe of a pure white color, and have scarcely any perceptible alimentary duct.

I found them best when cooked in Indian style, which is by roasting a number of them together on a wooden spit without any previous preparation whatever. They are so fat that they require no additional sauce, and I think them superior to any fish I have ever tasted, even more delicate and luscious than the white fish of the lakes which have heretofore formed my standard of excellence among fishes. I have heard the fresh anchovy much extolled, but I hope I shall be pardoned for believing this quite as good. The bones are so soft and fine that they form no obstruction in eating this fish.[388]

388. the candlefish, or eulachon (DeVoto)

13: March, 1806

The most remarkable trait in their physiognomy is the peculiar flatness and width of [the] *forehead which they artificially obtain by compressing the head between two boards while in a state of infancy, and from which it never afterwards perfectly recovers.*

Captain Meriwether Lewis,
March 19, 1806

Monday, March 3, 1806:

Lewis: No movement of the party today [was] worthy of notice. Everything moves on in the old way and we are counting the days which separate us from the first of April and which bind us to Fort Clatsop.

Tuesday, March 11, 1806:

Clark: The mule deer we have never found except in rough country. They prefer the open grounds and are seldom found in the woodlands near the river. When they are met with in the woodlands or river bottoms and pursued, they immediately run to the hills or open country as the elk do. The contrary happens with the common deer.

There are several differences between the mule and common deer, as well as in form as in habits. They are fully a third larger in general, and the male is particularly large. [I] think there is somewhat greater disparity of size between the male and the female of this species than there is between the male and female fallow deer. I am convinced I have seen a buck of this species twice the volume of a buck of the common deer.

The ears are peculiarly large. I measured those of a large buck which I found to be eleven inches long and three and a half [inches] in width at the widest part. They are not so delicately formed.

Their hair in winter is thicker, longer, and of a much darker grey. In summer, the hair is still coarser, longer, and of a paler red, more like that of the elk. In winter, they also have a considerable quantity of very fine wool intermixed with the hair and lying next to the skin, as the antelope has. The long hair which grows on the outer side of the first joint of the hind legs, and which in the common deer does not usually occupy more than two inches, in them occupies from six to eight.

Their horns also differ. Those in the common deer consist of two main beams gradually diminishing as the points proceed from it. With the mule deer, the horns consist of two beams which, at the distance of four or six inches from the head, divide themselves into two equal branches which again either divide into two other equal branches or terminate in a smaller and two equal ones, having either two, four, or six points on a beam. The horn is not so rough about the base as the common deer, and is invariably of a much darker color.

The most striking difference of all is the white rump and tail. From the root of the tail as a center, there is a circular spot, perfectly white, of about three and a half inches radius which occupies a part of the rump and the extremities of buttocks and joins the white of the belly underneath. The tail, which is usually from eight to nine inches long, for the first four or five inches from its upper extremity is covered with short, white hairs, much shorter, indeed, than those hairs of the body. From hence, for about one inch farther, the hair is still white but gradually becomes longer. The tail then terminates in a tissue of black hair of about three inches long.

From this black hair of the tail they have obtained, among the French engagés, the appellation of the "black-tailed deer," but this I conceive [is] by no means characteristic of the animal as much the larger portion of the tail is white. The ears and the tail of this animal, when compared with those of the common deer, so well comported with those of the mule when compared with the horse, that we have, by way of distinction, adapted the appellation of the mule deer which I think much more appropriate.

On the inner corner of each eye there is a drain (like the elk), or large receptacle which seems to answer as a drain to the eye, which gives it the appearance of weeping. This, in the common deer of the Atlantic states, is scarcely perceptible but becomes more conspicuous in the fallow deer, and still more so in the elk. This receptacle in the elk is larger than any of the Pecora order with which I am acquainted.

Saturday, March 15, 1806:

Lewis: This morning at 11:00 the hunters arrived, having killed four elk only. Labiche, it seems, was the only hunter who fell in with elk, and having by some accident lost the fore sight of his gun, shot a great number of times but killed only the number mentioned. As the elk were scattered, we sent two parties for them. They returned in the evening with four skins and the flesh of three elk, that of one of them having become putrid from the liver and pluck[389] having been carelessly left in the animal all night.

We were visited this afternoon by Delashelwilt, a Chinook chief, his wife, and six women of his nation which the old bawd, his wife, had brought for market. This was the same party that had communicated the venereal to so many of our party in November last, and of which they have finally recovered. I therefore gave the men a particular charge with respect to them, which they promised me to observe.

Late this evening we were also visited by Catel, a Clatsop man, and his family. He brought a canoe and a sea otter skin for sale, neither of which we purchased this evening.

The Clatsops who had brought a canoe for sale last evening left us early this morning.

Sunday, March 16, 1806:

Lewis: Drouillard and party did not return from the Clatsops this evening as we expected. We suppose he was detained by the hard winds of today.

The Indians remained with us all day but would not dispose of their canoes at a price which it was in our power to give consistently with the state of our stock of merchandise.

Two handkerchiefs would now contain all the small articles of merchandise which we possess. The balance of the stock consists of six blue robes, one scarlet do, one uniform, an artillerist's coat and hat, five robes made of our large flag, and a few old cloths trimmed with ribbon. On this stock we have wholly to depend for the purchase of horses and such portion of our subsistence from the Indians as it will be in our powers to obtain.

Monday, March 17, 1806:

Lewis: Old Delashelwilt and his women still remain. They have formed a camp near the fort and seem to be determined to lay close siege to us but, I believe, notwithstanding every effort of their winning graces, the men have preserved their constancy to the vow of celibacy which they made on this occasion to Captain Clark and myself.

We have had our pirogues prepared for our departure and shall set out as soon as the weather will permit. The weather is so precarious that we fear by waiting until the first of April that we might be detained several days longer before we could get from this to the Cathlahmahs, as it must be calm or we cannot accomplish that part of our route.

---

389. the heart, liver, windpipe, and lungs of a slaughtered animal

Drouillard returned late this evening from the Cathlahmahs with our canoe which Sergeant Pryor had left some days since, and also a canoe which he had purchased from those people. For this canoe he gave my uniform laced coat and nearly half a carrot of tobacco. It seems that nothing except this coat would induce them to dispose of a canoe which, in their mode of traffic, is an article of the greatest value except a wife, with whom it is equal, and is generally given in exchange to the father for his daughter.

I think the United States is indebted to me [for] another uniform coat, for that of which I have disposed on this occasion was but little worn. We yet want another canoe, and as the Clatsops will not sell us one at a price which we can afford to give, we will take one from them in lieu of the six elk which they stole from us in the winter.

Tuesday, March 18, 1806:

Lewis: Drouillard was taken last night with a violent pain in his side. Captain Clark bled him. Several of the men are complaining of being unwell. It is truly unfortunate that they should be sick at the moment of our departure.

We directed Sergeant Pryor to prepare the two canoes which Drouillard brought last evening for his mess. They wanted some knees to strengthen them and several cracks corked and payed. He completed them except the latter operation which the frequent showers in the course of the day prevented, as the canoes could not be made sufficiently dry even with the assistance of fire.

Comowool and two Cathlahmahs visited us today. We suffered them to remain all night.

This morning we gave Delashelwilt a certificate of his good deportment, etc., and also a list of our names, after which we dispatched him to his village with his female band. These lists of our names we have given to several of the natives and also pasted up a copy in our room. The object of these lists [which] we stated in the preamble of the same [is] as follows (viz.):

"The object of this list is that through the medium of some civilized person who may see the same, it may be made known to the informed world that the party consisting of the persons whose names are hereunto annexed, and who were sent out by the government of the United States in May, 1804, to explore the interior of the continent of North America, did penetrate the same by way of the Missouri and Columbia Rivers, to the discharge of the latter into the Pacific Ocean, where they arrived on the fourteenth of November, 1805, and from whence they departed the ____ day of March, 1806, on their return to the United States by the same route they had come out."

On the back of some of these lists we added a sketch of the connection of the upper branches of the Missouri with those of the Columbia, particularly of its main southeast branch, on which we also delineated the track we had come and that we meant to pursue on our return where the same happened to vary.

There seemed so many chances against our government ever obtaining a regular report through the medium of the savages and the traders of this coast that we declined making any.

Our party is also too small to think of leaving any of them to return to the United States by sea, particularly as we shall be necessarily divided into three or four parties on our return in order to accomplish the objects we have in view. And, at any rate, we shall reach the United States in all human probability much earlier than a man could who must, in the event of his being left here, depend for his passage to the United States on the traders of the coast who may not return immediately to the United States or, if they should, might probably spend the next summer in trading with the natives before they would set out on their return.

This evening Drouillard went in quest of his traps and took an otter.

Wednesday, March 19, 1806:

Lewis: It continued to rain and hail today in such [a] manner that nothing further could be done to the canoes.

The Killamucks, Clàtsops, Chinooks, Cathlahmahs, and Wâc-ki-a-cums resemble each other as well in their persons and dress as in their habits and manners. Their complexion is not remarkable, being the usual copper brown of most of the tribes of North America. They are low in stature, rather diminutive, and illy shaped, possessing thick, broad, flat feet, thick ankles, crooked legs, wide mouths, thick lips, noses moderately large, fleshy [and] wide at the extremity with large nostrils, black eyes, and black, coarse hair. Their eyes are sometimes of a dark yellowish-brown [and] the pupil black.

The most remarkable trait in their physiognomy is the peculiar flatness and width of [the] forehead which they artificially obtain by compressing the head between two boards while in a state of infancy, and from which it never afterwards perfectly recovers. This is a custom among all the nations we have met with west of the Rocky Mountains. I have observed the heads of many infants after this singular bandage had been dismissed, or about the age of ten or eleven months, that were not more than two inches thick about the upper edge of the forehead, and rather thinner still higher. From the top of the head to the extremity of the nose is one straight line. This is done in order to give a greater width to the forehead, which they much admire. This process seems to be continued longer with their female than their male children, and neither appears to suffer any pain from the operation. It is from this peculiar form of the head that the nations east of the Rocky Mountains call all the nations on this side, except the Aliohtans or Snake Indians, by the generic name of Flatheads.

The large or apparently swollen legs, particularly observable in the women, are obtained, in a great measure, by tying a cord tightly around the ankle. Their method of squatting or resting themselves on their hams, which they seem from habit to prefer to sitting, no doubt contributes much to this deformity of the legs by preventing free circulation of the blood.

The dress of the men consists of a small robe which reaches about as low as the middle of the thigh and is attached with a string across the breast and is, at pleasure, turned from side to side as they may have occasion to disencumber the right or left arm from the robe entirely, or when they have occasion for both hands. The fixture of the robe is in front with its corners loosely hanging over their arms. A mat is sometimes temporarily thrown over the shoulders to protect them from rain. They have no other article of clothing whatever, neither winter nor summer, and every part, except the shoulders and back, is exposed to view. They are very fond of the dress of the whites, which they wear in a similar manner when they can obtain them, except the shoe, which I have never seen worn by any of them.

The dress of the women consists of a robe, tissue, and sometimes, when the weather is uncommonly cold, a vest. Their robe is much smaller than that of the men, never reaching lower than the waist nor extending in front sufficiently for to cover the body. It is like that of the men, confined across the breast with a string, and hangs loosely over the shoulders and back. The most esteemed and valuable of these robes are made of strips of the skins of the sea otter net together with the bark of the white cedar or silk-grass. These strips are first twisted and laid parallel with each other a little distance asunder, and then net or woven together in such a manner that the fur appears equally on both sides and unites between the strands. It makes a warm and soft covering. Other robes are formed in a similar manner of the skin of the raccoon, beaver, etc. At other times the skin is dressed in the hair and worn without any further preparation.

The vest is always formed in the manner first described of their robes and covers the body from the armpits to the waist and is confined behind and [is] destitute of straps over the shoulder to keep it up. When this vest is worn, the breast of the woman is concealed, but without it, which is almost always the case, they are exposed, and from the habit of remaining loose and unsuspended, grow to great length, particularly in aged women in many of whom I have seen the bubby[390] reach as low as the waist.

The garment which occupies the waist, and from thence as low as nearly to the knee before and the ham behind, cannot properly be denominated a petticoat in the common acceptation of that term. It is a tissue of white cedar bark, bruised or broken into small shreds which are interwoven in the middle by means of several cords of the same materials, which serve as well for a girdle as to hold in place the shreds of bark which form the tissue, and which shreds confined in the middle hang with their ends pendulous from the waist, the whole being of sufficient thickness, when the female stands erect, to conceal those parts usually covered from familiar view, but when she stoops or places herself in many other attitudes, this battery of Venus is not altogether impervious to the inquisitive and penetrating eye of the amourite.

The favorite ornaments of both sexes are the common, coarse, blue and white beads which the men wear tightly wound around their wrists and ankles many times until they obtain the width of three or more inches. They also wear them in large rolls loosely around the neck, or pendulous from the cartilage of the nose or rims of the ears which are perforated for the purpose. The women wear them in a similar manner except in the nose, which they never perforate. They are also fond of a species of wampum which is furnished them by a trader whom they call Swipton. It seems to be the native form of the shell without any preparation. The men sometimes wear collars of bear claws, and the women and children the tusks of the elk, variously arranged on their necks, arms, etc. Both males and females wear bracelets on their wrists of copper, brass, or iron in various forms.

I think the most disgusting sight I have ever beheld is these dirty, naked wenches.

The men of these nations partake much more of the domestic drudgery than I had first supposed. They collect and prepare all the fuel, make the fires, assist in cleansing and preparing the fish, and always cook for the strangers who visit them. They also build their houses, construct their canoes, and make all their wooden utensils. The peculiar province of the woman seems to be to collect roots and manufacture various articles, which are prepared of rushes, flags, cedar bark, bear grass, or waytape. The management of the canoe for various purposes seems to be a duty common to both sexes.

390. variation of booby, or breast

Thursday, March 20, 1806:

Lewis: It continued to rain and blow so violently today that nothing could be done towards forwarding our departure. We intended to have dispatched Drouillard and the two Fields to hunt near the bay on this side of the Cathlahmahs until we joined them from hence, but the rain rendered our departure so uncertain that we declined this measure for the present.

Nothing remarkable happened during the day.

We have yet several days provision on hand which we hope will be sufficient to subsist us during the time we are compelled by the weather to remain at this place.

Although we have not fared sumptuously this winter and spring at Fort Clatsop, we have lived quite as comfortably as we had any reason to expect we should, and have accomplished every object which induced our remaining at this place except that of meeting with the traders who visit the entrance of this river. Our salt will be very sufficient to last us to the Missouri, where we have a stock in store.

It would have been very fortunate for us had some of those traders arrived previous to our departure from hence, as we should then have had it in our power to obtain an addition to our stock of merchandise which would have made our homeward- bound journey much more comfortable.

Many of our men are still complaining of being unwell. Willard and Bratton remain weak, principally, I believe, for the want of proper food. I expect when we get under way we shall be much more healthy. It has always had that effect on us heretofore.

The guns of Drouillard and Sergeant Pryor were both out of order. The first was repaired with a new lock, the old one having become unfit for use. The second had the cock screw broken which was replaced by a duplicate which had been prepared for the lock at Harper's Ferry where she was manufactured. But for the precaution taken in bringing on those extra locks and parts of locks, in addition to the ingenuity of John Shields, most of our guns would at this moment have been entirely unfit for use, but fortunately for us I have it in my power here to record that they are all in good order.

Gass: I made a calculation of the number of elk and deer killed by the party from the 1st of December, 1805, to the 20th of March, 1806, which gave 131 elk and twenty deer. There were a few smaller quadrupeds killed, such as otter and beaver, and one raccoon.

Friday, March 21, 1806:

Lewis: Our sick men, Willard and Bratton, do not seem to recover. The former was taken with a violent pain in his leg and thigh last night. Bratton is now so much reduced that I am somewhat uneasy with respect to his recovery. The pain of which he complains most seems to be seated in the small of his back and remains obstinate. I believe that it is the rheumatism with which they are both afflicted.

Sunday, March 23, 1806:

Clark: This morning proved so rainy and uncertain that we were undetermined for some time whether we had best set out and risk the tide, which appeared to be rising, or not.

The rain ceased and it became fair about meridian, at which time we loaded our canoes, and at 1:00 p.m. [we] left Fort Clatsop on our homeward bound journey. At this place we had wintered and remained from the seventh of December, 1805, to this day and have lived as well as we had any right to expect, and we can say that we were never one day without three meals of some kind a day, either poor elk meat or roots, notwithstanding the repeated fall of rain which has fallen almost constantly since we passed the Long Narrows.

Soon after we had set out from Fort Clatsop, we were met by Delashelwilt and eight men of the Chinook [tribe], and Delashelwilt's wife, the old bawd, and his six girls. They had a canoe, a sea otter skin, dried fish, and hats for sale. We purchased a sea otter skin and proceeded on through Meriwether's Bay.

There was a stiff breeze from the southwest which raised considerable swells around Meriwether's Point, which was as much as our canoes could ride. Above Point William we came to at the camp of Drouillard and the two Fields. Here we encamped for the night, having made sixteen miles.

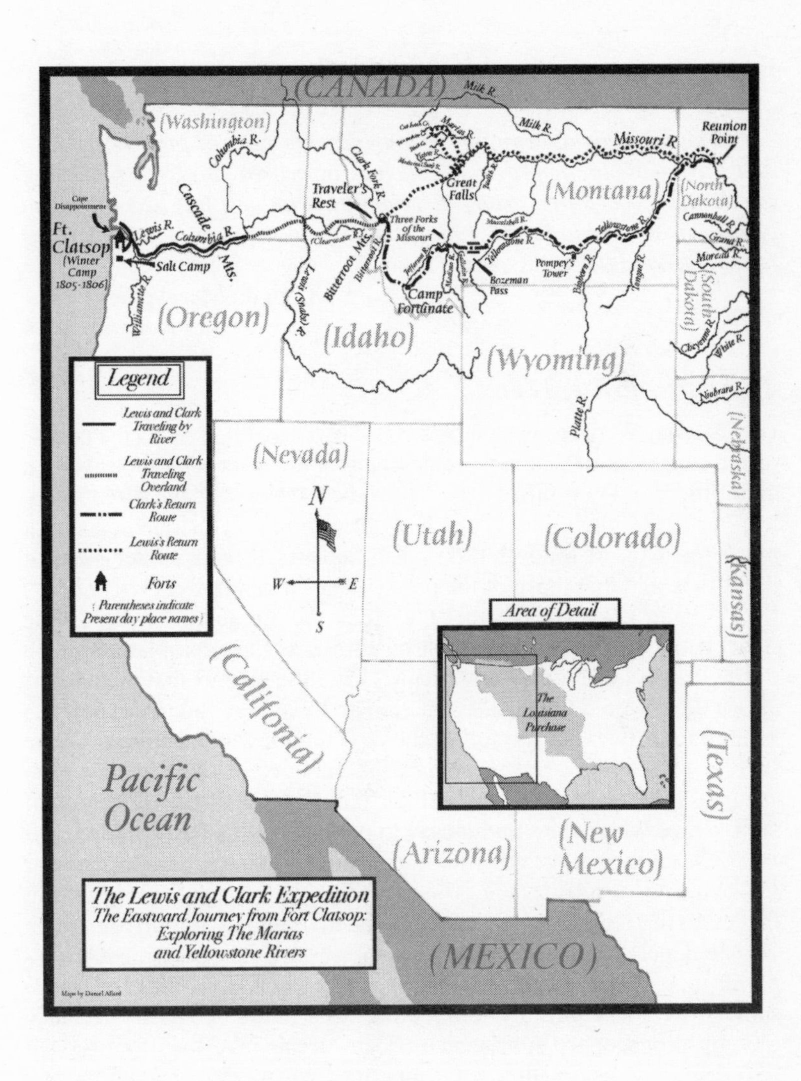
(CANADA)
Milk R.
(Washington)
Columbia R.
Marias R.
Milk R.
Missouri R.
Reunion Point
Clark Fork R.
Traveler's Rest
Great Falls
(Montana)
(North Dakota)
Cape Disappointment
Cascade Mts.
Ft. Clatsop
(Winter Camp 1805-1806)
Lewis R.
Columbia R.
Three Forks of the Missouri
Bitterroot Mts.
Yellowstone R.
Cannonball R.
Grand R.
Moreau R.
Salt Camp
Willamette R.
Pompey's Tower
Bozeman Pass
Camp Fortunate
(South Dakota)
Lewis (Snake) R.
(Oregon)
(Idaho)
(Wyoming)
Cheyenne R.
White R.
Niobrara R.
Platte R.
Legend
Lewis and Clark Traveling by River
Lewis and Clark Traveling Overland
Clark's Return Route
Lewis's Return Route
Forts
(Parentheses indicate Present day place names)
(Nevada)
(Nebraska)
N
W
E
S
(Utah)
(Colorado)
(Kansas)
Area of Detail
The Louisiana Purchase
(California)
(Texas)
Pacific Ocean
(Arizona)
(New Mexico)
The Lewis and Clark Expedition
The Eastward Journey from Fort Clatsop:
Exploring The Marias and Yellowstone Rivers
(MEXICO)
Maps by Daniel Allard

14: April, 1806

The dog now constitutes a considerable part of our subsistence and, with most of the party, has become a favorite food. Certain [as] *I am that it is a healthy, strong diet, and from habit it has become by no means disagreeable to me, I prefer it to lean venison or elk, and it is far superior to the horse in any state.*

Captain Meriwether Lewis,
April 13, 1806

Tuesday, April 1, 1806:

Lewis: We were visited by several canoes of natives in the course of the day, most of whom were descending the river with their women and children. They informed us that they resided at the Great Rapids[391] and that their relations at that place were much straitened at that place for want of food, that they had consumed their winter store of dried fish, and that those of the present season had not yet arrived.

I could not learn whether they took the sturgeon, but I presume [that] if they do it is in but small quantities as they complained much of the scarcity of food among them. They informed us that the nations above them were in the same situation and that they did not expect the salmon to arrive until the full of the next moon, which happens on the second of May. We did not doubt the veracity of these people who seemed to be on their way with their families and effects in search of subsistence which they find it easy to procure in this fertile valley.

This information gave us much uneasiness with respect to our future means of subsistence. Above the falls or through the plains from thence to the Nez Percé, there are no deer, antelope, nor elk on which we can depend for subsistence. Their horses are very poor most probably at this season and if they have no fish, their dogs must be in the same situation. Under these circumstances, there seems to be but a gloomy prospect for subsistence on any terms. We therefore took it into serious consideration what measures we were to pursue on this occasion.

---

391. The Dalles (DeVoto)

It was at once deemed inexpedient to wait the arrival of the salmon, as that would detain us so large a portion of the season that it is probable we should not reach the United States before the ice would close the Missouri or, at all events, would hazard our horses which we left in charge of the Nez Percé who informed us they intended passing the Rocky Mountains to the Missouri as early as the season would permit them which is, as we believe, about the beginning of May. Should these people leave their situation near Kooskooskee before our arrival, we may probably find much difficulty in recovering our horses, without which there will be little possibility of repassing the mountains. We are, therefore, determined to lose as little time as possible in getting to the Nez Percé village.

I purchased a canoe from an Indian today for which I gave him six fathoms of wampum beads. He seemed satisfied with his bargain and departed in another canoe, but shortly returned and canceled the bargain, took his canoe, and returned the beads. This is frequently the case in their method of trading and is deemed fair by them.

Wednesday, April 2, 1806:

Lewis: This morning we came to a resolution to remain at our present encampment, or somewhere in this neighborhood, until we have obtained as much dried meat as would be necessary for our voyage as far as the Nez Percé. [We intend] to exchange our pirogues for canoes with the natives on our way to the Great Falls of the Columbia, or purchase such canoes from them for elk skins and merchandise, as would answer our purposes. These canoes we intend exchanging with the natives of the plains for horses as we proceed until we obtain as many as will enable us to travel altogether by land.

At some convenient point, perhaps at the entrance of the southeast branch of the Columbia, we propose sending a party of four or five men ahead to collect our horses that they may be in readiness for us by our arrival at the Nez Percé, calculating [that] by thus acquiring a large stock of horses, we shall not only secure the means of transporting our baggage over the mountains, but that we will also have provided the means of subsisting, for we now view the horses as our only certain resource for food, nor do we look forward to it with any detestation or horror, so soon is the mind which is occupied with any interesting object reconciled to its situation.

We now informed the party of our intention of laying in a store of meat at this place and immediately dispatched two parties, consisting of nine men, to the opposite side of the river. We also sent out three others on this side, and those who remained in camp were employed in collecting wood, making a scaffold, and cutting up the meat in order to dry it.

About this time, several canoes of the natives arrived at our camp and, among others, one from below which had on board eight men of the "Shah-ha-la" nation. These men informed us that two young men they pointed out were Cashhooks and resided at the falls of a large river which discharges itself into the Columbia on its south side some miles below us. We readily prevailed on them to give us a sketch of this river, which they drew on a mat with a coal. It appeared that this river, which they called Multnomah,[392] discharged itself behind the island which we called the Image Canoe Island and as we had left this island to the south both in ascending and descending the river, we had never seen it. They informed us that it was a large river and ran a considerable distance to the south between the mountains.

Captain Clark determined to return and examine this river. Accordingly, he took a party of seven men and one of the pirogues and set out one-half after 11:00 a.m. He hired one of the Cashhooks, for a burning glass, to pilot him to the entrance of the Multnomah River and took him on board with him.

Clark: I had not proceeded far before I saw four large canoes at some distance above, descending and bending their course towards our camp which at this time is very weak, Captain Lewis having only ten men with him. I hesitated for a moment whether it would not be advisable for me to return and delay until a part of our hunters should return to add more strength to our camp, but on a second reflection, and reverting to the precautions always taken by my friend, Captain Lewis, on these occasions, banished all apprehensions and I proceeded on down.

At eight miles [we] passed a village on the south side. At this place, my pilot informed me [that] he resided and that the name of the tribe is "Ne-cha-co-lee." I proceeded on without landing.

At 3:00 p.m. I landed at a large double house of the "Ne-er-che-ki-oo" tribe of the Shahala nation. On the bank, at different places, I observed small canoes which the women make use of to gather wapatoo and roots in the slashes.[393] These canoes are from ten to fourteen feet long and from eighteen to twenty-three inches wide in the widest part, tapering from the center to both ends, and about nine inches deep, and so light that a woman may, with one hand, haul them with ease, and they are sufficient to carry a woman and some loading. I think one hundred of these canoes were piled up and scattered in different directions about in the woods in the vicinity of this house. The pilot

392. the Willamette (DeVoto)

393. wet or swampy ground overgrown with bushes and trees

informed me that these canoes were the property of the inhabitants of the Grand Rapids who used them occasionally to gather roots.

I entered one of the rooms of this house and offered several articles to the natives in exchange for wapatoo. They were sulky and they positively refused to sell any. I had a small piece of port fire match[394] in my pocket, off of which I cut a piece one inch in length and put it into the fire, and took out my pocket compass and sat myself down on a mat on one side of the fire, and also showed a magnet which was in the top of my ink stand. The port fire caught and burned vehemently, which changed the color of the fire. With the magnet, I turned the needle of the compass about very briskly, which astonished and alarmed the natives, and they laid several parcels of wapatoo at my feet and begged of me to take out the bad fire. To this I consented. At this moment the match being exhausted was, of course, extinguished, and I put up the magnet, etc. This measure alarmed them so much that the women and children took shelter in their beds and behind the men. All this time, a very old blind man was speaking with great vehemence, apparently imploring his god. I lit my pipe and gave them smoke, and gave the women the full amount of the roots which they had put at my feet. They appeared somewhat pacified and I left them and proceeded on.

On the south side of Image Canoe Island, which I found to be two islands, [I saw that the mouth was] hidden from the opposite side by one near the center of the river. The lower point of the upper and the upper point of the lower cannot be seen from the north side of the Columbia on which we had passed both descending and ascending, and had not observed the aperture between those islands.

At the distance of thirteen miles below the last village, and at the place I had supposed was the lower point of the Image Canoe Island, I entered this river which the natives had informed us of, called Multnomah River, so-called by the natives from a nation who reside on Wapatoo Island a little below the entrance of this river. Multnomah discharges itself in the Columbia on the southeast, and may be justly said to be one-fourth the size of that noble river. Multnomah had fallen eighteen inches from its greatest annual height. Three small islands are situated in its mouth which hides the river from view from the Columbia. From the entrance of this river, I can plainly see Mount Jefferson, which is high and covered with snow, southeast, Mount Hood east, Mount St. Helens, and a high humped mountain[395] to the east of Mount St. Helens.

394. fuse (DeVoto)

395. Mount Adams (DeVoto)

Thursday, April 3, 1806:

Clark: The water had fallen, in the course of last night, five inches. I set out and proceeded up a short distance and attempted a second time to fathom the river with my cord of five fathoms, but could find no bottom. The mist was so thick that I could see but a short distance up this river. When I left it, it was bending to the east of southeast. Being perfectly satisfied of the size and magnitude of this great river, which must water that vast tract of country between the western range of mountains and those on the seacoast and as far south as the waters of California, about latitude thirty-seven [degrees] north, I determined to return.

At 7:00 a.m. [I] set out on my return. The men exerted themselves and we arrived at the Neerchekioo house, in which the natives were so illy disposed yesterday, at 11:00 a.m.

I observed the wrecks of five houses remaining of a very large village, the houses of which had been built in the form of those we first saw at the Long Narrows of the E-lute nation, with whom these people are connected. I endeavored to obtain from these people of the situation of their nation, if scattered, or what had become of the natives who must have peopled this great town. An old man, who appeared [to be] of some note among them and father to my guide, brought forward a woman who was badly marked with the smallpox, and made signs that they all [had] died with the disorder which marked her face and which she was very near dying with when a girl. From the age of this woman, this destructive disorder, I judge, must have been about twenty-eight or thirty years past and [at] about the time the Clatsops informed us that this disorder raged in their towns and destroyed their nation.

These people speak a different language from those below, though in their dress, habits, and manners, etc., they differ but little from the Quathlahpohtle. Their women wear the truss, as those do of all the nations residing from the Quathlahpohtle to the entrance of Lewis's River and on the Columbia above for some distance. These people have some words the same with those below, but the air of their language is entirely different.

Their men are stouter and much better made, and their women wear larger and longer robes than those do below. These are most commonly made of deerskins dressed with the hair on them.

They pay great attention to their aged. Several men and women whom I observed in this village had arrived at a great age and appeared to be healthy though blind. I prevailed on an old man to draw me a sketch of the Multnomah River and give me the names of the nations residing on it, which he readily did, and gave me the names of four nations who reside on this river, two of them very numerous.

The entrance of Multnomah River is one hundred forty-two miles up the Columbia River from its entrance into the Pacific Ocean.

Sunday, April 6, 1806:

Lewis: This morning we had the dried meat secured in skins and the canoes loaded. We took breakfast and departed at 9:00 a.m.

We continued up the north side of the river, nearly to the place at which we had encamped on the third of November, when we passed the river to the south side in quest of the hunters we had sent up yesterday and the day before.

From the appearance of a rock near which we were encamped on the third of November last, I could judge better of the rise of the water than I could at any point below. I think the flood of this spring has been about twelve feet higher than it was at that time. The river here is about one and a half miles wide. Its general width from the Beacon Rock, which may be esteemed the head of the tide water, to the marshy islands is from one to two miles, though in many places it is still wider. It is only in the fall of the year, when the river is low, that the tides are perceptible as high as the Beacon Rock. This remarkable rock, which stands on the north shore of the river, is unconnected with the hills and rises to the height of seven hundred feet. It has some pine, or rather fir, timber on its northern side; the southern is a precipice of its whole height. It rises to a very sharp point, and is visible for twenty miles below on the river.

Tuesday, April 8, 1806:

Clark: This morning about daylight, I heard a considerable roaring like wind at a distance and, in the course of a short time, waves rose very high which appeared to come across the river and, in the course of an hour, became so high that we were obliged to unload the canoes.

At 7:00 a.m. the winds swelled and blew so hard and raised the waves so immensely high from the northeast and tossed our canoes against the shore in such a manner as to render it necessary to haul them up on the bank.

Finding from the appearance of the winds that it was probable that we may be detained all day, we sent out Drouillard, Shannon, Colter and Collins to hunt, with directions to return if the wind should lull [and] if not, to continue the hunt all day except [if] they killed elk or bear sooner, etc.

John Shields cut out my small rifle and brought her to shoot very well. The party owes much to the ingenuity of this man by whom their guns are repaired when they get out of order, which is very often.

I observed an Indian woman, who [had] visited us yesterday, blind of an eye, and a man who was nearly blind of both eyes. The loss of sight I have observed to be more common among all the nations inhabiting this river than among any people I [have] ever observed. They have almost invariably sore eyes at all stages of life. The loss of an eye is very common among them. Blindness in persons of middle age is by no means uncommon, and it is almost invariably a concomitant of old age. I know not to what cause to attribute this prevalent deficiency of the eye except it be their exposure to the reflection of the sun on the water, to which they are constantly exposed in the occupation of fishing.

About 1:00 p.m. Collins, Shannon, and Colter returned. Collins saw two bear but could not get a shot at them. Neither Shannon nor Colter saw anything worth shooting. Soon after, Drouillard returned, having only a summer duck. The elk are gone to the mountains, as the hunters suppose.

In the evening late an old man, his son, and grandson, and their wives, etc., came down during the time the waves raged with great fury. The wife of the grandson is a woman of different appearance from any we have seen on this river. She has a very round head and piercing black eyes. Soon after these people arrived, the old man was detected in stealing a spoon, and he was ordered away. At about two hundred yards below our camp, they built themselves a fire and did not return to our fires after.

The wind continued violently hard all day and threw our canoes with such force against the shore that one of them split before we could get it out.

Wednesday, April 9, 1806:

Clark: Last night at a late hour, the old emaciated Indian who was detected in stealing a spoon yesterday crept upon his belly with his hands and feet with a view, as I suppose, to take some of our baggage which was in several different parcels on the bank. The sentinel observed the motions of this old emaciated wretch until he got within a few feet of the baggage. At that, he hailed him and approached with his gun in a position as if [he was] going to shoot, which alarmed the old wretch in such a manner that he ran, with all his powers, tumbling over brush and everything in his way.

At 7:00 a.m. we set out and proceeded on to the camp of Joseph and Reubin Field. They had killed nothing.

Here we did not delay but proceeded on to Wahclellah[396] village on the north side and breakfasted. Here one of the men, Colter, observed the tomahawk which was stolen from me on the fourth of November last as we descended the Columbia. He took the tomahawk. The natives attempted to wrest it from him [but] he held fast [to] the tomahawk. These people attempted to excuse themselves from [the] odium of stealing it by making signs that they had purchased the tomahawk, but their neighbors informed me otherwise and made signs that they had taken it.

This village appears to be the wintering station of two bands of the Shahala nation. One band has already moved to the falls of the Multnomah, which is the place they take their salmon. The other band is now moving a few miles above to the foot of the first rapids on this river at which place they take their salmon. They take with them in their canoes, independent of all their household effects, the bark of their houses and boards.

These people were not hospitable, and with some difficulty we procured five dogs and a few wapatoo of them.

At 2:00 p.m. we set out and passed under the Beacon Rock on the north side of two small islands situated nearest the north side.

At 4:00 p.m. we arrived at the first rapids at the head of Strawberry Island at which place, on the northwest side of the Columbia, here we found the natives from the last village rebuilding their habitations of the bark of their old village. Sixteen huts are already completed and appear only temporary. It is most probable that they only reside here during the season of the salmon.

We could not pass with the large canoes up the northwest side for the rocks. The wind [was] high and [it was] a rainy, disagreeable evening. Our smallest canoe, being too low to cross through the high waves, we sent her up on the northwest side with Drouillard and the two Fields and, after purchasing two dogs, crossed and [went] into the sluice of a large, high island separated from the southeast side by a narrow channel. In this channel we found a good harbor and encamped on the lower side.

[The] evening [was] wet and disagreeable.

Thursday, April 10, 1806:

Clark: At 6:00 a.m. we set out and proceeded to the lower point of the island from whence we were compelled to draw our canoes up a rapids for about one-fourth mile, which we soon performed. In crossing the river, which at this place is not more than four hundred yards

396. a division of the Shahala tribe (Bakeless, p. 301)

wide, we fell down a great distance owing to the rapidity of the current.

We continued up on the north side of the river with great difficulty in consequence of the rapidity of the current and the large rocks which form this shore; the south side of the river is impassable. As we had but one sufficient tow rope and were obliged to employ the cord in getting our canoes the greater part of the way, we could only take them one at a time, which retarded our progress very much.

By evening we arrived at the portage on the north side where we landed and conveyed our baggage to the top of the hill, about two hundred paces distant, where we formed a camp. We had the canoes drawn on shore and secured.

The small canoe got loose from the hunters and went adrift with a tin cup and a tomahawk in her. The Indians caught her at the last village and brought her up this evening, for which we gave them two knives. The canoe overset and [we] lost the articles which were in her.

Friday, April 11, 1806:

Lewis: As the tents and skins which covered both our men and baggage were wet with the rain which fell last evening, and as it continued still raining this morning, we concluded to take our canoes first to the head of the rapids, hoping that by evening the rain would cease and afford us a fair afternoon to take our baggage over the portage. This portage is two thousand eight hundred yards along a narrow, rough, slippery road.

The duty of getting the canoes above the rapids was by mutual consent, confided to my friend, Captain Clark, who took with him for that purpose all the party except Bratton, who is yet so weak he is unable to work, three others who were lamed by various accidents, and one other to cook for the party. A few men were absolutely necessary, at any rate, to guard our baggage from the Wahclellahs who crowded about our camp in considerable numbers. These are the greatest thieves and scoundrels we have met with.

By the evening Captain Clark took four of our canoes above the rapids, though with much difficulty and labor. The canoes were much damaged by being driven against the rocks in despite of every precaution which could be taken to prevent it. The men complained of being so much fatigued in the evening that we postponed taking up our fifth canoe until tomorrow.

These rapids are much worse than they were in the fall when we passed them. At that time there were only three difficult points within seven miles. At present, the whole distance is extremely difficult of ascent, and it would be impracticable to descend except by letting down the empty vessels by a cord, and then even the risk would be greater than in taking them up by the same means. The water appears to be (considerably) upwards of twenty feet higher than when we descended the river.

Many of the natives crowded about the bank of the river where the men were engaged in taking up the canoes. One of them had the insolence to cast stones down the bank at two of the men who happened to be a little detached from the party at the time.

On the return of the party in the evening from the head of the rapids, they met with many natives on the road who seemed but illy disposed. Two of these fellows met with John Shields who had delayed some time in purchasing a dog and was a considerable distance behind the party on their return with Captain Clark. They attempted to take the dog from him and pushed him out of the road. He had nothing to defend himself with except a large knife, which he drew with an intention of putting one or both of them to death before they could get themselves in readiness to use their arrows, but discovering his design, they declined the combat and instantly fled through the woods.

Three of this same tribe of villains, the Wahclellahs, stole my dog this evening and took him towards their village. I was shortly afterwards informed of this transaction by an Indian who spoke the Clatsop language, some of which we had learned from them during the winter, and sent three men in pursuit of the thieves with orders, if they made the least resistance of difficulty in surrendering the dog, to fire on them. They overtook these fellows, or rather came within sight of them, at the distance of about two miles. The Indians, discovering the party in pursuit of them, left the dog and fled.

They also stole an ax from us but scarcely had it in their possession before Thompson detected them and wrested it from them.

We ordered the sentinel to keep them out of camp, and informed them by signs that if they made any further attempts to steal our property or insulted our men, we should put them to instant death.

A chief of the Wahclellah tribe informed us that there were two very bad men among the Wahclellahs who had been the principal actors in these scenes of outrage of which we complained, and that it was not the wish of the nation by any means to displease us. We told him that we hoped it might be the case, but we should certainly be as good as our words if they persisted in their insolence. I am convinced that no other consideration but our number at this moment protects us.

The chief had in his possession a very good pipe tomahawk which, he informed us, he had received as a present from a trader who visited him last winter over land, pointing to the northwest, whom he called Swipton. He was pleased with the tomahawk of Captain Clark in consequence of its having a brass bowl,[397] and Captain Clark gratified him by an exchange. As a further proof of his being esteemed by this white trader, he gave us a well-baked sailor's biscuit which, he also informed us, he had received from Swipton.

From these evidences I have no doubt but the traders who winter in some of the inlets to the north of us visit this part of the Columbia by land at certain seasons, most probably when they are confined to their winter harbor. And if so, some of those inlets are probably at no great distance from this place, as there seems to be but little inducement to entice the trader hither from any considerable distance, particularly as the difficulty in traveling on the borders of this mountainous country must be great at that season [and], as the natives informed me, their snows were frequently breast deep. I observe snowshoes in all the lodges of the natives above the Columbian valley.

I hope that the friendly interposition of this chief may prevent our being compelled to use some violence with these people. Our men seem well-disposed to kill a few of them. We keep ourselves perfectly on our guard.

Saturday, April 12, 1806:

Lewis: It rained the greater part of last night and still continued to rain this morning. I therefore determined to take up the remaining pirogue this morning, for which purpose I took with me every man that could be of any service.

A small distance above our camp there is one of the most difficult parts of the rapids. At this place the current sets with great violence against a projecting rock. In hauling the pirogue around this point, the bow unfortunately took the current at too great a distance from the rock. She turned her side to the stream and the utmost exertions of all the party were unable to resist the force with which she was driven by the current. They were compelled to let loose the cord and, of course, both pirogue and cord went adrift with the stream. The loss of this pirogue will, I fear, compel us to purchase one or more canoes of the Indians at an extravagant price.

After breakfast all hands were employed in taking our baggage over the portage. We caused all the men who had short rifles to carry them in order to be prepared for the natives should they make any attempts to rob or injure them. I went up to the head of the rapids and left Captain Clark below.

By 5:00 p.m. we had brought up all our baggage and Captain Clark joined me from the lower camp with the Wahclellah chief. I

397. Clark's hatchet was a pipe-tomahawk (DeVoto)

employed Sergeant Pryor the greater part of the day in repairing and corking the pirogue and canoes.

It continued to rain by showers all day. As the evening was rainy, cold, and far advanced, and ourselves wet, we determined to remain all night.

The mountains are high, steep, and rocky [and] the rock is principally black. They are covered with fir of several species and the white cedar. Near the river we find the cottonwood, sweet willow, broad-leafed ash, a species of maple, the purple haw, a small species of cherry, purple currant, gooseberry, red willow, vining, whiteberry,[398] honeysuckle, huckleberry, sacacommis, two species of mountain holly, and common ash.

For the three last days, this inclusive, we have made only seven miles.

Sunday, April 13, 1806:

Lewis: The loss of one of our pirogues rendered it necessary to distribute her crew and cargo among the two remaining pirogues and two canoes,[399] which being done, we loaded and set out at 8:00 a.m.

We passed the village immediately above the rapids where only one house at present remains entire, the other eight having been taken down and removed to the opposite side of the river as before mentioned.

We found [that] the additional lading which we had been compelled to put on board rendered our vessels extremely inconvenient to manage and, in short, rather unsafe in the event of high winds.

I therefore left Captain Clark with the two pirogues to proceed up the river on the north side, and with the two canoes and some additional hands [I] passed over the river above the rapids to the Yeh-huh village in order to purchase one or more canoes. I found the village consisting of eleven houses, crowded with inhabitants. It appeared to me that they could have mustered about sixty fighting men then present. They appeared very friendlily disposed, and I soon obtained two small canoes from them, for which I gave two robes and four elk skins. I also purchased four paddles and three dogs from them with deerskins.

The dog now constitutes a considerable part of our subsistence and, with most of the party, has become a favorite food. Certain [as] I am that it is a healthy, strong diet, and from habit it has become by no

398. white baneberry

399. Lewis called the two large canoes purchased from the Indians "pirogues" and the two remaining dugouts "canoes;" Clark called all four "canoes" (DeVoto)

means disagreeable to me, I prefer it to lean venison or elk, and it is far superior to the horse in any state.

After remaining about two hours at this village, I departed and continued my route with the four canoes along the south side of the river, the wind being too high to pass over to the entrance of Cruzatte's River[400] where I expected to have overtaken Captain Clark. Not seeing the pirogues on the opposite side, I ascended the river until 1:00, or about five miles above the entrance of Cruzatte's River. Being convinced that the pirogues were behind, I halted and directed the men to dress the dogs and cook one of them for dinner.

A little before we had completed our meal, Captain Clark arrived with the pirogues and landed opposite to us. After dinner, I passed the river to the pirogues and found that Captain Clark had halted for the evening and was himself hunting with three of the party.

Clark: The wind rose and raised the waves to such a height that I could not proceed any farther.

Monday, April 14, 1806:

Lewis: At 1:00 p.m. we arrived at a large village situated in a narrow bottom on the north side. Their houses are rather detached and extended for several miles. They are about twenty in number. These people differ but little in appearance, dress, etc., from those of the rapids. They have some good horses of which we saw ten or a dozen. These are the first horses we have met with since we left this neighborhood last fall.

In short, the country below this place will not permit the use of this valuable animal except in the Columbian valley, and there the present inhabitants have no use for them as they reside immediately on the river and the country is too thickly timbered to admit them to run the game with horses if they had them.

We halted at this village and dined. [We] purchased five dogs, some roots, shappellel, filberts, and dried berries of the inhabitants. These people appeared very friendly. Some of them informed us that they had lately returned from a war excursion against the Shoshone Indians who inhabit the upper part of the Multnomah River to the southeast of them, [and] that they had been fortunate in their expedition and had taken from their enemies most of the horses which we saw in their possession.

After dinner, we pursued our voyage to the entrance of a small run on the north side a little below a large village on the same side opposite the Sepulcher Rock.

---

400. today's Wind River (DeVoto) at present-day Carson, Washington

Ordway: We bought a number of dogs from the natives. They gave us such as they had to eat, which was pounded salmon, thistle roots, and wild onions.

Tuesday, April 15, 1806:

Lewis: We delayed this morning until after breakfast in order to purchase some horses of the Indians. Accordingly, we exposed some articles in exchange for horses. The natives were unwilling to barter. We therefore put up our merchandise and at 8:00 a.m. we set out.

We halted a few minutes at the Sepulcher Rock and examined the deposits of the dead at that place. There were thirteen sepulchers on this rock, which stands near the center of the river and has a surface of about two acres above [the] high water mark.

From hence we returned to the northern shore and continued up it about four miles to another village of the same nation with whom we remained last night. Here we halted and informed the natives of our wish to purchase horses. They produced us several for sale but would not take the articles which we had in exchange for them. They wanted an instrument which the northwest traders call an eyedagg[401] which we had not. We procured two dogs of them and departed.

Wednesday, April 16, 1806:

Clark: About 8:00 this morning, I passed the river with the two interpreters and nine men in order to trade with the natives for their horses, for which purpose I took with me a good part of our stock of merchandise.

Captain Lewis sent out the hunters and set several men at work making pack saddles. Twelve horses will be sufficient to transport our baggage and some pounded fish with our dried elk, which we intend taking with us as a reserved store for the plains and Rocky Mountains.

I formed a camp on the north side and sent Drouillard and Goodrich to the Skillute village, and Charbonneau and Frazier down to the Chilluckkittequaw village with directions to inform the natives that I had crossed the river for the purpose of purchasing horses, and if they had horses to sell us, to bring them to my camp. Great numbers of Indians came from both villages and delayed the greater part of the day without trading a single horse.

Drouillard returned with the principal chief of the Skillutes who was lame and could not walk. After his arrival some horses were offered for sale, but they asked [for] nearly half [of] the merchandise I had with me for one horse. This price I could not think of giving.

---

401. a short ax (DeVoto), or war club (Bakeless, p. 349)

The chief informed me [that] if I would go to his town with him, his people would sell me horses. I therefore concluded to accompany him to his village seven miles distant. We set out and arrived at the village at sunset.

After some ceremony, I entered the house of the chief. I then informed them that I would trade with them for their horses in the morning, for which I would give for each horse the articles which I had offered yesterday. The chief set before me a large platter of onions which had been sweated. I gave a part of those onions to all my party and we all ate of them. In this state, the root is very sweet and the tops tender. The natives requested the party to dance, [to] which they very readily consented, and Pierre Cruzatte played on the violin and the men danced several dances, and retired to rest in the houses of the first and second chiefs. This village had moved about three hundred yards below the spot it stood last fall at the time we passed down.

We observed many stacks of fish remaining untouched on either side of the river. This is the great mart of all this country. Ten different tribes visit these people for the purpose of purchasing their fish, and the Indians on the Columbia and Lewis's River quite to the Nez Percé nation visit them for the purpose of trading horses and buffalo robes for beads and such articles as they have not.

The Skillutes procure the most of their cloth, knives, axes, and beads from the Indians from the north of them who trade with white people who come into the inlets to the north at no great distance from the Tapteet. Their horses, of which I saw great numbers, they procure from the Indians who reside on the banks of the Columbia above, and what few they take from the Towarnihiooks or Shoshone Indians.

I smoked with all the principal men of this nation in the house of their great chief, and lay myself down on a mat to sleep, but was prevented by the mice and vermin with which this house abounded and which were very troublesome to me.

Ordway: Sergeant Gass and two men set at making pack saddles.

Thursday, April 17, 1806:

Clark: I rose early after a bad night's rest and took my merchandise to a rock which afforded an eligible situation for my purpose and at a short distance from the houses, and divided the articles of merchandise into parcels of such articles as I thought best calculated to please the Indians, and in each parcel I put as many articles as we could afford to give, and thus exposed them to view, informing the Indians that each parcel was intended for a horse.

They tantalized me the greater part of the day, saying that they had sent out for their horses and would trade as soon as they came.

Several parcels of merchandise were laid by, for which they told me they would bring horses. I made a bargain with the chief for two horses. About an hour after he canceled the bargain and we again bargained for three horses, which were brought forward. Only one of the three could be possibly used; the other two had such intolerable backs as to render them entirely unfit for service. I refused to take two of them, which displeased him, and he refused to part with the third.

I then packed up the articles and was about setting out for the village above when a man came and sold me two horses, and another man sold me one horse, and several others informed me that they would trade with me if I would continue [here] until their horses could be driven up. This induced me to continue at this village another day.

Many of the natives from different villages on the Columbia above offered to trade, but asked [for] such things as we had not and double as much of the articles which I had as we could afford to give. This was a very unfavorable circumstance as my dependence for procuring a sufficiency of horses rested on the success above where, I had reasons to believe, there was a greater abundance of these animals and was in hopes of getting them on better terms.

Before procuring the three horses, I dispatched Cruzatte, Willard, McNeal, and Peter Wiser to Captain Lewis at the Rock Fort Camp with a note informing him of my ill success in procuring horses and advising him to proceed on to this place as soon as possible, [and] that I would, in the meantime, proceed on to the Enesher nation above the Great Falls and try to purchase some horses of that people.

Soon after I had dispatched this party, the chief of the Eneshers and fifteen or twenty of his people visited me and appeared to be anxious to see the articles I offered for the horses. Several of them agreed to let me have horses if I would add sundry articles to those I offered, which I agreed to do, and they laid those bundles by and informed me [that] they would deliver me the horses in the morning. The chief informed me that their horses were all in the plains with their women gathering roots. They would send out and bring the horses to this place tomorrow. This intelligence was flattering, though I doubted the sincerity of these people who had several times disappointed me in a similar way. However, I determined to continue [here] until tomorrow.

Charbonneau purchased a very fine mare, for which he gave ermine, elk teeth, a belt, and some other articles of no great value. No other purchase was made in the course of this day.

In the evening, I received a note from Captain Lewis, by Shannon, informing me that he should set out early on tomorrow morning and should proceed up to the basin two miles below the Skillute village, and advising me to give double the prices which we had first agreed on for each horse.

I was invited into the house of the second chief where [I] concluded to sleep. This man was poor, [with] nothing to eat but dried fish, and no wood to burn. Although the night was cold, they could not raise as much wood as would make a fire.

Friday, April 18, 1806:

[Clark] Early this morning, I was awakened by an Indian man of the Nez Percé nation who informed me that he lived in the neighborhood of our horses. This man delivered [to] me a bag of powder and ball which he had picked up this morning at the place [where] the goods were exposed yesterday. I had a fire made of some poles purchased of the natives a short distance from the houses and the articles exposed as yesterday. [I] collected the four horses purchased yesterday and sent Frazier and Charbonneau with them to the basin where I expected they would meet Captain Lewis and commence the portage of the baggage on these horses.

About 10:00 a.m. the Indians came down from the Enesher villages and, I expected, would take the articles which they had laid by yesterday. But to my astonishment, not one would make the exchange today. Two other parcels of goods were laid by and the horses [were] promised at 2:00 p.m. I paid little attention to this bargain. However, [I] suffered the bundles to lie.

I dressed the sores of the principal chief, gave some small things to his children, and promised the chief some medicine for to cure his sores. His wife, who I found to be a sulky bitch, was somewhat afflicted with pains in her back. This I thought a good opportunity to get her on my side [by] giving her something for her back. I rubbed a little camphor on her temples and back and applied warm flannel to her back, which she thought had nearly restored her to her former feelings.

This I thought a favorable time to trade with the chief who had more horses than all the nation besides. I accordingly made him an offer which he expected, and [he] sold me two horses.

Great numbers of Indians from different directions visited me at this place today. None of them appeared willing to part with their horses, but told me that several were coming from the plains this evening.

At 3:00 p.m. Sergeant Ordway and three men arrived from Captain Lewis. They brought with them several elk skins, two of my coats, and four robes of the party to add to the stores I had with me for the purchase of horses. Sergeant Ordway informed me that Captain Lewis had arrived with all the canoes into the basin two miles below and wished some dogs to eat. I had three dogs purchased and sent down.

At 5:00 p.m. Captain Lewis came up. He informed me that he had passed the river to the basin with much difficulty and danger, having made one portage.

As I had not slept but very little for the two nights past on account of mice and vermin with which those Indian houses abounded, and having no blanket with me, and the means of keeping a fire sufficient to keep me warm out of doors was too expensive, I determined to proceed with Captain Lewis down to camp at the basin. I left the articles of merchandise, etc., with Drouillard, Werner, Shannon, and Goodrich until the morning. At the basin we cut up two of our canoes for firewood, very much to the chagrin of the natives, notwithstanding [that] they would give us nothing for them. Captain Lewis had twelve pack saddles completed and strings prepared of the elk skins for lashing the loads.

Saturday, April 19, 1806:

Clark: We determined to make the portage to the head of the Long Narrows. The two large canoes we could take no farther and therefore cut them up for fuel. We had our small canoes drawn up very early and employed all hands in transporting our baggage on their backs and, by means of four pack horses, over the portage. This labor we had accomplished by 3:00 p.m. and established our camp a little above the present Skillute village.

I left Captain Lewis at the basin and proceeded to the village early this morning with a view to receive the horses which were promised to be brought this morning for [the] articles laid by last evening. In the course of this day, I purchased four horses at the village, and Captain Lewis one at the basin before he left it.

After the baggage was all safely landed above the portage, all hands brought over the canoes in two loads, which was accomplished by 5:00 p.m. As we had not a sufficiency of horses to transport our baggage, we agreed that I should proceed on to the Enesher village at the Great Falls of the Columbia and, if possible, purchase as many horses as would transport the baggage from that place, and rid us of the trouble and difficulty of taking our canoes farther. I set out with Sergeant Pryor, George Shannon, Pierre Cruzatte, and Labiche at half past 5:00 p.m. for the Enesher village, at which place I arrived at 8:00 p.m.

[There were] several showers of rain in the afterpart of today and the southwest wind [was] very high.

There was great joy with the natives last night in consequence of the arrival of the salmon. One of these fish was caught. This was the harbinger of good news to them. They informed us that these fish would arrive in great quantities in the course of about five days. This fish was dressed and, being divided into small pieces, was given to each child in the village. This custom is founded on a superstitious opinion that it will hasten the arrival of the salmon.

We were obliged to dispense with two of our kettles in order to acquire two of the horses purchased today. We have now only one small kettle to a mess of eight men. These people are very faithless in contracts. They frequently receive the merchandise in exchange for their horses and, after some hours, insist on some additional article being given or revoke the exchange.

The Long Narrows are much more formidable than they were when we descended them last fall. There would be no possibility of passing either up or down them in any vessel at this time.

Sunday, April 20, 1806:

Lewis: This morning I was informed that the natives had pilfered six tomahawks and a knife from the party in the course of the last night. I spoke to the chief on this subject. He appeared angry with his people and addressed them, but the property was not restored. One horse which I purchased and paid for yesterday, and which could not be found when I ordered the horses into close confinement yesterday, I was now informed had been gambled away by the rascal who had sold it to me, and had been taken away by a man of another nation. I therefore took the goods back from this fellow.

I purchased a gun from the chief, for which I gave him two elk skins. In the course of the day, I obtained two other indifferent horses for which I gave an extravagant price. I found that I should get no more horses and therefore resolved to proceed tomorrow morning with those which I had and to convey the baggage in two small canoes that the horses could not carry. For this purpose I had a load made up for seven horses. The eighth Bratton was compelled to ride as he was yet unable to walk. I bartered my elk skins, old irons, and two canoes for beads. One of the canoes, for which they would give us but little, I had cut up for fuel. I had the horses grazed until evening and then picketed[402] and hobbled[403] within the limits of our camp.

I ordered the Indians from our camp this evening and informed them that if I caught them attempting to purloin any article from us I

402. tethered to posts

403. put a short rope around the legs to hamper, but not prevent, movement

would beat them severely. They went off in rather a bad humor, and I directed the party to examine their arms and be on their guard. They stole two spoons from us in the course of the day.

Clark: I showed the Eneshers the articles I had to give for their horses. They, without hesitation, informed me that they would not sell me any for the articles I had. If I would give them kettles, they would let me have horses, and not without that their horses were at a long ways off in the plains and they would not send for them, etc.

My offer was a blue robe, a calico shirt, a silk handkerchief, five parcels of paint, a knife, a wampum moon, eight yards of ribbon, several pieces of brass, a moccasin awl, and six braces of yellow beads. And to that amount for each horse, which is more than double what we gave either the Shoshone or first Flatheads we met with on Clark's River, I also offered my large blue blanket, my coat, sword, and plume, none of which seemed to entice these people to sell their horses. Notwithstanding every exertion, not a single horse could be procured of these people in the course of the day.

Monday, April 21, 1806:

Lewis: Notwithstanding all the precautions I had taken with respect to the horses, one of them had broken his cord of five strands of elk skin and had gone off spanceled.[404] I sent several men in search of the horse with orders to return at 10:00 a.m. with or without the horse, being determined to remain no longer with these villains.

They stole another tomahawk from us this morning. I searched many of them but could not find it. I ordered all the spare poles, paddles, and the balance of our canoes put on the fire as the morning was cold, and also that not a particle should be left for the benefit of the Indians. I detected a fellow in stealing an iron socket of a canoe pole and gave him several severe blows and made the men kick him out of camp.

I now informed the Indians that I would shoot the first of them that attempted to steal an article from us, that we were not afraid to fight them, that I had it in my power at that moment to kill them all and set fire to their houses, but it was not my wish to treat them with severity provided they would let my property alone, that I would take their horses if I could find out the persons who had stolen the tomahawks, but that I had rather lose the property altogether than take the horse of an innocent person. The chiefs who were present hung their heads and said nothing.

---

404. hobbled (Bakeless, p. 306)

At 9:00 a.m. Windsor returned with the lost horse. The others who were in search of the horse soon after returned, also. The Indian who [had] promised to accompany me as far as the Nez Percé country produced me two horses, one of which he politely gave me the liberty of packing.

We took breakfast and departed a few minutes after 10:00, having nine horses loaded and one which Bratton rode, not being able as yet to march. The two canoes I had dispatched early this morning.

At 1:00 p.m. I arrived at the Enesher village where I found Captain Clark and party. He had not purchased a single horse.

Gass: [We] made preparations for setting out from this place. While making preparations, an Indian stole some iron articles from among the men's hands, which so irritated Captain Lewis that he struck him, which was the first act of the kind that had happened during the expedition. The Indians, however, did not resent it.

Clark: I found it useless to make any further attempts to trade horses with these unfriendly people who only crowded about me to view and make their remarks and smoke. The latter I did not indulge them with today.

At 12:00 Captain Lewis and party came up from the Skillute village with nine horses packed and one which Bratton, who was yet too weak to walk, rode, and soon after the two small canoes, loaded with the residue of the baggage which could not be taken on [the] horses. We had everything immediately taken above the falls. In the meantime, [I] purchased two dogs, on which the party dined.

While I remained at the Enesher village I subsisted on two platters of roots, some pounded fish, and sunflower seed pounded, which an old man had the politeness to give me, in return for which I gave him several small articles.

The man who we had reason to believe had stolen the horse [that] he had given for the kettle we threatened a little, and he produced a very good horse in the place of that one, which we cheerfully received.

After dinner we proceeded on about four miles to a village of nine mat lodges of the Enesher. One of the canoes joined us. The other, not having observed us halt, continued on. We obtained two dogs and a small quantity of fuel of these people, for which we were obliged to give a higher price than usual.

Our guide continued with us. He appears to be an honest fellow. He tells us that the Indians above will treat us with much more hospitality than those we are now with.

We purchased another horse this evening but his back is in such a horrid state that we can put but little on him. We obtained him for a trifle, at least, for articles which might be procured in the United States for 10/ Virginia currency.

Tuesday, April 22, 1806:

Lewis: We had not arrived at the top of a hill over which the road leads opposite the village before Charbonneau's horse threw his load and, taking fright at the saddle and robe which still adhered, ran at full speed down the hill. Near the village, he disengaged himself from the saddle and robe. An Indian hid the robe in his lodge.

I sent our guide and one man who was with me in the rear to assist Charbonneau in retaking his horse which, having done, they returned to the village on the track of the horse in search of the lost articles. They found the saddle but could see nothing of the robe. The Indians denied having seen it. They then continued on the track of the horse to the place from whence he had set out, with the same success.

Being now confident that the Indians had taken it, I sent the Indian woman on to request Captain Clark to halt the party and send back some of the men to my assistance, being determined either to make the Indians deliver the robe or burn their houses. They have vexed me in such a manner by such repeated acts of villainy that I am quite disposed to treat them with every severity. Their defenseless state pleads forgiveness so far as [it] respects their lives. With this resolution I returned to their village which I had just reached as Labiche met me with the robe which, he informed me, he [had] found in an Indian lodge hidden behind their baggage. I now returned and joined Captain Clark who was waiting my arrival with the party.

We now made the following regulations as to our future order of march (viz.) that Captain Clark and I should divide the men who were disencumbered by horses and march alternately each day, the one in front and the other in [the] rear.

Having divided the party agreeably to this arrangement, we proceeded on through an open, plain country about eight miles to a village of six houses of the Enesher nation. Here we observed our two canoes passing up on the opposite side. The wind being too high for them to pass the river, they continued on.

We halted at a small run just above the village where we dined on some dogs which we purchased of the inhabitants, and suffered our horses to graze about three hours.

After dinner, we proceeded on up the river about four miles to a village of seven mat lodges of the last mentioned nation. Here our Nez Percé guide informed us that the next village was at a considerable distance and that we could not reach it tonight. A man belonging to the next village above proposed exchanging a horse for one of our canoes.

Just at this moment one of our canoes was passing. We hailed them and ordered them to come over, but the wind continued so high that they could not join us until after sunset, and the Indian who wished to exchange his horse for the canoe had gone on.

We obtained four dogs and as much wood as answered our purposes, on moderate terms. We can only afford ourselves one fire, and are obliged to lie without shelter.

The nights are cold and [the] days [are] warm.

Wednesday, April 23, 1806:

Lewis: At daylight this morning, we were informed that the two horses of our interpreter, Charbonneau, were absent. On enquiry it appeared that he had neglected to confine them to the pickets as had been directed last evening. We immediately dispatched Reubin Field and Labiche to assist Charbonneau in recovering his horses. One of them was found at no great distance, and the other was given over as lost.

We continued our march along a narrow, rocky bottom on the north side of the river about twelve miles to the Wahhowpum village of twelve temporary mat lodges near the Rock Rapids. These people appeared much pleased to see us [and] sold us four dogs and some wood for our small articles which we had previously prepared as our only resource to obtain fuel and food through these plains. These articles consisted of pewter buttons, strips of tin, iron and brass, twisted wire, etc.

Here we met with a Nez Percé man on his return up the river with his family and about thirteen head of horses, most of them young and unbroken. He offered to hire us some of them to pack as far as his nation, but we prefer buying, as by hiring his horses we shall have the whole of his family most probably to maintain.

At a little distance below this village, we passed five lodges of the same people who, like these, were waiting the arrival of the salmon.

After we had arranged our camp, we caused all the old and brave men to sit around and smoke with us. We had the violin played and some of the men danced, after which the natives entertained us with a dance after their method.

This dance differed from any I have yet seen. They formed a circle and all sang, as well the spectators as the dancers who performed within the circle. These placed their shoulders together, with their robes tightly drawn about them, and danced in a line from side to side. Several parties of from four to seven will be performing within the circle at the same time. The whole concluded with a promiscuous dance in which most of them sang and danced. These people speak a language very similar to the Nez Percé whom they also resemble in their dress. After the dance was ended, the Indians retired at our request and we retired to rest. We had all our horses side-hobbled and turned out to graze.

The river is by no means as rapid as when we descended, or at least not obstructed with those dangerous rapids. The water, at present, covers most of the rocks in the bed of the river. The natives promised to barter their horses with us in the morning. We therefore entertained a hope that we shall be enabled to proceed by land from hence with the whole of our party and baggage.

Thursday, April 24, 1806:

Clark: [We] rose early this morning and sent out after the horses, all of which were found except McNeal's, which I hired an Indian to find and gave him a tomahawk.

[We] had four pack saddles made ready to pack the horses which we may purchase.

We purchased three horses and hired three others of the Nez Percé man who accompanies us with his family, and at 1:00 p.m. set out and proceeded on through an open country, rugged and sandy, between some highlands and the river, to a village of five lodges of the Met-cow-we band, having passed four lodges at four miles, and two lodges at six miles.

Great numbers of the natives passed us on horseback. Many met us and continued with us to the lodges. We purchased three dogs which were poor but the fattest we could procure, and cooked them with straw and dry willow.

We sold our canoes for a few strands of beads. The natives had tantalized us with an exchange of horses for our canoes in the first instance, but when they found that we had made our arrangements to travel by land, they would give us nothing for them. We sent Drouillard to cut them up. He struck one and split her. They discovered that we were determined to destroy the canoes and offered us several strands of beads, which were accepted.

Most of the party complained of their feet and legs this evening being very sore. It is no doubt caused by walking over the rough stone and deep sand after being accustomed to a soft soil. My legs and feet give me much pain. I bathed them in cold water, from which I experienced considerable relief.

We directed that the three horses purchased yesterday should be hobbled and confined to pickets, and that the others should be hobbled and spanceled, and strictly attended to by the guard.

[We] made twelve miles today.

Sunday, April 27, 1806:

Lewis: This morning we were detained until 9:00 a.m. in consequence of the absence of one of Charbonneau's horses. The horse at length being recovered we set out and, at the distance of fifteen miles, passed through a country similar to that of yesterday. The hills at the extremity of this distance again approach the river and are rocky, abrupt, and three hundred feet high. We ascended the hill and marched through a high plain nine miles when we again returned to the river.

I now thought it best to halt as the horses and men were much fatigued although we had not reached the Wallawalla village as we had been led to believe by our guide who [had] informed us that the village was at the place [where] we should next return to the river, and the consideration of our having but little provision had been our inducement to make the march we had made this morning. We collected some of the dry stalks of weeds and stems of a shrub which resembles the southernwood. [We] made a small fire and boiled a small quantity of our jerked meat, on which we dined.

While here the principal chief of the Wallawallas joined us with six men of his nation. This chief, by [the] name [of] Yellept, had visited us on the morning of the nineteenth of October at our encampment a little below this place. We gave him, at that time, a small medal and promised him a larger one on our return. He appeared much gratified at seeing us return, invited us to remain at his village three of four days, and assured us that we should be furnished with a plenty of such food as they had themselves and some horses to assist us on our journey.

After our scanty repast we continued our march, accompanied by Yellept and his party, to the village which we found at the distance of six miles, situated on the north side of the river at the lower side of the low country, about twelve miles below the entrance of Lewis's River. This chief is a man of much influence, not only in his own nation, but also among the neighboring tribes and nations.

This village consists of fifteen large mat lodges. At present they seem to subsist principally on a species of mullet which weigh from one to three pounds, and roots of various descriptions which these plains furnish them in great abundance. They also take a few salmon trout of the white kind.

Yellept harangued his village in our favor [and] entreated them to furnish us with fuel and provisions, and set the example himself by bringing us an armful of wood and a platter of three roasted mullets. The others soon followed his example with respect to [the] fuel, and we soon found ourselves in possession of an ample stock. They burn the stems of the shrubs in the plains, there being no timber in their neighborhood of any description. We purchased four dogs of these people, on which the party supped heartily, having been on short allowance for nearly two days. The Indians retired when we requested them [to do so] this evening and behaved themselves, in every respect, extremely well.

The Indians informed us that there was a good road which passed from the Columbia opposite to this village to the entrance of the Kooskooskee on the south side of Lewis's River. They also informed us that there were plenty of deer and antelope on the road, with good water and grass. We knew that a road in that direction, if the country would permit it, would shorten our route [by] at least eighty miles. The Indians also informed us that the country was level and the road good. Under these circumstances, we did not hesitate in pursuing the route recommended by our guide, whose information was corroborated by Yellept and others.

Monday, April 28, 1806:

Clark: This morning early the Great Chief Yellept brought a very elegant white horse to our camp and presented him to me, signifying his wish to get a kettle, but being informed that we had already disposed of every kettle we could possibly spare, he said he was content with whatever I thought proper to give him. I gave him my sword, one hundred balls and powder, and some small articles, of which he appeared perfectly satisfied.

It was necessary, before we entered on [a] route through the plains where we were to meet with no lodges or resident Indians, that we should lay in a stock of provisions and not depend altogether on the gun. We directed Robert Frazier, to whom we have entrusted the duty of making the purchases, to lay in as many fat dogs as he could procure; he soon obtained ten.

Being anxious to depart, we requested the chief to furnish us with canoes to pass the river, but he insisted on our remaining with him this day at least, that he would be much pleased if we would consent to remain two or three days, but [that] he would not let us have canoes to leave him this day, that he had sent for the Chymnappos,[405] his neighbors, to come down and join his people this evening and dance for us. We urged the necessity of our proceeding on immediately in order that we might sooner return to them with the articles which they wished

405. the Yakima tribe; also called Chymnappum; part of the large Shahaptian group of tribes, which included the Salish and Nez Percé (Bakeless, p. 310)

brought to them, but this had no effect. He said that the time he asked could not make any considerable difference. At length [we] urged that there was no wind blowing, and that the river was consequently in good order to pass our horses, and [that] if he would furnish us with canoes for that purpose, we would remain all night at our present encampment. To this proposition he assented, and soon produced a canoe.

I saw a man who had his knee contracted who had previously applied to me for some medicine, [and I told him] that if he would furnish another canoe, I would give him some medicine. He readily consented and went himself with his canoe, by means of which we passed our horses over the river safely and hobbled them as usual.

We found a Shoshone woman, prisoner among these people, by means of whom and Sacagawea, Charbonneau's wife, we found [a] means of conversing with the Wallawallas. We conversed with them for several hours, and fully satisfied all their enquiries with respect to ourselves and the objects of our pursuit. They were much pleased.

They brought several disordered persons to us for whom they requested some medical aid, to all of whom we administered, much to the gratification of these poor wretches. We gave them some eye water which, I believe, will render them more essential service than any other article, in the medical way, which we had it in our power to bestow on them. Sore eyes seem to be a universal complaint among these people. I have no doubt but the fine sands of these plains, and the river, contribute much to the disorder.

A man who had his arm broken had it loosely bound in a piece of leather without anything to support it. I dressed the arm which was broken short above the wrist, supported it with broad sticks to keep it in place, put it in a sling, and furnished him with some lint bandages, etc., to dress it in [the] future.

A little before sunset the Chymnappos arrived. They were about one hundred men and a few women. They joined the Wallawallas, who were about one hundred fifty men, and formed a half-circle around our camp where they waited very patiently to see our party dance. The fiddle was played and the men amused themselves with dancing about an hour.

We then requested the Indians to dance, which they very cheerfully complied with. They continued their dance until 10:00 at night. The whole assemblage of Indians, about three hundred fifty men, women and children, sang and danced at the same time. Most of them danced in the same place they stood and merely jumped up to the time of their music. Some of the men, who were esteemed most brave, entered the space around which the main body was formed in [a] solid column and danced in a circular manner sideways. At 10:00 p.m., the dance ended and the natives retired. They were much gratified in seeing some of our party join them in their dance.

One of their party, who made himself the most conspicuous character in the dance and songs, we were told, was a medicine man and could foretell things, that he had told of our coming into their country, and was now about to consult his god, the Moon, if what we said was the truth, etc., etc.

Tuesday, April 29, 1806:

Clark: This morning Yellept furnished us with two canoes and we began to transport our baggage over the river. We also sent a party of the men over to collect our horses. We purchased some dogs and shappellel this morning. We now had a store of twelve dogs for our voyage through the plains.

By 11:00 a.m. we had passed the river with our party and baggage but were detained several hours in consequence of not being able to collect our horses. Our guide now informed us that it was too late in the evening to reach an eligible place to encamp, that we could not reach any water before night. We therefore thought it best to remain on the Walla Walla River about a mile from the Columbia until the morning.

The Walla Walla River discharges itself into the Columbia on its south side, fifteen miles below the entrance of Lewis's River, or the southeast branch. This [is] a handsome stream about four and a half feet deep and fifty yards wide. The Indians inform us that it has its source in the range of mountains[406] in view of us to the east and southeast.

The Shoshone Indian prisoner informed us that at some distance in the large plains to the south of those mountains, there was a large river[407] running to the northwest which was as wide as the Columbia at this place, which is nearly one mile. This account is no doubt somewhat exaggerated, but it serves to evince the certainty of the Multnomah being a very large river and that its waters are separated from the Columbia by those mountains, and that, with the aid of a southwardly branch of Lewis's River which passes around the eastern extremity of those mountains, it must water that vast tract of country extending from those mountains to the waters of the Gulf of California and no doubt heads with the Rochejhone[408] and Del Nord.

---

406. the Blue Mountains (DeVoto)
407. the Snake River (DeVoto)
408. Yellowstone

There are twelve other lodges of the Wallawalla nation on this river a short distance below our camp. These people, as well as the Chymnappos, are very well disposed, much more so particularly their women, than they were when we descended the river last fall. Most of them have long shirts and leggings, good robes, and moccasins. Their women wear the truss when they cannot procure the shirt, but very few are seen with the former at the present. I presume the success of their winter's hunt had produced this change in their attire.

They insisted on our dancing this evening but it rained a little, the wind blew hard, and the weather was cold. We therefore did not indulge them.

Several applied to me today for medical aid, one [with] a broken arm, another [with] inward fevers, and several with pains across their loins, and sore eyes. I administered as well as I could to all.

In the evening a man brought his wife and a horse both up to me. The horse he gave me as a present and his wife, who was very unwell [from] the effects of violent colds, was placed before me. I did not think her case a bad one and [I] gave [her] such medicine as would keep her body open, and wrapped her in flannel. [I] left some simple medicine to be taken. We also gave some eye water.

Wednesday, April 30, 1806:

Clark: This morning, we had some difficulty in collecting our horses, notwithstanding we had hobbled and picketed those we [had] obtained of these people. We purchased two other horses this morning and four dogs.

We exchanged one of our most indifferent horses for a very good one with the Nez Percé man who has his family with him. This man has a daughter now arrived at the age of puberty who, being [in] a certain situation, is not permitted to associate with the family but sleeps at a distance from her father's camp and, when traveling, follows at some distance behind. In this state, I am informed that the female is not permitted to eat, nor to touch, any article of a culinary nature or manly occupation.

At 10:00 a.m. we had collected all our horses except the white horse which Yellept, the Great Chief, had given me. The whole of the men having returned without being able to find this horse, I informed the chief and he mounted Captain Lewis's horse and went in search of the horse himself. About half an hour after the Nez Percé man brought my horse.

We determined to proceed on with the party, leaving one man to bring up Captain Lewis's horse when Yellept should return. We took leave of these honest, friendly people, the Wallawallas, and departed at

11:00 a.m., accompanied by our guide and the Nez Percé man and family.

15: May, 1806

My friend, Captain Clark, is their favorite physician.

Captain Meriwether Lewis,
May 5, 1806

Friday, May 2, 1806:

Gass: [It was] a fine morning.

Last night about 9:00, three of the Wallawallas came up with us and brought a steel trap that had been left at our camp on the north side of the Columbia. [This was] perhaps one of the greatest instances of honesty ever known among Indians.

Saturday, May 3, 1806:

Clark: This morning we set out at 7:00 a.m.

We met with Wearkkoomt, who we have usually distinguished by the name of the Big Horn Chief from the circumstance of his always wearing a horn of that animal suspended by a cord to his left arm. He is a first chief of a large band of the Nez Percé nation. He had ten of his young men with him. This man went down Lewis's River by land as we descended it by water last fall, quite to the Columbia and, I believe, was very instrumental in procuring us a hospitable and friendly reception among the natives. He had now come a considerable distance to meet us.

It rained, hailed, snowed, and blew with great violence the greater portion of the day. It was fortunate for us that this storm was from the southwest and, of course, on our backs. The air was very cold.

We divided the last of our dried meat at dinner when it was consumed, as well as the balance of our dogs nearly. We made but a scant supper and had not anything for tomorrow. However, Wearkkoomt consoled us with the information that there was an Indian lodge on the river at no great distance where we might supply ourselves with provisions tomorrow.

Ordway: [There was] a little rain the latter part of last night and [it] continues showery and cold. [There is] a little hail and snow intermixed.

[We] made twenty-eight miles this day.

Having nothing to eat, [we] bought the only dog the Indians had with them.

The air is very cold.

Sunday, May 4, 1806:

Lewis: [We] collected our horses and set out early. The morning was cold and disagreeable.

We ascended through a high, level plain to a ravine, which forms the source of a small creek, thence down this creek to its entrance into Lewis's River seven and a half miles below the entrance of the Kooskooskee.

On the river a little above this creek we arrived at a lodge of six families of which Wearkkoomt had spoken. We halted here for breakfast and, with much difficulty, purchased two lean dogs. The inhabitants were miserably poor. We obtained a few large cakes of half-cured bread made of a root which resembles the sweet potato. With these we made some soup and took breakfast.

A great portion of the Nez Percé, we are informed, are now distributed in small villages through this plain, collecting the quamash and cowas,[409] the salmon not yet having arrived to call them to the river.

The hills of the creek which we descended this morning are high and, in most parts, rocky and abrupt. One of our pack horses slipped from one of these heights and fell into the creek with its load, consisting principally of ammunition, but fortunately neither the horse nor load suffered any material injury. The ammunition, being secured in canisters, the water did not affect it.

After dinner we continued our route up the west side of the river three miles opposite to two lodges, the one containing three and the other two families of the Nez Percé nation. Here we met with Tetoharsky, the younger of the two chiefs who accompanied us last fall to the Great Falls of the Columbia. We also met with our pilot who descended the river with us as far as the Columbia. These Indians recommended our passing the river at this place and ascending the Kooskooskee on the northeast side. They said it was nearer and a better route to the forks of that river where the Twisted Hair resided, in whose charge we had left our horses. Thither they promised to conduct us.

We determined to take the advice of the Indians and immediately prepared to pass the river which, with the assistance of three Indian

---

409. biscuitroot

canoes, we effected in the course of the evening. [We] purchased a little wood and some bread of cowas from the natives and encamped, having traveled fifteen miles only today.

The evening was cold and disagreeable and the natives crowded about our fire in great numbers, insomuch that we could scarcely cook or keep ourselves warm.

At all these lodges of the Nez Percé, I observe an appendage of a small lodge with one fire, which seems to be the retreat of their women in a certain situation. The men are not permitted to approach this lodge within a certain distance, and if they have anything to convey to the occupants of this little hospital, they stand at the distance of fifty or sixty paces and throw it towards them as far as they can and retire.

Monday, May 5, 1806:

Clark: [We] collected our horses and set out at 7:00 a.m.

At four and a half miles we arrived at the entrance of the Kooskooskee, up the northeast side of which we continued our march twelve miles to a large lodge of ten families, having passed two other large mat lodges, the one at five and the other at eight miles from the mouth of the Kooskooskee, but not being able to obtain provisions at either of those lodges, [we] continued our march to the third, where we arrived at 1:00 p.m. and, with much difficulty, obtained two dogs and a small quantity of bread and dried roots.

At the second lodge of eight families Captain Lewis and I both entered [and] smoked with a man who appeared to be a principal man. As we were about to leave his lodge and proceed on our journey, he brought forward a very elegant, gray mare and gave her to me, requesting some eye water. I gave him a vial of eye water, a handkerchief, and some small articles, of which he appeared much pleased.

While we were encamped last fall at the entrance of [the] Nez Percé River, I gave an Indian man some volatile liniment to rub [on] his knee and thigh for a pain of which he complained. The fellow soon after recovered and has never ceased to extol the virtue of our medicines.

Near the entrance of the Kooskooskee, as we descended last fall, I met with a man who could not walk with a tumor on his thigh. This had been very bad and recovering fast. I gave this man a gentle purge, cleaned and dressed his sore, and left him some castile soap[410] to wash the sore, which soon got well. This man also assigned the restoration of his leg to me.

410. a hard, bland soap made from olive oil and sodium hydroxide

Those two cures have raised my reputation and given these natives an exalted opinion of my skill as a physician. I have already received many applications. In our present situation, I think it pardonable to continue this deception, for they will not give us any provisions without compensation in merchandise, and our stock is now reduced to a mere handful. We take care to give them no article which can possibly injure them and, in many cases, can administer and give such medicine and surgical aid as will effectually restore [them] in simple cases, etc.

Lewis: My friend, Captain Clark, is their favorite physician.

Clark: The Indians brought my horse, which was left at the place [where] we made canoes, from the opposite side and delivered him to me while here. This horse had, by some accident, separated from our other horses above and, agreeably to Indian information, had been in this neighborhood some weeks.

Gass: The old chief who is now with us says that the Shoshone guide[411] who deserted us last fall stole and took two of our horses with him.

Clark: While at dinner an Indian fellow very impertinently threw a half-starved puppy nearly into the plate of Captain Lewis by way of derision for our eating dogs, and laughed very heartily at his own impertinence. Captain Lewis was so provoked at the insolence that he caught the puppy and threw it with great violence at him and struck him in the breast and face, seized his tomahawk, and showed him by sign that if he repeated his insolence that he would tomahawk him. The fellow withdrew, apparently much mortified, and he continued his repast *on dog* without further molestation.

After dinner, we continued our route four miles to the entrance of Colter's Creek about half a mile above the rapids where we sank the first canoe as we descended the river last fall. We encamped on the lower side of this creek, a little distance from two lodges of the Nez Percé nation, having traveled twenty and a half miles today.

One of those lodges contained eight families. The other was much the largest we have yet seen. It is one hundred fifty-six feet long and about fifteen feet wide, built of mats and straw in the form of the roof of a house, having a number of small doors on each side, closed at the ends, and without divisions in the intermediate space. This lodges at least thirty families. Their fires are kindled in a row in the center of the lodge, and about ten feet asunder.[412]

We arrived here extremely hungry and much fatigued, but no articles of merchandise in our possession would induce them to let us

411. Old Toby (DeVoto)

412. apart from each other

have any article of provisions except a small quantity of bread of cowas and some of those roots dried. We had several applications to assist their sick, which we refused unless they would let us have some dogs or horses to eat.

A man whose wife had an abscess formed on the small of her back promised a horse in the morning provided we would administer to her. I examined the abscess and found it was too far advanced to be cured. I told them her case was desperate. Agreeably to their request, I opened the abscess. I then introduced a tent[413] and dressed it with bisilicon[414] and prepared some doses of the flour of sulphur and cream of tartar, which were given with directions to be taken on each morning. A little girl and sundry other patients were brought to me for cure but we postponed our operations until the morning.

They procured us several dogs but they were so poor that they were unfit to eat.

Tuesday, May 6, 1806:

Clark: This morning the husband of the sick woman was as good as his word. He produced us a young horse in tolerable order, which we immediately had killed and butchered. The inhabitants seemed more accommodating this morning. They sold us some bread.

We received a second horse for medicine and prescription to a little girl with the rheumatism whom I had bathed in warm water and anointed her a little with balsam capivia.[415] I dressed the woman again this morning who declared that she had rested better last night than she had since she had been sick. I was busily employed for several hours this morning in administering eye water to a crowd of applicants. We once more obtained a plentiful meal, much to the comfort of all the party.

Captain Lewis exchanged horses with Wearkkoomt and gave him a small flag with which he was much pleased and gratified. The sorrel which Captain Lewis obtained is a strong, active, well-broken horse.

The Kooskooskee River may be safely navigated at present. All the rocks of the shoals and rapids are perfectly covered. The current is strong, the water clear and cold. This river is rising fast. The timber of this river, which consists principally of the long-leafed pine, commences about two miles below our present encampment on Colter's Creek.

---

413. a small, cylindrical plug of lint or gauze used to keep open a wound

414. an ointment of wax, pitch, resin, and olive oil with "sovereign" healing powers (Bakeless, p. 313)

415. perhaps *copaiba balsam*, the oleoresin of the balsam

It was 2:00 p.m. this evening before we could collect our horses. At 3:00 p.m. we set out, accompanied by the brother of the Twisted Hair and Wearkkoomt. We directed the horse, which I had obtained for the purpose of eating to be led, as it was unbroken. In performing this duty, a quarrel ensued between Drouillard and Colter.

We continued our march along the river, on its north side, nine miles to a lodge of six families, built of sticks, mats and dried hay, of the same form of those heretofore described.

We passed a lodge of three families at four miles on the river. No provisions of any description were to be obtained of these people.

A little after dark our young horse broke the rope by which he was confined and made his escape, much to the chagrin of all who recollected the keenness of their appetites last evening. The brother of the Twisted Hair and Wearkkoomt, with ten others, encamped with us this evening. The natives have a considerable salmon fishery up Colter's Creek.

Wednesday, May 7, 1806:

Clark: This morning we collected our horses and set out early, accompanied by the brother of the Twisted Hair as a guide. Wearkkoomt and his party left us.

We proceeded up the river four miles to a lodge of six families just below the entrance of a small creek. Here our guide recommended our passing the river. He informed us that the road was better on the south side and that game was more abundant also on that side, near the entrance of [the] Nez Percé River. We determined to pursue the route recommended by the guide and, accordingly, unloaded our horses and prepared to pass the river, which we effected by means of one canoe in the course of four hours.

A man of this lodge produced us two canisters of powder which, he informed us, he had found by means of his dog where they had been buried in the bottom near the river a few miles above. They were the same which we had buried as we descended the river last fall. As he had kept them safe and had honesty enough to return them to us, we gave him a fire steel by way of compensation.

The spurs of the Rocky Mountains, which were in view from the high plains today, were perfectly covered with snow. The Indians inform us that the snow is yet so deep on the mountains that we shall not be able to pass them until after the next full moon, or about the first of June. Others set the time at a more distant period. This is unwelcome intelligence to men confirmed to a diet of horsebeef and roots, and who are as anxious as we are to return to the fat plains of the Missouri, and thence to our native homes.

I observed in all the lodges which we have passed since we crossed Lewis's River decoys, or stalking heads, as they are sometimes called. These decoys are for the deer and are formed of the skin of the head and upper portion of the neck of that animal, extended in the natural shape by means of a few little sticks placed within. The hunter, when he sees a deer, conceals himself and with his hand gives to the decoy the action of a deer at feed, and this induces the deer within arrowshot. In this mode the Indians near the woody country hunt on foot in such places where they cannot pursue the deer with horses, which is their favorite method when the grounds will permit.

The ornaments worn by the Nez Percé are: in their nose, a single shell of wampum; the pearl and beads are suspended from the ears; beads are worn around their wrists, neck, and over their shoulders crosswise in the form of a double sash. The hair of the men is queued in two rolls, which hang on each side in front of the body.

Collars of bear claws are also common, but the article of dress on which they appear to bestow most pains and ornaments is a kind of collar, or breastplate. This is most commonly a strip of otter skins of about six inches wide, taken out of the center of the skin, its whole length including the head. This is dressed with the hair on. This is tied around the neck and hangs in front of the body, the tail frequently reaching below their knees. On this skin, in front, are attached pieces of pearl, beads, wampum, pieces of red cloth and, in short, whatever they conceive most valuable or ornamental.

Thursday, May 8, 1806:

Clark: Drouillard and Pierre Cruzatte brought in a deer each and Collins wounded one which our dog caught near our camp. [The] total of our stock of provisions [is] four deer and some horse flesh.

On the small creek which passes our camp, the natives have lately encamped and, as we are informed, have been much distressed for provisions. They have felled a number of small pines in the vicinity of this encampment, for the seed which is in the burr of which they eat. We are informed that they were compelled to collect the moss of the pine, boil and eat it, in the latter part of the last winter.

On the creek near our camp I observed a kind of trap, which was made with great pains, to catch the small fish which pass down with the stream. This was a dam formed of stone so as to collect the water in a narrow part, not exceeding three feet wide, from which place the water shot with great force and scattered through some small willows closely connected and fastened with bark. This mat of willow switches was about four feet wide and six [feet] long, lying in a horizontal position, [and] fastened at the extremity. The small fish which fell on those willows were washed on the willows where they lay until taken off, etc. I caught, or took off those willows, nine small trout from three to seven inches in length.

Soon after I returned from the fishery, an Indian came from a fishery of a similar kind, a little above, with twelve small fish which he offered me, which I declined, accepting, as I found from his signs, that his house was a short distance above and that these fisheries afforded the principal part of the food for his children.

The great chief of the bands below, who has a cut nose, joined us this morning. We gave the entrails with four young fawns, which were in two of the deer killed today, to the Indians [and] also some of our deer and horse flesh. The paunches[416] of the deer they ate without any preparation further than washing them a little. The fawns they boiled and ate every part of them, even the skins with the hair. The Shoshone Indian was much displeased that he was not furnished with as much deer as he could eat. He refused to speak to the wife of Charbonneau, through whom we could understand the natives. We did not indulge him, and in the afterpart of the day, he came to and spoke very well.

We loaded up and set out on the road leading, as we were informed, to the lodge of the Twisted Hair, the chief in whose care we left our horses. We were accompanied by the Cut Nose chief, our old chief who had accompanied us down the river, and several men. We ascended the hills, which were steep and immensely high, to a level, rich country thinly timbered with pine.

We had not proceeded more than four miles before we met the Twisted Hair and several men meeting of us. We were very coolly received by the Twisted Hair. He spoke aloud and was answered by the Cut Nose. We could not learn what they said, but plainly discovered that a misunderstanding had taken place between them. We made signs to them that we should proceed on to the next water and encamp.

Accordingly, I set out and they all followed. We had not proceeded far before the road crossed a small, handsome stream, on which we encamped. The parties of these two chiefs took different positions at some distance from each other and all appeared sulky.

After we had formed our camp, we sent Drouillard with a pipe to smoke with the Twisted Hair and learn the cause of the dispute between him and the Cut Nose, and also to invite him to our fire to smoke with us. The Twisted Hair came to our fire to smoke. We then sent Drouillard to the Cut Nose's fire with the same directions. He returned and informed us that the Cut Nose said he would join us in a few minutes.

---

416. stomachs

It appears that the cause of the quarrel between these two men is about our horses and we cannot learn the particulars of this quarrel, which probably originated through jealousy on the part of the Cut Nose who blames the Twisted Hair for suffering our horses to be ridden and want water during the winter, etc. Twisted Hair says the horses were taken from him, etc.

The Cut Nose joined us in a short time. We smoked with all the party of both chiefs and told them that we were sorry to find them at variance with each other.

The Cut Nose said that the Twisted Hair was a bad man and wore two faces, that he had not taken care of our horses as was expected, that [he] himself and the Broken Arm had caused our horses to be watered in the winter and had them driven together, and that if we would proceed on to the village of the great chief for whom we had left a flag last fall, the Broken Arm, he would send for our horses, that he had himself three of them. He also informed us that the great chief, hearing of our distressed situation, had sent his son and four men to meet us and have furnished on the way, etc., that the young men had missed us and could never overtake us until this time, that the great chief had two bad horses for us and expected us to go to his lodge, which was near the river and about half a day's march above, etc.

The Twisted Hair told us that he wished to smoke with us at his lodge, which was on the road leading to the great chief's lodge and but a few miles ahead. If we would delay at his lodge tomorrow, he would go after our saddles and horses, which were near the place we made our canoes last fall.

Accordingly, we informed the Indians of our intentions. We all smoked and conversed until about 10:00 p.m. The Indians retired and we lay down.

[We] directed five hunters to turn out early in the morning to hunt and meet us at the Twisted Hair's lodge.

Friday, May 9, 1806:

Clark: We were detained until 9:00 a.m. for our horses, which were much scattered, at which time we collected our horses and set out and proceeded on through a beautiful, open, rich country for six miles to the camp of the Twisted Hair. This campment is formed of two lodges built in the usual form of mats and straw. The largest and principal lodge is calculated for two fires only. The second lodge is small and appears to be intended for the sick women who always retire to a separate lodge when they have the ____.

Before 2:00 p.m. all our hunters joined us, having killed only one deer, which was lost in the river, and a pheasant. Soon after we halted at the lodge of the Twisted Hair, he set out with two boys and Willard, with a pack horse, down to the river near the place we [had] made the canoes, for our saddles and a canister of powder and some lead buried there, [and] also a part of our horses, which resorted near that place.

Late in the evening they returned with twenty-one of our horses and about half our saddles with the powder and balls. The greater part of the horses were in fine order, though five of them had been ridden and worsted in such a manner last fall by the Indians that they had not recovered and are in very low order, and three with sore backs. We had all the recovered horses caught and hobbled.

We procured some pounded roots, of which a soup was made thick, on which we supped.

The wind blew hard from the southwest, accompanied with rain, until from 7:00 until 9:00 p.m. when it began to snow, and continued all night.

Saturday, May 10, 1806:

Clark: The air [was] keen and cold [and] the snow [was] eight inches deep on the plain.

We collected our horses and set out for the village of the chief with a flag, and proceeded on through an open plain. The road was slippery and the snow clogged and caused the horses to trip very frequently. The mud at the heads of the streams which we passed was deep and well-supplied with the camas.

At 4:00 p.m. we arrived at the village of Tin-nach-e-moo-toolt,[417] the chief whom we had left a flag. This flag was hoisted on a pole. Under the flag, the chief met me and conducted me to a spot near a small run about eighty paces from his lodges where he requested me to halt, which I did. Soon after, Captain Lewis, who was in the rear, came up and we smoked with and told this chief [of] our situation in respect to provisions.

They brought forward about two bushels of quamash, four cakes of bread made of roots, and a dried fish. We informed the chief that our party was not accustomed to eating roots without flesh and proposed to exchange some of our old horses for young ones to eat. They said that they would not exchange horses but would furnish us with such as we wished, and produced two, one of which we killed, and informed them that we did not wish to kill the other at this time.

We gave medals to the Broken Arm, or Tin-nach-e-moo-toolt, and Ho-hâst-ill-pilp, two principal chiefs of the Nez Percé nation, and

---

417. the Broken Arm

were informed that there was one other great chief (in all, four) who had but one eye. He would be here tomorrow.

A large lodge of leather was pitched, and Captain Lewis and I were invited into it. We entered and the chief and principal men came into the lodge and formed a circle. A parcel of wood was collected and laid at the door, and a fire [had been] made in this conic lodge before we entered it. The chief requested that we might make the lodge our homes while we remained with him. Here, after we had taken a repast on roots and horse beef, we resumed our council with the Indians which, together with smoking, took up the balance of the evening.

As these people had been liberal, I directed the men not to crowd their lodges in search of food [in] the manner hunger had compelled them to do at most lodges we have passed, and which the Twisted Hair had informed us was disagreeable to the natives, but their previous want of hospitality had induced us to consult their inclinations but little and suffered our men to obtain provisions from them on the best terms they could.

The village of the Broken Arm consists of one house, or lodge, only which is one hundred fifty feet in length, built in the usual form of sticks, mats, and dry grass. It contains twenty-four fires and about double that number of families. From appearance, I presume they could raise one hundred fighting men. The noise of their women pounding the cowas roots reminded me of a nail factory. The Indians appear well pleased, and I am confident that they are not more so than our men who have their stomachs once more well filled with horse beef and the bread of cowas.

These people have shown much greater acts of hospitality than we have witnessed from any nation or tribe since we have passed the Rocky Mountains. In short, be it spoken to their immortal honor, it is the only act which deserves the appellation of hospitality which we have witnessed in this quarter.

Sunday, May 11, 1806:

Clark: We were crowded in the lodge with the Indians who continued [with us] all night and this morning. Great numbers were around us.

The One-Eyed chief arrived and we gave him a medal of the small size, and spoke to the Indians through a Shoshone boy, Charbonneau, and his wife. We informed them who we were, where we came from, and our intentions towards them, which pleased them very much.

A young man, son to the great chief who was killed not long since by the Indians from the northeast, brought an elegant mare and colt and gave [them to] us, and said he had opened his ears to what we had said and his heart was glad, and requested us to take this mare and colt as a token of his determination to pursue our councils, etc. The Twisted Hair brought six of our horses, all in fine order.

Great numbers of Indians applied to us for medical aid which we gave them cheerfully, so far as our skill and store of medicine would enable us. Scrofula, ulcers, rheumatism, sore eyes, and the loss of the use of their limbs are the most common cases among them. The latter case is not very common, but we have seen three instances of it among the Nez Percé, a very extraordinary complaint.

About 3:00 p.m. George Drouillard arrived with two deer which he had killed. He informed us that the snow still continued to cover the plains.

We are now pretty well informed about the principal chiefs of the Nez Percé nation. As all these chiefs were present in our lodge, we thought it a favorable time to repeat what had been said and to enter more minutely into the views of our government with respect to the inhabitants of this western part of the continent, its intentions of establishing trading houses for their relief, its wish to restore peace and harmony among the natives, the strength, wealth and powers of our nation, etc.

To this end, we drew a map of the country with a coal on a mat in their way and, by the assistance of the Shoshone boy and our interpreters, were enabled to make ourselves understood by them, although it had to pass through French, Hidatsa, Shoshone, and Nez Percé languages. The interpretation being tedious, it occupied the greater part of the day before we had communicated to them what we wished. They appeared highly pleased.

After this council was over we amused ourselves with showing them the power of magnetism, the spyglass, compass, watch, air gun, and sundry other articles equally novel and incomprehensible to them. They informed us that after we left the Hidatsa last spring, that three of their people had visited that nation and that they had informed them of us, and had told them that we had such things in our possession, but that they could not place confidence in the information until they had now witnessed it themselves.

In the evening, a man was brought in a robe by four Indians and laid down near me. They informed me that this man was a chief of considerable note who has been in the situation I see him for five years. This man is incapable of moving a single limb but lies like a corpse in whatever position he is placed, yet he eats heartily, digests his food perfectly, [and] enjoys his understanding. His pulse is good and [he] has retained his flesh almost perfectly. In short, were it not that he appears a little pale from having been so long in the shade, he might well be taken for a man in good health.

I suspect that their confinement to a diet of roots may give rise to all the disorders of the natives of this quarter, except the rheumatism and sore eyes, and to the latter of those, the state of debility incident to a vegetable diet may measurably contribute.

The Nez Percé, notwithstanding they live in the crowded manner before mentioned, [yet] are much more cleanly in their persons and habitations than any nation we have seen since we left the Illinois.

Monday, May 12, 1806:

Clark: After breakfast I began to administer eye water and in a few minutes had nearly forty applicants with sore eyes, and many others with other complaints, most commonly rheumatic disorders and weaknesses in the back and loins, particularly the women.

The Indians had a grand council this morning, after which we were presented each with a horse by two young men at the instance[418] of the nation. We caused the chiefs to be seated and gave them each a flag, a pint of powder, and fifty balls. To the two young men who had presented the horses, we also gave powder and balls. The Broken Arm pulled off his leather shirt and gave [it to] me. In return, [I] gave him a shirt.

We retired to the lodge and the natives spoke to the following purport, i.e., [that] they had listened to our advice and that the whole nation was determined to follow it, [and] that they had only one heart and one tongue on this subject. They wished to be at peace with all nations, etc. Some of their men would accompany us to the Missouri, etc., etc.

As a great number of men, women, and children were waiting and requesting medical assistance, many of them with the most simple complaints which could be easily relieved, independent of many with disorders entirely out of the power of medicine, all requesting something, we agreed that I should administer and Captain Lewis to hear and answer the Indians.

I was closely employed until 2:00 p.m. administering eye water to about forty grown persons, some simple cooling medicines to the disabled chief, to several women with rheumatic afflictions, and a man who had a swelled hip, etc., etc.

In the evening three of our horses were brought, all in fine order. We have now only six remaining out.

---

418. request

These people are much afraid of the Blackfoot Indians, and the Hidatsa of Fort de Prairie establishment. Those Indians kill great numbers of this nation whenever they pass over to hunt on the Missouri.

One of our men bought a horse for a few small articles of an Indian. The Indians brought up a fat horse and requested us to kill and eat it as they had nothing else to offer us to eat. The Cut Nose made a present of a horse to Drouillard at the same time the two horses were offered to Captain Lewis and me.

The horses of these people are large, well-formed, and active [and] generally in fine order. Sore backs [are] caused by riding them either without saddles, or with pads, which do not prevent the weight of the rider pressing immediately on the backbone and withers of the horse.

The Indians formed two parties and plied for their beads. We gave the Twisted Hair a gun, powder, and one hundred balls, in part for taking care of our horses, etc., and wish him to camp near us until we cross the mountains, which he agreed to do and was much pleased. We have turned our attentions towards the Twisted Hair who has several sons grown who are well-acquainted, as well as himself, with the various roads through the Rocky Mountains and will answer very well as guides to us through those mountains.

In the council today the father of Hohâstillpilp said the Nez Percé were fully convinced of the advantages of peace and ardently wished to cultivate peace with their neighbors. Early last summer, three of their brave men were sent with a pipe to the Shoshones on the southeast fork of Lewis's River in the plains of [the] Columbia. Their pipe was disregarded and their three men murdered, which had given rise to the war expedition against that nation last fall, that their warriors had fallen in with and killed forty-two of the Shoshones with the loss of three men only on their part, that this had satisfied the blood of the deceased's friends, and they would never again make war against the Shoshones, but were willing to receive them as friends, [and] that as we had not seen the Indians towards Fort de Prairie they did not think it safe to venture over to the plains of the Missouri, where they would fondly go provided those nations would not kill them.

I gave a vial of eye water to the Broken Arm for to wash the eyes of all who applied to him and told him when it was out we would replenish it again.

Tuesday, May 13, 1806:

Clark: [It was] a fine morning.

I administered to the sick and gave directions.

We collected all our horses and set out at 1:00 p.m. and proceeded down the creek to the Flathead[419] River a short distance below the entrance of the creek. At this place, we expected to have met the canoe which was promised to be furnished [to] us, and for which an Indian set out very early this morning. We halted at the river and unloaded our horses and turned them out to feed. Several Indians accompanied us to the river and continued [with us] until evening. The man who set out early this morning to the forks of this river for a canoe did not arrive until after sunset.

We remained all night. In the evening, we tried the speed of several of our horses. These horses are strong, active, and well-formed. These people have immense numbers of them. Fifty or sixty or a hundred head is not unusual for an individual to possess.

The Nez Percé are, in general, stout, well-formed, active men. They have high noses, and many of them on the aquiline[420] order, with cheerful and agreeable countenances. Their complexions are not remarkable. In common with other Indian nations of America, they extract their beard; this is more particularly confined to the females. They appear to be cheerful, but not gay. They are fond of gambling and of their amusements, which consist principally in shooting their arrows at a target made of willow bark, and in riding and exercising themselves on horseback, racing, etc. They are expert marksmen and good riders.

They do not appear to be so much devoted to baubles as most of the nations we have met with, but seem anxious always to receive articles of utility, such as knives, axes, kettles, blankets, and moccasin awls. Blue beads, however, may form an exception to this remark. This article, among all the nations of this country, may be justly compared to gold and silver among civilized nations.

They are generally well-clothed in their style. Their dress consists of a long shirt which reaches to the middle of the leg, long leggings which reach as high as the waist, moccasins, and [a] robe. These are formed of various skins and are, in all respects, like those of the Shoshone. Their ornaments consist of beads, shells, and pieces of brass variously attached to their dress, to their ears, around their necks, wrists, arms, etc. A band of some kind usually surrounds the head. This is most frequently the skin of some fur animal [such] as the fox, otter, etc. I observed a tippet worn by Hohâstillpilp which was formed of human scalps and ornamented with the thumbs and fingers of several men which he had slain in battle. They also wear a collar, or breastplate, of otter skin ornamented with shells, beads, and quills. The

---

419. Clearwater (DeVoto)

420. curving like an eagle's beak

women braid their hair in two tresses[421] which hang in the same position of those of the men, which are queued and hang over each shoulder, etc.

Wednesday, May 14, 1806:

Clark: We had all our horses collected by 10:00 a.m. During that time, we had all our baggage crossed over the river, which is rapid and about one hundred fifty yards wide. After the baggage was over to the north side, we crossed our horses without much trouble and hobbled them in the bottom, after which we moved a short distance below to a convenient situation and formed a camp around a very convenient spot for defense.

This situation, we concluded, would be sufficiently convenient to hunt the woodlands for bear and deer, and for the salmon fish which, we were told, would be here in a few days, and also a good situation for our horses. The hills to the east and north of us are high, broken, and but partially timbered. The soil [is] rich and affords fine grass. In short, as we are compelled to reside a while in this neighborhood, I feel perfectly satisfied with our position.

Immediately after we had crossed the river, the chief called the Broken Arm and another principal chief arrived on the opposite side and began to sing. We sent the canoe over [for] those chiefs. The son of the Broken Arm and the son of a great chief who was killed last year by the Hidatsa of [the] Saskatchewan River, these two young men were the two who gave Captain Lewis and me each a horse with great ceremony in behalf of the nation a few days ago, and the latter a most elegant mare and colt the morning after we arrived at the village.

Hohâstillpilp, with much ceremony, presented Captain Lewis with an elegant gray horse, which he had brought for that purpose. Captain Lewis gave him in return a handkerchief, two hundred balls, and four pounds of powder, with which he appeared perfectly satisfied and appeared much pleased.

We made several attempts to exchange our stallions for geldings or mares without success. We even offered two for one. These horses are troublesome and cut each other very much and, as we can't exchange them, we think it best to castrate them and begin the operation this evening. One of the Indians present offered his services on this occasion. He cut them without tying the string of the stone, as is usual. He scraped it very clean and separated it before he cut it.

---

421. braids

About meridian Shannon came in with two grouse and two squirrels common to this country. His moccasins wore out [and] obliged [him] to come in early.

Collins returned in the evening with the two bears, which he had killed in the morning. One of them, an old he, was in fine order. The other, a female with cubs, was meager.

We gave the Indians about us, fifteen in number, two shoulders and a ham of the bear to eat, which they cooked in the following manner, to wit: On a brisk fire of dried wood, they threw a parcel of small stones from the river. When the fire had burned down and heated the stones, they placed them level and laid on a parcel of pine boughs. On those, they laid the flesh of the bear in flitches, placing boughs between each course of meat, and then covering it thickly with pine boughs. After this they poured on a small quantity of water, and covered the whole over with earth to the depth of four inches. In this situation, they suffered it to remain about three hours, when they took it out fit for use.

This nation esteems the killing of one of these tremendous animals equally great with that of an enemy in the field of action. We gave the claws of these bears, which Collins had killed, to Hohâstillpilp.

Thursday, May 15, 1806:

Clark: Reubin Field went out to hunt [on] his horse very early and saw a large bear, and at no great distance from camp. Several men went in pursuit of the bear and pursued his trail some time without getting sight of this monster.

Shannon went out with Labiche to hunt, and continued out three days. Gibson and Hall accompanied them for the meat Labiche [had] killed yesterday, which they brought in by 11:00 a.m. this morning.

The female bear was black with white hairs intermixed and a white spot [was] on the breast. The cubs were about the size of a dog [and] also poor. One of them [was] very black and the other a light reddish-brown or bay color. These bears give me a stronger evidence of the various colored bears of this country being [of] one species only than any I have heretofore had. Several other colors have been seen.

Frazier, Joseph Field, and Peter Wiser complained of a violent pain in their heads, [and] Howard and York with violent colics. The cause of these disorders we are unable to account for. Their diet and the sudden change of climate must contribute.

The Broken Arm and twelve of the young men of his nation left us today about 11:00 and crossed the river to his village. Hohâstillpilp and three old men continued with us until about 5:00 p.m. when they left us and returned to their village.

A party of fourteen Indians passed our camp about 1:00 p.m. on their way to the level uplands to run and kill the deer with their horses and bows and arrows. Some of them were also provided with deer heads cast for the purpose of decoying the deer. These men continued with us but a few minutes and proceeded on.

These people hunt most commonly on horseback, surround the deer or goat, which they find in the open plains, and kill them with their arrows, though they sometimes hunt the deer on foot and decoy them.

We had all of our horses driven together today with a view to familiarize them to each other. Those that were cut yesterday are stiff, and several of them much swelled. We had all our baggage secured and covered with a roof of straw. Our little fortification [is] also completely secured with brush, around which our camp is formed. The greater part of our security from the rains, etc., is the grass which is formed in a kind of ruff[422] so as to turn the rain completely, and is much the best tents we have. As the days are warm, etc., we have a bower made to write under, which we find not only comfortable but necessary to keep off the intense heat of the sun, which has [a] great effect in this low bottom.

On the high plains off the river, the climate is entirely different. [It is] cool, [with] some snow on the north hillsides near the top, and [the] vegetation [is] nearly three weeks later than in the river bottoms. The Rocky Mountains immediately in view [are] covered, several say four and five feet deep, with snow. Here I behold three different climates within a few miles.

Gass: From the Mandan nation to the Pacific Ocean, the arms of the Indians are generally bows and arrows and the war mallet. The war mallet is a club with a large head of wood or stone. Those of stone are generally covered with leather and fastened to the end of the club with thongs, or straps of leather, and the sinews of animals.

Friday, May 16, 1806:

Clark: The Indians of this country seldom kill the bear. They are much afraid of them and the killing of a white, or grizzly, bear is as great a feat as two of their enemy. The few of these animals which they chance to kill are found in the level, open lands and pursued on horses and killed with their arrows. They are fond of the flesh of this animal,

422. collar

and eat immoderately of it when they have a sufficiency to indulge themselves.

The men who were complaining of the headache and colic yesterday and last night are much better today.

Charbonneau's squaw gathered a quantity of fennel roots, which we find very palatable and nourishing food. The onion we also find in abundance and boil it with our meat.

Saturday, May 17, 1808:

Clark: [It] rained moderately all the last night and this morning until we are wet.

The rains, unfortunately, wet the chronometer in the fob[423] of Captain Lewis's breeches, which has never before been wet since we set out on this expedition. Her works were cautiously wiped and made dry by Captain Lewis, and I think she will receive no injury from this misfortune, etc.

We arranged the hunters and horses to each hunter and directed them to turn out in the morning early and continue out until they killed something. Others [were] arranged so as to take care of the hunters' horses in their absence.

[It] rained moderately all day [and], at the same time, [it] snowed on the mountains which are to the southeast of us.

No Indians visited us today, which is a singular circumstance as we have not been one day without Indians since we left the Long Narrows of the Columbia.

The few warm days which we have had have melted the snow in the mountains, and the river has risen considerably.

That icy barrier which separates me from my friends and country, from all which makes life estimable, is yet white with the snow, which is many feet deep. I frequently consult the natives on the subject of passing this tremendous barrier, which now presents [itself] to our view for a great extent. They all appear to agree as to the time these mountains may be passed, which is about the middle of June. Sergeant Pryor informs me that the snow on the high plains from the river was shoe deep this morning when he came down.

At the distance of eighteen miles from the river and on the eastern border of the high plains, the Rocky Mountains commence and present us with winter. Here we have summer, spring, and winter in the short space of twenty or thirty miles.

---

423. a small pocket at the front of trousers

Sunday, May 18, 1806:

Clark: The squaw wife to Charbonneau busied herself gathering the roots of the fennel, called by the Shoshone Indians "year-pah,"[424] for the purpose of drying, to eat on the Rocky Mountains. These roots are very palatable either fresh, roasted, boiled or dried, and are generally between the size of a quill and that of a man's finger, and about the length of the latter.

At 3:00 p.m. Joseph Field returned from the chase without killing anything. He complains of being unwell.

Soon after, an old man and a woman arrived, the man with sore eyes and the woman with a griping and rheumatic afflictions. I gave the woman a dose of cream of tartar and flour of sulphur, and the man some eye water.

Lepage took a salmon from an eagle at a short distance below our camp. This induces us to believe that the salmon are in this river and, most probably, will be here in great numbers in the course of a few days.

Monday, May 19, 1806:

Clark: We sent Charbonneau, Thompson, Potts, and Wiser over to the villages above to purchase some roots to eat with our poor bear meat, for which purchase we gave them a few awls, knitting pins and arm bands, and directed them to proceed up on this side of the river opposite to the village, and cross in the canoe which, we are informed, is at that place.

About 11:00 four men and eight women came to our camp with Thompson, who [had gone] to the village very early this morning. These men applied for eye water, and the women had a variety of complaints, though the most general complaints were the rheumatism, pains in the back, and the sore eyes. They also brought forward a very young child whom they said had been very sick. I administered eye water to all, [to] two of the women I gave a cathartic, [to] one, whose spirits were very low and much depressed, I gave thirty drops of laudanum,[425] and to the others, I had their backs, hips, legs, thighs, and arms well-rubbed with volatile liniment. All of these poor people thought themselves much benefited by what had been done for them and at 3:00 p.m. they all returned to their villages well-satisfied.

At 5:00 p.m. Potts, Charbonneau, etc., returned from the village with about six bushels of the root the natives call "cowas," and some bread of the same root.

---

424. yampa, or squawroot (DeVoto)
425. tincture of opium

Reubin and Joseph Field returned with the horse Captain Lewis rode across the Rocky Mountains. We had this horse immediately cut with two others, which we had not before thought proper to castrate.

We amused ourselves about an hour this afternoon looking at the men run their horses. Several of them would be thought swift horses in the Atlantic states.

Wednesday, May 21, 1806:

Clark: As our tent is not sufficient to keep off the rain, we are compelled to have some other resort for a security from the repeated showers which fall. We have a small, half-circular place made and covered with grass, which makes a very secure shelter for us to sleep under.

We divided our store of merchandise amongst our party for the purpose of procuring some roots, etc., of the natives. Each man's part amounted to about an awl, knitting pin, a little paint, and some thread and two needles, which is but a scanty dependence for roots to take us over those great snowy barriers (Rocky Mountains), which are and will be the cause of our detention in this neighborhood, probably, until the tenth or fifteenth of June. They are at this time covered deep with snow.

We ate the last of our meat for dinner today and our only certain dependence are the roots we can procure from the natives for the few articles we have left. Those roots, with what game we can procure from the woods, will probably last us until the arrival of the salmon. If they should not, we have a horse in store ready to be killed, which the Indians have offered to us.

Thursday, May 22, 1806:

Clark: [It was] a fine day. We exposed all our baggage to the sun to air and dry, [and] also our roots, which we have procured of the natives.

As the greater part of our men have not had any meat to eat for two days, and the roots they complain of, not being accustomed to live on them altogether, we directed a large colt, which was given to us by a young man with an elegant mare, to be killed. This colt was fat and was handsome-looking meat.

Late in the evening we were informed that the horse which Captain Lewis rode over the Rocky Mountains, and which was cut [the] day before yesterday, had his hip out of place since that time, and could not walk. Captain Lewis examined him and thought he could not recover.

At 5:00 p.m. two young men, highly decorated in their way, came to our camp and informed us that the fat fish were in great numbers in Lewis's River.

Charbonneau's son, a small child, is dangerously ill. His jaw and throat are much swelled. We applied a poultice of onions after giving him some cream of tartar, etc.

This day proved to be fine and fair, which afforded us an opportunity of drying our baggage, which had got a little wet.

Friday, May 23, 1806:

Clark: The child is something better this morning than it was last night. We applied a fresh poultice of the wild onion, which we repeated twice in the course of the day. The swelling does not appear to [have] increased any since yesterday.

The four Indians who visited us today informed us that they [had] come from their village on Lewis's River two days' ride from this place for the purpose of seeing us and getting a little eye water. I washed their eyes with some eye water and they all left us at 2:00 p.m. and returned to their villages on the opposite side of this river.

The hunters informed us that they had hunted with great industry all the country between the river and for some distance above and below without the smallest chance of killing any game. They informed us that the highlands are very cold with snow, which has fallen for every day or night for several days past.

Our horse which was cut is likely to do well.

Ordway: William Bratton, having been so long, better than three months, nearly helpless with a severe pain in his back, we now undertake sweating him nearly in the manner as the Indians do, only cover the hole with blankets, having bows bent over the hole. We expect this operation will help him.

Saturday, May 24, 1806:

Lewis: The child was very restless last night. Its jaw and the back of its neck are much more swollen than they were yesterday, though his fever has abated considerably. We gave it a dose of cream of tartar and applied a fresh poultice of onions.

William Bratton still continues very unwell. He eats heartily, digests his food well, and has recovered his flesh almost perfectly, yet [he] is so weak in the loins that he is scarcely able to walk, nor can he sit upright but with the greatest pain. We have tried every remedy which our ingenuity could devise with our stock of medicines furnished us, without effect. John Shields observed that he had seen men in a similar situation restored by violent sweats. Bratton requested that he might be sweated in the manner proposed by Shields, to which we consented.

Shields sunk a circular hole of three feet [in] diameter and four feet deep in the earth. He kindled a large fire in the hole and heated [it] well, after which the fire was taken out, a seat placed in the center of the hole for the patient, with a board at [the] bottom for his feet to rest on. Some hoops of willow poles were bent in an arch, crossing each over the hole. On these, several blankets were thrown, forming a secure and thick awning of about three feet high. The patient, being stripped naked, was seated under this awning in the hole, and the blankets [were] well-secured on every side. The patient was furnished with a vessel of water, which he sprinkled on the bottom and sides of the hole and, by that means, created as much steam or vapor as he could possibly bear. In this situation he was kept about twenty minutes, after which he was taken out and suddenly plunged in cold water twice, and was then immediately returned to the sweat hole where he was continued three-quarters of an hour longer, then taken out, covered up in several blankets, and suffered to cool gradually.

During the time of his being in the sweat hole, he drank copious draughts of a strong tea of horse mint. Shields says that he had previously seen the tea of Sinneca snake root used instead of the mint which was now employed for the want of the other, which is not to be found in this country.

This experiment was made yesterday. Bratton feels himself much better and is walking about today and says he is nearly free from pain.

At 11:00 a.m. a canoe arrived with three of the natives, one of them the sick man of whom I have before made mention as having lost the power of his limbs. He is a chief of considerable note among them, and they seem extremely anxious for his recovery. As he complains of no pain in any particular part, we conceive it cannot be the rheumatism, nor do we suppose that it can be a paralytic attack, or his limbs would have been more diminished. We have supposed that it was some disorder, which owed its origin to a diet of particular roots perhaps, and such as we have never before witnessed. While at the village of the Broken Arm, we had recommended a diet of fish or flesh for this man, and the cold bath every morning. We had also given him a few doses of cream of tartar and flour of sulphur, to be repeated every third day. This poor wretch thinks that he feels himself somewhat better, but to me, there appears to be no visible alteration. We are at a loss [as to] what to do for this unfortunate man. We gave him a few drops of laudanum and a little portable soup.

Four of our party passed the river and visited the lodge of the Broken Arm for the purpose of trading some awls, which they had made of the links of a small chain belonging to one of their steel traps, for some roots. They returned in the evening, having been very successful. They had obtained a good supply of roots and bread of cowas.

This day has proved warmer than any of the preceding since we have arrived here.

Sunday, May 25, 1806:

Clark: [It] rained moderately the greater part of last night and this morning until 6:00 a.m.

The child is not so well today as yesterday. I repeated the cream of tartar and the onion poultice.

I caused a sweat to be prepared for the Indian in the same hole which Bratton had been sweated in two days past.

One of our men purchased a bear skin of the natives which was nearly of a cream-colored white. This skin, which was the skin of an animal of the middle size of bears, together with the different sizes, colors, etc., of those which have been killed by our hunters, gives me a stronger evidence of the various colored bears of this country being one species only than any I have heretofore had. The poil[426] of these bears were infinitely longer, finer, and thicker than the black bear. Their talons [are] also longer and more blunt, as worn by digging roots. The bear here is far from being as passive as the common black bear. They have attacked and fought our hunters already, but not so fiercely as those of the Missouri. There are also some of the common black bear in this neighborhood, though not so common as the other species.

We attempted to sweat the sick Indian but could not succeed. He was not able either to sit up or be supported in the place prepared for him. I therefore determined to inform the natives that nothing but severe sweats would restore this disabled man, and even that [was] doubtful in his present situation.

Monday, May 26, 1806:

Clark: The child [was] something better this morning, though the swelling yet continues. We still apply the onion poultice.

I directed what should be done for the disabled man, gave him a few doses of cream of tartar and flour [of] sulphur and some portable soup, and directed that he should be taken home and sweated, etc.

---

426. French for *hair*

One of our men saw a salmon in the river today, and two others ate of salmon at the near village which were brought from Lewis's River.

Our canoe [was] finished and put into the water. It will carry twelve men.

The river [is] rising very fast and [the] snow appears to melt on the mountains.

Tuesday, May 27, 1806:

Lewis: Early this morning we sent Reubin Field in search of the horse which the Indians had given us to kill. At 10:00 in the morning he returned with the horse and we killed and butchered him. He was large and in good order.

Hohâstillpilp told us that most of the horses we saw running at large in this neighborhood belonged to him and his people, and whenever we were in want of meat, he requested that we would kill any of them we wished. This is a piece of liberality which would do honor to such as [those who] boast of civilization. Indeed, I doubt whether there are not a great number of our countrymen who would see us fast many days before their compassion would excite them to a similar act of liberality.

Charbonneau's son is much better today, though the swelling on the side of his neck, I believe, will terminate in an ugly imposthume[427] a little below the ear.

The Indians were so anxious that the sick chief should be sweated under our inspection that they requested [that] we would make a second attempt today. Accordingly, the hole was somewhat enlarged and his father, a very good looking old man, went into the hole with him and sustained him in a proper position during the operation. We could not make him sweat as copiously as we wished. After the operation, he complained of considerable pain. We gave him thirty drops of laudanum, which soon composed him and he rested very well.

This is, at least, a strong mark of parental affection. They all appear extremely attentive to this sick man, nor do they appear to relax. Their assiduity towards him notwithstanding, he has been sick and helpless upwards of three years. The Nez Percé appear to be very attentive and kind to their aged people, and treat their women with more respect than the nations of the Missouri.

427. abscess

Wednesday, May 28, 1806:

Clark: We sent Goodrich to the village of the Broken Arm for hair to stuff saddle pads.

Joseph and Reubin Field set out this morning to hunt towards the mountains.

At noon Charbonneau, York, and Lepage returned. They had obtained four bags of the dried roots of cowas and some bread.

In the evening Collins, Shannon, and Colter returned with eight deer. Deer were very abundant, they informed us, but there were not many bear.

The sick chief is much better this morning. He can use his hands and arms, and seems much pleased with the prospects of recovering. He says he feels much better than he has done for a great number of months. I sincerely wish that the sweats may restore him. I have consented to repeat the sweats.

The Nez Percé held a council in the morning of the twelfth among themselves in respect to the subject on which we had spoken to them the day before. The result, as we learned, was favorable. They placed confidence in the information they had received, and resolved to pursue our advice.

After this council was over, the principal chief, or the Broken Arm, took the flour of the roots of cowas and thickened the soup in the kettles and baskets of all his people.

This being ended, he made a harangue, the purport of which was making known the deliberations of their councils and impressing the necessity of unanimity among them, and a strict attention to the resolution which had been agreed on in council. He concluded by inviting all such men as had resolved to abide by the decree of the council to come and eat, and requested such [men] as would not be so bound to show themselves by not partaking of the feast.

I was told by one of our men who was present in the house that there was not a dissenting voice on this great national question, but all swallowed their objections, if any they had, very cheerfully with their mush. During the time of this loud, animated harangue of the chief, the women cried, wrung their hands, tore their hair, and appeared to be in the utmost distress.

After this ceremony was over, the chiefs and considerate men came in a body to where we were seated at a little distance from our tent, and two young men, at the instance of the nation, presented Captain Lewis and me each a fine horse, and informed us that they had listened with attention to what we had said and were resolved to pursue our councils, etc., that as we had not seen the Blackfoot Indians and the Hidatsa of Fort de Prairie, they did not think it safe to venture over to the plains of the Missouri, where they would fondly go provided those nations would not kill them, that when we had established a trading house on the Missouri as we had promised, they would come over and trade for arms, ammunition, etc., and live about us, that it would give them much pleasure to be at peace with those nations, although they had shed much of their blood.

They said that they were poor but their hearts were good [and] we might be assured of their sincerity. Some of the brave men would go over with us to the Missouri and bring them the news as we wished, and if we could make a peace between themselves and their enemies on the other side of the mountains, their nation would go over to the Missouri in the latter end of the summer. On the subject of one of their chiefs accompanying us to the land of the white men, they could not yet determine, but that they would let us know before we left them.

[They said] that the snow was yet so deep in the mountains that if we attempted to pass we would certainly perish, and advised us to remain until after the next full moon when the snow would disappear on the south hillsides and we would find grass for our horses.

Charbonneau's child is better this day than he was yesterday. He is free from fever. The imposthume is not so large but seems to be advancing to maturity.

Friday, May 30, 1806:

Clark: Lepage and Charbonneau set out early this morning to the Indian village in order to trade with them for roots.

Sergeant Gass was sent this morning to obtain some goat hair to stuff the pads of our saddles.

Shannon and Collins were permitted to pass the river in order to trade with the natives and lay in a store of roots and bread for themselves with their proportion of the merchandise, as others had done. On landing on the opposite shore, the canoe was driven broadside, with the full force of a very strong current, against some standing trees and instantly filled with water and sank. Potts, who was with them, is an indifferent swimmer; it was with difficulty he made the land. They lost three blankets and a blanket capote and their pittance of merchandise. In our bare state of clothing, this was a serious loss.

All our invalids are on the recovery. We gave the sick chief a severe sweat today, shortly after which he could move one of his legs and thighs and work his toes pretty well. The other leg he can move a little. His fingers and arms seem to be almost entirely restored. He seems highly delighted with his recovery. I begin to entertain strong hope of his recovering by these sweats.

One of the men brought me today some onions from the high plains of a different species from those near the borders of the river, as they are also from the chive, or small onion, noticed below the Falls of the Columbia. These onions were as large as a nutmeg. They generally grow double, or two, bulbs connected by the same tissue of radicals. Each bulb has two long, linear, flat, solid leaves. This onion is exceedingly crisp and delicately flavored, indeed. I think [it is] more sweet and less strong than any I ever tasted. It is not yet perfectly in bloom; the parts of the flower are not distinct.

16: June, 1806

Having exhausted all our merchandise, we were obliged to have recourse to every subterfuge in order to prepare, in the most ample manner in our power, to meet that wretched portion of our journey, the Rocky Mountains, where hunger and cold, in their most rigorous form, assail the wearied traveler. Not any of us have yet forgotten our sufferings in those mountains in September last, [and] *I think it probable we never shall.*

Captain William Clark,
June 2, 1806

Sunday, June 1, 1806:

Clark: This morning George Drouillard, accompanied by Hohâstillpilp, set out in search of [the] two tomahawks of ours which, we have understood, were in the possession of certain Indians residing at a distance in the plains on the south side of Flathead River. One is a pipe tomahawk which Captain Lewis left at our camp on Mosquito Creek, and the other was stolen from me while we lay at the forks of this and [the] Nez Percé River last fall.

Colter and Willard set out this morning on a hunting excursion towards the quamash grounds beyond Collins Creek.

We begin to feel some anxiety with respect to Sergeant Ordway and party who were sent to Lewis's River for salmon. We have received no intelligence of them since they set out.

We desired Drouillard to make some enquiry after the Twisted Hair. The old man has not been as good as his word with respect to encamping near us, and we fear we shall be at a loss to procure guides to conduct us by the different routes we wish to pursue from Traveller's Rest to the waters of the Missouri.

Monday, June 2, 1806:

Clark: McNeal and York were sent on a trading voyage over the river this morning. Having exhausted all our merchandise, we were obliged to have recourse to every subterfuge in order to prepare, in the most ample manner in our power, to meet that wretched portion of our journey, the Rocky Mountains, where hunger and cold, in their most rigorous form, assail the wearied traveler. Not any of us have yet forgotten our sufferings in those mountains in September last, [and] I think it probable we never shall. Our traders, McNeal and York, are furnished with the buttons which Captain Lewis and I cut off our coats, some eye water and bisilicon, which we made for that purpose, and some vials of eye water, and some tin boxes, which Captain Lewis had brought from Philadelphia.

In the evening, they returned with about three bushels of roots and some bread, having made a successful voyage, not much less pleasing to us than the return of a good cargo to an East India merchant.

Drouillard arrived this evening with the Cut Nose and Hohâstillpilp who had accompanied him to the lodge of the person who had our tomahawks. He obtained both the tomahawks, principally by the influence of the former of these chiefs. The one which had been stolen we prized most, as it was the private property of the late Sergeant Floyd, and I was desirous of returning it to his friends. The man who had this tomahawk had purchased it from the man who had stolen it and was himself, at the moment of their arrival, just expiring.

His relations were unwilling to give up the tomahawk, as they intended to bury it with the deceased owner but were, at length, induced to do so for the consideration of a handkerchief [and] two strands of beads which Drouillard gave them, and two horses, given by the chiefs, to be killed, agreeable to their custom, at the grave of the deceased. A wife of the Cut Nose died some short time since; he and her relations sacrificed twenty-eight horses to her.

About noon Sergeant Ordway, Frazier, and Wiser returned with seventeen salmon and some roots of the cowas. The distance was so great from whence they brought the fish that most of them were nearly spoiled. These fish were as fat as any I ever saw, sufficiently so to cook themselves without the addition of grease or butter. Those which were sound were extremely delicious. Their flesh is of a fine rose color with a small admixture of yellow.

Our horses are all recovering, and I have no hesitation in declaring that I believe that the Indian method of gelding is preferable to that practiced by ourselves.

Gass: About noon three men, who had gone over to Lewis's River, about two and a half days' journey distant, to get some fish, returned with a few very good salmon and some roots.

One of these men got two Spanish dollars from an Indian for an old razor. They said they got the dollars from about a Snake Indian's neck they had killed some time ago. There are several dollars among these people, which they get in some way. We suppose the Snake Indians, some of whom do not live very far from New Mexico, get them from the Spaniards in that quarter. The Snake Indians also get horses from the Spaniards.

Tuesday, June 3, 1806:

Clark: Our invalids are all on the recovery. Bratton is much stronger and can walk about with considerable ease. The Indian chief appears to be gradually recovering the use of his limbs, and the child is nearly well. The inflammation on his neck continues, but the swelling appears to [be] subsiding. We still continue the application of the onion poultice.

Today the Indians dispatched an express over the mountains to Traveller's Rest, or to the neighborhood of that creek on Clark's River, in order to learn from a band of Flatheads who inhabit that river and who have probably wintered on Clark's River near the entrance of Traveller's Rest Creek, the occurrences which have taken place on the east side of the mountains during last winter. This is the band which we first met with on that river.

The mountains being practicable for this express, we thought it probable that we could also pass, but the chiefs inform us that several of the creeks would yet swim our horses, that there was no grass, and that the road was extremely deep and slippery. They inform us that we may pass conveniently in twelve or fourteen days.

We have come to a resolution to remove from hence to the quamash grounds[428] beyond Collins Creek on the tenth, to hunt in that neighborhood a few days, if possible lay in a stock of meat, and then attempt the mountains about the middle of this month. I begin to lose all hope of any dependence on the salmon, as this river will not fall sufficiently to take them before we shall leave it, and as yet I see no appearance of their running near the shore as the Indians informed us they would in the course of a few days.

Thursday, June 5, 1806:

Clark: Colter and Bratton were permitted to visit the Indian village today for the purpose of trading for roots and bread. They were fortunate and made a good return.

We gave the Indian chief another sweat today, continuing it as long as he could bear it. In the evening he was very languid but still continued to improve in the use of his limbs.

The child is recovering fast. I applied a plaster of salve made of the resin of the long-leafed pine, beeswax, and bear oil mixed, which

---

428. Weippe Prairie (Schmidt, p. 116)

has subsided the inflammation entirely. The part is considerably swelled and hard.

In the evening, Reubin Field, George Shannon, and Collins returned from the chase and brought with them five deer and a brown bear.

Sunday, June 8, 1806:

Clark: The sick chief is much mended. He can bear his weight on his legs and recovers strength. The child has nearly recovered.

The Cut Nose and ten or twelve came over today to visit us. Two of these were of the tribes from the plains of Lewis's River whom we had not before seen. One of these men brought a horse for which I gave a tomahawk, which I had exchanged for with the chief of the Clahclahlah nation below the Great Rapids of [the] Columbia, and a broken-down horse which was not able to cross the mountains. We also exchanged two of our indifferent horses for sound back horses.

In the evening several foot races were run by the men of our party and the Indians, after which our party divided and played at prisoner's base until night. After dark, the fiddle was played and the party amused themselves in dancing.

One of these Indians informed us that we could not cross the mountains until the full of the next moon, or about the first of July. If we attempted it sooner, our horses would be three days without eating on top of the mountains. This information is disagreeable to us inasmuch as it admits of some doubt as to the time most proper for us to set out. At all events, we shall set out at or about the time which the Indians seem to be generally agreed would be the most proper, about the middle of this month.

Tuesday, June 10, 1806:

Clark: [We] rose early this morning and had all the horses collected except one of Whitehouse's horses, which could not be found. An Indian promised to find the horse and bring him on to us at the quamash fields, at which place we intend to delay a few days for the laying in [of] some meat, by which time we calculate that the snows will have melted more off the mountains and the grass raised to a sufficient height for our horses to live.

We set out with the party, each man being well-mounted, and a light load on a second horse, besides which we have several supernumerary horses in case of [an] accident or the want of provisions. We therefore feel ourselves perfectly equipped for the mountains.

We ascended the hills, which are very high and about three miles in extent. The pass of Collins Creek was deep and extremely difficult, though we passed without sustaining further injury than wetting some of our roots and bread.

The country through which we passed is extremely fertile and generally free from stone, is well-timbered with several species of fir, long-leafed pine, and larch. The undergrowth is choke cherry near the watercourses, black alder, a large species of red root now in bloom, a growth which resembles the pawpaw in its leaf and which bears a berry with five valves of a deep purple color, two species of shomake, seven bark, purple haw, serviceberry, gooseberry, wild rose, honeysuckle which bears a white berry, and a species of dwarf pine, which grows about ten or twelve feet high.

After we encamped this evening we sent out our hunters. Collins killed a doe on which we supped, much to our satisfaction.

We had not reached the top of the river hills before we were overtaken by a party of eight Indians who informed me that they were going to the quamash flats to hunt. Their object, I believe, is the expectation of being fed by us, in which, however, kind as they have been, we must disappoint them at this moment as it is necessary that we should use all frugality, as well as employ every exertion, to provide meat for our journey. They have encamped with us.

Thursday, June 12, 1806:

Clark: All our hunters except Gibson returned about noon. None of them had killed anything except Shields, who brought with him two deer.

The days are very warm and the mosquitoes, our old companions, have become very troublesome.

The Cut Nose informed us on the tenth before we left him that two young chiefs would overtake us with a view to accompany us to the Falls of the Missouri, and probably to the seat of our government.

Our camp is agreeably situated in a point of timbered land on the eastern borders of an extensive level and beautiful prairie, which is intersected by several small branches, near the bank of one of which our camp is placed. The quamash is now in bloom. At a short distance it resembles a lake of fine, clear water. So complete is this deception that on first sight, I could have sworn it was water.

Saturday, June 14, 1806:

Lewis: We had all our articles packed up and made ready for an early departure in the morning. Our horses were caught and most of them hobbled and otherwise confined in order that we might not be detained. From hence to Traveller's Rest we shall make a forced march. At that place we shall probably remain one or two days to rest ourselves and [the] horses, and procure some meat.

We have now been detained nearly five weeks in consequence of the snows, a serious loss of time at this delightful season for traveling. I am still apprehensive that the snow and the want of food for our horses will prove serious embarrassments to us, as at least four days [of the] journey of our route in these mountains lies over heights and along a ledge of mountains never entirely destitute of snow. Everybody seems anxious to be in motion, convinced that we have not now any time to delay if the calculation is to reach the United States this season. This I am determined to accomplish if within the compass of human power.

Sunday, June 15, 1806:

Clark: [We] collected our horses early with the intention of making an early start. Some hard showers of rain detained us. We took our final departure from the quamash fields and proceeded with much difficulty owing to the situation of the road, which was very slippery, and it was with great difficulty that the loaded horses could ascend the hills and mountains. They frequently slipped down both ascending and descending those steep hills.

The rain ceased and [the] sun shone out.

After detaining about two hours, we proceeded on, passing over some rugged hills, or spurs, of the Rocky Mountains, passing the creek on which I [had] encamped on the seventeenth [of] September last. We passed through bad, fallen timber and a high mountain this evening. From the top of this mountain, I had an extensive view of the Rocky Mountains to the south, and the Columbian plains for a great extent, [and] also the southwest mountains and a range of high mountains which divides the waters of Lewis's and Clark's Rivers, and seems to terminate [in] nearly a west course.

Monday, June 16, 1806:

Clark: [We] collected our horses early and set out [at] 7:00 a.m. [We] proceeded on up the creek through a gladey, swampy bottom covered with grass and quamash and through [the] most intolerably bad, fallen timber over a high mountain on which [a] great quantity of snow is yet lying promiscuously through the thick woods, and in many places the banks of snow are four feet deep.

We nooned it, or dined, on a small creek in a small, open valley where we found some grass for our horses to eat, although surrounded by snow.

This morning, Windsor burst his rifle near the muzzle.

Vegetation is proportionately backward. The dogtooth violet is just in bloom, [and] the honeysuckle, huckleberry, and a small species of white maple are beginning to put forth their leaves where they are clear of snow. These appearances, in this comparatively low region, auger but unfavorably with respect to the practicability of passing the mountains. However, we determined to proceed. Accordingly, after taking a hasty meal, we set out and continued our route through a thick woods, much obstructed with fallen timber and interrupted by many steep ravines and hills, which were very high.

The snow has increased in quantity so much that the greater part of our route this evening was over the snow, which has become sufficiently firm to bear our horses. Otherwise, it would have been impossible for us to proceed, as it lay in immense masses, in some places eight or ten feet deep. We found much difficulty in finding the road, as it was so frequently covered with snow.

We arrived early in the evening at the place I had killed and left the flesh of a horse for the party in my rear last September. Here is a small glade in which there is some grass, not a sufficiency for our horses, but we thought it advisable to remain here all night, as we apprehended [that] if we proceeded further, we should find less grass.

The air is pleasant in the course of the day, but becomes very cold before morning, notwithstanding the shortness of the night.

Tuesday, June 17, 1806:

Clark: We collected our horses and set out early. We found it difficult and dangerous to pass the creek in consequence of its depth and rapidity. We avoided two other passes of the creek by ascending a steep, rocky, and difficult hill. Beyond this creek, the road ascends the mountain to the height of the main leading ridges, which divide the waters of the Kooskooskee and Nez Percé rivers.

This mountain we ascended about three miles when we found ourselves enveloped in snow from eight to twelve feet deep, even on the south side of the mountain. I was in front and could only pursue the direction of the road by the trees, which had been peeled by the natives for the inner bark, of which they scraped and ate. As those peeled trees were only to be found scattered promiscuously, I with great difficulty pursued the direction of the road one mile farther to the top of the mountain where I found the snow from twelve to fifteen feet deep, but few trees with the fairest exposure to the sun.

Here was winter with all its rigors. The air was cold [and] my hands and feet were benumbed.

We knew that it would require four days to reach the fish [which] were at the entrance of Colt Creek, provided we were so fortunate as to be enabled to follow the proper ridge of the mountains to lead us to that place. Of this, all of our most expert woodsmen and principal guides were extremely doubtful. Short of that point, we could not hope for any food for our horses, not even underwood itself, as the whole was covered many feet deep in snow. If we proceeded and should get bewildered in those mountains, the certainty was that we should lose all of our horses, and consequently our baggage, instruments, perhaps our papers, and thus eventually risk the loss of our discoveries which we had already made, if we should be so fortunate as to escape with life.

The snow bore our horses very well, and the traveling was therefore infinitely better than the obstruction of rocks and fallen timber which we met with in our passage over last fall when the snow lay on this part of the ridge in detached spots only.

Under these circumstances, we conceived it madness in this stage of the expedition to proceed without a guide who could certainly conduct us to the fish weirs on the Kooskooskee, as our horses could not possibly sustain a journey of more than four or five days without food. We therefore came to the resolution to return with our horses while they were yet strong and in good order, and endeavor to keep them so until we could procure an Indian to conduct us over the snowy mountains, and again to proceed as soon as we could procure such a guide, knowing from the appearance of the snows that if we remained until it had dissolved sufficiently for us to follow the road, that we should not be enabled to return to the United States within this season.

Having come to this resolution, we ordered the party to make a deposit of all the baggage which we had not immediate use for, and also all the roots and bread of cowas which they had, except an allowance for a few days to enable them to return to some place at which we could subsist by hunting until we procured a guide. We left our instruments, and I even left the most of my papers, believing them safer here than to risk them on horseback over the road, rocks, and water which we had passed.

Our baggage being laid on scaffolds and well-covered, we began our retrograde march at 1:00 p.m., having remained about three hours on this snowy mountain. We returned by the route we had advanced to Hungry Creek, which we ascended about two miles and encamped. We had here more grass for our horses than the preceding evening, yet it was but scant.

The party was a good deal dejected, though not as much so as I had apprehended they would have been. This is the first time since we have been on this tour that we have ever been compelled to retreat or make a retrograde march.

Wednesday, June 18, 1806:

Clark: We dispatched Drouillard and Shannon to the Nez Percé Indians in the plains beyond the Kooskooskee in order to hasten the arrival of the Indians who promised to accompany us, or to procure a guide at all events, and rejoin us as soon as possible. We sent by them a rifle, which we offered as a reward to any of them who would engage to conduct us to Clark's River at the entrance of Traveller's Rest Creek. We also directed them, if they found difficulty in inducing any of them to accompany us, to offer the reward of two other guns to be given [to] them immediately, and ten horses, at the Falls of the Missouri.

We had not proceeded far this morning before John Potts cut his leg very badly with one of the large knives. He cut one of the large veins on the inner side of the leg.

Colter's horse fell with him in passing Hungry Creek, and he and [the] horse were driven down the creek a considerable distance, rolling over each other among the rocks. He fortunately escaped without much injury or the loss of his gun. He lost his blanket.

At 1:00 p.m. we returned to the glade on a branch of Hungry Creek where we had dined on the sixteenth instant. Here we again halted and dined.

After dinner, we proceeded on to the near fork of Collins Creek and encamped in a pleasant situation at the upper part of the meadows about two miles above our encampment of the fifteenth instant.

We sent out several hunters, but they returned without having killed anything. They saw a number of large fish in the creek and shot at them several times without success. We hope, by the means of the fish, together with what deer and bear we can kill, to be enabled to subsist until our guide arrives without the necessity of returning to the quamash flats. There is great abundance of good food here to sustain our horses.

We are in flattering expectations of the arrival of two young chiefs who informed us that they intended to accompany us to the United States, and should set out from their village in nine nights after we left them, or on the nineteenth instant. If they set out at that time, Drouillard and Shannon will meet them, and probably join us, on the twentieth or twenty-first.

[The] mosquitoes [are] troublesome.

Friday, June 20, 1806:

Clark: Labiche and Cruzatte returned late in the evening with one deer, which the former had killed. The hunters assured us that their greatest exertions would not enable them to support us here more than one or two days longer, from the great scarcity of game and the difficult access of the country, the underbrush being very thick and [the] great quantities of fallen timber. As we shall necessarily be compelled to remain more than two days for the return of Drouillard and Shannon, we determined to return in the morning as far as the quamash flats and endeavor to lay in another stock of meat for the mountains, our former stock now being nearly exhausted, as well as what we have killed on our route.

By returning to the quamash flats, we shall sooner be informed whether or not we can procure a guide to conduct us through the mountains. Should we fail in procuring one, we are determined to risk a passage on the following plan immediately because, should we wait much longer or until the snow dissolves in such a manner as to enable us to follow the road, we cannot expect to reach the United States this winter.

This is that Captain Lewis or I shall take four of our most expert woodsmen with three or four of our best horses and proceed two days in advance, taking a plentiful supply of provisions, [and] for this party to follow the road by the marks the Indians have made in many places with their baggage on the sides of the trees by rubbing against them, and to blaze the trees with a tomahawk as they proceed, [and] that after proceeding two days in advance of Hungry Creek, two of those men would be sent back to the party who, by the time of their return to Hungry Creek, would have reached that place. The men so returning would be enabled to inform the main party of the probable success of the proceeding party in finding the road and of their probable progress. In order that it should be necessary, the main party, by a delay of a day or two at Hungry Creek, should give the advance [party] time to make the road through before the main party could overtake them, and thus prevent delay on that part of the route where no food is to be obtained for our horses.

Should it so happen that the advance [party] should not find the road by the marks of the trees after attempting it for two days, the whole of them would return to the main party, in which case we would bring back our baggage and attempt a passage over the mountains through the country of the Shoshones farther to the south, by way of the main southwesterly fork of Lewis's River and Madison's or Gallatin's Rivers where, from the information of the Nez Percé, there is a passage which, at this season of the year, is not obstructed by snow, though the ground is very distant and would require at least a month in its performance. The Shoshones informed us when we first met with them that there was a passage across the mountains in that quarter, but represented the difficulties arising from steep, rugged, high mountains, and also an extensive and barren plain, which was to be passed without game, as infinitely more difficult than the route by which we came.

Saturday, June 21, 1806:

Clark: We collected our horses early and set out on our return to the flats. We all felt some mortification in being thus compelled to retrace our steps through this tedious and difficult part of our route, obstructed with brush and innumerable logs and fallen timber, which render the traveling distressing and even dangerous to our horses.

At the pass of Collins Creek, we met two Indians who were on their way over the mountains. They had brought with them the three horses and the mule which had left us and returned to the quamash ground. As well as we could understand the Indians, they informed us [that] they had seen George Drouillard and Shannon, and that they would not return until the expiration of two days. The cause [of] why Drouillard and Shannon did not return with these men we are at a loss to account for.

We pressed these Indians to remain with us and conduct us over the mountains on the return of Drouillard and Shannon. They consented to remain two nights for us and, accordingly, deposited their stores of roots and bread in the bushes at no great distance and, after dinner, returned with us as far as the little prairie about two miles distant from the creek. Here they halted with their horses and informed us [that] they would remain until we overtook them, or at least two nights.

At 7:00 in the evening we found ourselves once more at our old encampment where we shall anxiously await the return of Drouillard and Shannon.

Monday, June 23, 1806:

Clark: Apprehensive from Drouillard's and Shannon's delay, that they had met with some difficulty in procuring a guide, and also that the two Indians who had promised to wait two nights for us would set out today, we thought it most advisable to dispatch Wiser and Frazier to them this morning with a view, if possible, to detain them a day or two longer and directed, that in the event of their not being able to detain the Indians, that Sergeant Gass, Joseph and Reubin Field, and Wiser should accompany the Indians by whatever route they might take to Traveller's Rest, and blaze the trees well as they proceeded, and wait at that place until our arrival with the party.

At 4:00 p.m. Shannon, Drouillard, and Whitehouse returned. Shannon and Drouillard brought with them three Indians who had consented to accompany us to the Falls of the Missouri for the compensation of two guns. One of these men is the brother of the Cut Nose, and the other two are the same who presented Captain Lewis and myself with a horse on a former occasion at the lodge of the Broken Arm, and the two who promised to pursue us in nine nights after we left the river, or on the nineteenth instant. These are all young men of good character, and much respected by their nation.

Tuesday, June 24, 1806:

Clark: We collected our horses early this morning and set out accompanied by our three guides. Colter joined us this morning, having killed a bear which, from his description of its poverty and distance, we did not think proper to send after. We nooned it as usual at Collins Creek where we found Frazier solus,[429] the other four men having gone in pursuit of the two Indians who had set out from Collins Creek two hours before Frazier's arrival.

After dinner, we continued our route to Fish Creek. Here we found Sergeant Gass, Wiser, and the two Indian men whom they had prevailed on to remain at that place until our arrival.

Joseph and Reubin Field had killed one small deer only, and of this they had been liberal to the Indians insomuch that they had no provisions. They had gone on to the branch of Hungry Creek, at which we shall noon it tomorrow in order to hunt.

We had fine grass for our horses this evening.

Wednesday, June 25, 1806:

Clark: Last evening the Indians entertained us with setting the fir trees on fire. They have a great number of dry limbs near their bodies which, when set on fire, create a very sudden and immense blaze from bottom to top of those tall trees. They are a beautiful object in this situation at night. This exhibition reminded me of a display of fireworks. The natives told us that their object in setting those trees on fire was to bring fair weather for our journey.

We collected our horses and set out at an early hour this morning. One of our guides complained of being unwell, a symptom which I did not much like, as such complaints with an Indian are generally the prelude to his abandoning any enterprise with which he is not well

429. alone

pleased. We left four of these Indians at our encampment. They promised to pursue us in a few hours.

At 11:00 a.m. we arrived at the branch of Hungry Creek where we found Joseph and Reubin Field. They had not killed anything. Here we halted and dined, and our guides overtook us. At this place, the squaw collected a parcel of roots of which the Shoshones eat. It is a small knob root, a good deal in flavor and consistency like the Jerusalem artichoke.[430]

After dinner we continued our route to Hungry Creek and encamped about one and a half miles below our encampment of the sixteenth instant. The Indians all continue with us and, I believe, are disposed to be faithful to their engagements.

Captain Lewis gave the sick Indian a small buffalo robe, which he brought from the Missouri, this Indian having no other covering except his moccasins and a dressed elk skin without the hair.

Thursday, June 26, 1806:

Clark: We collected our horses and set out early and proceeded on down Hungry Creek a few miles and ascended to the summit of the mountain where we [had] deposited our baggage on the seventeenth instant [and] found everything safe and as we had left them. The snow, which was ten feet, ten inches deep on the top of the mountain had sunk to seven feet, though perfectly hard and firm. We made some fire, cooked dinner and dined while our horses stood on snow seven feet deep, at least.

After dinner we packed up and proceeded on. The Indians hastened us off and informed us that it was a considerable distance to the place they wished to reach this evening, where there was grass for our horses. Accordingly, we set out with our guides who led us over and along the steep sides of tremendous mountains entirely covered with snow except about the roots of the trees, where the snow was partially melted and exposed a small spot of earth. We ascended and descended several steep, lofty heights, but keeping on the dividing ridge of the Nez Percé and Kooskooskee rivers, we passed no stream of water.

Late in the evening, much to the satisfaction of ourselves and the comfort of the horses, we arrived at the desired spot and encamped on the steep side of a mountain convenient to a good spring. Here we found an abundance of fine grass for our horses. This situation was the side of an untimbered mountain with a fair southern aspect where the snow, from appearance, had been dissolved about ten days.

---

430. a perennial sunflower, cultivated for its tubers

The grass was young and tender, of course, and had much the appearance of the green sword. There is a great abundance of a species of beargrass which grows on every part of these mountains. Its growth is luxuriant and continues green all winter, but the horses will not eat it.

Soon after we had encamped, we were overtaken by a Nez Percé man who had pursued us with a view to accompany Captain Lewis to the Falls of [the] Missouri. We were now informed that the two young men we met on the twenty-first and detained several days were going on a party of pleasure merely to the Oatlashshoots or, as they call them, Sha-lees, a band of the Flathead nation who reside on Clark's River in the neighborhood of the mouth of Traveller's Rest.

I was taken yesterday with a violent pain in my head, which has tormented me ever since most violently.

Friday, June 27, 1806:

Clark: The road still continued on the heights of the dividing ridge on which we had traveled yesterday for nine miles, or to our encampment of the sixteenth [of] September last.

About one mile short of the encampment, we halted by the request of the guides a few minutes on an elevated point and smoked a pipe. On this eminence the natives have raised a conic mound of stones of six or eight feet high and erected a pine pole of fifteen feet long.

From this place, we had an extensive view of these stupendous mountains, principally covered with snow like that on which we stood. We were entirely surrounded by these mountains from which, to one unacquainted with them, it would have seemed impossible ever to have escaped. In short, without the assistance of our guides, I doubt whether we, who had once passed them, could find our way to Traveller's Rest in their present situation, for the marked trees on which we had placed considerable reliance are much fewer and more difficult to find than we had apprehended. These Indians are most admirable pilots. We find the road wherever the snow has disappeared, though it be only for a few paces.

After having smoked the pipe and contemplated this scene sufficiently to have dampened the spirits of any except such hardy travelers as we have become, we continued our march and, at the distance of three miles, descended a steep mountain and passed two small branches of the Nez Percé River just above their fork, and again ascended the ridge on which we passed.

At the distance of seven miles [we] arrived at our encampment of [the] sixteenth [of] September last. [We] passed three small branches, passed on a dividing ridge [which was] rugged, and we arrived at a situation very similar to our situation of last night, though as the ridge was somewhat higher and the snow had not been so long dissolved, of course there was but little grass. Here we encamped for the night, having traveled twenty-eight miles over these mountains without relieving the horses from their packs or their having any food.

Our meat being exhausted, we issued a pint of bear oil to a mess which, with their boiled roots, made an agreeable dish.

John Potts's leg, which had been much swelled and inflamed for several days, is much better this evening and gives him but little pain. We applied the pounded root and leaves of wild ginger, from which he found great relief.

My head has not pained me so much today as yesterday and last night.

Gass: The snow is so deep that we cannot wind along the sides of these steeps, but must slide straight down. The horses generally do not sink more than three inches in the snow, but sometimes they break through to their bellies.

The day was pleasant throughout but it appeared to me somewhat extraordinary to be traveling over snow six or eight feet deep in the latter end of June. The most of us, however, had saved our socks as we expected to find snow in these mountains.

Saturday, June 28, 1806:

Clark: We continued our route along the dividing ridge, over knobs and through deep hollows, past our encampment of the fourteenth [of] September last near the forks of the road, leaving the one on which we had come, [and following the] one leading to the fishery to our right, immediately on the dividing ridge.

At 12:00 we arrived at an untimbered side of a mountain with a southern aspect just above the fishery. Here we found an abundance of grass for our horses, as the guides had informed us. As our horses were hungry and much fatigued, and from information [that there was] no other place where we could obtain grass for them within the reach of this evening's travel, we determined to remain at this place all night, having come thirteen miles only. The water was distant from our encampment; we therefore melted snow and used the water.

The whole of the route of this day was over deep snow. We find the traveling on the snow [is] not worse than without it, as the easy passage it gives us over the rocks and fallen timber fully compensates for the inconvenience of slipping. Certain it is that we travel considerably faster on the snow than without it. The snow sinks from two to three inches with a horse, is course and firm, and seems to be formed of the larger particles of the snow. The surface of the snow is rather harder in the morning than after the sun shines on it a few hours, but it is not in that situation so dense as to prevent the horses from obtaining [a] good foothold.

Sunday, June 29, 1806:

Clark: We collected our horses and set out, having previously dispatched Drouillard and Reubin Field to the warm springs to hunt. We pursued the heights of the ridge on which we have been passing for several days. It terminated at the distance of five miles from our encampment and we descended to and passed the main branch of [the] Kooskooskee one and a half miles above the entrance of Glade Creek, which falls in on the northeast side. We bid adieu to the snow.

Near the river we found a deer, which the hunters had killed and left us. This was a fortunate supply as all our bear oil was now exhausted, and we were reduced to our roots alone, without salt.

Beyond this river we ascended a steep mountain about two miles to its summit where we found the old road, which we had passed on as we went out, coming in on our right. The road was now much plainer and much beaten.

At noon we arrived at the quamash flats on Valley Creek and halted to graze our horses and dined, having traveled twelve miles. Here is a pretty little plain of about fifty acres, plentifully stocked with quamash and, from appearance, this forms one of the principal stages of the Indians who pass the mountains on this road.

After dinner we continued our march seven miles farther to the warm springs, where we arrived early in the evening. These warm, or hot, springs are situated at the base of a hill of no considerable height, on the north side and near the bank of Traveller's Rest Creek which is, at this place, about ten yards wide.

These springs issue from the bottom and through the interstices of a grey freestone rock. The rock rises in irregular massy[431] cliffs in a circular range around the springs on their lower side. Immediately above the springs on the creek there is a handsome little quamash plain of about ten acres. The principal spring is about the temperature of the warmest baths used at the Hot Springs in Virginia.

In this bath, which had been prepared by the Indians by stopping the river with stone and mud, I bathed and remained in ten minutes. It was with difficulty [that] I could remain this long, and it caused a profuse sweat. Two other bold springs adjacent to this are much warmer, their heat being so great as to make the hand of a person smart

431. massive

extremely when immersed. We think the temperature of these springs [to be] about the same as that of the hottest of the hot springs of Virginia.

Both the men and the Indians amused themselves with the use of the bath this evening. I observed [that] after the Indians remain in the hot bath as long as they could bear it, [they] run and plunge themselves into the creek, the water of which is now as cold as ice can make it. After remaining there a few minutes, they return again to the warm bath, repeating the transition several times, but always ending with the warm bath.

[We] saw the tracks of two barefooted Indians.

Monday, June 30, 1806:

Clark: Just as we had prepared to set out at an early hour, a deer came in to lick at the springs and one of our hunters killed it. This secured to us our dinner.

We proceeded down the creek, sometimes in the bottoms and, at other times, on the tops or along the steep sides of the ridge to the north of the creek.

At one and a half miles, we passed our encampment of the twelfth of September last. We nooned it at the place we had on the twelfth of September last. While here, Shields killed a deer on the north fork near the road.

After dinner we resumed our march. Soon after setting out, Shields killed another deer and we picked up three others which George Drouillard had killed along the road. Deer are very abundant in the neighborhood of Traveller's Rest, of both species, [and] also some bighorn and elk.

A little before sunset we arrived at our old encampment on the south side of the creek, a little above its entrance into Clark's River.[432] Here we encamped with a view to remain two days in order to rest ourselves and [the] horses, and make our final arrangements for separation. We found no signs of the Oatlashshoots having been here lately. The Indians express much concern for them and apprehend that the Hidatsa of Fort de Prairie have destroyed them in the course of the last winter and spring, and mention the tracks of the barefooted Indians, which we saw yesterday as an evidence of their being much distressed.

Our horses have stood the journey surprisingly well and only want a few days rest to restore them.

---

432. Traveller's Rest, in Bitterroot Valley (DeVoto)

17: Lewis's Shortcut
(July and August, 1806)

One of them jumped behind a rock and spoke to the other, who turned around and stopped at the distance of thirty steps from me, and I shot him through the belly. He fell to his knees and on his right elbow, from which position he partly raised himself up and fired at me and, turning himself about, crawled in behind a rock which was a few feet from him. He [had] *overshot me. Being bareheaded, I felt the wind of his bullet very distinctly.*

Captain Meriwether Lewis,
July 27, 1806

Wednesday, July 2, 1806:

Lewis: In the course of the day we had much conversation with the Nez Percé Indians by signs, our only mode of communicating our ideas. They informed us that they wished to go in search of the Oat-lashshoots, their friends, and intended leaving us tomorrow morning. I prevailed on them to go with me as far as the east branch of Clark's River and put me on the road to the Missouri. I gave the chief a medal of the small size. He insisted on exchanging names with me according to their custom, which was accordingly done, and I was called "Yo-me-kol-lick" which, interpreted, is "The White Bearskin Folded."

In the evening, the Indians ran their horses and we had several foot races between the natives and our party, with various success. These are a race of hardy, strong, athletic, active men.

Goodrich and McNeal are both very unwell with the pox, which they contracted last winter with the Chinook women. This forms my inducement, principally, for taking them to the Falls of the Missouri where, during an interval of rest, they can use the mercury freely.

Clark: We gave the second gun to our guides, agreeable to our promise, and to each we gave powder and balls.

I had the greater part of the meat dried for to subsist my party in the mountains between the head of Jefferson's and Clark's Rivers where I do not expect to find any game to kill.

[I] had all of our arms put in the most prime order. Two of the rifles have, unfortunately, burst near the muzzle. Shields cut them off and they shoot tolerably well. One, which is very short, we exchanged with the Indian [to] whom we had given a longer gun, to induce them to pilot us across the mountains. We caused every man to fill his horn with powder and have a sufficiency of balls, etc.

The last day in passing down Traveller's Rest Creek, Captain Lewis fell down the side of a steep mountain nearly forty feet, but fortunately received no damage. His horse nearly fell on him, but fortunately recovered, and they both escaped unhurt.

Thursday, July 3, 1806:

On this date the Expedition divided. Lewis and his party of nine men proceeded from the Bitterroot River through the 'short route,' Lewis and Clark's Pass to the Falls of the Missouri, and an exploration of the headwaters of the Marias River. His purpose was to determine whether part of the Missouri River drainage might extend past the 49th parallel and thus include some of the profitable Canadian fur trade for the United States. (Eide, p. 187)

Clark followed the Yellowstone River and the two groups reunited on August 12. Clark's entries follow in Chapter 18.

Lewis: All arrangements being now completed for carrying into effect the several schemes we had planned for execution on our return, we saddled our horses and set out. I took leave of my worthy friend and companion, Captain Clark, and the party that accompanied him. I could not avoid feeling much concern on this occasion, although I hoped this separation was only momentary.

I proceeded down Clark's River[433] seven miles with my party of nine men[434] and five Indians. Here the Indians recommended our passing the river which was rapid and one hundred fifty yards wide. Two miles above this place, I passed the entrance of the east branch of Clark's River,[435] which discharges itself by two channels. The water of this river is more turbid than the main stream, and is from ninety to one hundred twenty yards wide.

As we had no other means of passing the river, we busied ourselves collecting dry timber for the purpose of constructing rafts. Timber being scarce, we found considerable difficulty in procuring as much as made three small rafts.

The Indians swam over their horses and drew over their baggage in little basins of deerskins, which they constructed in a very few min-

---

433. the Bitterroot (DeVoto)

434. Gass, Drouillard, Joseph and Reubin Field, Frazier, and Werner; Thompson, Goodrich, and McNeal will go as far as the Great Falls portage

435. the Hellgate: first called *Porte d'Enfer* (Gate of Hell) by Canadian trappers because the Blackfeet frequently ambushed the Flatheads and Nez Percé there (DeVoto)

utes for that purpose. We drove our horses in after them, and they followed to the opposite shore.

I remained myself with two men who could scarcely swim until the last. By this time the raft, by passing so frequently, had fallen a considerable distance down the river to a rapids and [a] difficult part of it crowded with several small islands and willow bars which were now overflowed. With these men I set out on the raft and was soon hurried down with the current a mile and a half before we made shore. On our approach to the shore the raft sank and I was drawn off the raft by a bush, and swam on shore. The two men remained on the raft and, fortunately, effected a landing at some little distance below.

I now joined the party and we proceeded with the Indians about three miles to a small creek, and encamped at sunset. I sent out the hunters who soon returned with three very fine deer, of which I gave the Indians half.

These people now informed me that the road which they showed me at no great distance from our camp would lead us up the east branch of Clark's River and to a river they called "Cokahlarishkit," or the River of the Road to Buffalo, and thence to Medicine River and the Falls of the Missouri, where we wished to go. They alleged that as the road was a well-beaten track, we could not now miss our way, and as they were afraid of meeting with their enemies, the Hidatsa, they could not think of continuing with us any longer, that they wished now to proceed down Clark's River in search of their friends, the Shalees.[436] They informed us that not far from the dividing ridge between the waters of this and the Missouri River, the road forked. They recommended the left hand[437] as the best route, but said they would both lead us to the Falls of the Missouri.

I directed the hunters to turn out early in the morning and endeavor to kill some more meat for these people whom I was unwilling to leave without giving them a good supply of provisions after their having been so obliging as to conduct us through these tremendous mountains.

The mosquitoes were so excessively troublesome this evening that we were obliged to kindle large fires for our horses. These insects torture them in such [a] manner [that] until they placed themselves in the smoke of the fires, I really thought they would become frantic.

We saw the fresh track of a horse this evening in the road near our camp which the Indians supposed to be a Shalee spy.

---

436. a branch of the Tushepaws and true "Flatheads" (Bakeless, p. 339)

437. today's Lewis and Clark's Pass (although Clark never saw it) across the Continental Divide (DeVoto)

We killed a prairie hen with the short, pointed tail. She had a number of young which could just fly.

Friday, July 4, 1806:

Lewis: At half after eleven, the hunters returned from the chase unsuccessful. I now ordered the horses saddled, smoked a pipe with these friendly people and at noon, bid them adieu. They had cut the meat, which I gave them last evening, thin and exposed it in the sun to dry, informing me that they should leave it in this neighborhood until they returned, as a store for their homeward journey.

It is worthy of remark that these people were about to return by the same pass by which they had conducted us through, the difficult part of the Rocky Mountains, although they were about to descend Clark's River several days journey in search of the Shalees, their relations, a circumstance which, to my mind, furnishes sufficient evidence that there is not so near or so good a route to the plains of Columbia by land along that river as that which we came.

The several war routes of the Hidatsa which fall into this valley of Clark's River concenter at Traveller's Rest, beyond which point they have never dared to venture in pursuit of the nations beyond the mountains. These affectionate people, our guides, betrayed every emotion of unfeigned regret at separating from us. They said that they were confidant that the Pahkees (the appellation they give to the Hidatsa) would cut us off.

The first five miles of our route was through a part of the extensive plain in which we were encamped. We then entered the mountains with the east fork of Clark's River through a narrow, confined pass on its north side, continuing up that river five miles farther to the entrance of the Cokahlarishkit River[438] which falls in on the northeast side, is sixty yards wide, deep, and rapid. The banks [are] bold, not very high, but never overflow. The east fork, below its junction with this stream, is one hundred yards wide, and above it, about ninety. The water of both is turbid, but the east branch much the most so. Their beds are composed of sand and gravel; the east fork possesses a large portion of the former. Neither of these streams is navigable in consequence of the rapids and shoals which obstruct their currents.

Thus far, a plain or untimbered country bordered the river which, near the junction of these streams, spread into a handsome level plain of no great extent. The hills were covered with long-leafed pine and fir.

---

438. today's Blackfoot

I now continued my route up the north side of the Cokahlarishkit River through a timbered country for eight miles and encamped in a handsome bottom on the river where there was an abundance of excellent grass for our horses. The evening was fine, [the] air pleasant, and [there were] no mosquitoes.

A few miles before we encamped, I killed a squirrel of the species common to the Rocky Mountains, and a ground squirrel of a species which I had never before seen. I preserved the skins of both of these animals.

Thursday, July 10, 1806:

Lewis: [There are] great quantities of prickly pear of two kinds on the plains. The ground is rendered so mirey by the rain which fell yesterday that it is excessively fatiguing to the horses to travel. We came ten miles and halted for dinner.

The wind blowing down the river in the forepart of the day was unfavorable to the hunters. They saw several gangs of elk but they, having the wind of them, ran off.

In the evening, the wind set from the west and we fell in with a few elk, of which Reubin Field and I killed three, one of which swam the river and fell on the opposite shore so we therefore lost its skin. I sent the pack horses on with Sergeant Gass, directing them to halt and encamp at the first timber, which proved to be about seven miles. I retained Frazier to assist in skinning the elk. We were, about this time, joined by Drouillard.

A large brown bear swam the river near where we were and Drouillard shot and killed it. By the time we butchered the two elk and [the] bear, it was near dark. We loaded our horses with the best of the meat and pursued the party and found them encamped, as they had been directed, in the first timber. We did not reach them until 9:00 p.m.

They informed us that they had seen a very large bear in the plains which had pursued Sergeant Gass and Thompson some distance but their horses enabled them to keep out of its reach. They were afraid to fire on the bear lest their horses should throw them, as they were unaccustomed to the gun.

We killed five deer, three elk, and a bear today. [We] saw vast herds of buffalo in the evening below us on the river. We heard them bellowing about us all night. [We saw] vast assemblages of wolves. [We] saw a large herd of elk making down the river. [We] passed a considerable rapids in Medicine River after dark. The river [is] about a hundred yards wide, is deep, and in many parts rapid, and today has been much crowded with islands.

Friday, July 11, 1806:

Lewis: I sent the hunters down Medicine River to hunt elk, and proceeded with the party across the plain to the White Bear Islands.

It is now the season at which the buffalo begin to copulate, and the bulls keep a tremendous roaring. We could hear them for many miles, and there are such numbers of them that there is one continual roar. Our horses had not been acquainted with the buffalo; they appeared much alarmed at their appearance and bellowing.

When I arrived in sight of the White Bear Islands, the Missouri bottoms on both sides of the river were crowded with buffalo. I sincerely believe that there were not less than ten thousand buffalo within a circle of two miles around that place. I directed the hunters to kill some buffalo, as well for the benefit of their skins to enable us to pass the river as for their meat for the men I meant to leave at this place.

We unloaded our horses and encamped opposite to the islands. [I] had some willow sticks collected to make canoes of the hides.

By 12:00 they [had] killed eleven buffalo, most of them in fine order. The bulls are now generally much fatter than the cows, and are fine beef.

By 3:00 in the evening we had brought in a large quantity of fine beef and as many hides as we wanted for canoes, shelters, and gear. I then set all hands to prepare two canoes. The one we made after the Mandan fashion with a single skin in the form of a basin, and the other we constructed of two skins on a plan of our own.

Saturday, July 12, 1806:

Lewis: We arose early and resumed our operations in completing our canoes, which we completed by 10:00 a.m. About this time, two of the men whom I had dispatched this morning in quest of the horses returned with seven of them only. The remaining ten of our best horses were absent and not to be found. I fear that they were stolen. I dispatched two men on horseback in search of them.

At noon Werner returned, having found three other horses. Sergeant Gass did not return until 3:00 p.m., not having found the horses. He had been about eight miles up Medicine River. I now dispatched Joseph Field and Drouillard in quest of them. The former returned at dark unsuccessful and the latter continued absent all night.

At 5:00 p.m. the wind abated and we transported our baggage and meat to the opposite shore in our canoes which we found answered even beyond our expectations. We swam our horses over also, and encamped at sunset.

The grass and weeds are much more luxuriant than they were when I left this place on the thirteenth of July, 1805.

Sunday, July 13, 1806:

Lewis: [We] removed above to my old station opposite the upper point of White Bear Island. [We] formed our camp and set Thompson, etc., at work to complete the gear for the horses.

[I] had the cache opened [and] found my bear skins entirely destroyed by the water, the river having risen so high that the water had penetrated. All my specimens of plants [were] also lost. The chart of the Missouri fortunately escaped. [I] opened my trunks and boxes and exposed the articles to dry. [I] found my papers damp and several articles damp. The stopper had come out of a vial of laudanum and the contents had run into the drawer and destroyed a great part of my medicine in such [a] manner that it was past recovery.

[We] waited very impatiently for the return of Drouillard. He did not arrive.

Monday, July 14, 1806:

Lewis: [I] had the carriage wheels dug up [and] found them in good order. The iron frame of the boat had not suffered materially. [I] had the meat cut thinner and exposed to dry in the sun.

The old cache being too damp to venture to deposit my trunks, etc., in, I sent them over to the large island and had them put on a high scaffold among some thick brush and covered with skins. I take this precaution lest some Indians may visit the men I leave here before the arrival of the main party, and rob them.

The hunters killed a couple of wolves. The buffalo have almost entirely disappeared. [I] saw the bee martin.[439] The wolves are in great numbers, howling around us and lolling about in the plains, in view at the distance of two or three hundred yards.

Tuesday, July 15, 1806:

Lewis: [I] dispatched McNeal early this morning to the lower part of the portage in order to learn whether the cache and white pirogue remained untouched, or in what state they were.

The men [were] employed in drying meat, dressing deerskins, and preparing for the reception of the canoes.

At 1:00 p.m. Drouillard returned without the horses and reported that after a diligent search of two days, he had discovered where the

439. kingbird

horses had passed Dearborn's River, at which place there were fifteen lodges that had been abandoned about the time our horses were taken. He pursued the tracks of a number of horses from these lodges to the road which we had traveled over the mountains, which they struck about three miles south of our encampment of the seventh instant, and had pursued this road westwardly. I have no doubt but they are a party of the Tushepaws who have been on a buffalo hunt. His horse being much fatigued with the ride he had given him, and finding that the Indians had at least two days the start of him, [he] thought it best to return.

His safe return has relieved me from great anxiety. I had already settled it in my mind that a white bear had killed him, and should have set out tomorrow in search of him, and if I could not find him, to continue my route to Maria's River. I knew that if he met with a bear in the plains, even he would attack him, and that if any accident should happen to separate him from his horse in that situation, the chances in favor of his being killed would be as nine to ten. I felt so perfectly satisfied that he had returned in safety that I thought but little of the horses, although they were seven of the best I had.

This loss, great as it is, is not entirely irreparable, or at least does not defeat my design of exploring Maria's River. I have yet ten horses remaining, two of the best and two of the worst of I [will] leave to assist the party in taking the canoes and baggage over the portage, and take the remaining six with me. These are but indifferent horses, most of them, but I hope they may answer our purposes. I shall leave three of my intended party, (viz.) Gass, Frazier and Werner, and take the two Fields and Drouillard. By having two spare horses, we can relieve those we ride.

Having made this arrangement, I gave orders for an early departure in the morning. Indeed, I should have set out instantly, but McNeal rode one of the horses which I intend to take, and has not yet returned.

A little before dark, McNeal returned with his musket broken off at the breech and informed me that on his arrival at Willow Run, he had approached a white bear within ten feet without discovering him, the bear being in the thick brush. The horse took the alarm and, turning short, threw him immediately under the bear. This animal raised himself on his hinder feet for battle and gave him time to recover from his fall, which he did in an instant, and with his clubbed musket, he struck the bear over the head and cut him with the guard of the gun and broke off the breech. The bear, stunned with the stroke, fell to the ground and began to scratch his head with his feet. This gave McNeal time to climb a willow tree which was near at hand, and thus fortunately made his escape. The bear waited at the foot of the tree until late in the evening before he left him, when McNeal ventured down and caught his horse which had by this time strayed off to the distance of two miles, and returned to camp.

These bears are most tremendous animals. It seems that the hand of Providence has been most wonderfully in our favor with respect to them, or some of us would long since have fallen a sacrifice to their ferocity. There seems to be a certain fatality attached to the neighborhood of these falls, for there is always a chapter of accidents prepared for us during our residence at them.

The mosquitoes continue to infest us in such [a] manner that we can scarcely exist. For my own part, I am confined by them to my bier at least three-fourths of my time. My dog even howls with the torture he experiences from them. They are almost insupportable. They are so numerous that we frequently get them in our throats as we breathe.

Wednesday, July 16, 1806:

Lewis: I dispatched a man early this morning to drive up the horses as usual. He returned at 8:00 a.m. with one of them only. Alarmed at this occurrence, I dispatched one of my best hands on horseback in search of them. He returned at 10:00 a.m. with them, and I immediately set out.

[I] sent Drouillard and Reubin Field with the horses to the lower side of Medicine River, and proceeded myself with all our baggage and Joseph Field down the Missouri to the Mouth of Medicine River in our canoe of buffalo skins. We were compelled to swim the horses above White Bear Island and again across Medicine River, as the Missouri is of great width below the mouth of that river.

Having arrived safely below Medicine River, we immediately saddled our horses and proceeded down the river to the handsome falls of forty-seven feet where I halted about two hours and took a hasty sketch of these falls. In the meantime, we had some meat cooked and took dinner, after which we proceeded to the grand falls where we arrived at sunset.

On our way, we saw two very large bears on the opposite side of the river. As we arrived in sight of the little woods before the falls, we saw two other bears enter it. This being the only woods in the neighborhood, we were compelled, of course, to contend with the bears for possession, and therefore left our horses in a place of security and entered the woods which we searched in vain for the bears. They had fled.

Here we encamped and, the evening having the appearance of rain, made our beds and slept under a shelving rock.

These falls have abated much of their grandeur since I first arrived at them in June, 1805, the water being much lower at present than it was at that moment. However, they are still a sublimely grand object.

Gass: When Captain Lewis left us he gave orders that we should wait at the mouth of Maria's River to the 1st of September at which time, should he not arrive, we were to proceed on and join Captain Clark at the mouth of the Yellowstone River, and then return home, but informed us that should his life and health be preserved, he would meet us at the mouth of Maria's River on the 5th of August.

Thursday, July 17, 1806:

Lewis: I arose early this morning and made a drawing of the falls, after which we took breakfast and departed, it being my design to strike Maria's River about the place at which I left it on my return to its mouth in the beginning of June, 1805.

I steered my course through the wide and level plains which have somewhat the appearance of an ocean: not a tree nor a shrub to be seen. The land is not fertile, at least far less so than the plains of the Columbia or those lower down this river.

We killed a buffalo cow as we passed through the plains, and took the hump and tongue which furnish ample rations for four men [for] one day.

At 5:00 p.m. we arrived at Rose[440] River where I proposed remaining all night as I could not reach Maria's River this evening, and unless I did, there would be but little probability of our finding any wood and, very probably, no water either.

On our arrival at the river, we saw where a wounded and bleeding buffalo had just passed and concluded [that] it was probable that the Indians had been running them and were near at hand. The Hidatsa of Fort de Prairie and the Blackfoot Indians rove through this quarter of the country and, as they are a vicious, lawless, and rather an abandoned set of wretches, I wish to avoid an interview with them, if possible. I have no doubt but they would steal our horses if they have it in their power and, finding us weak, should they happen to be numerous, will most probably attempt to rob us of our arms and baggage. At all events, I am determined to take every possible precaution to avoid them, if possible.

I hurried over the river to a thick woods and turned the horses to graze. [I] sent Drouillard to pursue and kill the wounded buffalo in order to determine whether it had been wounded by the Indians or not,

440. present-day Teton (DeVoto)

and proceeded myself to reconnoiter the adjacent country, having sent Reubin Field for the same purpose [on] a different route. I ascended the river hills and, by the help of my glass, examined the plains but could make no discovery.

In about an hour, I returned to camp where I met with the others who had been as unsuccessful as myself. Drouillard could not find the wounded buffalo. Joseph Field, whom I had left at camp, had already roasted some of the buffalo meat and we took dinner, after which I sent Drouillard and Reubin Field to resume their researches for the Indians, and sat myself down to record the transactions of the day.

The bed of this stream is small gravel and mud. Its banks are low but never overflow. The hills are about one hundred or one hundred fifty feet high. It possesses bluffs of earth like the lower part of the Missouri. Except [for] the depth and velocity of its stream, it is the Missouri in miniature. From the size of Rose River at this place, and its direction, I have no doubt but it takes its source within the first range of the Rocky Mountains.

Friday, July 18, 1806:

Lewis: We set out this morning a little before sunrise [and] ascended the river hills and continued our route as yesterday through the open plains. At about six miles we reached the top of an elevated plain which divides the waters of the Rose River from those of Maria's River. Our course led us nearly parallel with a creek of Maria's River which takes its rise in these high plains at the place we passed them.

At noon we struck this creek about six miles from its junction with Maria's River where we found some cottonwood timber. Here we halted to dine and graze our horses.

We passed immense herds of buffalo on our way. In short, for about twelve miles, it appeared as one herd only, the whole plains and valley of this creek being covered with them. [We] saw a number of wolves of both species [and] also antelope and some horses.

After dinner we proceeded about five miles across the plain to Maria's River where we arrived at 6:00 p.m. Being now convinced that we were above the point to which I had formerly ascended this river, and fearing that a fork of this stream might fall in on the north side between this place and the point to which I had ascended it, I directed Drouillard, who was with me on my former excursion, and Joseph Field to descend the river early in the morning to the place from whence I had returned and examine whether any stream fell in or not.

I keep a strict lookout every night. I take my tour of watch with the men.

Saturday, July 19, 1806:

Lewis: Drouillard and Joseph Field set out early this morning in conformity to my instructions last evening. They returned at one-half after 12:00 and informed me that the course of the river from hence downwards, as far as they were, is north eighty [degrees] east.

We set out [and] ascended the river hills, having passed the river, and proceeded through the open plains up the north side of the river twenty miles, and encamped. At fifteen miles, we passed a large creek on the north side a little above its entrance. There is but little running water in this creek at present. Its bed is about thirty yards wide, and appears to come from the Broken Mountains,[441] so-called from their ragged and irregular shape. There are three of them extending from east to west, almost unconnected. The center mountain terminates in a conic spire, and is that which I have called the Tower Mountain. They are destitute of timber. The plains are beautiful and level, but the soil is but thin.

Sunday, July 20, 1806:

Lewis: We set out at sunrise and proceeded through the open plain as yesterday, up the north side of the river. The plains are more broken than they were yesterday, and a great quantity of small gravel is everywhere distributed over the surface of the earth which renders traveling extremely painful to our barefoot horses. The mineral salts common to the plains of the Missouri have been more abundant today than usual.

The bluffs of the river are about two hundred feet high, steep, irregular, and formed of earth which readily dissolves with water, slips and precipitates itself into the river, as before mentioned frequently of the bluffs of the Missouri below, which they resemble in every particular, differing essentially from those of the Missouri above the entrance of this river, they being composed of firm, red or yellow clay, which does not yield readily to the rains, and a large quantity of rock.

The soil of the river bottom is fertile and well-timbered. I saw some trees today which would make small canoes.

From the apparent descent of the country to the north and above the Broken Mountains, I am induced to believe that the south branch of the Saskatchewan receives a part of its waters from the plain, even to the borders of this river, and from the breaks visible in the plains in a northern direction, [I] think that a branch of that river, descending from the Rocky Mountains, passes at no great distance from Maria's and to the northeast of the Broken Mountains.

---

441. the Sweetgrass Hills (DeVoto)

The day has proven [to be] excessively warm and we lay by four hours during the heat of it.

We traveled twenty-eight miles and encamped as usual in the river bottom on its north side.

There is scarcely any water at present in the plains, and what there is lies in small pools and is so strongly impregnated with the mineral salts that it is unfit for any purpose except the use of the buffalo. Those animals appear to prefer this water to that of the river.

Monday, July 21, 1806:

Lewis: We set out at sunrise and proceeded a short distance up the north side of the river. We found [that] the ravines which made in on this side were so steep and numerous that we passed the river, in doing which the pack horse which carried my instruments missed the ford and wet the instruments. This accident detained us about half an hour. I took the instruments out, wiped them, and dried their cases. They sustained no material injury.

At 2:00 p.m. we struck a northern branch of Maria's River,[442] about thirty yards wide at the distance of about eight miles from its entrance. This stream is closely confined between cliffs of freestone rocks, the bottom [is] narrow below us, and above the rocks confine it on each side. [There is] some little timber below but not any above. The water of this stream is nearly clear. From the appearance of this rock and the apparent height of the bed of the stream, I am induced to believe that there are falls in these rivers somewhere about their junction.

Being convinced that this stream came from the mountains, I determined to pursue it as it will lead me to the most northern point to which the waters of Maria's River extend, which I now fear will not be as far north as I wished and expected.

After dinner we set out up the north branch, keeping on its south side. We pursued it until dark and, not finding any timber, halted and made a fire of the dung of the buffalo. We lay on the south side in a narrow bottom under a cliff.

Our provisions are nearly out. We wounded a buffalo this evening but could not get him.

Tuesday, July 22, 1806:

Lewis: We continued up the river on its south side for seventeen miles when we halted to graze our horses and eat. There being no wood, we were compelled to make our fire with the buffalo dung

442. Cut Bank Creek (Schmidt, p. 148)

which I found answered the purpose very well. We cooked and ate all the meat we had except a small piece of buffalo meat which was a little tainted.

After dinner we passed the river and took our course through a level and beautiful plain on the north side. The country has now become level, the river bottoms wide, and the adjoining plains but little elevated above them. The banks of the river are not usually more than from three to four feet, yet it does not appear ever to overflow them. We found no timber until we had traveled twelve miles farther when we arrived at a clump of large cottonwood trees in a beautiful and extensive bottom of the river about ten miles below the foot of the Rocky Mountains where this river enters them. As I could see from hence very distinctly where the river entered the mountains, and the bearing of this point being south of west, I thought it unnecessary to proceed farther and therefore encamped, resolving to rest ourselves and [our] horses a couple of days at this place and take the necessary observations.

This plain on which we are is very high. The Rocky Mountains to the southwest of us[443] appear but low from their base up, yet are partially covered with snow nearly to their bases. There is no timber on those mountains within our view. They are very irregular and broken in their form, and seem to be composed principally of clay, with but little rock or stone.

The river appears to possess at least double the volume of water which it had where we first arrived on it below. This, no doubt, proceeds from the evaporation caused by the sun and air, and the absorbing of the earth in its passage through these open plains. I believe that the waters of the Saskatchewan approach the borders of this river very nearly. I now have lost all hope of the waters of this river ever extending to north latitude fifty degrees, though I still hope and think it [is] more than probable that both the White Earth River and Milk River extend as far north as latitude fifty degrees.

We have seen but few buffalo today, no deer, and very few antelope. Game of every description is extremely wild, which induces me to believe that the Indians are now, or have been lately, in this neighborhood. We wounded a buffalo this evening, but our horses were so much fatigued that we were unable to pursue it with success.

Wednesday, July 23, 1806:

Lewis: I dispatched Drouillard and Joseph Field this morning to hunt. I directed Drouillard, who went up the river, to observe its bear-

443. the Lewis Range (DeVoto)

ings and the point at which it entered the mountains. This he did, and on his return I observed the point at which the river entered to bear south fifty degrees west, distant about ten miles, the river making a considerable bend to the west just above us.

Drouillard informed us that there was an Indian camp of eleven leather lodges which appeared to have been abandoned about ten days; the poles only of the lodges remained. We are confident that these are the Hidatsa of Fort de Prairie, and suspect that they are probably at this time somewhere on the main branch of Maria's River on the borders of the buffalo. Under this impression, I shall not strike that river on my return until about the mouth of the north branch.

Thursday, July 24, 1806:

Lewis: At 8:00 a.m., the sun made its appearance for a few minutes and I took its altitude, but it shortly after clouded up again and continued to rain the balance of the day. I was therefore unable to complete the observations I wished to take at this place. I determined to remain another day in the hope of its being fair.

The air has become extremely cold which, in addition to the wind and rain, renders our situation extremely unpleasant.

Several wolves visited our camp today. I fired on and wounded one of them very badly. The small species of wolf barks like a dog. They frequently salute us with this note as we pass through the plains.

Friday, July 25, 1806:

Lewis: The weather still continues cold, cloudy, and rainy. The wind, also, has blown all day with more than usual violence from the northwest.

Late in the evening Drouillard and Joseph Field returned. The former had killed a fine buck on which we now fared sumptuously.

They informed me that it was about ten miles to the main branch of Maria's River [and] that the valley formed by the river in that quarter was wide, extensive, and level with a considerable quantity of timber. Here they found some wintering camps of the natives and a great number of others of a more recent date or that had, from appearance, been evacuated about six weeks. We consider ourselves extremely fortunate in not having met with these people.

I determined that if tomorrow [it] continued cloudy to set out, as I now begin to be apprehensive that I shall not reach the United States within this season unless I make every exertion in my power, which I shall certainly not omit when once I leave this place, which I shall do with much reluctance without having obtained the necessary data to establish its longitude. As if the fates were against me, my chronometer, from some unknown cause, stopped today. When I set her to going, she went as usual.

Saturday, July 26, 1806:

Lewis: The morning was cloudy and [it] continued to rain as usual, though the clouds seemed somewhat thinner. I therefore proposed [to delay] setting out until 9:00 a.m. in the hope that it would clear off, but finding the contrary result, I had the horses caught and we set out, bidding a last adieu to this place which I now call Camp Disappointment.

I took my route through the open plains southeast five miles, passing a small creek at two miles from the mountains, when I changed my direction to south seventy-five [degrees] east for seven miles farther, and struck a principal branch of Maria's River[444] sixty-five yards wide [and] not very deep. I passed this stream to its south side and continued down it two miles on the last mentioned course when another branch, of nearly the same dignity, formed a junction with it, coming from the southwest.

I passed the south branch just above its junction and continued down the river, which runs a little to the north of east, one mile and halted to dine and graze our horses. Here I found some Indian lodges, which appeared to have been inhabited last winter, in a large and fertile bottom well-stocked with cottonwood timber. During our stay at this place Reubin Field killed a buck, a part of the flesh of which we took with us.

After dinner I continued my route down the river to the north of east about three miles. When the hills [began] putting in close on the south side, I determined to ascend them to the high plain, which I did accordingly, keeping the Fields with me. Drouillard passed the river and kept down [in] the valley of the river. I had intended to descend this river with its course to its junction with the fork which I had ascended, and from thence have taken across the country obliquely to Rose River and descend that stream to its confluence with Maria's River. The country through which this portion of Maria's River passes, to the fork which I ascended, appears much more broken than that above and between this and the mountains.

I had scarcely ascended the hills before I discovered to my left at the distance of a mile an assemblage of about thirty horses. I halted and used my spyglass, by the help of which I discovered several Indians on the top of an eminence just above them who appeared to be

444. Two Medicine River

looking down towards the river, I presumed, at Drouillard. About half the horses were saddled. This was a very unpleasant sight.

However, I resolved to make the best of our situation and to approach them in a friendly manner. I directed Joseph Field to display the flag which I had brought for that purpose, and advanced slowly towards them. About this time they discovered us and appeared to run about in a very confused manner, as if much alarmed. Their attention had been previously so fixed on Drouillard that they did not discover us until we had begun to advance upon them.

Some of them descended the hill on which they were and drove their horses within shot of its summit and again returned to the height, as if to await our arrival or to defend themselves. I calculated on their number being nearly or quite equal to that of their horses, that our running would invite pursuit as it would convince them that we were their enemies, and [that] our horses were so indifferent that we could not hope to make our escape by flight. Added to this, Drouillard was separated from us and I feared that his not being apprised of the Indians, in the event of our attempting to escape, he would most probably fall a sacrifice.

Under these considerations, I still advanced towards them. When we had arrived within a quarter of a mile of them, one of them mounted his horse and rode full speed towards us, which when I discovered [this], I halted and alighted from my horse. He came within a hundred paces, halted, looked at us, and turned his horse about and returned as briskly to his party as he had advanced. While he halted near us I held out my hand and beckoned to him to approach, but he paid no attention to my overtures.

On his return to his party, they all descended the hill and mounted their horses and advanced towards us, leaving [the] other horses behind them. We also advanced to meet them. I counted eight of them but still supposed that there were others concealed, as there were several other horses saddled.

I told the men with me that I apprehended that these were the Hidatsa of Fort de Prairie, and [that] from their known character I expected that we were to have some difficulty with them, that if they thought themselves sufficiently strong I was convinced [that] they would attempt to rob us, in which case, be their numbers what they would, I should resist to the last extremity, preferring death to that of being deprived of my papers, instruments, and gun, and desired that they would form the same resolution and be alert and on their guard.

When we arrived within a hundred yards of each other, the Indians, except one, halted. I directed the two men with me to do the same, and advanced singly to meet the Indian, with whom I shook hands, and passed on to those in his rear, as he did also to the two men in my rear. We now all assembled and alighted from our horses.

The Indians soon asked to smoke with us, but I told them that the man whom they had seen pass down the river had my pipe, and we could not smoke until he joined us. I requested, as they had seen which way he went, that they would, one of them, go with one of my men in search of him. This they readily consented to, and a young man set out with Reubin Field in search of Drouillard.

I now asked them by signs if they were the Hidatsa of the north, which they answered in the affirmative.[445] I asked if there was any chief among them and they pointed out three. I did not believe them. However, I thought it best to please them and gave to one a medal, to a second a flag, and to the third a handkerchief, with which they appeared well satisfied.

They appeared much agitated with our first interview from which they had scarcely yet recovered. In fact, I believe they were more alarmed at this accidental interview than we were. From no more of them appearing, I now concluded [that] they were only eight in number and became much better satisfied with our situation, as I was convinced that we could manage that number should they attempt any hostile measures.

As it was growing late in the evening, I proposed that we should remove to the nearest part of the river and encamp together. I told them that I was glad to see them and had a great deal to say to them. We mounted our horses and rode towards the river which was at but a short distance. On our way, we were joined by Drouillard, Field, and the Indian.

We descended a very steep bluff, about two hundred fifty feet high, to the river where there was a small bottom of nearly one-half [a] mile in length and about two hundred fifty yards wide in the widest part. In this bottom there stood three solitary trees, near one of which the Indians formed a large semicircular camp of dressed buffalo skins, and invited us to partake of their shelter, which Drouillard and I accepted, and the Fields lay near the fire in front of the shelter.

With the assistance of Drouillard, I had much conversation with these people in the course of the evening. I learned from them that they were a part of a large band which lay encamped at present near the foot of the Rocky Mountains, on the main branch of Maria's River, one and a half day's march from our present encampment, that there was a white man with their band, that there was another large band of their nation hunting buffalo near the Broken Mountains and were on their way to the mouth of Maria's River where they would probably be in

445. actually Piegans, one of the three Blackfoot tribes (DeVoto)

the course of a few days. They also informed us that from hence to the establishment where they trade on the Saskatchewan River is only six days' easy march, or such as they usually travel with their women and children, which may be estimated at about one hundred fifty miles, that from these traders they obtain arms, ammunition, spirituous liquor, blankets, etc., in exchange for wolf and some beaver skins.

I told these people that I had come a great way from the east up the large river which runs towards the rising sun, that I had been to the great waters where the sun sets, and had seen a great many nations, all of whom I had invited to come and trade with me on the rivers on this side of the mountains, that I had found most of them at war with their neighbors and had succeeded in restoring peace among them, that I was now on my way home and had left my party at the Falls of the Missouri with orders to descend that river to the entrance of Maria's River and there await my arrival, and that I had come in search of them in order to prevail on them to be at peace with their neighbors, particularly those on the west side of the mountains, and to engage them to come and trade with me when the establishment is made at the entrance of this river, to all [of] which they readily gave their assent and declared it to be their wish to be at peace with the Tushepaws whom, they said, had killed a number of their relations lately, and pointed to several of those present who had cut their hair as an evidence of the truth of what they had asserted.

I found them extremely fond of smoking and plied them with the pipe until late at night. I told them that if they intended to do as I wished them, they would send some of their young men to their band with an invitation to their chiefs and warriors to bring the white man with them and come down and council with me at the entrance of Maria's River, and that the balance of them would accompany me to that place where I was anxious now to meet my men as I had been absent from them [for] some time and knew that they would be uneasy until they saw me, that if they would go with me I would give them ten horses and some tobacco. To this proposition they made no reply.

I took the first watch tonight and sat up until half after eleven. The Indians by this time were all asleep. I roused Reubin Fields and laid down myself. I directed Fields to watch the movements of the Indians and if any of them left the camp, to awaken us all as I apprehended [that] they would attempt to steal our horses. This being done, I fell into a profound sleep and did not awaken until the noise of the men and Indians awoke me a little after light in the morning.

Sunday, July 27, 1806:

Lewis: This morning at daylight the Indians got up and crowded around the fire. Joseph Fields, who was on post, had carelessly laid his gun down behind him where his brother was sleeping. One of the Indians, the fellow to whom I had given the medal last evening, slipped behind him and took his gun and that of his brother, unperceived by him. At the same instant, two others advanced and seized the guns of Drouillard and myself.

Joseph Fields, seeing this, turned about to look for his gun and saw the fellow just running off with her and his brother's. He called to his brother who instantly jumped up and pursued the Indian, with whom they overtook at the distance of fifty or sixty paces from the camp, seized their guns and wrested them from him, and Reubin Fields, as he seized his gun, stabbed the Indian to the heart with his knife. The fellow ran about fifteen steps and fell dead. Of this I did not know until afterwards. Having recovered their guns, they ran back instantly to the camp.

Drouillard, who was awake, saw the Indian take hold of his gun and instantly jumped up and seized her and wrested her from him, but the Indian still retained his pouch. His jumping up and crying, "Damn you! Let go my gun!" awakened me. I jumped up and asked what was the matter, which I quickly learned when I saw Drouillard in a scuffle with the Indian for his gun.

I reached to seize my gun but found her gone. I then drew a pistol from my holster and, turning myself about, saw the Indian making off with my gun. I ran at him with my pistol and bid him lay down my gun, which he was in the act of doing when the Fields returned and drew up their guns to shoot him, which I forbade, as he did not appear to be about to make any resistance or commit any offensive act. He dropped the gun and walked slowly off. I picked her up instantly.

Drouillard, having about this time recovered his gun and pouch, asked me if he might not kill the fellow, which I also forbade, as the Indian did not appear to wish to kill us.

As soon as they found us all in possession of our arms, they ran and endeavored to drive off all the horses. I now hollered to the men and told them to fire on them if they attempted to drive off our horses. They, accordingly, pursued the main party which was driving the horses up the river, and I pursued the man who had taken my gun who with another was driving off a part of the horses which were to the left of camp. I pursued them so closely that they could not take twelve of their own horses, but continued to drive mine with some others.

At the distance of three hundred paces, they entered one of those steep niches in the bluff with the horses before them. Being nearly out of breath, I could pursue no farther. I called to them, as I had done several times before, that I would shoot them if they did not give me back my horse, and raised my gun. One of them jumped behind a rock and spoke to the other, who turned around and stopped at the distance of thirty steps from me, and I shot him through the belly.

He fell to his knees and on his right elbow, from which position he partly raised himself up and fired at me and, turning himself about, crawled in behind a rock which was a few feet from him. He [had] overshot me. Being bareheaded, I felt the wind of his bullet very distinctly.

Not having my shot pouch I could not reload my piece, and as there were two of them behind good shelters from me, I did not think it prudent to rush on them with my pistol which I had discharged. I had not the means of reloading until I reached camp. I therefore returned leisurely towards camp.

On my way I met with Drouillard who, having heard the report of the guns, had returned in search of me and left the Fields to pursue the Indians. I desired him to hasten to the camp with me and assist in catching as many of the Indian horses as were necessary and to call to the Fields, if he could make them hear, to come back, that we still had a sufficient number of horses. This he did, but they were too far to hear him.

We reached the camp and began to catch the horses and saddle them and put on the packs.

The reason I had not my pouch with me was that I had not time to return about fifty yards to camp after getting my gun before I was obliged to pursue the Indians or suffer them to collect and drive off all the horses.

We had caught and saddled the horses and began to arrange the packs when the Fields returned with four of our horses. We left one of our horses and took four of the best of those of the Indians'.

While the men were preparing the horses, I put four shields and two bows and quivers of arrows, which had been left, on the fire with sundry other articles. They [had] left all their baggage at our mercy. They had but two guns, and one of them they left. The others were armed with bows and arrows and eyedaggs. The gun we took with us. I also retook the flag, but left the medal about the neck of the dead man that they might be informed who we were. We took some of their buffalo meat and set out ascending the bluffs by the same route we had descended last evening, leaving the balance of nine of their horses which we did not want.

The Fields told me that three of the Indians whom they pursued swam the river, one of them on my horse, and that two others ascended the hill and escaped from them with a part of their horses, two I had pursued into the niche, one lay dead near the camp, and the eighth we could not account for but supposed that he ran off early in the contest.

Having ascended the hill, we took our course through a beautiful, level plain a little to the south of east. My design was to hasten to the entrance of Maria's River as quickly as possible in the hope of meeting with the canoes and party at that place, having no doubt but that they would pursue us with a large party and, as there was a band near the Broken Mountains or probably between them and the mouth of that river, we might expect them to receive intelligence from us and arrive at that place nearly as soon as we could. No time was, therefore, to be lost, and we pushed our horses as hard as they would bear.

At eight miles, we passed a large branch, forty yards wide, which I called Battle River.

At 3:00 p.m. we arrived at Rose River about five miles above where we had passed it as we went out, having traveled, by my estimate compared with our former distances and courses, about sixty-three miles. Here we halted an hour and a half, took some refreshment, and suffered our horses to graze. The day proved warm, but the late rains had supplied the little reservoirs in the plains with water and had put them in fine order for traveling. Our whole route so far was as level as a bowling green, with but little stone and few prickly pears.

After dinner we pursued the bottoms of Rose River, but finding it inconvenient to pass the river so often, we again ascended the hills on the southwest side and took the open plains. By dark we had traveled about seventeen miles farther. We now halted to rest ourselves and [our] horses about two hours. We killed a buffalo cow and took a small quantity of meat.

After refreshing ourselves we again set out by moonlight and traveled leisurely. Heavy thunderclouds lowered around us on every quarter but that from which the moon gave us light. We continued to pass immense herds of buffalo all night as we had done in the latter part of the day. We traveled until 2:00 in the morning, having come, by my estimate, after dark about twenty miles.

We now turned out our horses and laid ourselves down to rest in the plain very much fatigued, as may be readily conceived. My Indian horse carried me very well, in short, much better than my own would have done, and leaves me with but little reason to complain of the robbery.

Monday, July 28, 1806:

Lewis: The morning proved fair. I slept soundly but fortunately awoke as daylight appeared. I awakened the men and directed the horses to be saddled.

I was so sore from my ride yesterday that I could scarcely stand, and the men complained of being in a similar situation. However, I encouraged them by telling them that our own lives, as well as those of our friends and fellow travelers, depended on our exertions at this moment. They were alert soon, prepared the horses, and we again resumed our march.

The men proposed to pass the Missouri at the grog spring[446] where Rose River approaches it so nearly, and pass down on the southwest side. To this I objected, as it would delay us almost all day to reach the point[447] by this circuitous route, and would give the enemy time to surprise and cut off the party at the point if they arrived there. I told them that we owed much to the safety of our friends and that we must risk our lives on this occasion, that I should proceed immediately to the point, and if the party had not arrived, that I would raft the Missouri a small distance above, hide our baggage, and march on foot up the river through the timber until I met the canoes or joined them at the falls.

I now told them that it was my determination that if we were attacked in the plains on our way to the point, that the bridles of the horses should be tied together, and we would stand and defend them, or sell our lives as dear as we could.

We had proceeded about twelve miles on an east course when we found ourselves near the Missouri. We heard a report which we took to be that of a gun, but we were not certain. Still continuing down the northeast bank of the Missouri about eight miles farther, being then within five miles of the grog spring, we heard the report of several rifles very distinctly on the river to our right.

We quickly repaired to this joyful sound, and on arriving at the bank of the river had the unspeakable satisfaction to see our canoes coming down. We hurried down from the bluff on which we were and joined them, stripped our horses, and gave them a final discharge, embarking without loss of time with our baggage.

I now learned that they had brought all things safely, having sustained no loss nor met with any accident of importance. Wiser had cut

---

446. on the outbound journey, some of the expedition had stopped here for "a good drink of grog" (Bakeless, p. 350)

447. the mouth of the Marias (DeVoto)

his leg badly with a knife opposite to our principal cache which we proceeded to open after reconnoitering the adjacent country.

We found that the cache had caved in and most of the articles buried therein were injured. I sustained the loss of two very large bearskins which I much regret. Most of the fur and baggage belonging to the men was injured. The gunpowder, corn, flour, pork, and salt had sustained but little injury. The parched meal was spoiled, or nearly so.

Having no time to air these things which they wanted, we dropped down to the point to take in the several articles which had been buried at that place in several smaller caches. These we found in good order, and recovered every article except three traps belonging to Drouillard which could not be found.

Here, as good fortune would have it, Sergeant Gass and Willard, who brought the horses from the falls, joined us at 1:00 p.m. I had ordered them to bring down the horses to this place in order to assist them in collecting meat, which I directed them to kill and dry here for our voyage, presuming that they would have arrived with the pirogue and canoes at this place several days before my return.

Having now nothing to detain us, we passed over immediately to the island in the entrance to Maria's River to launch the red pirogue, but found her so much decayed that it was impossible with the means we had to repair her, and [we] therefore merely took the nails and other ironworks about her which might be of service to us, and left her.

We now re-embarked on board the white pirogue and five small canoes and descended the river about fifteen miles and encamped on the southwest side near a few cottonwood trees.

Thursday, August 7, 1806:

Lewis: We set out early resolving, if possible, to reach the Yellowstone River today, which was at the distance of eighty-three miles from our encampment of last evening.

At 4:00 p.m. we arrived at the entrance of the Yellowstone River. I landed at the point and found that Captain Clark had been encamped at this place and, from appearances, had left it about seven or eight days [ago]. I found a paper on a pole at the point which merely contained my name in the handwriting of Captain Clark.

We also found the remnant of a note which had been attached to a piece of elk horn in the camp. From this fragment, I learned that game was scarce at the point and the mosquitoes troublesome, which were the reasons given for his going on. I also learned that he intended halting a few miles below where he intended, awaiting my arrival.

I now wrote a note directed to Colter and Collins, provided they were behind, ordering them to come on without loss of time. This note

I wrapped in leather and attached to the same pole which Captain Clark had planted at the point.

This being done, I instantly re-embarked and descended the river in the hope of reaching Captain Clark's camp before night. About seven miles below the point on the southwest shore, I saw some meat that had been lately fleeced and hung on a pole. I directed Sergeant Ordway to go on shore and examine the place. On his return, he reported that he saw the tracks of two men which appeared so recent that he believed they had been there today. The fire he found at the place was blazing and appeared to have been mended up afresh, or within the course of an hour past. He found at this place a part of a Chinook hat which my men recognized as the hat of Gibson.

From these circumstances we concluded that Captain Clark's camp could not be distant and pursued our route until dark, with the hope of reaching his camp. In this, however, we were disappointed, and night coming on compelled us to encamp on the northeast shore in the next bottom, above our encampment of the twenty-third and twenty-fourth of April, 1805.

As we came to, a herd of buffalo assembled on the shore, of which we killed a fat cow.

Gass: We discovered a few words written, or traced, in the sand, which were, "W. C. a few miles farther down on the right-hand side." At night we encamped, after coming above one hundred miles.

Friday, August 8, 1806:

Lewis: Believing from the recent appearances about the fire which we passed last evening that Captain Clark could be at no great distance below, I set out early. The wind [was] hard from the northeast, but by the force of the oars and current, we traveled at a good rate until 10:00 a.m., by which time we reached the center of the Beaver Bends about eight miles by water and three by land above the entrance of White Earth River.

Not finding Captain Clark, I knew not what calculation to make with respect to his halting, and therefore determined to proceed as though he was not before me and leave the rest to the chapter of accidents.

At this place I found a good beach for the purpose of drawing out the pirogue and one of the canoes which wanted corking and repairing. The men with me have not had leisure since we left the west side of the Rocky Mountains to dress any skins or make themselves clothes, and most of them are, therefore, extremely bare. I therefore determined to halt at this place until the pirogue and canoe could be repaired and the men dress skins and make themselves the necessary clothing. We encamped on the northeast side of the river. We found the mosquitoes extremely troublesome, but in this respect there is but little choice of camps from hence down to St. Louis.

From this place to the Little Missouri there is an abundance of game. I shall, therefore, when I leave this place, travel at my leisure and avail myself of every opportunity to collect and dry meat until I provide a sufficient quantity for our voyage, not knowing what provision Captain Clark had made in this respect.

I formed a camp, unloaded the canoes and pirogue, had the latter and one of the canoes drawn out to dry, fleeced what meat we had collected and hung it on poles in the sun, after which the men busied themselves in dressing skins and making themselves clothes.

Monday, August 11, 1806:

Lewis: We set out very early this morning. It being my wish to arrive at the Burnt Hills by noon in order to take the latitude of that place as it is the most northern point of the Missouri, I informed the party of my design and requested that they would exert themselves to reach the place in time, as it would save us the delay of nearly one day. Being as anxious to get forward as I was, they plied their oars faithfully and we proceeded rapidly.

We saw but little game until about 9:00 a.m. when we came up with a buffalo swimming the river, which I shot and killed. Leaving the small canoes to dress it and bring on the meat, I proceeded.

We had gone but little way before I saw a very large grizzly bear and put to in order to kill it, but it took wind of us and ran off. The small canoes overtook us and informed [us] that the flesh of the buffalo was unfit for use and that they had therefore left it.

[At] half after 11:00 a.m. we saw a large herd of elk on the northeast shore and I directed the men in the small canoes to halt and kill some of them, and continued on in the pirogue to the Burnt Hills. When I arrived there it was about twenty minutes after noon and, of course, the observation for the meridian altitude was lost.

Just opposite to the Burnt Hills there happened to be a herd of elk on a thick willow bar and, finding that my observation was lost for the present, I determined to land and kill some of them. Accordingly, we put to and I went out with Cruzatte only. We fired on the elk. I killed one and he wounded another. We reloaded our guns and took different routes through the thick willows in pursuit of the elk.

I was in the act of firing on the elk a second time when a ball struck my left thigh about an inch below my hip joint. Missing the bone, it passed through the left thigh and cut the thickness of the bullet across the hinder part of the right thigh. The stroke was very severe.

I instantly supposed that Cruzatte had shot me in mistake for an elk as I was dressed in brown leather and he cannot see very well. Under this impression, I called out to him, "Damn you! You have shot me!" and looked towards the place from whence the ball had come. Seeing nothing, I called Cruzatte several times as loud as I could, but received no answer.

I was now persuaded that it was an Indian that had shot me as the report of the gun did not appear to be more than forty paces from me, and Cruzatte appeared to be out of hearing of me.

In this situation, not knowing how many Indians there might be concealed in the bushes, I thought [it] best to make good my retreat to the pirogue. Calling out as I ran for the first hundred paces as loud as I could to Cruzatte to retreat, that there were Indians, hoping to alarm him in time to make his escape, also. I still retained the charge in my gun which I was about to discharge at the moment the ball struck me.

When I arrived in sight of the pirogue, I called the men to their arms to which they flew in an instant. I told them that I was wounded, but I hoped not mortally, by an Indian, I believed, and directed them to follow me, that I would return and give them battle and relieve Cruzatte, if possible, who, I feared, had fallen into their hands.

The men followed me as they were bidden, and I returned about a hundred paces when my wounds became so painful and my thigh so stiff that I could scarcely get on. In short, I was compelled to halt, and ordered the men to proceed and, if they found themselves overpowered by numbers, to retreat in order, keeping up a fire.

I now got back to the pirogue as well as I could and prepared myself with a pistol, my rifle, and air gun, being determined, as a retreat was impracticable, to sell my life as dearly as possible.

In this state of anxiety and suspense, I remained about twenty minutes when the party returned with Cruzatte and reported that there were no Indians nor the appearance of any. Cruzatte seemed much alarmed and declared [that] if he had shot me it was not his intention, that he had shot an elk in the willows after he left or separated from me. I asked him whether he did not hear me when I called to him so frequently, which he absolutely denied.

I do not believe that the fellow did it intentionally, but after finding that he had shot me, [he] was anxious to conceal his knowledge of having done so. The ball had lodged in my breeches which I knew to be the ball of the short rifles such as that he had and, there being no person out with me but him, and no Indians that we could discover, I have no doubt in my own mind of his having shot me.

With the assistance of Sergeant Gass, I took off my clothes and dressed my wounds myself as well as I could, introducing tents of patent lint into the ball holes. The wounds bled considerably, but I was happy to find that it had touched neither bone nor artery.

I sent the men to dress the two elk which Cruzatte and I had killed, which they did in a few minutes, and brought the meat to the river. The small canoes came up shortly after with the flesh of one elk. My wounds being so situated that I could not without infinite pain make an observation, I determined to relinquish it and proceeded on.

We came within eight miles of our encampment of the fifteenth of April, 1805, and encamped on the northeast side. As it was painful to me to be removed, I slept on board the pirogue. The pain I experienced excited a high fever and I had a very uncomfortable night.

At 4:00 p.m. we passed an encampment which had been evacuated this morning by Captain Clark. Here I found a note from Captain Clark informing me that he had left a letter for me at the entrance of the Yellowstone River but that Sergeant Pryor, who had passed that place since he left it, had taken the letter, that Sergeant Pryor, having been robbed of all his horses, had descended the Yellowstone River in skin canoes and had overtaken him at this encampment.

This, I fear, puts an end to our prospects of obtaining the Sioux chiefs to accompany us as we have not now leisure to send and engage Mr. Heney on this service, or at least he would not have time to engage them to go as early, as it is absolutely necessary we should descend the river.

Ordway: About 12:00 Captain Lewis halted at a bottom on [the] starboard side to kill some elk. Captain Lewis killed one and Cruzatte two and, as he still kept firing, one of his balls hit Captain Lewis in his back side. He instantly called to Pierre[448] but Pierre [was] not answering. He supposed it to be Indians and ran to the canoes and ordered the men to their arms.

Tuesday, August 12, 1806:

Lewis: Being anxious to overtake Captain Clark who from the appearance of his camps could be at no great distance before me, we set out early and proceeded with all possible expedition.

At 8:00 a.m. the bowman informed me that there was a canoe and a camp, he believed, of white men on the northeast shore. I directed the pirogue and canoes to come to at this place, and found it to be the camp of two hunters from the Illinois by the names [of] Joseph Dickson and Forest Hancock. These men informed me that Captain Clark had passed them about noon the day before. They also informed me that they had left the Illinois in the summer of 1804, since which time

448. Cruzatte

they had been ascending the Missouri, hunting and trapping beaver, that they had been robbed by the Indians and the former wounded last winter by the Tetons of the Burnt Woods, that they had hitherto been unsuccessful in their voyage, having as yet caught but little beaver, but were still determined to proceed.

I gave them a short description of the Missouri, a list of distances to the most conspicuous streams and remarkable places on the river above, and pointed out to them the places where the beaver most abounded. I also gave them a file and a couple of pounds of powder and some lead. These were articles which, they assured me, they were in great want of. I remained with these men an hour and a half when I took leave of them and proceeded.

While I halted with these men, Colter and Collins, who [had] separated from us on the third instant, rejoined us. They were well, no accident having happened. They informed me that after proceeding the first day and not overtaking us, that they had concluded that we were behind, and had delayed several days in waiting for us, and had thus been unable to join us until the present moment.

My wounds felt very stiff and sore this morning, but gave me no considerable pain. There was much less inflammation than I had reason to apprehend there would be. I had, last evening, applied a poultice of Peruvian barks.

At 1:00 p.m. I overtook Captain Clark and party and had the pleasure of finding them all well. As writing in my present situation is extremely painful to me, I shall desist until I recover and leave to my friend, Captain Clark, the continuation of our journal.

18: Clark on the Yellowstone
(July and August, 1806)

About 8:00 a.m. this morning, a bear of the large vicious species, being on a sand bar, raised himself up on his hind feet and looked at us as we passed down near the middle of the river. He plunged into the water and swam toward us, either from a disposition to attack or from the scent of the meat which was in the canoes. We shot him with three balls and he returned to shore badly wounded.

Captain William Clark,
August 2, 1806

Thursday, July 3, 1806:

Clark: We collected our horses and, after breakfast, I took my leave of Captain Lewis and the Indians and, at 8:00 a.m., set out with twenty men [and] interpreter Charbonneau and his wife and child (as an interpreter and interpretress for the Crow Indians, and the latter for the Shoshone) with fifty horses.

We proceeded on through the valley of Clark's River which we found more beautifully versified with small, open plains covered with a great variety of sweet-scented plants, flowers, and grass. Some snow is also to be seen on the high points and hollows of the mountains.

We encamped on the north side of a large creek where we found tolerable food for our horses. [The] mosquitoes [are] very troublesome.

One man, Joseph Potts, [is] very unwell this evening, owing to riding a hard trotting horse. I gave him a pill of opium, which soon relieved him.

Ordway: We got up our horses and both parties set out about one time. Captain Lewis parted here with their parties and proceeded on. I [went] with Captain Clark up the Flathead[449] River. We are now on our way to the head of the Missouri.

449. today's Bitterroot

Friday, July 4, 1806:

Clark: This being the day of the Declaration of Independence of the United States and a day commonly celebrated by my country, I had every disposition to celebrate this day and, therefore, halted early and partook of a sumptuous dinner of a fat saddle of venison and mush of cowas (roots).

We made thirty miles today.

Saturday, July 5, 1806:

Clark: I rose at daylight this morning, dispatched Labiche after a buck, which he [had] killed late last evening, and went with the three men whom I had sent in search of a ford across the west fork of Clark's River, and examined each ford. Neither of them, I thought, would answer to pass the fork without wetting all the loads. Near one of those places pointed out by Colter, I found a practicable ford and returned to camp.

[I] ordered everything packed up and, after breakfast, we set out. I saw fresh signs of two horses and a fire burning on the side of the road. I presume that these Indians are spies from the Shoshones.

Monday, July 7, 1806:

Clark: This morning our horses were very much scattered. I sent out men in every direction in search of them. They brought all except nine by 6:00, and informed me that they could not find those nine. I then ordered six men to take horses and go different directions and at a greater distance. These men all returned by 10:00 a.m. and informed me that they had made circles in every direction six or eight miles around camp and could not see any signs of them, that they had reasons to believe that the Indians had stolen them in the course of the night, and founded their reasons on the quality of the horses, all being the most valuable horses we had, and several of them so attached to horses of inferior quality which we have, they could not be separated from each other when driving with their loads on in the course of the day.

I thought it probable that they might be stolen by some skulking Shoshones, but as it was yet possible that they might have taken our back route or rambled to a greater distance, I determined to leave a small party to hunt for them today and proceeded on with the main party and all the baggage to the canoes, raise them out of the water, and expose them to the sun to dry by the time this party should overtake me.

I left Sergeant Ordway, Shannon, Gibson, Collins, and Labiche with directions to hunt this day for the horses without[450] they should discover that the Indians had taken them into the mountains, and pursue our trail, etc.

[We] entered an extensive open, level plain in which the Indian trail scattered in such a manner that we could not pursue it. The Indian woman, wife to Charbonneau, informed me that she had been in this plain frequently and knew it well. The squaw pointed to the gap through which she said we must pass, which was south fifty-six [degrees] east. She said we would pass the river before we reached the gap. This is the great plain where Shoshones gather quamash and roots, etc..

[The spring] has every appearance of boiling, too hot for a man to endure his hand in it three seconds. The [piece of meat] about the size of my three fingers cooked done in twenty-five minutes; the other, much thicker, was thirty-two minutes before it became sufficiently done.

Tuesday, July 8, 1806:

Clark: After dinner we proceeded on down the fork, which is here but small, nine miles to our encampment of 17 August,[451] at which place we sank our canoes and buried some articles as before mentioned. The most of the party with me, being chewers of tobacco, became so impatient to be chewing it that they scarcely gave themselves time to take their saddles off their horses before they were off to the deposit. I found every article safe, except a little damp.

I gave to each man who used tobacco about two feet off a part of a roll, took one-third of the balance myself, and put up two-thirds in a box to send down with the most of the articles which had been left at this place, by the canoes to Captain Lewis.

As it was late, nothing could be done with the canoes this evening. I examined them and found them all safe except one of the largest, which had a large hole in one side and [a] split in [the] bow.

The road which we have traveled from Traveller's Rest Creek to this place (this place is the head of the Jefferson River, where we left our canoes) [is] an excellent road. The distance is one hundred sixty-four miles.

---

450. meaning "unless"

451. 1805

Wednesday, July 9, 1806:

Clark: [I] set several men to work digging for the tobacco Captain Lewis informed me he had buried in the place the lodge stood when we lay here last summer. They searched diligently without finding anything.

At 10:00 a.m., Sergeant Ordway and party arrived with the horses we had lost. He reported that he found those horses near the head of the creek on which we encamped, making off as fast as they could, and much scattered.

Thursday, July 10, 1806:

Clark: Sergeant Ordway informed me that the party with him had come on very well, and he thought the canoes could go as fast as the horses. I determined to put all the baggage, etc., which I intend taking with me to the River Yellowstone in the canoes and proceed on to the Three Forks, or Madison and Gallatin rivers.

In passing down in the course of this day we saw great numbers of beaver. I saw several large rattlesnakes in passing the Rattlesnake Mountain; they were fierce.

Saturday, July 12, 1806:

Clark: Sergeant Pryor did not join me last night. He has proceeded on down.

The beaver were flapping their tails in the river about us all the last night.

This morning I was detained until 7:00 a.m. making paddles and drawing the nails of the canoe to be left at this place, and the one we had before left here. After completing the paddles, etc., and taking some breakfast, I set out.

Sunday, July 13, 1806:

Clark: [We] set out early this morning and proceeded on very well to the entrance of Madison's River at our old encampment of the 27th July last, at 12:00, where I found Sergeant Pryor and the party with the horses. They had arrived at this place one hour before us. His party had killed six deer and a white bear.

I had all the horses driven across Madison and Gallatin rivers and halted to dine and let the horses feed immediately below the entrance of Gallatin. [I] had all the baggage of the land party taken out of the canoes and, after dinner, the six canoes and the party of ten men under the direction of Sergeant Ordway set out. Previous to their departure, I gave instructions [on] how they were to proceed, etc. I also wrote to Captain Lewis by Sergeant Ordway.

My party now consists of the following party, viz., Sergeant Nathaniel Pryor, Joe Shields, George Shannon, William Bratton, Labiche, Windsor, Hugh Hall, Gibson, interpreter Charbonneau, his wife and child, and my man York, with forty-nine horses and a colt. The horses' feet are very sore and several of them can scarcely proceed on.

I observed several leading roads about eighteen or twenty miles distant. The Indian woman, who has been of great service to me as a pilot through this country, recommends a gap in the mountain[452] more south, which I shall cross.

Monday, July 14, 1806:

Clark: [I] sent Shields ahead to kill a deer for our breakfast, and at an early hour set out with the party.

[We] crossed Gallatin River, which makes a considerable bend to the northeast, and proceeded on nearly south seventy-eight degrees east through an open, level plain. At six miles I struck the river and crossed a part of it and attempted to proceed on through the river bottoms, which were several miles wide at this place. I crossed several channels of the river running through the bottom in different directions. I proceeded on about two miles, crossing those different channels, all of which were dammed with beaver in such a manner as to render the passage impracticable and, after being swamped, as I may say, in this bottom of beaver. I was compelled to turn short about to the right and, after some difficulty, made my way good to an open, low, but firm plain which was an island, and extended nearly the course I wished to proceed.

Here the squaw informed me that there was a large road passing through the upper part of this low plain from Madison River through the gap which I was steering my course to. I proceeded up this plain four miles and crossed the main channel of the river, having passed through a skirt of cotton timber to an open, low plain on the northeast side of the river, and nooned it. The river is much divided, and on all the small streams [are] innumerable quantities of beaver dams, though the river is yet navigable for canoes.

I overtook Shields soon after I set out. He had killed a large, fat buck. I saw elk, deer and antelopes, and a great deal of old signs of buffalo. Their roads are in every direction.

The Indian woman informs me that a few years ago buffalo were very plenty in these plains and valleys, quite as high as the head of Jef-

---

452. today's Bozeman Pass (Ambrose, *VD*, p. 216)

ferson's River, but few of them ever come into these valleys of late years, owing to the Shoshones, who are fearful of passing into the plains west of the mountains, and subsist on what game they take in the east fork of Lewis's River. Small parties of Shoshones do pass over to the plains for a few days at a time and kill buffalo for their skins and dried meat, and return immediately into the mountains.

[We] camped on a small branch of the middle fork[453] on the northeast side at the commencement of the gap of the mountain. The road leading up this branch, [and] several other roads, all old, come in from the right and left.

Tuesday, July 15, 1806:

Clark: We collected our horses and, after an early breakfast at 8:00 a.m., set out and proceeded over a low gap in the mountain [and] thence across the heads of the northeast branch of the fork of Gallatin River, which we camped near last night, passing over a low dividing ridge to the head of a water course, which runs into the Yellowstone, pursuing an old buffalo road, which enlarges by one which joins it from the most easterly branch of the east fork of Gallatin River, proceeding down the branch a little to the north of east, keeping on the north side of the branch to the River Yellowstone, at which place I arrived at 2:00 p.m.

The distance from the three forks of the easterly fork of Gallatin River (from whence it may be navigated down with small canoes) to the River Yellowstone is eighteen miles on an excellent high, dry, firm road with very inconsiderable hills.

In the evening, after the usual delay of three hours to give the horses time to feed and rest, and allowing ourselves time also to cook and eat dinner, I proceeded on down the river on an old buffalo road. The horses' feet are very sore; many of them can scarcely proceed on over the stone and gravel. In every other respect they are sound and in good spirits.

I saw two black bear on the side of the mountains this morning. Several gangs of elk, from one hundred to two hundred in a gang, [were] on the river. [There were] great numbers of beaver.

Wednesday, July 16, 1806:

Clark: [We] saw a large gang of about two hundred elk and nearly as many antelope [and] also two white, or gray, bears in the plains. One of them I chased on horseback about two miles to the rugged part of the plain where I was compelled to give up the chase. Two

---

453. Gallatin River (Eide, p. 209)

of the horses were so lame owing to their feet being worn quite smooth and to the quick. The hind feet were much the worse. I had moccasins made of green buffalo skin and put on their feet, which seems to relieve them very much in passing over the stony plains.

Thursday, July 17, 1806:

Clark: [We] passed an Indian fort built of logs and bark. This work is about fifty feet [in] diameter and nearly round. The squaw informed me that when the war parties (of Hidatsa, Crows, etc., who fight Shoshones) find themselves pursued, they make these forts to defend themselves.

Friday, July 18, 1806:

Clark: At 11:00 a.m. I observed a smoke rise to the south-south-east in the plains toward the termination of the Rocky Mountains in that direction (which are covered with snow). This smoke must be raised by the Crow Indians in that direction as a signal for us or other bands. I think it most probable that they have discovered our trail and, taking us to be Shoshones, etc., in search of them, the Crow Indians—now at peace with them—to trade, as is their custom, have made this smoke to show where they are or, otherwise, taking us to be their enemy, made this signal for other bands to be on their guard.

Saturday, July 19, 1806:

Clark: Immense swarms of grasshoppers have destroyed every sprig of grass for many miles on this side of the river.

Charbonneau informed me that he saw an Indian on the high lands on the opposite side of the river, at the time I was absent in the woods. I saw a smoke in the same direction with that which I had seen on the 7th instant. It appeared to be in the mountains.

Sunday, July 20, 1806:

Clark: I directed Sergeant Pryor and Shields, each of them good judges of timber, to proceed on down the river six or eight miles and examine the bottoms, if any larger trees than those near which we are encamped can be found, and return before 12:00. They set out at day-light.

I also sent Labiche, Charbonneau, and Hall to bring the skin and some of the flesh of the elk Labiche killed last evening. They returned with one skin, the wolves having eaten the most of the other four elk.

I also sent two men in search of wood suitable for ax handles. They found some chokecherry, which is the best wood which can be procured in this country.

[I] saw a bear on an island opposite, and several elk.

Sergeant Pryor and Shields returned at half past 11:00 a.m. and informed me that they had proceeded down the timbered bottoms of the river for about twelve miles without finding a tree better than those near my camp.

I determined to have two canoes made out of the largest of those trees and lash them together, which will cause them to be sturdy and fully sufficient to take my small party and self, with what little baggage we have, down this river. [I] had handles put in the three axes and, after sharpening them with a file, felled the two trees, which I intended for the two canoes. Those trees appeared tolerably sound and will make canoes of twenty-eight feet in length and about sixteen or eighteen inches deep and from sixteen to twenty-four inches wide.

The men with the three axes set in and worked until dark.

Monday, July 21, 1806:

Clark: This morning I was informed that half of our horses were absent. [I] sent out Shannon, Bratton, and Charbonneau to hunt them. Charbonneau went up the river, Shannon down, and Bratton in the bottom near the camp. Charbonneau and Bratton returned at 10:00 a.m. and informed me that they saw no signs of the horses.

Shannon proceeded on down the river about fourteen miles and did not return until late in the evening. He was equally unsuccessful. Shannon informed me that he saw a remarkably large lodge about twelve miles below, covered with bushes, and the top decorated with skins, etc., [that] had the appearance of having been built about two years.

I sent out two men on horseback to kill a fat cow, which they did, and returned in three hours. The men work very diligently on the canoes. One of them [is] nearly finished [and] ready to put in the water.

This evening late a very black cloud [came] from the southeast, accompanied with thunder and lightning with hard winds, which shifted about and was warm and disagreeable.

I am apprehensive that the Indians have stolen our horses, and probably [by] those who had made the smoke a few days past toward the southwest. I determined to have the balance of the horses guarded, and for that purpose sent out three men. On their approach near, the horses were so alarmed that they ran away and entered the woods, and the men returned.

Tuesday, July 22, 1806:

Clark: I sent Sergeant Pryor and Charbonneau in search of the horses with directions to proceed up the river as far as the first narrows and examine particularly for their tracks. They returned at 3:00 p.m. and informed me that they had proceeded up the distance I directed them to go and could see neither horses nor tracks. The plains immediately out from camp are so dry and hard that the track of a horse cannot be seen without close examination.

I therefore directed Sergeant Pryor, Shannon, Charbonneau, and Bratton to encircle the camp at some distance around and find the tracks of the horses and pursue them. They searched for tracks all evening without finding which course the horses had taken, the plains being so remarkably hard and dry as to render it impossible to see a track of a horse passing through the hard parts of them.

I began to suspect that they are taken by the Indians, and taken over the hard plains to prevent our following them. My suspicion is grounded on the improbability of the horses leaving the grass and rushes of the river bottoms, of which they are very fond, and taking immediately out into the open dry plains, where the grass is but short and dry. If they had continued in the bottoms, either up or down, their tracks could be followed very well. I directed Labiche, who understands tracking very well, to set out early in the morning and find what route the horses had taken, if possible.

Wednesday, July 23, 1806:

Clark: Last night the wolves or dogs came into our camp and ate the most of our dried meat, which was on a scaffold.

Labiche went out early, agreeable to my directions of last evening. Sergeant Pryor and Windsor also went out. Sergeant Pryor found an Indian moccasin and a small piece of robe, the moccasin worn out on the bottom and yet wet, and has every appearance of having been worn but a few hours before. These Indian signs are conclusive with me that they have taken the twenty-four horses which we lost on the night of the 20th instant, and that those who were about last night were in search of the balance of our horses, which they could not find, as they had fortunately got into a small prairie surrounded with thick timber in the bottom.

Labiche returned, having taken a great circle, and informed me that he saw the tracks of the horses making off into the open plains and were, by the tracks, going very fast. The Indians who took the horses bent their course rather down the river.

The men finished both canoes by 12:00 today, and I sent them to make oars and get poles, after which I sent Shields and Labiche to kill a fat buffalo out of a gang which has been within a few miles of us all day.

I gave Sergeant Pryor his instructions and a letter to Mr. Heney and directed that he, George Shannon, and Windsor take the remaining horses to the Mandans, where he is to inquire for Mr. Heney. If at the establishments on the Assiniboine River, to take twelve or fourteen horses and proceed on to that place, and deliver Mr. Heney the letter, which is with a view to engage Mr. Heney to prevail on some of the best informed and most influential chiefs of the different bands of Sioux to accompany us to the seat of government with a view to let them see our population and resources, etc., which, I believe, is the surest guarantee of savage fidelity to any nation—that of a government possessing the power of punishing promptly every aggression.

Sergeant Pryor is directed to leave the balance of the horses with the Grand Chief of the Mandans until our arrival at his village, [and] also to keep a journal of his route, with courses, distances, water courses, soil productions, and animals to be particularly noted.

Shields and Labiche killed three buffalo, two of them very fat. I had as much of the meat saved as we could conveniently carry. In the evening [I] had the two canoes put into the water and lashed together, oars and everything fixed ready to set out early in the morning, at which time I have directed Sergeant Pryor to set out with the horses and proceed on to the entrance of the Bighorn River (which we suppose to be at no great distance), at which place the canoes will meet him and set him across the Yellowstone, below the entrance of that river.

Thursday, July 24, 1806:

Clark: [I] had all our baggage put on board of the two small canoes which, when lashed together, are very sturdy and, I am convinced, will carry the party I intend taking down with me. At 8:00 a.m. we set out and proceeded on very well to a riffle. At this riffle the small canoes took a good deal of water, which obliged us to land to dry out articles and bail canoes. I also had a buffalo skin tacked on so as to prevent the water's flaking in between the two canoes.

After dinner I proceeded on past the entrance of a small creek and some wood on the starboard side, where I met with Sergeant Pryor, Shannon, and Windsor with the horses. They had but just arrived at that place.

Sergeant Pryor informed me that it would be impossible for the two men with him to drive on the horses after him without tiring all the good ones in pursuit of the more indifferent, to keep them on course [and] that in passing every gang of buffalo, several of which he had met with, the loose horses, as soon as they saw the buffalo, would immediately pursue them and run around them. All those that had speed sufficient would head the buffalo, and those of less speed would pursue on as fast as they could.

He at length found that the only practical method would be for one of them to proceed on and, whenever they saw a gang of buffalo, to scare them off before the horses got up.

This disposition in the horses is no doubt owing to their being frequently exercised in chasing different animals by their former owners, the Indians, as it is their custom to chase every species of wild animal with horses, for which purpose they train all their horses. I had the horses driven across the river, and set Sergeant Pryor and his party across. Hugh Hall, who cannot swim, expressed a willingness to proceed on with Sergeant Pryor by land and, as another man was necessary to assist in driving the horses. But observing [that] he was naked, I gave him one of my two remaining shirts, a pair of leather leggings, and three pairs of moccasins, which equipped him completely, and sent him on with the party by land to the Mandans.

I proceeded on the river[454] much better than above the entrance of the Clark's fork. [It is] deep and the current [is] regularly rapid, [and it is] from two to three hundred yards in width where it is all together, [and] much divided by islands, many of which are large and well-supplied with cottonwood trees, some of them large.

For me to mention or give an estimate of the different species of wild animals on this—particularly buffalo, elk, antelope, and wolves—would be incredible. I shall, therefore, be silent of the subject further. So it is, we have a great abundance of the best of meat.

We made seventy miles today. [The] current [was] rapid and much divided by islands.

Friday, July 25, 1806:

Clark: The wind continued high until 2:00 p.m.

I proceeded on after the rain lay a little, and at 4:00 p.m. arrived at a remarkable rock situated in an extensive bottom on the starboard side of the river and two hundred fifty paces from it. This rock I ascended and from its top had a most extensive view in every direction. This rock, which I shall call Pompy's Tower,[455] is two hundred feet high and four hundred paces in circumference, and only accessible

454. Yellowstone

on one side, which is from the northeast, the other parts of it being a perpendicular cliff of lightish-colored gritty rock.

On the top there is a tolerable soil about five or six feet thick covered with short grass. The Indians have made two piles of stone on the top of this tower. The natives have engraved on the face of this rock the figures of animals, etc., near which I marked my name and the day of the month and year. From the top of this tower I could discover two low mountains and the Rocky Mountains covered with snow southwest.

Sunday, July 27, 1806:

Clark: When we pass the Big Horn, I take my leave of the view of the tremendous chain of Rocky Mountains, white with snow, in view of which I have been since the 1st of May last.

Monday, July 28, 1806:

Clark: The elk on the banks of the river were so abundant that we have not been out of sight of them today.

Tuesday, July 29, 1806:

Clark: Below this river[456] at a few miles from the Yellowstone, the hills are high and rugged, containing coal in great quantities. Beaver are very plentiful in this part of the Yellowstone.

Friday, August 1, 1806:

Clark: My situation [was] a very disagreeable one: in an open canoe, wet, and without the possibility of keeping myself dry.

The country through which we passed is in every respect like that through which I passed yesterday.

At 2:00 p.m. I was obliged to land[457] to let the buffalo cross over.

Notwithstanding an island of a half a mile in width over which this gang of buffalo had to pass [and] the channel of the river on each side nearly one-fourth of a mile in width, this gang of buffalo was entirely across and as thick as they could swim. The channel on the side of the island [that] they went into the river was crowded with those animals for half an hour (I was obliged to lay to for one hour)

---

455. after Sacagawea's son, nicknamed "Pomp," a Shoshone word for "First Born" (Bakeless, p. 366); known as Pompeys Pillar (without an apostrophe) today (Schmidt, p. 153)

456. the Tongue River (Eide, p. 213)

457. near present-day Glendive, Montana (Schmidt, p. 155)

[and] the other side of the island for more than three-fourths of an hour.

I took four of the men and killed four fat cows for their fat and what portion of their flesh the small canoes could carry, that which we had killed a few days ago being nearly spoiled from the wet weather.

[We] encamped on an island close to the port shore. Two gangs of buffalo crossed a little below us, as numerous as the first.

Saturday, August 2, 1806:

Clark: About 8:00 a.m. this morning, a bear of the large vicious species, being on a sand bar, raised himself up on his hind feet and looked at us as we passed down near the middle of the river. He plunged into the water and swam toward us, either from a disposition to attack or from the scent of the meat which was in the canoes. We shot him with three balls and he returned to shore badly wounded.

In the evening I saw a very large bear take the water above us. I ordered the boat to land on the opposite side with a view to attack him when he came within shot of the shore. When the bear was in a few paces of the shore, I shot it in the head. The men hauled it on shore, and it proved to be an old she, which was so old that her tusks had worn smooth, and [was] much the largest female bear I ever saw.

Sunday, August 3, 1806:

Clark: Last night the mosquitoes were so troublesome that no one of the party slept half the night. For my part I did not sleep one hour. These tormenting insects found their way into my bier and tormented me the whole night.

At 8:00 a.m. I arrived at the junction of the Yellowstone with the Missouri and formed my camp immediately in the point between the two rivers, at which place the party had all encamped the 26th of April, 1805.

The distance from the Rocky Mountains at which place I struck the River Yellowstone to its entrance into the Missouri [is] eight hundred thirty-seven miles. Six hundred thirty-six miles of this distance I descended in two small canoes lashed together. The Rochejhone, or Yellowstone, River is large and navigable with but few obstructions quite into the Rocky Mountains. The color of the water differs from that of the Missouri, it being of a yellowish brown, whilst that of the Missouri is that of a deep, drab color, containing a greater portion of mud than the Yellowstone.

Monday, August 4, 1806:

Clark: [The] mosquitoes [are] excessively troublesome—so much so that the men complained that they could not work at their skins for those troublesome insects. And I find it entirely impossible to hunt in the bottoms, those insects being so numerous and tormenting as to render it impossible for a man to continue in the timbered lands, and our best retreat from those insects is on the sand bars in the river, and even those situations are only clear of them when the wind should happen to blow, which it did today for a few hours in the middle of the day. The evenings, nights, and mornings are almost unendurable, particularly by the party with me, who have no biers to keep them off at night and nothing to screen them but blankets, which are worn and have many holes.

The torments of those mosquitoes and the want of a sufficiency of buffalo meat to dry—those animals [are] not to be found in this neighborhood—induce me to determine to proceed on to a more eligible spot on the Missouri below, at which place the mosquitoes will be less troublesome and buffalo more plenty.

[I] wrote a note to Captain Lewis informing him of my intentions and tied it to a pole which I had stuck up in the point.

At 5:00 p.m. [we] set out and proceeded on down to the second point, which appeared to be an eligible situation for my purpose. On this point the mosquitoes were so abundant that we were tormented much worse than at the point.

The child of Charbonneau has been so much bitten by the mosquitoes that his face is much puffed up and swelled.

Tuesday, August 5, 1806:

Clark: The mosquitoes were so troublesome to the men last night that they slept but very little. Indeed, they were excessively troublesome to me. My mosquito bier has a number of small holes worn through which they pass in.

I set out at an early hour intending to proceed to some other situation. I had not proceeded on far before I saw a ram of the bighorn animal near the top of a port side bluff. I ascended the hill with a view to kill the ram. The mosquitoes were so numerous that I could not keep them off my gun long enough to take sight, and by that means missed.

I landed on a sand bar from the south point intending to form a camp at this place and continue until Captain Lewis should arrive.

Wednesday, August 6, 1806:

Clark: This morning a very large bear of the white species discovered us floating in the water and, taking us as I presume to be buffalo, immediately plunged into the river and pursued us. I directed the men to be still. This animal came within about forty yards of us and tacked about. We all fired into him without killing him, and the wind [was] so high that we could not pursue him, by which means he made his escape to the shore, badly wounded.

I have observed buffalo floating down, which I suppose must have been drowned in crossing above. More or less of these animals drown or mire in passing this river. I observed several floating buffalo on the River Yellowstone immediately below where large gangs had crossed.

Friday, August 8, 1806:

Clark: At 8:00 a.m. Sergeant Pryor, Shannon, Hall, and Windsor came down the river in two canoes made of buffalo skins. Sergeant Pryor informed me that the second night after he parted with me on the Yellowstone, he arrived about 4:00 p.m. on the banks of a large creek, which contained no running water. He halted to let the horses graze, during which time a heavy shower of rain raised the creek so high that several horses which had straggled across the channel of this creek were obliged to swim back. Here he determined to continue all night, it being in good food for the horses. In the morning he could see no horses.

In looking about their camp, they discovered several tracks within one hundred paces of their camp, which they pursued. [They] found where they[458] had caught and driven off all the horses. They pursued on five miles. The Indians there divided into two parties. They continued in pursuit of the largest party five miles farther. Finding that there was not the smallest chance of overtaking them, they returned to their camp and packed up their baggage on their backs, and steered a northeast course to the River Yellowstone, which they struck at Pompey's Tower. There they killed a buffalo bull and made a canoe in the form and shape of the Mandans and Arikaras—the form of a basin.

On the night of the 26th ult., the night after the horses had been stolen, a wolf bit Sergeant Pryor through his hand when asleep, and this animal was so vicious as to make an attempt to seize Windsor, when Shannon fortunately shot him. Sergeant Pryor's hand has nearly recovered.

---

458. the Indians

The country through which Sergeant Pryor passed after he parted with me is a broken, open country. He passed one small river, which I have called Pryor's River, which rises in a mountain to the south of Pompey's Tower. The note I left on a pole at the mouth of the Yellowstone, Sergeant Pryor, concluding that Captain Lewis had passed, took and brought with him. Captain Lewis, I expect, will be certain of my passing by the sign which I have made, and the encampment immediately in the point.

Sergeant Pryor, being anxious to overtake me, set out some time before the day this morning and forgot his saddlebags, which contain his papers, etc. I sent Bratton back with him in search of them. After dark, Sergeant Pryor returned with his saddlebags, etc. They were much farther up than he expected.

Monday, August 11, 1806:

Clark: At meridian I set out and had not proceeded more than two miles before I observed a canoe near the shore. I directed the canoes to land.

Here I found two men from the Illinois, Joseph Dixon[459] and Handcock.[460] These men are on a trapping expedition up the River Yellowstone. They informed me that they left the Illinois in the summer [of] 1804, that the Mandans and Hidatsa were at war with the Arikaras [and that] the Assiniboines were also at war with the Mandans, etc., and had prohibited the North West traders from coming to the Missouri to trade. These difficulties, if true, will, I fear, be a bar to our expectations of having the Mandan, Minnetaree, and Arikara chiefs to accompany us to the United States, though we shall endeavor to bring about a peace.

The last winter they spent with the Tetons, in company with Mr. Coartong,[461] who brought up goods to trade. The Tetons robbed him of the greater part of the goods and wounded this Dixon in the legs with a hard wad. The Tetons gave Mr. Coartong some few robes for the articles they took from him.

These men further informed me that they met the boat and party we sent down from Fort Mandan, near the Kansas River, on board of which was a chief of the Arikaras [and] that he met the Yankton chiefs with Mr. Dorion, McClellan, and several other traders on their way down.

---

459. Dickson (Eide, p. 215)

460. Forrest Hancock (DeVoto, and Eide, p. 215)

461. unknown

Tuesday, August 12, 1806:

Clark: At meridian Captain Lewis hove into sight with the party, which went by the way of the Missouri, as well as that which accompanied him from Traveller's Rest on Clark's River.

I was alarmed, on the landing of the canoes, to be informed that Captain Lewis was wounded by an accident. I found him lying in the pirogue. He informed me that his wound was slight and would be well in twenty or thirty days. This information relieved me very much. I examined the wound and found it [to be a] very bad flesh wound. The ball had passed through the fleshy part of his left thigh below the hip bone and cut the cheek of the right buttock for three inches in length and the depth of the ball. Captain Lewis informed me the accident happened the day before, by one of the men, Peter Cruzatte, mistaking him in the thick bushes to be an elk.

After Captain Lewis and myself parted at Traveller's Rest, he bore his course to the northeast until he struck Medicine River near where that river enters the Rocky Mountains and proceeded down Medicine River to the Missouri. This route is a very good one, though the best route would be from the falls of the Missouri by Fort Mountain to the gap through which the great road passes the dividing mountain. The total distance from the falls of the Missouri to Clark's River is only one hundred fifty miles of a tolerable road.

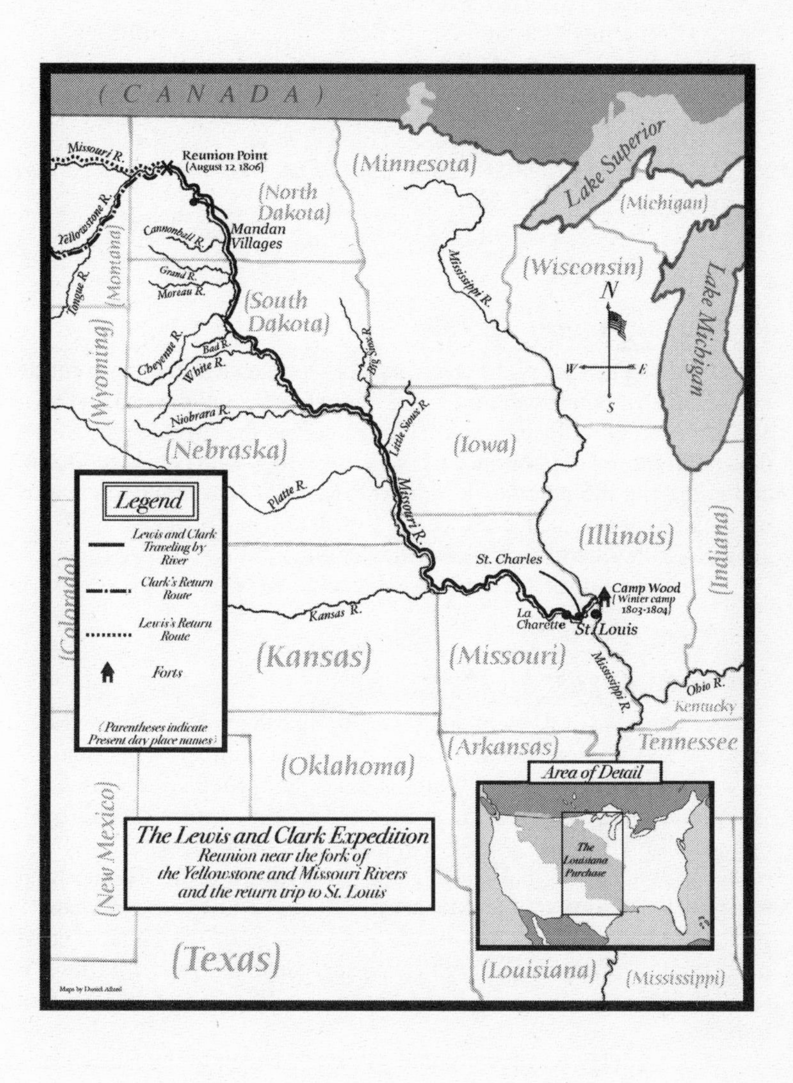

(C A N A D A)
Missouri R.
Reunion Point
(August 12 1806)
Yellowstone R.
Tongue R.
(Montana)
(Wyoming)
(Colorado)
(New Mexico)
(Minnesota)
(North Dakota)
Mandan Villages
Cannonball R.
Grand R.
Moreau R.
(South Dakota)
Cheyenne R.
Bad R.
White R.
Niobrara R.
(Nebraska)
Platte R.
Big Sioux R.
Little Sioux R.
Missouri R.
Mississippi R.
Lake Superior
(Michigan)
(Wisconsin)
Lake Michigan
N
W
E
S
(Iowa)
(Illinois)
(Indiana)
St. Charles
Camp Wood
(Winter camp 1803-1804)
La Charette
St. Louis
Kansas R.
(Kansas)
(Missouri)
Mississippi R.
Ohio R.
Kentucky
Tennessee
(Arkansas)
(Oklahoma)
(Texas)
(Louisiana)
(Mississippi)
Legend
Lewis and Clark Traveling by River
Clark's Return Route
Lewis's Return Route
Forts
(Parentheses indicate Present day place names)
Area of Detail
The Louisiana Purchase
The Lewis and Clark Expedition
Reunion near the fork of the Yellowstone and Missouri Rivers and the return trip to St. Louis
Maps by Daniel Alford

19: August, 1806

We invited them [the assembled chiefs] *to visit their Great Father, the President of the United States, and to hear his own councils and receive his gifts from his own hands.*

Captain William Clark,
August 15, 1806

Wednesday, August 13, 1806:

Clark: The last night was very cold with a stiff breeze from the northwest. All hands were on board and we set out at sunrise and proceeded on very well with a stiff breeze astern the greater part of the day. [We] passed the entrance of the Little Missouri River at 8:00 a.m. and arrived at the entrance of Myry[462] River at sunset and encamped on the northeast side, having come, by the assistance of the wind, the current and our oars, eighty-six miles.

The mosquitoes are not so troublesome this evening as they have been.

Thursday, August 14, 1806:

Clark: [We] set out at sunrise and proceeded on. When we were opposite the Hidatsa grand village, we saw a number of the natives viewing us. We directed the blunderbusses [and] fired several times.

Soon after, we came to at a crowd of the natives on the bank opposite the village of the Shoe Indians, or "Mah-har-has," at which place I saw the principal chief of the little village of the Hidatsa and the principal chief of the Maharhas. These people were extremely pleased to see us. The chief of the little village of the Hidatsa cried most immoderately. I enquired [into] the cause and was informed it was for the loss of his son who had been killed lately by the Blackfoot Indians.

After a delay of a few minutes, I proceeded on to the Black Cat's village on the northeast side of the Missouri where I intended to encamp, but the sand blew in such a manner that we determined not to continue on that side but return to the side we had left. Here we were

462. Big Muddy (Eide, p. 216)

visited by all the inhabitants of this village who appeared equally well-pleased to see us as those above. I walked up to the Black Cat's village and ate some simlins with him and smoked a pipe. This village, I discovered, had been rebuilt since I left it and [was] much smaller than it was. Enquiring into the cause, [I] was informed that a quarrel had taken place and a number of lodges had removed to the opposite side.

I had, [as] soon as I [had] landed, dispatched Charbonneau to the Hidatsa, inviting the chiefs to visit us, and Drouillard down to the lower village of the Mandans to ask Mr. Jessaume to come and interpret for us. Mr. Jessaume arrived and I spoke to the chief of the village informing them that we spoke to them as we had done when we were with them last, and we now repeated our invitation to the principal chiefs of all the villages to accompany us to the United States, etc., etc.

The Black Cat, Chief of the Mandans, spoke and informed me that he wished to visit the United States and his Great Father, but was afraid of the Sioux who were yet at war with them and were on the river below and would certainly kill him if he attempted to go down. I endeavored to do away with his objections by informing him that we would not suffer those Indians to hurt any of our red children who should think [it] proper to accompany us, and on their return they would be equally protected, and their presents, which would be very liberal, with themselves conveyed to their own country at the expense of the United States, etc., etc.

The chief of the Mah-har-has told me [that] if I would send [some men] with him, he would let me have some corn. I directed Sergeant Gass and two men to accompany him to his village. They soon returned loaded with corn.

Ordway: About 9:00 a.m. we arrived at our old neighbors, the Gros Ventres and Mandans. We saluted them by firing our swivel and blunderbusses a number of times. They were very glad to see us.

Captain Lewis fainted as Captain Clark was dressing his wound, but soon came to again.

Friday, August 15, 1806:

Clark: Mandan Village - After assembling the chiefs and smoking one pipe, I informed them that I still spoke the same words which we had spoken to them when we first arrived in their country in the fall of 1804. We then invited them to visit their Great Father, the President of the United States, and to hear his own councils and receive his gifts from his own hands, [and] also see the population of a government which can, at their pleasure, protect and secure you from all your enemies, and chastise all those who will shut their ears to his councils. We now offer to take you, at the expense of our government, and send you back to your country again with a considerable present in merchandise which you will receive of your Great Father.

The Great Chief of the Hidatsa spoke. He said he wished to go down and see his Great Father very much, but that the Sioux were in the road and would most certainly kill him or any others who should go down. They were bad people and would not listen to anything which was told them. When he saw us last, we told him that we had made peace with all the nations below. Since that time, the Sioux had killed eight of their people and stolen a number of their horses. He said that he had opened his ears and followed our councils. He had made peace with the Cheyenne and Rocky Mountain Indians, and repeated the same objections as mentioned. If the Sioux were at peace with them and could be depended on, he, as also the other chiefs of the villages, would be glad to go and see their Great Father, but as they were all afraid of the Sioux, they should not go down, etc.

The Black Cat, chief of the Mandan village on the north side of the Missouri, sent over and requested me to go over to his village. After taking a smoke, he informed me that as the Sioux were very troublesome and the road to his Great Father dangerous, none of the village would go down with us.

I told the chiefs and warriors of the village who were then present that we were anxious that some of the village should go and see their Great Father and hear his good words and receive his bountiful gifts, etc., and told them to pitch on some man on which they could rely and send him to see their Great Father.

They made the same objections which the chief had done before.

A young man offered to go down, and they all agreed for him to go down. The character of this young man I knew as a bad one and made an objection as to his age and character. At this time Gibson, who was with me, informed me that this young man had stolen his knife and had it then in his possession. This I informed the chief [of] and directed him to give up the knife. He delivered the knife with a very faint apology for his having it in his possession.

I then reproached these people for wishing to send such a man to see and hear the words of so great a man as their Great Father. They hung their heads and said nothing for some time when the chief spoke and said that they were afraid to send anyone for fear of their being killed by the Sioux.

Being informed by one of our interpreters that the second chief of the Mandans, commonly called the Little Crow, intended to accompany us down, I took Charbonneau and walked to the village to see this chief and talk with him on the subject. He told me he had determined to go down but wished to have a council first with his people, which would be in the afterpart of the day.

Colter, one of our men, expressed a desire to join some trappers, the two Illinois men we met and who now came down to us, who offered to become shearers with him and furnish traps, etc. The offer was a very advantageous one to him. His services could be dispensed with from this [place] down, and as we were disposed to be of service to anyone of our party who had performed their duty as well as Colter had done, we agreed to allow him the privilege, provided no one of the party would ask or expect a similar permission, to which they all agreed, that they wished Colter every success, and that as we did not wish any of them to separate until we should arrive at St. Louis, they would not apply or expect it, etc. Great numbers of the natives of the different villages came to view us and exchange robes with our men for their skins. We gave John Colter some small articles which we did not want, and some powder and lead. The party also gave him several articles which will be useful to him on his expedition.

This evening Charbonneau informed me that our back was scarcely turned before a war party from the two Hidatsa villages followed on and attacked and killed the Shoshone Indians whom we had seen and, in the engagement between them and the Shoshone Indians, they had lost two men, one of which was the son of the principal chief of the little village of the Hidatsa, that they had also gone to war from the Hidatsa and killed two Arikaras. He further informed me that a misunderstanding had taken place between the Mandans and Hidatsa and had very nearly come to blows about a woman. The Hidatsa, at length, presented a pipe and a reconciliation took place between them.

Ordway: [It was] a clear and pleasant morning.

Some of the party went at dressing themselves deerskins, etc.

The natives brought us corn and beans, etc. They brought us a breakfast of boiled simlins and beans, etc. The two villages of Mandans gave us considerable of corn and more than we would take away. The chiefs of the first village wished us to stay one or two days longer with them. We gave the swivel to the Big Bellies, or Gros Ventres.

Saturday, August 16, 1806:

Clark: As our swivel could no longer be serviceable to us, as it could not be fired on board the largest pirogue, we concluded to make a present of it to the Great Chief of the Hidatsa (the One Eye) with a view to ingratiate him more strongly in our favor. I had the swivel charged and collected the chiefs in a circle around it and addressed them with great ceremony.

[I] told them [that] I had listened with much attention to what the One Eye had said yesterday and believed that he was sincere and spoke from his heart. I reproached them very severely for not attending to what had been said to them by us in council in the fall of 1804 and at different times in the winter of 1804 and 1805, and told them our backs were scarcely turned before a party followed and killed the poor, defenseless Shoshone Indians whom we had taken by the hand and told them not to be afraid, that you would never strike them again, etc. [I] also mentioned the Arikaras, etc.

The little cheery old chief of the Hidatsa spoke as follows, viz.: "Father, we wish to go down with you to see our Great Father, but we know the nations below and are afraid of the Sioux who will be on the river and will kill us on our return home. The Sioux have stolen our horses and killed eight of our men since you left us, and the Arikaras have also struck us. We stayed at home and listened to what you have told us. We, at length, went to war against the Sioux and met with Arikaras and killed two of them. They were on their way to strike us. We will attend to your word and not hurt any people. All shall be welcome and we shall do as you direct." The One Eye said his ears would always be open to the word of his Great Father and shut against bad council, etc.

I then, with a good deal of ceremony, made a present of the swivel to the One Eye chief and told him when he fired this gun to remember the words of his Great Father which we had given him. After the council was over, the gun was fired and delivered. The chief appeared to be much pleased, and conveyed it immediately to his village, etc.

We settled with and discharged Colter. We sent for Mr. Jessaume and told him to use his influence to prevail on one of the chiefs to accompany us, and we would employ him. He informed us soon after that the Big White chief would go if we would take his wife and son, and Jessaume's wife and two children, which we were obliged to agree to do.

Sunday, August 17, 1806:

Clark: [We] settled with Toussaint Charbonneau for his services as an interpreter, the price of a horse and lodge purchased of him for public service, in all amounting to $500.33^{1}/_{3}$ cents.

[We] directed two of the largest of the canoes [to] be fastened together with poles tied across them so as to make them steady for the purpose of conveying the Indians and interpreter and their families.

We were visited by all the principal chiefs of the Hidatsa to take their leave of us. At 2:00 we left our encampment after taking leave of

Colter who also set out up the river in company with Messrs. Dickson and Hancock.

We also took our leave of Toussaint Charbonneau, his Shoshone Indian wife and their child, who had accompanied us on our route to the Pacific Ocean in the capacity of interpreter and interpretress. Toussaint Charbonneau wished much to accompany us in the said capacity if we could have prevailed upon the Hidatsa chief to descend the river with us to the United States, but as none of those chiefs, of whose language he was conversant, would accompany us, his services were no longer of use to the United States and he was therefore discharged and paid up. We offered to convey him down to the Illinois if he chose to go. He declined proceeding on at present, observing that he had no acquaintance or prospects of making a living below and must continue to live in the way that he had done.

I offered to take his little son, a beautiful promising child who is nineteen months old, to which they both, he and [his] wife, were willing provided the child had been weaned. They observed that in one year the boy would be sufficiently old to leave his mother, and he would then take him to me if I would be so friendly as to raise the child for him in such a manner as I thought proper, to which I agreed, etc.

We dropped down to the Big White chief's Mandan village a half a mile below on the south side. All the Indians proceeded on down by land and I walked to the lodge of the chief whom I found surrounded by his friends. The men were sitting in a circle smoking, and the women [were] crying. He sent his baggage with his wife and son, with the interpreter Jessaume and his wife and two children, to the canoes provided for them. After smoking one pipe and distributing some powder and lead which we had given him, he informed me that he was ready, and we were accompanied to the canoes by all the village. Many of them cried out aloud.

As I was about to shake with the Grand Chiefs of all the villages there assembled, they requested me to sit one minute longer with them, which I readily agreed to, and directed a pipe to be lit. The chiefs informed [me] that when we first came to their country, they did not believe all [that] we said, but they were now convinced that everything we had told them was true, that they should keep in memory everything which we had said to them and strictly attend to our advice, that their young men should stay at home and should not go again to war against any nation, that if any attacked them they should defend themselves, that we might depend on what they said, and requested us to inform their Great Father. They also requested me to tell the Arikaras to come and see them, not to be afraid, that no harm should be done them, [and] that they are anxious to be in peace with them.

The Sioux, they said, they had no dependence in and should kill them whenever they came into their country to do them harm, etc. I told them that we had always told them to defend themselves, but not to strike those nations we had taken by the hand. The Sioux, with whom they were at war, we had never seen.

On our return, we should inform their Great Father of their[463] conduct towards his faithful red children and he would take such steps as will bring about a lasting peace between them and his faithful red children. I informed them that we should inform the Arikaras [of] what they had requested, etc. The Grand Chief of the Hidatsa said that the Great Chief who was going down with us to see their Great Father was as well as if he went also, and on his return he would be fully informed of the words of his Great Father, and requested us to take care of this Great Chief.

We then saluted them with a gun and set out and proceeded on to Fort Mandan where I landed and went to view the old works. The houses, except one in the rear bastion [which] had been burned by accident, [and] some pickets, were standing in front next to the river.

Tuesday, August 19, 1806:

Clark: Captain Lewis's wounds are healing very fast. I am much in hope of his being able to walk in eight or ten days.

The wind rose and became very strong from the southeast and [with] a great appearance of rain.

Jessaume, the interpreter, let me have a piece of a lodge, and the squaws pitched or stretched it over some sticks. Under this piece of leather I slept dry. It is the only covering which I have had sufficient to keep off the rain since I left the Columbia.

It began to rain moderately soon after nightfall.

Wednesday, August 20, 1806:

Clark: I observed a great alteration in the current, course, and appearance of this point of the Missouri. In places where there were sand bars in the fall of 1804, at this time the main current passes, and where the current then passed, is now a sand bar. Sand bars which were then naked are now covered with willow several feet high. The entrances of some of the rivers and creeks [have] changed owing to the mud thrown into them, and a layer of mud [is] over some of the bottoms of eight inches thick.

---

463. the Sioux's

Thursday, August 21, 1806:

Clark: At 8:00 a.m. [we] met three Frenchmen coming up. They proved to be three men from the Arikaras, two of them Reeved and Greinyea, [who] wintered with us at the Mandans in 1804. We came to. These men informed us that they were on their way to the Mandans and intended to go down to the Illinois this fall. One of them, quite a young lad, requested a passage down to the Illinois. We consented, and he got into a canoe to ply an oar.

These men informed us that seven hundred Sioux had passed the Arikaras on their way to war with the Mandans and Hidatsa, and that their encampment where the squaws and children were was someplace near the big bend of this river below. They also informed us that no trader had arrived at the Arikaras this season, and that they were informed that the Pawnee, or Arikara chief, who went to the United States last spring was a year, died on his return at someplace near the Sioux River, etc.[464] These men had neither powder nor lead. We gave them a horn of powder and some balls and, after a delay of an hour, we parted from them.

At half past 11:00 a.m. we arrived in view of the upper Arikara villages. A great number of women [were] collecting wood on the banks. We saluted the village with four guns and they returned the salute by firing several guns in the village. I observed several very white lodges on the hill above the town which the Arikaras from the shore informed me were Cheyennes who had just arrived.

We landed opposite to the second village and were met by most of the men, women, and children of each village, as also the Cheyennes. They all appeared anxious to take us by the hand and much rejoiced to see us return. I was saluted by the two Great Chiefs whom we had met or given medals to as we ascended this river in 1804.

I sat myself down on the side of the bank and the chiefs and brave men of the Arikaras and Cheyennes formed a circle around me. After taking a smoke of Mandan tobacco which the Big White chief, who was seated on my left hand, furnished, I informed them, as I had before informed the Mandans and Hidatsa, where we had been, what we had done and said to the different nations in their favor, and invited some of their chiefs to accompany us down and see their Great Father and receive from his own mouth his good councils and from his own hands his bountiful gifts, etc., telling [them] pretty much the same which I had told the Mandans and Hidatsa. [I] told them not to be afraid of any nation below, that none would hurt them, etc.

---

464. the Arikara chief died in Washington in April, 1806 (DeVoto)

I also told the Arikaras that I was very sorry to hear that they were not on friendly terms with their neighbors, the Mandans and Hidatsa, and had not listened to what we had said to them, but had suffered their young men to join the Sioux who had killed eight Mandans, etc., that their young men had stolen the horses of the Hidatsa, [and] in retaliation for those injuries, the Mandans and Hidatsa had sent out a war party and killed two Arikaras. How could they expect [that] other nations would be at peace with them when they, themselves, would not listen to what their Great Father had told them?

I further informed them that the Mandans and Hidatsa had opened their ears to what we had said to them, but had stayed at home until they were struck, that they were still disposed to be friendly and on good terms with the Arikaras. They then saw the Great Chief of the Mandans by my side who was on his way to see his Great Father, and was directed by his nation and the Hidatsa and Omahas to smoke in the pipe of peace with you and to tell you not to be afraid to go to their towns or [to] take the birds in the plains, that their ears were open to our councils, and no harm should be done to an Arikara.

The sun being very hot, the Cheyenne chief invited us to his lodge which was pitched in the plain at no great distance from the river. I accepted the invitation and accompanied him to his lodge, which was new and much larger than any which I have seen. It was made of twenty dressed buffalo skins in the same form of the Sioux and lodges of other nations of this quarter. About this lodge were twenty others, several of them nearly the same size. I enquired for the balance of the nation and was informed that they were near at hand and would arrive on tomorrow, and when all together amounted to one hundred twenty lodges.

After smoking, I gave a medal of the small size to the Cheyenne chief, etc., which appeared to alarm him. He had a robe and a fleece of fat buffalo meat brought, and [he] gave me [them] with the medal back, and informed me that he knew that the white people were all "medicine" and that he was afraid of the medal or anything that white people gave to them. I had previously explained the cause of my giving him the medal and flag, and again told him the use of the medal and the cause of my giving it to him, and again put it about his neck, delivering him up his present of a robe and meat, informing him that this was the medicine which his Great Father directed me to deliver to all the Great Chiefs who listened to his word and followed his councils, that he had done so, and I should leave the medal with him as a token of his sincerity, etc. He doubled the quantity of meat and received the medal.

In the evening, the Great Chief requested that I would walk to his house, which I did. He gave me about two carrots of tobacco, two beaver skins, and a trencher of boiled corn and beans to eat (as it is the custom of all the nations on the Missouri to give to every white man who enters their lodges something to eat).

This chief informed me that none of his chiefs wished to go down with us, that they all wished to see the chief who went down return first, that the Cheyennes were a wild people and were afraid to go, that they should all listen to what I had said. The interpreter informed me that the chiefs of these villages had no intention of going down. One [of] the chiefs of the village on the island talked of going down.

I returned to the boat where I found the principal chief of the lower village who had cut part of his hair and disfigured himself in such a manner that I did not know him. He informed me [that] the Sioux had killed his nephew and that he was in tears for him, etc.

We determined to proceed down to the island and, accordingly, took the chief on board and proceeded on down to the island village, at which place we arrived a little before dark and were met, as before, by nearly every individual of the village.

The One Arm, [the] second chief of this village whom we had expected to accompany us down, spoke to the Mandan chief in a loud and threatening tone which caused me to be somewhat alarmed for the safety of that chief. I informed the Arikaras of this village that the Mandans had opened their ears to and followed our councils, that this chief was on his way to see their Great Father, the President of the United States, and was under our protection, that if any injury was done to him by any nation, that we should all die to a man.

I at length went to the Grand Chief's lodge by his particular invitation. The Mandan chief stuck close to me. The chief had prepared a supper of boiled young corn, beans, and squashes, of which he gave me in wooden bowls. He also gave me nearly two carrots of tobacco, and informed me he had always had his ears open to what we had said, that he was well convinced that the Sioux were the cause of all the trouble between the Mandans and them.

Friday, August 22, 1806:

Clark: As I was about to leave the Cheyenne chief's lodge, he requested me to send some traders to them, that their country was full of beaver and they would then be encouraged to kill beaver, but now they had no use for them as they could get nothing for their skins, and did not know well how to catch beaver. If the white people would come amongst them, they would learn [from] them how to take the beaver. I promised the nation that I would inform their Great Father, the President of the United States, and he would have them supplied with goods, and mentioned in what manner they would be supplied, etc., etc.

I am happy to have it in my power to say that my worthy friend, Captain Lewis, is recovering fast. He walked a little today for the first time. I have discontinued the tent in the hole [from which] the ball came out.

Tuesday, August 26, 1806:

Clark: At 8:00 [we] passed the place the Tetons were encamped at the time they attempted to stop us in September, 1804, and at 9:00 a.m. [we] passed the entrance of Teton River. [We] saw several black-tail, or mule, deer and sent out to kill them, but they were wild and the hunters could not get a shot at any of them.

A few miles below the Teton River, I observed a buffalo skin canoe lying on the south shore, and a short distance lower, a raft, which induces me to suspect that the Tetons are not on the Missouri at the big bend, as we were informed by the Arikaras, but up the Teton River.

At 5:00 p.m. we landed at Loisel's fort on Cedar Island. This fort is entire, and every part appears to be in the same state it was [in] when we passed it in September, 1804.

We proceeded on about ten miles lower and encamped on the southwest side. As we were now in the country where, we were informed, the Sioux were assembled, we were much on our guard, determined to put up with no insults from these bands of Sioux, [and] all the arms, etc., [were put] in perfect order.

Captain Lewis is still on the mending hand. He walks a little.

We made sixty miles today with the wind ahead [the] greater part of the day.

Saturday, August 30, 1806:

Clark: Captain Lewis is mending slowly.

I took three hunters and walked on the northeast shore with a view to kill some fat meat. We had not proceeded far before [we] saw a large plum orchard of the most delicious plums. Out of this orchard two large buck elk ran. The hunters killed them. I stopped the canoes and brought in the flesh which was fat and fine. Here the party collected as many plums as they could eat and several pecks of which they put by, etc. After a delay of nearly two hours, we again proceeded on downwards.

I saw several men on horseback which, with the help of a spy-glass, I found to be Indians on the high hills to the northeast. We landed on the southwest side and I sent out two men to a village of barking squirrels to kill some of those animals.

Immediately after landing, about twenty Indians were discovered on an eminence a little above us on the opposite side. One of these men I took to be a Frenchman from his having a blanket, capote, and a handkerchief around his head.

Immediately after, eighty or ninety Indian men, all armed with fusils and bows and arrows, came out of a woods on the opposite bank about one-fourth of a mile below us. They fired off their guns as a salute. We returned the salute with two rounds. We were at a loss to determine of what nation these Indians were. From their hostile appearance, we were apprehensive [that] they were Tetons, but from the country through which they roved, we were willing to believe them [to be] the Yanktons, Poncas, or Omahas, any of which nations are well-disposed towards the white people. I determined to find out who they were without running any risk of the party and Indians, and therefore took three Frenchmen who could speak the Omaha, Pawnee and some Sioux and, in a small canoe, I went over to a sand bar which extended sufficiently near the opposite shore to converse.

Immediately after I set out, three young men set out from the opposite side and swam next [to] me on the sand bar. I directed the men to speak to them in the Pawnee and Omaha languages first, neither of which they could understand. I then directed the man who could speak a few words of Sioux to enquire what nation or tribe they belong to. They informed me that they were Tetons and their chief was the Black Buffalo. This chief I knew very well to be the one we had seen with his band at Teton River, which band had attempted to detain us in the fall of 1804 as we ascended this river and with whom we were near coming to blows.

I told these Indians that they had been deaf to our councils and ill treated us as we ascended this river two years past, that they had abused all the whites who had visited them since. I believed them to be bad people and should not suffer them to cross to the side on which the party lay, and directed them to return with their band to their camp, that if any of them came near our camp we should kill them certainly. I left them on the bar and returned to the party and examined the arms, etc. These Indians, seeing some corn in the canoe, requested some of it, which I refused, being determined to have nothing to do with these people.

Several others swam across, one of which understood Pawnee and, as our Pawnee interpreter was a very good one, we had it in our power to inform [them of] what we wished. I told this man to inform his nation that we had not forgotten their treatment to us as we passed up this river, etc., that they had treated all the white people who had visited them very badly, robbed them of their goods, and had wounded one man whom I had seen. We viewed them as bad people and no more traders would be suffered to come to them, and whenever the white people wished to visit the nations above, they would come sufficiently strong to whip any villainous party who dared to oppose them, and words to the same purport.

I also told them that I was informed that a part of all their bands were going to war against the Mandans, etc., and that they would be well whipped, as the Mandans and Hidatsa, etc., had a plenty of guns, powder and ball, and we had given them a cannon to defend themselves, and directed them to return from the sand bar and inform their chiefs [of] what we had said to them, and to keep away from the river or we should kill every one of them, etc., etc.

These fellows requested to be allowed to come across and make comrades which we positively refused, and I directed them to return immediately, which they did, and after they had informed the chiefs, etc., of, I suppose, what we had said to them, they all set out on their return to their camps back of a high hill. Seven of them halted on the top of the hill and blackguarded[465] us, told us to come across and they would kill us all, etc., of which we took no notice.

We, all this time, were extremely anxious for the arrival of the two Fields and Shannon, whom we had left behind, and were somewhat concerned as to their safety. To our great joy, those men hove in sight at 6:00 p.m. Joseph Fields had killed three blacktail, or mule, deer. We then set out.

As I wished to see what those Indians on the hill would act, we steered across near the opposite shore. This notion put them in some agitation as to our intentions. Some set out on the direction towards their camps, others walked about on the top of the hill, and one man walked down the hill to meet us and invited us to land, to which invitation I paid no kind of attention. This man I knew to be the one who had, in the fall [of] 1804, accompanied us two days and is said to be the friend to the white people. After we passed him, he returned to the top of the hill and gave three strokes with the gun he had in his hand. This, I am informed, is a great oath among the Indians.

---

465. verbally abused

20: September, 1806

St. Louis

Mr. President:

It is with pleasure that I announce to you the safe arrival of myself and party at 12:00 today. In obedience to your orders, we have penetrated the Continent of North America to the Pacific Ocean.

I am with every sentiment of esteem your obedient and very humble servant,

Captain Meriwether Lewis,
September 23, 1806

Monday, September 1, 1806:

Clark: At 9:00 a.m., we passed the entrance of River Niobrara which had the same appearance it had when we passed up: water rapid and of a milky white color.

About two miles below the Niobrara, nine Indians ran down the bank and beckoned to us to land. They appeared to be a war party and I took them to be Tetons and paid no kind of attention to them further than an enquiry [as] to what tribe they belonged. They did not give me any answer. I presume they did not understand the man who spoke to them as he spoke but little of their language. As one canoe was yet behind, we landed in an open, commanding situation out of sight of the Indians, determined to delay until they came up.

About fifteen minutes after we had landed, several guns were fired by the Indians which, we expected, were at the three men behind. I called out fifteen men and ran up with a full determination to cover them, if possible, [and] let the number of the Indians be what it might. Captain Lewis hobbled up on a bank and formed the remainder of the party in a situation well-calculated to defend themselves and the canoes, etc.

When I had proceeded to the point about two hundred fifty yards, I discovered the canoe about one mile above and the Indians where we had left them. I then walked on the sand beach and the Indians came down to meet me. I gave them my hand and enquired of them what they were shooting at. They informed me that they were shooting off their guns at an old keg which we had thrown out of one of the canoes and was floating down. These Indians informed me [that] they were Yanktons. One of the men with me knew one of the Indians to be the brother of young Dorion's wife. Finding these Indians to be Yanktons, I invited them down to the boats to smoke.

When we arrived at the canoes, they all eagerly saluted the Mandan chief and we all sat and smoked several pipes. I told them that we took them to be a party of Tetons and the firing, I expected, was at the three men in the rear canoe, and I had gone up with a full intention to kill them all if they had been Tetons and [had] fired on the canoe as we first expected, but finding them Yanktons and good men, we were glad to see them and take them by the hand as faithful children who had opened their ears to our councils.

One of them spoke and said that their nation had opened their ears and [had] done as we had directed them ever since we gave the medal to their Great Chief, and should continue to do as we had told them.

We enquired if any of their chiefs had gone down with Mr. Dorion. They answered that their Great Chief and many of their brave men had gone down, that the white people had built a house near the Omaha village where they traded.

We tied a piece of ribbon to each man's hair and gave them some corn, of which they appeared much pleased. The Mandan chief gave a pair of elegant leggings to the principal man of the Indian party, which is an Indian fashion.

The canoe and three men having joined us, we took our leave of this party, telling them to return to their band and listen to our councils which we had before given to them. Their band of eighty lodges was on Plum Creek, a few miles to the north.

After we all came together, we again proceeded on down to a large sand bar immediately opposite to the place where we met the Yanktons in council at the Calumet Bluffs, and which place we left on the first of September, 1804. I observed our old flagstaff, or pole, standing as we left it.

Wednesday, September 3, 1806:

Clark: [We] passed the entrance of Redstone River on the northeast side at 11:00 a.m., and at half past 4:00 p.m. we spied two boats and several men. Our party plied their oars and we soon landed on the side of the boats. The men of these boats saluted us with their small arms.

I landed and was met by a Mr. James Aird[466] from the Mackinaw by way of Prairie de Chien[467] and St. Louis. This gentleman is of the house of Dickson and Company of Prairie de Chien who has a license to trade for one year with the Sioux. He has two bateaux loaded with merchandise for that purpose. This gentleman received both Captain Lewis and myself with every mark of friendship. He was himself at the time with a chill of the ague on him which he has had for several days. Our first enquiry was after the president of our country and then our friends and the state of the politics of our country, etc., and the state of Indian affairs, to all of which enquiries Mr. Aird gave us as [much] satisfactory information as he had it in his power to have collected in the Illinois, which was not a great deal.

Soon after we landed [there was] a violent storm of thunder, lightening, and rain from the northwest which was violent, with hard claps of thunder and sharp lightening which continued until 10:00 p.m., after which the wind blew hard. I sat up late and partook of the tent of Mr. Aird, which was dry.

Mr. Aird unfortunately had his boat sunk on the twenty-fifth of July last by a violent storm of wind and hail, by which accident he lost the most of his useful articles, as he informed us. This gentleman informed us of many changes and misfortunes which had taken place in the Illinois, amongst others the loss of Mr. Pierre Chouteau's house and furniture by fire. For this misfortune of our friend, Chouteau, I feel myself very much concerned, etc.

He also informed us that Gen. Wilkinson was the governor of the Louisiana and at St. Louis, [that] three hundred of the American troops had been cantoned[468] on the Missouri a few miles above its mouth, [that] some disturbance with the Spaniards in the Natchitoches[469] country is the cause of their being called down to that country, [that] the Spaniards had taken one of the United States' frigates in the Mediterranean,[470] [that] two British ships of the line had fired on an American ship[471] in the port of New York and killed the captain's brother, [that] two Indians had been hung in St. Louis for murder and several others [were] in jail, and that Mr. Burr and Gen. Hamilton [had] fought a duel[472] [and] the latter was killed, etc., etc.

---

466. a Scotch fur trader (Bakeless, p. 375)

467. in present-day Wisconsin

468. allotted quarters

469. in present-day Louisiana

470. the *President,* near Algeciras, Spain, in the fall of 1804 (Ambrose, *UC*, p. 401)

471. the merchant ship *Richard,* in April, 1806 (Ambrose, *UC*, p. 401)

472. on July 14, 1804

I am happy to find that my worthy friend, Captain Lewis, is so well as to walk about with ease to himself, etc.

We made sixty miles today.

The river [was] much crowded with sand bars which are very differently situated from what they were when we went up.

Thursday, September 4, 1806:

Clark: As we were in want of some tobacco, I proposed to Mr. Aird to furnish us with four carrots for which we would pay the amount [equal] to any merchant of St. Louis. He very readily agreed to furnish us with tobacco and gave to each man as much as it is necessary for them to use between this and St. Louis, an instance of generosity for which every man of the party appeared to acknowledge.

Mr. Aird also insisted on our accepting a barrel of flour. We gave to this gentleman what corn we could spare, amounting to about six bushels. This corn was well-calculated for his purpose as he was about to make his establishment, and would have it in his power to hull the corn, etc. The flour was very acceptable to us. We have yet a little flour, part of what we [had] carried up from the Illinois as high as Maria's River and buried it there until our return, etc.

At 8:00 a.m. we took our leave and set out and proceeded on very well.

At 11:00 a.m., [we] passed the entrance of the Big Sioux River, which is low, and at meridian we came to at Floyd's Bluff below the entrance of Floyd's River[473] and ascended the hill with Captain Lewis and several men. [We] found the grave had been opened by the natives and left half-covered. We had this grave completely filled up and returned to the canoes and proceeded on to the sand bar on which we encamped from the twelfth to the twentieth of August, 1804, near the Omaha village.

Here we came to and directed every wet article put out to dry, all the bedding of the party and skins being wet. As it was late in the evening, we determined to continue all night. [We] had issued to each man of the party a cup of flour. A little before night, several guns were heard below and in a direction towards the Omaha village which induced us to suspect that Mr. McClellan who, we were informed, was on his way up to trade with the Omahas, had arrived at the creek below and that those reports of guns were some of his party out hunting.

---

473. both rivers are at present-day Sioux City, Iowa

Friday, September 5, 1806:

Clark: The report of the guns which was heard must have been the Omahas who most probably have just arrived at their village from hunting the buffalo. This is a season they usually return to their village to secure their crops of corn, beans, pumpkins, etc., etc.

[We] proceeded on very well [and] passed the Blue Stone Bluff at 3:00 p.m.

Saturday, September 6, 1806:

Clark: At the lower point of Pelican Island, a little above the Petite River de Sioux, we met a trading boat of Mr. Auguste Chouteau of St. Louis bound to the River Jacques to trade with the Yanktons. This boat was in the care of a Mr. Henry Delorn.[474] He had exposed all his lading to dry and sent out five of his hands to hunt. They soon arrived with an elk.

We purchased a gallon of whiskey of this man and gave each man of the party a dram, which is the first spirituous liquor which had been tasted by any of them since the Fourth of July, 1805. Several of the party exchanged leather for linen shirts and beaver for cloth hats.

These men could inform us [of] nothing more than that all the troops had moved from the Illinois, and that Gen. Wilkinson was preparing to leave St. Louis.

We advised this trader to treat the Tetons with as much contempt as possible, and stated to him where he would be benefited by such treatment, etc., etc., and at 1:00 p.m. set out. These men gave us two shots from a swivel they had on the bow of their boat, which we returned in our turn.

The chief and the squaws and children are weary of their journey. [The] children cry, etc.

Sunday, September 7, 1806:

Clark: We proceeded on with a stiff breeze ahead. Note: the evaporation on this portion of the Missouri had been noticed as we ascended this river. I am obliged to replenish my ink stand every day with fresh ink, at least nine-tenths of which must evaporate.

We came forty-four miles today only.

Monday, September 8, 1806:

Clark: The Missouri at this place does not appear to contain more water than it did one thousand miles above this. The evaporation

474. Henry Delaunay, a fur trader working for Chouteau (Bakeless, p. 377)

must be immense. In the last one thousand miles, this river receives the water of twenty rivers and many creeks. Several of the rivers [are] large and the size of this river, or the quantity of water, does not appear to increase any.

Tuesday, September 9, 1806:

Clark: [We] passed the entrance of the great River Platte which is at this time low. The water [is] nearly clear [and] the current turbulent as usual. The sand bars, which choked up the Missouri and confined the river to a narrow, snaggy channel, are wasted away and nothing remains but a few small remains of the bar, which is covered with driftwood.

Below the River Platte, the current of the Missouri becomes evidently more rapid than above, and the snags [are] much more numerous and bad to pass.

Late in the evening, we arrived at the Bald Pated Prairie and encamped immediately opposite our encampment of the sixteenth and seventeenth of July, 1804. Our party appears extremely anxious to get on, and every day appears to produce new anxieties in them to get to their country and friends.

My worthy friend, Captain Lewis, has entirely recovered. His wounds are healed up and he can walk, and even run, nearly as well as ever he could. The parts are yet tender, etc., etc.

The climate is every day perceptibly warmer and [the] air more sultry than I have experienced for a long time. The nights are now so warm that I sleep comfortably under a thin blanket. A few days past, two were not more than sufficient.

Wednesday, September 10, 1806:

[Clark] At ____ p.m. we met a Mr. Alexander La Fass and three Frenchmen from St. Louis in a small pirogue on their way to the River Platte to trade with the Pawnee, Loup, or Wolf, Indians. This man was extremely friendly to us. He offered us anything he had. We accepted of a bottle of whiskey only, which we gave to our party. Mr. La Fass informed us that Gen. Wilkinson and all the troops had descended the Mississippi, and Mr. Pike[475] and young Mr. Wilkinson had set out on an expedition up the Arkansas River, or in that direction.

After a delay of half an hour, we proceeded on about three miles and met a large pirogue and seven men from St. Louis bound to the Omahas for the purpose of trade. This pirogue was in [the] charge of a Mr. La Croix. We made some few enquiries of this man and again pro-

475. Captain Zebulon Pike, of Pike's Peak fame

ceeded on through a very bad part of the river, crowded with snags and sawyers, and encamped on a sand bar about four miles above the Grand Nemahar.

We find the river in this timbered country narrower and [with] more moving sands, and [with] a much greater quantity of sawyers or snags, than above. Great caution and much attention are required to steer clear of all those difficulties in this low state of the water.

Friday, September 12, 1806:

Clark: We set out at sunrise, the usual hour, and proceeded on very well. At about seven miles, [we] met two pirogues from St. Louis. One contained the property of Mr. Chouteau bound to the Pawnees or River Platte, the other going up trapping as high as the Omahas. Here we met one of the Frenchmen who had accompanied us as high as the Mandans. He informed us that Mr. McClellan[476] was a few miles below.

The wind blew ahead.

Soon after we passed these pirogues, we saw a man on shore who informed us that he was one of Mr. McClellan's party and that he was a short distance below. We took this man on board and proceeded on and met Mr. McClellan at the St. Michael's Prairie. We came to. Here we found Mr. Joseph Gravelines, the Arikaras interpreter whom we had sent down with an Arikaras chief in the spring of 1805, and old Mr. Dorion, the Sioux interpreter.

We examined the instructions of these interpreters and found that Gravelines was ordered to the Arikaras with a speech from the President of the United States to that nation and some presents which had been given the Arikara chief who had visited the United States and unfortunately died at the city of Washington. He was instructed to teach the Arikaras agriculture and make every enquiry after Captain Lewis, myself, and the party.

Mr. Dorion was instructed to accompany Gravelines and, through his influence, pass him with his presents, etc., by the Teton bands of Sioux, and to prevail on some of the principal chiefs of those bands, not exceeding six, to visit the seat of the government next spring. He was also instructed to make every enquiry after us. We made some small addition to his instructions by extending the number of chiefs to ten or twelve, or three from each band, including the Yanktons, etc.

Mr. McClellan received us very politely and gave us all the news and occurrences which had taken place in the Illinois within his knowledge.

---

476. Robert McClellan, a fur trader (Bakeless, p. 378)

The evening proving to be wet and cloudy, we concluded to continue all night.

Saturday, September 13, 1806:

Clark: [We] rose early. Mr. McClellan gave each man a dram and a little. After sunrise we set out.

We landed at the camp of the five hunters whom we had sent ahead. They had killed nothing. The wind being too high for us to proceed in safety through the immensity of snags which were immediately below, we concluded to lay by and sent [some men] on the small canoes a short distance to hunt and kill some meat.

I felt myself very unwell and directed a little chocolate, which Mr. McClellan had given us, prepared, of which I drank about a pint and found great relief.

Sunday, September 14, 1806:

Clark: At 2:00 p.m., a little below the lower end of the old Kansas village, we met three large boats bound to the Yanktons and Omahas, the property of Mr. LaCroix, Mr. Aiten, and Mr. Chouteau, all from St. Louis. These young men received us with great friendship and pressed on us some whiskey for our men, biscuits, pork, and onions, and part of their stores.

We continued nearly two hours with these boats, making every enquiry into the state of our friends and country, etc. These men were much afraid of meeting with the Kansas.

We proceeded on to an island near the middle of the river below our encampment of the first of July, 1804, and encamped, having descended only fifty-three miles today. Our party received a dram and sang songs until 11:00 at night in the greatest harmony.

Tuesday, September 16, 1806:

Clark: The day proved excessively warm and disagreeable, so much so that the men rowed but little.

At 10:00 a.m. we met a large trading pirogue bound for the Pawnees. We continued but a short time with them.

At 11:00 a.m. we met young Mr. Robidoux with a large boat of six oars and two canoes. The license of this young man was to trade with the Pawnees, Omahas, and Otos, rather an extraordinary license for so young a man, and without the seal of the territory annexed. As Gen. Wilkinson's signature was not to this instrument, we were somewhat doubtful of it. Mr. Brown's signature we were not acquainted with without the territorial seal. We made some enquiries of this young man and cautioned him against pursuing the steps of his brother in attempting to degrade the American character in the eyes of the Indians.

Wednesday, September 17, 1806:

[Clark] At 11:00 a.m., we met a Captain McClallen,[477] [of] late a captain of artillery of the United States Army, ascending in a large boat. This gentleman, an acquaintance of my friend, Captain Lewis, was somewhat astonished to see us return and appeared rejoiced to meet us. We found him a man of information and from whom we received a partial account of the political state of our country. We were making enquiries and exchanging answers, etc., until nearly midnight.

This gentleman informed us that we had been long since given up by the people of the United States generally and almost forgotten. The President of the United States had yet hopes of us.

We received some civilities of Captain McClallen. He gave us some biscuits, chocolate, sugar, and whiskey, for which our party was in want and for which we made a return of a barrel of corn, and [were] much obliged to him.

Captain McClallen informed us that he was on a rather speculative expedition to the confines of New Spain, with a view to introduce a trade with those people. His plan is to proceed up this river to the entrance of the River Platte [and] there to form an establishment from which to trade partially with the Pawnees and Otos, to form an acquaintance with the Pawnees and prevail on some of their principal chiefs to accompany him to Santa Fe where he will appear in a style calculated to attract the Spanish government in that quarter and, through the influence of a handsome present, he expects to be permitted to exchange his merchandise for silver and gold, of which those people abound.

He has a kind of introductory speech from Gov. Wilkinson to the Pawnees and Ietans[478] with a view to gain their protection in the execution of his plans. If the Spanish government favors his plans, he proposes taking his merchandise on mules and horses, which can easily be procured of the Pawnees, to some point convenient to the Spanish settlements within the Louisiana Territory, to which place the inhabitants of New Mexico may meet him for the purpose of trade, etc.

Captain McClallen's plan [is], I think, a very good one if strictly pursued, etc.

---

477. John McClallen (DeVoto)

478. properly the Utes, but here probably meaning the Comanches (DeVoto)

Ordway: [We] met Mr. McClallen with a large keelboat. He was rejoiced to see us and gave our officers wine and the party as much whiskey as we all could drink. Mr. McClallen informed us that the people in general in the United States were concerned about us as they had heard that we were all killed. Then again, they heard that the Spaniards had us in the mines.[479]

Thursday, September 18, 1806:

Clark: Our party, entirely out of provisions, [is] subsisting on pawpaws.[480] We divided the biscuits which amounted to nearly one biscuit per man. This, in addition to the pawpaws, is to last us down to the settlements, which is one hundred fifty miles. The party appears perfectly contented and [they] tell us that they can live very well on the pawpaws.

We made fifty-two miles today only.

One of our party, John Potts, complains very much of one of his eyes which is burnt by the sun from exposing his face without a cover from the sun. Shannon also complains of his face and eyes, etc.

Friday, September 19, 1806:

Clark: We arrived at the entrance of Osage River at dark and encamped on the spot we had encamped on the first and second of June, 1804, having come seventy-two miles.

A very singular disorder is taking place amongst our party, that of sore eyes. Three of the party have their eyes inflamed and swelled in such a manner as to render them extremely painful, particularly when exposed to the light. The eyeball is much inflamed and the lid appears burnt with the sun. The cause of this complaint of the eye I can't account for. From its sudden appearance, I am willing to believe it may be owing to the reflection of the sun on the water.

Saturday, September 20, 1806:

Clark: As three of the party were unable to row from the state of their eyes, we found it necessary to leave one of our crafts and divide the men into the other canoes. We left the two canoes [which were] lashed together, which I had made high up the River Yellowstone. These canoes we set adrift, and a little after daylight we set out and proceeded on very well.

---

479. of Mexico (Duncan, p. 201)

480. plums (Ambrose, *UC*, p. 403)

At meridian we passed the entrance of the Gasconade River, below which we met a pirogue with five Frenchmen bound to the Osage ground village.

The party, being extremely anxious to get down, plies their oars very well. We saw some cows on the bank which was a joyful sight to the party and caused a shout to be raised for joy.

At ____ p.m. we came in sight of the little French village called La Charette. The men raised a shout and sprang upon their oars and we soon landed opposite to the village. Our party requested to be permitted to fire off their guns, which was allowed, and they discharged three rounds with a hearty cheer which was returned from five trading boats which lay opposite the village.

We landed and were very politely received by two young Scotsmen from Canada, one in the employ of Mr. Aird [and] a Mr. ____, and the other Mr. Reed. All of these boats were bound to the Osage and Otos. These two young Scotch gentlemen furnished us with beef, flour, and some pork for our men and gave us a very agreeable supper. As it was likely to rain, we accepted of a bed in one of their tents. We purchased of a citizen two gallons of whiskey for our party, for which we were obliged to give eight dollars in cash, an imposition on the part of the citizen.

Every person, both French and Americans, seem to express great pleasure at our return and acknowledged themselves much astonished in seeing us return. They informed us that we were supposed to have been lost long since and were entirely given up by every person, etc.

These boats are from Canada, in the bateau form, and wide in proportion to their length. Their length [is] about thirty feet and the width eight feet, and [they have a] pointed bow and stern, flat bottom, and row six oars only. These bottoms are prepared for the navigation of this river. I believe them to be the best calculated for the navigation of this river of any which I have seen. They are wide and flat, not subject to the dangers of the rolling sand which larger boats are on this river.

The American inhabitants express great disgust for the government of this territory. From what I can learn, it arises from a disappointment of getting all the Spanish grants confirmed.

Sunday, September 21, 1806:

Clark: [We] rose early this morning. [We] collected our men. Several of them had accepted of the invitation of the citizens and visited their families.

At half after 7:00 a.m. we set out. [We] passed twelve canoes of Kickapoos ascending on a hunting expedition. [We] saw several persons [and] also stock of different kinds on the bank which revived the party very much.

At 3:00 p.m. we met two large boats ascending.

At 4:00 p.m. we arrived in sight of St. Charles. The party rejoiced at the sight of this hospitable village, plied their oars with great dexterity, and we soon arrived opposite the town. This day being Sunday, we observed a number of gentlemen and ladies walking on the bank. We saluted the village by three rounds from our blunderbusses and the small arms of the party and landed near the lower part of the town.

We were met by great numbers of the inhabitants. We found them excessively polite. We received invitations from several of these gentlemen. Mr. Querie undertook to supply our party with provisions, etc. The inhabitants of this village appear much delighted at our return and seem to vie with each other in their politeness to us all.

We came only forty-eight miles today.

The banks of the river [are] thinly settled, etc.

Monday, September 22, 1806:

Clark: This morning being very wet and the rain still continuing hard and our party being all sheltered in the houses of these hospitable people, we did not think [it] proper to proceed on until after the rain was over, and continued at the house of Mr. Proulx. I took this opportunity of writing to my friends in Kentucky, etc.

At 10:00 a.m. it ceased raining and we collected our party and set out and proceeded on down to the cantonment at Coldwater Creek[481] about three miles up the Missouri on its southern banks.

At this place we found Col. Hunt and a Lt. Peters and one company of artillerists. We were kindly received by the gentlemen of this place. Mrs. Wilkinson, the lady of the governor and general, we were sorry to find in delicate health.

We were honored with a salute of ____ guns and a hearty welcome. At this place there is a public store kept in which, I am informed, the United States has 60,000$ worth of Indian goods.

Tuesday, September 23, 1806:

Clark: We rose early [and] took the chief to the public store and furnished him with some clothes, etc. [We] took an early breakfast with Col. Hunt and set out.

[We] descended to the Mississippi and down that river to St. Louis, at which place we arrived about 12:00. We suffered the party to

481. Fort Bellefontaine (Ambrose, *UC*, p. 403)

fire off their pieces as a salute to the town. We were met by all the village and received a hearty welcome from its inhabitants, etc.

Here I found my old acquaintance, Maj. William Christy, who had settled in this town in a public line as a tavern keeper. He furnished us with storerooms for our baggage and we accepted of the invitation of Mr. Peter Chouteau and took a room in his house. We paid a friendly visit to Mr. Auguste Chouteau and some of our old friends this evening.

As the post had departed from St. Louis, Captain Lewis wrote a note to Mr. Hay in Cahokia to detain the post at that place until 12:00 tomorrow which was rather later than his usual time of leaving it.

Ordway: [It was] a wet, disagreeable morning. We set out after breakfast and proceeded on. [We] soon arrived at the mouth of the Missouri. [We] entered the Mississippi River and landed at River Dubois where we wintered in 1804. We delayed a short time.

About 12:00 we arrived in sight of St. Louis. [We] fired three rounds as we approached and landed opposite the center of town. The people gathered on the shore and huzzahed three cheers.

We unloaded the canoes and carried the baggage all up to a storehouse in town. [We] drew out the canoes [and] then the party all considerably much rejoiced that we have the expedition completed.

And now we look for boarding in town and waiting for our settlement, and then we intend to return to our native homes to see our parents once more, as we have been so long from them.

Lewis:

St. Louis, September 23rd, 1806

Mr. President:

It is with pleasure that I announce to you the safe arrival of myself and party at 12:00 today. In obedience to your orders, we have penetrated the Continent of North America to the Pacific Ocean.

I am very anxious to learn the state of my friends at Albemarle, particularly whether my mother is yet living.

I am with every sentiment of esteem your obedient and very humble servant,

Meriwether Lewis

Wednesday, September 24, 1806:

Clark: I slept but little last night. However, we rose early and commenced writing our letters. Captain Lewis wrote one to the president and I wrote Gov. Harrison and my friends in Kentucky, and sent off George Drouillard with those letters to Cahokia and delivered them to Mr. Hays, etc.

We dined with Mr. Chouteau today. After dinner [we] went to a store and purchased some clothes which we gave to a tailor and directed to be made.

Captain Lewis, in opening his trunk, found all his papers wet and some seeds spoiled.

Thursday, September 25, 1806:

Clark: [We] had all of our skins, etc., sunned and stored away in a storeroom of Mr. Caddy Chouteau. [We] paid some visits of form to the gentlemen of St. Louis.

In the evening, [there was] a dinner and [a] ball.

Friday, September 26, 1806:

Clark: [It is] a fine morning.

We commenced writing, etc.

Glossary

acerose: shaped like a needle
acuminate: tapering to a slender point
air gun: a long-barreled rifle that fired by compressed air, like a BB gun
ambuscade: ambush
aquiline: curving like an eagle's beak
ascidia: pitcher-shaped
asunder: apart from each other
baie rouge: French for *red berry*
balsam capivia: *copaiba balsam,* perhaps, the oleoresin of balsam
barking squirrel: prairie dog
barks: probably a poultice of Peruvian bark
bawd: a madam for a house of prostitution
beargrass: of the lily family, with foliage resembling coarse blades of grass
bee martin: kingbird
bier: a framework for carrying
bisilicon: an ointment of wax, pitch, resin, and olive oil
blackguard: verbally abuse
blaireau: French for *badger*
blunderbuss: a short firearm with a large bore and flaring muzzle
bois roulé: kinninnik; Indian tobacco rolled with leaves or bark
bon pour manger: French for *good to eat*
boudin blanc: literally, French for *white black pudding*
bower: a shelter made with tree boughs or vines twined together
brace: an arm span's length
brant: small, dark wild goose, often with a black head and neck
breechclout: breechcloth or loincloth
bubby: variation of booby, or breast
bullboat: hide stretched over a bowl-shaped willow frame
bush drag: trout net
cabra: Spanish for *cabretta:* light, soft leather from sheepskins
caissee: cargo boat
cajaux: raft

camas: plants of the lily family with edible bulbs
cap à pie: head to toe
capote: a long, hooded, woolen blanket coat
canton: allot quarters
castile soap: a hard, bland soap made from olive oil and sodium hydroxide
castor: a bitter, strong-smelling creamy orange-brown substance consisting of the secretions of the perineal glands of the beaver
cataplasm: poultice
char: small-scaled trout
Corvus: genus of the black-billed magpie
cowas: biscuitroot
dead reckoning: a method of charting one's course using compass direction, time, and distance
decoction: reduction or extract
dram: an eighth of an ounce
draught: British variation of *draft*
espontoon: a spear and ax combined
eulachon: candlefish
eyedagg: a type of war hatchet
fascine: a long bundle of sticks bound together
fathom: six feet
flitches: like sides of pork
fowlers: wildfowl hunters
fusil: light flintlock musket
gage holes: drains
gill: four ounces
Glauber salts: a strong laxative
griping: sharp, spasmodic pains in the bowels
ground potato: "prairie turnip" or "Indian breadfruit;" turnip-like roots that could be eaten raw or cooked; usually braided into strings and dried
hackmatak: balsam poplar
haws: fruit of the hawthorn tree
hobble: put a short rope around the legs to hamper, but not prevent, movement
hollows: small valleys
imposthume: abscess
instance: occasionally meaning *request*
instant: the current month
jerking: cutting meat into long, thin strips and drying in the sun or curing by exposing to smoke

Jerusalem artichoke: a perennial sunflower, cultivated for its tubers

keelboat: a shallow, covered keeled riverboat; usually rowed, poled, or towed, but occasionally sailed

kinepox: medicine used for smallpox prevention

lamb's-quarters: goosefoot with a waxy or powdery coating

laudanum: tincture of opium

leader: tendon

league: three miles

lobelia: the leaves and tops of Indian tobacco

Lues venera: syphilis

lunated: crescent-shaped

making moccasins: preparing for war

massy: massive

maw: stomach

melt: spleen

meridian: when the sun is at its highest point in the sky (about noon)

meridian altitude: the angular measurement between the horizon and the sun at meridian

narrow dock: coarse, weedy plants in the buckwheat family

paunch: stomach

pawpaw: plum

payed: coated the seams

peltries: pelts, especially raw, undressed skins

pemmican: lean dried strips of meat pounded into a paste, mixed with fat and berries, and pressed into small cakes

pennyweight: 1.555 grams, or 0.05 ounces

petiolate: having a stalk or slender stem

picket: tether to a post

pied: patchy in color

pipe tomahawk: served as a weapon, camp ax, and tobacco pipe

pirogue: an open boat, often a dugout canoe

pluck: the heart, liver, windpipe, and lungs of a slaughtered animal

pog-gar-mag-gon: war club

poil: French for *hair*

polecat: skunk

port: left

portable soup: a thick paste concocted by boiling down beef, eggs, and vegetables

port fire match: fuse

prairie wolf: coyote

puncheon: wooden upright used in structural framing
punk: prostitute
quamash: *see* camas
riffle: a shallows extending across a stream bed causing broken water
rive: split, as in wood
Rochejhone: Yellowstone
ruff: collar
sand rush: a tufted marsh plant; stems are used in bottoming chairs and plaiting mats
sawyers: trees, or parts of trees, that protrude above the surface of a body of water
scrofula: tuberculosis of the lymph glands, especially in the neck
scuta: broad, thickened scales, usually on the belly of a snake
shappellel: a bread made of roots baked in the sun
she-blaireau: female badger
shomake: sumac, possibly
simlin: summer squash
simples: medicinal plants
slashes: wet or swampy ground overgrown with bushes and trees
snapped: misfired
snips: white or light marks on horses
solus: alone
sound: air bladder (of fish)
spancel: *see* hobble
splits: strips of flexible wood used in making baskets
spuck: infant otter
starboard: right
subulate: linear and tapering to a fine point
sun glass: magnifying glass
tab-ba-bone: thought by Lewis to mean "white man;" experts believe it meant "stranger," or possibly even "enemy"
taffee: rum
tent: a small, cylindrical plug of lint or gauze used to keep a wound open
thirtyweight: thirty pounds, perhaps
tippets: fur coverings for the shoulders with long ends that hang in front
trencher: a wooden platter for serving food
tresses: braids
tushes: long pointed teeth
ult.: abbreviation for *ultimo:* in the preceding month

viz.: abbreviation for *videlicet:* that is, or namely; used to introduce examples, lists, or items

wapatoo: the edible root of the arrowhead plant

wampum: beads of polished shells strung in strands, belts, or sashes

weir: a fence or enclosure set in a waterway for taking fish

white bear: grizzly; the captains also often used "brown" or "gray" for grizzly

whiteberry: white baneberry

without: occasionally meaning *unless*

yampa: squawroot

Lewis & Clark - Bibliography

Ambrose, Stephen E., *Lewis & Clark: Voyage of Discovery*, National Geographic Society, 1998.

Ambrose, Stephen E., *Undaunted Courage: Meriwether Lewis, Thomas Jefferson, and the Opening of the American West*, Simon & Schuster, 1996.

Bakeless, John, *The Journals of Lewis and Clark,* New American Library, 1964.

Burns, Ken, dir., *Lewis & Clark—The Journey of the Corps of Discovery,* PBS Home Video, 1997.

Chuinard, Eldon G., *Only One Man Died: The Medical Aspects of the Lewis and Clark Expedition,* Arthur Clark Company, 1980.

DeVoto, Bernard, ed., *The Journals of Lewis and Clark*, Houghton Mifflin, 1952.

Duncan, Dayton, *Lewis & Clark: The Journey of the Corps of Discovery*, Alfred A. Knopf, 1997.

Duncan, Dayton, *Out West: An American Journey*, Viking Penguin, 1987.

Dillon, Richard, *Meriwether Lewis: A Biography*, Coward-McCann, 1965.

Eide, Ingvard Henry, *American Odyssey: The Journey of Lewis and Clark*, Rand McNally & Co., 1979.

Jones, Landon Y., editor, *The Essential Lewis and Clark*, The Ecco Press, 2000.

Lavender, David, *The Way to the Western Sea: Lewis and Clark Across the Continent*, Harper & Row, 1988.

Mergault, Jean, *English-French Dictionary,* Librairie Larousse, 1983.

Moulton, Gary E., ed., *The Journals of the Lewis and Clark Expedition*, University of Nebraska Press, 1988.

Ronda, James P., *Lewis and Clark Among the Indians,* University of Nebraska Press, 1984.

Schmidt, Thomas, *The Lewis & Clark Trail,* National Geographic Society, 1998.

Thwaites, Reuben Gold, ed., *Original Journals of the Lewis and Clark Expedition*, Arno Press reprint, 1969.